THE ROUTLEDGE HANDBOOK OF LIFESTYLE JOURNALISM

Taking stock of research in an area that has long been starved of scholarly attention, *The Routledge Handbook of Lifestyle Journalism* brings together scholars from across journalism, communication, and media studies to offer the first substantial volume of its kind in this dynamic field.

This Handbook is divided into five major sections covering definitions; current trends; the relationship between lifestyle journalism and consumer culture; how lifestyle journalism interacts with matters of identity, emotion, politics, and society; and future directions. Featuring 30 contributions from authors at the cutting-edge of research around the world, each chapter provides an authoritative overview of key literature and debates and proposes a way forward for future scholarship.

The Routledge Handbook of Lifestyle Journalism is an essential companion for advanced students and researchers of lifestyle journalism and related beats including food, fashion, and travel writing.

Folker Hanusch is Professor of Journalism at the University of Vienna, Austria. He is editor-in-chief of *Journalism Studies* and Vice-Chair of the *Worlds of Journalism Study*. His research interests include comparative journalism studies, lifestyle journalism, transformations of journalism, and Indigenous journalism.

THE ROUTLEDGE HANDBOOK OF LIFESTYLE JOURNALISM

Edited by
Folker Hanusch

Designed cover image: Getty Images

First published 2025
by Routledge
4 Park Square, Milton Park, Abingdon, Oxon OX14 4RN

and by Routledge
605 Third Avenue, New York, NY 10158

Routledge is an imprint of the Taylor & Francis Group, an informa business

© 2025 selection and editorial matter, Folker Hanusch; individual chapters, the contributors

The right of Folker Hanusch to be identified as the author of the editorial material, and of the authors for their individual chapters, has been asserted in accordance with sections 77 and 78 of the Copyright, Designs and Patents Act 1988.

All rights reserved. No part of this book may be reprinted or reproduced or utilised in any form or by any electronic, mechanical, or other means, now known or hereafter invented, including photocopying and recording, or in any information storage or retrieval system, without permission in writing from the publishers.

Trademark notice: Product or corporate names may be trademarks or registered trademarks, and are used only for identification and explanation without intent to infringe.

British Library Cataloguing-in-Publication Data
A catalogue record for this book is available from the British Library

ISBN: 9781032500546 (hbk)
ISBN: 9781032500553 (pbk)
ISBN: 9781003396727 (ebk)

DOI: 10.4324/9781003396727

Typeset in Sabon
by codeMantra

CONTENTS

List of contributors ix

PART I
Conceptualizing lifestyle journalism 1

1 The making of a field? On the relevance of studying lifestyle journalism 3
Folker Hanusch

2 Defining lifestyle journalism: Cultural dimensions, commercial entanglements, and political relevance 13
Elfriede Fürsich and Nete Nørgaard Kristensen

3 The making of modern journalism, from coffeehouse capitalism (strategic news) to constitutional spectacle (market lifestyle) 28
John Hartley

4 Political and proprietorial interference in the food coverage of popular British newspapers between two world wars: A historical perspective 44
Sarah Lonsdale

5 Reviving contemporary journalism through narrative lifestyle coverage? 60
Annik Dubied

6 Journalism training and the status and dilemmas of lifestyle
 journalism practice in Southern Africa 74
 Nhamo Anthony Mhiripiri

PART II
Lifestyle journalism and consumption 91

7 Transforming journalistic genres on social media:
 Books and literary reviews as cultural consumption 93
 Unni From and Carsten Stage

8 Food journalism's commercial ingredients 108
 Peter English and David Fleischman

9 Aesthetics of lifestyle journalism 121
 Maarit Jaakkola

10 A voice of reason: Authenticity and journalistic authority
 in lifestyle journalism 136
 Joy Jenkins

11 Consumerism, popular culture, and religion between
 two continents: The Turkish case 151
 Nilüfer Türksoy

PART III
Lifestyle journalism, emotion and identity 169

12 Aspirational lifestyle journalism 171
 Sandra Banjac

13 Passion as profession? Lifestyle journalists between
 exceptionalism and cruel optimism 186
 Johana Kotišová

14 Wellness influencing in India: Ayurveda and identity on social media 202
 Anuja Premika and Sumana Kasturi

15 Bringing the world to us: Travel journalism and the mediation
 of others 219
 Ben Cocking

16 Role perceptions in lifestyle journalism *Folker Hanusch*	234
17 The role of experts in lifestyle journalism *Daniel Nölleke*	250

PART IV
The public utility of lifestyle journalism — 265

18 Popular and political: The radical origins of lifestyle journalism *Bethany Usher*	267
19 The political relevance of food journalism *Elizabeth Fakazis*	283
20 Green lifestyle journalism *Geoffrey Craig*	300
21 Lifestyle journalism practices in hard news: Dismantling the hard news versus soft news binary *Gregory P. Perreault and Ella Hackett*	313
22 How to be human: Turns in health, lifestyle, and wellness journalism *Mariah L. Wellman, Aly Hill and Avery E. Holton*	330
23 Ethical considerations in lifestyle journalism *Renita Coleman*	341

PART V
New horizons in lifestyle journalism studies — 359

24 Tastemakers or thought leaders? Lifestyle influencers and boundaries of lifestyle journalism *Phoebe Maares*	361
25 Digital technologies and change in the field of fashion journalism *Agnès Rocamora*	376

26 Coaches, gurus and influencers as self-help and lifestyle experts: From Insta therapy to becoming "that girl" on TikTok — 392
Stephanie Alice Baker

27 Everyday multiculturalism on Asian Australian food blogs — 407
Tisha Dejmanee

28 The new look of lifestyle guides: Rethinking brand journalism for the digital age — 423
Myles Ethan Lascity

29 Intimacy and community building in lifestyle journalism 'dialogues' — 439
Lucia Vodanovic

30 Precarity, algorithmic visibility and aspirational labour in the construction of lifestyle — 455
Rob Sharp

Index — 471

CONTRIBUTORS

Stephanie Alice Baker is Reader (Associate Professor) in Sociology at City St George's, University of London, UK. Her research examines the interplay between society, technology, and culture in the context of wellness and self-help. She is the author of several books on the topics including *Lifestyle Gurus* (2020), *Wellness Culture* (2022), and *Cults* (2024).

Sandra Banjac is Assistant Professor at the Centre for Media and Journalism Studies, University of Groningen, The Netherlands. She is also affiliated with the Journalism Studies Centre, University of Vienna, as research fellow on the FWF-funded project 'Audience Expectations of News in the Digital Age'. Her research relies on critical intersectional approaches to interrogate power and inequalities within journalism.

Ben Cocking is Reader in Journalism and Media at the Centre for Journalism, University of Kent, UK. His research interests include travel journalism; travel writing; media discourses on race, class, and culture wars; political communications.

Renita Coleman is Professor in the School of Journalism and Media at the University of Texas at Austin, USA, where she teaches courses in lifestyle journalism and popular culture and the media. She is an associate editor of *Journalism & Mass Communication Quarterly*. Her latest book is *Designing Experiments for the Social Sciences: How to Plan, Create and Execute Research Using Experiments*.

Geoffrey Craig is Professor in the School of Communication Studies at Auckland University of Technology (AUT), New Zealand. He is the author of *Media, Sustainability and Everyday Life* (Palgrave Macmillan).

Tisha Dejmanee is senior lecturer in Digital and Social Media at the University of Technology Sydney, Australia. She is the author of *Postfeminism, Postrace and Digital Politics in Asian American Food Blogs*.

Annik Dubied is Professor in Journalism and Communication at the University of Neuchâtel, Switzerland. Her field of interest focuses on narrative news genres (detective novels, celebrity news, crime news, and investigative reporting). She is currently vice-president of the Swiss Press Council (since 2021).

Peter English is senior lecturer in Journalism at the University of the Sunshine Coast, Australia. His research areas focus on journalism, media, and education, and he is the co-editor of *Australian Journalism Review*.

Elizabeth Fakazis is Professor of Media Studies in the School of Design & Communication at the University of Wisconsin-Stevens Point, USA. She earned a master's in journalism from the University of Missouri-Columbia and a PhD in journalism from the University of Indiana. Her research has centered on the everyday politics of food journalism and on the ways journalism as a profession maintains, polices, and challenges its boundaries. She has co-edited *The Political Relevance of Food Media and Journalism: Beyond Reviews and Recipes* (Routledge).

David Fleischman is senior lecturer in Marketing at the University of the Sunshine Coast, Australia. He researches in the field of services marketing, with a focus on the experience of consumers and the resulting marketing implications.

Unni From is Associate Professor of Media and Journalism and Head of the School of Communication and Culture, Aarhus University, Denmark. She specializes in research about cultural and lifestyle journalism and cultural criticism across media and has contributed with research on constructive journalism. Recent publications include *Heritage, Belonging, and Promotion: Food Journalism Reconsidered* (Routledge 2023) and *Rethinking Cultural Criticism: New Voices in the Digital Age* (Palgrave 2022).

Elfriede Fürsich is Associate Professor in the Department of Communication at the University of Pittsburgh, USA. Her research explores media representations, journalism, and popular culture, with a particular interest in lifestyle, travel, and food journalism. She co-edited *The Political Relevance of Food Media and Journalism: Beyond Reviews and Recipes* (Routledge).

Ella Hackett is a graduate student at the University of South Florida, USA, studying Mass Communications with a concentration in Media Literacy and Analytics. Ella is a writer and research scholar of journalism. Her research interests include gender representation in media, journalism leadership, and journalistic role performance.

Folker Hanusch is Professor of Journalism at the University of Vienna, Austria. He is currently editor-in-chief of *Journalism Studies* and Vice-Chair of the Worlds of Journalism Study and has co-edited the *International Encyclopedia of Journalism Studies* (Wiley). His research interests include comparative journalism studies, lifestyle journalism, transformations of journalism, boundaries of journalism, and Indigenous journalism.

John Hartley is Professor in Digital Media and Culture at the University of Sydney, Australia. His research and publications focus on media, culture, communication, journalism, creative industries, and digital culture. In *Make / Believe: We and They on a Digital Planet* (Bloomsbury 2025), he pursues the distinction between strategic and market stories to its logical conclusion—Barbenheimer.

Contributors

Aly Hill is a PhD student in the Department of Communication at the University of Utah, USA. Hill completed her MA in Communication (2022) at Johns Hopkins University and has collaborated with experts in academia, government, policy, journalism, and data science.

Avery E. Holton is Professor and Chair of the Department of Communication at the University of Utah, USA. His research engages social media, journalism, and identity. He is co-author/co-editor of *Happiness in Journalism* and *The Paradox of Connection: How Digital Media is Transforming Journalistic Labor*.

Maarit Jaakkola is Co-Director of Nordicom, a center for Nordic media research, and Associate Professor in Journalism in the Department of Journalism, Media and Communication at the University of Gothenburg, Sweden. She is also Adjunct Professor in Journalism at the Faculty of Information Technologies and Communication Sciences at Tampere University, Finland. Her research interests are focused on arts and cultural journalism, cultural criticism, platformized cultural practices related to arts and lifestyles, as well as media and cultural literacies.

Joy Jenkins is Assistant Professor of Journalism at the University of Missouri. Her research uses a sociological approach to examine changing organizational identities and practices in newsrooms, particularly among local media. She also studies gender and media. Jenkins serves as editor-in-chief of *The Journal of Magazine Media*. She is also a research associate for the Reuters Institute for the Study of Journalism at the University of Oxford, UK.

Sumana Kasturi is an independent scholar whose research interests include feminist media studies, children's communication, and digital cultures. She is the author of *Gender, Citizenship, and identity: Writing the Everyday* (Routledge, 2019) and co-editor of *Childscape, Mediascape: Children and Media in India* (Orient Blackswan, 2023). Her current research is in the area of food studies and lifestyle journalism. She lives in Mumbai, India.

Johana Kotišová is Assistant Professor in Documentary and Journalism in the Department of Media Studies at the University of Amsterdam, The Netherlands. Her recent publications focus on crisis and conflict reporting, cultural journalism, media professionals' emotional labor and mental well-being, applied research, and creative research methods.

Nete Nørgaard Kristensen is Professor of Media Studies in the Department of Communication at the University of Copenhagen, Denmark. She specializes in media, journalism, and popular culture, focusing on cultural and lifestyle journalism. Her recent co-edited volume is *Rethinking Cultural Criticism: New Voices in the Digital Age* (Palgrave Macmillan).

Myles Ethan Lascity is Assistant Professor and Director of Fashion Media at Southern Methodist University, USA, where his research examines fashion branding and popular culture. He is the author of *The Abercrombie Age: Millennial Aspiration and the Promise of Consumer Culture* and *Communicating Fashion: Clothing, Culture and Media*.

Sarah Lonsdale is senior lecturer in the Journalism Department at City Saint George's, University of London, UK. Her most recent book is *Wildly Different: How Five Women Reclaimed Nature in a Man's World* (MUP, 2025).

Contributors

Phoebe Maares is a postdoctoral researcher at the University of Vienna, Austria. Her research focuses on the boundaries of journalism, especially regarding lifestyle topics, as well as the socio-material conditions of journalistic work and the power relations within the journalistic field.

Nhamo Anthony Mhiripiri is Adjunct Professor in the Department of Journalism and Mass Communication at St Augustine's University of Tanzania. He now specializes in media and communication research and consultancy. He earned his PhD from the University of KwaZulu-Natal, South Africa, and has lectured at the University of KwaZulu-Natal, Midlands State University and Zimbabwe Open University. He was the associate editor in charge of Africa and the Middle East regions for the forthcoming *Oxford Encyclopedia on Race, Ethnicity and Communication*.

Daniel Nölleke is Assistant Professor for Sports Journalism and Public Relations at the Institute of Communication and Media Research at the German Sport University Cologne, Germany. His main areas of expertise include sports communication and journalism studies. He is acting Chair of the ECREA Temporary Working Group "Communication and Sport" and member of the editorial board of the *International Journal of Sport Communication*.

Gregory P. Perreault is Associate Professor of Media Literacy & Analytics at the University of South Florida, US. His work focuses on journalistic epistemology, hostility in journalism, and digital labor. He currently serves as reviews editor for *Journalism & Mass Communication Quarterly* and has served as Fulbright-Botstiber Professor of Austrian-American Studies at the University of Vienna. His book *Digital Journalism and the Facilitation of Hate* (Routledge) was published in 2023.

Anuja Premika is a PhD candidate in the Department of Communication at the University of Hyderabad, India. Her doctoral work examines the beauty media landscape in India, with a focus on the gendered labors—digital and otherwise—of the actors that produce it. Her research interests span the areas of digital cultures, feminist media studies, and cultural production.

Agnès Rocamora is Professor of Social and Cultural Studies at the London College of Fashion, University of the Arts London, UK. She is the author of *Fashioning the City: Paris, Fashion and the Media*. Her writing on the field of fashion and fashion media has appeared in a broad range of international journals, including *Fashion Theory*, *Journalism Practice*, the *Journal of Consumer Culture and Sociology*, as well as in many edited collections. She is a co-editor of *The Handbook of Fashion Studies, Fashion Media: Past and Present* and of *Thinking Through Fashion: A Guide to Key Theorists* (2nd Edition).

Rob Sharp is lecturer in Media and Cultural Studies at the University of Sussex, UK. His research has been published in *Journalism Studies*, *Media War and Conflict*, and the *International Communication Gazette*. His book *Refugee Voices: Performativity and the Struggle for Recognition* is published by Routledge, based on his PhD in Media and Communications from the London School of Economics. He is a former arts correspondent and features writer for the *Independent* (UK).

Contributors

Carsten Stage is Professor in the School of Communication and Culture, Aarhus University, Denmark. His research deals with affect and participatory media, digital health, and illness narratives. Recent books include *Methodologies of Affective Experimentation* (Palgrave 2022), *Quantified Storytelling* (Palgrave 2020), and *The Language of Illness and Death on Social Media* (Emerald 2018).

Nilüfer Türksoy currently serves as Vice Dean at the Faculty of Communication and Media Studies at Eastern Mediterranean University (EMU), Cyprus. She holds a PhD from Erasmus University Rotterdam and specializes in media representations of different social groups, power and politics in media, and news-making practices in Western societies. In June 2024, she was elected Chair of the Center for Research and Communication for Peace at EMU.

Bethany Usher is senior lecturer in Journalism and Director of Postgraduate Education for the School of Arts and Cultures at Newcastle University, UK. She is the author of *Journalism and Celebrity* (2020) and *Journalism and Crime* (2023) and continues to practice journalism. Find out more about her work at www.bethanyusher.com

Lucia Vodanovic is course leader of the MA Journalism degree at the London College of Communication, UK, and a committee member of the Association of Journalism Education. Her research about lifestyle media, social aesthetics, and expression and creativity in journalism has been published in journals such as *Journalism Studies* and *Journalism Practice*, among others. She is also the editor of *Lifestyle Journalism: Social Media, Consumption and Experience* (Routledge).

Mariah L. Wellman is Assistant Professor of Advertising & Public Relations at Michigan State University, USA. Her research interests include social media influencers and wellness. Her work has been published in outlets such as *New Media & Society*, *Social Media & Society*, and *Health Communication*.

PART I

Conceptualizing lifestyle journalism

1
THE MAKING OF A FIELD? ON THE RELEVANCE OF STUDYING LIFESTYLE JOURNALISM

Folker Hanusch

Introduction

As little as 20 years ago, terms such as service or lifestyle journalism, as well as specializations like travel, fashion or food journalism, were rarely encountered in journalism scholarship. Books, journal articles and presentations at academic conferences tended to heavily focus instead on areas of the news that were perceived to matter far more in terms of public import. When I presented some of my first studies on travel journalism around 15 years ago, it was certainly noticeable that such work was a little exotic – and maybe not always taken very seriously. Academic studies of journalism tended to revolve almost exclusively around journalism's role in elections or political processes more generally. This was not surprising given the historical trajectory of much journalism scholarship, which has looked far more frequently at journalism's core – its relationship with political life (Hanitzsch & Vos, 2018).

The center of power in the journalistic field still lies squarely in so-called hard news, an area associated with the highest level of prestige. While names like Christiane Amanpour, Robert Fisk, Laura Kuenssberg, Anna Politkovskaya or Barbara Walters are known to many around the world, far fewer might be able to name a famous lifestyle journalist. Soft news beats typically tend to hold far less power in newsrooms around the world (Harrington, 1997), even if these areas often contribute substantially to the financial success of news organizations. Yet, there continues to be a perception in many corners that lifestyle journalists are free-loading, unethical 'hacks' who are too beholden to the PR and marketing machines of private companies. One example of such perceptions was the response of a journalist who worked in what I had identified as the broader area of lifestyle journalism to an invitation to take part in a survey of lifestyle journalists (Hanusch, 2019). They were outraged by my invitation, saying they certainly did not regard what they did as lifestyle journalism but instead took their work very seriously. Scholarship often had similar views, with Franklin (1997, p. 5) famously noting that the shift toward market-oriented journalism had meant that the "task of journalism has become merely to deliver and serve up what the customer wants; rather like a deep-pan pizza". Lifestyle journalism, it seems, has historically always been measured against the yardstick of political journalism. Not surprisingly, it has often been found wanting in this comparison. But perhaps lifestyle journalism really is "a different animal – one that does not necessarily lend itself to the norms entertained in the realm of political communication"? (Hanusch et al., 2017, p. 156).

Over the past 20 years, there has been a notable shift in the approach of both the journalistic profession and journalism scholarship to lifestyle journalism. In the news industry, some of this may have to do with the fact that the softer forms of journalism have been increasingly successful in attracting eyeballs. At a time when journalism is increasingly measurable (Carlson, 2019) and financial success is closely tied to such measures, hard news journalists are beginning to realize that their soft news counterparts draw in substantial audiences, which may help the long-term survival of their organizations. Lifestyle journalists we spoke to around a decade ago reported that their counterparts in hard news beats did show some level of respect, admiration and even envy (Hanusch & Hanitzsch, 2013). Of course, this is not a new phenomenon – lifestyle journalism experienced enormous growth since the 1980s (Bell & Hollows, 2005) and had been responsible for substantial revenues given the close association many of its beats have with advertising interests. One only needs to think of weekend newspaper lifestyle supplements as recently as ten years ago, which accounted for a large degree of newspapers' overall number of pages (Hanusch, 2014).

Journalism scholarship has also increasingly recognized the relevance of studying lifestyle journalism in order to better understand the breadth of journalism's contribution to a whole range of societal processes. Increasingly, scholars have come to the conclusion that the journalism studies' historical preoccupation with hard news and political life has led to too narrow a narrow vision of journalism. Notably, influential journalism scholar Barbie Zelizer has pointed out that past scholarship, strongly influenced by political communication and political science, had created an unrealistic vision of journalism. "In other words, in political communication's push for largely one version of the aspired, desired, and subjunctive – the normatively hoped for – much of the focus on the multiple journalisms evident on the ground has been lost" (Zelizer, 2011, p. 9). As a result, these other forms of journalism had "become denigrated, relativized, and reduced in value alongside aspirations for something better" (Zelizer, 2011, p. 9). In a similar vein, in their attempt to reconcile different forms of journalism when studying journalistic roles, Hanitzsch and Vos (2018, p. 147) have argued that "other forms of journalism, such as service or lifestyle news, have been marginalized in scholarly discourse and occasionally discredited as an unworthy other".

In fact, scholarship has come up with strong arguments for why we should take forms such as lifestyle journalism more seriously. Thomas Hanitzsch and I have previously identified three key developments in society that are related to the rise in lifestyle journalistic content and its relevance: individualization; social value change; and mediatization (Hanusch & Hanitzsch, 2013). Individualization processes are a global phenomenon, related to traditional institutions' grip on people's lives waning and a resulting need for other institutions – such as the media – to provide a sense of direction for people to engage in identity work. In addition, social values around the world are moving away from a focus on survival to self-expression, leading to societies placing a stronger focus on subjective well-being and quality of life, rather than their economic and physical security (Inglehart, 1997). A focus on consumption is the result of this process. Finally, media are playing an increasingly central role in people's lives, replacing traditional institutions like family, school or the church, with media now the most important storytellers in societies (Hjarvard, 2008).

This makes media and journalism inseparable from personal experiences and everyday life. Taken together, these developments demonstrate that lifestyle journalism has an important function that, while perhaps different from hard news journalism, is no less relevant or important for people's lives. In fact, John Hartley argued 25 years ago already that soft news formats are "the ones who extend the reach of the media, who teach audiences the pleasures of staying tuned, who popularize knowledge" (Hartley, 2000, p. 40).

Taking stock

The past 20 years have thus witnessed a substantial growth in scholarship on a vast range of issues that can be grouped under the umbrella of lifestyle journalism. While such research is still mostly conducted in the Global North – an issue I return to late – there has been a phenomenal variety of studies that inquire into historical, technological, political, economic and social dimensions of lifestyle journalism. Recent years have seen a range of book-length analyses of the field, or at least sub-fields. This includes, for example, Lucia Vodanovic's (2019) superb edited collection on lifestyle journalism, which provides an excellent, global array of case studies into key aspects of the field. There have also been books on sub-beats like food journalism (Fakazis & Fürsich, 2023), travel journalism (Hanusch & Fürsich, 2014) or fashion journalism (Rocamora, 2009), as well as volumes focusing on more practical aspects of lifestyle journalism (Turner & Orange, 2013). Works such as these, in addition to the large number of journal articles that now exist, demonstrate the success that the study of lifestyle journalism is enjoying.

It would therefore seem that the field has slowly reached a certain level of maturity that forces us to take stock of what we know about lifestyle journalism and to identify key areas for future work. This volume is an attempt to do so. The title of this book plays an important role in this context: being able to present *The Routledge Handbook of Lifestyle Journalism* fills me with a sense of pride about the recognition for the field that comes with being published in an esteemed book series such as this. It is, I believe, a significant moment for all scholars who are dedicated to the study of lifestyle journalism. I would like to think that lifestyle journalism has come a long way over the past 20 or so years to be able to call itself at least a sub-field of journalism studies. As the chapters in this book demonstrate, scholars of lifestyle journalism study deploy a large variety of approaches to studying all kinds of aspects that surround the production, distribution, content and reception of lifestyle journalism, and I am particularly honored to have been able to edit this eclectic collection that overviews the state of our field. The variety of ideas, methodologies and insights presented within the covers of this book point to a vibrant and dynamic field that, while it may have reached some level of maturity, is also still growing. The ideas that chapter authors present for future work demonstrate that there are still vast areas to explore further and in more detail, and I hope the chapters provide ample food for thought for future inquiries. Lifestyle journalism is a young field, and emerging scholars play a particularly important role in it. I, therefore, hope that the overviews and analyses presented here will benefit particularly advanced undergraduate and graduate students, as well as more established scholars.

The book is divided into five major sections, each of which addresses an important area of current debates in the field. The first section focuses on conceptualizations of what we actually understand by lifestyle journalism – a term that appears to have come into use only recently. The chapters in this section deal with definitional debates on the topic, as well as contextualize lifestyle journalism historically, tracing its roots and subsequent evolution. The second section examines lifestyle journalism's relationship with consumer culture – a key facet of the genre, as identified in one definition that views lifestyle journalism as "the journalistic coverage of the expressive values and practices that help create and signify a specific identity within the realm of consumption and everyday life" (Hanusch & Hanitzsch, 2013, p. 947). The third section examines the second part of that definition, which relates to matters of identity, as well as emotion, considered a particularly relevant area in recent journalism scholarship more broadly. In the fourth section, chapters engage with a key critique of lifestyle journalism, which is that the field has no political relevance or public utility. To show that this is actually not the case, contributions highlight not only the instances of critical lifestyle journalism and the contributions this can make to society but also the tensions that arise. Finally, the fifth section examines current trends and future projections on lifestyle journalism by dealing primarily with digital developments in the field, which lead to a number of opportunities and challenges. Of particular note here is the role that audiences and outside actors who are increasingly engaging in lifestyle journalism play in impacting on lifestyle journalism.

Conceptualizing lifestyle journalism

While lifestyle journalism is a term that is increasingly used in scholarship, the underlying phenomenon is invariably studied under different guises, making it difficult to conceptualize. What is referred to here as lifestyle journalism has, for example, also been examined under different umbrella terms such as the aforementioned soft news, service journalism (Eide & Knight, 1999) and infotainment (McNair, 2006) or through its subfields such as travel, fashion, style, health, fitness, wellness, entertainment, leisure, lifestyle, food, music, arts, gardening and living (Hanusch, 2012). Definitional debates are critical for the field, and the chapters in this section approach these issues from a variety of viewpoints. Elfriede Fürsich & Nete Nørgaard Kristensen (Chapter 2) engage with the growing literature on the topic, looking particularly at the commercial, cultural and political impacts that lifestyle journalism has in society. Crucially, their analysis takes issue with the traditional binary that is often drawn between hard and soft news, and they argue for a more continuum-based view in scholarship to better understand the role lifestyle journalism – but also journalism more broadly – plays in society. In a similar vein, John Hartley (Chapter 3) takes a historical approach and through an analysis of British journalism argues that the preference for what he calls 'strategic' news emerged from the context of a time when predominantly men gathered in coffeehouses to discuss business and public affairs. Thus, a certain kind of journalism was privileged at the expense of other forms like 'market' journalism, which in his view explains the relegation of lifestyle to subordinate and gendered consumer status.

Staying with a historical perspective on lifestyle journalism, Sarah Lonsdale (Chapter 4) explores British newspapers' coverage of food during the 1920s and 1930s. Her analysis demonstrates convincingly how the public/private binary cannot easily be upheld when we consider how even during these times, media owners' influence and political ambition played a strong role in affecting how newspapers reported on lifestyle matter. Such accounts, as other chapters in this book also do, demonstrate that even 100 years ago, lifestyle journalism had clear political or public relevance. Moving to the modern day, Annik Dubied (Chapter 5) focuses on two somewhat cognate fields of lifestyle journalism – crime and celebrity news – with the aim of identifying how such forms can contribute to reinvigorate the public sphere. Rather than simply following traditional narratives of such journalistic forms, leading to the dumbing down or downfall of journalism, she turns around the perspective by asking what everyday life forms of journalism can contribute to helping traditional journalism, which is faced with its own range of challenges. Such an analysis is important in the context of how everyday journalism forms that focus on popular, common, person-centered and emotional narratives can help us rethink journalism at large. The final chapter in this section provides a perspective on lifestyle journalism that is still extremely rare in the field. Scholarship has almost exclusive focused on advanced economies in the Global North and parts of Asia, but we still have little understanding of how the issues resonate on the African continent. To this extent, Nhamo Mhiripiri (Chapter 6) provides crucial insights into the standing of the field among African scholars and journalism training institutions, where lifestyle journalism is still largely denigrated. Yet, he points particularly to the critical cultural work by renowned scholar Keyan Tomaselli as a way to spur on more research in this direction.

Lifestyle journalism and consumption

The link between lifestyle journalism and matters of consumption is the one debated perhaps most regularly and arguably the launching pad for most critical assessments of its practice. As was already pointed out earlier, lifestyle journalism is closely tied to consumption, especially given its regular focus on consumer goods, whether they include fashion items, technological gadgets, restaurant meals or tourist experiences. The chapters in this section thus engage closely with various aspects of consumption. Unni From and Carsten Stage (Chapter 7) explore the issue in relation to the genre of book reviews, which straddles boundaries of cultural and lifestyle journalism. Through an analysis of two exemplary literary works and their reviews in Danish legacy media and on Instagram, they demonstrate the ways in which not only are the two genres increasingly blurred but also how they offer ways to understand book reviews' role in cultural consumption. Reviews also regularly play a role in food journalism, and Peter English and David Fleischman's analysis (Chapter 8) of this genre and its commercial imperatives nicely exposes how commercial consideration are a key component here. They provide an incisive commentary on the difficulty of aligning commercial motives with ethical considerations.

The chapter is followed up by Maarit Jakkola's examination of aesthetics (Chapter 9), an aspect that resonates with food journalism but also more broadly with lifestyle journalism at large. As she points out, aesthetics play a key role in how culture is consumed, and it is shaped by social structures of class and taste. Closely related are matters of authenticity and authority, which are crucial considerations when it comes to asserting lifestyle journalism's relevance for audiences and its commercial success as a result. To this end, Joy Jenkins (Chapter 10) explores the role of authenticity when lifestyle journalism aims to provide orientation and a service to its audiences. Her analysis provides us with a highly useful overview across different genres and platforms, in order to better understand the relationship between authenticity and journalistic authority. To round off the section, Nilüfer Türksoy (Chapter 11) explores the case of lifestyle journalism in Turkey, strategically located at the intersection between East and West. Her fascinating account of the commodification of both secular and Islamic lifestyles, which increasingly blur and overlap, creating and negotiating hybrid identities, illuminates also matters of identity, an aspect that nicely transitions into the following section of the book.

Lifestyle journalism, emotion and identity

With the societal changes that have occurred over past decades, journalism at large, but especially lifestyle journalism, has become an important resource for audiences in order to craft their identity. As social origin and background have become less important determinants of people's identity, the media's role in providing orientation and developing a sense of identification has become more relevant (Hanitzsch & Vos, 2018). Similarly, emotion has become an important consideration for journalism studies, so much so that many argue that we are witnessing an emotional turn of the field (Wahl-Jorgensen, 2020). Scholars have noted emotion's centrality in both journalistic practice and consumption, and lifestyle journalism specifically plays a key role in helping people manage their emotional well-being (Hanitzsch & Vos, 2018). The chapters in this section thus provide fascinating insights into the processes through which lifestyle journalism becomes involved in identity work and emotions.

A key concept related to identity work is aspiration, and in engaging with this topic, Sandra Banjac (Chapter 12) provides us with an in-depth overview of how lifestyle journalism can act as a tool for envisioning alternative futures and form aspirations. Her critical account highlights, however, the need to keep in mind social disparities, which can act as barriers to aspiration. These structural inequalities constitute tensions in how lifestyle journalism can be produced, as well as consumed. Similarly, there are differing ways in which lifestyle journalism speaks to emotions, a topic that Johana Kotišová explores (Chapter 13). Through a systematic analysis of 25 key works on lifestyle and cultural journalism, she outlines the ways in which such scholarship has dealt with emotions. Here, she is able to draw parallels with broader work in journalism studies, outlining the value of such research not merely for lifestyle journalism but also scholars in other fields.

Identity is a key theme that also runs through the following chapters. Anuja Premika and Sumana Kasturi (Chapter 14) explore the concept from the perspective of wellness influencing in India, specifically as related to the role of Ayurveda. Theirs is an important account of how post-colonial imperatives, tied in with modern-day political ambitions in the world's largest democracy, shape the construction of wellness culture, with important lessons for lifestyle journalism's role in identity work. Importantly, too, we can see the intersection of identity work, consumption and political considerations, demonstrating the multi-faceted nature of lifestyle media. Identity is also often a concern for scholars who study travel journalism, perhaps one of the more widely examined genres of lifestyle journalism. To this end, Ben Cocking (Chapter 15) gives an overall account of a form that plays a crucial role in cultural mediation, providing images of 'others', and thus of ourselves. Travel journalism has long been found to provide stereotypical cultural discourse and exoticize others, and the case study presented here demonstrates that even in an age of differing commercial models on various online platforms, such problems persist, albeit with important caveats around notions of identity.

Identities are also a topic of my own chapter, but here we shift focus to the journalists themselves and the ways in which we can analyze lifestyle journalists' role perceptions (Chapter 16). The chapter provides an overview of existing work on journalistic roles and outlines four key areas that will require further attention, in relation to how these roles are enacted, more international comparative work, the impact of new actors on the field and the need to go beyond binaries that persist in conceptualizing these roles. The concluding chapter of this section focuses on the sourcing of lifestyle journalism, in particular the role that experts and expertise play. Daniel Nölleke (Chapter 17) surveys the scholarship on experts in journalism in general, arguing that the need for advice has led to a veritable explosion of expertise in lifestyle media. He argues that lifestyle journalism's focus on the ordinary helps contribute to a democratization of knowledge, opening up the field for new forms of experts.

The public utility of lifestyle journalism

As has already been pointed out multiple times, lifestyle journalism has often been denigrated for supposedly dealing with inconsequential topics, and its role has been relegated to having little relevance for political life. But increasingly scholars, including various authors in this book, have pointed to such dichotomies as being unhelpful, with Eide and Knight (1999, p. 536), for example, arguing that they "underestimate both the ways in which consumerism is implicated in citizenship and the extent to which the identity and subjectivity of the consumer are also complex and problematic". The chapters in this section speak to these issues and provide some important insights into the political relevance and public utility of lifestyle journalism.

To begin this section, Bethany Usher (Chapter 18) provides a fascinating historical account of how lifestyle journalism – largely overlooked in histories of journalism – contributes to a better understanding of the development of capitalist democracies. Her analysis of nineteenth-century British journalism convincingly argues that through focusing on lifestyle issues, journalists brought together middle-class audiences around political issues and citizenship. Such themes are also taken up in Elizabeth Fakazis' (Chapter 19) expansive account of food journalism's political relevance. She notes that despite its association with soft news, this field has during its history always engaged with politics, particularly during times of crisis or war. Even today, there are clear connections with political themes such as agricultural sustainability, food justice and in relation to social identities. Such issues are also taken up by Geoffrey Craig (Chapter 20), who focuses specifically on the topic of green lifestyle journalism. At the intersection of consumption and politics, this field engages with individual lifestyles that result from or are in response to public policy, particularly around sustainability.

The binary between the political and the private is also taken up by Gregory Perreault and Ella Hackett (Chapter 21). They aim to turn the debate on its head, by arguing that rather than looking for hard news practices in lifestyle journalism, we can actually also identify many lifestyle practices in hard news. Their exploration of aspects such as social cohesion, advocacy and audience commitment in hard news challenges us to rethink the binary even further. Mariah Wellman, Aly Hill and Avery Holton (Chapter 22) also explore such binary assumptions in their analysis of the boundaries between health, lifestyle and wellness journalism. Their critical overview outlines some of the key tensions between traditional hard news health journalists and wellness influencers in particular. Such issues became particularly important in the context of the COVID-19 pandemic, and the increasingly blurred lines will no doubt be an ongoing concern. Another aspect of the binary often noted in scholarship is the perception that while hard news tries to closely follow ethical guidelines, lifestyle journalism has a more cavalier relationship with journalistic ethics. This is a topic Renita Coleman picks up in her analysis of ethical considerations of lifestyle journalism (Chapter 23). Grounded in philosophical underpinnings of journalistic ethics and surveying the field of existing research, she concludes that while lifestyle journalists often claim they are rarely influenced by commercial pressures, empirical evidence suggests there may still be a long way to go to be able to support such claims.

New horizons in lifestyle journalism studies

The rapid development of new technologies over the past 30 or so years have had a profound impact on the practice and study of journalism worldwide, and the digital transformation of journalism is at the top of the agenda of the vast majority of scholarships today. This is no less the case in the study of lifestyle journalism, where these technological transformations have opened up opportunities for deeper audience engagement and the arrival of a vast range of new actors in the journalistic field. But they have also contributed to substantial challenges such as job losses and higher precarity in journalism. Hence, chapters in this section take stock of not only the various challenges but also opportunities that lifestyle journalism is confronted with today.

The phenomenon of new or different kinds of actors in lifestyle journalism is the focus of Phoebe Maares' contribution, which provides a detailed account of the role that social media influencers play in challenging established lifestyle journalism (Chapter 24). While influencers are often considered a group, Chapter 24 reminds us that it is important to differentiate, and Maares demonstrates ways in which such influencers may not only challenge but also complement lifestyle journalism. The theory of boundary work is particularly important to understand these tensions and is also taken up in Agnès Rocamora's analysis of how the field of fashion journalism engages deeply with a changed environment where bloggers and influencers threaten established fashion journalists (Chapter 25). Using a Bourdieuan field theory perspective, she identifies and studies the differing kinds of actors that have emerged in the field in recent times, including bloggers, TikTokers, fashion brands and technology companies. In keeping with these themes, Stephanie Baker (Chapter 26) focuses on influencers and provides an overview of how these self-help 'gurus', particularly on short video platforms like TikTok and Instagram, impact on identity work. Her work critically examines the blurring of boundaries between influence and expertise and fact and opinion, providing important lessons for the study of lifestyle journalism more broadly.

The digital environment is also the focus of Tisha Dejmanee's analysis of Asian Australian food blogs (Chapter 27), which draws together a range of themes presented in this book. By focusing on these blogs and their activities, she demonstrates how bloggers challenge existing racial stereotypes in mainstream food journalism, providing an alternative of multiculturalism that centers on non-white Australian perspectives. Lifestyle guides who compete with traditional lifestyle journalism are also fast emerging in other areas. Myles Ethan Lascity takes a closer look at brand journalism (Chapter 28), the phenomenon of corporate communication or advertising that masquerades as journalism. While such forms have always existed, the digital environment has increasingly enabled its use by companies and further blurred the lines between journalism and public relations. Lascity points out that the modern affordances of the digital environment mean that the role of brand journalism has evolved more into educating shoppers rather than building brand meaning.

Another important development brought on by the digital age is the ability for journalists to know more about and engage directly with their audiences. Taking this 'audience turn' in the profession and in scholarship as her starting point, Lucia Vodanovic explores the ways in which engaging with commenters can bring about notions of intimacy and community in lifestyle journalism (Chapter 29). These issues are important because despite scholarship increasingly studying audiences, research on lifestyle journalism has so far rarely engaged with these aspects. She also notes important implications for precariously employed lifestyle journalists, a topic that is more closely examined in the final contribution to this section. Here, Rob Sharp explores the role that precarity and financial disruption play in the field, particularly as it is faced with threats from influencers (Chapter 30). There are important consequences that emerge both for the profession and for future research into these issues.

Concluding thoughts

This book aims to be an authoritative overview of the state of the art of lifestyle journalism. Across 30 different chapters, eminent scholars from across the globe have provided fascinating insights into a scholarly field that is quickly growing, but which – due to the relative neglect until recently – still has ample opportunities for growth. As I hope readers will note when reading the various chapters, there exists a plethora of perspectives and lenses through which we can study lifestyle journalism. Its relevance should be clear by now and is increasingly noticed in the field. But at the same time, while the publication of this volume represents somewhat of a seminal moment for the field, there is still a lot of unfinished work. We continue to battle with a range of blindspots, which are partly of a structural nature. This field is still maturing, and despite its growth, its prestige among wider scholarship may not be as high as one might like it to be, limiting the number of scholars who engage with it. This is, of course, to some extent natural, and a growth in emerging researchers will allow them to continue to carve away at persisting perceptions that relegate lifestyle journalism to a lesser form of journalism. Norms – whether in journalism itself or in academia – do not change quickly, but rather extremely slowly.

Another blindspot persists that is somewhat related, and it is an aspect I tried to address as much as possible, but fear I may not have been as successful in as I wished. The field of lifestyle journalism scholarship is still heavily dominated by perspectives from the Global North. In some way, this is a result of the broader Western bias in journalism studies (Wasserman & de Beer, 2009). In other ways, one might argue that lifestyle journalism is more a Western phenomenon, given it is closely tied to growing consumption cultures and individualization processes, which are simply larger or more advanced in the industrialized, wealthy countries of the Global North. But as some evidence has already shown (Banjac & Hanusch, 2022), it is not automatically true that poverty equals less consumption of or interest in lifestyle journalistic content. And the chapters in this book, particularly those by Nhamo Mhiripiri, Nilüfer Türksoy, Tisha Dejmanee as well Anuja Premika and Sumana Kasturi show the enormous benefit a non-Western view can have on the field in various ways. Much like it is crucial to de-westernize the broader field of journalism studies, so is the case in relation to lifestyle journalism. There is so much to gain from exploring and including these contexts, particularly with a view to comparing different forms of lifestyle journalism across different countries. I tried very hard to recruit authors from all over the world, including particularly from the Global South, and also asked all authors to try to be as global in their analyses as possible. But much of the literature and case studies are based on the experience of lifestyle journalism in the Global North, thus limiting how global this volume can be in its outlook. We have still some way to go in achieving this more global understanding of lifestyle journalism, I fear. I am hopeful that this book may contribute to spawning new studies across all parts of the globe and that it can act as a resource for those who do so. Yet, it is one that also needs to be challenged and tested against the experience of other societal, economic, cultural, political and even technological contexts. Lifestyle journalism thus continues to be a field that still offers vast and rich opportunities for research aimed at understanding the role of journalism in society more broadly.

References

Banjac, S., & Hanusch, F. (2022). Aspirational lifestyle journalism: The impact of social class on producers' and audiences' views in the context of socio-economic inequality. *Journalism*, 23(8), 1607–1625.
Bell, D., & Hollows, J. (Eds.) (2005). *Ordinary lifestyles: Popular media, consumption and taste*. Open University Press.
Carlson, M. (2019). *Measurable journalism*. Routledge.
Eide, M., & Knight, G. (1999). Public/private service. Service journalism and the problems of everyday life. *European Journal of Communication*, 14(4), 525–547.
Fakazis, E., & Fürsich, E. (2023). *The political relevance of food media and journalism*. Routledge.
Fanklin, B. (1997). *Newszak and News Media*. Arnold.
Hanitzsch, T., & Vos, T. P. (2018). Journalism beyond democracy: A new look into journalistic roles in political and everyday life. *Journalism*, 19(2), 146–164.
Hanusch, F. (2019). Journalistic roles and everyday life: An empirical account of lifestyle journalists' professional views. *Journalism Studies*, 20(2), 193–211.
Hanusch, F. (2014). The geography of travel journalism: Mapping the flow of travel stories about foreign countries. *International Communication Gazette*, 76(1), 47–66.
Hanusch, F. (2012). Broadening the focus: The case for lifestyle journalism as a field of scholarly inquiry. *Journalism Practice*, 6(1), 2–11.
Hanusch, F., & Fürsich, E. (Eds.) (2014). *Travel journalism: Exploring production, impact and culture*. Springer.
Hanusch, F., Hanitzsch, T., & Lauerer, C. (2017). 'How much love are you going to give this brand?' Lifestyle journalists on commercial influences in their work. *Journalism*, 18(2), 141–158.
Hanusch, F., & Hanitzsch, T. (2013). Mediating orientation and self-expression in the world of consumption: Australian and German lifestyle journalists' professional views. *Media, Culture & Society*, 35(8), 943–959.
Harrington, W. (1997). *Intimate journalism: The art and craft of reporting everyday life*. Routledge.
Hartley, J. (2000). Communicative democracy in a redactional society: The future of journalism studies. *Journalism Studies*, 1(1), 39–48.
Hjarvard, S. (2008). The mediatization of religion: A theory of the media as agents of religious change. *Northern Lights: Film & Media Studies Yearbook*, 6(1), 9–26.
Inglehart, R. (1997). *Modernization and Postmodernization: Cultural, Economic and Political Change in 43 Societies*. Princeton University Press.
McNair, B. (2006). What is journalism? In H. de Burgh (Ed.), *Making journalists: Diverse models, global issues* (pp. 25–43). London: Routledge.
Rocamora, A. (2009). *Fashioning the city: Paris, fashion and the media*. Bloomsbury Publishing.
Turner, B., & Orange, R. (Eds.) (2013). *Specialist journalism*. Routledge.
Vodanovic, L. (Ed.) (2019). *Lifestyle journalism: Social media, consumption and experience*. Routledge.
Wahl-Jorgensen, K. (2020). An emotional turn in journalism studies? *Digital Journalism*, 8(2), 175–194.
Wasserman, H., & de Beer, A. S. (2009). Towards de-westernizing journalism studies. In K. Wahl-Jorgensen & T. Hanitzsch (Eds.), *The handbook of journalism studies* (pp. 448–458). Routledge.
Zelizer, B. (2011). Journalism in the service of communication. *Journal of Communication*, 61(1), 1–21.

2
DEFINING LIFESTYLE JOURNALISM

Cultural dimensions, commercial entanglements, and political relevance

Elfriede Fürsich and Nete Nørgaard Kristensen

Introduction

Defining lifestyle journalism proves challenging due to various dimensions contributing to this type of journalism. The blurred boundaries of what constitutes lifestyle, as well as the evolving transformation of journalistic and media work in the digital era, add layers of complexity. While Merriam Webster traced the first known use of the English term 'lifestyle' back to 1915, Google's Books Ngram Viewer reveals a notable surge in its popularity around 1970, experiencing exponential growth from 1980 to 2013, with a slight decline thereafter. The term 'lifestyle journalism' is even more recent, gaining significant traction since 2011, particularly in the years leading up to 2016. This coincides with lifestyle journalism increasingly gaining scholarly attention in media and journalism studies. Since the 2000s, media scholars have, at book length, engaged with lifestyle *media* and, for example, their historicizing of lifestyle (Bell & Hollows, 2006), their communication of expertise (Lewis, 2008), their role in the formation of the self (Raisborough, 2011), their connection to neoliberalism (Ouellette, 2016), and their broader sociocultural significance (Ryan, 2018). A special issue of *Journalism Practice* (Hanusch, 2012) marked the emergence of lifestyle *journalism* as a distinct subfield within journalism studies. While few academic books have interrogated lifestyle journalism broadly (e.g., Vodanovic, 2019), several scholars have examined subtypes such as travel journalism (e.g., Pirolli, 2019), fashion journalism (e.g., Bradford, 2019), and food journalism (e.g., Fakazis & Fürsich, 2023).

The surge in lifestyle content across media, particularly its remarkable growth over the past three decades, can be attributed to several factors. Technological advancements in media, notably the development of the printing press, enabled newspapers to publish more pages, starting in the 1960s. Publishers sought soft news to fill this expanded content space (see Hanusch, 2013). Increased competition on the print market led to niche marketing opportunities, advantaging lifestyle magazines. Additionally, the proliferation of satellite and cable channels worldwide in the 1990s resulted in a similar expansion in lifestyle programming on television. This increase was often linked to public service journalism mandates or fueled by archives of public broadcasters, exemplified by the success of Discovery International (Fürsich, 2003). The Internet and its inclination toward personal, domestic, and entrepreneurial content provided an ideal platform in the early 21st century for the growth of lifestyle content. All these trends coincided with the rise of consumer societies, initially in the West and progressively across the globe (Ouellette, 2016).

According to Hanusch's definition (2012), lifestyle journalism is "a distinct journalistic field that primarily addresses its audiences as consumers, providing them with factual information and advice, often in entertaining ways, about goods and services they can use in their daily lives" (p. 4). Specific beats are "travel, fashion, style, health, fitness, wellness, entertainment, leisure, lifestyle, food, music, arts, personal technology, gardening and living" (p. 4). Today, the genre extends across multiple forms of media, including magazines, TV, and radio shows, print sections, blogs, and influencer content on visually driven social media platforms like Instagram and TikTok. Content producers can be diverse, ranging from traditional journalists employed by major media corporations to freelancers, native advertising-supported social media producers, and comment uploading users. These content providers may hold full-time or part-time positions, working professionally in regulated roles, but they also include entrepreneurial journalists or amateur producers in more precarious labor positions.

In this chapter, we chart the broader cultural, commercial, and political significance of lifestyle journalism – an ever-expanding type of journalism that is most often criticized for its commercial anchorage. Our focus is professionally produced lifestyle journalism in institutionalized (news) media, but connections to the significantly expanding influencer field on digital platforms are also included. First, we point to the cultural dimensions of lifestyle journalism, which emphasize the broader societal significance of this type of reporting and content production. Second, we outline the commercial entanglements of lifestyle journalism, which have been a key point in professional and academic debates so far, connecting lifestyle journalism mainly to advising and the commercial logics of the media industry and journalism. Third, we highlight the public and political impacts of lifestyle journalism by situating it within a wider framework rooted in cultural dimensions of citizenship and national belonging. On this basis, we end this chapter by plotting the field of lifestyle journalism on a continuum by highlighting the predecessors and contemporaries of lifestyle journalism, such as service journalism and constructive journalism. Our argument posits that lifestyle dimensions have long been integral to journalism in various forms. More recently, journalism as a whole has increasingly adopted a lifestyle-oriented approach, bridging perceptions between public and private and, importantly, acknowledging audiences as both collectives and individuals, encompassing their roles as citizens and consumers. Ultimately, we advocate that journalism studies would benefit from giving up the binary definitions of hard versus soft news and instead see journalism on a continuum between the two with lifestyle journalism as key example.

Cultural dimensions of lifestyle journalism

Lifestyle journalism is often grouped under the soft news umbrella term with adjacent, culturally oriented types of journalism such as arts journalism (e.g., Chong, 2019) and cultural journalism (e.g., Kristensen, 2019), especially those types that engage with aesthetics, popular culture, the cultural industries, and cultural participation and consumption. Kristensen and From (2012) argued that the boundaries of lifestyle journalism and cultural journalism are in fact blurred and do not represent distinct categories. There are theoretical and historical reasons for this lack of clear delineation.

Theoretical context for the cultural dimensions of lifestyle journalism

A theoretical reason for the difficult demarcations between lifestyle journalism and cultural journalism is the diffuse definitions of the terms 'lifestyle' and 'culture'. Even if these polysemantic, complex, and historically contingent concepts may connote different issues depending on the theoretical lenses applied, their meanings overlap. Both concepts are also omnipresent in contemporary societies and everyday talk (Purhonen et al., 2023; Ryan, 2018), where they are often used interchangeably.

The extensive literature on the concept of culture often emphasizes two primary perspectives (e.g., Gans, 1999). A narrower or hierarchical conceptualization views culture in a more limited and exclusive manner, associating it primarily with arts and aesthetics. In this understanding, culture is perceived as a distinct realm, separate from the political sphere and everyday practices (Fornäs, 2017, p. 35). Arts journalism and certain segments of cultural journalism adopt this conceptualization, treating arts and culture as isolated spheres. A broader and more inclusive perspective understands culture "as a whole way of life" (Williams, 1960). Here culture and lifestyle intertwine as culture is perceived as "a particular way of life, whether of a people, a period, a group, or humanity in general" (Williams, 1983, p. 90).

The literature on lifestyle as a concept, informed especially by marketing and psychology, often examines lifestyle in relation to both individual and group consumption, as well as consumer patterns (e.g., Featherstone, 1987). Scholars in cultural sociology and cultural studies, however, also point to close associations of lifestyle to cultural practices, status, and participation. Especially Bourdieu's work on cultural distinction has become a key reference when highlighting the interplay between lifestyle choices and cultural taste. Accordingly, studies on the social stratification of lifestyles assess a wide range of cultural, lifestyle, and consumer-oriented elements. These may include music preferences, sports activities, cooking habits, movie choices, and media consumption (e.g., Flemmen et al., 2018). This debate illustrates that the meanings of 'lifestyle' and 'culture' can be closely intertwined, posing challenges in drawing distinctions in the professional work of journalists.

Research on lifestyle journalism and cultural journalism further exemplifies these blurred conceptual and subject boundaries. Whipple (2023, p. 7), for example, interviewed 66 US 'cultural journalists' with titles ranging from arts writer and food critic to travel editor. Fürsich (2012, p. 13) pointed to subareas of lifestyle journalism "such as travel, food, music or other arts journalism" arguing that this type of journalism is "distinguished by the dimensions of review, advice and consumerism", thereby highlighting aspects that are also commonly used in research to define cultural journalism (e.g., Kristensen, 2019). The cultural dimensions of lifestyle journalism are evident in the evolving relationship between (news) media and journalism with lifestyle, reflecting changes influenced by various cultural shifts over time.

The historical evolution of lifestyle journalism

Niche media dedicated to everyday life and everyday culture have existed since the 17th and 18th century, with women's magazines being a key example (Chambers, 2015). The early phase of consumer society, during the late 19th and early 20th century, saw a gradual democratization of consumption. Evolving from being an elite marker of status to becoming accessible for the developing middle class, this shift led to the emergence of designated lifestyle media and culturally oriented niche media and magazines. Examples of such publications that have survived in a print and/or digital form to this day include *Harper's Bazaar* (1867), *Variety* (1905), and *Esquire* (1933), offering a broad spectrum of stories pertaining to lifestyle, consumption, leisure, culture, and entertainment. The number and diversity of such niche media and magazines only increased from the late 1950s and onward (Weiss, 2020, p. 167) with the intertwined broadening and democratization of culture as a concept, the expansion of the cultural industries and mass consumption, the commercialization of the media industry itself, and the aestheticization of everyday life (Ryan, 2018). Even as lifestyle journalism has long been gendered, targeting first and foremost a female audience, it brought about more specialization and segmentation of the magazine industry in terms of both lifestyle and consumer goods, cultural goods, and audience identity markers such as gender and age (Weiss, 2020).

Since the early 20th century, stories on lifestyle and culture have also been part of the daily news mix and content repertoire of Western print and later digital newspapers as well as the emergent broadcast media, first radio and later television. Lifestyle topics gained increasing precedence and were gradually allocated designated spaces, e.g., in specialized newspaper supplements. In the US context, Nerone and Barnhurst (1995) date this compartmentalization of the newspaper to the 1920s and 1930s, linking it to the rising role of advertising in the news industry. In Europe, such sectioning became more common in newspapers from the 1970s and 1980s onward (Heikkilä et al., 2018; Kristensen & From, 2012), and television produced more lifestyle programming from the 1990s (Brunsdon, 2003). Overall, lifestyle content is tailored to appeal to increasingly specific and diverse audiences. These audiences are characterized by having more leisure time (Lewis, 2008) and exhibit a growing appreciation for a wide range of leisure and cultural forms (Peterson & Kern, 1996). These developments reflect not only changes in lifestyles, cultural participation, and everyday culture but also its commercialization within institutional media logics. With reference to Hartley's work on popular journalism, From (2018) argued that the development of lifestyle journalism can be understood as part of the development of modern journalism, i.e., as offering audiences – in their capacity of citizens, cultural consumers, and media users – ways to make sense of the world, not only politically but also culturally and in their everyday lives. Accordingly, topics on lifestyle and culture continue to remain significant and coexist in various media forms, most recently on digital platforms.

Impact on societal norms and values

Journalistic engagement with lifestyle and culture has played a key role in legitimating both lifestyle practices and cultural expressions in society broadly and in the everyday lives of individual consumers and citizens specifically. The literature on women's magazines, for example, has shown how such magazines have presented historically contingent – and increasingly commercialized – views of the role of women in society, their identities, and status (Chambers, 2015). Bourdieu (2002/1979) coined the term 'cultural intermediaries' to designate journalists as one professional group among others (such as PR and marketing) that serve as arbiters of good taste by negotiating and legitimizing cultural values and lifestyles. Since then, numerous studies have demonstrated how media content and journalism ascribe cultural value by representing, reproducing, legitimizing, and contesting (certain) cultural artifacts and trends (e.g., Purhonen et al., 2019). Similarly, lifestyle media and lifestyle journalism present particular – aestheticized and stylized – versions of ways of life that can potentially shape audiences' expectations of everyday living. Similarly, Hanusch and Hanitzsch (2013, p. 947) argue that lifestyle journalism engages with "expressive values and practices that help create and signify a specific identity within the realm of consumption and everyday life".

Niche and mainstream media have for more than a century educated and informed publics as well as entertained audiences about consumer lifestyles and culture. The aestheticization of everyday life, or the increasing significance of the aesthetic representation and perception of everyday activities (Southerton, 2011), especially since the 1980s and 1990s, has further been amplified in digital media as culture, lifestyles, and consumption are increasingly mediated and mediatized. Some warn of a cultural turn toward lifestyle in the media (especially on television) during the past three decades at the expense of other cultural forms (Ryan, 2018). The boom in lifestyle content produced by digital creators and influencers has intensified the conceptual and practical ambiguity of lifestyle, culture, and aesthetics in the mediated and journalistic realm.

Commercial entanglements of lifestyle journalism

The blurred line between editorial and commercial interests and transparency

The intertwined relationship between lifestyle journalism and commercial influences has been a subject of significant criticism within the profession. A typical example is travel journalism, particularly its reliance on complimentary trips and giveaways, which has been extensively discussed by practitioners themselves since the inception of travel sections in newspapers during the 1970s. Critics highlight the materialistic inclination of journalists in this field, the overly optimistic tone, and the blurring of lines between editorial and advertorial content (e.g., Eliot, 1994). Addressing these professional shortcomings, critics often advocate ethical or regulatory disclosure of financial arrangements, authenticity, or a shift toward traditional news practices, including objectivity and a rational and critical perspective.

Ethical dilemmas in lifestyle journalism have often led to calls for direct or indirect regulation and transparency. Journalists are encouraged to disclose conflicts of interest while maintaining editorial integrity. Existing regulatory frameworks and industry standards typically take the form of ethics statements from professional organizations. However, enforcement is challenging, relying on media companies or individual journalists. The rise of online lifestyle influencers has complicated these efforts further.

More binding regulations in some countries address advertising content distinctions in print and broadcast media. In the United States, for example, the Federal Trade Commission (FTC) mandates influencers to disclose any material in connection with a brand (e.g., Carpenter & Bonin, 2021). Similar guidelines exist in the United Kingdom and Canada. Within the European Union, consumer protection laws focus on a clear separation of advertising and editorial content and financial transparency in legacy media and extend this logic to online influencers, ensuring they reveal commercial affiliations with brands. Enforcement of disclosure rules and transparency regulations poses challenges, however. For traditional media, the effectiveness of the regulations in mitigating commercial pressures and maintaining journalistic integrity is undermined by the current decline in profits in the traditional media industries, making them even more responsive to direct or covert sponsorship, brandvertising, or other forms of commercial–editorial interconnections.

Enforcing rules and regulations in the influencer marketing landscape also presents challenges. The global reach of social media, key platforms in the influencer ecosystem, contributes to the complexity of coordination and enforcement efforts across jurisdictions. While some platforms have their own policies, e.g., Instagram requiring the use of the 'Paid Partnership' tag for sponsored content, the dynamic and evolving features of social media platforms complicate the task as regulators struggle to keep pace with emerging trends and technologies.

Beyond undisclosed arrangements, the field of lifestyle journalism has always accepted collaborations and partnerships with commercial entities. Corporate public relations have long utilized these collaborations to imitate journalistic discourse in paid content to increase the credibility and probably also to make audiences believe that the content is news (e.g., Wojdynski, 2019). It is exactly this type of content creation, however, that has led to the charge of inauthentic content. Moreover, it is difficult for lifestyle creators to maintain independence while working directly with external partners.

An often-voiced recommendation for lifestyle journalism to following more accurately the standards of objective journalism as a cure for commercial influence is limited as well. First, online lifestyle influencers have all but given up on any distinction between editorial content and advertising. Followers do not seem to be bothered by the overt pitching of products and native advertising (e.g., Kolo & Haumer, 2018). Audience engagement in lifestyle journalism online is of a new quality – a symbiotic relationship between content producers, brands, and consumers. On social media platforms, influencers and user-generated content shape the editorial direction and commercial interests of lifestyle journalism anew. Second, traditional objective news journalism also faces increased commodification in product placement, direct marketing, and promotional efforts by the public relations and marketing industry (e.g., Hardy, 2021). Financial struggles and technological advancements contribute to this predicament. Identifying instances of non-compliance and ensuring responsible and transparent practices require addressing these complex dynamics within lifestyle journalism and news journalism alike.

Lifestyle journalism, the new economy, and neoliberalism

Beyond lamenting the direct commercial influence over lifestyle content, researchers also analyze its connection to the current overall sociopolitical landscape shaped by a 'new' economy and neoliberal globalization. Societal norms are evolving, with traditional distinctions between private, public, and commercial spheres becoming increasingly blurred in this era of 'liquid modernity' (Bauman, 2000). This development inspired Deuze (2007) to interrogate the current interconnectedness of consumer culture and civic engagement, suggesting a need for a 'liquid journalism' that embraces human agency and user participation in the face of this changing socioeconomic situation.

This transformation also impacts the producers of lifestyle journalism, often part of the 'flexible' workforce characteristic of the new economy. These professionals, working as interns, part-timers, or freelancers without job security or benefits, face challenges in a field where traditional institutions are giving way to online platforms. The rise of 'content mills' further complicates matters, utilizing crowdsourcing, repurposing of free online content, and underpaid freelancers to generate content. Such precarious work situations are becoming increasingly common in the media and cultural industries (e.g., Hesmondhalgh & Baker, 2011). Adding to these challenges is the advent of Artificial Intelligence (AI), posing a further threat to the authenticity of lifestyle content. The success of AI, especially in generating generic and non-authentic lifestyle content and imagery, raises concerns about the replicability and originality of journalistic work.

To draw an even wider circle of ideological impact, the success of lifestyle content has been linked to the rise of the economic ideology of neoliberalism. Ouellette (2016), echoing others, links the success of lifestyle media to a problematic neoliberal ideology that weakens the state, public institutions, and the common good. This ideology emphasizes private institutions, individual choice, and self-empowerment in citizenship. Ouellette's work on governmentality and lifestyle television illustrated how this genre perfectly fits the requirement of this ideology as it transforms citizens into self-entrepreneurs responsible for their own welfare, particularly in an era of underfunded, privatized, or abandoned collective systems and the public good. Lewis (2008) similarly emphasized the individualistic and consumption-oriented nature of lifestyle, where traditional identity constraints are replaced by a focus on endless choice and transformation. She questions whether the shift of public concerns to private, domestic consumption signifies a more intricate redefinition of civic life or the demise of a common public culture.

In this complex scenario, the situation of lifestyle journalists within this evolving precarious workforce and the text genre as a whole can serve as a lens through which the complexities of cultural production in a society characterized by uncertainty, risk, and shifting norms can be examined.

Political and public dimensions of lifestyle journalism

While the connection of lifestyle to the economic and cultural *Zeitgeist* seems understandable, the political dimension of lifestyle journalism is another important aspect of the genre that needs explanation. The genre that traditionalists would not even call 'journalism' because of its lack of objectivity seems incompatible with political and civic public functions. Schudson (2008), for example, was somewhat torn between these poles as he observed that there is a fine line between journalism that instills authentic social empathy necessary for democracy and narcissistic and frivolous consumer journalism covering "fluffy topics of a self-absorbed society and can be a distraction from public life rather than an expansion of it. Still, all of these topics are potentially doors into public life" (Schudson, 2008, p. 20).

However, directly connecting lifestyle content to the political and civil sphere can be grounded in the work of scholars who have emphasized the cultural dimension of civic belonging. The concept of cultural citizenship has been used by communication scholars (e.g., Klaus & Lünenborg, 2004) to explain that national belonging is not only connected to civic duties such as voting or paying taxes but also to aspects of culture such as media representation and participation. Similarly, pioneering work especially by Hartley (1996) and Zelizer (1993) repositioned journalism studies and foregrounded the interpretive, semiotic, and discursive dimensions of news journalism. Acknowledging a significant transformation in the dynamic between audiences, the public sphere, and media, as well as citizenship in recent decades, McKay (1998) and Hartley (1999) took this a step further by detailing how individuals foster a sense of civic belonging. Utilizing the concept of DIY culture and journalism, they explained how audiences tap into a diverse range of media content and popular culture to mobilize the popular for political action. Acknowledging that people use a wide variety of media content to engage in civic issues provides the basis for scholars to interrogate the public and political relevance of the seemingly trivial and innocuous content produced by lifestyle journalism. Fürsich (2012) used the work of Fiske and Costera Meijer to create a framework for evaluating these aspects and developed a list of criteria that can be used in these types of analyses.

Theoretical foundation of the public and political dimensions of lifestyle journalism

Fiske (1989) was among the early scholars to explore the notion of the popular in the context of news and journalism, particularly advocating for popular news. While his observations primarily addressed television news, they can be extrapolated to other journalistic forms such as lifestyle journalism. Fiske criticized the flawed dichotomy that assigned education and social responsibility to traditional news, leaving emotionality and pleasure for trivial popular taste. He contended that traditional TV news failed to meaningfully engage the audience due to the construction of semiotically closed texts. To address these issues, Fiske proposed the strategies of 'productivity' and 'relevance' as alternatives to traditional news routines. He argued that a productive news program should exhibit "a high level of formal openness" and an "internal interrogatory" form, fostering heightened interest and discussion, similar to quiz shows or sports programs. Relevance, according to Fiske, could be achieved by selecting and narrating topics in alignment with the audience's experiences. By integrating production strategies from popular television formats, he envisioned a type of popular news that would undermine social hierarchies, provoke discussion, and make journalism matter (Fiske, 1989, p. 190).

Taking the exploration beyond the traditional versus popular journalism dichotomy, Costera Meijer (2001) challenged the binary concept of quality versus popular journalism. She proposed a third category termed 'public quality' to help analyze if ostensibly trivial media content (e.g., talk shows on commercial channels) contributes constructively to a democratic public sphere. Costera Meijer's 'public quality' introduces a normative category, allowing scholars to assess journalism beyond its objective role as a textual representation of issues of public concern. It also reconnects analysis of popular media formats to a public and democratic notion of the public sphere. Costera Meijer emphasized that for media content to have a public quality, it needs to acknowledge people's immediate world, including family, friendships, neighborhood, town, or country, which traditional journalism often overlooks. Public-oriented journalism, as she argued, treats people as active citizens valuing information that can be used for both personal and social life (Costera Meijer, 2001, p. 194).

By extending Fiske's and Meijer's concepts to lifestyle journalism, researchers can evaluate the extent to which specific examples of this journalism meet the requirements of being productive, relevant, and of public quality. The crucial question is to identify the concepts of public or political life established and positively sanctioned in the coverage and which aspects, topics, and groups are left behind. Investigating lifestyle journalism as a profession and unique popular discourse can challenge binary distinctions and outdated concepts, providing insights into contemporary social, political, and economic changes. By abandoning the dichotomy between news journalism and popular journalism in favor of a more integral concept of 'public quality', research on lifestyle journalism can contribute to developing complex models of how public concerns are addressed and negotiated in the media more effectively. This approach views lifestyle journalism as both a symptom and symbol of the evolving public sphere in times of liquid modernity.

Lifestyle media's role in addressing issues of public concern

Researchers examining lifestyle journalism, encompassing genres like food, music, and travel reporting, have confirmed its dual role in both facilitating and hindering the navigation of ongoing global, political, and environmental transformations. An exploration of travel journalism, for instance, revealed a tendency for travel shows to grapple with a problematic approach, as they are caught in the pursuit of diversity and difference while simultaneously exoticizing other cultures (Fürsich, 2003). In another study on world music, reviewers, hesitant to relinquish static, national notions of culture, eventually acknowledged global culture as a dynamic, hybrid, and transnational phenomenon (Fürsich & Avant-Mier, 2013). Critical food journalism, addressing issues related to foodways, supply chains, and nutritional disparities, originally found its platform in social media outlets with precarious financial stability. Over time, this type of coverage has spilled over to traditional food media and led to a markedly different coverage of concerns in the food industry such as the environment, labor, identity politics, and unfettered consumerism (Fakazis & Fürsich, 2023). Craig (2019) evaluated the inclusion of sustainability issues in lifestyle media, elucidating that media emphasizing green lifestyles often depict sustainability primarily in commercial contexts and consumption processes. He argued that this is not inherently problematic as cultivating a sustainable daily life necessitates active engagement with material culture. Individuals passionate about environmental concerns leverage various media channels, particularly social media, to construct a sustainable identity. Green lifestyle media trace the everyday networks of sustainability, spanning from domestic and local levels to broader societal contexts.

Overall, despite some qualifications, many examples within lifestyle journalism suggest a shift in professional journalistic processes, as manifested in the gradual breakdown of traditional dichotomies between hard and soft news and the incorporation of more dynamic and hybrid concepts concerning cultural exchange, diversity, international relations, and climate change. During its 'public' moments, such lifestyle journalism constructs a pertinent and constructive discourse on important political concerns, disrupting polarized, limited, or stereotypical representations in traditional news journalism. Its close connection to the audience's lives, commitment to following trends, and the blurring of traditional news and entertainment boundaries position lifestyle journalism as a valuable space for active cultural negotiation.

Characterizing lifestyle journalism as popular journalism with public value should not lead researchers to presume an inherent democratic and anti-hierarchical potential across all types of lifestyle coverage. Examining the lived experiences and attitudes of audiences becomes crucial as a counterbalance to overly optimistic portrayals. Nonetheless, a growing body of research underscores the corrective role that lifestyle journalism can play for journalists and audiences facing compassion fatigue, polarization, and political alienation from traditional news sources, at least in Western countries (e.g., Banjac & Hanusch, 2023; Fakazis & Fürsich, 2023).

The concepts of relevance, productivity, and public quality provide avenues for a critical assessment of lifestyle journalism's democratic role amid contemporary social changes. The analysis of lifestyle journalism inevitably straddles the line between celebrating its democratic potential as a popular media text and denouncing it as an overly commercialized format. Nevertheless, lifestyle journalism has become so integral to media output that scholars would be remiss not to investigate its political relevance.

Lifestyle journalism on a historical continuum

Some research on lifestyle journalism has pointed to its associations with other types of journalism that approach the social world in different ways than traditional news journalism, such as service journalism and constructive journalism (e.g., Elgesem et al., 2024; From & Kristensen, 2019). A common denominator is the ways in which these types of journalism address audiences as both individuals, by proving guidance, service, and empowerment, and as citizens, by coupling everyday problem-solving to broader political and economic structures and issues of public relevance. Another commonality is that service journalism and constructive journalism – like lifestyle journalism – can be seen as a response to transformations in contemporary societies and the role of the news industry in this context. From and Kristensen (2018) argued that service journalism could be "seen as a response to other societal institutions' loss of authority with journalism taking on new expert and advisory roles to help citizen–consumer clients", whereas constructive journalism "is an addition to journalism in a digitalized society, where the authority and gatekeeping role of professional journalism is highly contested" (p. 724). In similar ways, the success of lifestyle journalism across time and media, as outlined in the previous sections, is not only a result of the development of consumer society and the commercialization of the news industry but also a sign of their politicized dimensions urging journalism to pursue new paths to engage, inform, and support audiences.

Service journalism as a precursor to contemporary lifestyle reporting

Service journalism is not a new phenomenon, but Eide and Knight (1999) argued that it expanded in the 1980s and 1990s along the increasing trend of 'news you can use'. According to them, this type of journalism emerged in the second half of the 20th century to support audiences in coping with grievances and risks in an increasingly complex society and, by extension, in their everyday lives. They linked service journalism to both tabloid journalism, pointing at how tabloid journalists address audiences in their ordinariness, and to public service media, emphasizing how commercialization toward the end of the 20th century entailed a shift in public service media from a paternalistic, educational approach to publicly addressing the concerns of everyday life (Eide & Knight, 1999, p. 529). Service journalism primarily connects with audiences' lifeworlds rather than broader systemic structures, providing private rather than public service. Their main contention is that audiences are viewed as a hybrid social unit, not strictly as collectives or individuals, citizens, or consumers. They are perceived as "part citizen, part consumer, part client", and the reporting focuses on addressing everyday problems through a combination of individualistic and collective, political responses (Eide & Knight, 1999, p. 527). Since the concept of service journalism was coined in the late 1990s in the scholarly literature, journalism scholars have increasingly engaged with studies of lifestyle journalism and everyday life and linked these to issues of consumption, identity, and emotion (Hanitzsch & Vos, 2018), but often also to their elements of service to audiences in coping with everyday life.

Constructive journalism and its connections to lifestyle reporting strategies

In contemporary journalism studies and practice, there is a continual acknowledgment of the role of journalism in offering positive problem-solving approaches, often referred to as 'constructive journalism'. McIntyre and Gyldensted (2018, p. 20) described constructive journalism as applying "positive psychology techniques to news processes and production in an effort to create productive and engaging coverage while holding true to journalism's core functions". Bro (2024) saw constructive journalism as a

> Call on journalists, editors, and others in the news media to present problems as well as potentials … to reflect the world more accurately. For some constructive journalists presenting potentials is an end in itself, for others this is simply the means to another end, namely, to help society solve its problem.
>
> *(2024, p. 87)*

The constructive journalism movement is driven by the belief that it can counteract the negativity and conflict biases prevalent in news reporting, thereby addressing the rise in news avoidance among citizens (Overgaard, 2023). However, constructive journalism, rooted more in practical application than research, faces a challenge due to the absence of a clear definition (Ahva & Hautakangas, 2018). A related problem is defining *what type of problems* to cover and, by extension, solve (Bro, 2024, p. 68). Some argue that in contrast to service journalism, constructive journalism engages with systemic issues and problems in the public sphere, otherwise covered by hard news rather than issues related to the domain of everyday life or the private sphere (e.g., From & Kristensen, 2019; Bro, 2024). Scholars and practitioners engaging in constructive journalism emphasize a fundamental goal: contributing to democracy. Accordingly, constructive journalism is not understood as different from traditional journalism but as a supplementary approach (Bro, 2024). Emphasizing the significance of constructive journalism for democracy serves as a legitimization strategy among practitioners and scholars. This approach helps deflect criticism for the positive orientation and advocacy for problem-solving that is characteristic of constructive journalism while establishing a separation from issues directly connected to everyday life, often found in service journalism and lifestyle journalism.

This self-understanding in constructive journalism implies that soft news, such as lifestyle journalism and service journalism, does not contribute to democracy – an assumption that this chapter challenges, as exemplified by the political dimensions of lifestyle journalism as a genre. Recent research demonstrates the diminishing validity of this previously established dichotomy between constructive journalism, typically associated with public or hard news, and service and lifestyle journalism, traditionally centered around private or soft news. Using the climate issue as a case, Bro (2024) illustrated that what is acceptable to report on in constructive journalism has changed over time. Based on From and Kristensen's (2019) broader argument about constructive journalism's commonalities with both lifestyle journalism and service journalism, Elgesem, Knudsen, and Fløttum (2024) similarly used the issue of climate change to elucidate the conceptual connection between lifestyle journalism and constructive journalism. Their survey data from Norwegian journalists and editors indicated substantial support among these practitioners for adopting a constructive approach in the coverage of climate and lifestyles.

Our objective of delineating the evolution of lifestyle journalism in relation to late 20th-century service journalism and early 21st-century constructive journalism is to underscore that these journalistic forms constitute a spectrum rather than stark opposites. They all encompass lifeworld and systemic aspects – addressing both every day and political dimensions. This line of argumentation ultimately contests the dichotomy that dictates reporting on such issues strictly as either hard or soft news.

Conclusion and future directions

This chapter explored the expansive cultural, commercial, and political implications of lifestyle journalism. We argued that it is important not to overlook the relevance of this ever-expanding genre and to disparage it for its commercial moorings and presumably trivial content. Instead, we first illuminated the cultural facets of lifestyle journalism, underscoring its broader sociocultural impact extending beyond mere commercial dimensions. The goal was to highlight the distinctions, but especially the commonalities to and blurred boundaries with traditional arts and cultural journalism. Understanding the overlapping genre characteristics is a sign of an increasing acceptance that culture happens in edified areas as well mundane processes. Despite this recognition, lifestyle journalism is frequently ignored as a force that could contribute to a broader public discourse due to its commercial underpinnings. For that reason, we delineated the intricate commercial associations of lifestyle journalism, emphasizing issues of ethics and transparency as essential concerns in professional and academic debates. By linking lifestyle journalism to current advertising practices and the commercial rationale of the media industry, we emphasized that concerns about authenticity and integrity are now pertinent across all kinds of media production due to increasing commercialization and algorithm-driven hyper-marketing in the digitalized media era. Moving beyond the criticism of lifestyle journalism as shallow, we underscored its direct public and political reverberations and contextualized the genre with a broader framework rooted in popular and public qualities related to the cultural dimensions of citizenship and national identity.

Building on these lines of argumentation, we conclude this chapter by mapping the landscape of lifestyle journalism alongside its predecessors and contemporary counterparts, especially service journalism and constructive journalism. Our assertion was that lifestyle dimensions have been ingrained in journalism across diverse forms throughout history. The ongoing decline in reach and returns for traditional journalism have prompted a growing inclination for the whole field of journalism toward adopting a lifestyle- and every day-oriented perspective. This has involved a deliberate blending of the distinctions between public and private domains, recognizing audiences as both groups and individuals with dual roles as citizens and consumers. The importance of lifestyle journalism lies in this nuanced approach and its willingness to take audiences' everyday lives as a starting point. We ultimately advocate a flexible continuum approach in journalism studies, moving away from rigid categorizations such as hard versus soft news. Within this framework, well-executed lifestyle journalism can serve as a notable model for other forms of journalism, showcasing effective strategies in their continuous efforts to remain pertinent and engaging to audiences in their multiple capacities.

Future scholarship in lifestyle journalism should focus on key areas that demand urgent attention. These include investigating the role, potential, and constraints of lifestyle journalism in debates surrounding sustainability and the climate crisis, as well as activism and (in)equality. Moreover, culture wars often connect to lifestyle journalism as they revolve around the politicized and divisive aspects of everyday life, culture, and consumption patterns. Lifestyle journalism is constantly navigating inherent paradoxes, particularly when portraying both individual and collective lifestyles, while also promoting potential shifts toward more sustainable and inclusive ways of living. However, these efforts can sometimes conflict with the individualistic and promotional nature of the culture that lifestyle journalism itself promotes. Additionally, there is a crucial need for genuine, systematic, and large-scale comparative research on lifestyle journalism. Such research should extend beyond Western contexts to encompass a global perspective. By doing so, we can better understand the potentials and limitations of this form of journalism, which has expanded significantly over the past century and continues to evolve within the digital media landscape of the 21st century.

Further reading

Fakazis, E., & Fürsich, E. (Eds.) (2023). *The political relevance of food media and journalism: Beyond reviews and recipes*. Routledge. https://doi.org/10.4324/9781003283942

Fürsich, E. (2012). Lifestyle journalism as popular journalism: Strategies for evaluating its public role. *Journalism Practice*, 6(1), 12–25. https://doi.org/10.1080/17512786.2011.622894

Hanusch, F. (Ed.) (2013). *Lifestyle journalism*. Routledge.

Kristensen, N. N., & From, U. (2012). Lifestyle journalism. *Journalism Practice*, 6(1), 26–41. https://doi.org/10.1080/17512786.2011.622898

Vodanovic, L. (Ed.) (2019). *Lifestyle journalism: Social media, consumption and experience* (1st ed.). Routledge.

References

Ahva, L., & Hautakangas, M. (2018). Why do we suddenly talk so much about constructiveness? *Journalism Practice*, 12(6), 657–661. https://doi.org/10.1080/17512786.2018.1470474

Banjac, S., & Hanusch, F. (2023). The struggle for authority and legitimacy: Lifestyle and political journalists' discursive boundary work. *Journalism*, 24(10), 2155–2173. https://doi.org/10.1177/14648849221125702

Bauman, Z. (2000). *Liquid modernity*. Polity Press.

Bell, D., & Hollows, J. (Eds.) (2006). *Historicizing lifestyle. Mediating taste, consumption, and identity from the 1900s to 1970s*. Routledge.

Bourdieu, P. (2002, org. 1979). *Distinction: A social critique of the judgement of taste* (11. print). Harvard University Press.

Bradford, J. (2019). *Fashion journalism* (2nd ed.). Routledge. https://doi.org/10.4324/9781351174626

Bro, P. (2024). *Constructive journalism: Precedents, principles, and practices* (Vol. 2024). Routledge. https://www.routledge.com/Constructive-Journalism-Precedents-Principles-and-Practices/Bro/p/book/9781032516097

Brunsdon, C. (2003). Lifestyling Britain: The 8–9 slot on British television. *International Journal of Cultural Studies*, 6(1), 5–23. https://doi.org/10.1177/1367877903006001001

Carpenter, C. C., & Bonin, M. II. (2021). To win friends and influence people: Regulations and enforcement of influencer marketing after ten years of the endorsement guides. *Vanderbilt Journal of Entertainment & Technology Law*, 23(3), 253–278. https://scholarship.law.vanderbilt.edu/jetlaw/vol23/iss2/1

Chambers, D. (2015). Contexts and developments in women's magazines. In M. Conboy & J. Steel (Eds.), *The Routledge companion to British media history* (pp. 285–296). Routledge.

Chong, P. (2019). Valuing subjectivity in journalism: Bias, emotions, and self-interest as tools in arts reporting. *Journalism*, 20(3), 427–443. https://doi.org/10.1177/1464884917722453

Costera Meijer, I. (2001). The public quality of popular journalism: Developing a normative framework. *Journalism Studies*, 2(2), 189–205. https://doi.org/10.1080/14616700120042079

Craig, G. (2019). *Media, sustainability and everyday life*. Palgrave Macmillan UK. https://doi.org/10.1057/978-1-137-53469-9

Deuze, M. (2007). *Media work*. Polity.

Eide, M., & Knight, G. (1999). Public/private service: Service journalism and the problems of everyday life. *European Journal of Communication*, 14(4), 525–547. https://doi.org/10.1177/0267323199014004004

Elgesem, D., Knudsen, E., & Fløttum, K. (2024). The impact of climate change on lifestyle journalism. *Journalism Studies*, 25(4), 337–357. https://doi.org/10.1080/1461670X.2023.2299463

Eliot, A. (1994). A cure for skepticism about travel journalism. *Editor & Publisher*, 127(46), 56.

Fakazis, E., & Fürsich, E. (Eds.) (2023). *The political relevance of food media and journalism: Beyond reviews and recipes*. Routledge. https://doi.org/10.4324/9781003283942

Featherstone, M. (1987). Lifestyle and consumer culture. *Theory, Culture & Society*, 4(1), 55–70. https://doi.org/10.1177/026327687004001003

Fiske, J. (1989). *Reading the popular*. Unwin Hyman.

Flemmen, M., Jarness, V., & Rosenlund, L. (2018). Social space and cultural class divisions: The forms of capital and contemporary lifestyle differentiation. *The British Journal of Sociology*, 69(1), 124–153. https://doi.org/10.1111/1468-4446.12295

Fornäs, J. (2017). *Defending culture*. Springer International Publishing. https://doi.org/10.1007/978-3-319-57810-1

From, U. (2018). Lifestyle journalism. In *Oxford research encyclopedia of communication*. https://doi.org/10.1093/acrefore/9780190228613.013.835

From, U., & Kristensen, N. N. (2018). Rethinking Constructive Journalism by Means of Service Journalism. *Journalism Practice*, 12(6), 714–729. https://doi.org/10.1080/17512786.2018.1470475

From, U., & Kristensen, N. N. (2019). Unpacking lifestyle journalism via service journalism and constructive journalism. In L. Vodanovic (Ed.), *Lifestyle journalism* (1st ed., pp. 13–25). Routledge. https://doi.org/10.4324/9781351123389

Fürsich, E. (2012). Lifestyle journalism as popular journalism: Strategies for evaluating its public role. *Journalism Practice*, 6(1), 12–25. https://doi.org/10.1080/17512786.2011.622894

Fürsich, E. (2003). Between credibility and commodification: Nonfiction entertainment as a global media genre. *International Journal of Cultural Studies*, 6(2), 131–153. https://doi.org/10.1177/13678779030062001

Fürsich, E., & Avant-Mier, R. (2013). Popular journalism and cultural change: The discourse of globalization in world music reviews. *International Journal of Cultural Studies*, 16(2), 101–118. https://doi.org/10.1177/1367877912452481

Gans, H. J. (1999). *Popular culture and high culture: An analysis and evaluation of taste* (2nd ed.). Basic Books.

Hanitzsch, T., & Vos, T. P. (2018). Journalism beyond democracy: A new look into journalistic roles in political and everyday life. *Journalism*, 19(2), 146–164. https://doi.org/10.1177/1464884916673386

Hanusch, F. (Ed.) (2013). *Lifestyle journalism*. Routledge.

Hanusch, F. (2012). Broadening the focus. *Journalism Practice*, 6(1), 2–11. https://doi.org/10.1080/17512786.2011.622895

Hanusch, F., & Hanitzsch, T. (2013). Mediating orientation and self-expression in the world of consumption: Australian and German lifestyle journalists' professional views. *Media, Culture & Society*, 35(8), 943–959. https://doi.org/10.1177/0163443713501931

Hardy, J. (2021). Sponsored editorial content in digital journalism: Mapping the merging of media and marketing, *Digital Journalism*, 9(7), 865–886. https://doi.org/10.1080/21670811.2021.1957970

Hartley, J. (1999). *Uses of television*. Routledge.

Hartley, J. (1996). *Popular reality: Journalism, modernity, popular culture*. Arnold.

Heikkilä, R., Lauronen, T., & Purhonen, S. (2018). The crisis of cultural journalism revisited: The space and place of culture in quality European newspapers from 1960 to 2010. *European Journal of Cultural Studies*, 21(6), 669–686. https://doi.org/10.1177/1367549416682970

Hesmondhalgh, D. (2011). *Creative labour: Media work in three cultural industries*. Routledge.

Klaus, E., & Lünenborg, M. (2004). Cultural citizenship. Ein kommunikationswissenschaftliches Konzept zur Bestimmung kultureller Teilhabe in der Mediengesellschaft. *M&K - Medien und Kommunikationswissenschaft*, 52(2), 193–213.

Kolo, C., & Haumer, F. (2018). Social media celebrities as influencers in brand communication: An empirical study on influencer content, its advertising relevance and audience expectations. *Journal of Digital & Social Media Marketing*, 6(3), 273–282.

Kristensen, N. N. (2019). Cultural journalism—Journalism about culture. *Sociology Compass*, 13(6), e12701. https://doi.org/10.1111/soc4.12701

Kristensen, N. N., & From, U. (2012). Lifestyle journalism. *Journalism Practice*, 6(1), 26–41. https://doi.org/10.1080/17512786.2011.622898

Lewis, T. (2008). *Smart living: Lifestyle media and popular expertise*. Peter Lang.

McIntyre, K., & Gyldensted, C. (2018). Constructive journalism: An introduction and practical guide for applying positive psychology techniques to news production. *The Journal of Media Innovations*, 4(2), Article 2. https://doi.org/10.5617/jomi.v4i2.2403

McKay, G. (1998). *DiY culture: Party & protest in Nineties Britain*. Verso.

Nerone, J., & Barnhurst, K. G. (1995). Visual mapping and cultural authority: Design changes in U.S. newspapers, 1920–1940. *Journal of Communication*, 45(2), 9–43. https://doi.org/10.1111/j.1460-2466.1995.tb00726.x

Ouellette, L. (2016). *Lifestyle TV*. Routledge.

Overgaard, C. S. B. (2023). Mitigating the consequences of negative news: How constructive journalism enhances self-efficacy and news credibility. *Journalism*, 24(7), 1424–1441. https://doi.org/10.1177/14648849211062738

Peterson, R. A., & Kern, R. M. (1996). Changing highbrow taste: From snob to omnivore. *American Sociological Review*, 61(5), 900–907. https://doi.org/10.2307/2096460

Pirolli, B. (2019). *Travel journalism: Informing tourists in the digital age*. Routledge.

Purhonen, S., Lauronen, T., & Heikkilä, R. (2019). Between legitimization and popularization: The rise and reception of U.S. cultural products in culture sections of quality European newspapers, 1960–2010. *American Journal of Cultural Sociology*, 7(3), 382–411. https://doi.org/10.1057/s41290-018-0064-z

Purhonen, S., Verboord, M., Sirkka, O., Kristensen, N. N., & Janssen, S. (2023). Definitely (not) belonging to culture: Europeans' evaluations of the contents and limits of culture. *Poetics*, 101, 101840. https://doi.org/10.1016/j.poetic.2023.101840

Raisborough, J. (2011). *Lifestyle media and the formation of the self*. Palgrave Macmillan UK. https://doi.org/10.1057/9780230297555

Ryan, M. E. (2018). *Lifestyle media in American culture: Gender, class, and the politics of ordinariness*. Routledge. https://doi.org/10.4324/9781315464978

Schudson, M. (2008). *Why democracies need an unlovable press*. Polity.

Southerton, D. (2011). Aestheticization of everyday life. In D. Southeron (Ed.), *Encyclopedia of consumer culture* (1–3, pp. 16–19). Sage. https://doi.org/10.4135/9781412994248

Vodanovic, L. (Ed.) (2019). *Lifestyle journalism: Social media, consumption and experience* (1st ed.). Routledge.

Weiss, D. (2020). Magazines and the construction of consumer lifestyles. In M. Sternadori & T. Holmes (Eds.), *The Handbook of Magazine Studies* (pp. 163–179). John Wiley & Sons. https://doi.org/10.1002/9781119168102.ch13

Whipple, K. (2023). Contextualizing the art and the artist: How U.S. arts and culture journalists perceive the impact of cancel culture practices and discourses. *Journalism Practice*, 0(0), 1–19. https://doi.org/10.1080/17512786.2023.2180653

Williams, R. (1983). *Keywords* (Vol. 1983). Oxford University Press.

Williams, R. (1960). *Culture & society 1780–1950*. Doubleday & Company, Inc. https://archive.org/details/culturesociety17001850mbp

Wojdynski, B. W. (2019). Advertorials and native advertising. In T. P. Vos, F. Hanusch, D. Dimitrakopoulou, M. Geertsema-Sligh, & A. Sehl (Eds.), *The international encyclopedia of journalism studies* (1st ed., pp. 1–6). Wiley. https://doi.org/10.1002/9781118841570.iejs0062

Zelizer, B. (1993). Journalists as interpretive communities. *Critical Studies in Mass Communication*, 10(3), 219–237. https://doi.org/10.1080/15295039309366865

3
THE MAKING OF MODERN JOURNALISM, FROM COFFEEHOUSE CAPITALISM (STRATEGIC NEWS) TO CONSTITUTIONAL SPECTACLE (MARKET LIFESTYLE)

John Hartley

Textual modernity

As a form of writing, journalism is 'the textual system of modernity'. It emerged in the early modern era, at a time when the three great textual systems of modernity – fiction, journalism, and science – were sorting themselves into different houses, as it were, while differentiating themselves from their premodern predecessors – poesy, monarchy, and divinity (Hartley, 1996). Journalism took shape in contradistinction from (and in relations with) other textual systems. It retains the shapes and shadows of its embryonic form to this day.

As a textual system, it is subject to the Saussurian principle of negative definition: it must be identified in relation to *what it is not*:

1 Not *religious sermonising*, because journalism acknowledges empirical rather than 'revealed' truths; its lessons are addressed to policy and public administration, not to salvation of the soul.
2 Not *state-sanctioned knowledge*, because official propaganda could only prevail by suppressing unofficial expression through censorship, taxes, and repression; journalism requires a 'free and open encounter' if falsehood is to be defeated (Milton, 1644).
3 Not *literary fiction*, because it is composed in 'plain style' prose (Bennett, 2019); and not *commercial fiction*, because journalism reports real events (externally checked); its storytelling purports to be rhetorically unadorned and true.
4 Not *scientific method*, because journalism is not an expert method but a human right (Hartley, 2008a); to practice it you need a pen, not a PhD.

Inevitably, the boundaries between journalism and its discursive neighbours remain mobile. Each form spilled into the others, even as each also developed its own specialist codes and rules. Neighbouring systems like science and statecraft readily assumed a journalistic guise when addressing larger publics, and publicists used every ruse to achieve 'product placement' in news or editorial content rather than in ads, so journalism's territory was regularly poached by other agents for other purposes. Journalism has remained unstable and prone to infection with fiction, rhetoric, religiosity, propaganda, partisanship, and exclusivity.

Early journalism was addressed to the 'common reader', a secular, modern, male, geographically proximate adult, with the means to buy or subscribe to the paper, untutored in specialist protocols or professional rules, looking for enlightenment and the satisfaction of curiosity. Journalism quickly proved popular among the reading public as a source of entertainment. In that guise, especially after the expansion of literacy with industrialisation, it was an increasingly prominent component of popular culture. As the press gave way to broadcasting and then to digital screen media, it was increasingly subsumed within visual and narrative entertainment. In other words, over a period of 300+ years, mainstream journalism took on the attributes of its media competitors, until the prime purpose of the popular press was entertaining a market, unlike the 'quality' press, which continued to inform the select readership of those who were active in public affairs. For the uncommitted common reader, what mattered was a good story. It may not have mattered whether it came from journalism, propaganda, fiction, faith, or science or from other components of media entertainment, including sports, comedy, kids' shows, drama, and 'such fields as travel, fashion, style, health, fitness, wellness, entertainment, leisure, lifestyle, food, music, arts, gardening and living', which are the components of lifestyle journalism, according to Folker Hanusch (2012).

Journalism as market entertainment was, by definition, *unserious*, in contrast to the 'serious' press, which remained the core paradigm for professional journalists and 'hard news' and the basis of their social repute. This centre/periphery configuration conforms to Yuri Lotman's concept of a semiosphere (Lotman, 1990). The distinctive identity of journalism is most marked at its core, while its peripheral margins are zones of dialogue, translation, theft, and trade. Defining what counts as journalism does not depend on what's popular with readers, but on the enforcement of its semiotic borders, to ensure that insiders know their limits and outsiders can be excluded (see also Chapter 24 on boundary struggles). Such definitional work is an everyday practice among journalists themselves. For example, the Ethical Journalism Network (EJN, 2018) identifies five 'core principles of ethical journalism':

1 *Accuracy* (check the facts).
2 *Independence* (avoid conflicts of interest).
3 *Impartiality* (every story has 'two sides').
4 *Humanity* (do no harm to your subjects).
5 *Accountability* (practice self-correction).

The need to assert and defend journalism's core values is only urgent when they are breached. But, once promulgated, they may be appropriated by others. For example, the Association for Science in Autism Treatment has applied the EJN's five core principles to news stories about autism, precisely because so much coverage of that condition is: (1) false or inaccurate; (2) motivated by vested interests; (3) driven by fads; (4) careless of negative effects; (5) irresponsible (Celiberti, Sniezyk and Leif, 2020). This is a positive example of how the subjects of reporting can hold journalism to account by adopting its own code of ethics. On the negative side, state actors can use the law or regulation to decide that criticism of themselves is not journalism at all but subversion, from John Wilkes to

Julian Assange. Historically, journalistic writing evolved into a tangled web, remaining epistemologically uncertain and open to constant adaptation at its border zones, raids by knowledge-neighbours, subject to official interference, and in competition for audiences who are untutored in its values, practices, and limits.

Insider/outsider distinction

This 'inside/outside' tension sustains two very different forms of journalism. The difference between them is not textual or even professional; it is in their purposes and hence in the 'ideal readers' they address, namely, insiders or outsiders in the conduct of public life. Insiders are imagined/addressed as players in the decisions of government or trade; outsiders are private citizens, who are positioned as pleasure-seeking consumers of entertainment. That distinction underlies the asymmetric status of public vs private life; business vs household; empire-building vs character-building. Novelist E.M. Forster memorably criticised 'this outer life of telegrams and anger' as inimical to the inner truths of 'personal relations', which are 'the important thing for ever and ever' (Forster, 1910: Chapter XIX), but journalism had already taken the 'telegrams and anger' path.

Samuel Johnson, the great Enlightenment rationalist and journalist, was among the first to provide journalism with a code of ethics. Writing in 1758, he reserved his strongest criticism for those 'writers of news' who 'relate on one day, what they know not to be true, because they hope it will please' and 'contradict it on the next day, when they find that it will please no longer' because 'they know ... that what is desired will be credited without nice examination'. He declared that journalists must obey 'the first law of History, the Obligation to tell Truth' (Johnson, 1758). Johnson contrasted 'what will *please*' and 'what is *desired*' with the truth. He warned against indulging 'the current of a *popular clamour*' (Hartley, 1992: 159–163).

This prescription was especially important for those who operated in 'this outer life' of government and business and who relied on accurate information – as well as the disclosure of secretive intelligence (a.k.a. gossip) – in order to compete. Like football (Borge, 2019), journalism is a 'destructive-constructive sport'; the object of the game is to identify winners by producing losers. It seeks to justify the veracity of the reporter's craft by reference only to destructive criteria – conflict, cruelty, and war – without recognition for the rival claims of lifestyle, including connectivity, nature, sustainability, and personal relations. For those in the game of 'telegrams and anger', unpalatable truths were of the highest value.

For those in private life with private affairs, journalism could only offer a true story with a lesson. According to Dr Johnson, journalism's duty was to educate the 'lower orders of mankind' in 'how the world goes'. For good reason and good government, good journalism is also showbiz:

> A Journalist ... is to consider himself not as writing to students or statesmen alone, but to women, shopkeepers and artisans, who have little time to bestow upon mental attainments, but desire, upon easy terms, to know how the world goes; who rises, and who falls; who triumphs, and who is defeated.
>
> *(Johnson, 1758)*

Those aiming for larger readerships soon found the formula for 'how the world goes' in 'true crime', which sustained the 'penny dreadfuls' and the 'yellow press' as newspapers extended their reach into the homes of urban artisans and the industrial classes. Thus was established, throughout the career of modern journalism, a distinction between what I will call *strategic journalism* and *market journalism*; stories for action and stories for edification.

That distinction was strongly gendered, both textually and professionally. Journalism's internal mythology has *lionised* the war correspondent and the attack reporter, whose line of questioning is 'why is this lying bastard lying to me?' (Burley, 2023), but it has *loathed* the gossip columnist, publicist, and lifestyle journalist. You could tell them apart very easily: the lion was male; the loathsome was female. The daily press in its heyday practiced a kind of narrative gender apartheid. The front pages were reserved for news of conflict, action, and decision; the back pages were reserved for the same qualities in pure, abstract, balletic form, i.e., male contact/conflict sports. Bracketed between them on the inside pages, well away from public combat, was a 'women's page' (when finally introduced). It might feature 'human interest' stories, 'gossip', advice, and even fiction, set in the private worlds of home, consumption, leisure, wellbeing, travel, fashion, performance, and the arts. Along with opinion columns and cartoons for the kids, these features occupied a subordinate position in the paper (the inside pages), in journalistic hierarchies (its own lower orders), and in the political value of readers (unenfranchised).

The male-coded attachment to truth as a product of binary polarity, whose highest forms are conflict and war, could only be achieved by *cutting off* lifestyle journalism. Adding contempt for female-coded embodiment and experience confirms that what is really going on here is a staged conflict between cruelty and hope, in which cruelty is always the winner. You can't be a proper journalist until you've abandoned hope and joined the cynics who fear the worst but take no action to change it. The 'common reader' was simply excluded from public life, being assigned the position of target – or victim – of decisions made over their heads.

Constitutional spectacle

For the outsiders, the press became a chief source of what Thorstein Veblen (1899) called the practice of 'invidious comparison', whereby the lives of the rich and famous intersected with the lives of ordinary populations only in the form of spectatorship. That quality of 'visibility' was seen as a 'constitutional' component of modern nations by Walter Bagehot (owner-editor of *The Economist*), who wrote *The English Constitution* (1872; and see Hartley, 2008b). He claimed that this was 'the great quality which rules the multitude, though philosophers can see nothing in it—visibility' (Bagehot, 1872: No. VIII). For Bagehot, the common people:

> Defer to what we may call the THEATRICAL show of society. A certain state passes before them; a certain pomp of great men; a certain spectacle of beautiful women; a wonderful scene of wealth and enjoyment is displayed, and they are coerced by it.
> *(Bagehot, 1872: No. VIII)*

For Bagehot and his successors, the (unwritten) Constitution of what was then the largest empire in world history, founded on maritime power, global colonialism, the slave trade, and industrial capital, had an 'efficient' or useful component (running the country) and a 'dignified' or ceremonial component (ruling the multitude), which was populated by the monarchy, aristocracy, high society, and high fashion, to keep the deferential eyes of the populace on the show of rule.

Of course, the quotidian vehicle for communicating that spectacle was the popular press, which performed its constitutional function by adopting the very techniques that persons of quality professed to despise, such as sensationalism, gossip, personality politics, tribal partisanship, populist nationalism, and the triumph of style over substance. The popular press eavesdropped on the lifestyles of the rich and famous to keep the masses in their place, thereby keeping the decisions and strategies of 'persons of quality' safely out of sight, away from critical scrutiny by their peers (if not by the tabloid phone tappers). Thus, Bagehot's own publication, *The Economist*, was addressed to few but decisive agents of productive industry and economics, leaving the powerless multitudes to the mercy of the emergent tabloids, which were transitioning from the radical 'pauper' press of the first Reform Act of 1832 to the commercial popular press of the second Reform Act of 1867 to which *The English Constitution* was a response. The tabloids came into their own at the turn of the 20th century, with the rotary steam press, improved photo-reproduction, and the 'press barons'. In Britain, these were epitomised by the Harmsworth brothers (Lords Northcliffe and Rothermere) and the Berry brothers (Lords Buckland, Kemsley, and Camrose); and on the other side of the Atlantic, by W.R. Hearst, immortalised by Orson Welles in 1940 as *Citizen Kane*.

Modern industrial and capitalist society was far from equal, despite widespread attempts to modernise political and cultural as well as industrial and economic life. Honours were granted to 'captains of industry' and press proprietors, but not to those in 'trade'; industrial magnates were ennobled, but urban industrial workers were feared as a dangerous 'mob'. To gain 'constitutional' acceptance and status, those who made big money needed to translate wealth into aristocratic show – the stately home, landed property, conspicuous charity, and marriage to the daughter of a peer.

In other words, the cultural honorific system was out of step with the productive apparatus. Conceptions of how to be a worthy winner were derived not from productivity or popularity but from values inherited from premodern societies going back to medieval times and the Bronze Age. For the Ancient Greeks, honours were distributed to warriors according to their performance in battle. Homer reserved fame for those who amassed the most '*geras*' – spoils of war, including captives. Honour went to the predator/perpetrator and shame to the prey/victim. Warriors and hunters trumped labourers and farmers, whose rights and lands could be trampled for sport. Aristocratic honour was signalled by the maximum possible avoidance of productive/useful labour, while at the same time displaying the maximum possible expenditure on conspicuous consumption/waste (Veblen, 1899).

Invidious comparison

These predatory, unproductive, and wasteful signs of supremacy were not abolished along with the *ancient regime*, despite the vigorous decapitatory efforts of the French Revolution. Instead, they returned (not as tragedy but as farce, if you like), successively resurfacing in imperial, 'Gilded Age', and now 'big tech' forms of capitalism to sort the winners from the losers, as President Trump has liked to phrase it (Goldberg, 2020; NPR, 2024) Olaf Kaltmeier (2019) uses Veblen's concept of 'invidious comparison' to characterise the contemporary era of 'a global elite of hyper-rich people', arguing that the present shares this characteristic with the American 'Gilded Age' critiqued by Veblen, as well as with premodern models based on feudal and monarchical societies.

Journalism is an essential participant in the game of invidious comparison, not only by sensationalising politics and power as a spectator sport for outsiders but also in its own self-image and organisation. Some journalism is cast as honorific – the 'quality press' and the truth-warrior war reporter; some is scorned as shameful – consumerist publicity and 'the PR girl' (Yeomans, 2019). Even though journalism is a product of modernity, Kaltmeier (2019) argues that it is not exempt from currents of 'refeudalization' that show up periodically in both sociological forms (resurgence of aristocracies) and cultural aesthetics (a politics of invidious comparison).

Thus, early modern merchant-adventurers and industrial entrepreneurs were dedicated to enterprise and the expansion of trade and production, with a working ethic and anti-feudal sensibilities. But in the present era of financialised markets, 'big tech', and platform-capitalism, (Srnicek, 2017), where certain individuals may rapidly gain exorbitant wealth, the sign of a winner is not rule over but emancipation from the rest of society:

> In the contemporary Gilded Age driven by financial capitalism, the popular classes are mainly conceptualized as a "waste" – and not even an exploitable working force. In this sense, the aristocratic leisure based lifestyle undermines a fundamental capitalist value based on meritocracy. Instead, the aristocratic habitus relies on practices of comparing that establish a categorial difference to the popular classes.
>
> *(Kaltmeier, 2019: 37)*

As industrialisation gathered pace in the eighteenth and nineteenth centuries, the increasingly enfranchised labouring and productive masses and their families were only addressed directly when running the country could be presented as a combination of spectacle, sermonising, and spectator sport, converting decision-making to mass entertainment, integrated with the constitutional apparatus to keep the 'ignorant' classes apart from 'educated' active citizens (Hartley, 2008b). Individual media proprietors responded to this division by specialising or by publishing multiple mastheads with a highbrow title for strategic players and populist tabloids for the lifestyle market.

However, it was the mass market that supplied proprietors with direct political influence or, as the Murdoch *Sun* (UK) famously put it, 'IT'S THE SUN WOT WON IT' (Thomas, 2005). Emblematic of the present generation of this 'Citizen Kane' type of press baron, Rupert Murdoch made his money from populist scandal, shock, and sensationalism across three continents. Like rival moguls, he devoted some of the profits to buying prestige mastheads, as a platform for political lobbying for allies, and pillorying for adversaries. He launched *The Australian* in 1964; bought *The Times* and *Sunday Times* (UK) in 1981; and in 2007 added the *US Wall St. Journal*. He wanted strategic influence as well as lifestyle profits, and he wanted to escape national constraints to strut the global stage:

> *The reasons why press barons want to own newspapers remain much the same today as they did for Northcliffe, Beaverbrook, and Black: making money, securing a place in the national (or global) economic and social elite, generating political influence, and delivering the thrill of the great corporate deal.*
>
> *(Potter, 2023)*

For the billionaires, owning a 'quality' title and gaining a place at the societal decision-making table is a manifestation of ultra-conspicuous consumption. But profiting from market journalism is what gets them their seat at this exclusive table.

Lifestyle

Out of journalism's path-dependent historical and societal process, a new category has achieved late recognition – that of 'lifestyle journalism'. This was long neglected in media and journalism studies. Folker Hanusch made one of the first attempts to bring it into scholarly coherence (Hanusch, 2012). He isolated from the various genres a general definition of the form. Lifestyle journalism is

> A distinct journalistic field that primarily addresses its audiences as consumers, providing them with factual information and advice, often in entertaining ways, about goods and services they can use in their daily lives.
>
> *(Hanusch, 2012: 4)*

Given the historic fissures and divisions outlined above, the question from the start – certainly in anglophone media – was whether this counted as journalism at all. As a creature of the journalistic margins, lifestyle had grown without planning, design, or recognition. Unsurprisingly, 'core' news reporters were slow to accept its significance, adopting dismissal and contempt, often cast in gender terms, to divide 'hacks' (journos) from 'flaks' (publicists) (Hargreaves, 2014: Chapter 6). This prejudicial and exclusionary language masks the very obvious fact that both 'hacks' and 'flaks' accept payment for writing material at the proprietor's behest. Nobody is free, and news is itself a trade, as well as promoting commodities. Professional publicists target 'hard news' for their campaigns, knowing that an editorial story is worth any number of ads (Kahn, 2023). Many a news item is released by interested parties, from police and military footage to the PR and marketing offices of companies, organisations, and thinktanks. These handouts are routinely published as supplied, where they magically count as news not publicity, even when the video footage is watermarked with a police or military logo. But that may not come as a surprise since public relations personnel outnumber journalists by a wide margin, and they earn more too (Williams, 2014).

Separating journalists from publicists represents an institutional barrier that is meant to differentiate what I've called *strategic* from *market journalism*. This conceptual binarism is not a direct response to contemporary conditions but is rooted in history because strategic journalism developed as a trade to expand trade, to participate in governmental decisions, and to advance national interest, while market journalism developed to expand domestic and eventually global markets. Along the way, the term 'news' prevailed, while all the other types that are now gathered under the umbrella of 'lifestyle' were relegated to dependent status ('features') or even to parasitic status (PR). The publicity trade ended up with higher numbers and paygrades, while news reporters vied for the top rung of repute. This was reserved for investigative and exposé reporters, personified by the war correspondent and 'truth warrior'. The same distinction between profitability and repute marked news organisations. 'Quality' and public service media were notoriously strapped for cash but could rely on greater public trust. However, in the way of these things, it wasn't long before the very term 'truth warrior' was hijacked by the alt-right fringe, further eroding the trust granted to journalism as a whole (Maly, 2024). As Marx had pointed out, 'the first freedom of the press consists in it not being a trade' (cited Harrison, 1974: 237). This freedom was never achieved, except in the Soviet Union (Levitsky, 1956).

The expansion of market journalism

With the digital revolution, 'the press' lost its pre-eminence in politics. Once able to put governments to the sword, while advancing their own proprietorial interests (Potter, 2023), the 'press barons' and 'media moguls' found their entire business model was in jeopardy, thanks to the upstart internet and corporate platforms that soon domesticated it in the 'internet of shopping' (Elon University, 2023) and psychographically targeted advertising (Bakir, 2020). Led by the Murdoch press, legacy and analogue media outlets systematically badmouthed the internet for quite a while (Hartley, 2010), but they eventually joined what they could not beat. Indeed, the expansion of markets both globally and digitally was just what incumbent media firms needed. Lifestyle journalism was perhaps the last invention, one might say the last gasp, of 'the press' as a coherent industry. It expanded journalism's role as a cultural intermediary (Smith Maguire and Matthews, 2014: 16–24) from the political to the consumer domain, expanding its own 'inside page' features into a kind of brokerage for shoppers to gain market information about desirable and undesirable lifestyle enhancements, organised around self, family, home, and domestic life, guided by recommenders, reviewers, influencers, and publicists – and algorithms – under the banner of favoured media brands.

But the threat posed by the tech giants was existential for the 'imagined communities' the analogue media had sustained, such as nations (Anderson, 2006). For global digital platforms, countries and their web of institutions were an impediment to the expansion of trade. Digital and social media soon abandoned collective identities like 'the nation', 'the public', 'the citizen', and 'the audience' altogether, in favour of an abstract individual consumer with no cultural or political baggage, only a 'globule of desire', as Veblen had put it (1898: 389–390), whose scope for agency is reduced to a pecuniary decision: buy *this* or buy *that*. Platforms did not invest in content, as news media had; they were interested in traffic. Success was calculated by the number of eyeballs an item attracted, no matter where it originated. The economics of looking came to maturity in the age of social media because eyeball-data can be monetised in marketing, which explains the relentless quest for corporate analytic data about user eyeballs, which could be disembodied, disaggregated, and stripped of meaning, to be digitally reassembled via 'black box' algorithms for on-sale in a data economy. Anderson's 'imagined community' was reduced to algorithmic ashes (Schäfer and van Es, 2017). Libertarian market fundamentalism replaced collective identities with the 'sovereign' individual, personified in the billionaire proprietor not the consumer–user.

In such an environment, no one is safe, especially sacred cows. The position of the journalist as a 'cultural intermediary' is usurped by the 'influencer' (Arnesson, 2023), a super-consumer whose emotional attachment to a brand or product becomes a bankable commodity in the competition for eyeballs, dethroning the journalist – no matter what kind – as the symbolic representative of a given 'we' community. The evidence of the 'eyewitness' is replaced by the 'experience' of the celebrity and the 'lifestyle' of the shopper. Once mighty mastheads gave way to household brands, which themselves vie for global reach in search of market scale, a game where US companies gained first-mover advantage.

Journalism lost its privileged position as a *strategic* discourse for nation-building and for holding public affairs to account on behalf of national reader-citizens (Fischer and Jarren, 2024). It was used for strategic purposes, by corporate, state, and partisan agencies, but it no longer had an independent voice of its own. Lifestyle journalism, on the other hand, seemed a good proposition for bringing together producers (advertisers) and populations (markets). Where the digital platforms led (taking their sources of income with them), news journalism was obliged to follow.

Insider countries

During the three or four centuries of its modern career, journalism was far from universal. It was confined to linguistic, national, and sectarian boundaries, often of its own making. While some countries developed a rich journalistic landscape very early in the process, some did not, while others had foreign versions imposed over their heads. Inevitably, the international growth of journalism followed patterns of international trade and conflict, culminating in the 19th-century epoch of European imperial rivalry and expansion.

As a maritime power, Britain looms large in that history, with not one but two successive empires to its name: the American, established under Elizabeth I and 'lost' in 1776, and the British, which gained truly global extent in the 19th century. As a result, for both European colonisers and the typically non-European colonised peoples, the model of journalism that took root globally was a ready-made import, marked with national, linguistic, and generic characteristics that continued to follow the currents of strategic power and trade.

Fiction was yoked to the colonial project through a growing domestic 'reading public', who could follow the career of the coloniser in drama and novels, from Shakespeare's 1611 *The Tempest* at the outset, via Defoe's 1719 *Robinson Crusoe* and Swift's 1726 *Gulliver's Travels* at the time of optimistic expansion, to Conrad's 1899 *Heart of Darkness* and J.G. Farrell's 1970s *Empire* trilogy as imperialism decayed from within.

Despite its national origins, journalism history is important globally because the vision of a 'free press' offered something to both colonisers and the colonised. For colonisers, it was a vehicle for 'free trade' and open markets. For the colonised, it was the standard-bearer for political and personal freedoms, on the principle that what's sauce for the colonising goose is sauce for the colonised gander. In the context of the Indian independence movement, the 1913 Nobel laureate Rabindranath Tagore:

> Recalls what India has gained from "discussions centred upon Shakespeare's drama and Byron's poetry and above all … the large-hearted liberalism of nineteenth-century English politics."
>
> *(Sen, 2001)*

Journalism and freedom seemed inseparable, which explains why radical journalists like John Wilkes and Tom Paine were of such interest to the American rebels, who installed freedom of speech and of the press into their modern Constitution, before taking over the global policing functions of the European empires after World War II.

In the post-war and Cold War era, the frontier myth of rugged individual freedom was Americanised and weaponised to force global markets to open up to American goods and services, including media. It was broadcast systematically to rivals, enemies, and markets (e.g., through Voice of America; Radio Free Europe/Radio Liberty) and at arm's length through Pentagon-assisted Hollywood movies, to the extent that critical commentators have coined the successive terms 'cultural imperialism', 'media imperialism', and 'platform imperialism' to track the globalisation, commodification, and digitisation of media content, journalism included (Jin, 2015; Mirrlees, 2023). Again, the strategic importance of a particular version of 'free speech' assists the world's most powerful countries, markets, and media to maintain their sway over the semiosphere. The individual digital user is thought to pose little more threat to these platforms than farmed creatures do to agribusiness, which was exactly the status accorded to Indigenous, enslaved, and colonised people during the Imperial Era.

Empires of the sign

It has seemed important to emphasise the local origins of journalistic categories, because the history of journalism owes a great deal to two successive world-trading empires, the British and American (Hickel, 2018). Along the way, the English language supplanted French as the lingua franca of the global traveller, if not the European diplomat. News journalism emerged, not as an abstract category indifferent to place or time but as a social and textual institution that followed economic, political, and social forces: nation, class, gender, race, imperial colonialism, and the competitive interests of business and states.

Of course, colonialism was not confined to the anglosphere; countries across Europe founded empires in the Americas, Africa, Asia, and Oceania, where the interests of imperial modernity were conducted in Portuguese, Spanish, French, Dutch, Swedish, German, Russian, Italian, Belgian, and Danish. Thus, my restriction of the story to the anglosphere is merely a result of limits of space and my own knowledge. What can be said, however, is that journalism 'as we know it' did not arise autochthonously in any of the great civilisations that flourished beyond the bounds of modernising Europe in the Americas, Africa, and Asia. Thus, although I live and work in the anglosphere, considering journalism as a European and specifically anglophone artefact is not mere ethnocentrism; it is an account of how inequality was exported and enforced globally by geostrategic means (see Ueda, 2021; Zhang, 2007).

Strategic coffeehouses

Journalism, for its part, was not so much an observer as a tool of colonial and imperial expansion. It offered strategic and market information to men of affairs in public life, enabling those interested in policy, government, and trade to calculate the risk/reward ratio for their investments, at the time when trade followed European expansionism around the world. Useful knowledge was pooled where men gathered to keep up with the news – the tavern, coffeehouse, and the club (often dedicated to an exclusive sport: horse-racing, hunting–shooting–fishing, yachts, polo, and golf). In this respect, journalism was invented for those who sought pecuniary or political advantage from being in the know. Furthermore, it was a feature of a particular lifestyle, that of the mercantile players who gathered in coffeehouses in the City of London, which explains not only its distinction between 'strategic' and 'market' information but also its strongly gendered preference for negative news for men and domestic lifestyle for women and its alignment with imperial trade but not with home-grown dissent.

It was not designed for home consumption or general entertainment but for a mixed clientele of nascent modern professions, each of which tended to gather in their own premises, especially the coffeehouse. Historian Richard Dale has identified different coffeehouses for literary 'wits', learned scholars and scientists, politicians (sorted by faction), lawyers, clergy, and the 'commercial classes', including marine underwriters, insurance brokers, shipping agents, and stockjobbers (2004: 8). He concludes: 'The London coffee houses fulfilled several important functions. First and foremost, they were a source of political, economic and financial information':

> Eighteenth century traders and investors had to rely very largely on the coffee house and the press for information about investments and market movements. These two sources of information were interdependent, since journalists obtained much of their news from the coffee house, and one of the main attractions of the latter were the newspapers provided to its clientele.
>
> *(Dale, 2004: 7–8)*

The coffeehouses' formula of maximised sociability, critical judgement, and relative sobriety (compared with the alehouse) proved a catalyst for creativity and innovation. Collectively, they were an early example of what institutional economist Jason Potts (2019) calls an 'innovation commons'. Matthew Green explains:

> Coffeehouses encouraged political debate, which paved the way for the expansion of the electorate in the 19th century. The City coffeehouses spawned capitalist innovations that shaped the modern world. Other coffeehouses sparked journalistic innovation.
>
> *(Green, 2013)*

Encouraging political debate made coffeehouses the progenitors of the 'public sphere' (Habermas, 1991), but they were not democratic in the modern sense. Members of the labouring classes, women, persons of colour, and radicals like Tom Paine would doubtless have been barred from entry, if not arrested, had they shown up for a 'political debate'; and participants in coffeehouse culture included slaveowners and slave traders. Lloyd's of London, for instance, started life in a coffeehouse of the same name in 1652. It became a major global insurance agency, and among those enriched as a result were slavers: 'During this time many involved with Lloyd's amassed fortunes through the economics of empire and the slave economy' (Lloyd's, n.d.). Lloyd's has posted this statement on the company website:

> From 1640 to the early 19th century, an estimated 3.2 million enslaved African people were transported by Britain's vast shipping industry. Lloyd's was the global centre for insuring that industry. We are deeply sorry for the Lloyd's market's participation in the transatlantic slave trade. It is part of our shared history that caused enormous suffering and continues to have a negative impact on Black and ethnically diverse communities today.
>
> *(Lloyd's, n.d.)*

The hundreds of London coffeehouses and the lively periodicals they sustained (including Dr Johnson's *Rambler* and *Idler* and Addison's *Spectator*) were not harbingers of democracy but of the capitalist innovations that shaped the modern world, the City of London itself, and literary expression as a whole. They hosted and sparked journalistic innovation that textualised and abstracted the public sphere for wider readerships (Green, 2013; Films

Media Group, 2016). Journalism has had coffee stains all over it ever since. As it took its modern shape, the distinction between strategic and lifestyle journalism was already in place. Strategic journalism was indeed a manifestation of one particular lifestyle, that of the coffeehouse, where the technicians of merchant capitalism – insurers, traders, stockbrokers, and 'scribblers' – could gather, gossip, and globalise their market strategies.

Feeding on a dead duck

Coming up to date, amidst epochal changes, journalism has necessarily had to reinvent itself again. Some of its most cherished imaginings about itself have been swept aside, leaving emergent practice out of step with its own symbolic and ideological imaginary. Even as journalism theory has started to become more self-aware, it has continued to laud 'the normative relationship between journalism and democracy, which has dominated political science perspectives on journalism' (Steensen and Ahva, 2015). Meanwhile, the newspaper format is a 'dead duck' (Holmes, 2016).

The prospect of a 'free press', one that criticises its own leaders in the name of democratic values and an open society, is in continuous recession around the world (International IDEA, 2023). Media historian Simon Potter concurs:

> We are still a long way from the dream of a democratic utopia promoted by 19th-century campaigners for press freedom. They believed that the free market would liberate the press and, by doing so, liberate us all. Sadly, it seems like Logan Roy [the 'dark heart' of HBO's series Succession] was closer to the truth when he said to his wannabe successors: "Money wins. Here's to us."
>
> *(Potter, 2023)*

In this context, 'lifestyle journalism' is not a champion of democratic participation but a survival strategy for corporate media proprietors. In other words, corporate, state, and populist actors still have a use for it, but not to sustain a democratic free press. Instead, commerce, state, and populism continue to feed on the dead duck:

1. *Media moguls* have already turned media platforms into a global market, vying with each other to buy up respectable brands and innovative digital start-ups, which they can then put behind paywalls, while they themselves exert maximum political and market control in the name of their multimillion digital subscribers. Those subscribers are reduced to the status of individual shoppers, with no say in how proprietors use their numbers to influence powerbrokers and political events.
2. *State agencies* are active in the influencer game too because 'strategic narrative' is now part of the weaponry of great powers and mid-sized countries alike. The results of that game can be seen daily in news coverage of global conflict, in the Middle East, NATO vs. Russia and the war in Ukraine, and US–China rivalry for Indo-Pacific sway. Each 'side' has captured and harnessed the local news and comment media to its cause, such that in the West we hear plenty about Russian, Palestinian, or Chinese aggression, but little or nothing about NATO provocations, or the encirclement of rival powers with military hardware (Suny, 2022). Thus, news journalism is now a partisan 'non-state agent' in global warfare. This is a 'game' the Global South cannot play on a level field, so conflicts in Africa, Asia, and Latin America are routinely neglected, except insofar as they precipitate refugee and

migrant 'crises' in more affluent countries. As a result, the 'globalisation' of journalism and social media is not even-handed, but follows the contours of strategic power, which itself has a long history, going back to rivalries among 19th-century empires.

3 *Populist partisans* are gaining traction in many countries, using the electoral process to undermine elective democracy, denouncing public administration as an elite swamp while seeking to capture and dominate it, and interfering with opponents' media infrastructure via hacking and cyberwarfare, while crying 'fake news' to criticism of themselves. These are the tactics of extremist 'entryism' (Campion, 2020). In Europe and Asia as well as the United States, far-right populist authoritarianism is a significant force (Huq and Ginsburg, 2018: 123–137), while traditional political parties are atrophying, leaving them open to extremist entryism, even as they squander social trust among the public, prioritising ideological tit-for-tat over good government, while environmental and climate crises accelerate without the prospect of concerted remedial action by governments, corporations, or consumers.

Strategic and market journalism have staked out different claims on the reader–consumer. Strategic journalism lays claim to truth because it is an axiomatic news value that truth is a product of struggle between 'two sides', of which war is the highest expression. Market journalism lays claim to lifestyle because that's the commodity form of planetary markets. An unforeseen consequence of this polarity is that lifestyle is not considered to belong to the domain of truth, only to that of publicity, while war is not considered to belong to the category of lifestyle, only to its destruction.

Further consequences are that journalism began and has remained as a strongly gendered and raced profession and discursive form. Front-page strategic news has long been personified as a white male domain; inside-page journalism is feminised, with room for people of colour in music, sports, entertainment, and – belatedly – fashion. The only place where combat and lifestyle coincide is on the back page, in sports reporting, but this too is conceptualised as make-believe masculine warfare, and sports reporting is typically confined to team contact sports of the home country; its enjoyment represented as a male-bonding culture of booze, betting, and 'biffo'. Sport is mediated as conflict (Borge, 2019), which is a news value that lifestyle journalism does not use.

On the contrary, lifestyle topics steer clear of conflict. But it is not enough to argue that lifestyle journalism is 'just as good' as its grim sibling. That lets journalism (as a form) off the hook because it leaves intact the presumption that lifestyle is OK *in its place*, i.e., not the front page. In that case, the very concept of 'lifestyle journalism' is an affront to equality, because it would maintain the hierarchy of gendered truth.

Therefore, I'm not here to defend lifestyle journalism but to argue that its marginal, peripheral, and discounted status allows for newness, adaptation, and change, possibly pointing the way to a preferable future for journalism in general. This supposedly inconsequential form has proven fertile ground for alternative voices and practices, especially those associated with the 'new social movements' that burgeoned in the 1960s. These include feminism, the peace movement, anti-colonialism, environmentalism, non-binary sexuality, intersectionality, and neurodivergence, more recently joined by #MeToo, #Black Lives Matter, and the recognition of privileged 'positionality', not least in journalism itself (Khalid, 2023). They have found a welcome in lifestyle formats, even where they have been strongly contested in news (see also Chapters 24–28).

But equally, market journalism steers clear of *collective action* of any kind, especially protests and demonstrations. 'Lifestyle' is construed as an individual consumer choice, not as an acceptable and sustainable life for collective groups, from cities and nations to gender, ethnic, and human demographics taken together. This means that direct action, protest, and collective resistance on such urgent topics as sexism, racism, multiculturalism, ethnic and Indigenous rights, climate crisis, destruction of natural ecosystems, pollution, extinction, waste, refugee and migration crises, and the global exploitation of labour in goods and services are coded as deviance in strategic journalism and are only patchily gaining acceptance, as compatible with lifestyle journalism (as recorded elsewhere in this volume), even though they impact on the lifestyle of every consumer.

Is there time for journalists and their allies to mend their own house?

Further reading

Asseraf, A. (2022) Mass media and the colonial informant: Messaoud Djebari and the French Empire, 1880–1901. *Past & Present*, 254(1), 161–192. https://doi.org/10.1093/pastj/gtab008

Carter, S., Steiner, L., & Allan, S. (Eds.) (2019). *Journalism, Gender and Power*. London: Routledge. https://doi.org/10.4324/9781315179520

Hanusch, F. (Ed.) (2013). *Lifestyle Journalism*. Routledge.

Hartley, J. (2025). *Make/Believe: We and They on a Digital Planet*. Bloomsbury.

References

Anderson, B. (2006). *Imagined Communities: Reflections on the Origin and Spread of Nationalism*, Revised edn. Verso.

Arnesson, J. (2023). Influencers as ideological intermediaries: Promotional politics and authenticity labour in influencer collaborations. *Media, Culture & Society*, 45(3), 528–544. https://doi.org/10.1177/01634437221117505

Bagehot, W. (1872). *The English Constitution*, 2nd edn. Project Gutenberg. https://www.gutenberg.org/files/4351/4351-h/4351-h.htm

Bakir, V. (2020). Psychological operations in digital political campaigns: Assessing Cambridge Analytica's psychographic profiling and targeting. *Frontiers of Communication*, 5, Article 67. https://doi.org/10.3389/fcomm.2020.00067

Bennett, K. (2019). Plain English: The "rhetoric of anti-rhetoric" and its consequences for anglophone culture. *English Studies*, 100(6), 688–709. https://doi.org/10.1080/0013838X.2019.1613104

Borge, S. (2019). *The Philosophy of Football*. Routledge.

Burley, R. (2023). *Why Is This Lying Bastard Lying to Me: 25 Years of Searching for the Truth on Political TV*. HarperCollins.

Campion, K. (2020). Infiltrating democracy: Non-violent strategies serving violent ideologies. *Open Democracy*, 16 July. https://www.opendemocracy.net/en/countering-radical-right/infiltrating-democracy-non-violent-strategies-serving-violent-ideologies/

Celiberti, D., Sniezyk, C., & Leif, E. (2020). Five principles of ethical journalism: Implications for media representations of autism treatment. *Science in Autism Treatment*, 18(2). https://asatonline.org/for-media-professionals/ethical-journalism-autism-treatment/

Dale, R. (2004). *The First Crash: Lessons from the South Sea Bubble*. Princeton University Press.

EJN. (2018). Our five core principles of ethical journalism. *Ethical Journalism Network*. https://ethicaljournalismnetwork.org/who-we-are

Elon University. (2023). Predicting the best and worst of digital life by 2035. *Imagining the Internet: A History and Forecast*. https://www.elon.edu/u/imagining/surveys/xvi2023/the-best-worst-digital-future-2035/

Films Media Group. (2016). *Ancient Bean: Global Journey*. Episode 1. *The Story of Coffee*, 3-part documentary. https://www.films.com/ecTitleDetail.aspx?TitleID=211691

Fischer, R., & Jarren, O. (2024). The platformization of the public sphere and its challenge to democracy. *Philosophy & Social Criticism*, 50(1), 200–215. https://doi.org/10.1177/01914537231203535

Forster, E. M. (1910). *Howard's End*. Project Gutenberg: https://www.gutenberg.org/files/2946/2946-h/2946-h.htm

Goldberg, J. (2020). Trump: Americans who died in war are 'losers' and 'suckers'. *The Atlantic*, 3 September. https://www.theatlantic.com/politics/archive/2020/09/trump-americans-who-died-at-war-are-losers-and-suckers/615997/

Green, M. (2013). The lost world of the London coffeehouse. *The Public Domain Review*. https://publicdomainreview.org/essay/the-lost-world-of-the-london-coffeehouse/

Habermas, J. (1991). *The Structural Transformation of the Public Sphere: An Inquiry into a Category of Bourgeois Society*. MIT Press.

Hanusch, F. (2012). Broadening the focus: The case for lifestyle journalism as a field of scholarly inquiry. *Journalism Practice*, 6(1), 2–11. https://doi.org/10.1080/17512786.2011.622895

Hargreaves, I. (2014). *Journalism: A Very Short Introduction*, 2nd edn. Oxford University Press.

Harrison, S. (1974). *Poor Men's Guardians*. Lawrence and Wishart.

Hartley, J. (1992). *The Politics of Pictures: The Creation of the Public in the Age of Popular Media*. Routledge.

Hartley, J. (1996). *Popular Reality: Journalism, Modernity, Popular Culture*. Arnold [now Bloomsbury].

Hartley, J. (2008a). Journalism as a human right: The cultural approach to journalism. In Löffelholz, M. & Weaver, D. (Eds.) *Global Journalism Research: Theories, Methods, Findings, Future*. Peter Lang, 39–51.

Hartley, J. (2008b). "The supremacy of ignorance over instruction and of numbers over knowledge": Journalism, popular culture, and the English constitution. *Journalism Studies*, 9(5), 679–691. https://doi.org/10.1080/14616700802207607

Hartley, J. (2010). Attack of the creationist reverberators! Or: The end of the world (As We Know It). *Popular Communication*, 8(3), 180–185. https://doi.org/10.1080/15405702.2010.493434

Hickel, J. (2018). *The Divide: Global Inequality from Conquest to Free Markets*. W. W. Norton & Co.

Holmes, J. (2016). Can you cut journalists and still keep quality? *Sydney Morning Herald*, 23 March. https://www.smh.com.au/opinion/fairfax-medias-pursuit-of-mass-digital-audience-at-odds-with-quality-journalism-claims-20160322-gnnwh9.html

Huq, A. & Ginsburg, T. (2018) *How to Lose a Constitutional Democracy*. 65 UCLA Law Review, 78. https://chicagounbound.uchicago.edu/cgi/viewcontent.cgi?article=13666&context=journal_articles

International IDEA. (2023). *The Global State of Democracy 2023: New Checks and Balances*. International Institute for Democracy and Electoral Assistance. https://www.idea.int/sites/default/files/2024-02/the-global-state-of-democracy-2023-the-new-checks-and-balances.pdf

Jin, D. Y. (2015). *Digital Platforms, Imperialism and Political Culture*. Routledge.

Johnson, S. (1758). Of the duty of a journalist. *Universal Chronicle*, 8 April. Reprinted in Womersley, D. (Ed.) (2020). *Samuel Johnson: Selected Writings*. Oxford University Press.

Kahn, D. (2023). As the media becomes less centralized, PR professionals should focus on building relationships. *Forbes Agency Council*, 19 April. https://www.forbes.com/sites/forbesagencycouncil/2023/04/19/as-the-media-becomes-less-centralized-pr-professionals-should-focus-on-building-relationships/

Kaltmeier, O. (2019). Invidious comparison and the new global leisure class: On the refeudalization of consumption in the old and new gilded age. *Forum for Inter-American Research*, 12(1), 29–42.

Khalid, H. (2023). How do we decolonise journalism? *Al Jazeera Media Institute*. https://institute.aljazeera.net/en/ajr/article/2128

Levitsky, S. (1956). The Soviet Press and copyright legislation: Some legal concepts. *Fordham Law Review*, 25(3). https://ir.lawnet.fordham.edu/cgi/viewcontent.cgi?article=1521&context=flr

Lloyd's (n.d.). *The Transatlantic Slave Trade*. Lloyd's. https://www.lloyds.com/about-lloyds/history/the-trans-atlantic-slave-trade

Lotman, Y. (1990). *The Universe of the Mind: A Semiotic Theory of Culture*. I. B. Tauris; Indiana University Press.

Maly, I. (2024). *Metapolitics, Algorithms and Violence New Right Activism and Terrorism in the Attention Economy*. Routledge Studies in Fascism and the Far Right.

Milton, J. (1644). *Areopagitica: A Speech of Mr. John Milton for the Liberty of Unlicenc'd Printing, to the Parliament of England*. John Milton Reading Room. https://milton.host.dartmouth.edu/reading_room/areopagitica/text.shtml

Mirrlees, T. (2023). Ten postulates of a media imperialism framework: For critical research on China's media power and influence in the Global South. *Global Media and China*, 9(4), 433–450. https://doi.org/10.1177/20594364231195934

NPR. (2024). Biden is using one of Trump's insults — 'loser' — against him. *All Things Considered*, 12 January. https://www.npr.org/2024/01/12/1224546711/biden-is-using-one-of-trumps-insults-loser-against-him

Potter, S. (2023). Rupert Murdoch and the rise and fall of the press barons: How much power do newspapers still have? *The Conversation*, 22 September. https://theconversation.com/rupert-murdoch-and-the-rise-and-fall-of-the-press-barons-how-much-power-do-newspapers-still-have-213283

Potts, J. (2019). *Innovation Commons: The Origin of Economic Growth*. Oxford University Press.

Schäfer, M. T., & van Es, K. (Eds.) (2017). *The Datafied Society: Studying Culture through Data*. Amsterdam University Press. https://library.oapen.org/handle/20.500.12657/31843

Sen, A. (2001). Tagore and his India. *The Nobel Prize in Literature*. https://www.nobelprize.org/prizes/literature/1913/tagore/article/

Smith Maguire, J., & Matthews, J. (Eds.) (2014). *The Cultural Intermediaries Reader*. Sage Publications.

Srnicek, N. (2017). *Platform Capitalism*. Polity. https://mudancatecnologicaedinamicacapitalista.files.wordpress.com/2019/02/platform-capitalism.pdf

Steensen, S., & Ahva, L. (2015). Theories of journalism in a digital age: An exploration and introduction. *Journalism Practice*, 9(1), 1–18. https://doi.org/10.1080/17512786.2014.928454

Suny, R. (2022). Ukraine war follows decades of warnings that NATO expansion into Eastern Europe could provoke Russia. *The Conversation*, 1 March. https://theconversation.com/ukraine-war-follows-decades-of-warnings-that-nato-expansion-into-eastern-europe-could-provoke-russia-177999

Thomas, J. (2005). *Popular Newspapers, the Labour Party and British Politics*. Routledge.

Ueda, K. (Ed.) (2021). *Fanning the Flames: Propaganda in Modern Japan*. Hoover Institution. https://fanningtheflames.hoover.org/shorthand-story/9

Veblen, T. (1898). Why is economics not an evolutionary science? *Quarterly Journal of Economics*, 12(4), 373–397.

Veblen, T. (1899). *The Theory of the Leisure Class: An Economic Study in the Evolution of Institutions*. Project Gutenberg. https://gutenberg.org/cache/epub/833/pg833-images.html

Williams, A. (2014). The growing pay gap between journalism and public relations. *Pew Research Center*, 11 March. https://www.pewresearch.org/short-reads/2014/08/11/the-growing-pay-gap-between-journalism-and-public-relations/

Yeomans, L. (2019). Is a 'new feminist visibility' emerging in the UK PR industry? Senior women's discourse and performativity within the neoliberal PR firm. *Public Relations Inquiry*, 8(2), 127–147. https://doi.org/10.1177/2046147X19842909

Zhang, X. (2007). *The Origins of the Modern Chinese Press: The Influence of the Protestant Missionary Press in Late Qing China*. Routledge.

4
POLITICAL AND PROPRIETORIAL INTERFERENCE IN THE FOOD COVERAGE OF POPULAR BRITISH NEWSPAPERS BETWEEN TWO WORLD WARS

A historical perspective

Sarah Lonsdale

Introduction

Food and journalism about food have always occupied a special location in lifestyle journalism. Scholars consistently point to the subject of food, essential to life, as being part of wider discourses about politics and national identity (Duffy and Ashley, 2013; Jones and Taylor, 2013; Teughels, 2021; Lonsdale, 2022) (see also Chapters 8 and 19). As Liz Fakazis and Elfriede Fürsich recently pointed out, quoting celebrity chef and film-maker Anthony Bourdain, 'There's nothing more political than food' (Fakazis and Fürsich, 2022, p. 1). Food journalism can often be found outside of so-called lifestyle sections of newspapers and television networks as journalistic, and thus public, 'interest in food is not restricted to recipe columns and restaurant reviews' (Jones and Taylor, 2013, p. 96). Jones and Taylor contend that this emergence of food journalism from newspaper and magazine women's and lifestyle pages, celebrity food shows and cookery columns has been a relatively modern phenomenon. However, more recent (and not-so-recent) scholarship provides evidence that food has, since the First World War at least, been a moveable feast, occupying news pages and letters columns and investigative television documentary programmes particularly during times of national crisis and political change. These periods of crisis and change include wartime when food literally becomes a life or death issue (Lonsdale, 2022); postwar periods when a nation seeks to recover from trauma and when there are large numbers of invalids to care for (Lyon and Kautto, 2021). Other moments of economic and political crisis include the Great Depression, when the nation and its identity are under immense stress, or the Black Lives Matter movement in the summer of 2020 (Dejmanee, 2022), and in nation-building in the postcolonial world (Cusack, 2000).

Food journalism bleeds into many genres of journalism, from 'service' journalism', helping consumers navigate the problems of everyday life (Kristensen and From, 2013; Eide and Knight, 1999), to political journalism, when agricultural and environmental policy affects food production and consumption (Jones and Taylor, 2013). Food is also about taste and luxury and pleasure (Johnston and Goodman, 2015). Food is also bound up with a country's ideas of nationhood, built into symbols such as 'national dishes' and 'national cuisine' (Teughels, 2021). While there is much, if belated, scholarship on the political significance of food journalism, there is still much work to be done on the editorial choices made by journalism platforms in carrying specific items or promoting specific ways of cooking or ingredients. In Liz Fakazis and Elfriede Fürsich's foundational recent edited volume (2022), there has been a start. Elfriede Fürsich's examination of the *New York Times'* approach to food and cooking during the coronavirus pandemic reveals how careful consideration of readers' needs at this time emerged as a 'significant driver of subscription gains' (Fürsich, 2022, p. 102). In Britain, the pro-Brexit media's fixation with so-called Bendy Bananas in the run-up to the EU Referendum in June 2016 is seen to have contributed to Euro-scepticism amongst readers of the *Daily Mail* (Irwin and Tominc, 2022). This latter work, however, deals specifically with news, rather than lifestyle, articles about bananas and cucumbers. This chapter takes us back to another highly political newspaper campaign in the late 1920s and early 1930s and examines the food coverage, in both the news, and 'lifestyle' or women's pages.

The British newspaper press emerged from the First World War with a very mixed reputation. On the one hand, there was the generally held view amongst the reading public that over the four years of conflict they had been lied to on an industrial scale by newspapers caught between censorship laws and a misplaced patriotism that covered up the sordid realities of the trenches (Knightley, 2000; Buitenhuis, 1989; Ponsonby, 1928; Montague, 1922). On the other hand, 'softer', prototype newspaper 'lifestyle' features advising readers how to navigate the traumatic and unfamiliar conditions they were living through created a bond between the reader and newspaper that editors saw had enormous possibilities (Lonsdale, 2015, 2022). This wartime advice ranged from how to care for invalids and feed a family on limited ingredients, how to break the worst news to relatives about the death of a much-loved family member and how to refresh clothes with upcycled materials at a time of national privation (Lonsdale, 2015). Food, the most vital of family concerns, obtained a powerful status in newspapers during the war years. The specially created *Daily Mail* Food Bureau, for example, responded to queries from millions of readers about how to cook palatable meals during the period of rationing (Peel, 1933). Even the lofty *Daily Telegraph* and *Times* advised their middle-class readership on how to fish for pike and save on fuel by cooking with a hay box (Lonsdale, 2015).

Reduced pagination during wartime meant that fledgling newspaper women's pages, which had been developing during the pre-war period, were cut back, and food and recipe articles were published in the main body of the slimline newspapers, expanding interest and readership beyond wives and mothers and other inhabitants of the domestic sphere. Once restrictions on newsprint were lifted, most major national newspapers increased their women's page offerings, investing in more specialist and female writers better attuned to the interests of women readers (Bingham, 2018). During the interwar years, food coverage in popular newspapers, on average, occupied around a quarter of space allocated to the 'Women's Page', or 'Home Page', as it was called in the London *Evening Standard,* although within this average, there was a wide variety in both content and pagination. Moving away from the dreary offering of wartime rationing, aspirational middle-market newspapers, the *Daily Mail* and *Daily Express,* catered for housewives, often now without domestic staff, anxious about issues such as taste and variety (Bingham, 2018). With the rising numbers of young working women and the interwar phenomenon, 'the bachelor girl' created further complexities for newspapers offering advice on planning daily menus for readers who had less time to prepare meals at the end of the working day (Lonsdale, 2020). How would lifestyle features and in particular, coverage of food develop during peacetime, now that editors and proprietors had seen the circulation gains and reader loyalty that helping their readers tackle 'the problems of everyday life' could bring? (Eide and Knight, 1999).

This chapter examines the food coverage of three middle-market British newspapers during the late 1920s and early 1930s and attempts to trace how newspaper food writers identified and responded to their readers' concerns. In addition, this was the time when the 'press barons', the proprietors of the *Daily Mail*, *Daily Express* and London *Evening Standard* aspired to gain power and political influence through the substantial circulation of their papers. By reading these papers' food coverage in the context of the turbulent social and political upheavals of the interwar years, this chapter identifies how proprietorial interference and the political ambitions of powerful men found their way into the larders and shopping lists of interwar British housewives. My findings sadly conclude that there is no such thing as an innocent avocado or grapefruit in a newspaper food feature.

Empire trade

Britain's economy struggled for most of this period to recover from the costs of financing the First World War. Unemployment was rising, there were hunger marches through the 1920s and 30s and competition from overseas, particularly an increasingly protectionist United States and Japan, threatened Britain's export markets in South America and Asia, respectively (Gardiner, 2010; Graham, 2022). In those uncertain years after 1918, it was increasingly believed that Britain's continued prosperity and status relied on keeping her Empire intact. It was also recognised that the sacrifices made by Empire troops (some 200,000 dead and half a million wounded) required a more collaborative approach to dominions and dependencies than jingoistic flag-waving (Maguire, 2021). One way of knitting Britain's colonies closer to her was through trade (Trentmann, 2007). While several countries in the Empire, particularly New Zealand, Australia, Canada and South Africa had implemented a preferential system towards imports from Britain, the 'mother country' as yet offered no reciprocal trade preference in return (Varian, 2022). A strengthened, better-connected Empire would also dampen the ideas of independence or self-government in the aftermath of the Irish Republican War, which resulted in independence for the 26 counties of the Irish Free State in 1921 (Cannadine, 2001).[1] Agitations for independence were particularly strong in India and Egypt. "If we lose India, the Empire will collapse", was a common imperialist refrain during these years (this warning was published in an *Evening Standard* leader 16 May1930). As far as food was concerned, the Empire focus was multifaceted. In addition to the concern to bridge the geographical distance between Britain and her colonies, there was a nascent protectionism, no small degree of racism (the 'cleanliness' of the white farmers cross the Empire was often emphasised in marketing slogans), and the desire amongst British housewives to relieve the tedium of a diet that even amongst the middle classes encompassed a narrow range of foods (Trentmann, 2007; Lyon and Kautto, 2021). The commercial food canning and cold storage industries had enabled the processing, preservation and transportation of exotic fruit and vegetables such as peaches and pineapples and frozen fish and meat from the colonies and Dominions to Britain (Trentmann, 2007; Lyon and Kautto, 2021; Barnes and Higgins, 2020). Development of pesticides during the First World War had tackled the problems of spoiling of grains and other dried and unprocessed foods from countries as far away as Australia during their long boat journeys around the world (Empire Marketing Board, 1932). Cook book and cookery column writers offered fresh looks at favourite dishes from the Empire such as curries and kedgerees. Although there was certainly an element of racism behind the Empire Shopping campaigns, there was also an element of benign cosmopolitanism towards the different peoples of the Empire combined with a patronising attitude towards white colonials who had emigrated from the Mother Land to Australia, New Zealand and Canada, particularly (Cannadine, 2001). As the Great Depression set in and agrarian economies such as Australia, Canada and New Zealand suffered a terrible slump in exports and mass unemployment, there entered an element of patriotism in the call to housewives to buy Empire products (Fishback, 2012). Readers of newspapers were left in no doubt that the Dominions needed their help. Ideas of patriotism became inextricably linked with shopping and cooking: 'Much depends on the housewife to make sure that her purchases for the larder are of Empire origin', readers of the *Daily Mail* were told in May 1930 ('The Home and Empire', 24 May 1930, p. 6); 'To our women readers: Buy Empire Foodstuffs' (*Daily Express* 19 February 1930, p. 8); 'Canada facing a crisis: buy Canadian flour' (*Daily Express* 8 February 1930, p. 1).

The Empire Marketing Board (E. M. B.), a government-funded body founded in 1926 to promote trade between Britain and countries of the Empire, advertised in newspapers and cinemas, showing, for example, a (white) South African farmer holding a basket of luscious juicy oranges 'ripening in South African sunshine' (*Daily Express* 1 July 1929, p. 2). In predominantly conservative newspapers, food columns became sites of international exchange as they introduced suburban housewives to guava jelly, avocadoes and other exotic ingredients. Housewives were encouraged to experiment with such new taste sensations as Jamaican rum and sultanas from Australia (O'Connor, 2009). Particular focus was given to events and promotions around Empire Shopping Week during the third week in May and, in December, during the run-up to Christmas when patriotic citizens were encouraged to buy gifts from Empire countries. 'The King's Christmas Pudding', made entirely from Empire ingredients, became a festive regular after 1927, with recipes published in most major newspapers (O'Connor, 2009). Newspaper food columns such as those by the first 'celebrity' food columnist Elizabeth Craig taught women how to negotiate exotic ingredients imported from across the Empire, as trade routes reopened and the larder became interesting again. The E. M. B was credited with successes in encouraging the popularity of certain Empire foods, including New Zealand butter, and South African and Jamaican grapefruits. The grapefruit, particularly, enjoyed enormous popularity during the interwar years, with commentators noting that it had gone from a rare and expensive delicacy to a breakfast table staple in just a few years ('Covent Garden's Strange Fruits' *Observer,* 13 July, 1930, p. 8). In 1929, The Empire Marketing Board announced that imports of grapefruit from Jamaica had increased from 2 million pieces in 1921 to 36 million in 1927 ('Grapefruit Marmalade' *Daily Mail* 24 January 1929). Much of its popularity stemmed from its association with weight loss, an association that still exists today, even though there is no scientific evidence for it (Vester, 2023).

The empire crusade

The interwar period was a time of rapid press expansion, with newspaper circulations more than doubling 1919–1939 (Bingham, 2018, p. 225). The pre-eminent popular newspapers were the *Daily Express*, which had reached a circulation of 2.3 million by 1938, and the *Daily Mail* with a circulation of nearly 1.6 million; the *Daily Mail* had outsold the *Daily Express* for most of this period but lost circulation following its early support for Hitler and the Nazis 1933–1934 (Cockett, 1989). Each of these papers was owned by the so-called 'Press Lords': Lord Beaverbrook (Max Aitken) owned the *Daily Express* and Lord Rothermere (Harold Harmsworth) the *Daily Mail*. The latter had taken over ownership and control of the *Daily Mail* after his brother Lord Northcliffe's death in 1922. Beaverbrook, Rothermere and Northcliffe saw ownership of their hugely influential newspapers as a means of connecting with the powerful and steering government policy. Their papers had been instrumental in removing Prime Minister Herbert Asquith halfway through the First World War and replacing him with David Lloyd George (Taylor, 1998, p. 179). In addition, the press barons, as they were disparagingly called, had been elevated to government positions, with Rothermere being made Secretary of State for Air, Beaverbrook Minister of Information and Northcliffe Director of Propaganda in Enemy Countries (Northcliffe declined a Cabinet role, preferring to keep his image as a critical outsider) (Taylor, 1998, pp. 187, 229). Rothermere and Beaverbrook became close friends, and both shared similar political outlooks. These were conservative and nationalist, verging on protectionist, and at their heart, celebrating and upholding British imperialism (Chisholm and Davie, 1993). This culminated in the years 1929–1931 with the peers' 'British Empire Crusade', a campaign for tariff-free trading within the Empire, and the creation of a new political party, the United Empire Party, with its aim of splitting the Conservative Party after their General Election defeat in May 1929 (Chisholm and Davie, 1993). The campaign argued for reducing tariffs to zero between Britain and its colonies, protectorates, dominions and dependencies and raising them against all countries in the rest of the world. While raw materials, coal, pig iron and steel, were amongst its industrial targets, preferential treatment of foods from across the Empire – sugar from the Caribbean, pineapples from Malaya (Malaysia) and oranges from South Africa – would be a way of eliciting support from a public desperate to expand its imagined horizons and real taste experiences.

Beaverbrook and Rothermere (especially the former) saw their newspapers' enormous circulations, and thus influence, as a means of steering Britain's political direction. Beaverbrook had seen the success of Northcliffe's food tax campaign of 1911 when 'the power of the independent popular press' had forced the government into humiliating retreat over a major economic policy (Chisolm and Davie, 1993, p. 275). A Canadian national, Beaverbrook was a passionate imperialist and was deeply suspicious of US hegemony in North America (Chisolm and Davie, 1993). Beaverbrook was interested to see how far he could go, using the combined firepower of his and Rothermere's newspapers in changing the direction of the Conservative Party in forcing it to adopt the policy of Empire Free Trade or indeed propelling Beaverbrook 'to high office' (Taylor, 1998, p. 274). Both men could dictate the content of their eight national newspapers to their respective editors, creating 'a joint barrage scarcely paralleled in newspaper history' (Chisolm and Davie, 1993, p. 294; Taylor, 1998). Their efforts combined speeches, electioneering and advertising and political stories and leaders in their papers. In a bid to emulate Northcliffe's food tax campaign, Beaverbrook launched the 'Empire Loaf' campaign in his *Daily Express* in May 1930, urging British housewives to demand the Empire Loaf from their bakers (Chisolm and Davie, 1993, p. 295). Made with 'nutritious' 'Empire wheat, British milled in British bread' (*Daily Express*, 8 May 1930, p. 1), the loaf merged news and food journalism with political activism on the front page of a major daily newspaper. What was the relationship between these papers' lifestyle journalism promoting shopping for Empire ingredients and their proprietors' political ambitions? Were recipes using South African pears and avocados, nutmeg from the Straits Settlements or canned salmon from Canada, attempting to provoke a desire in British housewives for Empire produce? Or were they simply responding to an appetite amongst a patriotic, pro-protectionist section of society, for ideas of Imperial Preference, as well as the desire for greater variation in domestic menus? While there has been much recent scholarly work on Britain's interwar trade and economic policy, and the Empire Marketing Board (e.g., Graham, 2022; Chattopadhyay, 2024; Varian, 2022), there has been less work on how these great global winds of political, social and economic changes eddied into the so-called 'Small Spaces of Empire': ordinary people's breakfast tables, their larders and the lifestyle pages of interwar newspapers: overlooked but vital cogs in the vast imperial machine.[2] The lifestyle pages of these major national influencers, whose campaigns for Empire trade reached such a pitch of high intensity in 1929–1932 that they dominated their front pages and leaders, have so far been ignored by scholars. What was the link between concerns about economic and imperial collapse, for example, and an article in the *Daily Mail* in November 1929, painting for its readers an enticing image of the high seas populated with ships bearing Empire delicacies to the ports of Britain: 'Oranges from Africa, spices from India, apples from Canada…the Empire Ocean routes at this moment are literally marked out in delicacies' (*Daily Mail* 25 November 1929, p. 4). This chapter examines how the food coverage of the *Daily Mail*, *Daily Express* and *Evening Standard* (also owned by Beaverbrook) combined these meddlesome proprietors' astute understanding of their readers' interests and needs during the interwar era with their own political and commercial aims during a time of major economic upheaval.

The case study

This chapter uses qualitative content analysis of a range of food journalism types, from news articles to recipes and features. The period covered is the four years from 1 January 1929 to 31 December 1932, that is, the period immediately before the launch of the Empire Crusade and ending just after the signing of the Ottawa Agreements that ushered in a modified form of Imperial Preference between Britain and several countries within her Empire. This period also includes the Wall Street crash of 1929, the first years of the Great Depression, the British pound being forced off the Gold Standard in 1931 and the stirrings of unease, following the 'roaring twenties', over the stability of peace in Europe. A digitised copy of the *Daily Mail* was available to me, through my institution. Combinations of search terms were used to generate texts. These terms employed generic words, for example, 'recipe, dish, menu, cookery', or ingredients, such as 'grapefruit' or 'guava' or 'nutmeg'. Dish names such as 'curry' or 'Kedgeree' were also used to identify foods from countries in the Empire. The period of research for this chapter coincided with the catastrophic outage at the British Library caused by a cyber-attack, and copies of the *Daily Express* and London *Evening Standard* were available only on old-style microfilm using mechanical readers. These two newspapers were 'read' from cover to cover, although for efficiency, when 'women's' or other 'lifestyle' pages were identified as regular sections, these were focused on. While this latter method was more laborious, it enabled a more holistic approach to viewing the newspapers' content and connections to be made between commercial and political concerns. So, for example, on 1 July 1929, the Monday following the launch of Lord Beaverbrook's 'Empire Crusade', an advertisement placed by the Empire Marketing Board, promoting South African oranges, appeared on page 2, and a few pages later, the 'leader' thundered in capital letters: 'Who is for the Empire?' Irrelevant items such as imperial nature notes on guava tree flowers, short stories set in exotic locations and advice on how to make bird-feeders out of half a grapefruit skin, although interesting, were discarded. 'Lifestyle' articles were divided into two broad and occasionally overlapping categories: recipes and menus on the one hand and more discursive food features on the other. The former category by far dwarfed the latter in numerical terms, for reasons discussed below. The remaining articles were read and sorted into four distinct themes that emerged: 'monotony/variety', 'thrift/economy', 'slimming/health' and 'novelty/luxury'.

The newspapers

Readers of the *Daily Mail*, *Daily Express* and *Evening Standard* were exposed to saturation coverage of the Empire Free Trade issue during these years. The subject was rarely off the front page and was a regular topic in the leading articles. Readers also received vast quantities of information about food trade and export policies of the Dominions: 'Rescuing the Agriculture in the Transvaal' (*Daily Express* 11 February 1930, p. 9); 'Ontario ready to tax foreign foodstuffs' (*Evening Standard* 29 May 1930, p. 1); 'The Empire sending us food of all kinds' (*Evening Standard* 14 August 1929, p. 2; 'Our bread is buttered on the Empire side' *Daily Mail* 30 January 1929, p. 4). This latter article listed all the Empire countries and the food they provided: lamb, pork and butter from New Zealand; apples and pears from Australia; wheat from Canada; oranges, grapefruit, peaches and grapes from South Africa; coffee from British East Africa and tea from India and Ceylon. At the launch of the Empire Crusade several articles in the *Daily Express* provided helpful world maps to show readers exactly where the Dominions were and which foods came across the world to the British larder, with their colour shading, the same as the mother country, marking them as British as opposed to 'foreign'. During this time, the *Daily Express* was an average of 20–24 pages long; the *Evening Standard* 28 pages; the *Daily Mail* 20–24 pages; all three were priced at one penny. (For contrast, the more upmarket *Times* and *Manchester Guardian* cost four pence and two pence, respectively).

Daily Express

At the start of the survey period, the *Daily Express* carried the lowest number of articles on food in its 'Lifestyle' pages. These occupied pages 4 and 5 every weekday. Their main contents consisted of lengthy and detailed health features on issues such as mending broken bones, coping with childhood rheumatism and recovering from tuberculosis. Other articles ranged from advice on cleaning the home, beauty and self-care and interior decorations. There was often a cartoon and part of a serialised story. Later, page 4 became a children's page. Food items appeared rarely, but when they did were clearly pegged to news or seasonal interest, so articles on jam-making, iced juices and fruit bottling appeared in the summer. From February 1930, page 5 introduced a weekly menu, 'Seven Days' Catering', by-lined Catherine Ives. The menus, she told readers, "are designed to help every woman who wishes to give her household interesting, nourishing and economical food" ('Seven Days' Catering', 7 February 1930, p. 4). Of all the papers' food coverage, Ives' recipes most noticeably linked cooking with specific Empire ingredients, as will be seen later. In addition, the paper regularly carried articles on Empire food as an interesting or exotic ingredient in its news pages, sometimes combining the news item with a short recipe. For example, a news page article about the success of a new experiment in cultivating avocado in South Africa came with a recipe for avocado and pineapple salad ('Avocados All Year Round' *Daily Express* 25 June 1929, p. 5).

Daily Mail

The Daily Mail had by far the most comprehensive food coverage of all three papers. It combined recipes and menus, with longer, more discursive articles about food and cookery in its lifestyle pages. These appeared towards the back of the paper, usually on pages 19 or 23 depending on whether the paper was 20 or 24 pages long. Their names varied from 'A Woman about Town' and 'A Woman's Household Diary', but often there was no sub-title to the page at all. Lifestyle feature coverage was the usual women's page fare of fashion, children's health, interior decorations and food. There was a strong association between food and the need for weight loss, particularly in its popular '18-days-diet', promoted in 1929 and 1930, which included eating grapefruit every day. The 'Woman's Household Diary' column gave readers regular peeks into the food choices of the wealthy and aristocratic, often with an Empire theme, with connotations of aspirational luxury: "grapefruit, peaches, wines and liqueurs from South Africa [have] taken a prominent places among the wines served at several banquets recently" (January 1930, p. 15). Outside of the lifestyle section, a wide range of food items could be found, many focusing on Empire trade and many emphasising Empire food's quality and exoticism. The *Daily Mail* also carried the highest number of 'advertorials' about food and Empire, which merged apparently independent articles about interesting foods from abroad, with advertisements from Empire producers.

Evening Standard

The *Evening Standard* carried very few discursive articles on food as a cooking ingredient. The paper was geared towards busy London workers and prided itself on its intellectual coverage with contributors like the novelist Arnold Bennett and the commentator Dean Inge as well as famous women MPs such as Ellen Wilkinson and Mary Agnes Hamilton. To reflect its busy readership, its 'Home Page' (usually page 18) carried a daily 'menu' feature initially by the food journalist Elizabeth Craig. She was later replaced by an unnamed male cookery writer with the initials 'G. H. B. B'. Readers had complained that Craig's recipes were too difficult, requiring them to make complicated sauces with anchovies, vanilla and curry spices ('My Menus: Elizabeth Craig explains, *Evening Standard* 16 July 1929, p. 22). Craig hugely favoured grapefruit and pineapple, adding these to meals as breakfast or pudding on average more than 20 times a month. These fruits were virtually extinguished from G. H. B. B.'s menus when he took over. On the other hand, G. H. B. B. was clearly a fan of curries, kedgerees, mulligatawny and other Indian dishes, as well as banana-based dishes, including these on average ten times a month. Beginning after the Wall Street Crash in November 1929, G. H. B. B.'s recipes were sub-titled 'Economy Menus', reflecting readers' anxieties over household budgets as the economic crisis deepened. These menus, often no more than a few lines long, but carried each day, meant that in terms of quantity, the *Evening Standard* carried the largest number of menu articles, on average 300 each year. The paper did carry articles about food in its news pages, but mostly of trade or technological interest, such as new chilling methods to enable 'bringing chilled beef as easily from Australia as the Argentine' ('The Empire and its Food', *Evening Standard* 5 August, 1929, p. 6).

The themes

Monotony/variety

There could be no doubt in the minds of housewives and cooks reading their newspapers in the 1920s and 1930s that one of their chief responsibilities was to avoid monotony in the meals they provided for their families and guests. The interwar diet was restricted, even amongst middle classes, and carbohydrate-rich stomach fillers, particularly bread and potatoes, were the mainstay of family menus (Lyon and Kautto, 2021, p. 350). A healthy appetite was something to be aimed for in children, in busy working husbands and also in the tens of thousands of invalids and war-wounded who had returned from the War with amputations and severe lung disease caused by gas attacks (Cohen, 2001). Housewives were urged to avoid 'insipid', 'drab', 'stodgy' and 'monotonous' dishes ('Why do people put up with insipid dishes?' *Daily Mail* 26 January 1931, p. 15; 'Must our Meals be Monotonous?' *Evening Standard* 31 August 1929, p. 7; 'What's wrong with these menus' *Daily Mail* 22 September 1931, p. 19). Instead, they were told not to be afraid to introduce 'novel items – give them a trial to prevent monotonous meals'. The Empire could offer novel ingredients, once only reserved for the dinner tables of the wealthy. This women's page feature suggested serving guava jelly or Cape gooseberry jelly with cheese to guests, as opposed to the usual pickles ('Shopping – The Key to Good Meals', *Daily Mail* 19 April 1932, p. 19). Tinned food from the Empire was offered as a way of keeping mealtimes interesting all year round. The fruit and vegetable tinning industry was flourishing both in Britain and within Empire countries, so much that 'with the tinned products of the Dominions it is now possible to meet any requirements for such goods without going outside the Empire' ('Boom in British fruit Tinning' *Daily Mail* 23 October 1930, p. 7). This latter is one of many articles combining ideas around variety, taste and exotic foodstuffs, with ideas of buying Empire products. Tinned apricots, pineapples, grapefruit and pears from South Africa were all offered as ways of lifting dull British diets. In May 1930, readers of the *Daily Mail* were informed that: "50 cases of tinned blackberries have been sent over from Tasmania as an experiment. They have such good flavour that only 4 remain to be sold" ('A Woman's Household Diary', *Daily Mail* 21 May, 1930, p. 19). Another article published to mark the 70th anniversary of the famous Mrs *Beeton's Book of Household Management* marvelled at the 'delicious variety' available in 1930, as opposed to the 1860s. This was all thanks to the 'Empire larder', a heady phrase incorporating ideas of taste, variety and patriotism ('Cookery has improved' *Daily Mail* 5 December 1930, p. 19). Similarly, Empire honey could sweeten the British diet, with the memory of sugar rationing still strong in the nation's memory ('Honey as money-maker' *Daily Express* 14 May, 1930, p. 8). In his daily menu item, the cookery writer 'G.H.B.B.' tried to combine thrift with variety. He told readers specifically the origins of some of the foods he used, such as 'South African pears' ('Friday's Economy Menu' *Evening Standard* 8 May 1930, p. 22) and Bombay toast, made with Indian spices ('Weekend Menu' *Evening Standard* 2 May 1930, p, 22).

Political and proprietorial interference in the food coverage

Thrift/economy

Despite the cheery and uplifting ideas around variety versus monotony, food security was a real issue during this time. Social commentators and nutritionists became deeply concerned about the diets of the unemployed and working poor (Gazeley et al., 2022). While later reassessments speculate that diets were not as marginal as once feared, one survey conducted in 1937–1939 concluded that half the adult population was not getting the nutrients it needed for a healthy life (Shave, 2015). Empire produce tended to be slightly cheaper than food from other parts of the world, so in late 1929, Jamaican grapefruits were selling at London's Covent Garden for 18 shillings per case, whereas Florida grapefruit was 24 shillings per case. Similarly, South African oranges were 17–22 shillings per case, whereas Californian oranges were 18–23 shillings per case. ('Produce Markets' *Daily Mail* 20 November 1929, p. 4). Women were encouraged to keep their eyes out for food bargains, especially as the period wore on and the economy worsened ('Wives who watched the food prices and saved' *Daily Mail* 25 January 1932, p. 9). Just in case housewives didn't read the market pages, the *Daily Mail* spelled it out for them in the women's page: "It pays to buy Empire goods because we usually get better value for money" ('The Eighteen-day diet' *Daily Mail* 5 December 1929, p. 19). Governments from countries across the Empire delivered savings to British consumers through deliberate preference policies (Varian, 2022). The Australian Government, for example, paid import duty imposed by Britain on its wines in the form of an 'Export Bounty', which made a bottle of Australian wine 1/6 shillings cheaper than wines from Europe ('Australian Wine', advertorial, *Daily Mail* 5 December 1929, p. 19). Similarly, an advertisement for Australian Kangaroo butter, 'full of sunshine sweetness', was trumpeted as being 'cheaper than foreign butter' (*Daily Mail* 13 February 1931, p. 18). While the three newspapers' food coverage remained determinedly aspirational and upbeat, there were a notable number of recipes using leftovers and advice on how to make a dish or cut of meat last through the week through various iterations from roast, to cold, to minced to including remains in salads and macaroni sauces. Kedgeree, a recipe from India using rice, fish and chopped eggs, was regularly proposed as a way of using leftover fish (for example 'Why Should There be Bacon for breakfast?' *Daily Mail* 20 April 1929, p. 23).

Catherine Ives in her *Daily Express* weekly menus proposed use of salmon in four different ways in one week to make it last. Here, she specifically recommends housewives buy Newfoundland salmon, "a really excellent food at moderate cost which has been provided by modern methods of storage and cold transport. One of the greatest bargains on the market just now is Newfoundland chilled salmon" ('Seven Days' Catering' 20 May 1930, p. 5). On another occasion, she told women to buy Canadian salmon because it is "really cheap now and it seems a pity not to take advantage of the fact" ('Salmon in Shells' *Daily Express* 8 May 1930, p. 5). A particular favourite ingredient of hers was 'Canterbury Lamb', the brand name for New Zealand lamb frozen in the Canterbury area of New Zealand and shipped to Britain (Barnes and Higgins, 2020). She recommended it several times a month, each time advising housewives to order the correct cuts, so it could be used through the week in cutlets, casseroles and with the bones cooked up in Scotch Broth ('Seven Days Catering' *Daily Express* 21 February 1930, p. 5; 16 May 1930, p. 5). Canned food offered economy as well as variety too. Tinned food extended its shelf life, made it easier to transport across the world and kept it fresher. Grapefruits, previously a luxury, were now seen in working class homes, thanks to canning, the *Daily Mail* told its readers ('London's luxury Diets' *Daily Mail* 27 July 1929, p. 11). After *Evening Standard* readers had admonished her for proposing too complicated and too expensive meals, Elizabeth Craig began introducing cheaper and easier dishes from July 1929. In August 1929, for example, she proposed recipes using tinned pineapple 12 times in one month, including pineapple slices, pineapple sauce, a fruit salad with tinned pineapple and grapefruit and pineapple trifle. After he took over from Craig, G. H. B. B.'s favourite recipes for household economy combined cheap foods with spices or unusual ways of cooking them. Curried prawns on toast for a light supper, kedgeree and fried bacon with banana for a cheap and filling breakfasts were regular suggestions ('Tuesdays Economy Menus' *Evening Standard* 12 May 1930; 'Weekend Economy Menu' 9 May 1930, p. 22; 'Wednesday's Economy Menu' 22 May 1930, p. 22).

Slimming/health

In late 1929, a famous new celebrity diet, the 'Hollywood Diet' swept into the pages of the *Daily Mail*, from the United States. The so-called '18-days-diet' promised miraculous results. Based on no scientific or medical evidence, it called for half a grapefruit to be eaten with every meal (Vester, 2023). For several months, the *Daily Mail* carried recipes and features for the 'Eighteen Days Diet', telling readers demands for the diet were flooding into the newspaper (*Daily Mail* 5 December 1929), although it did also publish a reader letter complaining that they were advised to eat grapefruit 'so often' that could it please suggest other ingredients (15 November 1929, p. 23). Even when the 18-Day Diet was not being promoted, *Daily Mail* readers were regularly told that if they wanted to lose weight, they should eat grapefruit for breakfast ('The ideal diet' 7 April 1930, p. 21; 'Slimming without starvation', *Daily Mail* 16 June, 1932). While the paper never specifically recommended using Empire grapefruit, its regular 'Produce Markets' feature told readers that Jamaican grapefruits were cheaper than those from Florida.

Keeping a family healthy was also a major responsibility of the housewife. The *Daily Express* health pages hammered this message home day in day out. By the middle of the interwar period, the role of vitamins in food, in helping prevent illnesses like scurvy and rickets and also generally improving health and vitality was established and widely known (Stark, 2018). Grapefruit and oranges as well as raw vegetables like carrots were regularly proposed in the lifestyle and news pages for their high vitamin quantities and their abilities to ward off diseases like scurvy and rickets ('Vitamins and our summer diet' *Daily Mail* 22 June, 1929, p. 18; 'Salads that make a meal' *Daily Mail* 24 June 1932, p. 17; 'Diet at Age of 40' *Daily Mail* 4 August 1932, p. 5). While most of the *Daily Express* health page articles were of medical nature, the importance of vitamins and 'nourishing' food was also stressed ('Seven Days' Catering' *Daily Express*, 7 February 1930). Similarly, the *Daily Mail* made the link between children's health and carefully planned meals that contained fresh fruit and vegetables ('Planning those nursery menus' *Daily Mail* 21 October 1932, p. 21). Empire food advertisers also emphasised this point: New Zealand Anchor butter regularly pointed out that its vitamin content was not impaired during transportation, thanks to cold storage, and Del Monte canned fruits from a range of Empire countries, claimed tests, showed that canned fruit retained its vitamins. Advertisements aside, the link with specific Empire foods and *editorial* content was weakest in this theme apart from the major exception of Beaverbrook's 'Empire Loaf' campaign. When the *Daily Express* launched its campaign in May 1930, the high nutrient content of Canadian flour was one of its chief selling points since the bread was no cheaper than bread made from wheat grown in Britain. Various experts were rolled out to trumpet the nutritional qualities of the flour ('More Empire

Grist' *Daily Express* 14 May 1930, p. 11; 'Finest Bread in the World' *Daily Express* 9 May 1930, p. 1). In another campaign launched by Lord Rothermere in 1932, to try to 'save' the British fishing industry, the 'One fish day a week' promised that not only would eating more fish improve the nation's trade balance, but also fish would 'improve the nation's health' ('One fish day a week' 30 May 1932, p. 10).

Novelty/luxury

While sticking to the household budget, avoiding monotony and keeping a family healthy were the reader of interwar food journalism's major concerns, and occasionally ideas of luxury and gourmet cooking crept in. French cookery was still the apogee of taste in the 1920s and 30s. It was the food of the elite, and the best chefs in London were French, such as Maitre Pagot of Claridges, Maitre Guillier of the Berkeley and Maitre Verlogieux of the Savoy Grill (Lyon, 2020). French chefs in London were often consulted by newspaper women's pages for their top cookery tips ('Women's Grouse Rush' *Daily Mail* 12 August, 1929, p. 7; 'French Methods with English Vegetables' *Daily Mail* 4 April 1930, p. 23). These French chefs always used butter, sometimes several ounces in a recipe. With Empire butter, English housewives no longer had the excuse that it was too expensive, they were told. 'Nothing horrifies the intelligent foreigner more than the fact we do not cook with butter. We no longer have the excuse that butter is dear. It is not, and Empire butter is the cheapest of all.' ('Oh if only they'd Cook!' *Daily Mail* 26 January 1931, p. 15). English cooks were told that the Empire was sending Britain its butter in record quantities: 42,000 tons from Australia in 1929, double the quantity it had sent just two years earlier ('The Empire sending us more food of all kinds' *Evening Standard* 14 August 1929, p. 2).

At Christmas particularly, the Empire could add that extra sparkle of flavour: 'Nutmeg from the Straits settlements, lemons from South Africa, Demerara sugar from the West Indies' would make a Christmas pudding to remember ('Try this Christmas Pudding' *Daily Mail* 9 November 1931, p. 23). Exotic fruits such as the mangosteen, goldenberry and jelly melons, imbued with the sun from the Dominions, brightened English newspaper lifestyle pages and occasionally dinner tables ('Looking at Life' *Daily Mail* 24 May 1931, p. 8). Even lobster, the height of luxury now, came within the ordinary middle-class budget thanks to tinned lobster from Canada ('The Empire Food Lure', *Daily Mail* 5 April 1930, p. 7). Narratives around the hardworking Dominion producers helping to add something special to the suburban larder was a common theme. Fishermen working the monstrous seas around Cape Breton Island, between Newfoundland and Nova Scotia, were able to provide British consumers with swordfish, which had a 'delightful flavour' and was becoming 'more popular each year', thanks to the brave men who risked their lives in the waves ('Swordfish as a delicacy' *Daily Express* 2 December 1929, p. 11). Indeed, the Empire farmer's whole aim in life, it seemed, was to create tempting delicacies for the British housewife: passion fruit from South Africa, the 'beautifully coloured red dessert apple' from Canada, the pineapple from Malaya and 'astonishing variety from every country in the Empire' ('Foreign Vintages' *Daily Mail* 24 October 1932, p. 3). After Britain came off the Gold Standard in September 1931, newspaper readers were reassured that this would not lead to food shortages; still an unpleasant memory for so many and the Empire would step up: 'The national larder is fully stocked' and 'The Dominions are increasing their shipments' the *Daily Mail* informed its readers ('Empire Imports to Increase' 23 September 1931, p. 6).

Conclusion

By 1932, the growth in the demand for Empire goods had reached record levels. The Annual Report of the Empire Marketing Board for the year that ended May 1932 announced records for West Indian bananas, Malayan canned pineapples, Cyprus oranges and East African coffee. The Annual report also announced that the bulk of the board's income had been invested in research into tropical diseases and pesticides for crop-destroying insects such as locusts (Empire Marketing Board, 1932). In 1929, the British Empire had accounted for 30 percent of UK imports; by 1938, it accounted for 42 percent, a significant increase (de Bromhead, 2019). In 1932, with the signing of the Ottawa Agreements, a modified form of Empire Preference between Britain and Australia, New Zealand, Canada, India, Newfoundland, South Africa and Southern Rhodesia was instigated (ibid). This was greeted with triumph in the *Daily Express* and *Daily Mail*, even though the United Empire Party had collapsed part-way through 1931, and the 'Press Lords' were ridiculed in a famous speech by Stanley Baldwin. The speech, oft-quoted in relation to Britain's popular press, accused Beaverbrook and Rothermere of exercising 'power without responsibility – the prerogative of the harlot throughout the ages' (Chisolm and Davie, 1993, p. 305). But in a way, they had won. How much of a role had their newspapers played in convincing patriotic housewives to support Empire farmers and producers? In the news pages, the messaging could hardly have been clearer, and the lifestyle pages certainly promoted Empire foods, with the exotic delights of South African avocado, Straits Settlements nutmeg and plump sultanas from Australia, all name-checked with approval. As well as sunshine-filled luxuries from the Empire, these newspapers also promoted frozen Canterbury lamb from New Zealand, and Canadian and Newfoundland salmon, on the grounds of cost. With the new technology of canning, luxury and economy could go hand in hand, with Tasmanian blackberries and South African grapefruit lasting for months on larder shelves. While in this particular study, the impetus for this specific promotion of certain foods appears to have been political, these findings foreshadow the blurring of lines between editorial and advertising in newspaper and magazine lifestyle sections, where often travel and food coverage are positioned adjacent to each other, and culinary tourism is pushed by overseas destinations with the promise of the exotic in every bite (Brien, 2014). Whether or not British housewives made the connection between their shopping basket and the owner of their newspaper's political ambitions, these recipes and general larder advice offered helpful ideas for hard-pressed housewives concerned about a wide range of food problems, from monotony to nutrition at a time of economic and political anxiety.

Future directions

This chapter has identified trends in historical lifestyle pages that foreshadow much modern food coverage. From cooking on a budget, which is echoed in contemporary lifestyle pages that address the cost-of-living crisis, to cooking during times of national anxiety, be it the anxious interwar years or the anxious years of the pandemic, we can see the origins of modern food and cooking advice in newspapers of 100 years ago (Fürsich, 2022). This chapter has of necessity covered only a fraction of themes that emerged during the interwar years, and there is much scope for further research particularly, as the 1930s wore on, when once again people began to worry about another War and fiercer political winds blew into larders and pantries. What advice did newspapers give on issues such as food preserving and hoarding, and grow-your-own and self-sufficiency that would emerge in the late 1930s?

How would these issues be linked to ideas of patriotism? Judging from the findings here, we may find much that foreshadows modern day anxieties of food security, biodiversity and food miles as climate change poses an even more existential threat than war.

Notes

1 Although the Irish Free State became self-governing in 1921, it remained a dominion of the British Empire until 1937
2 I have to thank Swati Chattopadhyay (2024) for this delightful metaphor

Further reading

Clay, Catherine, DiCenzo, Maria, Green, Barbara and Hackney, Fiona (eds.) (2018). *Women's Periodicals and Print Culture in Britain 1918–1939: The Interwar Period*. Edinburgh: Edinburgh University Press.
De Bromhead et al. (2019). When Britain Turned Inward. *American Economic Review* 109/2, pp. 325–352.
Eide, Martine and Knight, Graham (1999). Public/Private. Service Journalism and the Problems of Everyday Life. *European Journal of Communication* 14/4, pp. 525–547.
Fakazis, Liz and Fürsich, Elfriede (eds.) (2023). *The Political Relevance of Food Media and Journalism: Beyond Reviews and Recipes*. London: Routledge.
Trentmann, Frank (2007). Before 'Fair Trade': Empire, Free Trade and the Moral Economies of Food in the Modern World. *Environment and Planning D* 25, pp. 1079–1102.

Bibliography

Barnes, Felicity and Higgins, David (2020). Brand Image, Cultural Association and marketing: 'New Zealand' Butter and Lamb Exports to Britain, c. 1920–1938. *Business History* 62/1, pp. 70–97.
Bingham, Adrian (2018). Modern Housecraft? Women's Pages in the National Daily Press. Clay et al. (eds.) *Women's Periodicals and Print Culture in Britain 1918–1939: The Interwar Period*. Edinburgh: Edinburgh University Press, pp. 225-237.
Brien, Donna Lee (2014). A Taste of Singapore: Singapore Foord Writing and Culinary Tourism. *Media Culture Journal* 17/1, p. 3. https://doi.org/10.5204/mcj.767
Buitenhuis, Peter (1989). *The Great War of Words: Literature as Propaganda 1914–1918 and After*. London: B. T. Batsford.
Cannadine, David (2001). *Ornamentalism: How the British Saw their Empire*. London: Allen Lane.
Chattopadhyay, Swati (2024). The Small Spaces of Empire: Long-Distance Trade, Anglo-Indian Foodways and the *Bottlekhana*. *The Journal of Imperial and Commonwealth History* 52/1, pp. 1–44.
Chevalier, Natacha (2018). Iconic Dishes, Culture and Identity: The Christmas pudding and its hundred years' journey in the USA, Australia and New Zealand. *Food, Culture and Society* 21/3, pp. 367–383.
Chisholm, Anne and Davie, Michael (1993). *Lord Beaverbrook: A Life*. New York: Alfred A. Knopf.
Cockett, Richard (1989). *Twilight of Truth*. London: Weidenfeld and Nicolson.
Cohen, Deborah (2001). *The War Came Home: Disabled Veterans in Britain and Germany 1914–1938*. Berkeley: University of California Press.
Cusack, Igor (2000). African Cuisines: Recipes for Nationbuilding? *Journal of African Cultural Studies* 13/2, pp. 207–225.
De Bromhead et al. (2019). When Britain Turned Inward. *American Economic Review* 109/2, pp. 325–352.
Dejmanee, Tisha (2022). Influencer Activism: Visibility, Strategy, and #BlackLivesMatter Discourse on Food Instagram. Fakazis, Liz and Fürsich, Elfriede (eds.) *The Political Relevance of Food Media and Journalism: Beyond Reviews and Recipes*. London: Routledge, pp. 19–33.
Driberg, Tom (1956). *Beaverbrook: A Study in Power and Frustration*. London: Weidenfeld and Nicolson.

Duffy, Andrew and Ashley, Yang Yuhong (2013). Bread and Circuses: Food Meets Politics in the Singapore Media. Hanusch, Folker (ed.) *Lifestyle Journalism*. London: Routledge, pp. 58–73.
Eide, Martine and Knight, Graham (1999). Public/Private. Service Journalism and the Problems of Everyday Life. *European Journal of Communication* 14/4, pp. 525–547.
Empire Marketing Board (1932). *Annual Report*. London: HMSO.
Fakazis, Liz and Fürsich, Elfriede (2022). Introduction. Fakazis, Liz and Fürsich, Elfriede (eds.) *The Political Relevance of Food Media and Journalism: Beyond Reviews and Recipes*. London: Routledge, pp. 1–16.
Fishback, Price (2012). Relief during the Great Depression in Australia and America. *Australian Economic History Review* 52/3, pp. 221–249.
Fürsich, Elfriede (2022). Cooking in the Time of Corona: The Politicized Domesticity of Food Journalism in the New York Times. Fakazis, Liz and Fürsich, Elfriede (eds.) *The Political Relevance of Food Media and Journalism: Beyond Reviews and Recipes*. London: Routledge, pp. 100–114.
Gardiner, Juliet (2010). *The Thirties: An Intimate History*. London: Harper.
Gazeley, Ian et al. (2022). How Hungry Were the Poor in late 1930s Britain? *Economic History Review* 75/1, pp. 80–110.
Graham, Daniel (2022). Advertising Empire: Consumerism and the Spatial Imaginary of the British Empire. *Journal of Colonialism and Colonial History*, 23/2. https://dx.doi.org/10.1353/cch.2022.0013.
Irwin, Mary and Tominc, Ana (2022). How the Bendy Banana Became a Symbol of Anti-EU Sentiment: British Media, Poitical Mythology and Populism. Fakazis, Liz and Fürsich, Elfriede (eds.) *The Political Relevance of Food Media and Journalism: Beyond Reviews and Recipes*. London: Routledge, pp. 153–166.
Johnston, Josee and Goodman, Michael (2015). Spectacular Foodscapes: Food Celebrities and the politics of Lifestyle Mediation in an Age of Inequality. *Food, Culture and Society* 18/2, pp. 205–222.
Jones, Steve and Taylor, Ben (2013). Food Journalism. Orange, Richard, Turner, Barry and Wheeler, Sharon (eds.) *Specialist Journalism*. London: Routledge, pp. 96–106.
Knightley, Phillip (2000). *The First Casualty: The War Correspondent as Myth-Maker from the Crimea to Kosovo*. London: Prion Books.
Kristensen, Nete Nørgaard and From, Unni (2013). Lifestyle Journalism: Blurring Boundaries. Hanusch, Folker (ed.) *Lifestyle Journalism*. London: Routledge, pp. 25–40.
Lonsdale, Sarah (2015). Roast Seagull and other Quaint Bird Dishes: The Development of Features and Lifestyle Journalism in British Newspapers during the First World War. *Journalism Studies* 16/6, pp. 800–815.
Lonsdale, Sarah (2020). *Rebel Women between the Wars: Fearless Writers and Adventurers*. Manchester: Manchester University Press.
Lonsdale, Sarah (2022). Patriotic Hens, Tomato Turbans, and Mock Fish: The Daily Mail Food Bureau and National Identity during the First World War. Fakazis, Liz and Fürsich, Elfriede (eds.) *The Political Relevance of Food Media and Journalism: Beyond Reviews and Recipes*. London: Routledge, pp. 183–198.
Lyon, Phil (2020). Dining Out: Restaurants and British Society in the 1930s. *Journal of Culinary Science and Technology* 18/3, pp. 177–191.
Lyon, Phil and Kautto, Ethel (2021). Half the Battle Is Fought in the Kitchen: Convalescence and Cookery in 1920s and 1930s Britain. *Food, Culture and Society* 24/3, pp. 345–367.
Maguire, Anna (2021). *Contact Zones of the First World War: Cultural Encounters across the British Empire*. Cambridge: Cambridge University Press.
Montague, Charles Edward (1922). *Disenchantment*. London: Chatto and Windus.
Peel, Dorothy (1933). *Life's Enchanted Cup*. London: John Lane and the Bodley Head.
Ponsonby, Arthur (1928). *Falsehood in Wartime*. London: George Allen and Unwin.Shave, Samantha (2015). The Carnegie Dietary Survey of Interwar Britain. *Local Population Studies* 94, pp. 71–79.
Stark, James (2018). Replace them by Salads and Vegetables: Dietary Innovation, Youthfulness and Authority 1900–1939. *Global Food History* 4/2, pp. 130–151.
Taylor, S. (1998). *The Great Outsiders: Northcliffe, Rothermere and the Daily Mail*. London: Orion.
Teughels, Nelleke (2021). Politics at the Table: Food and Power Relations at the 1935 Brussels International Exposition. *Food, Culture and Society* 24/2, pp. 227–243.

Trentmann, Frank (2007). Before 'Fair Trade': Empire, Free Trade and the Moral Economies of Food in the Modern World. *Environment and Planning D* 25, pp. 1079–1102.

Varian, Brian (2022). Imperial Preference before the Ottawa Agreements: Evidence from New Zealand's Preferential and Reciprocal Trade Act of 1903. *Economic History Review* 75, pp. 1214–1241.

Vester, Katharina (2023). How Dare You Hoard Fat When Our Nation Needs it? Weight Loss Advice and Female Citizenship during World War One and the 1920s. *Subjectivity* 30/3, pp. 297–316.

5
REVIVING CONTEMPORARY JOURNALISM THROUGH NARRATIVE LIFESTYLE COVERAGE?

Annik Dubied

Introduction

Over the past decades, numerous attempts have been made to define lifestyle journalism and to identify its (narrow and broad) contours. At the same time, lifestyle journalism has been rightly promoted for its little-known and neglected ability to rethink the field of journalism studies from scratch (Hanusch, 2012, 2020; Fürsich, 2012). Several authors have succeeded in thinking beyond a normative model of journalism conceived solely in its narrow (and contestable, see Neveu, 2001) role of a watchdog and political tool in the strict or institutional sense of the terms (From & Kristensen, 2018; Hanusch, 2020). The (arguable!) tendency of lifestyle journalism to focus on audiences and their often consumerist expectations (From, 2020) has been emphasised, as has its ability to challenge a normative conviction of 'original' and 'pure' information free from commercial imperatives (Hanusch, 2012).

I take these statements as premises and propose that we should think about lifestyle journalism and its study from two viewpoints: its ability to challenge normative visions and make sense politically and democratically and the important questions this raises (albeit perhaps poorly) about audiences and their everyday concerns. It is about "(…) challeng[ing] problematic binaries such as public/private, altruistic/hedonistic, rational/ irrational or civic/personal that tend to inform discussions on the public sphere" (Fürsich, 2012, p. 19) and considering journalism as a tool to "empower the individual, provide orientation in a highly complex world and, by doing so, strengthen the collective in modernity" (From & Kristensen, 2018, p. 715, synthesising Giddens). These premises are in line with the results of a recent study on the available scientific literature on journalistic relevance, which highlights the crisis journalism is facing today (Amigo et al., 2023). Literature on the subject outlines two ideas for consideration:

- Thinking about journalism beyond its explicitly democratic or political role
- Taking account of the public, its concerns, and its possible involvement

This chapter explores these issues by taking a historical look at two cousins of lifestyle journalism that, while seemingly different, have yet developed along similar lines: crime news on the one hand and celebrity news on the other. In doing so, I argue for a broader approach to study lifestyle journalism that includes such 'everyday-life journalism'. The chapter further highlights the issues raised by this historical parallel and goes on to examine the avenues for research and for professional practice renewal that it suggests. Finally, I take a wider look at the ability of predominantly narrative genres such as lifestyle journalism, crime news journalism, celebrity news journalism, and everyday-life news more generally to raise essential questions for the current field of journalism, for the public space, and for journalism studies.

Crime news, public concerns, and mass press

Crime news is a cousin of lifestyle journalism: a number of similarities, both historical and ontological, emerge from their comparison. Their respective origins are ontologically linked to the commercial dimension of news coverage; both of them are everyday-life-oriented; both are emotion-driven genres; and their study, therefore, points to the question of cultural (il)legitimacy.

Historically, lifestyle journalism has been growing because of news organisations' desire to sell more products to larger publics. On the other hand, the birth of the mass press in Western countries has been relying on crime news[1] (Dubied, 2004). An interesting parallel can then be drawn between lifestyle journalism and crime news. Its emergence, in the European French-speaking world and beyond, confirms Banjac and Hanusch's (2022) observations for lifestyle journalism. "Fait divers", or crime news, has been considered, from the beginning, as a popular, commercial, desperately individual genre, that contributes to the degeneration of news. The elites and institutional powers first (Perrot, 1981; Schudson, 1978), but also journalists themselves, and scholars later, have tirelessly worked to confirm its cultural illegitimacy (Bourdieu, 1996; Mattelart & Neveu, 2003).

However, crime news has made a decisive and essential contribution to the success of the "presse à un sou" in the Western French-speaking world (Perrot, 1981; Kalifa, 1995; Dubied, 2004), and of the penny press in the United States (Schudson, 1978). Clearly, these stories of ordinary people surprised in their daily lives by extraordinary events were touching audiences to such an extent that they were willing to devote part of their income to buying newspapers – newspapers that previously catered only for a very economically, culturally, and socially privileged part of the population. The 'rhetorics of the specific case' (Dubied, 2009), which focusses the story on individual figure and governs crime news, clearly made it possible to attract the interest of people who usually feel unconcerned by institutional news. And even if crime news was emotional and sensational, they were clearly able to generate discussion on public interest concerns: at the end of the 19th century, in France, crime news brought up the issue of attacks on private property or physical integrity, at a time when these issues were of concern to a population that had recently regrouped in large urban centres (Kalifa, 1995). In the same way, lifestyle journalism during the First World War enabled people to find out about their daily lives (Lonsdale, 2015).

This contribution goes beyond Hanusch's observation that with "(…) the arrival of the penny press, as well as the illustrated press, came increasing focus on matters of everyday life, in an attempt by newspapers to attract new audiences, such as workers and women, to their products" (2020, p. 409). Coverage of everyday concerns by the mass press, through crime news, simply enabled the media to become 'mass media' and to offer news to a large public (that is, beyond the elites). The 'new audiences' mentioned by Hanusch were quite simply the general public, previously excluded from what the elite considered to be the legitimate press. Without crime news, which reflected and discussed the strong concerns of the time (promiscuity and insecurity) through individual and dramatic stories (Kalifa, 1995; Dubied, 2004, pp. 81–82), publics attracted by the media would have been much more limited to elites. Whatever the criticisms that may be addressed at such often sensationalist coverage, it seems, nevertheless, difficult to maintain that a mass press can exist without it.

Of course, crime news alone did not generate such considerable social change: at the same time, literacy had reached a satisfying level to make it possible, just as transport made it by now possible to drive printed newspapers to their readers within a reasonable timeframe; and printers were now working with rotary presses, enabling mass production of newspaper copies (Mollier, 2006, pp. 65–67; Schudson, 1978). Be that as it may, several famous news stories (the Troppman affair in Paris, or the "poisoners of Marseilles affair" in the south of France) undoubtedly contributed to an exponential growth in the circulation of the media that reported them in French-speaking Europe (Dubied, 2004, p. 23). These news items were often covered in a sensational way to attract the attention of a large public, which was as entertained as it was interested by the portrayal of a widely shared feeling of insecurity brought about by the structural changes of the time (urbanisation, industrialisation, and promiscuity).

In any case, crime news focussed on individuals, and valued also for its commercial dimension, contributed to the birth and survival of the Western mass press. This is, indeed, hardly compatible with a traditional, normative, and theoretical vision of the historical role of journalism in a democracy. But it is worth recalling, as Hanusch does, that "[e]ven the forerunners of newspapers, while focused primarily on matters of political and civic life, quickly included accounts that belong mostly to the private sphere" (2020, p. 409). Researchers and journalists themselves should, therefore, question the hierarchy between hard news and soft news and between institutional and everyday-life journalism afresh. What if these long-denigrated genres – crime news but also celebrity news and lifestyle journalism and everyday-life journalism in general – were an intrinsic part of the information system, contributing in a roundabout, implicit, and delegated way to public debate? And the question that follows would be how are they treated, handled, and trained to finally take them seriously?

As for researchers, the issue is more or less settled, even if studies and publications on the subject are still less valued than those on "legitimate" genres. But there is now a consensus that studies on crime news, like studies on lifestyle journalism "(…) are exciting terrain for cultural-critical media scholars in their project to examine the negotiation of ideologies in relation to lived experiences" (Fürsich, 2012, p. 17), even if there are still few of them and if most of these studies "will always straddle the duality between the naive celebration of [their] democratic potential as a popular media text and the undifferentiated denunciation as a hyper-commercial format" (Fürsich, 2012, p. 23). However, it is now recognised that crime news history is an excellent way of understanding the mentality, values, and representations of an era through the 'rhetoric of the specific case'.

It remains to be seen what the above observation could mean for journalistic practices themselves: like lifestyle columns (Banjac & Hanusch, 2022), crime news is denigrated, scorned, and shunned by professionals who see it as a voyeuristic, commercial, and overly emotional genre (Dubied, 2005b, p. 60). As a result, crime news stories are not taken seriously enough and are often handled by people who are ill-trained or ill-prepared and who consequently have poor command of the 'strike force' of the genre (2005b, 61ss). When they are taken seriously and well-handled, their ability to reflect and even discuss the issues of the everyday life is, nevertheless, remarkable. Poorly executed, however, the intrinsically sensational and emotional nature of crime news makes it difficult to handle, resulting in potentially serious ethical violations.

Celebrity news, everyday life, and consumerism

This first historical comparison confirms the interest of defining and studying lifestyle journalism and everyday-life news beyond the normative and sometimes rigid definitions of journalism and to highlight (with all due precautions!) the ability of this type of journalism to deal with public interest concerns, without being explicitly political. The French sociologist Edgar Morin, in his seminal work on mass culture *L'Esprit du temps* (1962), suggested that crime news represents the "negative polarity" (my translation) of mass culture, the utility of which is to enable the rejection of tragedy on the periphery of a normal, pacific life. Crime news allows the audience, in short, to experience transgression. In line with Morin's work, I suggest taking now into consideration the "positive polarity" of mass culture; that is to say, celebrity news. Morin argues that celebrity news represents, in contrast, "super-individuals" who embody, positively or negatively, the values of mass culture (glorification of the individual and personal success until the 1970s, or crisis of these values thereafter; see Gorin & Dubied, 2011). Following Morin, both positive and negative polarities of mass culture, which we suggested earlier as being cousins to lifestyle journalism, deserve to be considered in order to understand the kind of importance everyday-life journalism can have in the public space.

From the beginning, reporting on celebrities' extraordinary and ordinary lives was designed by the Hollywood studios to keep the public's involvement through these double-sided figures (extraordinary–ordinary), while waiting for the next film (Dyer, 1979). This relentless and highly effective management of the 'attention economy' was adjusted beyond the Hollywood studios, but the principle remained the same: stars and their entourage continued to put themselves in the spotlight outside the works to which they contributed, in order to attract attention beyond their work and to achieve, above all, commercial objectives. Celebrity news was soon divided between complacent reports conceded by the celebrities themselves and stolen news or images (or presented as such) that were less advantageous (see, for instance, Conboy, 2014). The effect was, and remains, the same: retain attention, enhance reputation (whatever that may be), and make the 'super-individual's' figure work in addition to/in the service of the artworks. These figures were and are still presented as "idols of consumption" (Lowenthal, 2004 (1961), p. 130): the 'celebrity sphere' is a world of leisure, holidays, and sports, and the stars themselves are often depicted as consumers, if they are not directly promoting products in advertisements or on social networks. Whatever the case, celebrity news captivates the general public, who can observe, compare, negotiate, or weigh up issues encountered in their own daily lives (health, family, consumerism, moral limits, etc.) (Gorin & Dubied, 2011).

In this context, how can celebrity journalism help us think about journalism? One can first argue that celebrity journalism, by its very nature described above, is over-exposed to pressure from sources; it experiences, in an intensified way, what journalism in general encounters in a more diffuse way. Like lifestyle journalists (Hanusch et al., 2017), celebrity news journalists are aware of their vulnerability but nevertheless claim to belong fully to the professional group and to respect its ethical standards (Dubey & Dubied, 2014, p. 68). In this regard, "difficulties they meet are of the same kind as those encountered by the rest of the profession; however, they experience them in an exacerbated and particularly virulent form, finding 'themselves in the front line of an evolving profession'" (Dubey & Dubied, 2014, p. 81). The increasingly harsh power relations experienced by these journalists, faced with the professionalisation of their sources and the growing desire of the latter to control information about them, represent undoubtedly one of the major challenges facing journalism in the 21st century. If celebrity news journalists, like lifestyle journalists, are particularly affected by these pressures, they are also in the best position to know how and to what extent they can resist them and, at best, safeguard what constitutes the essence of their profession.

Celebrity news journalism is then ontologically concerned with its audiences, for commercial reasons – as lifestyle journalism is (Usher, 2012). What can be seen as a weakness is nevertheless interesting for professional practice as for research, for we know that the public is traditionally rarely taken into account in the practices and research studies and is not part of journalist's culture, nor appears in traditional training courses (Swart et al., 2022). To whom are the journalists talking? What subjects are audiences interested in? How can they get involved? These are questions for which the importance is highlighted by surveys on audience confidence and media quality (see, e.g., Newman et al., 2023 for the annual report of the Reuters Institute, or the occasional report by Gault & Medioni, 2022 on the news fatigue phenomenon in France), but journalists do not ask them as a priority. In this respect, lifestyle journalism and celebrity news journalism have a head start. Even if their approach to audiences is based on ontologically commercial intentions, as we have seen, they, nevertheless, inject the question of public concerns and the usual standards of journalism in practice. In any case, then, this commercial nature points at what allows including and interesting the general public and to "invite people to participate in the making of public meaning" (Costera Meijer, 2001, p. 192).

By dealing with everyday life and what is at stake in it, through the lives of celebrities or ordinary people, or the common uses of health, fashion, or well-being, everyday-life journalists in general automatically put on the agenda concerns that are more connected, more involving, and less detached than their colleagues in traditional news beats. As they have "a sense of common experience and a basis for social cohesion" (Fürsich, 2012, p. 18), they are in some way participants in everyday lives, they develop an ability for community building (From & Kristensen, 2018, pp. 723–724), and are likely to help repair "the torn social fabric" (Hanusch, 2020, p. 416, discussing Harrington, 1997). And they know the difference between a purely commercial and sensationalist coverage and news geared towards the public interest. All in all

> [J]ournalistic routines of celebrity news are therefore exemplary case studies for those who wish to understand the contemporary changes in journalism. In this regard, celebrity news seems to offer a fruitful path to identifying emerging trends in the sociology of journalism.
>
> *(Dubey & Dubied, 2014, p. 68)*

As for practices, these discredited skills raise, paradoxically, sound and essential questions and even sketch out some answers. Does journalism have a daily orientation function in addition to its role as the fourth estate? Does everyday life deserve media attention, whether it be that of ordinary people or celebrities? Can individual issues make sense for the collective? etc. To all these questions, the study of crime news and celebrity news offers a 'yes' – even if it's not an unconditional or naïve 'yes'. On a broader scale, these genres are driving "(…) scholarly attention to the ways in which news may engage people rather than being exclusive and elitist" (From & Kristensen, 2018, p. 724). It is, therefore, interesting to look at the way they do this – that is to say, narrative.

Everyday-life journalism and narrative

The study of crime/celebrity news, and of everyday-life journalism in general, draws our attention to the importance of journalism's day-to-day orientation role and to some shortcomings in the traditional coverage of public concerns. The analysis of crime and celebrity news adds then another dimension to these findings: both use mainly the narrative form. And narrative is precisely reputed to enable people making sense of reality and help them understand their role and their identity in it, as Paul Ricoeur puts in his seminal work on the subject (Time and Narrative, 1983–1985, Oneself as another, 1991, and Memory, history, and forgetting[2]). Crime news and celebrity news draw then our attention to the importance and relevance of narratives news centred on individual stories.

The outbreak of crime news in European French-speaking press at the end of the 19th century represented a radical break, bringing the existing media into the age of masses. These news items now offered on a large scale stories that reflected the everyday concerns in which publics would recognise their reality, through figures and situations they could identify with. In that sense, the narrative form helped turn "complex social discussions and issues into issues with clear options" (Costera Meijer, 2001, p. 201), through its figures, narrative causalities, and *mimesis* (Ricoeur, 1983–1985). For Costera Meijer, an ability to raise "consciousness", together with creating "common experience" and enabling "dialogue" (2001, p. 202), constitutes the basis for rethinking and renewing the quality of journalism. And yet, narrative is precisely what makes it possible to share experience, to read one's own story through that of others (Oneself as another, Ricoeur, 1990), and to allow, if not dialogue, at least comparison and the putting into perspective of experiences.

Similarly, the success of celebrity-centred news stories, from the invention of the star system (Dyer, 1979) to the beginning of the 21st century (Dubied & Hanitzsch, 2014), underlined the interest of stories focussed on individual destinies and the public negotiations that these narratives allow (Morin, 1962; Gorin & Dubied, 2011) through individual stories.

The narrative, as format, has (also!) long been delegitimised in the news media, considered as it is as too emotional and entertaining. However, it is now well-recognised that narrative enables us to make sense of reality. Even before Ricoeur's definitive theorisation, qualitative methods in social sciences (which can usefully be compared to journalistic approaches) had already emphasised, in their methodological reflections on the Chicago school contribution to the field, the extent to which life stories, as a method, made possible an "intimate understanding of the lives of others", which provides an "insight into the subjective side of much-studied institutional processes" (Becker, 1966, p. XII). Howard Becker already pointed out in 1966 that the lifestory approach was relevant beyond sociology since it

> Describes to people the ways of life of segments of their society with which they would never otherwise come in contact. (…) it's a live and vibrant message from 'down there', telling us what it means to be a kind of person we have never met face

to face [and allow us to] feel and become aware of the deep biases about such people that ordinarily permeate our thinking and shape the kind of problems we investigate.

(1966, XIV–XV)

The relevance of narrative, when used in a thoughtful way, has, therefore, been widely emphasised, before journalists and researchers in Journalism Studies began to address the issue.[3] Ricoeurs' and Becker's statements are promising enough, as Neveu underlines:

> In exploring the emotional experiences and subjectivities of individuals and groups, [narrative reporting of new (new) journalism] do much more than move readers: they provide access to the subjective dimensions of life and experience. They simultaneously supply an 'objectifying' dimension, revealing aspects of social life hitherto unseen, whether hidden or visible. Their effect is panoptic, rendering more of the social world visible and developing in-depth perception of the details of lifestyles, social interactions and urban scapes. [T]hese two dimensions of knowledge (objective and subjective) create remarkable opportunities for making sense of the varied forms of 'otherness'.
>
> *(2017, p. 9)*

Talking about collective problems through individual stories and thus enabling an intimate understanding of unknown or inaccessible realities or allowing the negotiation of 'living-together' through shared stories – all these qualities are recognised in narrative. And this ability goes well beyond other questionable aspects, such as personalisation and spectacularisation, which have been readily put forward for criticism and devaluation of storytelling as a whole. On the contrary, Ricoeur, Becker, Neveu, and even Bourdieu are suggesting that good use of narrative makes possible what no other form of coverage makes possible. Schudson, in advocating "social empathy", says nothing different: "Personal trouble as entrée to a public issue seemed almost inescapable by the 1980s (…) Learning about our neighbours through the mass media, both news and entertainment (…) serves a vital democratic function" (2008, pp. 18–20). Clearly, narrative constitutes the optimal media for these 'personal troubles' and seems even the only way to gain access to the reality of these 'neighbours'.

Crime news, celebrity news, or even lifestyle journalism, therefore, invite us to think afresh about the place of individual daily lives stories in contemporary media coverage. This type of journalism has long been underestimated, even scorned, both within the profession (Dubied, 2005a; Dubey & Dubied, 2014; Hanusch et al., 2017) and beyond. Often learnt on the job, by imitation and adjustment, taught little or not at all in journalism training courses, and practised 'for want of anything better' by professionals who condemn themselves to being categorised as bad journalists, everyday-life journalism, in general, certainly raises important ethical questions (personification and problematic exposure of individuals to public knowledge, spectacularisation, commercialisation, etc.) that have to be studied (Neveu, 2016) and taught, rather than treating them as a negligible quantity. And because they are concerned with individuals, their emotions, their legitimate concerns, and their daily joys and difficulties, these genres are worth practising.

Considering (lifestyle) journalism through the lens of everyday-life journalism tends then to highlight the ability of these news genres to cover individual, everyday life, and prosaic concerns, in a very accessible way, while being eminently political – without being directly institutional. It has already been suggested (Hanusch, 2012, p. 8) and even demonstrated (see e.g. Lonsdale, 2015) by others, but the examples from crime and celebrity news allow us to rethink things from scratch. Obviously, news covering the "existing real world" (Hanusch, 2012, p. 4) like health, education, wellbeing, consumption, security, or (celebrities) private life and "meltdowns" (Gorin & Dubied, 2011) are intrinsically political, are of public interest, and have a real "democratic potential" (Hanusch, 2012, p. 8). Moreover, the above observations confirm Hanusch's call "to explore the ways in which journalism that operates supposedly on the margins may in fact also be a critical influence on other journalistic fields" (2012, p. 9). I suggest that the use of narrative form, sometimes experienced with in questionable ways in crime and celebrity news, is one such way. This is confirmed by the reflection of Edgar Morin (1962), which considered everyday-life genres such as crime or celebrity news to be central to how mass culture works.

The perceived illegitimacy of these genres prevented them from inclusion in any consideration of what journalism can or should be. But dismissing them out of disgust or modesty prejudices reflection and ultimately proves counterproductive. News that reports everyday life, recounts reality in a form that is accessible and familiar to everyone (the narrative), and leaves room for emotions not only seems to have always existed in the mass press but seems also essential for citizens to find their way in their daily lives, something that traditional conceptions of journalism fail to remember. An entire journalistic culture is challenged here: one can observe many recent examples of journalists failing to understand and cover everyday concerns that seemed essential to their audiences, with the result of leaving these journalists bereft, dumbfounded, and discredited. The current crisis of traditional journalism as a Fourth Estate (Amigo et al., 2023) requires thinking beyond prescriptive visions that sometimes become rigid.

As Western journalism is going through a profound crisis, it needs to reinvent itself and its relationship with its audiences. It is then relevant to question the most traditional and prescriptive of its definitions, in the light of genres that have always been considered and used as repellents. In other words, journalism must put its myths to the test because these myths tend to inhibit all kinds of constructive thinking.

> The uncertain and ambiguous nature of the crisis means that its outcome is uncertain. As the crisis sees the joint emergence of forces of disintegration and regeneration (of 'death' and 'life'), as it brings into play 'healthy' (research, strategy, invention) and 'pathological' (myth, magic, ritual) processes, as it both awakens and puts to sleep, the crisis can have a regressive or progressive outcome.
>
> *(Morin, 1976, p. 149; my translation)*

If journalism wants to reinvent itself, it has to stop mythologising and classifying, take seriously its history, and open a discussion on the values, power relationships, and social stratifications that underpin its (il-)legitimacies.

Hard news is itself, by no means, exempt from sensationalism, emotion, or personalisation, while everyday-life journalism and soft news have long demonstrated their ability to tackle general, institutional, and eminently political subjects through narrative, an individual and emotional approach, putting on the agenda the day-to-day concerns about which institutional journalism seems sometimes blind or unconcerned. It is only a short step from saying, in a Bourdieusian vein (Neveu, 2007), that journalists are unable of stepping out of the comfort zone of their own social class in order to understand what does not emerge from it. Even if I do not fully agree with this statement, I feel like questioning the agenda, as constructive journalism (From & Kristensen, 2018) does from another angle, is necessary. In any case, crime news, celebrity news, and lifestyle journalism have long practiced a different agenda – even if we can and should discuss the relevance of their coverage.

This is not about glorifying soft news or adopting a naïve stance that would tend to rehabilitate 'all emotional' and 'all narrative' for news and advocating to replace hard news with soft news. Instead, I support Eide and Knight's statement that

> The idea of a dichotomy between citizenship and consumerism is problematic inasmuch as it tends to reify both terms, and underestimate both the ways in which consumerism is implicated in citizenship and the extent to which the identity and subjectivity of the consumer are also complex and problematic.
>
> *(1999, p. 536)*

In the same perspective, the idea of a well-established dichotomy between the rational and the emotional seems neither relevant nor productive, but rather rigid. As Costera Meijer argued (2001, p. 202), we need to go beyond this dichotomy and rethink the quality of journalistic coverage in terms of its ability to promote the 'living-together'. In this line, I argued above that narratives offer incomparable advantages in terms of the ability to reflect on 'living together'. The result is an ability for journalism to open in-depth discussion, with the help of the scientific field, on what underpins its values, priorities, and reasons for being. In this perspective,

> Journalists are social actors whose primary purpose is to serve the public interest. To do so, they must assume certain responsibilities that are recognised as conducive to achieving this objective: in particular, to seek out and disseminate, fairly and rigorously, truthful and relevant information that will help all citizens of a society to make informed choices in all areas of contemporary life, with a view to improving their living conditions.
>
> *(Bernier, 2014, p. 8, my translation)*

Therefore, soft news and everyday-life journalism can be considered as having a political and public interest potential, maybe as essential as explicit hard news coverage. It goes certainly beyond definitions of lifestyle journalism that are strictly limited to news that "focuses on audiences as consumers, providing them with factual information and advice, often in entertaining ways, about goods and services they can use in their daily lives" (Hanusch, 2012, 2), but includes it in a wider reflection on legitimate journalism and its quality.

Future directions

Thinking about journalism through some of its most reviled illegitimate genres seems then a beneficial approach. How can lifestyle journalism and its cousins contribute to (the reflection on) the renewal and health of contemporary journalism? Could that kind of popular, everyday, person-centred, narrative and emotional news contribute, under certain conditions, to the wellbeing of the public sphere? And how? I suggest five directions.

First, it can work as a *counterpoint to an overly institutional journalism*, problematised by the barometers of public confidence in the media ("journalists are not interested in my life/my opinions"), as well as by the criticisms of journalists in the recent social movements (Gault & Medioni, 2022; Barbosa de Almeida, 2023, Souillard et al., 2020). If current news is dramatically removed from the day-to-day realities of the public, what about lifestyle journalism, celebrity journalism, or crime news journalism in this context? About lifestyle journalism during World War I, Lonsdale claims: "These articles do not solely focus on the reader as passive consumer but as social actor whose minute decisions on how to tackle the problems that everyday life raises have political consequences" (2015, p. 813) – an observation that could partly be extended to celebrity news, which allows publics to negotiate social values (Gorin & Dubied, 2011). As for crime news, historians note that it disappears in situations of crisis or political authoritarianism (Dubied, 2004, 29), as it has a subversive potential, even if its power of 'diversion' (Bourdieu, 1996; Foucault, 1975) should not be underestimated either. Of course, "Understanding lifestyle journalism as popular journalism of public value should not lead researchers to assume an automatic democratic and anti-hierarchical potential of all types of lifestyle coverage" (Fürsich, 2012, p. 23). But the ability of such genres to report everyday-life matters has been underestimated for far too long.

Second, lifestyle, crime, and celebrity journalism can operate, under certain conditions, as a counterpoint to the *highly polarised and agonistic journalism* the same media barometers problematise. That kind of agonistic news minimises the contribution of journalism to the day-to-day orientation of audiences and to their 'living-together', beyond the political choices that are often presented in a simplistic way. If current news neglects social link and daily guidance, does everyday-life journalism restore balance, and on what conditions? Although eminently political (health, mobility, leisure, lifestyle choices, and individual trajectories), the subjects of everyday-life journalism lay on the fringes of the myths and stereotypes in vogue about the profession (neutrality and objectivity) and beyond the reach of the recent political attacks (Christin & Motironi, 2024; Mabut, 2024). Attacks have moreover chosen to target journalists precisely in their role as the Fourth Estate, forgetting in the process its ability to provide day-to-day guidance on subjects, which, even if they are not explicitly political, are so in the broadest sense, which, in this case, is both significant and undoubtedly interesting for the media, bogged down as they are in simplistic debates about their 'mythological' role as the Fourth Estate.

Third, everyday-life journalism in its broadest sense contributes to question the existence of mass media that can only *find their audience by opening up to everyday and irreducibly individual themes*. Accepting this evidence, rather than mourning and spitting at some genres that are considered responsible for a degeneration of news, avoids falling back on sclerotic myths and enables the field of journalism to take these genres seriously and provide them with a better framework. Mass press has been able to reach its audiences because it has broadened its range of subjects and interests, particularly to include crime news items. To take this historical evidence seriously means accepting that it was not only due to a regrettable spectacularisation and emotionalisation of news, but that it can also be explained, to a large extent, for more respectable reasons – namely, the ability to handle issues of everyday life, for example. It means also to take into account the part of this condemnation that was due to the anger and contempt of the literate elite, who was deprived of certain privileges, and did attack what was beyond its reach (Perrot, 1981; Schudson, 1978).

Fourth, everyday-life journalism, through crime and celebrity news, raises at new costs crucial questions about its reception: *what are audiences looking for in this particular kind of news*? To what extent are they critical, detached, or aware of the limits of independence of this type of journalism? To what extent is their confidence in the media in general (Amigo et al., 2023) affected or, on the contrary, strengthened? Beyond value judgements and cultural legitimacies, everyday-life journalism in its broadest sense is at the forefront of the challenges the field of journalism is facing (changing business models, anti-elitism, public disaffection, and so on). And it provides interesting and productive questions, in line, for instance, with Fürsich's argument that "the main goal of any type of journalism with a public quality ultimately would be to empower all audiences to live and act in a democratic system" (Fürsich, 2012, p. 19).

Fifth, everyday-life journalism, through crime and celebrity news, is part, albeit peripherally, of the narratives that have developed in recent years, such as narrative podcasts or witnessing journalism. These narratives focus on individuals in an emotional way and make in-depth use of the *narrative form's potential to give sense to reality, to help people understand themselves, and to reflect on human actions*. In doing so, they appear to fill a kind of gap in terms of understanding individual motivations and trajectories. If "'current journalism fails to acknowledge fully the significance of people's immediate world: their family, friendships, neighbourhood, town, or country'" (Costera Meijer, 2001, p. 198), crime, celebrity, and lifestyle journalism does. The question is: how can it be done correctly and in the public interest (which it currently does not do systematically)? This already implies serious training in the practice of these genres.

Conclusion

In short, I am calling for an "update [of] our classification and typification of journalistic templates and styles" (Neveu, 2017, p. 2). The frontier is of course thin between "narcissistic consumer journalism and journalism that instills authentic 'social empathy'" (Fürsich, 2012, p. 18, mentioning the 'social empathy' conceptualised by Schudson, 2008, p. 17), and it requires a thoughtful reflection on the fundamental values that guide Western journalism. In short: search for truth, independence, and respect for the individual, all in the service of the public interest.

Clearly, lifestyle journalism is constantly living on the edge of independence from its sources and advertisers. The same is true of celebrity news, which also raises legitimate suspicions about its independence in relation to its famous sources, as well as about its quest for truth, which is undermined by accommodation, 'bidonnages', and collusion. For its part, crime news raises nagging questions about respect for individuals, who are often sacrificed for the sake of the emotion and sensation that their misfortunes can arouse.

Nothing new, even if the same kind of concern can more or less be found in the practice of more legitimate journalistic genres, like political journalism. For example, in France, the interdependence of the latter with its sources has already been demonstrated (Lemieux, 2000), and the search for truth has been the subject of highly questionable choices (e.g., the concerted concealment of important information about the private lives of several presidents of the Republic, finally revealed by… the celebrity press, see, for instance, Dubied, 2005a).

The public interest dimension is rather the focus of attention here: how is everyday-life journalism able to put on the agenda concerns that drive the interest of the publics and enable them to find their way in their daily lives and make 'informed choices' (to use Bernier's words quoted earlier)? It seems that the potential for 'making good use of everyday-life news' in this area has been neglected. We definitely need to rethink journalism from a fresh perspective, looking beyond rigid classifications, and taking everyday-life genres as seriously as any others. It requires us also to take audiences seriously, without immediately denigrating their choices in the name of cultural legitimacies that flirt with the elite's contempt for the general public.

Finally, it implies to help everyday-life journalism to become "citizen-oriented" (Costera Meijer, 2001, p. 190), by resolutely including its learning in the journalism education. This involves training in crisis situations, learning emotional skills, offering reflective tools for delicate situations in terms of respect for people or conflicts of interest, mastering the narrative and its explosive potential, and learning about the audiences journalists are talking to, and their concerns.

Notes

1 I use here the expression "crime news", even if the French expression "fait divers" is improperly and only partly translated by it; the "fait divers" goes beyond crime stories, to include coverage about events that transgress and challenge the existing order (surprising, unusual, unnatural events, etc.). The genre is nevertheless dominated by crime stories, particularly in the 19th century. This translation, albeit incomplete, is therefore nevertheless relevant.
2 The dates mentioned here are those of the original edition in French: *Temps et récit*, 1983–1985, *Soi-même comme un autre*, 1991, and *La mémoire, l'histoire, l'oubli*
3 Becker's argument on lifestory was so relevant to Pierre Bourdieu that he had it translated in French and published (with a critical response from himself) in his journal: Becker, H. (1986). Biographie et mosaïque scientifique, *Actes de la recherche en sciences sociales*. 62/63, 105–110 and Bourdieu's answer : Bourdieu, P. (1986). L'illusion biographique. *Actes de la recherche en sciences sociales*. 62/63, 69–72

Further readings

Amigo, L., et al. (2023). *Pertinence du journalisme. Une revue de la littérature*. Swiss Confederation: Federal Media Commission. https://www.emek.admin.ch/inhalte/Pertinence_Rapport_COFEM.pdf
Becker, H. (1970 (1966). The Life-story and the scientific Mosaïc. *Sociological Work*. Hawthorne.
Fürsich, E. (2012). Lifestyle journalism as a popular journalism. *Journalism Practice*, 6(1), 12–25.
Neveu, E. (2017). Revisiting the "Story vs. Information" model. *Journalism Studies*, 18(10), 1293–1306.

References

Amigo, L., Détraz, C., Pignard-Cheynel, N., & Dubied, A. (2023). *Pertinence du journalisme. Une revue de la littérature*. Federal Media Commission of the Swiss Confederation. https://www.emek.admin.ch/inhalte/Pertinence_Rapport_COFEM.pdf
Banjac, S., & Hanusch, F. (2022). Aspirational lifestyle journalism: The impact of social class on producers' and audiences' views in the context of socio-economic inequality. *Journalism*, 23(8), 1607–1627.
Barbosa de Almeida, T. (2023). *Lula en prison: une analyse multimédiatique de la polémique publique au Brésil dans la presse et sur Twitter autour de l'affaire Triplex (2016–2018)* [PhD thesis, Université de Limoges and Universidade Federal do Paraná]. HAL theses. https://theses.hal.science/tel-04397325
Becker, H. (1970 (1966). *The Life-Story and the Scientific Mosaïc. Sociological Work*. Hawthorne.
Bernier, M.-F. (2014, 3rd edition). *Ethique et déontologie du journalisme*. Presses Universitaires de Laval.
Bourdieu, P. (1996). *Sur la télévision / L'emprise du journalisme*. Liber.

Christin, P., & Motironi, H.-P. (2024). *Taisez-vous! Le débat démocratique est-il mort?* Le bord de l'eau.
Conboy, M. (2014). Celebrity journalism, an oxymoron? Forms and functions of a genre. *Journalism*, 15(2), 171–185. https://doi.org/10.1177/1464884913488722
Costera Meijer, I. (2001). The public quality of popular journalism: Developing a normative framework. *Journalism Studies*, 2(2), 189–205.
Dubey, M., & Dubied, A. (2014). Celebrity news journalism. The storytelling injunction. In Broersma, M. & Peeters, C. (eds.), *Retelling Journalism. Conveying Stories in a Digital Age*. Peeters, 67–85.
Dubied, A. (2004). *Les dits et les scènes du fait divers*. Droz.
Dubied, A. (2005a). La polémique-people, emblème d'une nouvelle forme de polémique journalistique? *Médiatiques. Récit et Société*, 37, 36–41.
Dubied, A. (2005b). Quand les journalistes de presse parlent du fait divers. Une lecture exploratoire de leurs représentations et de leurs récits de pratiques. *Les cahiers du journalisme*, 14, 58–75. http://www.cahiersdujournalisme.net/pdf/14/04_Dubied.pdf
Dubied, A. (2009). L'information people, entre rhétorique du cas particulier et récit de l'intimité. *Communication*, 27(1), 54–65. https://doi.org/10.4000/communication.1257
Dubied, A., & Hanitzsch, T. (2014). Studying celebrity news (introduction). *Journalism*, 15(2), 137–143. https://doi.org/10.1177/1464884913488717
Dyer, R. (1979). *Stars*. British Film Institute.
Eide, M., & Knight, G. (1999). Service journalism and the problems of everyday life. *European Journal of Communication*, 14(4), 525–547.
Foucault, M. (1975). Illégalisme et délinquance. Naissance de la prison. In Foucault, M. (ed.), *Surveiller et punir*. Gallimard, 292–299.
From, U. (2020). *Lifestyle Journalism*. Oxford Research Encyclopedia of Communication. https://oxfordre.com/communication/display/10.1093/acrefore/9780190228613.001.0001/acrefore-9780190228613-e-835?rskey=ZyfIDc&result=1. 1–16.
From, U., & Kristensen, N. (2018). Rethinking constructive journalism by means of service journalism. *Journalism Practice*, 12(6), 714–729.
Fürsich, E. (2012). Lifestyle journalism as a popular journalism. *Journalism Practice*, 6(1), 12–25.
Gault, G., & Medioni, D. (2022). *Les Français et la fatigue informationnelle. Mutations et tensions dans notre rapport à l'information*. Institut Jean Jaurès. https://www.jean-jaures.org/publication/les-francais-et-la-fatigue-informationnelle-mutations-et-tensions-dans-notre-rapport-a-linformation/
Gorin, V. & Dubied, A. (2011). Desirable people: Identifying social values through celebrity news'. *Media, Culture and Society*, 33(4), 599–618.
Hanusch, F. (2020). Journalism and everyday life. In Hanitzsch, T. & Wahl-Joergensen, K. (eds.), *Handbook of Journalism Studies*. Routledge, 406–419.
Hanusch, F. (2012). Broadening the focus. *Journalism Practice*, 6(1), 2–11.
Hanusch, F., et al. (2017). 'How much love are you going to give this brand?' Lifestyle journalists on commercial influences in their work. *Journalism*, 18(2), 141–158.
Harrington, W. (1997). *Intimate journalism: The art and craft of reporting everyday life*. London: Routledge.
Kalifa, D. (1995). *L'encre et le sang. Récit de crimes et sociétés à la Belle Epoque*. Fayard.
Lemieux, C. (2000). *Mauvaise presse. Une sociologie compréhensive du travail journalistique et de ses critiques*. Métailié.
Lonsdale, S. (2015). Roast Seagull and other Quaint Bird Dishes. *Journalism Studies*, 16(6), 800–815.
Lowenthal, L. (2004 (1961)). The Triumph of mass idols. In Marshall, D. P. (ed.), *The Celebrity Culture Reader*. Sage, 124–152.
Mabut, T. (journalist) (2024). Quand l'AFP est prise pour cible. *Discussion avec Fabrice Fries* [video]. https://fr.ejo.ch/regards-dexperts/quand-lafp-est-prise-pour-cible-discussion-avec-fabrice-fries
Mattelart, A., & Neveu, E. (2003). *Introduction aux Cultural Studies*. La Découverte.
Mollier, J.-Y. (2006). L'émergence de la culture de masse dans le monde. In Mollier, J.- Y. et al. (eds.), *Culture de masse et culture médiatique en Europe et dans les Amériques 1860–1940*, 65–81. Presses Universitaires de France.
Morin, E. (1976). Pour une crisologie. *Communications*, 25, 149–163. https://www.persee.fr/web/revues/home/prescript/article/comm_0588-8018_1976_num_25_1_1388

Morin, E. (1962). *L'esprit du temps*. Grasset.
Neveu, E. (2017). Revisiting the 'story vs. information' model. *Journalism Studies*, 18(10), 1293–1306.
Neveu, E. (2016). On not going too fast with slow journalism. *Journalism Practice*, 10(4), 448–460. https://doi.org/10.1080/17512786.2015.1114897.
Neveu, E. (2007). Pierre Bourdieu, sociologist of media, or sociologist for media scholars? *Journalism Studies*, 8(2), 335–347.
Neveu, E. (2001). *Sociologie du journalisme*. La Découverte.
Newman, N., et al. (2023). *Digital News Report*. Reuters Institute. https://doi.org/10.60625/risj-p6es-hb13
Perrot, M. (1981). L'affaire Troppman, 1869. *L'Histoire*, 30, 28–37.
Ricoeur, P. (1990). *Soi-même comme un autre*. Seuil.
Ricoeur, P. (1983–1985). *Temps et récit*. Seuil.
Schudson, M. (2008). *Why Democracies Need an Unlovable Press*. Polity.Schudson, M. (1978). *Discovering the News. A Social History of American Newspapers*. Basic Books.
Souillard, N. et al. (2020). Les gilets jaunes, étude d'un mouvement social au prisme de ses arènes médiatiques. *Terminal. Technologies de l'information, culture et société*, 127, 1–19. https://doi.org/10.4000/terminal.5671
Swart, J., et al. (2022). Advancing a radical audience turn in journalism. Fundamental dilemmas for journalism studies. *Digital Journalism*, 10(1), 8–22. https://doi.org/10.1080/21670811.2021.2024764
Usher, N. (2012). Service journalism as a community experience. *Journalism Practice*, 6(1), 107–121.

6
JOURNALISM TRAINING AND THE STATUS AND DILEMMAS OF LIFESTYLE JOURNALISM PRACTICE IN SOUTHERN AFRICA

Nhamo Anthony Mhiripiri

Introduction

Academic research and appreciation of lifestyle journalism per se in Africa are sparse, although there is a growing body of literature on tabloid journalism that treats lifestyle journalism as the latter's subset (Chama 2017, 2019; Wasserman 2010). This is partly because academic curricula at journalism training institutions such as polytechnic colleges and universities rarely give space to the area. There are also few journalists who easily and comfortably claim to be lifestyle journalists, in spite of many who specialize on sports and entertainment. Hard political news, news on business, finance, agriculture, industries and technologies appear to wield more prestige as compared to the arts and culture sections, which often specialize on lifestyle journalism. To shed more light on these issues, this chapter investigates the practices and attitudes of Africa-based media, journalism and cultural studies academics and Africa-based journalists, all selected from representative southern African countries. The underlying assumptions are that African journalists perceive lifestyle journalism as "light" and not "serious" enough for the development demands for Africa. It is also possibly the perception that lifestyle journalism deals with superficial and banal material that pervades low regard for news on travel, fashion, fitness, leisure, food and cuisines, arts and artefacts, luxury houses and hotels, fashion, beauty products, shopping malls, Christmas decor, clothing, ethnic cultures and tourism and fishing, among others. Apart from the perceptions and preoccupation of media academics and professional practicing journalists, there is the stark and robust terrain of lifestyle influencers who have taken space on social media with hundreds of followers. The latter are a ubiquitous reality, who are slowly gaining attention in university dissertations written by younger media and cultural studies students, who appreciate them more perhaps because social media influencers' articulations often do not smoothly comply with the pedantic strictures of journalistic standards.

In spite of the assumptions about class and tastes embodied in these seemingly innocuous topics, this chapter argues that there are political and identity issues implied in them.

Indeed, some academics have tried to extricate the political dynamics in travel journalism, especially when the citizens of the Global North visit and encounter inhabitants and citizens of the Global South who supposedly live in their natural states that are not remarkably tainted with industrial and postindustrial influences (Fabian 2006; Tomaselli 2012; Taylor 2018; Elbarbary 2022). The chapter will attempt to provide a link between African journalism training and practice and the reasons for why lifestyle journalism is treated as a low level and inconsequential type of journalism, or conversely, if it is regarded as too elitist and embarrassing for a continent that is still preoccupied with raising the standards of life for the majority of its people. It also tries to identify missed opportunities in lifestyle journalism that can still spur the promotion of African cultures and their development, especially when used within the context of travel journalism and cultural tourism. Interviews were conducted with African academics teaching media, journalism and cultural studies as well as print journalists from the mainstream media to ascertain their attitudes and opinions on lifestyle journalism.

Ambiguities of defining lifestyle journalism

Studies on lifestyle journalism are still preoccupied with issues of definition of this broad journalistic practice. This confirms its emergence and epistemological assertion as a proper critical field of study. Most literature on lifestyle journalism places it within a media institutional context that locates its interface and synergies with commercialization, individualization and digitalization (Fürsich 2012; From and Kristensten 2019).

Some scholars prefer conceptual and definitional boundaries to what is lifestyle journalism. While it remains broad in what it contains, there are attempts to particularize it so that it becomes a distinct genre. Thus, From (2019) enunciates this definitional ambiguity and complexity of lifestyle journalism. It is often defined in contradistinction to the normative ideal of journalism, hence acquiring its identity and value from "what it is not". Taking examples from studies on travel and music journalism, Fürsich (2012: 12) posits that lifestyle journalism as a "seemingly trivial journalism" can still be evaluated for its political and civil potential. Its journalistic qualities of review, advice and commercialism can sustain journalistic research that analyses deeper social and cultural facets of life. This is journalism with a potential public role, and "its discourse is worth analyzing for its ideological dimensions". Using Fiske's (1989: 1992) notion of "popular news" and Costera Meijer's (2001) "public quality", Fürsich argues that even this seemingly trivial journalism can be evaluated for its political and civil potential. She further notes how the journalistic dimensions of review, advice and commercialism can be transformed into approaches for journalism research that probes the social and cultural aspects of lifestyle journalism, while analysing lifestyle journalism's ideological dimensions. (Fürsich 2012).

Lifestyle journalism's definition cross-cuts other prominent journalistic practices, adopting and amalgamating elements such as soft news, service journalism, consumer journalism, popular journalism or even cultural journalism. From (2018: 1) further describes lifestyle journalism as "an umbrella term for more specialized beats of journalism such as travel journalism, fashion journalism or food journalism". A conflation of "soft news" and "hard news" genres typifies lifestyle journalism, and there is a blurring of boundaries of genre. The distinctions of hard or soft news are stemmed more on what topics are addressed, how they are presented and the "modes of addressing the audiences" (From 2018: 3). For example, when goods or services are marketed openly or subliminally within a lifestyle story, that story immediately acquires a key characteristic of lifestyle journalism. Quite often, lifestyle journalism is criticized for doing public relations work for organizations or advertising goods and services for market interests (Fürsich 2012; From 2018; From and Kristensten 2019). Sabrina Faramarzi (2021) writes that lifestyle journalism's "complex dynamics" shift "between traditional journalistic practices and consumerism, entertainment and cosmopolitanism". It presents a myriad of content from food, fashion, technology, sexuality, identity, gardening, photography, knitting, motoring, tourism, computer programming, etc. It is, therefore, important for any pedagogical work and professional journalistic practice on lifestyle journalism to carry a clear consciousness of the power dynamics embedded in narratives and language (Gramsci 2007; Bourdieu 2008).

Some scholars regard human interest stories as a key component of lifestyle reporting. Such stories use the experiences of ordinary people, incorporating 'a human face' in the narrative in order to present an event, issue or problem (Figenschou et al. 2023; Semetko and Valkenburg 2000: 95). They aim for audience engagement, the influence of public opinion and, more importantly, attraction of revenue for media organizations (Figenschou et al. 2023; Zillmann 2002). Since elitist critics and professional journalists have often viewed lifestyle journalism with condescension, largely due to its commercial imperative (Wasserman 2010), the current predicament that traditional journalism faces due to declining audiences and aggressive innovations in social media might be a vindication for lifestyle journalism. A fastidious adherence to editorial autonomy is now precarious as traditional journalism resorts to stories that are interwoven with advertisements, marketing and public relations in order to attract revenue, something it previously frowned at (Fürsich 2012: 15).

A cursory survey of academic literature on lifestyle journalism reveals that the dominant analysis of lifestyle journalism is that it is relegated to the periphery of media and communications research throughout the world (Fürsich 2012; Banjac and Hanush 2022; From 2018, 2019). It is even worse in African scholarly literature, although there is growing optimism about its potential. Literature on tabloid journalism in Africa often lacks in aspects of lifestyle journalism, especially when it pays attention to the "infotainment genres" in Africa's emerging democracies (Chama 2017, 2019; Wasserman 2010). With the social mobility that shaped out after the demise of apartheid in South Africa, lifestyle journalism in tabloid newspapers acts as a resource for guidance for both the Black elites and the poor and working class so that they could visualize their aspirations for a better life. Tabloids provide "an ostensibly apolitical focus of everyday life" that appeals to readers "who feel disconnected from formal politics" (Wasserman 2010: 95).

Such papers give a veritable menu of "tips and advice on 'lifestyle', homeownership, and financial matters'". This appeals well to the young Black wannabes "who prefer to express their identities by means of conspicuous consumption rather than through the old identity categories" (Wasserman 2010: 34). Concealed in these stories is a free-market discourse that props up liberal individualist ideology. In spite of the gem snippets on lifestyle journalism gleaned from scholarly literature on tabloid journalism and journalism in general, this chapter lobbies for a self-conscious scholarship that puts lifestyle journalism at the centre and not as a subset of other constitutive genres.

While it is not necessarily concerned directly with lifestyle journalism, the most insightful literature on lifestyles and identities is largely associated with the radical Cultural Studies scholarship produced under the leadership of Keyan Tomaselli at the University of KwaZulu-Natal. Tomaselli's team focuses more on cultural tourism, identity politics and its interface with traveling researchers, a process Tomaselli (2012) has termed "anthro-tourism".

This is a systematic analysis of group identities of selected communities, especially the San and the Zulu, the commercialization and commodification of these identities within the global capitalist and tourism markets (McLennan-Dodd 2003; Tomaselli 1999; 2005, 2012; Mhiripiri 2008, 2012; Mhiripiri and Tomaselli 2010; Dyll-Myklebust 2014). There are the usual tourists who embark on leisure travels to visit other places and other people. And there are also researchers who also travel for leisure and academic work as well. Both sets of travelers exhibit traits of "anthropological tourists" fascinated with gazing upon the other. Tomaselli's group applies the Goffman's theory of front-stage and back-stage, with the front-stage as where choreographed performances are exhibited for the tourist gaze (Dyll 2003; Mhiripiri 2012). Patron–Client relations are forged here, with the Zulu and San willing to sell pristine images about themselves to mostly 'Western' tourists whose imaginations about these African groups are mostly drawn from dominant mass-mediated myths. The backstage is where the frontstage actors retreat at the end of the act and live their ordinary lives away from the tourist gaze. In their writings, the Tomaselli-led group juxtaposes the popular public spectacles (and the economic reasons behind them), with the back-stage quotidian lives normally concealed from clients. Documentary and fictional films – some made by Tomaselli's students and colleagues – have occupied a reasonable part of the studies (Mlauzi 2002; Reinhardt 2002a, 2002b). Few of the materials are drawn from the mainstream media such as newspapers, TV and radio. This is mainly due to the methodology applied by the UKZN team, where they preferred interacting with people and performers in their spaces of existence, rather than rely predominantly on the raw copy produced in newsrooms.

It is tempting to write that there is a scarcity of serious scholarship on lifestyle journalism, but there is a need to make a concerted exploration of studies that have so far catered for the broader field of travel, tourism, culture and identities. Indeed, there is no clear-cut media and communication discipline or school that has systematically studied professional journalism as commonly known and understood and how lifestyles are studied. The formidable *The Palgrave Handbook on Media and Communication Research in Africa* reveals that African-centred researchers do not often give priority to lifestyle journalism in its general sense (Mutsvairo 2018). Rather, such scholars are preoccupied with topics perceived to be complex and more serious such as politics and the media, gender and class. Examples they draw or the content they examine is not deemed as "light" and "light-hearted". All major contributions on lifestyle journalism note how it is neglected as a field of study, despite the fact that there are decades of production of journalistic content that substantiates the existence of lifestyle journalism (Fürsich 2012; From 2018; Banjac and Hanusch 2022). Notwithstanding literature on mainly African tabloid journalism that occasionally gives minimal space to lifestyle journalism (Chama 2017; Wasserman 2010), there is still very minimal self-conscious academic work that ascribes itself as specializing on African lifestyle journalism per se. The scarcity of scholarly research on the lifestyle journalistic topics on the African continent arguably makes researchers like Banjac and Hanusch (2022) pacesetters beside the "anthro-tourism" works from Tomaselli's stable.

Banjac and Hanusch (2022) focus on the state of lifestyle journalism in South Africa, covering the perceptions of both journalists and audiences on the significance of lifestyle stories. The title of the article is very telling, "Aspirational lifestyle journalism: The impact of social class on producers' and audiences' views in the context of socio-economic inequality". South Africa is a very poignant case study of the phenomenon of lifestyle journalism due to the country's well-researched and publicized socioeconomic disparities, where the rich and elites live lives with qualities comparable to those of the wealthiest in the Global North. However, the poor majority's lives can be as poor and depressing as those of many that wallow in poverty throughout the African continent. Hence, the case choice is quite representative of African conditions. Banjac and Hanusch's (2022) research on lifestyle journalism provides a promising and optimistic outlook of the future of lifestyle journalism in countries with struggling economies and serious economic disparities across social classes such as South Africa. Both journalists and audiences have identifiable sources of inspiration and aspirations from various kinds of content produced under the rubric of lifestyle journalism. The rich appeal to certain content and the distressed to other content that suits their circumstances, but some of their expectations are similar. Journalists are also aware of the public service role of lifestyle journalism. Such awareness is important for projections of the industry into the future. However, there is a missing gap, in that academia has not consistently addressed the purpose and significance of lifestyle journalism, not only as necessary "soft" news but also as purveyors of ideological sensibilities. All types of news legitimate ideology, and news professionalism and news organizations also have ways of legitimating specific economic systems such as capitalism (Tuchman 1978).

South African journalists interviewed by Banjac and Hanusch (2022) were aware that all stories are inherently political; hence, lifestyle was not separate from politics. Journalists were "very aware of social class divisions among their audiences" (Banjac and Hanusch 2022: 1617). They understood class differences and how the rich and those with less disposal income had different aspirations and desires. Journalists thus shaped their news content to suit appropriate living standard measure desires. Stories provided "affluent South Africans with ideas to go away for the weekend or for holiday", while aspiration was targeted at people "who aren't necessarily rich … not in the luxury market, but […] are working and they still have things that they want to acquire, but they are not kind of low LSM (Living Standard Measures) where they can't afford certain things", while "people from fully disadvantaged backgrounds whose key purpose is to put food on the table" were not targeted (Banjac and Hanusch 2022: 1618).

Locating lifestyle journalism within the theory of value

The concept of 'value' is crucial to the understanding of the operation and professionalization and organization of the field of lifestyle journalism. Research that is rooted in media studies not only focuses on media texts or news "as the construction of social reality" but also analyses the constraints of content production or news work and the resources available to content producers or news workers. Content producers or news workers are studied as professionals, and their newspapers and television stations are studied as complex media organizations, among other areas of enquiry (Tuchman 1978: ix). This chapter sets out to study the role and value of lifestyle journalism to overall professional journalism. Of particular significance is how the field of lifestyle journalism is taught in tertiary education institutions and what values are attached to the field in the actual newsrooms. The chapter uses value in at least a binary form, one where the value is 'measurable' and statistical or numerical figures quantifying it possible. That is the value in terms of how much the area of lifestyle journalism is apparently earning, that is, if its monetary and financial contributions are being systematically collated and presented. On this first approach, there are further perspectival complexities that are embedded in the historicization of the notion of value. Economist Mazzucato explains:

> Originally, the objective theory of value was tied to the conditions in which goods and services are produced, the time spent to produce them, the quality of the labour employed; the determinants of 'value' actually shaped the price of the goods and services. Later, the new thinking among economists was that the value of things was determined by the price paid on the 'market' – what the consumer was prepared to pay.
>
> *(2019: 7)*

Generally, the first approach makes the concept of 'value' interchangeable with 'wealth'. However, wealth appears as more monetary, while value is a more social concept, involving not only *value* but *values* (Mazzucato 2019: 7). Analytics and metrics are, therefore, important here, just as in other genres of journalism (Nelson 2021; Lawrence and Napoli 2023; Shin 2023), although this study does not present these for lifestyle journalism but only argues that they are necessary in order to justify the elevation of the genre to a deserved status. Another approach is nearly *subjective* as it signifies 'standards', attitudes, perceptions, sense and sensibilities pertaining to lifestyle journalism. The latter can be an expression of news values of one type of news – let's say hard news – over another, soft news. News stories usually reveal the value of their newsworthiness. Some readers are interested in the newness or timeliness of the news, but other values pertain to the ideological slant of the news, that is to say, which class, gender or age group is being promoted at the detriment of another or others. Of course, the subjective value is still intricately linked to the political economic system, in that some preferences are normalized as more prestigious or more 'civilized' as compared to others depending on the social actors that promote them. Values are legitimized through systems of production of cultural goods and services such as the media industry and its production of lifestyle journalism. To sum it up, Henry Giroux argues:

> Within neoliberalism's market-driven discourse, corporate power marks the space of a new kind of public pedagogy, one in which the production, dissemination, and circulation of ideas emerges from the educational force of the larger culture. Public pedagogy in this sense refers to a powerful ensemble of ideological and institutional forces whose aim is to produce competitive, self-interested individuals vying for their own material and ideological gain. The culture of corporate public pedagogy largely cancels out or *devalues* gender, class-specific, and racial injustices in the existing social order by absorbing the democratic impulses and practices of civil society within narrow economic relations.
>
> *(2004: 106)(emphasis added)*

The status quo hence uses (lifestyle) journalists within bureaucratic structures designed to prop up the values and interests of the elite classes at the expense of marginalized majorities. A new lifestyle journalism that is – like Steenveld (2006: 20) suggests for tabloid journalism – "multivarigated" and attentive to "textual exploration", "audience responses" and the political economy of newsrooms should therefore inform the operations and production of lifestyle stories. Similarly, its critique should be responsive to these, especially when analysing how and why Africa's lower class majorities have unique preferences for some lifestyle stories regardless of their low purchasing power for commoditized goods and services. Since journalism is a form of communication, it addresses cultural issues that carry different people's value preferences, and lifestyle journalism can provide the critique for such preferences, in the same manner that academic research and pedagogics do more or less the same with scientific exploration and analysis (Zelizer 2008)

Exploring African academics' views of lifestyle journalism

The chapter reports results from a study that sought academics' opinions on the presence or absence of explicit modular curricular of lifestyle journalism or its related offshoots like Arts and Culture, Entertainment or Human Interest reporting. Academics lecturing at purposively selected universities in Zimbabwe, South Africa, Botswana and Malawi responded to questions on the value and scope of lifestyle journalism in their respective university's curricular. Incidentally, one of the academics has previously practiced as a journalist, namely, Professor Oswelled Ureke of the University of Johannesburg. Dr Lyton Ncube gave responses about the curriculum of the University of Botswana, and Mr Lee Ajussa commented on the Malawi University of Business and Applied Sciences (MUBAS). Oswelled Ureke, formerly of the now defunct Zimbabwean *The Mirror* – former News Editor of Zimbabwe's tabloid *Hmetro* Mr. Tatenda Chipungudzanye, News editor of Botswana's *Mmengi*, Mr Mompati Tlhankane, and a practicing journalist from Malawi Sam Juniour Banda of the *Daily Times* of Malawi were interviewed for their perceptions on the status and value of lifestyle journalism. Ureke was purposively selected due to the complexity of his experience where he is both an academic and a former journalist, thus possessing cross-sectional insights into some of the critical aspects of journalism in general.

This chapter's main assumption is that lifestyle journalism attracts millions of readers and audiences due to its entertainment and human interest qualities, as compared to other beats. Studies are confirming the growing significance of lifestyle journalism, attested by the 'softening' and tabloidization of journalism and the transition from the hard news tradition (Wasserman 2010, 2019). More and more consumer-driven formats combining information and entertainment now conflate the hard news and "soft" news boundaries (Fürsich 2012: 12). The incorporation of consumerism and service journalism that advises people on what to do in life makes the content attractive to different types of readers/audiences across classes, race and gender. That being the case, it also attracts a lot of revenue for the media organizations. Unfortunately, actual statistics on audience research are still scarce to justify the general assumption that lifestyle journalism attracts audiences to newspapers that carry other genres and content. Global and African media research institutions such as the South African Audience Research Foundation (SAARF) and Zimbabwe All Media Research Foundation should produce overviews of media performance focusing more on the statistics on this arguably very important but neglected field of lifestyle journalism.

To avoid imposing a set of terms and concepts on respondents concerning the critical issues that lifestyle journalism is associated with in the emerging critical scholarship, the questions deliberately did not include words like "consumers/consumerism", "commercialization", "commodification", "personal" and "intimate". These words are now common in serious scholarship on lifestyle journalism. Their exclusion from the questionnaire was intended to avoid leading both academics and journalists into using them, whereas on their own, they probably would not have associated lifestyle journalism with such concepts, ways of thinking and ways of making sense. The pitfalls of using more generalized non-leading statements like what is the "value of lifestyle journalism" are that respondents tended to provide equally generalized answers without a direct focus on the discursive or 'critical' nature of lifestyle journalism. All respondents are holders of postgraduate qualifications and have most likely been exposed to critical appreciation in their previous studies; hence, they could most likely use the same discourse. Just because the critical discourse is not directly incorporated in the questions could solicit casual and general answers.

This chapter refers to the works produced by Keyan Tomaselli and his colleagues and students starting from when he was at the University of Natal (now University of KwaZulu-Natal) before he moved to the University of Johannesburg (see Mhiripiri et al. 2024). Tomaselli has influenced the majority of media and cultural studies scholars writing on journalism, media and communication studies in Africa today. His work is embedded in Critical Cultural Studies with inflections from neo-Marxism. The work from the Tomaselli stable is critically and conveniently located to offer an African-based source of conscious inspiration to the emerging studies on lifestyle journalism with a focus on Africa.

When we explore the interviewed academics' views, there is consensus that lifestyle journalism is a vital component of popular journalism. In spite of its popular appeal to people of different classes and backgrounds, it is generally regarded lowly as compared to other beats. While there are academic modules on specialized reporting, there is no university that is specifically offering courses with the nomenclature "lifestyle journalism" or its equivalent. Curricula contain some period of internship variously known as "Industrial Attachment", "Internship" or "Work Related Learning" that stretch for periods ranging from six months to a full year. This is when journalism, media and communications students get placements in media organizations usually in the year preceding their final year of undergraduate studies. University academic assessors and industry-based assessors examine the students on their internships. Quite often, the students write examinable reports on their internship stint. The internship is supposed to bridge the gap between academic study and the actual professional working environment, preferably to satisfy the industry expectations for their future professionals before they graduate. Students are placed under different desks, and the majority – assessing from my more than 20-year experience in university education – write reports on the so-called prestigious sections such as politics, business and health.

South African-based Zimbabwean academic Oswelled Ureke who has practised print journalism in Zimbabwe at the now defunct *The Mirror*, a documentary film maker of note, who has taught at Zimbabwe's Midlands State University and is now lecturing at the University of Johannesburg concurs that Lifestyle journalism or Arts and Entertainment journalism is not regarded "a serious beat", so it tends to be "peripheralized" for that reason. He observes:

> Even in newsrooms you may find out the arts and lifestyle desk falls under the purview of the features editor or sometimes even under the news editor… It doesn't have a line editor dedicated to it. In newsrooms that have a line editor dedicated to that desk, you may find that the editor is the reporter or are the sole staff that's reporting about lifestyle and arts. But sometimes it is implicated in other forms of journalism.

Studies of journalism content realize that no journalism genre is self-enclosed and topics straddle boundaries. For instance, sports news is now much more complex and quite often delve beyond the performance of sports persons on the sporting fields alone. It includes economics and business, politics and identity, race and gender and health. News beats of all sorts are increasingly intersecting, and lifestyle journalism is not an exception. At times, components of lifestyle journalism emerge in beats or genres whose focal point is not essentially about lifestyle. Ureke notes this pattern especially when he is using trendy social media platforms or tools such as podcasting. He says:

> I realise that these days when we teach podcasting, most examples or even most of the podcasting that's happening tends to be on light-hearted cultural lifestyle issues. So for that reason, you may find that examples that are deployed when teaching may also lean towards lifestyle journalism. But in general I get a sense that lifestyle journalism is not given serious attention like other beats such as financial reporting, investigative reporting, and style and other beats like that.

Curricula of the University of Zimbabwe, Midlands State University, University of Botswana, University of Johannesburg, Malawi University of Business and Applied Sciences (MUBAS) (formerly the Malawi Polytech) all have journalism, media and communications departments with degree programmes that do not explicitly provide modules for lifestyle reporting. While they have specialized modules for journalism practice in general, political communication, business and financial reporting, investigative journalism, and so forth, they do not have anything tantamount to lifestyle journalism. Lee Ajussa from MUBAS teaches the module Specialized Writing for Print but notes that the module content shows that lifestyle content is "less prioritized". He says the obscure status of this type of journalism "is largely because it wears a very social (read casual) face – it's not given ... serious attention". This, he says, is in spite of the "multi-billion industry" that lifestyle journalism supports in its own right, a financial backbone that is now further enhanced with the rise of social media platforms and a new techno-savvy generation of "Ama2K[1]" producers and consumers of content, products and services. Ureke reiterates the sparseness of lifestyle content in curricula where financial and political reporting issues dominate. Lifestyle issues are peripheral or "simply implicated", like when one is teaching collaborative global investigative journalism. For instance, the Panama Papers scandal mentions icons from the world of entertainment such as film star Jackie Chan or footballer Lionel Messi.

> And so when you are then giving examples in that topic which is not essentially about lifestyle journalism, that's where you may end up making inferences to issues of lifestyle, or to icons that are known in the world of entertainment.

explains Ureke.

According to University of Botswana (UB) media educationist and researcher Dr Lyton Ncube, both media and journalism educators and learners apparently undervalue lifestyle journalism which "suffers the 'fluff'" tag. Lifestyle reporting modules are offered as elective or optional. It is not unusual to go for a semester or two without offering them. Whenever the department thinks that students have been overburdened with workload, such optional modules are sacrificed. Ncube says:

> I have also observed that in most cases students do not select/choose lifestyle modules due to a number of reasons. Some of my fourth year students informed me that during their internship, they observed that lifestyle reporting/journalism departments are framed as 'toy departments' in most newsrooms.

Ncube posits that the political economy of higher education in Africa is directly implicated in the sparse or outright neglect and marginalization of the teaching of lifestyle journalism at Africa's universities.

> Due to shrinking or reduced government spending on higher education in Africa, as elsewhere, universities are under pressure to find a third stream of income. Corporates are more interested in funding journalism curricula focusing on business and financial reporting rather than injecting their money to fund entertainment, leisure, cuisine, etc., issues. Therefore journalism/media training departments model their curricula to suit the demands and expectations of potential funders. To some extent, journalism educators lack an appreciation of the importance of lifestyle journalism. Therefore, some naively assume that students do not need training on lifestyle journalism aspects, but can always apply the techniques learnt in political journalism, business and financial journalism, etc. (to lifestyle journalism).

While Ncube lambasts the shortsightedness of training departments, the lifestyle desks and those corporate organizations that fund goods and services through lifestyle stories are equally to blame. According to him, they should realize how the broad lifestyle genre is supporting their business, corporate and civil service endeavours, hence the need to finance the training of lifestyle journalism in tertiary education institutions.

While I concur with the general observations of my academic peers, as an educationist, I believe there is room to harness lifestyle journalism and infuse it with the critical inflection. Nearly all the curricula at selected universities mentioned in this chapter contain modules on critical media theory or political economy of the media and discourse analysis (including semiotics) that are necessary for a conscious lifestyle journalism pedagogy and praxis. The works of Keyan Tomaselli's stable are also a very good starting or comparative point for an Africa-centred lifestyle journalism, much as it is not essentially about conventional lifestyle journalism (Mhiripiri et al. 2024: Sehume 2020: Tomaselli 1995, 1996, 1999; 2005, 2006, 2012).

Semiotics and lifestyle journalism

As already mentioned, the Tomaselli stable of academics has produced works that analyse lifestyles of selected African ethnic groups through an approach they call "anthro-tourism". This approach is rooted in Cultural Studies with its eclectic methodological and theoretical approaches that straddle politics, sociology, literary studies, anthropology and ethnography, economics, etc. Their major input has been the adoption of semiotics in identifying dominant tropes and archetypes used to describe African ethnic groups in the cultural tourism industry (Tomaselli 2005, 2012; Mhiripiri 2008, 2012). The mediation and commodification of the tropes and archetypes is then critiqued to understand whether it is empowering or dehumanizing the concerned African peoples. Most of the tropes and archetypes are residual from the epistemic violence associated with colonialism. While the Tomaselli stable has been remarkable in attending to lifestyle presented as fictional or documentary content in films such as *Gods Must be Crazy* (Uys 1980) and *The Hunters* (Marshal 1967), the work has only made inferences to print journalism texts. However, the stable provides rich analytical tools for lifestyle journalism in both print, broadcasting and digital media (see Mhiripiri 2008; Tomaselli 2012). The performative use of ethnic identities for the purposes of attracting clients in the cultural tourism industry is notable among the San and Zulu of South Africa, who often repackage and sell back to their Western visitors the popular stereotypes that the visitors already hold about their hosts (Mhiripiri and Tomaselli 2010).

Journalists' perceptions on African lifestyle journalism

Mompati Tlhankane, News Editor for Botswana daily *Mmengi*, gives interesting insights into the sociology of news production at the newspaper. Joining the newspaper as an intern, he was never formally trained on lifestyle journalism whether at college or at the media organization. However, *Mmengi* believes that for one to "become a complete reporter", one was "rotated around desks" and along the way was exposed to lifestyle journalism. Coincidentally, Tlhankane "loved writing lifestyle articles" when he joined *Mmengi*. He was a lifestyle reporter from 2015 to 2021, starting as a junior reporter on the lifestyle desk and rising to Arts and Culture Editor before he attained his current position. He still writes lifestyle pieces "now and then", although he has since switched to "general hard news". There are ambivalent perceptions on the valorization of lifestyle news reporting at *Mmengi*, both among journalists and in the institutional structure. Tlhankane has internalized this ambiguity in his own personal responses to the value of lifestyle reporting, when he shows both love for the beat and its opportunities and some discomfort about its low regard. He says

> Although generally some reporters from other desks in the newsroom don't take lifestyle reporting seriously, I think my organization does cherish the significance of the entertainment desk. In terms of daily needs of the desk, I can say the desk has full support of the organization. I think I am also a living example that one can progress from being cub lifestyle reporter to overseeing the whole newsroom including the so-called core desks of the newsroom.

My interviews produced several denigrating and belittling names and adjectives signifying lifestyle journalism and its various sub-sets of arts and entertainment reporting, human interest stories, and so forth. These include reference to the lifestyle desk as "a filler in some newspapers", "a toy department", "'pink ghetto' of the newsroom", "minority desk", "fluff news", "trivial", "not serious", etc. The derision and condescension impose a heavy tag on the genre and brand; hence, Tlhankane's disconcerting advice is as follows: "For growth, I think lifestyle reporting is a start but as one progresses in the field, they should try out something different". This is a disturbing view from one who has "loved" lifestyle journalism from his internship, one who has been recognized and rewarded with career mobility to a senior News Editor post and who continues to write such stories "now and then". His promotion to News Editor is a vindication that lifestyle journalism can be rewarding and worthwhile as one scales the professional heights, but a reader cannot help sense some defensive inferiority complex in his tone arising from the institutionalized and normalized bludgeoning of the origins, legitimacy and trajectory of the profession. It is also daunting to realize that in Botswana, editors "don't give much attention to the desk and it is regarded as some sort of a filler in some newspapers" and "the desk is mostly dominated by women". This genderization of the desk not only demeans working women but also disregards that lifestyle reporters are often young and "work odd hours and sometimes they even put their lives at risk covering music festivals and other night life activities". The young reporters, however, like the desk due to what Tlhankane describes as "some of the perks like fun trips, entertainment and mingling with celebrities". No mention is made of how the desk attracts revenue for the media establishment or whether journalists benefit from the money that is accrued from other individuals and organizations' sale of services and commodities presented subliminally as infotainment. Tlhankane says:

> Also most editors don't give much attention to the desk and it is regarded as some sort of a filler in some newspapers. Editors could never take their best reporters to report lifestyle and the desk is mostly dominated by women. Overall lifestyle reporting is one of the most demanding jobs in the newsroom because reporters work odd hours and sometimes they even put their lives at risk covering music festivals and other night life activities. Most young reporters like the desk because of some of the perks like fun trips, entertainment and mingling with celebrities.

Former News Editor for the Zimbabwean tabloid, *Hmetro* Mr Tatenda Chipungudzanye holds a Master's degree in Media and Society Studies and claims he "was trained as an overall journalist" who is comfortable with any news desk. Like most of the journalists, he is a media generalist by training and had to hone his lifestyle journalism skills on the job. As News Editor at *Hmetro*, he was in charge of all the content in the paper.

To him, the value of lifestyle journalism lies in its provision of news about consumer goods and services in an entertaining tone. He says: "Being reliant on advertiser revenue, it has taken marketing and PR stunts: he who pays the piper calls the tune type of journalism". According to him, lifestyle journalism is better placed to satisfy audience expectations for the future. The biggest dilemma is that while lifestyle journalism is popular and people interact with it every day, there is still daily resistance in both professional and audience circles that it is authentic journalism. Chipungudzanye is, nonetheless, optimistic that such attitudes will change in future as "people will cope with time". While the status and legitimacy of lifestyle journalism within the journalism profession remain controversial, it competes with and complements newer but similarly popular lifestyle digital media content platforms such as blogs and vlogs. Audience and reader demographics favour the new tastes for soft media content. Chipungudzanye observes: "We are getting to a generation where hard news is becoming less important to late 90s and ama2000 generation. They fall for lifestyle journalism". The lifestyle genre attains special status as it also etches avenues for future career opportunities, not only in broader mainstream media but also for public relations and marketing professions. As a critical component of broader journalism, *Hmetro* brought a "new type of (sensational) journalism" that thrives on what is trending in people's everyday lives. Its success was not only in the number of readers it attracted, but according to Chipungudzanye, in its substantial economic viability within the larger Zimpapers media organization.

Prominent *Daily Times* of Malawi journalist Sam Junior Banda says "arts and culture news" that he writes are "taken as fillers". He has fought for editorial space and respect of the genre within the print media profession. Lifestyle and arts productions are accorded low value within the print media industry. In the absence of proper studies of both the economic and financial and public service values of lifestyle journalism, wrong perceptions and stereotypes might continue to bedevil this important sector. The measurable business and financial contributions of lifestyle journalism to news organizations' coffers need to be calculated properly and compared to financial flows contributed from other news desks and activities. Limited appreciation and understanding of the genre due to proper scientific studies result in low regard for lifestyle journalism; hence, more space is allocated news beats that are considered more prestigious. That is where the "filler" tag for lifestyle journalism arises. This "filler" subordinate status in the news genre terrain is not dissimilar to what Unni From (2018: 1) terms the "supplement" role of lifestyle journalism to its more prestigious counterparts of "breaking news, political news, and news on social and cultural conflicts". That filler or supplement status is largely due to the fact that lifestyle journalism and its focus on "private, intimate and cultural matters" is perceived as supplementing traditional hard news. Classifying the genre as lowly might overlook measurable economic and intangible social, societal and public value of lifestyle stories to news stables.

In their responses to "what is lifestyle journalism" and "what is its value and purpose", both academics and journalists barely used the common critical terms or concepts that are now found in the emerging scholarship on lifestyle journalism. There is no direct mention of how lifestyle journalism is a discursive tool for marketing products and services to consumers, nor is commodification, and the politics of consumption ever mentioned. These perspectives on the role of lifestyle journalism in a globalized capitalist market system are not as vividly spelt out in responses.

This is arguably due to the absence of such discourse in the measly curricula on lifestyle journalism. Curricula tend to create an order and quality of knowledge which becomes common parlance among those exposed to it. Such parlance and ways of thinking then drift in the collective professional psyche and consciousness. Such discursive parlance will, thus, easily get expressed in interviews of the nature of those conducted for the purposes of this study. Emerging scholarship on media and communication pedagogy in Africa is mostly taking a decolonial turn (Mutsvairo 2018; Mudavanhu et al. 2024). However, it is arguable that academic institutions usually design their curricula in response to the strategic visions that the political leadership spells out in their development plans. Most tertiary education institutions are publicly owned or state-controlled; thus, they are likely to adopt government and ruling party strategic plans. Media training and curricula hence follow suit. A quick scan of curricula across the continent shows a preponderance for programmes in science and health communication, development communication or communication for development, and so on. Academics appear to be isolating lifestyle journalism as a self-contained area of study that is not capable of addressing deeper issues on science, technology, health or development.

But it is possible to repackage hard news factual and analytical content within the "soft" news genre of lifestyle journalism. The Tomaselli school has succeeded in giving a human face and flavor to stories about the San deprivation, marginalization and exploitation within a neo-liberal market economy. Using individuals such as Dawid Kruiper, Veitkat Kruiper and Silikat van Wyn, the academic travel narratives give voices and personalities to ordinary persons, who then become the prism for analysis of local and global sociostructural relations within a global market economy. Nearly all aspects of African lifestyles and beliefs are now commodified and commercialized in obvious or subliminal forms, and audiences show a readiness to consume lifestyle narratives.

Analytics and metrics on lifestyle journalism must be used to justify their inclusion in the African media curricula and also to elevate their status within the political economies of newsrooms. Admittedly, lifestyle journalism is more popular in the Global North because people there can afford the products advertised, but in the Global South, people are also consuming stories that are relatable and relevant to their cultural contexts, especially stories that make them aspire for new forms of life. The so-called "fillers" of lifestyle journalism are generally present in the newspapers, and more so in social media platforms that report on African "celebrities". Metrics and analytics on audience preferences and tastes should, therefore, inform the salience of this genre just as they are now readily available for social media and other mainstream media (Lawrence and Napoli 2023; Nelson 2021).

Concluding critical reflection

The critical inflection adopted from radical semiotics and critical discourse analysis can make lifestyle, arts, entertainment and human interest stories draw better attention from Africa-centred media and communications academics. Existent research and literature on African journalism, communication, media and cultural studies already reveal a preference for leftist neo-Marxian approaches that aspire to unravel all social and economic disparities and imbalances, while advocating for equity, equality, human dignity and justice. When lifestyle content is distilled through the discursive prisms of representations of voices across classes, gender, classes, age and other critical demographics and their nexus with power relations, the epistemic treatment of lifestyle content becomes challenging and exciting. Discourses should not just legitimize and normalize social and technological systems without the normative justifications for the retention and sustenance of such power structures or systems. Lifestyle journalism content certainly has a serious import that is further-reaching than the trivializing it currently gets not only in newsrooms but as a pedagogical, theoretical and methodological topic of critical significance.

Critical and decolonial scholars have long provided some of the broader critical tools of studying some of these seemingly mundane and "soft" content such as movies and popular art. However, they infused in their studies critical appreciations that elevated that mundane and "soft" content to a heightened level that enlightens the consciousness of deeper structural and socioeconomic, political and cultural dynamics (Hokheimer and Adorno 2002). Technological interventions of all sorts were clearly implicated in the (re)production of dominant ideological positions promoted by capitalism and the elite classes in order to maintain a status quo that exploited and marginalized the working classes and peasantry (Gramsci 2007: Benjamin 2008). Other scholars such as Bourdieu (2008), Giroux (2004), Mbembe (2001), wa Thiongo (1986) and the contemporary generation of African critical media studies have asked important questions about language and media within the matrix of political economy and power dynamics (Wasserman 2010; Steenveld and Strelitz 2010).

It is now time for Africa-centred scholars to take cue from Banjac and Hanusch (2022) and infuse the critical pedagogical tools that they already possess and implement in other fields and topics of enquiry into what type of lifestyle journalism is being produced and whose interests it serves. The works of Tomaselli's stable on cultural tourism or anthro-tourism offer a good insight into possibilities and opportunities of studying and applying critical lifestyle journalism in Africa. Such works, complemented with what Banjac and Hanusch (2022) have done, show the ubiquity of commodification of culture and individual personalities. Lifestyle journalism, thus, tends to serve the interests of a market economy that supports global capitalism. A new scholarship is needed to explore further how, where, when and why Africans from different social classes, races, gender, age, religious and other ethnic groups access and consume lifestyle journalism content. The preferences and tastes of demographic groups should be supported with incisive critique, metrics and analysis without deriding both the genre and its professional producers and consumers as people who are merely distracted from discussing critical public issues necessary in a democracy.

A radical or decolonial turn in the production and critique of lifestyle journalism can still be realized from a thorough understanding of the reasons for people's preferences, tastes and aspirations. Lifestyle journalism is both a practical and intellectual activity in which pedagogics impart into the news worker's skills and consciousness that which should assist him or her to tell stories which enhance a new higher humanism (Gramsci 2007). Multi-dimensional approaches already suggested for the study of tabloid journalism (Steenveld 2006) can be employed to study the texts, production processes, audience preferences and consumption and the political economy of lifestyle journalism. Perhaps much more important is the critical analysis of the metrics and analytics arising out of the production, marketing and consumption of lifestyle journalism.

Note

1 Those born since the year 2000.

Further reading

Banjac, S., & Hanusch, F. (2022) Aspirational lifestyle journalism: The impact of social class on producers' and audiences' views in the context of socio-economic inequality. *Journalism* 23(8): 1607–1625. https://doi.org/10.1177/1464884920956823

From, U. (2018) Lifestyle journalism. *Oxford Research Encyclopedias, Communication.* https://doi.org/10.1093/acrefore/9780190228613.013.835

Mutsvairo, B. (2018) *The Palgrave Handbook of Media and Communication Research in Africa.* London: Springer Nature.

Tomaselli, K. G. (2005) *Where Global Contradictions Are Sharpest: Research Stories from the Kalahari.* Amsterdam: Rozenberg.

Wasserman, H. (2010) *Tabloid Journalism in South Africa: True Story!* Indiana University Press.

References

Banjac, S., & Hanusch, F. (2022) Aspirational lifestyle journalism: The impact of social class on producers' and audiences' views in the context of socio-economic inequality. *Journalism* 23(8): 1607–1625. https://doi.org/10.1177/1464884920956823

Benjamin, W. (2008) *The Work of Art in the Age of Mechanical Reproduction.* London: Penguin.

Bourdieu, P. (2008) *Political Interventions: Social Science and Political Action.* London: Verso.

Chama, B. (2017) *Tabloid Journalism in Africa.* Cham: Palgrave MacMillan.

Chama, B. (2019) *Anti-Corruption Tabloid Journalism in Africa.* Cham: Springer Nature.

Costera Meijer, I. (2001) The public quality of popular journalism: Developing a normative framework. *Journalism Studies* 2(2): 189–205.

Dyll, L. (2003) In the Sun with Silikat. *Current Writing: Text and Reception in Southern Africa* 15(Special issue): 135–150.

Dyll-Myklebust, L. (2014) Development narratives: The value of multiple voices and ontologies in Kalahari research. *Critical Arts: South-North Cultural Studies* 28(1): 521–538.

Elbarbary, A. S. (2022) *Othering and Ideology in Travel Writing.* https://paaljapan.org/files/uploads/SelectedPaperPAAL2022_3.pdf (Accessed 1 July 2024).

Fabian, J. (2006) Forgetting Africa. In M. Ntarangwi, D. Mills & M. Babiker (Eds.), *African Anthropologies: History, Critique and Practice.* Dakar: CODESRIA.

Faramarzi, S. (2021) The power of data storytelling for lifestyle journalism. *Datajournalism.com.* https://datajournalism.com/read/longreads/the-power-of-data-storytelling-for-lifestyle-journalism (Accessed 5 February 2024).

Figenschou, T. U., Thorbjørnsrud, K., & Hallin, D. C. (2023) Whose stories are told and who is made responsible? Human-interest framing in health journalism in Norway, Spain, the U.K. and the U.S. *Journalism* 24(1): 3–21. https://doi.org/10.1177/14648849211041516.

Fiske, J. (1989) *Reading the Popular*. London: Routledge.
Fiske, J. (1992) Popularity and the politics of information. In P. Dahlgren and C. Sparks (Eds.), *Journalism and Popular Culture*. London: Sage, pp. 45–63.
From, U. (2018) Lifestyle journalism. *Oxford Research Encyclopedias, Communication*. Retrieved 27 Jan. 2025, from https://oxfordre.com/communication/view/10.1093/acrefore/9780190228613.001.0001/acrefore-9780190228613-e-835.
From, U., & Kristensten, N. N. (2019) Unpacking lifestyle journalism via service journalism and constructive journalism. In L. Vodonovic (Ed.), *Lifestyle Journalism: Social Media, Consumption and Experience*. London: Routledge, pp. 13–25.
Fürsich, E. (2012) Lifestyle journalism as popular journalism. *Journalism Practice* 6(1): 12–25. https://doi.org/10.1080/17512786.2011.622894
Giroux, H. A. (2004) *The Terror of Neoliberalism: Authoritarianism and the Eclipse of Democracy*. London: Paradigm Publishers.
Gramsci, A. (2007) *Selections from the Prison Notebooks*. London: Lawrence and Wishart.
Hokheimer, M. & Adorno, T. (2002). *Dialectic of Enlightenment*, edited by G. S. Noerr. California: Stanford University Press.
Lawrence, R. G., & Napoli, P. M. (2023) *News Quality in the Digital Age*. London: Routledge.
Mazzucato, M. (2019) *The Value of Everything: Making and Taking in the Global Economy*. London: Penguin Books.
Mbembe, A. (2001) *On the Postcolony*. California: University of California Press.
McLennan-Dodd, V. (2003) Hotel Kalahari: You can check out any time you like, but you can never leave. *Cultural Studies<=>Critical Methodologies* 3(4): 448–469.
Mhiripiri, N. A. (2008) *The Tourist-Viewer, the Bushmen and the Zulu: Imaging and (re) Invention of Identities through Contemporary Cultural Productions* [Doctoral dissertation, University of KwaZulu-Natal].
Mhiripiri, N.A. (2012). A Performative Encounter with ≠Khomani Ethnographic Artist Silikat van Wyk in the Kalahari. *Critical Arts: a journal of south-north cultural and media studies* 26(2): 375-400.
Mhiripiri, N., & Tomaselli, K. (2010) Language ambiguities, cultural tourism and the ≠Khomani. In K. Luger & K. Wohler (Eds.), *Kulturelless erbe und tourismus: Rituale, traditionen, inszenierungen*. Innsbruck: StudeinVerlag, pp. 285–296.
Mhiripiri, N. A., Tomaselli, K., & Grant, J. (2024) Articulation and recognition of San Firstness in Southern Africa and the contestation over citizenship. *Communication: Oxford University Encyclopedias*. https://doi.org/10.1093/acrefore/9780190228613.013.1337
Mudavanhu, S. Mpofu, S., & Batisai, K. (2024) *Decolonising Media and Communications Studies Education in Sub-Saharan Africa*. New York: Routledge.
Mutsvairo, B. (2018) *The Palgrave Handbook of Media and Communication Research in Africa*. Cham: Springer Nature.
Nelson, T. (2021) *Journalism and Digital Labour*. London: Routledge.
Sehume, J. (2020) *A Transdisciplinary Appraisal of the "Rethinking Indigeneity" Research Project* [Doctoral dissertation, University of Johannesburg].
Semetko, H. A., & Valkenburg, P. M. (2000) Framing European politics: A content analysis of press and television news. *Journal of Communication* 50: 93–109.
Shin, J. (2023) Social media metrics and news quality. In R. G. Lawrence and P. M. Napoli (Eds.), *News Quality in the Digital Age*. London: Routledge, pp. 33–48.
Steenveld, L. (2006) Tabloids a social phenomenon. In S. Bulbulia (Ed.), *The Tabloid Challenge*. Johannesburg: Institute for the Advancement of Journalism, pp. 18–21.
Steenveld, L., & Strelitz, L. (2010) Trash or popular journalism? The case of South Africa's Daily Sun. *Journalism* 11(5): 531–547.
Taylor, B. (2018) *Travels in Arabia*. Frankfurt: Salzwasser-Verlag Gmbh.
Tomaselli, K. G. (Ed.) (1995) Recuperating the San [Special issue]. *Critical Arts*, 9(2): 1–153.
Tomaselli, K. G. (Ed.) (1999) Encounters in the Kalahari [Special issue]. *Visual Anthropology* 12(2–3): 131–364.
Tomaselli, K. G. (2005) *Where Global Contradictions Are Sharpest: Research Stories from the Kalahari*. Amsterdam: Rozenberg Publishers.
Tomaselli, K. G. (2006) Rereading the *Gods Must be Crazy* films. *Visual Anthropology* 19(2): 171–200.

Tomaselli, K. G. (Ed.) (2012) *Cultural Tourism and Identity: Rethinking Indigeneity*. Leiden: Brill.
Tuchman, G. (1978) *Making News: A Study in the Construction of Reality*. New York: The Free Press.
Wasserman, H. (2010) *Tabloid Journalism in South Africa: True Story!* Bloomington: Indiana University Press.
Wasserman, H. (2019) Tabloidization of news. In Wahl-Jorgensen & T. Hanitzsch (Eds.), *The Handbook of Journalism Studies*. London: Routledge.
Wa Thiongo, N. (1986) *Decolonising the Mind: The Politics and Language in African Literature*. London: Heinemann.
Zelizer, B. (2008) How communication, culture, and critique intersect in the study of journalism, *Communication, Culture and Critique* 1(1): 86–91. https://doi.org/10.1111/j.1753-9137.2007.00009.x
Zillmann, D. (2002) Exemplification theory of media influence. In J. Bryant, D. Zillmann and M. B. Oliver (Eds.), *Media Effects*. London: Routledge, pp. 29–52.

Filmography

Mlauzi, M. Linje. (2002) *Reading Photographs in the Kalahari*. Cultural, Communication and Media Studies, University of Natal, Durban.
Reinhardt, T. (2002a) *A Guy, a Camera, a Journey*. Cultural, Communication and Media Studies, University of Natal, Durban.
Reinhardt, T. (2002b) *Vetkat*. Cultural, Communication and Media Studies, University of Natal, Durban.

PART II

Lifestyle journalism and consumption

7
TRANSFORMING JOURNALISTIC GENRES ON SOCIAL MEDIA

Books and literary reviews as cultural consumption

Unni From and Carsten Stage

Introduction

In this chapter, we examine how books and literature have been and are being reviewed in legacy media, how the review genre is transformed and re-moulded in a social media context and how these developments reflect processes in which books are increasingly communicated as lifestyle items. We have included a historical perspective to be able to trace how the evolution of the coverage of books and literature reflects central societal and cultural changes, not least the emergence of a consumer culture, but also to show how the (book) review genre has always served a dual goal by having both educational and marketing aims.

Typically, the literary review genre is associated with academic journals or journalistic coverage of literature in cultural sections in legacy media. However, the review genre has also travelled to and developed in lifestyle sections and on social media concurrently with an expanding consumer culture where reading has been and remains a central cultural activity (Thumala Olave, 2020). We examine not only how the review genre rests on defining features embedded in an aesthetic tradition but also how it has transformed and now includes more emotional and subjective strategies (Koreman et al., 2024) as it moves on to, for instance, the social media platform of Instagram, which provides a "novel dimension for reviewing" (Jaakkola, 2022, p. 139). We argue that the visual infrastructure and the multiple voices exposed on Instagram offer new spaces for the intermediation of books (e.g., Dezuanni et al., 2022) and for the interaction between, e.g., professional media institutions, public institutions such as libraries, the publishing industry, influencers and consumers.

This chapter first provides a historical overview of the (book) review genre in cultural and lifestyle journalism to make the argument that even though the genre has expanded considerably, it also carries defining features developed mainly in legacy media lifestyle and cultural sections. Secondly, it outlines and discusses how the historical roots and defining features of reviews are transformed in the social media context of Instagram. One of the key arguments of this chapter is that Instagram accelerates transformations of the review genre. These transformations entail the increased *entanglement of lifestyle communication with reviewing*, the tendency that *reviewing is articulated through a more subjective or affectively involved voice* and that *the materiality of books* plays a more central communicative role. Thus, this chapter contributes to exploring the blurred boundaries between culture and lifestyle and between professional media institutions, commercial agents and book enthusiasts in relation to contemporary reviewing practices.

Finally, it discusses to what extent Instagram reviews challenge the traditional defining features of the review genre by developing their own distinctive genre modes in which literature is increasingly linked to lifestyle, affect and identity rather than evaluative argumentation. As an example, book reviews on Instagram are characterized by a profound preoccupation with the materiality of the book as review authors

> are, above all, making use of the perceived visual affordances of Instagram's interface and the patterns of the review genre, and by doing this they are to some extent re-inventing the review genre in the specific visually imbued online environment of Instagram.
>
> *(Jaakkola, 2022, p. 153)*

The key arguments will be developed in dialogue with Danish reviews of two illustrative cases/literary works: French Nobel prize winner Annie Ernaux's book *The Years* (2008) and the Danish author Kim Blæsbjerg's book *The Best Families* (2023). The two cases were chosen not only because they prompted substantial reviewing activity across both social and legacy media but also because Ernaux is highly endorsed by the traditional literary system, while Blæsbjerg is an upcoming Danish author. In that way, the cases allow us to compare reviewing practices across media and how different degrees of canonization or systemic endorsement are reflected within these reviewing practices. The aim of this chapter is, however, not to provide a systematic empirical analysis of the cases but rather to use them to discuss and exemplify current transformations of the book review as a genre, and as different ways of understanding the book as cultural consumption.

Book reviewing and taste-making in a (media) historical perspective

Reviews have historically fostered and stimulated cultural consumption, and legacy media have had a dominant role as cultural gatekeepers, tastemakers and cultural intermediaries (e.g., Jaakkola, 2022; Janssen & Verboord, 2015). Scholars have pointed out that contemporary criticism is currently produced by a heterogeneous cultural critic (Kristensen & From, 2015a) that includes at least four different agents: the intellectual cultural critic, whose authority is linked to more elitist traditions and aesthetic expertise; the professional journalist, whose expertise is linked to journalism as a profession; the media-made arbiter of taste, whose legitimacy is linked to and secured by repeated media performances; and last but not the least, the everyday amateur expert, whose authority is linked to formulating a bottom–up perspective and subjective opinions. Book reviewing in the contemporary media landscape is shaped by all these different agents – sometimes all of them at the same time. This heterogeneity also blurs the boundaries between different traditions of reviewing in legacy media in general and cultural and lifestyle journalism more specifically, in marketing material with the book industry as a central driver and in book blogging and review-like posts produced by social media influencers. To be able to understand the roots and innovations of contemporary reviewing practices, we briefly outline how reviews have developed historically.

The review genre dates back to the emergence of literary periodicals in the early 18th century (e.g., Carroll, 2009; McDonald, 2007; see From, 2019) where intellectuals announced new literary books and writings, often with many and lengthy quotes. Jost (2022, p. 140) argues that this type of announcements "sought to equip readers to make up their own minds". They transformed into more opinionated pieces in, for example, the magazine *Monthly Review* in 1749, which meant that two of the defining features of the review genre – the announcement and the judgement – had been introduced, continuing still today to be key in the classification of a review (Kristensen & From, 2024).

Critics succeeded in establishing themselves as authorities, and their work was, for instance, used by booksellers and authors who included excerpts from reviews in the advertisements of books. In this sense, the strong link between, and dual purpose of, reviewing as education and marketing was established early in history. However, at first, the genre was dominated by intellectuals (Shrum, 1991), who used the review as a platform for elitist dialogues between authors and academics, with a focus on how society and culture needed radical change. In this sense, marketing and the understanding of literature as cultural consumption did not fully develop until later.

During the 19th century, the institutions of the book market, the newspaper industry and professional journalism changed significantly, and ordinary people's access to books increased as more bookstores opened and many countries established public libraries (e.g., Deutsch, 2022). The Industrial Revolution led to advancements in mass production and increased the availability and affordability of consumer goods, making them more accessible to a wider population. The relevance of the review was accentuated by the fact that reading as a cultural activity proliferated and developed into an everyday practice.

At the beginning of the 20th century, the advent of radio had a sweeping impact on the public dissemination of knowledge about books and literature, and book programmes became an integrated part of the broadcasting. In the beginning of the radio era, book reviewing was rather closely linked to traditions derived from the printed press, but it steadily transformed into more conversational formats (Crowl et al., 2017) based on interviews with authors and dialogues with listeners. In continuation of this transformation, scholarly work has identified two central periods in the 20th century in trying to grasp the transformation of the review genre (Verboord & Janssen, 2015, see From, 2019). One defining period is the 1950s and 1960s, when a consumer-oriented culture and a rise in consumer goods and services broadened the topics covered by newspapers in general and in arts and culture more specifically. Moreover, newspapers began to develop separate culture sections (Verboord, Koreman & Janssen, 2020), and the review genre was used to address new cultural objects such as television shows (e.g., Rixon, 2018). However, in the culture pages, the classification and evaluation of cultural products were based on rather clear distinctions between highbrow and lowbrow culture and between fine arts and popular culture and entertainment and appraised high art as more valuable than popular culture (e.g., Kristensen & From, 2015b; Verboord, 2010).

These distinctions were increasingly blurred during the other defining period – the 1980s and 1990s – in which books were simultaneously covered in accordance with traditional aesthetic traditions and as part of a more popular aesthetics (Koreman et al., 2024) focused on function and utility to fulfil the purposes of reading. Thus, it can be argued that in this period, the traditional review was supplemented by review practices taking their point of departure in the lives of readers and their needs for different reading experiences associated with specific reading contexts (relaxation, knowledge, personal interests, etc.). In this period, taste evolved into a much broader and more diverse concept, not least due to globalization and the deepening impact of commercialization (see also Purhonen et al., 2019). The traditional boundaries between highbrow and popular culture were, thus, redefined due to the expansion of consumerism, popular culture and a much more profound cultural pluralism. As a reflection of these processes, lifestyle sections and content flourished across media platforms, including television, radio and newspapers, and it can be argued that this expansion was emblematic of a consumer culture characterized by omnivore consumption patterns (Koreman et al., 2024; Verboord, 2014). Thus, the cultural pages of newspapers were complemented by lifestyle supplements, and traditional cultural content – including literature – was increasingly assessed as lifestyle content or service journalism (Eide & Knight, 1999; Kristensen & From, 2012).

This expansion of cultural and lifestyle content and reviews has been accelerated by the advent of the internet and social media, which challenged or diversified a traditional and institutionalized form of criticism (Jaakkola, 2022, p. 3). Reviews on digital media platforms span traditional criticism, blogging, aggregates and participatory communities, where voices "from the ivory tower" (Kristensen & From, 2015) are constantly mixed with layperson perspectives.

To sum up, in the past, reviews in the cultural pages were typically authored by strong intellectual and professional authorities who aimed to educate their audience, but these authorities were increasingly supplemented by generalists with ambitions to guide and entertain with reviews focusing on cultural consumption and cultural activities linked to a wider array of lifestyle practices. With the advent of the internet and social media, reviewing practices diversified even further, and today, book reviews are found on all media platforms, dedicated cultural pages, programming and forums and spaces reserved for lifestyle content.

It is, however, important to stress that we cannot understand this evolution as a linear process; rather, book reviewing in the contemporary media landscape is a complex conglomerate of voices, agents and platforms characterized by a mix of approaches, but paradoxically also by traditional and recognizable features of the review genre. The reviews of the two novels we use as empirical examples in this chapter are in line with this argument. The novels were both reviewed in traditional cultural pages, on TV programmes and on radio/in podcasts and also appeared in lifestyle magazines and sections and on multiple personal profiles and communities on social media.

Defining features of book reviews in cultural and lifestyle journalism

As we have argued, the review genre, and other coverage of books, has undergone significant changes throughout history, closely intertwined with the rise of consumer culture and a broadened spectrum of genres and cultural products, media formats and communication technologies. Moreover, it has been shaped by the many different agents producing reviews of different cultural products including intellectuals, artists, professional journalists, marketing agents and everyday consumers of culture. However, the genre is also characterized by a set of strong and defining features developed in different ways in cultural journalism on the one hand and lifestyle journalism on the other. These defining features make the review relatively recognizable, despite the plurality of voices and platforms that produce them.

In the following, we draw on empirical material that was sampled manually on Instagram by searching the author's surname and the Danish title of the book (date of search and archiving: 13/4–2023). All posts that included an evaluation of the book were then included in the sample (Ernaux: 12 posts; Blæsbjerg: 17 posts). These posts are supplemented by readings of more traditional reviews (12 of *The Years* and eight of *The Best Families*), which were sampled from the Danish database of reviews called www.bog.nu. Both literary works were reviewed in five Danish broadsheets (*Information, Politiken, Weekendavisen, Jyllands-Posten* and *Kristeligt Dagblad*), while *The Years* was also reviewed in the broadsheet *Berlingske*. We found no reviews of the books in tabloids. The rest of the reviews were found in magazines and online fora.

The traditional book review developed in cultural journalism is often associated with defining elements such as description, classification, contextualization, elucidation, interpretation and analysis (Carroll, 2009, see also From, 2018). This system of evaluating cultural products – not least literature – was shaped according to high-art criteria (Koreman et al., 2024) and primarily focused on the artistic quality of the literary work. Yet, the most distinctive feature of a review is the evaluative judgement. Without this feature, the text would most often be characterized as, e.g., a book essay or a column (Jaakkola, 2023, p. 6). Not surprisingly, the reviews published in legacy media on the two novels by Ernaux and Blæsbjerg include many of these defining elements, but, as we will demonstrate, they also integrate some of the more subjective descriptions of reading experiences that often dominate social media reviewing practices. Thus, all reviews of the books in legacy media describe and introduce plot and themes and make literary judgements by using the other elements mentioned as part of a literary analysis, leading to an evaluation. One example is the reviewer in the Danish broadsheet *Kristeligt Dagblad* (30/7–2021, Jonas Krogsgaard Christensen), who produces a traditional classification by stating that:

> A brilliant technique can be experienced in Annie Ernaux's *The Years*, which is a narrative about the development in France and the life of a French woman from 1941 to 2006. It is an immensely vast and unwieldy subject, but instead of using a classic first-person narrator, Ernaux employs a 'we' and a 'one'.
>
> *(Krogsgaard Christensen, 2021)*

Arguably, the reviews of the two books are mainly based on academic argumentation, leading to a judgement. Accordingly, the consumption value relates to a more elitist approach to culture and the position of the critic as a professional authority. However, in line with Chong (2019), subjectivity is often integrated in reviews through three elements: bias, emotion or self-interest. All reviewers add elements to their evaluations that reflect some aspect of a personal and subjective reading experience – for instance, when including adjectives such as brilliant, fantastic or surprising. As mentioned, the reviewers in some cases also include their own reading experience to build the argument. One example comes from the reviewer in the broadsheet *Weekendavisen* (08/04–2021, Linea Maja Ernst), who is slightly underwhelmed and writes:

> THE YEARS IS OBVIOUSLY a colossal effort; the novel's intricate details and overview are impressive, and I wish I were more enraptured. However, the reading often feels enumerative, almost dutifully myopic, preoccupied with obscure details. One must be prepared to Google a sea of long-forgotten trademarks, politicians, actors, and hit songs. And even if one becomes acquainted with the mentioned personalities and artifacts, is it intimacy? Is it a true triumph over forgetfulness?
>
> *(Ernst, 2021)*

This point confirms existing scholarly work, in which it is argued that cultural criticism is linked to aesthetic traditions, but also, and perhaps increasingly so, to emotions and subjective experiences (Kristensen, 2021).

Lifestyle journalism is not only often associated with the coverage of subareas such as travel; fashion and beauty; health, wellness and fitness; food, cuisine and cooking; living and gardening; parenting and family; people and celebrities; and personal technology (Hanusch & Hanitzsch, 2013, see also From, 2018) but also includes coverage of more traditional cultural topics (Kristensen & From, 2012) such as books. However, the academic aesthetic tradition of reviewing is more subdued in review practices in lifestyle journalism, which rely on a more consumer-oriented version of the review genre. Reviews in lifestyle journalism and supplements often integrate guides and tests, thereby embracing the receiver as a cultural consumer and linking (cultural) activities and taste-making to lifestyle issues. The guides and tests share the common feature of employing evaluative formats, but they are different from the more traditional review by using other evaluative formats compared to traditional aesthetic argumentation.

Grant Blanks differentiates between connoisseurial reviews and procedural reviews (Blank, 2007). The connoisseurial review relies on the unique skills and expertise of the reviewer. In this form of review, the evaluator's subjective judgment, refined taste and deep knowledge of the subject matter are of vital importance. These reviews are often associated with expert assessment and the ability to discern nuances that may broaden the perspective of the average consumer. In contrast, procedural reviews are rooted in the outcomes of standardized assessments or tests. These reviews do not rely primarily on the subjective opinions of individual reviewers but are instead based on systematic procedures and/or quantifiable results. They often involve objective criteria such as measurements, ratings or test scores, which are used to evaluate and compare products, services or performances. Procedural reviews, in that sense, prioritize a more empirical and data-driven approach to evaluation. Blank, however, acknowledges that the two categories often overlap. He highlights the book review as an example. Traditionally, the book review would be considered connoisseurial, but because book reviews often include information on, e.g., price, place of publication and length, they also incorporate elements associated with procedural review formats.

An important point is, however, that book reviewing in lifestyle journalism first and foremost includes guiding elements and relates the practice of reading – and the decision about which book to choose – to situational contexts (e.g., holiday reading). In lifestyle sections, reviews not only acknowledge the literary aspects of the cultural product but also highlight the practical relevance of the book for an individual's life, thereby incorporating a more immediate and functional perspective.

As mentioned, the novel *The Years* has, for example, been the object of traditional reviewing and discussions in the cultural pages of the printed press but also framed as lifestyle content in, for example, women's magazines. In the latter, the novel is not presented through lengthy analysis and judgement but briefly categorized as worth your time and money. As an example, the novel is included in a practical guide of must-reads for the summer vacation: "This year's 25 best books that you should bring on your summer vacation. Whether you're lounging by the water or enjoying the tranquillity of a summer cottage, you should have these books as companions" (*Alt for Damerne* 11/7–2022). The guide is accompanied by a picture of a woman by the sea with a book in her hand. Thus, the guide associates the idea of the perfect holiday with reading.

Nevertheless, the presentation of the book in the guide also contains traces of the traditional book review as it contextualizes and briefly links the theme of the book to the work of Marcel Proust. Still, the dominant feature is the short announcement, the guide and the creation of a link between the affective idea of holiday and reading. Accordingly, it can be argued that seasonal journalism is an often-used context for lifestyle guides on what to read. Moreover, it should be added that these guides in their minimalistic formats somehow re-integrate the short announcement that also characterized early reviewing practices.

Book(ish) and affective reviews on Instagram

The entanglement of book reviewing and lifestyle communication is intensified and accelerated on social media, where an embodied and affectively passionate reviewer position seems to dominate. Instagram is a dynamic photo-sharing platform that allows for a diverse range of content and a mix of professional and amateur voices, as well as new media influencers or micro-celebrities (Abidin, 2016; Marwick, 2015; Lobinger, 2016). This eclectic space bears witness to an evolution in how reviews are presented. Instagram, thus, accommodates more visually engaging formats such as image-driven critique and video reviews. These multimedia approaches enhance the viewers' engagement and allow them to appreciate the nuances and merits of a product, experience or work of art in a more immersive manner than traditional approaches.

However, social media also challenge the notion and definition of a review, and it can be argued that much of the evaluative communication about books on social media is not necessarily reviews. Thus, Jaakkola (2022, p. 7) takes literature as a point of departure in arguing that the book review is different from other formats such as the book discussion (Boot, 2011), book blogging (Steiner, 2010) and bookish online engagement (Rodger, 2019). A slightly different angle would be to argue that the book review on social media is partly aligned with the traditional defining features of reviews, partly a renegotiation of the genre that takes a much more affective, collective, embodied and material approach to evaluating books. This stance implies that lifestyle communication and book reviews become even more difficult – or even often impossible – to distinguish from one another on social media because a general love of, and interest in, books and book culture constantly intertwine with practices of recommending and evaluating specific books (Thumala Olave, 2020).

Jaakkola (2022) claims that the visual affordances of reviewing practices on Instagram and in vlogs have created a new preoccupation with the materiality, spaces, atmospheres and embodiments linked to reading, consuming and reviewing books:

> Material artefacts are portrayed and put into contexts of private spaces of reception in another way than what has been common in the cultures of reviewing before the internet, and visual and audiovisual practices such as vlogging and Instagramming foreground the reviewer as a human body, placed in the context of home or family, in a new way.
>
> *(Jaakkola, 2022, p. 157)*

Jaakkola argues that this has created a new visual style of book reviewing through which a particular atmosphere is communicated by focusing on (1) "the book as a material artefact" (by, e.g., taking photos of the book with various backdrops), (2) "anchoring the book-reading experience in its reception context" (by, e.g., documenting the reader's actual or potential reading environment such as a living room, bedroom, library and café) and on (3) "atmosphere-creating props" (by, e.g., photographing books as parts of arrangements with cups, flowers, shells, carpets, etc.) (Jaakkola, 2022, pp. 157–158).

These stylistic choices can be combined and merged in different ways. Jaakkola outlines four basic and often used styles by bookstagrammers or book vloggers: (1) compositions where a book is presented as part of a carefully crafted constellation of multiple objects, (2) arranged still lifes where a number of books are used to produce a particular structure or shape, (3) an environment-focused style where the books are documented with a particular spatial setting as the backdrop (e.g., a park or a scenic view) and (4) photos showing the body of the reader with a book (Jaakkola, 2022, pp. 159–160). These styles are popular and widely used, but sometimes supplemented with the alternative and more basic style of just sharing an image of the front cover or spine of the book being reviewed.

If we compare the Instagram reviews of Ernaux's and Blæsbjerg's novels, all of the four styles are present in the material, but the reviews of *The Years* by Ernaux seem to involve more embodied readers (eight out of 17 posts reveal the body of the reader in one way or other), while Blæsbjerg's novel is treated more as a demarcated book object presented on a table as part of a composition with other objects or in front of bookshelves (only two out of 12 posts depict the actual reader). One potential explanation could be that the cover of Blæsbjerg's novel is quite closely connected to the plot (uncovering how chemical pollution affected a local environment in Denmark in dramatic ways) and thus works as a natural illustration of the storyline when trying to communicate what the book is about. The reviews of Blæsbjerg also seem to focus on the plot of this large novel, while Ernaux's novel – which is itself focused on sensations, memories and material culture – is treated more as a trigger for the reviewers' personal reflections on life and the everyday. This is somehow mirrored in the depictions of Ernaux's book on Instagram, which focus less on the book as an isolated, plot-containing object and more as entangled with the lifeworld and subjective experiences of readers. In that way, the actual choices involved in producing a composition of text and image for Instagram reviews are also intertwined with the specificities of the content and materiality of the book in question.

What unites the two samples of Instagram reviews is their explicit love of books (Thumala Olave, 2020) and their fascination with the book as a visual and tangible object and with the sheer joy of being around books. The concept of bookishness has been introduced to grasp a particular type of engagement with material book culture that seems to thrive in the era of digital media. Pressman argues that:

> At the moment of the book's foretold obsolescence because of digital technologies—around the turn of the millennium—we saw something surprising: the emergence of a creative movement invested in exploring and demonstrating love for the book as symbol, art form, and artifact. This is what I describe as "bookishness": creative acts that engage the physicality of the book within a digital culture.
>
> *(Pressman, 2020, p. 15)*

Bookishness, in other words, refers to a certain approach to the print book where its (documented) materiality is fetishized as an attractive object that the reader wants to be near and consume – not least to signal their identity as a book person (Pressman, 2020; Rodger, 2019), which is "an identity derived from a physical *nearness* to books, not just from the 'reading' of them in the conventional sense" (Pressman, 2020, p. 18). In that way, digital technologies – which could intuitively be said to threaten a more traditional material engagement with books (due to, e.g., audiobook or screen reading) – also "help to maintain a 'nearness' to books in a digital realm that is becoming ever more an extension of our intimate living and personal spaces, a process that makes evaluating what counts as 'near' ever more complex" (p. 18).

It can be discussed to what extent book reviewing practices on social media are inherently bookish or rather characterized by a more traditional approach to literature considering that the actual reading of books is still key (Jaakkola, 2022, p. 169). When looking at the reviews of Ernaux's and Blæsbjerg's novels, it is, however, difficult to draw clear boundaries between the book as a traditional literary reading-object and a more bookish fascination with the novel as a lifestyle object. The act of reading and reviewing specific books seems to be intertwined with a communicated desire to be around and near books and with having them as crucial material dimensions of the private sphere or home. Being a social media book reviewer and a book person, in other words, seems to be two sides of the same coin because social media reviewing is intricately connected to the lifestyle of being a book lover.

The general love of books often mentioned as a crucial dimension of bookishness can also be a challenge for the Instagram reviewer. Explicit critique or less immersive reading experiences can simply become a communicative problem for reviewers who position themselves as book lovers. Therefore – we argue – a set of alternative evaluative strategies to avoid explicit negative judgement have been developed. One strategy is to focus on the negative reading experience as not necessarily indicative of the book's quality, but rather of the reader's lacking literary competences. One reviewer, for instance, explains that it can be anxiety-provoking to review a book that is perceived as a French literary masterpiece (@bibliotikaren, 05/04–2021). Another reader–reviewer shares her initial impression of *The Years* as she is reading the novel for a book club meeting "on Thursday": "I am very enthusiastic, but I also have to admit that I have been a little challenged due to my lack of skills and knowledge about French history, politics and cultural life" (@justfollowmyread, 20/11–2022). This strategy indicates a departure from the historically founded evaluative practices of professionals using objective criteria in their judgement of the quality of a given book. Another strategy is to present critique as linked to a lack of intense engagement or to what could be called an affectively ambiguous or flat assessment of the book in question. A reviewer in an online book community, for instance, communicates a somewhat hesitant experience, but quickly takes on responsibility for not being Francophile enough to appreciate the book:

> *The Years* is perceived as a main work in modern literature, and it is a big and ambitious memory novel. The style is minimalistic and maybe it is a bit difficult to really get to know it. I certainly struggled a bit, but this is probably just a matter of taste. Here you will find a myriad of details and references that anyone with Francophile tendencies would love to dive into.
>
> *(@bbcs.bogunivers, 18/05–2022)*

Many of the posts mention that *The Years* is considered a masterpiece and thus frame an established judgement made by the literary establishment as a point of reference for their own reading experience. This is potentially caused by the fact that the contextual motivation for reviewing the novel is that Ernaux received the Nobel Prize in 2022. The reviewers on Instagram in that way seem to assess the book from a rather humble reading perspective and blame themselves if the novel occasionally feels a little too cramped with French details. By doing so, the reviewers avoid framing their assessments as traditional connoisseurial judgements, presenting them instead as reports on a more subjective encounter between a book lover and a piece of literature that is highly praised by the literary establishment.

An interesting comparison can be made to the review by Linea Ernst previously cited in this chapter. Ernst also notes that the reader ends up googling a lot of details during the reading of *The Years*, but she blames the lack of immersion and readability on the novel and author, not on herself. In other words, she trusts her own authority as a connoisseur and positions the novel as failing according to aesthetic standards, while the Instagram readers seem to frame themselves as unable to immerse in – and appreciate the quality of – the novel. An important point, however, is that the judgements of the latter group are still quite clear. They are just communicated through non-enthusiasm, affective flatness, hesitation and insecurity with regard to their personal reading experience, rather than through an analytical and self-confident assessment of the novel as a cultural object. Their judgements are in that way primarily affective and measured according to a standard of immersion and enthusiasm.

Changing interaction between market, cultural institutions and consumers

In a post-industrial society, cultural mediation is, as already demonstrated, performed in many different formats and by an array of agents including the intellectual cultural critic, the professional journalist, the media-made arbiter of taste and the everyday amateur expert, as well as the cultural industry itself. Instagram seems to inspire an amplification of various combinations of cultural intermediaries who stimulate cultural consumption – a point that is also reflected in the reception of the two different literary works included here. Thus, the reviews of the books are circulated, liked and re-posted by publishers, sponsored readers (who get free copies of literature) and libraries.

In our sample, we also see examples of bookstores and libraries creating posts drawing on the review genre to stimulate cultural consumption. The examples of bookstores using reviews to promote the two literary works merge different communicative practices. In a post from the 22/12–2022, showing the cover of Kim Blæsbjerg's novel with a note saying "Kristian F. Møller recommends", this Danish bookstore, for instance, announces:

Kristian F. Møller recommends
   Kim Blæsbjerg's new novel *The best families* resonates strongly with me and is an excellent portrayal of the human, societal and environmental consequences of the chemical factory Cheminova establishing itself in West Jutland in the 1950s. It is a well-written and engaging story that I highly recommend.

- Margrethe

In their physical store, the bookseller collects different reader responses and shares them on a huge shelf, but they also use these subjective opinion pieces as part of their marketing and promotion strategy on Instagram. Margrethe is an ordinary – but to most readers of the Instagram post also completely abstract or unknown – reader, and the use of her quote is in that way a reflection of how booksellers assume that ordinary readers convey a certain and important legitimacy (even without an actual interpersonal relation). This trend mirrors the use of reviews in movie promotion (see, for example, Kristensen & From, 2015b), but with the important difference that it is primarily legacy media reviews that are integrated into movie posters and commercials. In the case of Margrethe, it is instead (and presumably) a layperson who has the authority to make a recommendation simply because she is an ordinary reader. The picture of the book cover in the post is moreover accompanied by several hashtags – for example, #welovebooks and #readreadread – thus confirming that Instagram is a space for book lovers (Thumala Olave, 2020) and for reading as a form of cultural consumption.

A similar case is found in a post published by Copenhagen Libraries from 8/11–2021. It is rather comprehensive and contains elements of the traditional review known from legacy media, such as a thematic reading and a contextualization drawing on the readers' knowledge about consumer society. It is originally produced by the profile "One chapter a day" and then shared by the library:

> But it hasn't diminished the reading experience, and since I turned the last page of *The Years*, I have only become happier to have read it. It doesn't resemble anything else I've read, and I have a feeling that I will return to it and keep it as a historical document, a philosophical breather and a genuine Francophile exile.
> Guest recommendation by Lise @etkapitelomdagen
> Borrow the book from the library.
> #copenhagenlibraries #lillianmunkrösing #gadsforlag #bookstagram #booktalk #bookish #readmore #theyears #gadsforlag #francophile #literature #frenchauthors #annieernaux @gads_forlag

The first-person perspective and a dominating subjective approach are central features in social media in general, but as already indicated, it is also a growing tendency in cultural reviewing in relation to contemporary forms of criticism (Kristensen, 2021). Moreover, it is worth noting that this type of review has the traditional traits of the review genre but promotes both the products (the artwork), an industrial agency (the publisher called Gad) and a cultural institution (Copenhagen Libraries). By using Instagram, the library also facilitates and engages in an informal dialogue with their followers – and in line with this, the comments are very personal: "this sounds as a relevant book for me". To this the library replies: "@doktormor yay, one more on the list ♥📚 Happy reading, regards Louise".

A final trend of changing interaction and promotion is related to journalists' self-promotion and communication with readers. One example is journalist Malou Wedell Brun, who shares a book review of *The Years* on her Instagram profile and includes a link to her review published the same day in the Danish newspaper *Berlingske*, 04/04–2021. In that way, a review that was previously presented in a newspaper is recirculated on Instagram, thereby reinforcing the stable characteristics of the genre across platforms.

Simultaneously, the comment thread enables a more direct dialogue between the journalist and the readers. Readers react to the recommendation of the book with comments like: "I'm looking forward to reading the book", to which the journalist replies: "She is truly special! She analyses, drills, investigates, turns and twists, and peels off layers, and one feels so enriched and seen. That one is not alone in one's female life". This interactive dynamic adds an extra dimension to the review and the experience of consuming books together with others by making the review livelier and more engaging for the audience.

It is not just a one-sided presentation of the review but a more open conversation that can contribute to shaping the readers' perception and understanding of the book. Thus, the review is not only reproduced but also transformed when shared on social media like Instagram. It not only gains extra visibility but also acquires a new interactive and affective quality that can influence readers' perception and engagement. This point confirms existing scholarly work, arguing that cultural criticism is not only linked to aesthetic traditions but also increasingly connected to emotions and subjective experiences (Kristensen, 2021).

The examples in this section show how the book review is entangled with changing patterns of cultural consumption and interaction between consumers, cultural institutions and market and thus how the production of book reviews on social media is characterized by increasingly blurred boundaries between professional and lay readers.

Future directions

In this chapter, we have addressed how the review genre has developed over time, how it reflects a transformation of cultural consumption and how books are perceived and valued. Thus, the historical development of the book review shows how books traditionally belonged to the lifeworld of writing and the reading elite and was reviewed in short announcements. As the press developed, books were increasingly reviewed by professional voices in the omnibus press, while book reviewing in the current social media landscape is practiced by a diverse range of voices that represent and blur the boundaries between layperson, professional, semi-professional and commercial perspectives.

Our readings underpin how the value of the book as literary experience and material object has changed and how contemporary reviews combine and remix historical practices and features. Across media and agents, books are reviewed with a focus on content and aesthetic quality, material surface and the specific reading experience or atmosphere that the book produces. In consequence, the review genre is becoming increasingly hybrid and engaged in complex combinations of lifestyle components and cultural consumption and of communicative practices of informing, educating and entertaining.

We have shown how Instagram accelerates transformations of the review genre and how it has traditionally been presented in legacy media. These transformations include the increased *entanglement of lifestyle communication with reviewing*, the tendency that *reviewing is articulated through a more subjective or affectively involved voice* and that *the materiality of books* plays a more central communicative role. All these tendencies emphasize reading and the valuation of books as an embodied and material everyday experience. We have, thus, shown that book reviewing in a contemporary setting demonstrates "how materiality matters by offering an interpretation of attachment to cultural objects that integrates shared cultural valuations and the experiential, nonrepresentational dimension of meaning-making" (Thumala Olave, 2020, p. 24).

This chapter has combined existing scholarly contributions from literary studies, media and journalism studies and cultural sociology. Future studies could elaborate and develop these interdisciplinary insights and more systematically address the review ecosystem through empirical analyses. As Thumala Olave (2020) argues, it would also be relevant and interesting to include more in-depth analyses of the diversity of voices producing reviews. How are the patterns of reviewing and book-related experiences, for instance, related to issues of gender? Remarkably, all the posts in our small (non-representative) sample are created by women, while the professional reviews represent both men and women.

Our analysis links book reviewing practices to the reading of books and literature and the enjoyment of the materiality of books. Other studies have been more hesitant in making this connection, and scholars have instead argued "that Instagram and TikTok content about books is constructed to elicit very specific responses which are only sometimes focused on promoting reading. Collecting and displaying books does not equate to reading them" (Dezuanni et al., 2022, p. 370). This points to an empirical lack of knowledge regarding the potential relation between reading practices and book-posting, and research must be developed to examine how reading dispositions are (or are not) stimulated by reviews and review-like posts on social media. We encourage such studies that may combine interdisciplinary historical knowledge and theoretical perspectives with complex empirical analysis.

Further readings

Blank, G. (2007). *Critics, Ratings, and Society: The Sociology of Reviews*. Rowman & Littlefield.
From, U. (2019). Criticism and Reviews. In T. P. Vos & F. Hanusch (Eds.), *The International Encyclopedia of Journalism Studies*, 1–9. Wiley. https://doi.org/10.1002/9781118841570.iejs0203
Jaakkola, M. (2022). *Reviewing Culture Online*. Cham: Palgrave Macmillan.
Kristensen, N. N. (2021). Critical Emotions: Cultural Criticism as an Intrinsically Emotional Type of Journalism. *Journalism Studies*, 22(12), 1590–1607. https://doi.org/10.1080/1461670X.2021.1910544
Pressman, J. (2020). *Bookishness: Loving Books in a Digital Age*. New York: Columbia University Press.

References

Abidin, C. (2016). "Aren't These Just Young, Rich Women Doing Vain Things Online?": Influencer Selfies as Subversive Frivolity. *Social Media + Society*, 2(2), 1–17.
Blank, G. (2007). *Critics, Ratings, and Society: The Sociology of Reviews*. Lanham: Rowman & Littlefield.
Boot, P. (2011). Towards a Genre Analysis of Online Book Discussion: Socializing, Participation and Publication in the Dutch Booksphere. Aoir Selected Papers of Internet Research, 1–16. https://doi.org/10.5210/spir.v1i0.9076.
Carroll, N. (2009). *On Criticism*. London: Routledge.
Chong, P. (2019). Valuing Subjectivity in Journalism: Bias, Emotions, and Self-Interest as Tools in Arts Reporting. *Journalism*, 20(3), 427–443.
Crowl, L. Fisher, S., Webby, E., & Wevers, L. (2017). Newspapers and Journals. In C. A. Howells, P. Sharrad & G. Turcotte (Eds.), *The Oxford History of the Novel in English: Volume 12: The Novel in Australia, Canada, New Zealand, and the South Pacific Since 1950*, Oxford History of the Novel in English, online edn. Oxford: Oxford Academic, 21 June 2018. https://doi-org.ez.statsbiblioteket.dk/10.1093/oso/9780199679775.003.0037.
Deutsch, J. (2022). *In Praise of Good Bookstores*. Princeton: Princeton University Press. https://doi-org.ez.statsbiblioteket.dk/10.1515/9780691229669
Dezuanni, M., Reddan, B., Rutherford, L., & Schoonens, A. (2022). Selfies and Shelfies on #Bookstagram and #Booktok – Social Media and the Mediation of Australian Teen Reading. *Learning, Media and Technology*, 47(3), 355–372. https://doi.org/10.1080/17439884.2022.2068575
Eide, M., & Knight, G. (1999). Public/Private: Service Journalism and the Problems of Everyday Life. *European Journal of Communication*, 14(4), 525–547.
Ernst, L. (09/04–2021).Man skulle nok have været der? Weekendavisen
From, U. (2019). Criticism and Reviews. In T. P. Vos & F. Hanusch (Eds.), *The International Encyclopedia of Journalism Studies*, 1–9. https://doi.org/10.1002/9781118841570

From, U. (2018). Lifestyle Journalism. *Oxford Research Encyclopedia of Communication*. Oxford University Press. doi:10.1093/acrefore/9780190228613.013.835.
Hanusch, F., & Hanitzsch, T. (2013). Mediating Orientation and Self-Expression in the World of Consumption: Australian and German Lifestyle Journalists' Professional Views. *Media, Culture & Society*, 35(8), 943–959. https://doi.org/10.1177/016344371350
Jaakkola, M. (2022). *Reviewing Culture Online*. Cham: Palgrave Macmillan.
Jaakkola, M. (2023). Community-first Criticism: Reviewing of Art and Culture in Local Newspapers. *Journalism Studies*, 24(9), 1214–1236. https://doi.org/10.1080/1461670X.2023.2205526
Janssen, S., & Verboord, M. (2015). Cultural Mediators and Gatekeepers. In J. D. Wright (Ed.), *International Encyclopedia of the Social & Behavioral Sciences* (pp. 440–446). Oxford: Elsevier.
Jost, J. S. (2022). Eighteenth-Century British Literary. In T. Lanzendörfer (Ed.), *The Routledge Companion to the British and North American Literary Magazine* (pp. 135–142). https://doi-org.ez.statsbiblioteket.dk/10.4324/9780429274244
Koreman, R., Verboord, M., & Janssen, S. (2024). Constructing Authority in the Digital Age: Comparing Book Reviews of Professional and Amateur Critics. *European Journal of Cultural Studies*, 27(4), 736–753. https://doi.org/10.1177/13675494231187472
Kristensen, N. N. (2021). Critical Emotions: Cultural Criticism as an Intrinsically Emotional Type of Journalism. *Journalism Studies*, 22(12), 1590–1607. https://doi.org/10.1080/1461670X.2021.1910544
Kristensen, N. N., & From, U. (2024). The Development of Criticism in the Intersection between Objective and Subjective Rhetorical Strategies [Anmeldelsens udvikling i krydsfeltet mellem objektive og subjektive retoriske greb]. In E. Skyum-Nielsen & N. D. Lund (Eds.), *Reading Pleasure & the Urge to Write: Danish Cultural Journalism and Literary History [Læselyst & skrivekløe: Dansk kulturjournalistik og litteraturhistorie]* (pp. 55–63). Hellerup: Spring.
Kristensen, N. N., & From, U. (2015a). From Ivory Tower to Cross-Media Personas: The Heterogeneous Cultural Critic in the Media. *Journalism Practice*, 9(6), 853–871. https://doi.org/10.1080/17512786.2015.1051370
Kristensen, N. N., & From, U. (2015b). Publicity, News Content, and Cultural Debate: The Changing Coverage of Blockbuster Movies in Cultural Journalism. *Communication, Culture & Critique*, 8(2015), 484–501. https://doi.org/10.1111/cccr.12094
Kristensen, N. N., & From, U. (2012). Lifestyle Journalism: Blurring Boundaries. *Journalism Practice*, 6(1), 26–41. https://doi.org/10.1080/17512786.2011.622898Krogsgaard Christensen, J. (31/07-2021).Fabelagtigt fransk mesterværk kan nu endelig læses på dansk. Kristeligt Dagblad.
Lobinger, K. (2016). Photographs as Things – Photographs of Things. A Texto-Material Perspective on Photo-Sharing Practices. *Information, Communication & Society*, 19(4), 475–488.
Marwick, A. (2015). Instafame: Luxury Selfies in the Attention Economy. *Public Culture*, 27(1), 137–160.
McDonald, R. (2007). *The Death of the Critic*. London: Continuum.
Pressman, J. (2020). *Bookishness: Loving Books in a Digital Age*. New York: Columbia University Press.
Purhonen, S., Heikkilä, R., Karademir Hazir, I. K., Lauronen, T., Fernández Rodríguez, C. J., & Gronow, J. (2019). *Enter Culture, Exit Arts? In the Transformation of Cultural Hierarchies in European Newspaper Culture Sections,1960–2010*. London: Routledge.
Rixon, P. (2018). *Radio Critics and Popular Culture: A History of British Radio Criticism*. London: Palgrave Macmillan.
Rodger, N. (2019). From Bookshelf Porn and Shelfies to #Bookfacefriday: How Readers Use Pinterest to Promote their Bookishness. *Participations*, 16(1), 473–495.
Shrum, W. (1991). Critics and Publics: Cultural Mediation in Highbrow and Popular Performing Arts. *American Journal of Sociology*, 97, 347–375.
Steiner, A. (2010). Personal readings and public texts: Book blogs and online writing about literature. *Culture Unbound: Journal of Current Cultural Research*, 2(2), 471–494.
Thumala Olave, M. A. (2020). Book Love. A Cultural Sociological Interpretation of the Attachment to Books. *Poetics*, 81(101440), 1–11. https://doi.org/10.1016/j.poetic.2020.101440
Verboord, M. (2014). The Impact of Peer-Produced Criticism on Cultural Evaluation: A Multilevel Analysis of Discourse Employment in Online and Offline Film Reviews. *New Media & Society*, 16(6), 921–940. https://doi.org/10.1177/1461444813495164

Verboord, M. (2010). The Legitimacy of Book Critics in the Age of the Internet and Omnivorousness: Expert Critics, Internet Critics and Peer Critics in Flanders and the Netherlands. *European Sociological Review*, 26(6), 623–637. https://doi.org/10.1093/esr/jcp039

Verboord, M., & Janssen, S. (2015). Arts Journalism and Its Packaging in France, Germany, The Netherlands and The United States, 1955–2005. *Journalism Practice*, Vol.9 (6), 829–852. https://doi.org/10.1080/17512786.2015.1051369

Verboord, M, Koreman, K., & Janssen, S. (2020). Where to Look Next for a Shot of Culture? In N. N. Kristensen, U. From, & H. Haastrup (Eds.), *Rethinking Cultural Criticism*. (pp. 235-259). Singapore: Palgrave Macmillan.

Wedell Bruun, M. L. (04/04–2021). Fransk feminist: Jeg skulle have kæmpet de muslimske kvinders kamp. Berlingske.

8
FOOD JOURNALISM'S COMMERCIAL INGREDIENTS

Peter English and David Fleischman

Introduction

Food journalism is a commercially conflicted area of lifestyle journalism, and these murky aspects are usually hidden from the eyes of consumers and audiences. Often focused on the high-profile areas of fine dining and commercial television, coverage of food in media highlights the curated plates, delicate desserts and aspiration of the audience. Reviewers usually examine the best restaurants and focus on middle-class aspects (see Brüggemann, Kunert & Sprengelmeyer, 2024; Jenkins & Hinnant, 2020; Wood, 1996), food shows are often shot in exotic or luxury locations and glossy reality show contestants pretend to be hatted television chefs. The pervasive commercial influences and consumerism focus are reflected in lifestyle journalism more broadly, with its market-driven and entertainment functions (see Hanusch, Banjac & Maares, 2020).

Behind the glamour of the gastronomy and "gastroporn" (Jenkins & Hinnant, 2020, p. 32) are stories that do not always fit the lifestyle narrative: underpaid and abused staff; restaurants on the brink of financial collapse; and bad food or experiences that are not called out or written about. Food journalism can often be awarded five stars for ignoring hard news. Key reasons behind this approach are the commercial influences and conflicts within the industry and the way the media does – or does not – cover an issue, restaurant or story. These financial elements come both from the broader food industry's marketing and public relations influence and news organisation tensions between editorial and advertising departments and subsequent decisions (English & Fleischman, 2019; Hanusch, Banjac & Maares, 2020; Titz, Lanza-Abbott & Cordúa y Cruz, 2004; Wood, 1996).

In this environment, it is important to examine the role of journalists in food journalism and the various commercial influences in food journalism. Economic conflict can occur in many places, including reviews and ratings of restaurants, where tensions exist between the demands of media publications' editorial and advertising considerations, along with the potential damage a poor review can generate. There is also evidence of commercial issues over transparency in reviews and whether the reporter is operating independently of the restaurant and delivering a more detached judgement or as someone with the support of the business and being provided with a free dining experience. These elements raise ethical issues and questions over professional standards, especially in comparison with traditional journalism and factors of promotion rather than reporting, as well as highlighting the impact of commercial influences on professional roles.

Food journalism also includes a range of content providers, from established food critics and journalists in broadsheet and tabloid publications to the growing digital sphere of bloggers and social media influencers, which include different approaches to both commercial and ethical factors. These elements are explored in an analysis of restaurant reviews and the role of ratings in this process and the value of news in food journalism. It is important to recognise that food journalism is not restricted to text-based publications and has expanded dramatically in television and digital spaces. Food TV is associated with food journalism, even though its primary role is often entertainment rather than information or education, and the hosts are more likely to be presenters rather than reporters. This sector of the food industry highlights how the boundaries between journalism and media are increasingly blurred. A case study on the evolution of food TV complements the academic analysis in this chapter and highlights the development of this high-profile area of the media industry.

Journalists in food and lifestyle journalism

The rise of food journalism, particularly since the 1990s, has occurred across media and in markets throughout the world (Brüggemann, Kunert & Sprengelmeyer, 2024; Brown, 2004; Davis, 2009; Hollows, 2022; Naulin, 2020; Phillipov, 2016). Kirkwood (2023) links the increase in the number of shows and coverage of food with the expanding presence of the celebrity chef from the late 20th century. The focus on these figures has led to some, such as the UK's Jamie Oliver, becoming "global opinion leaders", whose comments are covered by journalists in similar ways to how they would report on politicians or royals (Kirkwood, 2023, p. 115). Fakazis and Fürsich (2023, p. 1) state the volatility, competitiveness and technological shifts of the media in the early 21st century further "jolted the field" of food journalism, creating both anxiety and "an infusion of creative energy birthing new publications and platforms, story structures, production practices, and framing strategies". These changes included the introduction of different styles of social and digital media, such as bloggers, vloggers and influencers, in conjunction with the more traditional elements of food media, including reviews, cookbooks and television programmes (see Kirkwood, 2023; Naulin, 2020; Phillipov, 2022). Historically, Lonsdale (2015) notes how food coverage achieved significance in newspapers, including the *Daily Mail* and *The Guardian*, during WW1 in Britain (see also Chapter 4). Lonsdale (2015) found two types of food articles during this time: practical stories with recipes which were often limited to the *Woman's Page* and a newer form of writing providing pleasure and knowledge about food. She outlines a history in which this genre of journalism developed much earlier than the generally accepted claims that food and cooking writing emerged in women's magazines later in the 20th century or through television in the United States, starting with *I Love to Eat* in 1946 (see Collins, 2009; Kirkwood, 2023).

In contrast to the rapid recent rise of food journalism and media, there has been limited research on lifestyle journalism that includes food (see Fürsich, 2012; Hanusch, 2012; Hanusch, Hanitzsch & Laurer, 2017; Kristensen & From, 2012), and food journalism specifically, such as reviews and writing about food (Duffy & Ashley, 2012; Fakazis & Fürsich, 2023; English & Fleischman, 2019; Kirkwood, 2023; Titz, Lanza-Abbott, & Cordúa y Cruz, 2004; Williamson et al., 2009). Fakazis and Fürsich (2023, p. 3) note how lifestyle journalism deals with audiences as consumers and, subsequently, "contributes to the construction of consumer societies". They state that this shift has created more fluid boundaries between hard and soft news, as well as information and elements of entertainment, advocacy and advertising. In a Bourdieusian context, lifestyle journalism sits within the economic field (Hanusch, Banjac & Maares, 2020; Hanusch, Hanitzsch & Lauerer, 2017), with a strong market orientation (see also Fürsich, 2012), and reflects the increasing commercialisation of the media more broadly in recent decades (Picard, 2004). English and Fleischman (2019) state that food journalism is a valuable area of media, including lifestyle journalism and softer forms of journalism; has a greater focus on entertainment and information; and is more market-driven when examined within traditional journalistic functions (see also Hanusch, Banjac & Maares, 2020). They argue food journalism is more closely aligned with aspects of promotion (see Davis, 2009; Wood, 1996) than the public-interest revelations that occur more regularly in news reporting. This includes food media having strong ties with commercial influences, similar to other lifestyle journalism areas (see Fürsich, 2012; Hanusch, Hanitzsch & Lauerer, 2017), and links with PR, marketing and advertising, both from outside and inside news organisations.

Hanusch, Banjac and Maares (2020) note that commercial influences are prevalent across lifestyle journalism, which can include pressure from PR people, demands from advertisers or conflicts of interest over journalists being provided with freebies (see also Titz, Lanza-Abbott & Cordúa y Cruz, 2004; Wood, 1996). Hanusch, Hanitzsch and Lauerer (2017) also outline how public relations companies can try to attract positive attention and pressurise reviewers to eat at specific restaurants and provide reports, which are given "the appearance of unbiased assessment" but are influenced by commercial factors (Hanusch, Hanitzsch & Lauerer, 2017, p. 151; see also Hanusch, Banjac & Maares, 2020). They argue there has been an expectation that lifestyle journalists were "obviously influenced" by commercial factors (Hanusch, Banjac & Maares, 2020, p. 1030). With news organisations undergoing substantial change, including difficulties in generating revenues, these conditions have led to a greater perception of commercial influences impacting on the individual and organisational levels of journalism (Hanusch, Banjac & Maares, 2020; see also Fürsich, 2012). Hanusch, Banjac and Maares (2020) outline how lifestyle journalists build a rapport with the industry and figures within it, such as food journalists and restaurants, which can lead to an uneasy and dependent relationship. Importantly, however, they state that "commercialism hasn't necessarily posed a threat to journalistic professionalism" (Hanusch, Banjac & Maares, 2020, p. 1033). They mention the example of China provided by Li (2012), where lifestyle magazine journalists working within broader state-based frameworks have gained more freedom to exercise professionalism, including through their news organisations' partnerships with international publications.

Food journalism is, therefore, an important part of the broader industry, but one that is often on the periphery of traditional journalism due to the roles and routines and commercial and industry pressures that influence the work of the journalists and the content they produce. Journalists in other areas of journalism, including news reporting, can also be influenced by commercial elements (see McManus, 2009; Obijiofor & Hanusch, 2011; Picard, 2004). Ownership models can impact on the stories that are reported on more regularly – or ignored entirely – while organisational elements including conflict between the demands of editorial and advertising departments can also determine what the journalists as gatekeepers are encouraged – or compelled – to publish or avoid (Obijiofor & Hanusch, 2011; Shoemaker & Vos, 2009). In lifestyle journalism, as in other areas of journalism considered less serious, these elements may not be viewed as vital, partly due to the entertainment and market-focused functions already outlined (see Hanusch, Banjac & Maares, 2020). Fakazis and Fürsich (2023, p. 8) state journalism continues to hold relevant standards unique to the field of food and "must continue to be defined by its accuracy, information, and watchdog functions, in addition to its many other possible roles such as entertainment, advocacy, literary, or community building". They note the importance of a balance between these often-competing elements of traditional approaches and those suiting more contemporary outlooks, including aspects found in lifestyle journalism. Food journalism itself has some differing norms to other areas of lifestyle journalism. While areas such as travel describe experiences or places that currently have sales or deals, food journalism is similar to music and entertainment where reviews and ratings are established modes of content.

Reviews

Food reviews are a core feature of food journalism, especially in newspapers and news websites (Davis, 2009; English & Fleischman, 2019) but can involve conflict with commercial interests, hindering attempts for an independent appraisal of a restaurant. Journalistic reviewers and critics can uphold professional standards, such as not announcing their arrival and paying for meals (Hanusch, Banjac & Maares, 2020; Hanusch, Hanitzsch & Lauerer, 2017; *The Guardian*, 2016). However, the pressures of public relations, advertising and the law, along with personal ethics and approaches to commercial influences, can create tension (Davis, 2009; English & Fleischman, 2019; Hanusch, Banjac & Maares, 2020; Hanusch, Hanitzsch & Lauerer, 2017; Titz, Lanza-Abbott & Cordúa y Cruz, 2004; Wood, 1996). It is in this space where the commercial aspects of a review can come into conflict. Reviews can help or crush a restaurant (Crouch, 2016; Davis, 2009; Lethlean, 2016b; Titz, Lanza-Abbott & Cordúa y Cruz, 2004) and, depending on the content, can be both a form of promotion and a journalistic account of strengths and weaknesses.

Davis (2009, p. 1) argues reviews are "the most obvious, direct, and effective form of public relations", while Wood (1996) stated more than two decades earlier that food journalists performed a "promotional task". At the pure journalism end of reviews, journalists and reviewers do not tell the restaurant they will be dining and pay through their news company for the experience. For example, *The Guardian Weekend's* former restaurant critic Marina O'Loughlin reviewed anonymously, and her face was obscured by a plate in her profile picture (*The Guardian* 2016). However, even when reviews are conducted in this way, Davis (2009, pp. 102–103) argues there is a relationship between advertising and publicity instead of the content being "part of a subset of cultural criticism that has a long-standing tradition in journalism". Commercial influences on reviewers can come from PR and marketing companies and include pressuring them to review a place or inducements to produce positive comments (see Titz, Lanza-Abbott & Cordúa y Cruz, 2004; Wood, 1996).

Reviews are, of course, subjective and in contrast with the traditional journalism approach of objectivity – or, at least, attempts at detachment or independence. Reviewers and critics are also catering to a more middle-class, aspirational market, targeting the people who are likely be to be able to afford a restaurant with higher prices (see Brüggemann, Kunert & Sprengelmeyer, 2024; Jenkins & Hinnant, 2020; Rayner, 2023; Wood, 1996). However, if journalists apply their professional and news industry values, it has been found that commercial influences are not necessarily a threat to their professionalism

(Hanusch, Banjac & Maares, 2020). In terms of transparency of the information provided to audiences, it is important to determine whether a review is promotional and aligned with the restaurant's public relations and marketing or journalistic and accounting for the pluses and minuses of a dining experience (see English & Fleischman, 2019). As mentioned above, this can occur through reviewers not telegraphing their intention to dine at a particular place and paying for the experience rather than accepting it for free (see Hanusch, Banjac & Maares, 2020; Hanusch, Hanitzsch & Lauerer, 2017; *The Guardian,* 2016). Another key point raised by Titz, Lanza-Abbott and Cordúa y Cruz (2004) is that reviewers "train themselves to be critical of eating in restaurants", which can create unrealistic expectations. Jones and Taylor (2013, p. 101) state the food critic's job is "to proclaim publicly and authoritatively on matters of taste". However, it is important to note that the training, in conjunction with ethical obligations of journalists, can set them apart from the roles performed by bloggers, social media reviewers or influencers (English & Fleischman, 2019).

The growing phenomenon of social media usage across traditional lifestyle journalism is also evident in food media and reviewing (see also Chapter 7). Social media influencers have been exposed for touting for free meals, agreeing to a review if their expenses are paid by the restaurant (see Lethlean, 2016b). This can provide an inflated economy where only pleasant – or glowing – reviews are published or posted, giving the reader – and eater – a false view of the dining experience. Reviews of restaurants started in gastronomic literature (Davis, 2009) and have expanded into new spheres, which has raised ethical questions, especially in relation to commercial conflicts of interest. John Lethlean (2016b) is a former restaurant reviewer for *The Australian* newspaper, who has written about the problems of the "cheerleading media" who provide promotional stories. He has also highlighted requests by influencers for free meals for coverage on their platforms through #couscousforcomment on Instagram (see Glover, 2022). Naulin (2020, p. 104), who surveyed and interviewed food bloggers in France, describes them as amateurs, "passionate hobbyists" who consider themselves different from food journalists, but are still seen by audiences as providing information and influence. In noting a key issue around "who is legitimated to give advice concerning food and cooking", Naulin (2020, p. 103) outlines how both bloggers and journalists can be classed as influencers, but this description is based on different foundations of amateurism and professionalism. For example, food journalists assigned to the round may not have a passion for food but apply journalistic standards to their reporting (Naulin, 2020). Alternatively, Lethlean (2016b) explains how the PR companies working for restaurants do not tell the chefs and managers about the "traditional arms-length media practices" for food journalists that can lead to unflattering reviews, and raise expectations of positive coverage. The absence of professional standards for bloggers and social media influencers highlights their differing approaches to reviews and reports.

Reviewer ratings of restaurants

A common way for reviews to provide a subjective determination of a restaurant's quality is giving them a rating. It is another place in the food field where commercial influences are apparent, with the final score unlikely to be low. A positive or negative review and rating can impact a restaurant considerably (Titz, Lanza-Abbott & Cordúa y Cruz, 2004). Titz, Lanza-Abbott and Cordúa y Cruz (2004, p. 50) concluded from a content analysis of 38 restaurant reviews in newspapers in five US cities that most "reflect a good or at least average experience", although negative experiences were included at times. English and

Fleischman (2019) examined restaurant reviews in four broadsheet newspapers in Australia and the United Kingdom over three years, finding the average mark out of 10 ranged from 6.74 to 7.26. They outlined how the figure indicated more supportive judgements than critical ones, reflecting the softer side of journalism. They also noted the reviews were generally of high-end restaurants, so the expectation was they would be good – or at least better than average. "While there were negative reviews and critiques that offered evidence of detached accounts of the dining experience, the overall tone of positive results indicates the influence of marketing, commercial and promotional elements" (English & Fleischman, 2019, p. 101). They did not argue that there was "widespread cheerleading" but that "reviewers consistently marked the establishments favourably" and were "more inclined to praise in their ratings than dismiss" (English & Fleischman, 2019, p. 101).

Giles Coren (2015), a restaurant reviewer for *The Times* since 1993, has written about his difficulties in producing negative reviews, stating his average score was around 6.3. At the time, he also wrote about having expenses to go to restaurants but not review them if they were unsuitable. Macro-factor aspects such as defamation laws can influence the ferocity – or honesty – of a review. While Coren (2015) stated that no food reviewer had been sued in Britain, Australian reviewers have been, including *The Sydney Morning Herald* being forced to pay damages for its coverage of the restaurants Coco Roco in 2003 and Blue Angel in 1984 (Crouch, 2016). Six months after Coco Roco's 9/20 rating, it went into administration (AAP, 2009), highlighting the dangers for the business – and the broader industry – of a poor review. More recently, Lethlean (2016a) was criticised and legal action threatened (Crouch, 2016) for a review of Adelaide's Hill of Grace restaurant, after giving it zero stars out of five. Among the scathing descriptions were a "brown, mucoid gloop that passes for a pig liver sauce" and a summary that the critic was "trying hard to think of someone I'd recommended" the restaurant to (Lethlean, 2016a). Lethlean (2016b) subsequently wrote he was surprised by criticism that "fell into the 'if you don't have something nice to say' category", when his job as a mainstream reviewer was to "follow up with honest, independent appraisal".

News stories in food journalism

There are many potential hard news stories in the food industry, but constraints, including commercial influences, can prevent reporters from providing the full story. If the middle-class audience wants content involving reviews and food trends, food journalism and the associated lifestyle sections are very capable of providing them. Fakazis and Fürsich (2023) note an increase in important stories about food that engage with social, political or cultural elements and have been encouraged by media outlets supporting complex and risky reporting about food. However, other scholars and critics have argued there is limited traditional news coverage on topics such as underpayment and treatment of staff, the stagiaire experiences of mostly younger chefs working for free, issues around food scarcity or problems with people of lower classes actually being able to afford food (Jenkins & Hinnant, 2020). Brüggemann, Kunert and Sprengelmeyer (2024), who examined 10,022 articles in elite newspapers in Germany, the United States and India from 2016 to 2018, found that the reporting of food is frequent, but it is rarely covered in terms of ecological problems and does not reflect critical or investigate scrutiny. Writing about the serious issues of food is not popular. There is space for these critical items to appear in the food pages, as well as the PR-focused pieces on a restaurant's food miles and the procuring of produce. Instead, these sections are more likely to be a site for the "gastroporn" (Jenkins & Hinnant, 2020, p. 32) of photos of well-crafted dining plates. These conclusions can also apply to lifestyle journalism more broadly, with hard-hitting issues not always reported in a critical way and often written or produced by journalists who are more likely to be involved in general news or rounds away from the lifestyle sections.

The Observer's restaurant critic, Jay Rayner (for example, see 2014 and 2017), is well known for harsh restaurant reviews and has detoured from the usual fare to outline some of the problems with fine dining, which have expanded to include broader environmental and financial issues. A piece in 2023 was in response to Copenhagen's regular world's best restaurant, Noma, revealing it would close in 2024 because the business was not sustainable. As Rayner (2023) wrote: "Too many have long survived on battalions of unpaid interns, or stagiaires, who are expected to be grateful for the opportunity to do menial tasks for free so they can list it on their CV". Noma said it would start paying interns in 2023 as reported in an in-depth investigation by the *FT Magazine's* Imogen West-Knights (2022). Focusing on Danish restaurants but reflecting on many global industry conditions, West-Knights (2022) said there were two stories in fine-dining.

> The first is in the dining room, a perfectly choreographed show of luxury and excellence, a performance so fine-tuned, down to the decor, the staff uniforms, the music, the crockery, that in some ways the food itself is the least important element. And then there is the story that you, as a diner, are never supposed to hear. The story of what happens on the other side of the kitchen wall.
>
> *(West-Knights, 2022)*

West-Knights (2022) wrote these experiences involved violence, fear and abuse – including post-traumatic stress for some – low pay, high hours and exploitation. Workers in the story said they were speaking to let the public know what was happening. It is notable that this story was written by a freelance journalist and writer who operated within lifestyle topics but was not a food critic. She, therefore, sits outside the domain of a rounds journalist being conflicted by the commercial pressures of the industry. Similar to other areas of lifestyle journalism, this watchdog-style reporting is done more easily by the outsider, not the reviewer or writer who knows who butters their bread. Rayner (2023) also writes of the contradiction of chefs promoting their restaurant's sustainability while catering for the financial elite travelling in business class or limousines "because those are the only ones who can afford it". "The carbon footprint of the people you attract becomes part of the carbon footprint of your business" (Raynor, 2023). West-Knights (2022) notes the same approaches in relation to the sustainability of restaurant staff and their working conditions.

Verification of claims provided by authors, PR companies and chefs is another journalistic technique that is often overlooked in food journalism in favour of following the commercial line. The example of Jock Zonfrillo, the late celebrity chef and judge on television reality show *MasterChef*, stands out following the release of his memoir in 2021. It includes, as *The Sydney Morning Herald's Good Weekend Magazine* journalist Tim Elliott (2021) writes, tales of "drug abuse, violence and kitchen chaos" but "many of the stories that Zonfrillo tells about himself in the book and elsewhere differ markedly" from other witnesses' recollections. The in-depth feature fact-checked many of Zonfrillo's claims, including noting there were 159 mentions of Marco Pierre White, an English chef who gained three Michelin stars by his 30s. White is quoted as saying, "the only problem is that almost everything he has written about me is untrue" (Elliott, 2021).

Again, the story is compiled by a senior writer, rather than a food critic, highlighting the journalistic freedom for facts that occurs more easily outside the food industry clique. These types of critical reporting examples are not often seen among the positive reviews of the new, shiny restaurants. But this reporting is still a valuable part of food journalism – arguably more important than praiseworthy reviews – and satisfies the public interest goals of traditional reporting. Instead, so much of food journalism focuses on the food and the saffron tastes and caviar bursts while hiding the heat in the kitchen. The gritty reality, where there is often more traditional news that audiences across publications and class divides deserve, is crucial to expose, along with the elements crafted by commercial and financial influences.

The rise of food television

Food-based TV has evolved significantly to influence and shape how society perceives, prepares and enjoys food. From the early beginnings in the mid-20th century, a diverse array of programmes initially distributed via traditional broadcasting and now streamed on-demand have played a pivotal role in shaping culinary trends and consumer perceptions, promoting cultural diversity and transforming the viewers' relationship with food. This case study unpacks the evolution of food TV shows in television, shedding light on their historical progression. From simple beginnings to genre-specific shows shot in beautiful high definition, food TV does more than allow people to eat with their eyes; it drives a multi-faceted experience associated with all aspects of food. In the context of this chapter, food TV is linked with lifestyle journalism due to its focus on providing information about experiences, including elements of travel (see Kirkwood, 2023). While entertainment is a primary aim of these broadcasts, which are often not hosted by journalists, there are informative aspects in programmes that highlight blurring of boundaries between food TV and food journalism.

Food TV shows first aired in the mid-20th century when TV started to become a prominent medium for entertainment. James Beard's show, *I Love to Eat*, was one of the first to bring cooking to household TV sets in the United States in 1946 (Collins, 2009; Kirkwood, 2023). Beard's programme laid the foundation, with his name now synonymous with the prestigious James Beard Foundation Awards, which recognise the best chefs, restaurateurs, authors and journalists in the nation. Julia Child is another pioneer of food TV and one of the most famous chef personalities (see Collins, 2009). Her eccentric personality was contagious and captivated audiences from the 1960s to 1990s. Her show, *The French Chef*, gained a prominent public following and eventually led to pop-culture movies such as *Julie and Julia* (2009).

From the groundwork laid by Child and Beard, the 1990s experienced an explosion of food-based TV (Hollows, 2022). Moving beyond networks airing in dedicated time slots, entire food-centred TV stations such as the Food Network and the Cooking Channel were launched. TV networks shined the light on chefs and food personalities through personal cooking shows, including Marco Pierre White, Jamie Oliver, Martha Stewart, Curtis Stone, Gordon Ramsay, Nigella Lawson, Emeril Lagasse, Rachel Ray, Morimoto, Madhur Jaffrey and Bobby Flay (see Hollows, 2022). Celebrity chefs and food personalities soon created a large wave of gastronomic momentum in popular culture (Fuste-Forne &

Masip, 2019). Networks responded by expanding and producing a variety of reality food TV shows. By the early 2000s, competitive reality cooking was viewed, among many others, on *Iron Chef*, *MasterChef*, *Top Chef*, *Hell's Kitchen*, *Kitchen Nightmares* and *My Kitchen Rules*, which often occupied prime-time spots. These shows provided a spectacle for the high level of professionalism needed to be successful in the culinary industry and inspired a generation of home cooks to explore, experiment and enjoy a variety of food. While the PR-laden curation and mediation of food TV is not without criticism, it has become baked into global pop culture as a lifestyle phenomenon worthy of further research (Goodman et al., 2017).

Food TV continued to evolve in line with popular society. The late 2000s and early 2010s saw a shift in societal behaviour. Younger generations sought cultural experiences over material possessions, as a means of self-identity, expression and growth (Sthapit et al., 2019). Combining food and travel was the perfect recipe to satisfy the appetites of novelty-seeking, intrinsically driven young adults (Kim et al., 2010) – driving the popularity of shows focused on food and travel exploration. Food media's links with tourism (see, for example, Ellis et al., 2018) are another commercial element within the industry. Nobody transformed the fusion of food and travel more than the late Anthony Bourdain. Through *No Reservations* and *Parts Unknown*, Bourdain unlocked the beauty of life and learning through food and travel, while also shining a light on the darker realities of the culinary world. Whether he was fine dining in France, eating street food in Vietnam, taking a boat ride to a remote part of Cambodia, enjoying a New York hotdog or wandering the streets of Spain snacking on pinchos, Bourdain had the unique ability to draw audiences together by authentically showcasing the learning, understanding, adventure and humility achieved through enjoying food – whether it was alone, with a friend or a stranger. Although some academic research notes the commercial underpinnings of Bourdain's shows (Beattie, 2023), his legacy continues, particularly in the power of food to transcend borders and socio-political differences, reminding society of what brings people together. Bourdain's approach was a testament to developing the richness of what food TV could offer, helping the evolution for the next wave of food shows.

It is important to note again that many high-profile food TV presenters are not journalists and therefore not required to adhere – or even consider – the professional roles and ethical considerations of journalistic conduct. However, they are integrating elements of food journalism through their informational offerings and descriptions of dishes and experiences, and, as a result, parts of these programmes can be considered in this context. For example, towards the end of Bourdain's life, he began discussing political issues, including Palestine, immigrant labour exploitation, sexual harassment and violence in restaurants, and even described his "auxiliary role as a political journalist" (Fakazis & Fürsich, 2023, p. 1). Despite being told by critics to stay out of politics and talk only about food, Bourdain (in Fakazis & Fürsich, 2023) argued that food itself was political, with issues needing to be debated including who was and was not able to eat. Fakazis and Fürsich (2023, p. 1) note Bourdain's desires to discuss "issues at the margins or even outside the expected boundaries of food journalism and entertainment food media's 'beat'" and how this approach earned him awards, recognition and kudos (see also Chapter 19).

From the 2010s to the present, food TV has largely evolved via digital media platforms. The anywhere, anytime notion of digital platforms like YouTube not only allowed for more widespread exposure to professional chefs and food personalities, but it also ensured 'everyday' people could record and share their passion for various aspects of food, building an organic following without large TV networks (Hollows, 2022). Thousands of short videos showcase recipes, restaurants, eateries, travel and health. Food reviews continue to provide TV-like content on digital platforms that audiences have an appetite for, but are not being picked up by mainstream media. As platforms like Instagram and TikTok have gained traction, they have also become prominent media for food TV-style content for well-known celebrity chefs and personalities, including 'every day' cooks, who have become widely followed influencers. These platforms offer the ability to interact directly and in real-time with food personalities and influencers, through live-streamed cooking shows or food reviews and tours. Such platforms also help 'amateur' cooks be discovered and provide them with avenues into the culinary industry that they may not have had before the digitisation of food television. On the surface, digital TV democratised food shows and entertainment by connecting audiences worldwide at a scale of distribution and personalisation that traditional TV broadcast networks could not. However, this democratisation should be considered at times along with a grain of sea salt as it can often be turned into free labour (i.e., content creation) to leverage larger corporate interests (Lewis, 2018).

Alongside the uptake of social media, subscription streaming platforms backed by legacy media, including Netflix, Disney+, Hulu and Paramount Plus, and free-to-air TV streaming (e.g., Australian Broadcasting Corporation and Special Broadcast Service) have also become prominent mediums for digital food programmes. Again, appealing to shifts in sociocultural tastes, the streaming platforms catered to viewers' desires to engage with food more deeply. Shows on streaming platforms moved beyond pure entertainment, incorporating elements of educational documentaries and docu-dramas, profiling unique individuals and current challenges across the food landscape. For example, shows like Netflix's *Chef's Table* are shot in high definition, showcasing the artistry and eccentricity of chefs whose core ethos is defined by the food they create and share with others, which some argue creates a sense of comfort for viewers, while masking the labour needed to support such an ethos, with leisure lifestyle choices (Phillipov, 2022; Willis, 2023). Other shows like Hulu's *The Bear* won acclaim as a docu-comedic drama series based on the real-life story of a decorated executive chef returning to his hometown to manage the chaotic day-to-day operations of a sandwich shop.

Free-to-air docu-series like Matthew Evans' *Fat Pig Farm* highlight the hard work and dedication in food production and the importance and satisfaction of supporting smaller-scale local food. With a similar flavour, Netflix series, *Live to 100 – Secrets of Blue Zones*, chronicles the keys to longevity associated with dietary awareness in specific geographic regions. Documentaries like *Food, Inc*, which was streamed across a variety of subscription platforms, expose some of the startling realities of mass food productions. While not without criticism (see Phillipov, 2022), streaming platforms have exposed viewers to food TV ranging from the journeys of visionary chefs to growing awareness of how food fits into and impacts everyday lives and environments (see also Willis, 2023).

Unsurprisingly, food TV continues to evolve with society. Whether for entertainment, education, escape, exposure or interaction, food TV provides a sense of satiety with one of the simple pleasures of being and existing as a human. As food remains central to individuals, families, communities and societies, food TV will continue to showcase the fabric of the culinary tapestry from inspiring chefs, passionate home cooks, dynamic influencers, soul-searching travellers and a variety of cultures – continuously reaffirming itself as a staple of TV no matter what the next medium of distribution may be. In this way, it will continue to develop within the blurred lines between a purely entertainment focus of food TV and the more informational elements of lifestyle journalism. By highlighting aspects which can be considered important to the lives of audiences and providing them with information to assist in their choices or aspirations for culinary adventure, food TV can be considered part of the lifestyle journalism kitchen.

Conclusion

Food journalism has developed as an accepted and growing area of journalism, but it contains many areas of conflict with the historical roots of the profession. The tension exists between the entertainment, market and lifestyle elements of food media and the search for a palatable truth. While food journalists who operate towards the more pure end of journalism do not announce their visits and pay for the meals, there are many instances where writers, reviewers and bloggers are in ethical conflict with the restaurants they review, especially if the restaurant is providing them with a free dinner and associated perks.

In food TV, the positioning of the programme can be key in relation to how to view it journalistically. If it is a reality show on commercial television, then there is a greater expectation that it would not be independent, or reported in a more tabloid style, with conflict storylines heightened and sponsored products being promoted. Food travel shows blur the boundaries further, and while they reflect the experiences of the restaurants or regions, the segments are often pre-arranged, including being organised at times through tourism agencies or public relations companies. Alternatively, in line with ethical approaches, commercial conflicts can be ethically navigated, including if there is a disclaimer in the article outlining who paid for the meal. A simple sentence indicates the rules of this eating game to the audience.

Across food journalism, the beautiful stories are often told, but many important ones that are unpopular to the financial powers in the industry can be ignored. There are many places to look for news about food, but in journalism and media, the writers, reviewers and producers do not always find them. Further reporting – and greater academic research – can highlight these issues so that audiences receive public-interest information as well as entertainment. In its current form, food journalism serves a commercial focus in promoting gloss and floss over grit and loss.

Further scholarship focusing on the views of the audiences would be beneficial, particularly in relation to how much they are actually influenced by elements such as reviews and ratings, as well as understanding the appetite for how important journalistic transparency is in relation to independence and financial detachment from restaurants. A closer examination of journalistic elements provided by the hosts and the content within food TV programmes is another strand of research that could assist in explaining the blurred lines between journalism and media. Finally, mapping of the food journalism field, including understanding in greater depth the different versions of writers, producers and digital media content providers, would be relevant, locating this field's contemporary developments within the greater spaces of lifestyle journalism.

Further reading

Fakazis, E., & Fürsich, E. (2023). *The Political Relevance of Food Media and Journalism: Beyond Reviews and Recipes*, Routledge, London.

Hollows, J. (2022). *Celebrity Chefs, Food Media and the Politics of Eating*, Bloomsbury Publishing, London.

References

AAP. (2009). Sued food critic confirms bad restaurant review in court, *The Sydney Morning Herald*, November 13. Retrieved from https://www.smh.com.au/national/sued-food-critic-confirms-badrestaurant-review-in-court-20091113-ieh0.html

Beattie, M. (2023). 'That's good': An industrial, ethics-focused analysis of the televised works of Anthony Bourdain, *Critical Studies in Television,* 18(4). https://doi.org/10.1177/17496020231168067.

Brown, D. (2004). Haute cuisine, *American Journalism Review*, 26(1), 50–55.

Brüggemann, B., Kunert, J., & Sprengelmeyer, L. (2024). Framing food in the news: Still keeping the politics out of the broccoli, *Journalism Practice*, 18(10), 2712–2734. https://doi.org/10.1080/17512786.2022.2153074

Collins, K. (2009). *Watching What We Eat: The Evolution of Television Cooking Shows*, Continuum, New York.

Coren, G. (2015, August 8). Giles Coren reviews Oldroyd, London, *The Times*. Retrieved from https://www.thetimes.co.uk/article/giles-coren-reviews-oldroyd-london-b7wtvb8cp9b

Crouch, B. (2016, February 20). Adelaide Oval's fine dining restaurant Hill of Grace savaged by *The Australian* food critic John Lethlean, *The Advertiser*. Retrieved from https://www.adelaidenow.com.au/news/south-australia/adelaide-ovals-fine-dining-restaurant-hill-of-grace-savaged-by-the-australian-food-critic-john-lethlean/news-story/00da12f6295e8a1c62b4d4713f8e29d3

Davis, M. (2009). *A Taste for New York: Restaurant Reviews, Food Discourse, and the Field of Gastronomy in America*, PhD thesis, New York University.

Duffy, A., & Ashley, Y. (2012). Bread and circuses: Food meets politics in Singapore, *Journalism Practice*, 6(1), 59–74.

Elliott, T. (2021). 'He's very nice. The only problem is…': chef Marco Pierre White on Jock Zonfrillo, *The Sydney Morning Herald's Good Weekend Magazine*, August 7. Retrieved from https://www.smh.com.au/national/he-s-very-nice-the-only-problem-is-chef-marco-pierre-white-on-jock-zonfrillo-20210714-p589q3.html

Ellis, A., Park, E., Kim, S., & Yeoman, I. (2018). What is food tourism? *Tourism Management*, 68, 250–263.

English, P., & Fleischman, D. (2019). Food for thought in restaurant reviews, *Journalism Practice*, 13(1), 90–104.

Ephron, N. (2009). Julia & Julia, Sony Pictures.

Fürsich, E. (2012). Lifestyle journalism as popular journalism, *Journalism Practice*, 6(1), 12–25.

Fusté-Forné, F., & Masip, P. (2019). Food and journalism: Storytelling about gastronomy in newspapers from the U.S., and Spain, in L. Vodanovic (Ed.), *Lifestyle Journalism: Social Media, Consumption and Experience* (pp. 129–40). Abingdon: Routledge.

Glover, A. (2022). Australian café owner shares brutal response to influencer who asked for a 'collab', *Kitchen*, February 26. Retrieved from https://kitchen.nine.com.au/latest/australian-restaurant-owner-slams-influencer-for-asking-for-free-food-couscous-for-comment/c04403ff-3d31-4dab-9e6c-628ea66b9891

Goodman, M. K., Johnston, J., & Cairns, K. (2017). Food, media and space: The mediated biopolitics of eating, *Geoforum*, 84, 161–168.Hanusch, F. (2012). Broadening the focus, *Journalism Practice*, 6(1), 2–11.

Hanusch, F., Banjac, S., & Maares, P. (2020). The power of commercial influences: How lifestyle journalists experience pressure from advertising and public relations, *Journalism Practice*, 14(9), 1029–1046.

Hanusch, F., Hanitzsch, T., & Lauerer, C. (2017). How much love are you going to give this brand?' Lifestyle journalists on commercial influences in their work, *Journalism*, 18(2), 141–158.

Hollows, J. (2022). *Celebrity Chefs, Food Media and the Politics of Eating*, Bloomsbury Publishing, London.

Jenkins, J., & Hinnant, A. (2020). Idealised authenticity. Analysing Jean Baudrillard's Theory of Simulation and its applicability to food coverage in city magazines, in L. Vodanovic (Ed.), *Lifestyle Journalism: Social Media, Consumption and Experience* (pp. 26–37), Routledge, London.

Jones, S., & Taylor, B. (2013). Food Journalism, in B. Turner & R. Orange (Eds.), *Specialist Journalism* (pp. 96–106), Routledge, Abingdon.

Kim, Y., Suh, B., & Eve, A. (2010). The relationships between food-related personality traits, satisfaction, and loyalty among visitors attending food events and festivals, *International Journal of Hospitality Management*, 29(2), 216–226.

Kirkwood, K. (2023). Paleo and pain free: Reporting on scandals of food celebrities, in E. Fakazis & E. Fürsich (Eds.), *The Political Relevance of Food Media and Journalism: Beyond Reviews and Recipes* (pp. 115–131), Routledge, London.

Kristensen, N. N., & From, U. (2012). Lifestyle journalism, *Journalism Practice*, 6(1), 26–41.

Lethlean, J. (2016a, February 20). Hill of Grace, Adelaide Oval: restaurant review, *The Weekend Australian*. Retrieved from https://www.theaustralian.com.au/life/food-wine/restaurants/hill-of-grace-adelaide-oval-restaurant-review/news-story/5349ebb200ac7623fdc2395aef041eb8

Lethlean, J. (2016b, March 26). Restaurant reviews: Bloggers don't cut the mustard, *The Weekend Australian*. Retrieved from https://www.theaustralian.com.au/life/food-wine/restaurant-reviews-bloggers-dont-cut-the-mustard/news-story/480db526e3ff92c9264cebe7efbdd2a3

Lewis, T. (2018). Digital food: From paddock to platform, *Communication Research and Practice*, 4(3), 212–228.

Li, S. (2012). A new generation of lifestyle magazine journalism in China, *Journalism Practice* 6(1), 122–137.

Lonsdale, S. (2015). Roast seagull and other quaint bird dishes, *Journalism Studies*, 16(6), 800–815, DOI: 10.1080/1461670X.2014.950474

McManus, J. (2009). The commercialisation of news, in K. Wahl-Jorgensen & T. Hanitzsch (Eds.), *The Handbook of Journalism Studies* (pp. 218–234), Routledge, New York.

Naulin, S. (2020). Are food bloggers a new kind of influencer? in L. Vodanovic (Ed.), *Lifestyle Journalism: Social Media, Consumption and Experience* (pp. 102–125), Routledge, London.

Obijiofor, L., & Hanusch, F. (2011). *Journalism Across Cultures: An Introduction*, Palgrave MacMillan, Basingstoke.

Phillipov, M. (2016). The new politics of food: Television and the media/food industries, *Media International Australia*, 158(1), 90–98.

Phillipov, M. (2022). Loving neoliberalism? Digital labour and aspirational work on streaming food TV, *Communication Research and Practice*, 8(2), 152–165.

Picard, R. (2004). Commercialisation and newspaper quality, *Newspaper Research Journal*, 25(1), 54–65.

Rayner, J. (2014). Beast: Restaurant review, *The Observer*, October 19. Retrieved from https://www.theguardian.com/lifeandstyle/2014/oct/19/beast-restaurant-review-jay-rayner

Rayner, J. (2017). Le Cinq, Paris: restaurant review, *The Observer*, April 9. Retrieved from https://www.theguardian.com/lifeandstyle/2017/apr/09/le-cinq-paris-restaurant-review-jay-rayner

Rayner, J. (2023). Twenty-six courses, £400 bills, artichoke creme brulee … I won't miss super-luxe restaurants, *The Observer*, January 16. Retrieved from https://www.theguardian.com/commentisfree/2023/jan/15/twenty-six-courses-400-bills-artichoke-creme-brulee-i-wont-miss-fine-dining

Shoemaker, P., & Vos, T. (2009). *Gatekeeping Theory*, Routledge, New York.

Sthapit, E., Coudounaris, D., & Björk, P. (2019). Extending the memorable tourism experience construct: an investigation of memories of local food experiences, *Scandinavian Journal of Hospitality and Tourism*, 19(4–5), 333–353.

The Guardian. (2016). Marina O'Loughlin. Retrieved from https://www.theguardian.com/profile/marina-oloughlin

Titz, K., Lanza-Abbott, J., & Cordúa y Cruz, G. (2004). The anatomy of restaurant reviews, *International Journal of Hospitality & Tourism Administration*, 5(1), 49–65.

West-Knights, I. (2022). Fine dining faces its dark truths in Copenhagen, *FT Magazine*, June 2. Retrieved from https://www.ft.com/content/a62a96b8-2db2-44ec-ac80-67fcf83d86ef

Williamson, D., Tregidga, H., Harris, C., & Keen, C. (2009). The working engines of distinction: Discourse for main course in restaurant reviews. *Journal of Hospitality and Tourism Management* 16(1), 55–61. doi: 10.1375/jhtm.16.1.55.

Willis, D. (2023). Chefs table and a collective past: Netflix, food media, and cultural memories, in E. Fakazis & E. Fürsich (Eds.), *The Political Relevance of Food Media and Journalism: Beyond Reviews and Recipes* (pp. 210–223), Routledge, London.

Wood, R. (1996). Talking to themselves: food commentators, food snobbery and market reality, *British Food Journal*, 98(10), 5–11.

9
AESTHETICS OF LIFESTYLE JOURNALISM

Maarit Jaakkola

Introduction

Lifestyle journalism refers to diverse fields of journalism across different types of media that address cultural citizenship and consumption (Vodanovic, 2019; From, 2018; Hanusch, 2013; Kristensen & From, 2013). In the ways or styles of life, which are, at an individual level, based on choice, difference, and symbolic expression, or "distinctive configurations of cultural identity and practice which are associated particularly with forms of cultural consumption" (O'Sullivan et al., 1994, p. 167), aesthetics play a central role. Questions of visual appearance, design, and mood – essentially, how things look and feel – play a crucial role in the consumption of culture. Also, lifestyle journalism, by its nature, is partly consumed for its aesthetic appeal. This suggests that aesthetics are conveyed in multiple ways in journalism. Firstly, the aesthetics of the objects featured in journalism, like consumer products, home decorations, or travel destinations, are mediated through journalism. Secondly, journalism itself generates its own aesthetic. The perception of aesthetic dimensions is inherently subjective and contingent upon the individual receiver's apprehension. Nonetheless, aesthetic experiences are always to some extent intersubjective and shaped by the social structures of class and taste in which individuals are situated and therefore shareable.

Professional journalistic production, as understood in the production of culture perspective, refers to the shared principles and norms regarding aesthetics applied across different media and subfields of lifestyle journalism (Peterson & Anand, 2004; Fine, 1992). As the subfields of lifestyle journalism are diverse, spanning across the highbrow and lowbrow forms of culture (Gans, 1974/1999) and ranging from consumption of arts to consumer products (Gronow & Warde, 2001), different lifestyle-journalistic genres display different aesthetic preconditions and endeavours, patterns, and challenges. In general, the field of aesthetics provides a framework for examining and understanding the role of textual organization, artistic expression, and aesthetic experiences in audience behaviour, related to ideas of beauty, taste, and need. They are often said to present the "surface", yet the understanding of aesthetics needs to underlie an analysis of "deeper" structures both in production and reception of messages. Aesthetic analysis, thus, requires an interdisciplinary approach, supported by research fields discussing journalism as different, as in cultural sociology and sociology of arts, literary studies and criticism, studies of film, theatre, music and other cultural forms, visual analysis, and media linguistics. Whereas arts and cultural journalism have traditionally been conceived as the highbrow space in journalism, lifestyle journalism has emerged as a grey zone between the arts and everyday experiences (Jaakkola, 2015). However, today, the changes in newsroom development, which point to a journalistification (Jaakkola, 2015), and audience behaviour, where cultural omnivorousness has become prevalent (Peterson & Kern, 1996; Wright, 2016), result in the consumption of lifestyle journalism fields being less stratified; the public sphere of lifestyle issues is followed and produced by a number of heterogeneous actors, and the audience mobility across fields has increased (Kristensen & From, 2015).

Aesthetics in the context of journalism

Aesthetics, as a field and tradition of philosophy, is devoted to conceptual and theoretical inquiry into aesthetic experience. The analytic aesthetics has traditionally had a strong focus on "pure arts", differentiated from "life", and the institution of arts (see Levinson, 2003), while pragmatic aesthetics have been willing to extend the conception, suggesting that all visible phenomena have aesthetic significance (Shusterman, 2000). In media, aesthetics has been mostly developed in the context of visual studies, such as the study of films, television, visual arts, journalistic photography, and photojournalism (Corner, 2005; Hausken, 2013), and in literary journalism, where the creation of an aesthetic experience lies at the fore (Hartsock, 2016). In general, departing from the German 18th-century philosopher Alexander Baumgarten's (1735, cited in Levinson, 2003, p. 7) original definition of aesthetics as "the science of how things are cognized by means of the senses", aesthetics has to do with perception, and it is thus closely connected to the visual, visible, multimodal, and perceivable dimensions of storytelling. Key questions include what kind of aesthetic properties manifest in an object or practice and how they are experienced by humans.

In the context of journalism, aesthetics can be understood in a restricted and broad sense. In the restricted sense, aesthetics deals with the way of presentation, tightly connected to genres, formats, and conventions of journalism in general. The aesthetic inquiry is predominantly interested in the mediatic and sometimes even material dimensions of the object that is studied. In print journalism, aesthetical dimensions become manifested in the publication design, which includes the permanent design of ground layout (publication size, that is, whether the publication is a broadsheet, tabloid, or another size format; the number of columns, selection of fonts, etc.), as well as the publication's formats, graphical elements, and other choices described in the stylebook (Frost, 2011). Aesthetics are also important with regard to the illustrations that are selected and presented within the limitations and possibilities of the publication design each time a new issue is produced. Alternatively, in audiovisual formats such as television programmes and online videos, the design choices deal, above all, with programme length and structuration. The design, thus, constitutes the framework where certain affordances are available for presentation. Aesthetics hold high relevance for other fields that deal with appreciation of objects, such as stylistics, poetics, and critique (in journalism, see, e.g., Jaakkola, 2015, 2018), as well as modes and politics of presentation. For example, studies inquiring into affects and emotions in lifestyle journalism, resonating with the emotional turn of such journalism (Wahl-Jorgensen & Pantti, 2021), have captured confessional and subjectivity-anchored modes in discourse, re-focussing journalism aesthetics. In a similar fashion, studies analysing the narratives of presenting non-normative bodies or bodies with disabilities (Dyer, 2003; Meeuf, 2014) conform to aesthetics of what is normalized.

In the broad sense, the area of aesthetics includes choices that deliver certain impressions and experiences, while at the same time directing the audience's experience in a way that hides and excludes some dimensions of reality. Aesthetical choices shape the message, which means the representations and discourses of reality, and the audiences' experiences about the provided content – for example, regional aesthetics as a sense of place or place-bound identity (Chignell et al., 2020). For journalism, the connection to reality has always been and continues to be a crucial component as journalism is expected to report on the world, in contrast to fictional forms of storytelling that, accordingly, have more freedom to experiment with and develop aesthetics regardless of how reality looks. Despite the realism requirement, audiences relate to, understand, interpret, and use content in different and unanticipated ways, which is especially true of lifestyle journalism that is not supposed to primarily convey fact-based information about current events but support individuals in their lifestyle work.

The two definitions of aesthetics are interconnected, and the broader definition of aesthetics is highly relevant for the ways that lifestyle journalism provides surfaces of projection for audience members to reflect upon, maintain and develop their lifestyles, or to adopt entirely new lifestyles. Lifestyle journalism is aspirational (Banjac & Hanusch, 2022; Ashe, 2023), which means that it intends to capture qualities, goals, or lifestyles that individuals desire to attain, even if they have not yet reached that level. Aspirational elements are often associated with positive values, success, or a higher standard of living. Aesthetic dimensions of journalistic storytelling essentially support the aspirational character of this type of journalism. Aesthetics comes into being in dual ways: on the one hand, journalism may support the existing aesthetic dimensions of lifestyles, and on the other, they can create new aesthetics to provide material for maintaining a certain type of life. In lifestyle coverage, audiences can discover a source of inspiration or motivation for personal improvement or achievement.

The role of aesthetics comes into being in very different ways in different genres of lifestyle journalism. To give some examples, in female and family magazine journalism, fashion, beauty, and health journalism, the aesthetics of home – such as the home decoration, garments, and accessories – and wellbeing products and services play an important role. In celebrity journalism, the aesthetics that are presented are encountered in terms of extraordinariness and ordinariness, the key question being about the accessibility of the aesthetic choices made by well-known persons. In nature and outdoor life, the properties of photos and videos that capture the essence of places and spaces, or create them visually, constitute a key dimension. In journalistic genres related to leisure time and hobbies, ranging from sailing to motorsport or from fitness to cooking, there are also expectations to create a visual sphere that engages the audience.

The field of lifestyle journalism being diverse and its conceptualizations heterogeneous, it would be impossible to give an exhaustive account for the "lifestyle journalism aesthetics" as a field. Therefore, I first focus on conceptualizing the aesthetics by presenting two conceptualizations that many subfields of the diverse and heterogeneous field of lifestyle journalism share: first, the cultural objects, services, venues, and actions that are presented as aspirational objects in journalism and second, lifestyle work that describes the ongoing activities of an individual related to their "life project", which lifestyle journalism can and is expected to support. Thereafter, I discuss with examples from some selected fields that can be regarded as central to lifestyle journalism on how these two concepts manifest and have been studied in their aesthetical aspirations.

Aspirational objects

Aspirational objects are commodities that are framed as acquirable or desirable. Similar to Pepper's (1946, 1952) concept of an aesthetic object, aspirational objects are entities selected from the world for observation, but in contrast to aesthetic objects, aspirational objects are projections for desires, dreams, hopes, and fantasies. In the same way as it is important in artistic aesthetics to identify certain objects as being *art*, in lifestyle journalism, certain objects are presented as access or entry points into a certain lifestyle. Aspirational objects do not need to be tangible; an object can be an artefact, such as a material piece of arts (sculpture) or crafts (tablecloth), a consumer product (lipstick), or a person (a film actor), but it can also be a service (massage), process (visiting amusement parks), an idea or ingredient of a larger entity (green colour), or a physical place (realistic Paris) or imaginative space (romantic Paris). Lifestyle journalism works by selecting and framing these objects in different ways. Aspirational objects also always belong to someone – either actually or potentially owned by someone. They are part of someone's lifestyle, and here, the question is often about the intended consumer.

Aspirational objects are treated journalistically in different ways. Based on the privileged access that the journalist has to these objects, journalists select, expose, describe, explain, interpret, frame, and judge aspirational objects, functioning as gatekeepers and tastemakers in the chain of cultural intermediation (Jaakkola, 2022). Visualizing plays a major role in creating aspirational objects in public. Here, different degrees of judgemental commitment and critical intervention can be observed: to begin with, journalists describe, show, and present selected aspirational objects, in which the visual appearance often draws attention and is of interest to the audiences, who may not have access to the objects themselves. Here, journalists are public pre-experiencers of the objects, and their externalized aesthetic experience helps audiences make a choice about whether the objects in question are interesting to them. While exposing objects, journalists may also interpret and make sense of them, placing them into a context where they are understandable and become interesting, motivating, empowering, inspiring, and raising pleasure around the objects. Further, similar to reviewing and criticism, as well as consumer or service journalism, lifestyle journalism is also often occupied with testing, ranking, rating, and recommending objects to discover their worth. Evaluating, criticizing, and finding alternatives are yet stronger in reviewing and criticism than in lifestyle journalism, which often stays at the stage of constructing an aspiration, leaving the ultimate choice and judgement to the consumer.

Lifestyle work

The maintenance of lifestyle implies making constant choices regarding one's everyday life, also with, through, and in journalistic media: making consumption choices, and choices of learning and being exposed to new things, departing from the habitus and dispositions of the positioning in the sociological field that the individual is located in because of these dispositions and forms of capital (Bourdieu, 1979/2010; Bolin, 2011). In opting for certain lifestyles and lifestyle issues and excluding others, consumers conduct aesthetic work – or, broader, lifestyle work – that involves their aims of expressing identity, community belonging, and taste (Jaakkola, 2022; Vlahos et al., 2022). Aesthetic questions include, for example, how one wants to look or be perceived by others, both in terms of appearance and outfits and in which material, social, and symbolic environments they want to live. Lifestyle journalism can also be a source for individuals to pursue dreams that are not fully possible in real life: Living in luxury, a tidy home, or travelling far away may not be possible for most of the audience members, yet – or because of that – they feel pleasure by following lifestyle journalism. Furthermore, lifestyle journalism with environmental or ethical consciousness, or social responsibility, can guide individuals in concrete ways to make choices in their everyday lives that are more sustainable.

The processes and activities of lifestyle work contribute to personal fulfilment, relaxation, and the pursuit of individual interests outside of work, formal education, and obligatory responsibilities, and they can be as diverse as reading, painting and drawing, cooking, yoga, hiking, birdwatching, stargazing, following motorsports, or volunteering – equally, even sitting on the couch, killing time, and disengagement count as processes with similar functions. Against this backdrop, lifestyle journalism works as a channel of translating lifestyle ideas from the symbolic repertoires offered by consumer culture to individuals' life spheres, also by attracting and persuading individuals to invest in lifestyle politics in areas they are engaged in. Even if lifestyle journalism may be a central constituent of the lifestyle work that individuals conduct, it is, however, not the only source of information, motivation, and inspiration, but individuals are today following multiple channels with relevance for lifestyle work, as well as producing public messages of their own. Content and engagement – mostly online, but with offline effects – are intermixed and used as fuel for lifestyle work. Communities on social networking sites and platforms, such as the Bookstagram, cottagecore, or dark academy communities, to name but a few, develop special aesthetics of their own that intend to satisfy aspirational needs. The aesthetics of online communities and related platforms increasingly influence the discussion of those matters in journalism – possibly, for example, by exposing more ordinary individuals who initially become popular in the amateur spheres of content production – but the aesthetics of lifestyle journalism itself do not necessarily follow the aesthetical norms and conventions of their objects of coverage, instead being aligned with those of journalism.

Aesthetic genre traits from previous studies

The aesthetics dimensions of lifestyle journalism have been more often studied in printed publications and their online editions – that is, in newspapers (Turner & Orange, 2012) and magazines (Holmes, 2013) – than in broadcasting, in which the aspect of journalism has been less studied in lifestyle issues (see, e.g., Palmer, 2008). Traditionally, the landscape of magazines displays a gendered division, which indicates that the women's magazines (Duffy, 2013) and men's magazines (Waling et al., 2018) also develop different aesthetics. In television, lifestyle issues are often located in the category of factual programming, and lifestyle journalism is distinguished from lifestyle entertainment. This emphasis in scholarship is partly because the scholarly work on lifestyle journalism has been carried out in relation to arts and cultural journalism, defining lifestyle journalism as a specialized form of journalism, vis-á-vis cultural journalism, thus influenced by the study of cultural journalism that has been strongly focused on the culture sections of print newspapers (Jaakkola, 2015). In this line of thought, lifestyle journalism has been seen through the detachment from arts journalism, resulting in discussions on lifestyle journalism from perspectives of blurring boundaries (Kristensen & From, 2013), widening the field (Hanusch, 2013), and moving towards the more popular (Fürsich, 2012). Accordingly, the shift from arts-related aesthetics towards an everyday-based aesthetics has been the key scholarly question: *in difference from* arts journalism, including arts criticism, that is typically restricted by (the institutional) boundaries of arts, object-related and evaluation-based lifestyle journalism has been seen as more process- and audience-oriented. Another distinction is made between news features (for example, news magazines that are more connected to the genre and documentation form of news and produced about news occurrences with an intention to interpret and contextualize them) and identifying new trends for cultural consumers and focusing on the aspirational framing, which lies at the heart of lifestyle journalism. Many patterns of presentation are, however, shared between these genres. Lifestyle and cultural journalism both draw partly from the staged, product- and event-centred modus operandi of pseudo-events and are dependent on promotional material. The news- and occurrence-oriented ways of feature reporting – as evident in the seminal Snowfall reportage (Dowling & Vogan, 2015) – benefit lifestyle journalism aesthetics in bringing lifestyle issues into life on screen.

Historically, many magazine genres that are nowadays considered to represent the lifestyle genre underlie the fundamental need to inform and educate citizens – for example, family magazines were supposed to assist women in improving family life and becoming engaged in the literary culture of their time (Phegley, 2016) – but along with the technological development, the aesthetic dimensions have become prevalent. The study of the aesthetics of lifestyle journalism has rather organically revolved around subfields of lifestyle journalism where aesthetic properties are the most prevalent, such as forms that are visually oriented or entertaining in their character or the principles of organizing a text and the experiences they produce are developed. Within the first category, aesthetics has been a concern in arts- and fiction-oriented journalism, such as literary journalism (Hartsock, 2016) or documentary journalism (Cramerotti, 2009), where the aesthetics of experience, by stressing the narrative and richness of details and attention to everyday life, typically constitutes the signature characteristics of the genre. Some aesthetic aspects have been covered in celebrity, beauty, wellbeing, and fashion journalism, in which outfits and appearance occupy a central place (Conboy, 2014); consumer and service journalism, where the testing of products and services plays a central role (Eide, 2017); and service material that is not journalistic per se, such as newspaper comics (Glascock & Preston-Schreck, 2004).

Audiovisual and cross-media aesthetics have been mostly studied in news features, reality television, and journalistic documentary, subordinated to factual programming (Hill, 2007; Corner, 2005). Within the latter category, the internet has created new possibilities for expression through digital longform stories, understood as complex journalistic presentations rich in text and multimedia elements (Planer & Godulla, 2021) and aesthetic hybridization. It has been argued that online video form owes more to the aesthetics of cinema than journalism (Fasolo, 2015; Canella, 2023). Media and genre convergence, in which lifestyle journalism acquires hybridized forms and becomes increasingly blended with non-journalistic areas, has been observed to produce new aesthetic opportunities in so-called "i-docs", interactive documentaries located at the intersection of journalism, film, and digital games (Dowling, 2022). In the same fashion, it has been observed that journalistic documentary films are being simultaneously consumed as both journalistic and film products on online subscription services platforms such as Netflix (Camarero, 2021; Goldson, 2015). Factual entertainment, partly rooted in tabloid lifestyle journalism, also mixes aesthetic elements of journalism and lifestyle television or YouTube culture (Hill, 2007; Roscoe, 2001). In some cases, the aesthetic features of storytelling methods and the discourse of lifestyle journalism are harnessed as a means of masqueradization of aesthetics for fictional entertainment or propaganda purposes (Roscoe, 2001; Farkas & Neumayer, 2020).

Aesthetic aspects of lifestyle journalism are targeting groups that want to identify with, construct, and maintain certain identities. Lifestyle journalism has been observed to operate in proximity of its audiences and, in this way, promote identity-shaping consumption, for example, among females (Ytre-Arne, 2011); teenagers, particularly girls (Carter, 2005); and males (Huybers-Withers & Livingston, 2010). Consumption-oriented genres give guidance in using products and services to satisfy needs and wants; for example, the style-oriented geek and gaming magazines (Kirkpatrick, 2017) and fashion journalism (Miller & McNeil, 2018) deliver suggestions and ideas regarding what to draw attention to and purchase at a given moment, in conjunction with judging and predicting which content, trends, and persons are worth noticing; parenting and family journalism – actually written for mothers – provide advice on home decoration and acquisitions (e.g., Sunderland, 2006) and gardening (Taylor, 2002); food journalism (Jones & Taylor, 2013) inspires home cooking and uses of restaurant services; and travel journalism (Hanusch & Fürsich, 2014) presents tourist destinations worth visiting. Suggestions are made by editorial curation of artefacts and services, often adapted to the socioeconomic conditions of the target audience, or more indirectly through well-known or elite people and their choices. Journalism also tells audiences what kind of language to use, in terms of a socio- or fanlect, how to behave, and what kind of attitudes to cherish.

Recently, scholarly attention has been drawn to the tightening relationship between lifestyle journalism and social media, which has become an established channel to support lifestyles (Cheng & Chew, 2022; Perreault & Stanfield, 2019; Perreault & Hanusch, 2022; Cheng & Tandoc, 2022; Maares & Hanusch, 2020; Vodanovic, 2019). It has been observed that lifestyle journalists are maintaining a distance from the diverse groups of communicators in social media addressing lifestyle issues, as part of safeguarding their professional boundaries. However, it is likely that the aesthetics of lifestyle communication beyond journalistic contexts will continue to influence journalism. Evidence of that may be the increase in subjective accounts in journalism (see, e.g., Steensen, 2016), which is a prevalent mode of storytelling among both lifestyle influencers (Khamis et al., 2017) and commercial lifestyle sites (Frig & Jaakkola, 2023) where personalization of issues, self-branding, and celebrification as well as parasociality based on self-disclosure, intimacy, and confessionality are essential communication strategies of aspirational labour and cultural co-consumption (Duffy, 2017; Khamis et al., 2017; Jaakkola, 2022).

Critical issues and topics

A central question, related more generally to the politics of representation and based on processes of journalistic gatekeeping and framing, is how lifestyle is presented and what is *not* presented in the subgenres of lifestyle journalism. Formats convey a certain politics of (re)presentation by exposing selected cultural objects and venues, while strategically hiding some of them, which is an important matter, especially in highly formalized productions and formats. Visuals, along with other elements in coverage, also convey gendered thinking and narrow portrayals of gender roles (Huybers-Withers & Livingston, 2010). The crucial questions include whose aesthetics are presented, that is, whose gaze is applied, whose ordinariness is constructed, or how the intended spectator is positioned.

As for (re)presentation, boundaries between fact and fiction are at stake when playing with aesthetic possibilities that may possibly blur the distinction between constructed media text and reality. This question has mainly manifested in a tension between journalistic representation of authenticity and staging of reality. In travel journalism, many tourist destinations per se are already constructed for tourism, stripped of local populations, and the journalistic coverage, often pursuing authenticity to tell about the culture and people of a country, is a crafted and mediated picture of "reality" (Ashe, 2023). As observed in nature or a historical audiovisual documentary, the certain "aesthetic of reality" that is constructed to give audiences access to the "truth" may, as such, be a manipulation of reality; while the classical cinematic procedures of montage, editing, manipulation of temporality, masking, and so on, are all part of the language of audiovisual storytelling, the use of dramaturgical elements in camera, sound, and edit design can lead to the manipulation of the temporality and undermine epistemological foundations of presentation (Capdevila, 2015).

When creating atmospheres through aesthetic means, wellbeing journalism – with genres that align with it, such as coverage on physical and mental health, self-care, and home and family life – has been alleged to prefer the pursuit of balance and happiness as overshadowing any other aspects of life (see also Chapters 14 and 22). Moeran (2010) remarks that women's fashion magazines adopt a special "technology of enchantment" that invests beauty and fashion products with magical qualities and ritualistic power, which is further supported by advertisements. The visibility and invisibility of certain kinds of bodies has been a central issue in lifestyle coverage research, addressing the invisibility of obese, disabled, and deviant bodies (Reynolds & LoRusso, 2016; Hardin et al., 2006), objectification, sexualization, youthification or adultification of bodies (Gerding Speno & Aubrey, 2018), and commodification and fetishization of certain products (Bhalla & Moscowitz, 2020). Accordingly, lifestyle journalism forms have been heavily criticized for hiding critical aspects behind the aspirationality and, instead, reifying values of commodity, consumerism, and divisive exclusionary identity. Instead of providing audiences with tools for empowerment and transformative learning, they may give false promises and hopes, as well as "provoke self-absorbed, distractive anxiety" (Farkas, 2010, p. 130) or a commodified view of "constructed certitude" of identities (Jackson et al., 1999). Lifestyle journalism has been stated to blur class-consciousness; contribute to content confusion between journalism and commerciality by establishing ties to producers, sellers, marketers, and lobbyists through advertorials, branded journalism, product placement, and other partnerships in production; promote unreflexive consumption or overconsumption instead of raising critical thoughts of sustainability; and collapse into hypocritical constellations of greenwashing and green-wishing (Frig & Jaakkola, 2023; Bhalla et al., 2022; Farkas, 2010).

Current contributions and research

Studies on lifestyle journalism have greatly benefited from the recent elaboration of critical perspectives on journalism and media coverage related to gender, geocentrism, race, language, religion, and so on, asking for more inclusion, diversity, and alternatives. The calls for decolonizing and postcolonial, de-westernizing and non-Western, transnational, queer, racial, and minority perspectives (see, e.g., Mohammed, 2022; Wasserman & De Beer, 2009) have highlighted the need to question and deconstruct the biased façade that is constructed by focusing on aspirations. Alternative lifestyle magazines have existed for a long time, as local newsletters or fanzines, as part of different movements, as well as a vehicle for them (Metcalf & Vanclay, 1984), but the current contributions to transforming presentations of lifestyle are most often attempts to mainstream more marginal ideas within the institutional structures. Increased gender, linguistic, and ethnic diversity in lifestyle journalism can contribute to the visibility of groups of people who are marginalized, vulnerable, and less empowered in society. Lifestyle journalism can be said to become more multi-voiced in terms of whose aesthetics is described, if celebrity and expert lifestyle and consumption choices are increasingly contrasted and complemented with ordinary, non-elite, and minoritized people's choices.

Many attempts to change have dealt with making conscious choices in illustration and article design when it comes to individual human properties that are typically visible, such as gender, age, and skin colour, or audible, such as language. Scholars have highlighted the need for traditionally male-dominated genres such as popular culture journalism, sports journalism, as well as tech, innovation, and gaming journalism – which suffer from a gender-bias and even ethnicity bias, even in their production structures – to become enriched by a wider framing of masculinity and female perspectives, as well as visual and textual practices avoiding structuralized sexism, misogyny, and homophobia (Kirkpatrick, 2017; Hardin et al., 2006). Exposure to non-normative bodies and visual appearances has been considered a measure to combat too-restricted gender and body normativity as well as ableism (Meeuf, 2014; Saucier & Caron, 2008). Ethnic and cultural diversity has been advanced by developing the visibility of minorities and their experiences (Lewis, 2019). The objectification of bodies and exclusion of certain bodies in journalistic coverage have been broadened by efforts drawing insights from the societal movements of LGBTQ+, body positivism, anti-ageism, and so on. Sustainability thinking has been advanced by addressing consumption choices through green lifestyle journalism and consumerism (Craig, 2016; Smith, 2010). In all these areas, the influence of the paradigms of constructive and positive journalism (From & Kristensen, 2018) continues to assist journalists in finding solutions that would reflect a wider variety of values, also at the aesthetic level of presentation.

Future directions

The future directions regarding the aesthetic dimensions of lifestyle journalism are dependent on how journalism is going to develop in the next decades, adopting new technologies that carry along new aesthetic affordances. The technological development of journalism is likely to extend the study of aesthetics beyond texts, new modes and methods of creation, and the traditional institutions. As the methodology of studying visual, audiovisual, and multimodal materials is becoming more advanced, more aesthetic dimensions can be captured, not only when studying coverage but also audience reception and behaviour. The recent theoretical and conceptual development of lifestyle journalism scholarship indicates that lifestyle journalism will and must be addressed in increasingly nuanced ways when it comes to the constitutive elements of civic and cultural citizenship, consumership, and critical approaches to these. Developing self-critical approaches to addressing aspirational objects in a way that supports informed ways of lifestyle work needs to be considered a necessary goal for future research which will be conducted in different contexts, including beyond the dominating Anglo-American frame. As journalists are more engaged in shaping the social reality in the postmodern or liquid journalism (Jaakkola et al., 2015), more transparency is needed. This may mean a lead into the increased personification of journalism as the subjective accounts of journalists need to be explained.

Journalism is becoming less detached from the form of a traditional written text, extending to processes of engagement such as newsletters, onstage narratives and live publishing, as well as educational events (Vodanovic, 2022; Adams, 2021; Larson, 2015). These re-configurations provide opportunities for lifestyle journalism to support individuals' lifestyle work in the milieus in which they are living. As journalistic production is becoming increasingly decentralized and carried out in connection with more entrepreneurial, small-scale, and non-institutionalized environments (Deuze & Witschge, 2020), lifestyle journalism may continue to dilute its boundaries and approach co-creation in multistakeholder networks involving companies and product sellers, as well as brand and fan communities, which are relevant for lifestyle journalism genres.

The rise of artificial intelligence (AI) raises questions about the new aesthetic possibilities of the posthuman condition (Lewis et al., 2019), in which interactions between humans and intelligent agents (that is, non-human actors that can be robots, bots, and machine-learning technologies) become common and where the processes of storytelling can be more effective, validated, and diverse, but also reinforce stereotypical patterns and aesthetic biases, as computer systems are trained and learn from existing materials (Broussard et al., 2019). The automatic generation of material by AI-powered technologies results in computational or artificial aesthetics where new realities can be created through synthetic media (Manovich & Arielli, 2023). The first journalistic experiments with AI have testified how people who do not speak a language are attributed a voice in a foreign language or a voice is attributed to a late person. Further, milieus and experiences, either such that never existed or do no longer exist, can be reconstructed. Augmented realities and human–computer interaction add the possibility of immersive journalism to gain first-person experiences of the aspirational objects and enhancing the aesthetic experience with somaesthetic experiences (Greber et al., 2023). Moreover, because of developing technologies, inclusion can potentially be approached as a question of accessibility to online media and media content, instead of being restricted to beauty and visual pleasure.

Finally, the technological, economic, and social evolvements can potentially entail enhanced possibilities and increased pressures towards commercialism. When commercial dynamics are integrated into journalism at its aesthetic surface in increasingly advanced ways, critical approaches are needed to maintain the integrity and autonomy of journalism. Critical approaches, as noted by Nothstine and colleagues (2002), are investments in consuming audiences to help them develop alternatives in pursuing their own interests and self-understanding. Metacriticism and metareflection in lifestyle journalism can come into being as counterintuitive, alternative aesthetics by replacing the normalized, routinized, or ordinarized aspirational objects with deviating ones and developing parallel perspectives to approach choices of consumption. By critically inspecting lifestyle issues, lifestyle journalists can contest aspirationality and find individual-centred paths to it, which will, paradoxically, not undermine the very essence of lifestyle journalism but make it stronger, by defending its contours against non-journalistic forms of lifestyle communication.

Further readings

Dowling, D. O. (2017). Toward a new aesthetic of digital literary journalism: Charting the fierce evolution of the "supreme nonfiction". *Literary Journalism Studies*, 9(1), 100–116.

Jacobs, J., & Peacock, S. (Eds.) (2013). *Television aesthetics and style*. Bloomsbury.

Lamberg, J. J. J. (2016). *Clothing the paper: On the state of newspaper design, redesigns, and art directors' perspectives in contemporary quality and popular newspapers.* Doctoral thesis. University of Reading.

Ritzer, I. (Ed.) (2022). *Media and genre: Dialogues in aesthetics and cultural analysis.* Palgrave Macmillan.

Taylor, P. C. (2016). *Black is beautiful: A philosophy of black aesthetics.* Wiley Blackwell.

References

Adams, C. (2021). News on stage: Towards re-configuring journalism through theatre to a public sphere. *Journalism Practice*, 15(8), 1163–1180. https://doi.org/10.1080/17512786.2020.1771754

Ashe, I. (2023, August 9). Time to go: Aspirational framing and place-making in domestic travel journalism. *Journalism Practice.* Advance online publication. https://doi.org/10.1080/17512786.2023.2244931

Banjac, S., & Hanusch, F. (2022). Aspirational lifestyle journalism: The impact of social class on producers' and audiences' views in the context of socio-economic inequality. *Journalism*, 23(8), 1607–1625. https://doi.org/10.1177/1464884920956823

Bhalla, N., & Moscowitz, D. (2020). Yoga and female objectification: Commodity and exclusionary identity in U.S. women's magazines. *Journal of Communication Inquiry*, 44(1), 90–108. https://doi.org/10.1177/0196859919830357

Bhalla, N., O'Boyle, J., & Moscowitz, L. (2022, September 15). Selling yoga 'off the mat': A 10-year analysis of lifestyle advertorials in yoga journal magazine. *Journal of Communication Inquiry.* Advance online publication. https://doi.org/10.1177/01968599221118646

Bolin, G. (2011). *Value and the media: Cultural production and consumption in digital markets.* Ashgate.

Bourdieu, P. (2010). *Distinction: A social critique of the judgement of taste.* Routledge. (Original work published 1979)

Broussard, M., Diakopoulos, N., Guzman, A. L., Abebe, R., Dupagne, M., & Chuan, C.-H. (2019). Artificial intelligence and journalism. *Journalism & Mass Communication Quarterly*, 96(3), 673–695. https://doi.org/10.1177/1077699019859901

Camarero, E. (2021). A media format on the rise: The journalistic investigation documentary on Netflix and Prime Video. *Media Education (Mediaobrazovanie)*, 17(3), 415–425.

Canella, G. (2023, October 24). Cinematic journalism: The political economy and "emotional truth" of documentary film. *Studies in Documentary Film.* Advance online publication. https://doi.org/10.1080/17503280.2023.2270988

Capdevila, P. (2015). The objectifying documentary: Realism, aesthetics and temporality. *Communication & Society*, 28(4), 67–85. https://doi.org/10.15581/003.28.4.67-85

Carter, F. (2005). It's a girl thing: Teenage magazines, lifestyle and consumer culture. In D. Bell & J. Hollows (Eds.), *Ordinary lifestyles: Popular media, consumption and taste* (pp. 173–186). Open University Press.

Cheng, L., & Chew, M. (2022, December 2). Functional interlopers: Lifestyle journalists' discursive construction of boundaries against digital lifestyle influencers. *Journalism.* Advance online publication. https://doi.org/10.1177/14648849221143875

Cheng, L., & Tandoc, E. C. (2022). From magazines to blogs: The shifting boundaries of fashion journalism. *Journalism*, 23(6), 1213–1232. https://doi.org/10.1177/1464884920988183

Chignell, H., Franklin, I., & Skooh, K. (Eds.) (2020). *Regional aesthetics: Mapping UK media cultures.* Palgrave Macmillan.

Conboy, M. (2014). Celebrity journalism – An oxymoron? Forms and functions of a genre. *Journalism*, 15(2), 171–185. https://doi.org/10.1177/1464884913488722

Corner, J. (2005). Television, documentary and the category of the aesthetic. In A. Rosenthal, & J. Corner (Eds.), *New challenges for documentary* (2nd ed., pp. 48–58). Manchester University Press.

Craig, G. (2016). Political participation and pleasure in green lifestyle journalism. *Environmental Communication*, 10(1), 122–141. https://doi.org/10.1080/17524032.2014.991412

Cramerotti, A. (2009). *Aesthetic journalism: How to inform without informing.* Intellect.

Deuze, M., & Witschge, T. (2020). *Beyond journalism*. Polity Press.
Dowling, D. O. (2022). Interactive documentary and the reinvention of digital journalism, 2015–2020. *Convergence, 28*(3), 905–924. https://doi.org/10.1177/13548565211059426
Dowling, D., & Vogan, T. (2015). Can we "snowfall" this? *Digital Journalism, 3*(2), 209–224. https://doi.org/10.1080/21670811.2014.930250
Duffy, B. E. (2013). *Remake, remodel: Women's magazines in the digital age*. University of Illinois Press.
Duffy, B. E. (2017). *(Not) getting paid to do what you love: Gender, social media, and aspirational work*. Yale University Press.
Dyer, R. (2003). *Heavenly bodies: Film stars and society*. Routledge. https://doi.org/10.4324/9780203605516 (Original work published 1986)
Eide, M. (2017). The culture of service journalism. In N. N. Kristensen, & K. Riegert (Eds.), *Cultural journalism in the Nordic Countries* (pp. 195–204). Nordicom, University of Gothenburg. https://urn.kb.se/resolve?urn=urn:nbn:se:norden:org:diva-5073
Farkas, C.-A. (2010). "Tons of useful stuff": Defining wellness in popular magazines. *Studies in Popular Culture, 33*(1), 113–132. https://www.jstor.org/stable/23416322
Farkas, J., & Neumayer, C. (2020). Mimicking news: How the credibility of an established tabloid is used when disseminating racism. *Nordicom Review, 41*(1), 1–17. https://doi.org/10.2478/nor-2020-0001
Fasolo, D. (2015). The case for cinematic aesthetics in online video journalism: The BBC news authored story. *Культура/Culture, 5*(11), 43–53. https://journals.cultcenter.net/index.php/culture/article/view/163
Fine, G. A. (1992). The culture of production: Aesthetic choices and constraints in culinary work. *American Journal of Sociology, 97*(5), 1268–1294. https://www.jstor.org/stable/2781416
Frig, M.-M., & Jaakkola, M. (2023, April 17). Between conspicuous and conscious consumption: The sustainability paradox in the intermediary promotional work of an online lifestyle site. *Journal of Consumer Culture*. Advance online publication. https://doi.org/10.1177/14695405231170684
From, U. (2018). Lifestyle journalism. *Oxford Encyclopedia of Communication*. https://doi.org/10.1093/acrefore/9780190228613.013.835
From, U., & Kristensen, N. N. (2018). Rethinking constructive journalism by means of service journalism. *Journalism Practice, 12*(6), 714–729. https://doi.org/10.1080/17512786.2018.1470475
Frost, C. (2011). *Designing for newspapers and magazines*. Routledge. https://doi.org/10.4324/9780203181089
Fürsich, E. (2012). Lifestyle journalism as popular journalism: Strategies for evaluating its public role. *Journalism Practice, 6*(1), 12–25. https://doi.org/10.1080/17512786.2011.622894
Gans, H. (1999). *Popular culture and high culture: An analysis and evaluation of taste* (Rev. ed.). Basic. (Original work published 1974)
Gerding Speno, A., & Aubrey, J. S. (2018). Sexualization, youthification, and adultification: A content analysis of images of girls and women in popular magazines. *Journalism & Mass Communication Quarterly, 95*(3), 625–646. https://doi.org/10.1177/1077699017728918
Glascock, J., & Preston-Schreck, C. (2004). Gender and racial stereotypes in daily newspaper comics: A time-honored tradition? *Sex Roles, 51*, 423–431. https://doi.org/10.1023/B:SERS.0000049231.67432.a9
Goldson, A. (2015). Journalism plus? The resurgence of creative documentary. *Pacific Journalism Review, 21*(2), 86–98.
Greber, H., Aaldering, L., & Lecheler, S. (2023, February 15). The worthwhileness of immersive journalism: Taking on an audience perspective. *Journalism Practice*. Advance online publication. https://doi.org/10.1080/17512786.2023.2177711
Gronow, J., & Warde, A. (Eds.) (2001). *Ordinary consumption*. Routledge. https://doi.org/10.4324/9780203381502
Hardin, M., Lynn, S., & Walsdorf, K. (2006). Depicting the sporting body: The intersection of gender, race and disability in women's sport/fitness magazines. *Journal of Magazine Media, 8*(1), 1–17. https://doi.org/10.1353/jmm.2006.0006
Hartsock, J. C. (2016). *Literary journalism and the aesthetics of experience*. University of Massachusetts Press.

Hanusch, F. (2013a). Broadening the focus: The case for lifestyle journalism as a field of scholarly inquiry. In F. Hanusch (Ed.), *Lifestyle journalism* (pp. 1–10). Routledge. https://doi.org/10.4324/9781315829470

Hanusch, F. (Ed.) (2013b). *Lifestyle journalism*. Routledge. https://doi.org/10.4324/9781315829470

Hanusch, F., & Fürsich, E. (Eds.) (2014). *Travel journalism: Exploring production, impact and culture*. Springer. https://doi.org/10.1057/9781137325983

Hausken, L. (2013). *Thinking media aesthetics: Media studies, film studies and the arts*. PL Academic Research.

Hill, A. (2007). *Restyling factual TV: Audiences and news, documentary and reality genres*. Routledge. https://doi.org/10.4324/9780203099735

Holmes, T. (Ed.) (2013). *Mapping the magazine: Comparative studies in magazine journalism*. Routledge.

Huybers-Withers, S. M., & Livingston, L. A. (2010). Mountain biking is for men: Consumption practices and identity portrayed by a niche magazine. *Sport in Society*, *13*(7–8), 1204–1222. https://doi.org/10.1080/17430431003780195

Jaakkola, M. (2015). *The contested autonomy of arts and journalism: Change and continuity of the dual professionalism of cultural journalism*. Tampere University Press.

Jaakkola, M. (2018). Journalistic style and writing. In H. Örnebring (Ed.), *Oxford encyclopedia of journalism studies*. https://doi.org/10.1093/acrefore/9780190694166.001.0001

Jaakkola, M. (2022). *Reviewing culture online: Post-institutional cultural critique across platforms*. Palgrave Macmillan. https://doi.org/10.1007/978-3-030-84848-4

Jaakkola, M., Hellman, H., Koljonen, K., & Väliverronen, J. (2015). Liquid modern journalism with a difference: The changing professional ethos of cultural journalism. *Journalism Practice*, *9*(6), 811–828. https://doi.org/10.1080/17512786.2015.1051361

Jackson, P., Brooks, K., & Stevenson, N. (1999). Making sense of men's lifestyle magazines. *Environment and Planning D: Society and Space*, *17*(3), 353–368. https://doi.org/10.1068/d170353

Jones, S., & Taylor, B. (2013). Food journalism. In B. Turner & R. Orange (Eds.), *Specialist journalism* (pp. 96–106). Routledge.

Khamis, S., Ang, L., & Welling, R. (2017). Self-branding, "micro-celebrity" and the rise of social media influencers. *Celebrity Studies*, *8*(2), 191–208. https://doi.org/10.1080/19392397.2016.1218292

Kirkpatrick, G. (2017). How gaming became sexist: A study of UK gaming magazines 1981–1995. *Media, Culture & Society*, *39*(4), 453–468. https://doi.org/10.1177/0163443716646177

Kristensen, N. N., & From, U. (2013). Lifestyle journalism: Blurring boundaries. In F. Hanusch (Ed.), *Lifestyle journalism* (pp. 25–40). Routledge. https://doi.org/10.4324/9781315829470

Kristensen, N. N., & From, U. (2015). From ivory tower to cross-media personas: The heterogeneous cultural critic in the media. *Journalism Practice*, *9*(6), 853–871. https://doi.org/10.1080/17512786.2015.1051370

Larson, C. (2015). Live publishing: The onstage redeployment of journalistic authority. *Media, Culture & Society*, *37*(3), 440–459. https://doi.org/10.1177/0163443714567016

Levinson, J. (Ed.) (2003). *The Oxford handbook of aesthetics*. Oxford University Press.

Lewis, S. C., Guzman, A. L., & Schmidt, T. R. (2019). Automation, journalism, and human–machine communication: Rethinking roles and relationships of humans and machines in news. *Digital Journalism*, *7*(4), 409–427. https://doi.org/10.1080/21670811.2019.1577147

Lewis, S. K. (2019). Pushing the limits in black girl-centred research: Exploring the methodological possibilities of *Melt* Magazine. In A. S. Halliday (Ed.), *The black girlhood studies collection* (pp. 157–180). Women's Press.

Maares, P., & Hanusch, F. (2020). Exploring the boundaries of journalism: Instagram micro-bloggers in the twilight zone of lifestyle journalism. *Journalism*, *21*(2), 262–278. https://doi.org/10.1177/1464884918801400

Manovich, L., & Arielli, E. (2023). *Artificial aesthetics: A critical guide to AI, media and design*. Manovich. https://manovich.net/index.php/projects/artificial-aesthetics

Meeuf, R. (2014). The nonnormative celebrity body and the meritocracy of the star system: Constructing Peter Dinklage in entertainment journalism. *Journal of Communication Inquiry*, *38*(3), 204–222. https://doi.org/10.1177/0196859914532947

Metcalf, B., & Vanclay, F. (1984). Alternative lifestyle magazines. *Media International Australia*, *33*(1), 45–53. https://doi.org/10.1177/1329878X8403300105

Miller, S., & McNeil, P. (2018). *Fashion journalism: History, theory, and practice*. Bloomsbury Publishing.
Moeran, B. (2010). The portrayal of beauty in women's fashion magazines. *Fashion Theory*, 14(4), 491–510. https://doi.org/10.2752/175174110X12792058833933
Mohammed, W. F. (2022). Dismantling the Western canon in media studies. *Communication Theory*, 32(2), 273–280. https://doi.org/10.1093/ct/qtac001
Nothstine, W. L., Blair, C., & Copeland, G. A. (2002). *Critical questions: Invention, creativity, and the criticism of discourse and media*. McGraw-Hill Education.
O'Sullivan, T., Hartley, J., Saunders, D., Montgomery, M., & Fiske, J. (1994). *Key concepts in communication and cultural studies* (2nd ed.). Routledge.
Palmer, G. (Ed.) (2008). *Exposing lifestyle television: The big reveal*. Routledge. https://doi.org/10.4324/9781315581743
Perreault, G., & Hanusch, F. (2022). Field insurgency in lifestyle journalism: How lifestyle journalists marginalize Instagram influencers and protect their autonomy. *New Media & Society*, published online on June 23, 2023. https://doi.org/10.1177/14614448221104233
Perreault, G., & Stanfield, K. (2019). Mobile journalism as lifestyle journalism? Field theory in the integration of mobile in the newsroom and mobile journalist role conception. *Journalism Practice*, 13(3), 331–348. https://doi.org/10.1080/17512786.2018.1424021
Peterson, R. A., & Anand, N. (2004). The production of culture perspective. *Annual Review of Sociology*, 30(1), 311–334. https://doi.org/10.1146/annurev.soc.30.012703.110557
Peterson, R. A., & Kern, R. M. (1996). Changing highbrow taste: From snob to omnivore. *American Sociological Review*, 61(1), 900–909. https://doi.org/10.2307/2096460
Pepper, S. C. (1946). *The basis of criticism in the arts*. Harvard University Press.
Pepper, S. C. (1952). Further consideration of the aesthetic work of art. *Journal of Philosophy*, XLIX(8), 274–279. https://doi.org/10.2307/2020802
Phegley, J. (2016). Family magazines. In A. King, A. Easley, & J. Morton (Eds.), *The Routledge handbook to nineteenth-century British periodicals and newspapers* (pp. 276–292). Routledge. https://doi.org/10.4324/9781315613345
Planer, R., & Godulla, A. (2021). Longform journalism in the USA and Germany: Patterns in award-winning digital storytelling productions. *Journalism Practice*, 15(4), 566–582. https://doi.org/10.1080/17512786.2020.1742771
Reynolds, C., & LoRusso, S. (2016). The women's magazine diet: Frames and sources in nutrition and fitness articles. *Journal of Magazine Media*, 17(1), 1–23. https://doi.org/10.1353/jmm.2016.0001
Roscoe, J. (2001). Real entertainment: New factual hybrid television. *Media International Australia*, 100(1), 9–20. https://doi.org/10.1177/1329878X0110000104
Saucier, J. A., & Caron, S. L. (2008). An investigation of content and media images in gay men's magazines. *Journal of Homosexuality*, 55(3), 504–523. https://doi.org/10.1080/00918360802345297
Shusterman, R. (2000). *Pragmatist aesthetics: Living beauty, rethinking art* (2nd ed.). Rowman & Littlefield.
Smith, A. N. (2010). The ecofetish: Green consumerism in women's magazines. *Women's Studies Quarterly*, 38(3–4), 66–83.
Steensen, S. (2016). The intimization of journalism. In T. Witschge, C. W. Anderson, D. Domingo, & A. Hermida (Eds.), *The Sage handbook of digital journalism* (pp. 113–127). Sage.
Sunderland, J. (2006). "Parenting" or "mothering"? The case of modern childcare magazines. *Discourse & Society*, 17(4), 503–528. https://doi.org/10.1177/0957926506063126
Taylor, L. (2002). From ways of life to lifestyle: The 'ordinari-ization' of British gardening lifestyle television. *European Journal of Communication*, 17(4), 479–493. https://doi.org/10.1177/02673231020170040501
Turner, B., & Orange, R. (Eds.) (2012). *Specialist journalism*. Routledge. https://doi.org/10.4324/9780203146644
Vlahos, A., Hartman, A. E., & Ozanne, J. L. (2022). Aesthetic work as cultural competence: Chasing beauty in the coproduction of aesthetic services. *Journal of Service Research*, 25(1), 126–142. https://doi.org/10.1177/10946705211047983
Vodanovic, L. (Ed.) (2019). *Lifestyle journalism: Social media, consumption and experience*. Routledge. https://doi.org/10.4324/9781351123389

Vodanovic, L. (2022). Aesthetic experience, news content, and critique in live journalism events. *Journalism Practice*, *16*(1), 161–177. https://doi.org/10.1080/17512786.2020.1796763

Wahl-Jorgensen, K., & Pantti, M. (2021). Introduction: The emotional turn in journalism. *Journalism*, *22*(5), 1147–1154. https://doi.org/10.1177/1464884920985704

Waling, A., Duncan, D., Angelides, S., & Dowsett, G. W. (2018). Men and masculinity in men's magazines: A review. *Sociology Compass*, *12*(7), e12593. https://doi.org/10.1111/soc4.12593

Wasserman, H., & De Beer, A. (2009). Towards de-westernizing journalism studies. In K. Wahl-Jorgensen, & T. Hanitzsch (Eds.), *The handbook of journalism studies* (pp. 428–438). Routledge. https://doi.org/10.4324/9781315167497

Wright, D. (2016). Cultural consumption and cultural omnivorousness. In D. Inglis, & A.-M. Almila (Eds.), *The Sage handbook of cultural sociology* (pp. 567–577). Sage. https://doi.org/10.4135/9781473957886

Ytre-Arne, B. (2011). Women's magazines and their readers: The relationship between textual features and practices of reading. *European Journal of Cultural Studies*, *14*(2) 213–228. https://doi.org/10.1177/1367549410389928

10

A VOICE OF REASON

Authenticity and journalistic authority in lifestyle journalism

Joy Jenkins

Introduction

In November 2023, the Merriam-Webster dictionary announced its word of the year: *authentic*. An article explaining the decision proclaimed that "authentic" is something "we're thinking about, writing about, aspiring to, and judging more than ever" (Merriam-Webster, 2023, para. 1). Merriam-Webster attributed the interest to concerns around artificial intelligence, celebrity culture's emphasis on an "authentic voice" or "authentic self," social media seeking to offer "real" experiences, and shifting notions of identity. Although synonyms for "authenticity" abound – real, pure, actual, genuine, and original – and it is seen as a universally desirable quality, even the dictionary has trouble defining it.

The surge of interest in "authenticity" has largely been associated with the rise of digital culture. In particular, content creators and influencers have become their own economy as advertisers have shifted their focus to amateur marketers to connect with young consumers who largely learn about brands on social media (Jones, 2023). An array of news articles has examined the fascination with authenticity online. A *Forbes* article instructing readers how to create an "authentic social media presence" (Licano, 2019) emphasized being open and honest, avoiding "fake or photoshopped images" and posting "real updates that reflect your genuine personality and the brand." Another *Forbes* article suggested that content that is "raw, unfiltered, and even amateurish" can go viral as long as it is genuine and heartfelt, with raw footage providing a "distinctive authenticity" that can instill confidence and trust from viewers (Varricchio, 2023).

Although intertwined with digital culture, authenticity has been an important concept in older forms of media as well. This chapter explores the role of authenticity in lifestyle journalism. Lifestyle journalism has been an important facet of journalism for centuries. From the rise of women's magazines in the 19th century instructing readers on how to cook, clean, buy goods, and care for their children and homes to the popularity of newspaper gossip columns and tabloids in the 20th century to the 21st century emergence of digital-native outlets and blogs focused on topics ranging from food to travel to clothing to relationships, the public has often turned to news outlets to learn how to navigate the world around them. As Fürsich (2012) described, those who produce lifestyle journalism on topics such as food, music, and the arts not only aim to inform audiences about events or products but also offer criticism and evaluation. Indeed, assessments of journalistic roles have broadened from political roles to the realm of everyday life, including *marketer, service provider, friend, connector, mood manager, inspirator*, and *guide* (Hanitzsch & Vos, 2017).These emphases reflect elements of authenticity and its connection to values such as sincerity, truth, honesty, originality, perfection, purity, and naturalness (Lindholm, 2013).

Scholars have examined the role of authenticity in journalism, including how it intersects with the perceived roles of lifestyle journalists, including offering "judgments of taste" (Fürsich, 2012) and aspirational narratives to connect with and influence readers, as well as the emphasis on authenticity among digital lifestyle bloggers and influencers, who use personal anecdotes and testimonies to appear more genuine and relatable to audiences. In these ways, authenticity helps legitimize the content that lifestyle journalists embrace, including a focus on service, guidance, advocacy, and entertainment (Hanusch, 2019). Personal anecdotes, true-life stories, opinions, community advocacy, and cultivating relationships with readers online – lifestyle journalists draw from these strategies and more to cultivate audience trust and loyalty.

This chapter explores the connections between journalistic authenticity and journalistic authority. I begin by defining "authenticity" and summarizing how it has been studied. I then shift to the role of authenticity as a concept in journalism studies. Next, I examine the importance of authenticity to lifestyle media, from newspapers to magazines to digital media, elucidating the relationship between authenticity and journalistic authority. I then assess the ways authenticity has been studied in the context of digital media, with a particular focus on digital labor and "influencers." Lastly, I present challenges and directions for future research.

What is authenticity?

Authenticity is connected to principles such as being sincere, essential, natural, original, and real (Lindholm, 2013). Lindholm traces the roots of authenticity to the value of sincerity, which arose during the 16th century as face-to-face feudal relationships began to disappear in European society. While medieval Europe was defined by hierarchal social relations evident in church and familial relations, the move to modernity and urban environments meant that people could challenge these prescribed roles and pursue other types of aims, some through false claims and deceit. Therefore, sincerity (or someone doing what they say they will do) was highly desired. Eventually, sincerity was also questioned – could it result less from moral intentions and more from pride – and the rise of scientific reason made way for an increased emphasis on discovering an authentic and divine being. Today, authenticity can be considered a collective arrangement, in that it gathers people who are seen to be "real, essential, and vital, providing participants with meaning, unity, and a surpassing sense of belonging," as well as an internal process achieved through transformative experiences or consuming goods that "symbolize the really real" (Lindholm, 2013, p. 1).

Scholars across disciplines have conceptualized authenticity in terms of individuals recognizing their true self, which emphasizes the socially constructed and performative nature of the idea (Luebke, 2021). This emphasis also distinguishes authenticity from more personalized concepts such as sincerity or integrity (Luebke, 2021). Authenticity can be associated with other factors, such as ethical behavior, consciousness, subjectivity, self-processes, and social or relational contexts (Balaban & Szambolics, 2022). It has been contrasted with "whatever is fake, unreal, or false" (Enli, 2015, p. 2).

Peterson (2005) describes authenticity as "a claim that is made by or for someone, thing, or performance and either accepted or rejected by relevant others" (p. 1086). Peterson cites Goffman's (1959) "face work" — or individuals behaving as if they are acting in a play and maintaining the characters others have created for them, as well as reconciling impressions when their communication deviates from those expectations. Peterson (2005) also describes "authenticity work," efforts to appear more authentic through ethnicity/culture identity, group identity, status identity, authenticity experiences, and mediated authenticity – including in-person connections and online communication. Enli (2015) also focused on the socially constructed nature of authenticity, noting that it is defined through a communicative process, and the degree "depends on symbolic negotiations between the main participants in the communication" (p. 3).

A socially constructed understanding of authenticity connects to performed political authenticity, which, as Luebke (2021) describes, does not reside in politicians publicly presenting their real selves but in constructing an authentic image for the audience. Luebke identifies important components of political authenticity, including consistency (similar appearances and actions over time), intimacy (disclosing personal information), ordinariness (fulfilling the role of a politicians and a normal person), and immediacy (real-time communication of spontaneous and true thoughts). Authenticity assessments can vary based on qualities such as the gender of a political candidate, with women being perceived as less authentic than men as a result of the lack of women in these roles (Enli & Rosenberg, 2018, as cited in Luebke & Steffan, 2023). However, the authors found that on social media, these assessments can vary, with an analysis of tweets finding that gender did not affect the authenticity ratings of candidates, and self-presentation strategies might play a role.

Authenticity in journalism

Expectations of authenticity in journalism take multiple forms. For journalists, authenticity can represent a dedication to accurately and objectively representing an event, topic, source, or other information. There is also the notion of "mediated authenticity," which addresses the relationship between media and authenticity and reflects conventions of media production, or "authenticity illusions," such as live reporting and eyewitness interviews (Enli, 2015). Audiences, through an authenticity contract, accept these illusions based on norms and practices associated with various media genres. In terms of media, this contract relies on assumptions of trustworthiness, particularly for news coverage of crises and the value in providing answers and forums for public discussion, as well as originality and spontaneity (Enli, 2015).

According to Vodanovic (2024), a focus on authenticity is a new phenomenon in journalism that "points to other features, such as genuineness, intimacy, and, notoriously, trust, derived from what is perceived as an honest self" (p. 4). Tulloch (2014) suggested that trust, which emphasizes directness, immediacy, and intimacy, is associated with journalists presenting an "authentic narrative voice" (p. 630). Hayes, Singer, and Ceppos (2007) explored the relationship between authenticity and credibility, highlighting the role of journalistic autonomy and accountability, as well as institutional authenticity and the need to preserve credibility amid competition from digital actors.

Eyewitnessing is a key element of authenticity in journalism. It is rooted in both the personal and narrative authority of journalists directly experiencing events on the front lines (Gregory, 2022). As Zelizer (1990) described in the context of TV journalists discussing coverage of US President John F. Kennedy Jr.'s assassination, journalists assert and legitimize their authority using narrative strategies such as *synecdoche*, or covering related events to stand in for those they did not cover; *omission*, or downplaying their role in events; and *personalization*, or recollecting events they did not witness through a focus on their own experiences. This authority has been jeopardized, as Gregory (2022) argues, by discourse around deepfakes, misinformation, and media manipulation that creates questions about all types of images – whether edited or not. A possible solution is "authenticity infrastructure," as Gregory termed, which aims to track the origins of media and whether manipulation has occurred for reference both in publication and sharing.

As an extension of eyewitnessing, lived experiences have become an important part of journalism practice, with connections to conversations around trust, engagement, and relating to audiences (Vodanovic, 2024). This shift was evident in the emergence of "j-blogs," which allowed journalists to adapt their reporting to an online audience through nonlinear, interactive formats and through challenging norms of independence, verification, news judgment, and truth (Robinson, 2006). As Robinson concluded,

> Compared to the real world of objective reporting where every single detail must be verified and the reporter invisible, the j-blog allows the reporter to let loose in some creative writing – all verified because the reporter is both source and the subject.
>
> *(p. 79)*

Lived experiences can also be tied to a recent scholarly focus on emotion, which has become increasingly important to news production and consumption and can, as Beckett and Deuze (2016) argued, drive attention, encourage engagement, and facilitate better understanding of audiences and their behaviors toward news (see also Chapter 13). Rather than eschewing norms like objectivity, this form of journalism links news with emotion, connects with communities, suggests solutions, and supports social-network sharing. Wahl-Jorgensen (2020) examined the "emotional turn in journalism studies," including studies assessing the role of emotion in journalistic production, texts, and audience engagement. In particular, the rise of digital media has led to citizen journalism, user-generated content, and other ways for audiences to create "new ways of knowing, through personalized and embodied accounts of news events" (Wahl-Jorgensen, 2020, p. 189). Social media have continued this focus through promoting affect and connection and spurring journalists to draw upon emotion and personalization.

Coward (2009) tracked the rise of autobiographical journalism, which values authenticity as a "holy grail of a culture needing to see how real people react to real difficulties" (p. 241); it is also an attribute that journalism, by nature of its approach to capturing accurate and trustworthy accounts, can provide. This focus on subjectivity and emotions reflects a feminization of journalism, with women bringing in a more confessional voice. Additionally, by emphasizing reflexivity, particularity, and lived experiences, authenticity could be seen as a feminist practice (Steiner, 2018). Vodanovic (2024) analyzed the role of the narration of lived experiences in reporting on the Abortion Referendum in Irish newspapers, a topic that has led to multiple examples of autobiographical reporting. The articles, which were split nearly evenly between those in support of the referendum and those opposing it, largely featured the experiences of older adults. Personal stories also tended to focus on other people's abortions, including relatives, partners, and daughters, differentiating them from personal essays – a strategy Vodanovic associated with journalism's normative emphasis on "bearing witness." This approach, she argued, relates to authenticity, in that the journalist's presence reinforces the authority of the text. That is, "the bearing witness is often expressed in the writing, retelling, and sharing of stories that foster a dialogue between the lived experiences of the authors and that of the readers, and therefore is not just about individual self-expression" (Vodanovic, 2024, p. 584).

Holt (2012) addressed authenticity in the form of "existential journalism," which draws from Merrill's (1995, 1996) focus on journalists living authentically as both private individuals and professionals. Existential authenticity requires journalists to challenge newsroom conformity so that they can stay true to themselves, embracing a uniqueness and originality that allows them to perform according to their own ethical ideals, rather than being controlled by institutional norms. However, embracing authenticity as an ethical ideal creates challenges – that is, because it prioritizes an individual's freedom to choose what stories to cover and how, it may "encourage a more narcissistic and cynical focus on individual career-achievements than stimulating closer scrutiny of journalists' inner conscience" (Holt, 2012, p. 13).

Similarly, Markham (2012) discussed authenticity in the context of journalistic creativity or "more personalized ways of doing journalism" (p. 188). A valorization of creativity can lead to exploitation of expression, such as for freelance journalists, as well as a shift from professional expertise to something to which all individuals have access. Markham also explored the perceptions of creativity, which can suggest that the act of self-expression is more important than the content itself, as long as it is genuine. However, understanding the rules of what counts as genuine is more apparent to some journalists than others, and journalists cannot control how their work is received; therefore, only a few creative practices are seen as authorized, which can also be seen as a form of de-authorization.

Images are important to perceived authenticity in journalism because "they appear consonant with what audiences believe to be firsthand recordings of events as they truly unfolded" (Borges-Rey, 2015, p. 573). The use of social media to present journalistic work, however, has complicated these roles. Borges-Rey examined how professional and citizen photojournalists use Instagram, particularly how the norms of the platform's use challenge the emphasis on realism and objectivity typically associated with photojournalism. As Borges-Rey suggested, online photo-sharing platforms have become spaces where citizens, citizen journalists, and professional journalists document daily life, creating aesthetics that complicate the understandings of authenticity. In particular,

> The more citizen photojournalists try to emulate professional standards when creating their simulations, the more they risk distancing themselves from the aura of authenticity perceived by news audiences in other modalities of citizen and amateur witnessing imagery, and to be catalogued by the public as presenting the same detached and artificial frames that are subject to criticism.
>
> *(Borges-Rey, 2015, p. 588)*

Other emerging technologies shape the relationship between journalists and authenticity. For example, news organizations have experimented with augmented reality in visual storytelling, which reflects journalism's emphasis, providing a realistic portrait of the world and supplementing it with an accuracy, authenticity, and credibility that comes through the audience's perceived presence in the image (Aitamurto, Aymerich-Franch, Saldivar, Kircos, Sadeghi, & Sakshuwong, 2022). Although augmented-reality tools can heighten these perceptions, they can also be disrupted if viewers do not see the images as real or authentic enough.

Lifestyle journalism: Connecting authenticity and authority

Lifestyle journalism, which includes reporting on topics such as food, travel, fashion, celebrities, wellness, and parenting, can be defined as the coverage of "the expressive values and practices that help create and signify a specific identity within the realm of consumption and everyday life" (Hanusch & Hanitzsch, 2013, p. 947). While traditional journalism tends to prioritize collective, public approaches to defining problems and solutions, lifestyle journalism emphasizes individual, personal approaches. Lifestyle journalists embrace distinctive roles, with a survey of Australian lifestyle journalists finding that they focused on providing fun and inspiring content to offer audiences a relaxing experience (the Inspiring Entertainer), particularly those working in travel, fashion, and beauty, as well as embraced roles such as service provider, life coach, and community advocate (Hanusch, 2019). Readers also embrace these roles, which suggests that lifestyle journalism should be held to the same standards as traditional journalism, combining a focus (notably) on authenticity with objectivity, ethics, and rational and critical perspectives (Fürsich, 2012). However, as Fürsich argued, even traditional journalism faces challenges reconciling the blurred lines between editorial, marketing, and advertising, and lifestyle journalism should be evaluated on its own accord.

Authenticity is a longstanding feature of lifestyle reporting, evident in journalists who seek not just to inform readers but also to provide "judgments of taste" (Fürsich, 2012, p. 13) based on their expertise, experience, and authority. This point reinforces the need to consider authenticity as an important component of journalistic authority. Journalistic authority is "the ability of journalists to promote themselves as authoritative and credible spokespersons of 'real-life' events" (Zelizer, 1992, p. 8). Examining the ways authority has been studied, including a focus on professionalization, narratives, and field theory, Anderson (2008) suggested that the journalistic project requires considering journalism as a system of knowledge production, a source of expertise, and a cultural authority, all of which are encapsulated in efforts to assert control over newsgathering, particularly in light of the rising competition from bloggers and others. Journalistic authority is also relational, in that audiences "expect journalists to know and to communicate their knowing" (Carlson, 2017, p. 7) through recording, sharing, and interpreting world events.

Authority, as Carlson and others have suggested, is always open to contestation and change, evident in efforts of journalists to maintain their boundaries. According to Vos and Thomas (2018), journalistic authority is constituted through discourse, where anxieties facing journalists had become evident over time. Vos and Thomas cited the rise of bloggers and the overall blurring of the lines between amateurs and professionals as news moved online, which led journalists to distinguish themselves through their public-service roles and impact. Similar boundary work has occurred with current affairs programs in TV news, which emphasize journalists addressing the camera/audience directly, making judgments to summarize a situation, telling the "stories behind the news" (p. 87), or even becoming a character in the story or getting involved in the events they report on – all of which contributes to journalistic authenticity (Holland, 2014).

Lifestyle journalists are often drawn to the profession because of personal connections to the topics and people they cover, although they must also negotiate institutional expectations for their work (Perreault & Bélair-Gagnon, 2024). In contrast, lifestyle bloggers can take an "intensely personal" approach to their writing, such as through incorporating personal narratives, personal style, and personal thoughts to "connect with their readers in 'real authentic ways'" and appear useful, relatable, and accessible (Cheng & Tandoc, 2022). This practice allows bloggers to distinguish themselves from mainstream news organizations, which tend to emphasize their history, authority, and exclusivity, although some strive to achieve reader loyalty through developing intimate connections and inclusive communities (Cheng & Tandoc, 2022). Travel bloggers, similarly, reinforce their authority and expertise through strategies such as focusing on the cities they cover as "beats," offering insider scoops because they know the culture and language, and providing "boots on the ground" perspectives (Pirolli, 2017, p. 746). Travel journalists recognized the value of personalizing their work, including incorporating their own voices, opinions, and anecdotes and using first-person narratives, although they distanced themselves from the need to interact with reader feedback (Pirolli, 2017).

Lifestyle journalists also compete with digital influencers, who are seen as more authentic than traditional media, to draw advertising (Cheng & Tandoc, 2022) (see also Chapters 24 and 26). Influencers, such as professional lifestyle Instagrammers, can be seen as "interlopers" who place themselves at the margins of the journalistic field but value normative journalistic ideals and fulfill similar roles, including offering advice, inspiration, entertainment, and relaxation (Maares & Hanusch, 2020). These influencers include digital lifestyle gurus: non-experts who rely on narratives of self-transformation, anecdotes, and testimonies – supported by highly curated social media feeds – to offer health advice to fans and followers (Baker & Rojek, 2020). Here, influence is measured by follower counts and engagement, as well as media attention, challenging the authority of journalists and other experts.

This competition is evident in the discursive strategies through which lifestyle journalists describe their relationship with influencers. Austrian and U.S. lifestyle journalists engaged in boundary work in reference to influencers on Instagram, a platform frequently associated with notions of genuineness and authenticity, suggesting that influencers could take a more casual tone and serve a smaller, more niche audience, as well as pursue more personal connections with audiences (Perreault & Hanusch, 2024). Ultimately, journalists suggested that their work was more professionalized and focused on audience needs than that of most influencers. Interviews with lifestyle journalists in Singapore revealed that they emphasize the legitimacy of legacy publications, which they describe as more credible, trustworthy, and prestigious, and suggest that the influencers they choose to collaborate with also benefit from this authority (Cheng & Chew, 2024). However, the journalists sought to replicate the authentic practices of influencers through building their social media presence – and communities (Cheng & Chew, 2024).

Ashe (2023) identified authenticity as a component of the aspirational focus of lifestyle journalism, alongside accessibility, advice, and aesthetics. Drawing from other scholarship, Ashe connected authenticity to aesthetics, in that goods and experiences are perceived as better if they are more authentic, as well as genuineness, a value judgment that shapes consumer choices. Through interviews with American travel media producers, Ashe found that they aimed to achieve authenticity through strategies such as incorporating friends and family into their writing, discussing their own leisure interests, and including local voices.

Aspirational lifestyle journalism reflects assumptions related to social class, on the part of journalists, and differing needs from audiences, which can challenge the perceptions of authenticity. Drawing from Bourdieu's concept of "taste" and the symbolic struggles between authentic and imitational culture, Banjac and Hanusch (2022) explored the perspectives of South African lifestyle journalists and audiences. Journalists emphasized their role in providing aspiration through the stories and goods they featured, largely focusing on middle-class and newly affluent audiences, rather than the economically disadvantaged – what the authors called a "mindful marketer" role. Aspiration manifested in different ways for audiences, with aspiration through consumption appealing across classes, while the working class identified with aspiration through motivation and hope. This focus emerged through "true-life stories" that allowed working-class audiences to, as the authors described, "recognize themselves in other people's struggles and potential future successes" (Banjac & Hanusch, 2022, p. 1621).

In this way, lifestyle journalists can function as community advocates, such as through providing a forum for readers, offering reader service, advocating for audience's interests, and investigating the ethical and moral dimensions of certain lifestyles and experiences (Hanusch, 2019). Depictions in U.S. city magazines reflected idealized, consumption-driven versions of cities to appeal to an imagined community of affluent, educated, engaged readers, largely neglecting opportunities to explore topics that challenge these dominant understandings (Jenkins, 2016a). Lifestyle journalists at city and regional magazines also balance a focus on "private-service" content offering insights and advice for how readers can experience their cities through consumption with public-service content that "supports editors' desire to educate and empower readers and improve cities" (Jenkins, 2016b, p. 631). These negotiations reflect a tension between presenting an "authentic" version of a city while desiring to reflect the perceived needs and interests of news organizations and segments of readers.

Authenticity and digital media

Authenticity has become a particularly complex and important concept in the social media environment, where content creators and lifestyle journalists co-mingle and the lines between marketing and journalism are blurred. Authenticity permeates political, cultural, and social life through brands seeking to build affective connections with consumers (Banet-Weiser, 2021), which many have sought to achieve through embracing digital content creators or "influencers." Perceived authenticity for social media influencers consists of five dimensions: sincerity, truthful endorsements, visibility, expertise, and uniqueness (Lee & Eastin, 2021). Banet-Weiser (2021) proposed that concerns around misinformation, "fake news," and deepfakes have complicated the idea of "truth" and made the need to be authentic both more important and more difficult to achieve. For social media influencers, "positioning oneself as authentic has been a necessity. […] Influencers promise their followers authenticity, where their selves are mediated apparently by us rather than by content-producing media institutions" (Banet-Weiser, 2021, p. 142).

On social media, authenticity is "subjective, personally defined, and socially constructed" (Balaban & Szambolics, 2022, p. 237). Influencers tend to associate authenticity with sincerity, realness, transparency, and genuineness. This involves presenting themselves as they are and not how audiences expect them to be, as well as upholding personal principles and values – both in their messaging and in the brands they endorse. They also prioritize offering high-quality and relevant content that draws upon their expertise and allows them to appear unique. This "realness," though, is limited.

Authenticity is also an industrial construction shaped by a "sophisticated and complicated profit-making enterprise whose decisions about what expressions of reality are valuable help determine what types of content and tools for communication and self-expression are available to the world's billions of social media users" (Hund, 2023, p. 18). This understanding of authenticity reflects the ways that media industries, including legacy and social media, have idealized a focus on "realness" in ways that affect both amateur creators and professional journalists, among others.

For digital lifestyle gurus, authenticity comes through appearing genuine and "real," as well as sharing intimate details of their personal lives, which represents a contrast to mass media. As Baker and Rojek (2020) argue, "Whereas the media is criticized for manufacturing the news, spinning stories and airbrushing images for ratings and profit, lifestyle gurus perform authenticity through managed self-disclosure" (p. 59). Authenticity, then, is a form of social capital allowing lifestyle gurus to cultivate trust with their followers. Lee and Johnson (2022) found that two-sided messages – those including both positive and negative evaluations of products – could increase the credibility and interactivity with followers, allowing influencers to be seen as authentic without revealing too much personal information.

Arriagada and Bishop (2021) suggested the term "influencer imaginary" to explain how influencers reconcile their dual interest in appearing authentic with embracing the commerciality of representing a particular brand or product. The authors argue that cultural workers have had to navigate the authentic and the commercial as binaries, as developing an authentic artistic identity is often key to achieving success in the creative industries. This tension reflects the inherent amateur nature of digital media production – what Burgess and Green (2018) called an "ideology of authenticity" (p. 39) – which rewards those who earn their experience outside of the traditional Hollywood system. As influencers have become more prevalent in digital culture, however, authenticity has become intertwined with a "calibrated amateurism" emphasizing intentional behaviors in everyday scenarios (Arriagada & Bishop, 2021, p. 571).

Influencers rely on discursive strategies to present brands in ways that feel as natural as possible. This includes describing their followers as "friends" whom they are helping through using their expertise to help them make informed purchasing decisions (Arriagada & Bishop, 2021). They also position themselves in opposition to other types of media that fulfill the same functions, such as suggesting that magazines feature products that are not accessible to "common people." Similarly, they use everyday language and emotion to build community and reinforce their "luxury-ordinary" lifestyle while welcoming their followers to respond.

Considering the relationship between authenticity labor ("how producers intend to be perceived") and authenticity consumption ("how audiences perceive authenticity") as an interactive and relational process is also valuable (Maares et al., 2021, p. 8). Interviews with 19 Instagrammers focused on lifestyle topics (fashion, food, and beauty) and 11 focus group discussions showed that creators valued authenticity – particularly a "true to their inner self" presentation (p. 6) – and desired to connect with their audiences (Maares et al., 2021). While audience members approached creators' work with skepticism, they also valued honest and credible portrayals of their "imperfection and the negative aspects of life" (Maares et al., 2021, p. 8).

As in journalism, authenticity is a gendered concept in the realm of digital media. Women face bigger risks when making themselves visible on social media platforms (Duffy & Hund, 2019), and they often experience more severe ramifications when they are not authentic enough. As Banet-Weiser (2021) wrote:

> Women have been historically told (through all sorts of media and institutions) that their "real" selves are not good enough, and certainly not to be trusted. So within institutions (such as politics, media, and the law) women are routinely not believed, and on social media, the media platforms continually authorize how to "fake" one's identity to make it, ironically, more believable—and more profitable.
>
> *(p. 142)*

This "labor of authenticity" requires women to communicate the failures, pressures, depression, and vulnerabilities they experience in the pursuit of crafting a version of "apparently effortless authenticity," all of which operates according to an "endless feedback loop" (Banet-Weiser, 2021, p. 143) that can be challenging to maintain. As Arriagada and Bishop (2021) wrote, "Feminine authenticity encompasses deep expectations and pressures—a bricolage of intimate confession, aesthetic labor shared with audiences, and discourses that sustain relatability" (p. 572).

Duffy and Hund (2019) explored the "authenticity bind" (Pooley, 2010) for Instagram content creators in the United States and Canada. The creators described a pressure to present themselves as "real" on social media "without stepping into territory that could be perceived as too real" (p. 4989). This involved incorporating candid and relatable moments into posts; making themselves seem approachable; featuring only brands they like; and reflecting gendered norms related to motherhood, home life, and beauty. These efforts carried tangible implications, as creators said that being perceived as too real or not real enough could result in criticism, causing emotional or financial harm. Ultimately, "influencers' projections of authenticity were narrowly defined. That is, these boundary definitions were firmly entrenched in a capitalist economy that privileges creators' 'organic' endorsements and expressions of 'real beauty'" (p. 4996).

Influencers are also subject to gendered authenticity policing, which seeks to critique capitalist patriarchy, but rather than targeting broader systems, "hatebloggers" focus on individual influencers who emphasize certain gendered norms and practices (Duffy et al., 2022). An analysis of antifans' posts on GOMIBLOG revealed an emphasis on the ideals of realness, truth, and sincerity, including women influencers' efforts to present an unrealistic image of "having it all"; promoting products that did not align with their aesthetic or ethos; and offering performative or exploitative images of their relationships, parenting, and friendships. According to these reactions, these "'fake' projections of career/relational/aesthetic perfection perpetuate unachievable expectations for women and, further, that such ideals are consequently regressive or un-feminist" (Duffy et al., 2022, p. 1670).

Conclusion

The idea of having authenticity or being authentic has existed for centuries and can be considered both an internal process and a source of collective meaning-making. Humans have long manipulated discourses around who they are, what they do, and what they want to achieve. Today, this "face work" (Goffman, 1959) occurs largely in digitally mediated spaces, rather than in person, creating renewed interest around what it means to be authentic, the value of authenticity, and how to recognize authenticity across personalities and platforms. These conversations reference multiple elements of authenticity as identified by scholars, including values such as sincerity, truth, honesty, originality, perfection, purity, and naturalness (Lindholm, 2013). Of course, concerns around the opposite characteristics – or "whatever is fake, unreal, or false" (Enli, 2015, p. 2) – remain prominent.

Authenticity has emerged as an important concept in journalism studies. Journalists have long prioritized being seen as independent, credible, and reliable interpreters of events. These values represent a form of "mediated authenticity" shaped by conventions of journalistic practice, including the role of live reporting and eyewitness interviews – "authenticity illusions" (Enli, 2015). Audiences, in turn, accept these illusions based on their trust in the journalist and news organization, as well as their recognition of the norms and practices commonly associated with different media genres. A focus on authenticity is a new phenomenon in journalism; however, that connects to an increased desire among journalists to appear genuine, intimate, and honest to build trust (Vodanovic, 2024). This development is spurred by a need to more effectively connect with audiences to build community and support for journalism, as well as combat news avoidance and the decline of openly participatory news users online (Newman, Fletcher, Eddy, Robertson, & Nielsen, 2023). It also reflects journalists' and audiences' interest in journalism that presents emotional responses to events, suggests solutions, and encourages engagement and participation (Beckett & Deuze, 2016).

Authenticity is a form of social capital for digital content creators, who draw fans and followers through appearing genuine, real, and accessible, as well as sharing personal insights in a process of "managed self-disclosure" (Baker & Rojek, 2020, p. 59). Brands increasingly seek these influencers to promote their products and connect them with digital media-oriented younger audiences. Therefore, rather than relying on traditional media institutions to manage these "authentic" selves, they rely on the public (Banet-Weiser, 2021).

Although the rise of digital influencers has been associated with marketing and branding, their tactics have affected the journalistic field, particularly lifestyle journalism. Studies have explored how lifestyle journalists engage in boundary work to differentiate their editorial practices and impact from influencers (Perreault & Hanusch, 2024). Lifestyle journalists also reinforce the credibility, trustworthiness, and prestige of their legacy media organizations and suggest that when they collaborate with influencers, influencers benefit from that authority (Cheng & Chew, 2024).

Journalistic authority and boundary work are intertwined concepts. The "journalistic project" recognizes journalism as a source of knowledge, expertise, and cultural authority (Anderson, 2008), roles that journalists have defended from bloggers, citizen journalists, and others seeking to participate in newsgathering. Journalists' authority comes through the ways they reinforce their ability to reliably represent "real-life events" (Zelizer, 1992, p. 8), as well as the ways they reinforce their distinctive public-service roles (Vos & Thomas, 2018). As Carlson (2017) argues, when considering journalistic authority, journalistic practice is not a monolith. Rather, epistemological approaches differ across the field.

Lifestyle journalists reinforce their authority – and, by extension, their authenticity – through providing "judgments of taste" (Fürsich, 2012); highlighting their personal connections to topics (Perreault & Bélair-Gagnon, 2024); incorporating their own experiences into accounts and interviewing sources they see as authentic (Ashe, 2023); providing fun, entertainment, and relaxation (Hanusch, 2019); and offering motivation and hope through aspirational content and "true-life stories" (Banjac & Hanusch, 2022), among other roles. Digital influencers in the lifestyle area have embraced these roles as well while differentiating themselves from their legacy media counterparts (Maares & Hanusch, 2020). Similarly, journalists have pursued community-building on social media using the same authenticity-driven tactics as digital content creators.

As these strategies and goals continue to influence one another, authenticity will remain a highly sought after – and debated – element of journalistic practice. Journalistic authenticity, particularly in the context of lifestyle journalism, remains a rich area for exploration, including ways authenticity can contribute to building audience trust and interest; authenticity's role in reinforcing what characteristics, practices, and ideals make journalism meaningful and relevant; the relationship between authenticity and audience engagement and community-building; how a focus on authenticity can contribute to journalists' sense of joy and fulfillment in their work; and how authenticity differs across news platforms, geographic focus, beats, political focus, and other areas. Research should also consider authenticity in the context of new and emerging technologies, particularly the use of AI in news production and the continued impact of mobile, digital, and social media. How to define what is genuine, real, and original remains subjective and highly contextual – a question in which journalism is not only involved but also to which it is subject.

Further reading

Baker, S. A., & Rojek, C. (2020). *Lifestyle gurus: Constructing authority and influence online*. Wiley.
Carlson, M. (2017). *Journalistic authority: Legitimating news in the digital era*. Columbia University Press.
Enli, G. (2015). *Mediated authenticity: How the media constructs reality*. Peter Lang.
Hund, E. (2023). *The influencer industry: The quest for authenticity on social media*. Princeton University Press.

References

Aitamurto, T., Aymerich-Franch, L., Saldivar, J., Kircos, C., Sadeghi, Y., & Sakshuwong, S. (2022). Examining augmented reality in journalism: Presence, knowledge gain, and perceived visual authenticity. *New Media & Society*, 24(6), 1281–1302. https://doi.org/10.1177/1461444820951925
Anderson, C. (2008). Journalism: Expertise, authority, and power in democratic life. In D. Hesmondhalgh & J. Toynbee (Eds.), *The media and social theory* (pp. 262–278). Routledge.
Arriagada, A., & Bishop, S. (2021). Between commerciality and authenticity: The imaginary of social media influencers in the platform economy. *Communication, Culture and Critique*, 14(4), 568–586. https://doi.org/10.1093/ccc/tcab050
Ashe, I. (2023). Time to go: Aspirational framing and place-making in domestic travel journalism. *Journalism Practice*, 1–18. https://doi.org/10.1080/17512786.2023.2244931
Baker, S. A., & Rojek, C. (2020). *Lifestyle gurus: Constructing authority and influence online*. John Wiley & Sons.
Balaban, D. C., & Szambolics, J. (2022). A proposed model of self-perceived authenticity of social media influencers. *Media and Communication*, 10(1), 235–246. https://doi.org/10.17645/mac.v10i1.4765
Banet-Weiser, S. (2021). Gender, social media, and the labor of authenticity. *American Quarterly*, 73(1), 141–144. https://doi.org/10.1353/aq.2021.0008
Banjac, S., & Hanusch, F. (2022). Aspirational lifestyle journalism: The impact of social class on producers' and audiences' views in the context of socio-economic inequality. *Journalism*, 23(8), 1607–1625. https://doi.org/10.1177/1464884920956823
Beckett, C., & Deuze, M. (2016). On the role of emotion in the future of journalism. *Social Media+ Society*, 2(3), 1–6. https://doi.org/10.1177/2056305116662395

Borges-Rey, E. (2015). News images on Instagram: The paradox of authenticity in hyperreal photo reportage. *Digital Journalism*, 3(4), 571–593. https://doi.org/10.1080/21670811.2015.1034526

Burgess, J., & Green, J. (2018). *YouTube: Online video and participatory culture*. John Wiley & Sons.

Carlson, M. (2017). *Journalistic authority: Legitimating news in the digital era*. Columbia University Press.

Cheng, L., & Chew, M. (2024). Functional interlopers: Lifestyle journalists' discursive construction of boundaries against digital lifestyle influencers. *Journalism*, 25(2), 372–390. https://doi.org/10.1177/14648849221143875

Cheng, L., & Tandoc Jr, E. C. (2022). From magazines to blogs: The shifting boundaries of fashion journalism. *Journalism*, 23(6), 1213–1232. https://doi.org/10.1177/1464884920988183

Coward, R. (2009). Me, me, me: The rise and rise of autobiographical journalism. *The Routledge Companion to News and Journalism*, 234.

Duffy, B. E., & Hund, E. (2019). Gendered visibility on social media: Navigating Instagram's authenticity bind. *International Journal of Communication*, 13, 20.

Duffy, B. E., Miltner, K. M., & Wahlstedt, A. (2022). Policing "fake" femininity: Authenticity, accountability, and influencer antifandom. *New Media & Society*, 24(7), 1657–1676. https://doi.org/10.1177/146144482210992

Enli, G. (2015). *Mediated authenticity: How the media constructs reality*. Peter Lang Inc.

Enli, G., & Rosenberg, L. T. (2018). Trust in the age of social media: Populist politicians seem more authentic. *Social Media+ Society*, 4(1), 1–11. https://doi.org/2056305118764430

Fürsich, E. (2012). Lifestyle journalism as popular journalism: Strategies for evaluating its public role. *Journalism Practice*, 6(1), 12–25. https://doi.org/10.1080/17512786.2011.622894

Goffman, E. (1959). *The presentation of self in everyday life*. New York: Anchor

Gregory, S. (2022). Deepfakes, misinformation and disinformation and authenticity infrastructure responses: Impacts on frontline witnessing, distant witnessing, and civic journalism. *Journalism*, 23(3), 708–729. https://doi.org/10.1177/14648849211060644

Hanitzsch, T., & Vos, T. P. (2017). Journalistic roles and the struggle over institutional identity: The discursive constitution of journalism. *Communication Theory*, 27(2), 115–135. https://doi.org/10.1111/comt.12112

Hanusch, F. (2019). Journalistic roles and everyday life: An empirical account of lifestyle journalists' professional views. *Journalism Studies*, 20(2), 193–211. https://doi.org/10.1080/1461670X.2017.1370977

Hanusch, F., & Hanitzsch, T. (2013). Mediating orientation and self-expression in the world of consumption: Australian and German lifestyle journalists' professional views. *Media, Culture & Society*, 35(8), 943–959. https://doi.org/10.1177/0163443713501931

Hayes, A. S., Singer, J. B., & Ceppos, J. (2007). Shifting roles, enduring values: The credible journalist in a digital age. *Journal of Mass Media Ethics*, 22(4), 262–279. https://doi.org/10.1080/08900520701583545

Holland, P. (2014). Authority and authenticity: Redefining television current affairs. In M. Bromley (Ed.), *No news is bad news* (pp. 80–95). Routledge.

Holt, K. (2012). Authentic journalism? A critical discussion about existential authenticity in journalism ethics. *Journal of Mass Media Ethics*, 27(1), 2–14. https://doi.org/10.1080/08900523.2012.636244

Hund, E. (2023). *The influencer industry: The quest for authenticity on social media*. Princeton University Press.

Jenkins, J. (2016a). The good life: The construction of imagined communities in city magazines. *Journalism Studies*, 17(3), 319–336. https://doi.org/10.1080/1461670X.2014.982942

Jenkins, J. (2016b). Public roles and private negotiations: Considering city magazines' public service and market functions. *Journalism*, 17(5), 619–635. https://doi.org/10.1177/146488491557673

Jones, R. (2023, 15 February). As companies cut traditional advertising, social media influencers are taking advantage. *Observer*. https://observer.com/2023/02/as-companies-cut-traditional-advertising-social-media-influencers-are-taking-advantage/

Lee, J. A., & Eastin, M. S. (2021). Perceived authenticity of social media influencers: Scale development and validation. *Journal of Research in Interactive Marketing*, 15(4), 822–841. https://doi.org/10.1108/JRIM-12-2020-0253

Lee, S. S., & Johnson, B. K. (2022). Are they being authentic? The effects of self-disclosure and message sidedness on sponsored post effectiveness. *International Journal of Advertising*, 41(1), 30–53. https://doi.org/10.1080/02650487.2021.1986257

Licano, L. (2019, 13 September). Keeping it real: The importance of having an authentic social media presence. *Forbes*. https://www.forbes.com/sites/forbesagencycouncil/2019/09/13/keeping-it-real-the-importance-of-having-an-authentic-social-media-presence/?sh=aa0ad39110fd

Lindholm, C. (2013). The rise of expressive authenticity. *Anthropological Quarterly*, 86(2), 361–395. https://www.jstor.org/stable/41857330

Luebke, S. M. (2021). Political authenticity: Conceptualization of a popular term. *The International Journal of Press/Politics*, 26(3), 635–653. https://doi.org/10.1177/1940161220948013

Luebke, S. M., & Steffan, D. (2023). Pathway to authenticity? The influence of politicians' gender and multimodal self-presentation in social media on perceived authenticity. *New Media & Society*, 1–20. https://doi.org/10.1177/14614448231208920

Maares, P., Banjac, S., & Hanusch, F. (2021). The labour of visual authenticity on social media: Exploring producers' and audiences' perceptions on Instagram. *Poetics*, 84, 1–20. https://doi.org/10.1016/j.poetic.2020.101502

Maares, P., & Hanusch, F. (2020). Exploring the boundaries of journalism: Instagram micro bloggers in the twilight zone of lifestyle journalism. *Journalism*, 21(2), 262–278. https://doi.org/10.1177/1464884918188014

Markham, T. (2012). The politics of journalistic creativity: Expressiveness, authenticity and de-authorization. *Journalism Practice*, 6(2), 187–200 https://doi.org/10.1080/17512786.2011.616651

Merriam-Webster. (2023). Word of the year 2023. https://www.merriam-webster.com/wordplay/word-of-the-year#:~:text=Authentic%20has%20a%20number%20of,many%20people%20to%20the%20dictionary

Merrill, J. C. (1995). *Existential journalism*, rev. ed. Ames, IA: Iowa State University Press.

Merrill, J. C. (1996). *Existential journalism*, rev. ed. Ames, IA: Iowa State University Press.

Newman, N., Fletcher, R., Eddy, K., Robertson, C., & Nielsen, R. K. (2023). Digital news report. *Reuters Institute for the Study of Journalism*. https://reutersinstitute.politics.ox.ac.uk/digital-news-report/2023

Perreault, G. P., & Bélair-Gagnon, V. (2024). The lifestyle of lifestyle journalism: How reporters discursively manage their aspirations in their daily work. *Journalism Practice*, 18(7), 1641–1659. https://doi.org/10.1080/17512786.2022.2111697

Perreault, G., & Hanusch, F. (2024). Field insurgency in lifestyle journalism: How lifestyle journalists marginalize Instagram influencers and protect their autonomy. *New Media & Society*, 26(7), 3767–3785. https://doi.org/10.1177/14614448221104233

Peterson, R. A. (2005). In search of authenticity. *Journal of Management Studies*, 42(5), 1083–1098. https://doi.org/10.1111/j.1467-6486.2005.00533.x

Pirolli, B. (2017). Travel journalists and professional identity: Ideology and evolution in an online era. *Journalism Practice*, 11(6), 740–759. https://doi.org/10.1080/17512786.2016.1193821

Pooley, J. (2010). The consuming self: From flappers to Facebook. In M. Aronczyk & D. Powers (Eds.), *Blowing up the brand* (pp. 71–89). New York: Peter Lang.

Robinson, S. (2006). The mission of the j-blog: Recapturing journalistic authority online. *Journalism*, 7(1), 65–83. https://doi.org/10.1177/1464884906059421

Steiner, L. (2018). Solving journalism's post-truth crisis with feminist standpoint epistemology. *Journalism Studies*, 19(13), 1854–1865. https://doi.org/10.1080/1461670X.2018.1498749

Tulloch, J. (2014). Ethics, trust and the first person in the narration of long-form journalism. *Journalism*, 15(5), 629–638. https://doi.org/10.1177/1464884914523233

Varricchio, E. (2023, 31 May). How authentic content creators build social media trust. *Forbes*. https://www.forbes.com/sites/forbesbusinesscouncil/2023/05/31/how-authentic-content-creators-build-social-media-trust/?sh=532e703363d7

Vodanovic, L. (2024). Confessional journalism, authenticity and lived experiences: A case study of news stories published during the Irish abortion referendum. *Journalism Practice*, 18(3), 571–586. https://doi.org/10.1080/17512786.2022.2049012

Vos, T. P., & Thomas, R. J. (2018). The discursive construction of journalistic authority in a post truth age. *Journalism Studies*, 19(13), 2001–2010. https://doi.org/10.1080/1461670X.2018.1492879

Wahl-Jorgensen, K. (2020). An emotional turn in journalism studies? *Digital Journalism*, 8(2), 175–194. https://doi.org/10.1080/21670811.2019.1697626

Zelizer, B. (1990). Achieving journalistic authority through narrative. *Critical Studies in Media Communication*, 7(4), 366–376. https://doi.org/10.1080/15295039009360185

Zelizer, B. (1992). *Covering the body: The Kennedy assassination, the media, and the shaping of collective memory*. University of Chicago Press.

11
CONSUMERISM, POPULAR CULTURE, AND RELIGION BETWEEN TWO CONTINENTS
The Turkish case

Nilüfer Türksoy

Introduction

A significant portion of the existing academic literature on the field of lifestyle journalism studies has primarily focused on contexts within the Western world or the Global North. This has left a considerable gap in our understanding of how lifestyle journalism is practiced and/or perceived in other regions. Most of the studies in this area have examined the production, content, and consumption of lifestyle journalism in countries like Australia, Germany, the United Kingdom, the United States, and other developed nations (see, Fusté-Forné & Masip, 2019; Rodrigues-Blanco & Cardenas-Hernandez, 2019; Hanusch & Hanitzsch, 2013). A small proportion of research has focused on Asia (see, Duffy & Ashley, 2012; Li, 2012) and the Middle East (see, Sayan-Cengiz, 2019; Hamid-Turksoy, Kuipers & Van Zoonen, 2014; Cocking, 2009). While these studies offer valuable insights into the practices and trends within their specific contexts, it is important to acknowledge that they might not comprehensively include the complexities present in different cultural, political, social, and economic environments. There is, then, a need for scholars to consider contexts outside the West or the Global North when studying lifestyle journalism. Since different cultures and societies may have different perspectives and approaches to lifestyle journalism, by exploring non-Western contexts, we can gain a more comprehensive understanding of the cultural factors that shape this genre of journalism. Turkey stands out as a case *par excellence* in this regard.

As Morris (2006, p. 3) points out, "Turkey remains mysterious to most outsiders. It's a complex country, hard to understand: secular and Muslim, Western and Eastern, all at the same time. It's modern and traditional, democratic and still authoritarian". It is "located at the geographical crossroads between Europe and Asia, but it is also a crossroads between extremely diverse, and sometimes contradictory, cultural and political models" (Roy, 2005, p. 11). This multifaceted image of the country provides an ideal context to examine whether there are any themes and characteristics that might differ from the established lifestyle journalism practices in the Global North or whether any commonalities are incorporated about contemporary global lifestyle trends and influences. By looking at the secular and Islamic lifestyle media outlets in Turkey, I focus on the patterns of consumption and hedonistic pleasure of Turkish people nowadays. Choosing Turkey as a case aligns with the observation made by Banjac and Hanusch (2022, p. 1607) that "the existing literature has tended to focus on countries with relatively prosperous economies, neglecting to explore those with greater socio-economic inequality". Gürgen (2022, p. 21) points out that Turkey has higher income inequality than European countries, while Ergul and Cakir (2019) note that there are serious wage, income, and consumption inequalities in Turkey. Since the socioeconomic conditions, media landscapes, and consumer behaviours in Turkey are different from those in the Global North, studying lifestyle journalism in the Turkish contexts can shed light on how it reflects the realities of diverse economic and social environments.

Background

By focusing on lifestyle journalism practices in Turkey, this chapter aims to uncover the main topics, practices, and experiences of this journalistic genre, dedicated to representing a wide range of themes relevant to the daily lives of Turkish people, including fashion, beauty, family life, relationships, travel, food, health, fitness, or mental well-being and spirituality. With its predominantly Muslim population, lifestyle journalism in Turkey serves as a platform to provide information, guidance, and inspiration to readers seeking to lead a Turkish lifestyle. Therefore, the overarching aim here is to provide a platform for cultural analysis and to expand our comprehension of the role of lifestyle journalism within the Turkish context. Drawing from the existing literature on popular culture, consumption practices, and lifestyle preferences among both secular and Muslim Turks, it explores how distinct identities are presented to various segments of society, through different media outlets with diverse political orientations, be it mainstream/commercial or conservative/Islamist. Here, lifestyle journalism reflects the cultural values, lifestyle choices, pleasures, and consumption patterns influenced by a particular culture (Hanusch, 2019; Hanusch & Hanitzsch, 2013). This form of popular news writing practice differs structurally from hard news in terms of language, pictorial content, and readership.

Turkey is a case in point as it occupies a contested and problematic position between the West and the East, at the same time representing the symbolic tensions between the modern/secular and traditional/conservative Turks. Despite the fact that "Turkey set her direction, unconditionally to the West" since the establishment of the Republic in 1923 (Sandikci & Ger, 2002, p. 465), the country often finds itself portrayed as the traditional 'oriental Muslim other' (Strasser, 2008; Wimmel, 2009), simultaneously inside and outside of Europe, as well as an underdeveloped nation on the European Union's doorstep (Strasser, 2008). Given Turkey is struggling to be a Westernized and modern country, it is, nevertheless, located outside the European Union borders and considered, by some (i.e., Haller, 2013; Tekin, 2010), as part of the Middle Eastern territory. Following the Muslim way of life, it is also largely constructed in the European imagination as uncivilized, patriarchal, and traditional (Wimmel, 2009). This tendency to view Muslims through an Islamophobic lens is not new and is documented in the works by Saeed (2007) and Poole and Richardson (2006). Turkey is no exception to this trend (Kaya, 2020). Framing Turkey predominantly through its Islamic identity reinforces existing biases and misconceptions. For instance, Öztürkmen (2005) notes in her research that some European tourists, especially those without higher education, "at times classify Turkey as 'backward' or among the classic 'Islamic Arab countries'" (p. 612).

Usually written in a light, fun, inspiring, and entertaining tone, the goods and services promoted through Turkish lifestyle media can reflect Turkish people's personal style, values, and aspirations. By choosing specific brands, products, or experiences that are being introduced to Turkish readers, individuals may seek to communicate their individuality, social status, or belonging to a particular group or sub-culture. Through the lenses of lifestyle journalistic practices in a Muslim-majority country (Muchtar et al., 2017), this chapter sets out to decipher what has been encouraged and what has been featured as a lifestyle in conservative media (supportive of Islamist ideology) and commercial media (supportive of Kemalist ideology) outlets.

This chapter makes two noteworthy contributions to the existing literature. Firstly, while academic circles have shown some interest in lifestyle journalism practices within Turkish media (Meşe, 2015; Bali, 2013; Arık, 2008), whether modern/secularist or traditional/Islamist, there is still a notable gap in scholarship regarding a comparative analysis. This analysis would draw from lifestyle journalism practices across both commercial and conservative media outlets. Secondly, it is generally agreed that the current landscape of Turkish politics is characterized by the ideological conflict between secularist/civilized/Westernized and conservative/pro-Islamic parties (Bayazit, 2016; Kejanlıoğlu, 2001). We see the same polarization and dualism in the contemporary Turkish media landscape, as Islamic media is competing with the secular media (Kaya & Çakmur, 2010). In Turkey, media is

> Characterized by a high level of concentration (that) is sharply divided into two major camps. On one side, there is the mainstream media, primarily concerned with increasing its commercial value through higher circulations/ratings; on the other side, there is a conservative/Islamist/pro-government media, chiefly involved in the dissemination of their viewpoints.
>
> *(Kaya & Çakmur, 2010, p. 533)*

From this perspective, the study undertakes the task of mapping the sociocultural transformation within the dichotomy of secularists versus Islamists, while also exploring their respective lifestyle and consumption patterns.

Here, it is important to highlight that Islamic modesty, in its new sense, is an urban and modern phenomenon. It is a symbol of the element of elegance, of the demand for distinctiveness. It has emerged as a characteristic of urban, modern, educated, middle and upper class, and devout and conservative women, replacing the traditional veiling that was previously linked with the dark face of Islam and stigmatized in the Western mindset with perceptions that included connotations of Islamic fundamentalism, oppression, extremism, rural areas, underdevelopment, backwardness, ugliness, exoticism, and lack of education (Meşe, 2015). Some of the major textile companies, owned by the Islamic bourgeoisie (Muslim high society or the green rich), merged veiling and modesty with fashion. In doing so, they not only sold clothing but also marketed an image and identity of how a veiled woman should appear through that clothing (Meşe, 2015). They meticulously constructed the modern and civilized face of Islam.

Given everyday life is, to some extent, shaped in connection with industrially encoded networks of commodity signs (Jansson, 2002), my examination of mainstream and Islamist media extends to a wide range of everyday consumption habits in various fields including fashion, culinary culture, artistic preferences, entertainment choices, urban lifestyle, and tourism patterns. By investigating the portrayal of these dimensions in secular and Islamic lifestyle media, this study offers a comprehensive and in-depth examination of different societal groups and their evolving identities, preferences, and consumption practices in non-Western contexts.

The succeeding sections provide an in-depth exploration of the evolution of lifestyle journalism, examining its production, editorial content, and its complex connection with consumer culture. I then turn my attention to the evolution of consumer capitalism and its impact on the current Turkish media landscape. I subsequently discuss the presentation of lifestyle in secular media. Lastly, I explore the portrayal of Islamic consumerism in the Islamic lifestyle media, simultaneously highlighting the symbolic content covered by these distinct media institutions.

Defining lifestyle journalism, consumer culture and the politics of lifestyle

There is a universal consensus that the media plays a pivotal and defining role in politics (Kaya & Çakmur, 2010). Numerous studies provide enough evidence that investigative journalists of the Western world perform crucial dissemination, analyst, watchdog, and gatekeeper roles in society (Hanitzsch, Hanusch, Ramaprasad & de Beer, 2019; Hanitzsch, 2007; Schudson, 2003; Harcup & O'Neill, 2001); they offer an independent critique of society and its institutions (McQuail, 2000). But, as confirmed by Hanitzsch and Vos (2017), journalism is not inherently a political institution. The majority of journalists do not exclusively cover political affairs and hard news; they also delve into culture, sports, fashion, lifestyle, and celebrities and cover good news (Hanusch, 2019, 2012; Campbell, 2004).

> The rise of celebrity and lifestyle journalism along with the blurring of news with public relations, advertising, image management, and entertainment has changed the nature of the field and now mainstream media no longer have a monopoly on the field of journalism.
>
> *(Brennen, 2009, p. 300)*

Journalists, thus, play significant roles in two domains: political life and everyday life (Hanitzsch & Vos, 2018).

There is a sizeable scholarship on lifestyle journalism, indicating that this form predominantly serves as a mediator of culture and the leisure industry. It holds ideological power to guide readers and provide help, advice, and information in various aspects of their daily lives (Hanusch & Hanitzsch, 2013; Stone, 2018). Lifestyle journalists may not always live up to professional expectations from their hard news counterparts, which is why their profession is open to questions of credibility. "The roles of journalism in everyday life map onto three interrelated spaces of everyday needs: consumption, identity, and emotion" (Hanitzsch & Vos, 2018, p. 157). Lifestyle journalism is considered integral to consumer culture, and it offers discussions on taste and aesthetics that guide consumers in shaping their way of life (Vodanovic, 2019; Kristensen & From, 2012; Featherstone, 1991). Here, it is significant to mention that consumption is not merely an act that fulfils basic needs (Ülken, 2015; Veblen, 1994). Instead, it addresses emotional, psychological, and social needs, while simultaneously carrying a symbolic value that signifies the pursuit of wealth, status, group belonging, personal gratification, and the desire to feel special and exclusive. Pierre Bourdieu (1984) comprehensively explores how social class influences individual preferences and aesthetic tastes and argues that individuals from higher social classes are more likely to possess and appreciate certain higher cultural tastes, while those from lower classes may have different and cheaper preferences.

Hanusch (2019) has revealed that lifestyle journalists aim to fulfil four key roles: they want to be service providers, life coaches, community advocates, and inspiring entertainers. There are similarities here to cultural journalism, service journalism, and consumer journalism. "Both lifestyle journalism and cultural journalism fall within the 'soft news' category, since both usually concern matters relating to the private sphere and do not represent breaking news" (Kristensen & From, 2012, p. 28). While the traditional notion of journalism has a close link with political affairs, lifestyle journalism is intertwined with the day-to-day lives of people (Hanusch, 2012). It provides judgments of taste (Fürsich, 2012); it offers readers guidance on matters of consumption and choices related to the softer aspects of life in an increasingly complex society (Kristensen & From, 2012). In doing so, lifestyle journalism addresses the reader as consumers rather than as citizens (Hanusch, 2012; Hanusch & Hanitzsch, 2013).

Another branch of studies has focused more on lifestyle journalism's close connection to commercial interests (Hanusch, Hanitzsch & Lauerer, 2017). For Fürsich, (2012, p. 17), there is a serious "duality between media that are important for an informed citizenry and popular media which frivolously focus on individual pleasure and consumption". Lifestyle journalism's intimate connection with the audience, its essential focus on current trends, and its tendency to blur the conventional boundaries between news and entertainment position it as a dynamic space for active cultural negotiation (Fürsich, 2012).

In Turkish academic literature, lifestyle is defined as a phenomenon consisting of symbolic values, such as dining in quality restaurants, emphasizing clothing and fashion, smoking the finest cigars, and possessing wine knowledge, all contributing to a culture of luxury consumption (Bali, 2013). Lifestyle journalism in Turkey has flourished in the aftermath of the coup d'état in September 1980. The dominant discourse within lifestyle journalism revolves around the sanctification of consumption (Dağtaş & Dağtaş, 2009). Arık (2008), who wrote the first master thesis on the topic in Turkey, titled *The Development of Lifestyle Journalism and the Fundamental Dynamics Behind It,* listed the characteristics of lifestyle journalism as the following (Arık, 2008, pp. 59–63): (1) It encourages consumption by attributing cultural and status values to goods; (2) It has an instructive style, guiding individuals towards specific actions; (3) it rationalizes leisure time by offering alternatives; (4) it creates an image, builds identity, and promises social prestige and status through the quality of life; (5) it advocates the promotion of companies through hidden or explicit advertising; (6) it targets a reader base with high spending capacity, capable of consumption, urbanized, and open to change; (7) it uses fashion as a tool; (8) it carries traces of the changes experienced by Western media and global culture; (9) it manifests itself in non-political areas; (10) it has elite role models; and (11) while advocating freedom and individuality, it essentially aligns individuals with the system and renders them passive.

The development of consumer capitalism and the contemporary Turkish media landscape

Neoliberal policies and practices, which took root in the mid-1980s, led to a profound transformation in the Turkish economy. The country entered a restructuring process characterized by a dominant free-market economy, limited state intervention in the market, the presence of an a-politicized social order, and the glorification of consumption (Pınar &

Dağtaş, 2023). As a result, Bali (2013) argues that passive readers were pushed into the position of active consumers.

Known as the Özal period (1983–1993), this era also witnessed rapid economic growth and expanded international trade (Dinç, 2014). Starting with this period, "many small- or medium-scale, mostly family-owned and Anatolian-based businesses that claim an Islamic identity were founded in this new economic environment. Most veiling-fashion companies fall into this category" (Gökarıksel & Secor, 2009, p. 11; also, in Demir, Acar & Toprak, 2004). Following these developments, the Turkish textile industry underwent rapid development. The liberalization and privatization of the economy during this period not only changed the lifestyle of urban secular elites but also gave rise to an Islamic bourgeoisie (professional, urban, upper/middle class, well-educated, and upwardly mobile young, religious people), inevitably paving the way for the commodification of Islam (Sandikci & Ger, 2002; Bali, 2013). Like new secular business establishments, new Islamic enterprises experienced rapid growth, providing an alternative market for individuals who held religious and conservative values, yet welcomed avant-garde consumption practices (Sandikci & Ger, 2002). The new religious elite Turks found conspicuous consumption to be the primary way to express their wealth and social status symbolically. Social status significantly influences consumption practices (Veblen, 1994). Historically, class stratification has also been manifested through the consumption of items such as cell phones, cars, and fashion. Consumption started to play a crucial role in the construction and expression of personal identity. Consumption, identity, and emotion, thus, influence one another (Banjac & Hanusch, 2022).

The economic consciousness established by old secular elites in society was also displayed in the media. Between the 1980s and 1990s, especially,

> The number of pornographic magazines published increased, television culture came to dominate, art became commodified with the sponsorship of big capital, and lifestyle magazines boomed, on food, entertainment, holidays, home styling, fashion and so on, disseminating the ideology of consumerism.
>
> *(Gencel Bek, 2004, p. 375)*

Magazines targeting young and solo individuals, taste and pleasure magazines, current affairs, and high-society magazines also started to be published in this period (Bali, 2013).

In the 1990s, another significant development unfolded as domestic private commercial channels began broadcasting via satellites from Europe: "Turkey has moved from a scarcity of images directly controlled by the state to an abundance of them, fueled by the competition among increasing numbers of commercial channels" (Öncü, 1995, p. 51). Commercial media began broadcasting a Western style of consumption characterized by massive, standardized, uniform culture (Öncü, 1995). Business norms entered the newsrooms (Bayazit, 2016). The notion of public broadcasting considering the public interest, which was active in media in the past, declined, and a commercial broadcasting approach began to be embraced in every aspect of the media (Pınar & Dağtaş, 2023). Today, "Turkish media markets are dominated by a handful of vertically integrated conglomerates with cross-ownership in almost every segment, supported by influential religious sects. These interests control more than 90% of advertising revenues" (Bayazit, 2016, p. 415). This new ownership structure is the driving force behind the profit-oriented and entertainment or relaxation-based content in the community press, where a popular and tabloid publishing concept is adopted (Pınar & Dağtaş, 2023). The media's close relationship with global capitalism has inevitably influenced its content, leading to increased sensationalism (Pınar & Dağtaş, 2023; Sayan-Cengiz, 2019; Gencel Bek, 2004).

Journalistic monitoring of society and of the social life of the upper and upper-middle class, well-defined as the "new elites", "new rich", or "Islamic bourgeois" by Bali (2013), has become widespread. Many Turkish commercial media outlets exclusively started to highlight "the values of a consumerist culture and promote a lifestyle that is practiced in the capitalist West" (Algan, 2003, p. 188). This view is also shared by Sandikci and Ger (2002), who maintain that in many developing countries, the proliferation of communication technologies and the growing exchange of goods and information pave the way for the adoption of pro-Western consumption values and practices. Lifestyles driven by consumption also incorporate values such as "Westernization", "modernization", and "improvement n" (Dağtaş & Erol, 2009, p. 171).

In today's Turkish media landscape, like in some other parts of the modern world, commercial media is full of articles on consumerism and a focus on lifestyle. Newspaper and magazine articles, entertainment programmes, and popular series and movies portray the luxurious and comfortable lives of local and international celebrities, encouraging individuals to engage in consumerism. The audience is encouraged to follow these celebrities by visiting the same restaurants, dressing like them, and spending their leisure time or engaging in similar activities (Baş, 2022). Torlak (2010) uncovers that individuals are guided by programmes, magazine supplements, columns, and headlines on matters such as how to dress, where to vacation, which activities to prefer, and where to dine (also in Stone, 2018). This means that the emergence of a commercialized popular press that largely focuses on entertainment also signifies the increasing dominance of consumerist content. The growing influx of popular Western brands and products has prominently featured in the private TV channels and the lifestyle sections of Turkish media, actively encouraging readers to adopt Western lifestyles. The growing number of lifestyle magazines and newspaper columnists covering popular topics such as dining, travel, and fashion is further proof of this ongoing trend.

Lifestyle portrayal in commercial Turkish media

In consumer society, consumption is regarded as a means of revealing and shaping individual identities. When the Turkish media employs the products and services it offers to the audience, it conveys subliminal messages about social status, prestige, personal identity, often emphasizing distinctiveness, and group belonging (Dağtaş, 2009; Baş, 2022).

The role of high-circulation newspapers in the 1990s

During the 1990s, high-circulation secular newspapers like *Hürriyet* and *Zaman* played a crucial role in shaping a cosmopolitan lifestyle through their weekend supplements. These publications delivered content that often encourages consumption as a status symbol and portrayed a lifestyle indicating social class. Notably, Ülken's (2012) research that analysed the content of the Friday supplements of the newspapers *Hürriyet* (with a secular ideology) and *Zaman* (with an Islamic ideology) uncovered that the *Hürriyet Friday* supplement suggested a Western style of consumption (e.g., the conversation revolved around dishes from world cuisines, entertainment in bars/night clubs, and alcohol). On the other hand, the *Zaman Friday* supplement prioritized traditional values with an emphasis on Islamic practices (e.g., the presence of mosques, masjids, worshiping places, emphasis on Turkish cuisine, and the use of halal-slaughtered meats where food is prepared according to Islamic rules).

In a separate study, Ülken (2015) examined lifestyle and consumer culture representations in the *Istanbul Life* magazine, which was established in 1996 and considered a significant example of lifestyle journalism. *Istanbul Life* covers a broad range of topics from stylish fashion and entertainment to sophisticated cultural events, thereby promoting a lifestyle associated with Western consumption (Ülken, 2015). Publications like *Istanbul Life* magazine have been instrumental in this regard, offering readers guidance on high-end living and upscale entertainment options which symbolize social privilege. Wine was presented as a symbol of nobility. Having a culture of alcoholic beverages was portrayed as a means of acquiring social privilege and status. The culture of drinks emerged as another expression of an exclusive lifestyle and was presented as an indispensable part of nightlife.

Consumer culture and lifestyle journalism

Studies from various scholars like Bali (2013) and Silsüpür (2016) highlight how lifestyle journalism has been shaped by and continues to reinforce consumer culture in Turkey. Festivals, for instance, stand out as a sign of civilized living. Social events are portrayed as markers of an elite lifestyle, thus fostering an exclusive image that aligns with capitalist interests (Bali, 2013). "While classical Western music emerges as a symbol of modern and Western lifestyle in Turkey, there is a common belief that jazz music also appeals to a culturally sophisticated segment," Bali (2013, pp. 163–165) argued.

Media's advertising influence and consumerism

Recent research points out that the content of lifestyle sections is heavily influenced by advertising pressures, with a significant emphasis on consumer goods and services that indicate luxury and exclusivity (Baş, 2022; Pınar & Dağtaş, 2023). This influence suggests a mutual relationship between media producers and advertisers in Turkey, aimed at crafting a consumerist narrative that aligns with the interests of capitalist groups. Silsüpür (2016), for instance, found out that a profound number of messages guided readers towards consumption, shopping, and to-do lists, conveying the message that by following their recommendations, readers could raise their status to the upper class and embrace a more elite, luxurious, and affluent lifestyle. The study by Utkan (2015) and Sine (2017) also concluded that the texts in the weekend supplements carried more advertising value than news value; they deliberately encourage consumption; just like the clothing brands, the venues target the elite with their prices, showcasing the exclusive lifestyle of this group. One of the most recent studies, conducted by Pınar and Dağtaş (2023), on two secular society magazines – *Alem* and *Şamdan Plus* – concluded that society magazines play an important role in shaping and popularizing consumer culture and lifestyles in Turkey. The authors observe that the structures and editorial processes of society magazines are dependent on advertisers, and the content is also shaped by the demands of advertisers. Consequently, these magazines serve as a market where they promote famous luxury consumption patterns, lifestyles, and items. In doing so, they serve the interests of capitalist groups (Pınar & Dağtaş, 2023). All these findings align well with the study of Hanusch, Hanitzsch, and Lauerer (2017), which found that lifestyle journalists are attractive to a broader range of advertisers, and they experience high pressure to meet advertisers' demands.

What these authors most stridently indicate is that mainstream newspapers' weekend supplements aim to provide exclusive content and present luxury consumer goods to readers. Lifestyle journalism in Turkey is used to present the lifestyle of an exclusive segment to the readers.

Portrayal of Islamic consumerism in Turkey's Islamic lifestyle media

The emergence of a group of new Islamist elites in Turkey during the 1980s, alternatively labelled as "Islamic capital", "Green capital", or "Anatolian tigers" (Mumyakmaz, 2014; Demir, Acar & Toprak, 2004), paved the way for the development of an Islamic consumer market, Islamic fashion, and the Islamization of urban lifestyles in the 2000s. Restaurants, supermarkets, fashion shows, banks, and new designs for veiling, all aligning with Islamic principles, became widespread. Gender-segregated luxury hotels and spas respecting the praying hours also gained prominence (Kılıçbay & Binark, 2002). The liberalization policies during the Özal period had an accelerating impact on the development of the Anatolian capital, and its rise led to the formation of a new class of religious–conservative consumers (Demir, Acar & Toprak, 2004). This, in turn, led to the rise of Islamic modesty as a commercial commodity, the growth of Islamic popular culture, and the simultaneous release of several Islamic fashion magazines at the end of 2011. This group of new religious elites aims to position itself as an alternative to the historically dominant Westernized and secular elite in the Turkish public sphere. This elite group crafts "new consumption practices – modern, casual and trendy clothes, natural goods, traditional cuisine, Ottoman culture and artifacts, alternative vacation and traveling […] – In an attempt to differentiate itself from the secularist moderns and other groups of Islamists" (Sandikci & Ger, 2002, p. 468).

In 2011, several Islamic lifestyle and fashion magazines covering clothing, health issues, and childcare from the Islamic perspective began publication to empower the voice of the Islamic community and serve the needs and expectations of the Islamic consumer market. The first Islamic women's magazine, *Âlâ*, often referred to as the Vogue for the veiled, has attracted 30,000 subscribers since its establishment in June 2011. Subsequently, there was an increase in the number of conservative and lifestyle magazines: *Hesna, Enda, Şems-i Tuba, İkra,* and *Aysha* commence their issues. This trend reflects the emergence of an Islamic bourgeoisie in Turkey. Some of these have evolved into online magazines (*İkra* and *Hesna*); some strive to be both women's and men's magazines, featuring relatively more conservative themes and visuals (*Semsi-i Tuba*); *Enda* tries to emphasize its identity more as a woman's and family or home magazine; *Âlâ* and *Aysha* stand out as the most popular fashion magazines, covering beauty, while often focusing on modest clothing styles, veiled fashion, and health tips following Islamic guidelines (Sayan-Cengiz, 2019). These magazines, as emphasized by Turkish sociologist Erkilet (2012), have significantly influenced the values of Muslims concerning class-based social differentiation, modesty, and piety. For example, when Dan Bilefsky from the *New York Times* covered *Âlâ* magazine, he used the following headline: "A fashion magazine unshy about baring a bit of piety" (29 March 2012).

The depiction of the relationship between women and fashion in Islamic women's magazines is controversial and paradoxical as it reveals a conflict between a lifestyle rooted in Islamic principles and a contemporary capitalist lifestyle (Kılıçbay & Binark, 2002). *Aysha* magazine, for instance, serves as a platform that unites the veiling industry and consumers, shaping them in alignment with class and aesthetic pleasures (Sandıkcı & Ger, 2010). It outlines an elite Muslim woman's identity by appealing to middle and upper-class women with its stylish and expensive clothing designs (Meşe, 2015). *Aysha* promises that readers can stay updated on the latest news in conservative and women's issues, lifestyle, latest fashion trends, style tips, health, religion, spirituality, children and motherhood, travel, food, and beauty topics. The magazine also features articles that support traditional gender roles as a reflection of a conservative lifestyle (Sayan-Cengiz, 2019; Meşe, 2015). The majority of advertisements both in Aysha and *Âlâ* feature well-known luxury consumer goods, including luxury leisure and Islamic tourism consumption (Sayan-Cengiz, 2019; Meşe, 2015). In this context, these two magazines not only integrate Muslim women into modern life through fashion but also, simultaneously, deconstruct their identity by presenting an exclusive narrative (Meşe, 2015).

Interestingly, and as noted by Meşe (2015), *Aysha* is full of interviews with Islamic clothing manufacturers and designers, but

> There is no mention of Islamic principles, rules, ethics, or aesthetic understanding. The discussions solely revolve around the terminology of capitalist economy, focusing on how to enhance the quality of Islamic clothing and transform it into an upper-class brand and a globally desirable fashion.
>
> *(Meşe, 2015, p. 150)*

Despite presenting fashion products with the same sales strategies and sharing similarities with secular media in terms of the targeted classes in the market, *Aysha* and *Âlâ* distinguish themselves by featuring topics such as dressing models with headscarves, having conservative clothing, discussing religious topics, and issues related to children and motherhood (Sayan-Cengiz, 2018; Meşe, 2015; Dinç, 2014). Moreover, many articles in these magazines emphasize that the man is the head of the family and that the woman should be a modest and virtuous mother and wife. At the same time, she should not "neglect her role and duty in maintaining the order of the household, ensuring family unity, and raising children" (Meşe, 2015, p. 150). *Aysha* distinguishes itself from secular media by not primarily emphasizing the inclusion of women in work life. Instead, it provides content aligned with Islamic teachings, promoting values such as modesty, piety, motherhood, and moral conduct that specifically resonate with women.

Applying a critical discourse analysis to the content in *Âlâ* magazine, Dinç (2014) found that the content presented in *Âlâ* was similarly targeted towards fashion-conscious Muslim women. In her study of the eroding symbolic significance of veiling, Sayan-Cengiz (2018) had found that *Âlâ* endeavours to harmonize piety, modesty, and beauty. "*Âlâ* uses the same language of style as other secular magazines", employing lexical terms such as stylish, pure, elegant, trend, natural, and harmonious outlook, to describe clothing and accessories featured in the magazine (Dinç, 2014, p. 655). Another aspect involves the photo shoot sections. Similar to other secular and glossy fashion magazines like *Vogue*, *Âlâ* features a photo shoot section, centred around a specific theme. In this section, veiled models with confident poses present various expensive fashions in a unique and glamourous urban setting (Dinç, 2014), transforming the veil into a chic, elegant, and even fetishized and seductive commodity. In the images found in *Âlâ*, women "look straight into the eyes of the spectator" (Sayan-Cengiz, 2018, p. 166).

While Islamic lifestyle and women's magazines continue their publications, specific criticisms have emerged, particularly from Islamic thinkers, suggesting that Islam and capitalism are inherently antithetical. According to Meşe (2015, p. 152), these criticisms revolve around points such as

> The corruption of modesty, the lack of attention to modesty principles, models being adorned with makeup and striking provocative poses, not reflecting Islamic ethics, presenting incorrect role models to the youth, and causing damage to the reputation of the religion.
>
> *Sayan-Cengiz (2018, p. 160)*

It is also discovered that "Âlâ is criticized for blurring the symbolic distinctions between what are marked as 'Islamic' and 'secular' identities in Turkey" and faced accusations of sexualizing the veil. The debate raises concerns about the intersection of media, ideology, and faith. Muslim intellectuals criticize lifestyle and women's magazines especially for undermining Islamic values by objectifying the Islamic conservative woman's body, which is a violation against the established Islamic values and principles that hold human dignity and modesty in high regard (Günenç, 2022; Pınar & Dağtaş, 2023). They criticize the modern capitalist system and consumer society, which are seen as consequences of Western civilization (Kılıçbay & Binark, 2002). This issue becomes even more sensitive when the *hijab* (headscarf) – a religious symbol – is used in commercial context, as it is an expression of identity and carries deeper political and religious significance. Therefore, when such symbols are presented in a way that is considered in line with commercial or capitalist aesthetics, it presents a challenge to the established status quo of Islamic religious practices in Turkey. It seems that lifestyle media distorts the religious symbol's intended meaning. Thus, it is fair to say that the commodification promoted via lifestyle magazines is potentially reshaping the understanding of faith and threatening the Muslim identity.

From a slightly different critical point of view, one of the founders of clothing sociology, Thorstein Veblen (2006), confirmed that a woman is an indicator of her husband's status. Veblen (2006) argues that engaging in conspicuous consumption serves as a demonstration of social status, and clothing is the area where this behaviour is best represented. He emphasises that "a Muslim woman image is emerging in which it is expected for her to dress in a way that showcases her spouse's wealth/status/class and display it in public" (cited in Erkilet, 2012, p. 38). Then, the products presented and advertised in Islamist women magazines are intended not for covering but for displaying (Erkilet, 2012). Thus, as acknowledged by Erkilet (2012), the image of women that Islamic women's magazines attempt to create refers to a Muslim woman who is expected to dress in a way that reflects her spouse's wealth, status, and class, displayed in public. Simultaneously, she is depicted as a passive entity devoid of freedom, serving as an indicator of her husband's status (Erkilet, 2012). This perspective aligns with Sandikci and Ger (2010, p. 18), who emphasize that "veiling indicates compliance to a patriarchal authority and signifies Muslim women's sub-ordination and lack of agency".

Conclusions

It is widely accepted that consumerism often leads to excessive waste, contributing to environmental degradation and resource depletion. Critics suggest that consumerism promotes a materialistic mindset, where personal worth and happiness are often tied to the possession of material goods (Trentmann, 2016). This can exacerbate social inequalities and can contribute to social stratification, particularly by creating a gap between those who can afford the products and those who cannot (Keeley, 2015; Bourdieu, 1984). Contrary to these criticisms, in their renowned book *The World of Goods*, Douglas and Isherwood (1978, p. 62) suggest focusing on consumerism's "capacity to make sense" and treat the material environment as an "information system" that provides us information about a particular society. In this chapter, my goal was to uncover the consumerist culture depicted in both commercial and Islamic lifestyle media. I treated lifestyle texts of mainstream and Islamic media as an information system that will enlighten the reader on how Turkish popular culture, taste, identity, and social class are embodied and represented within the discourse of consumerism and capitalism.

Lifestyle journalism practices in Turkey, just like in South Africa, are "mediating the worlds of luxury and inequalities" (Banjac & Hanusch, 2022, p. 1607). This genre of journalism predominantly focuses on crafting narratives tailored for heterogeneous audiences with a conservative and/or secular perspective, typically belonging to the middle, upper-middle, and high socioeconomic classes. Both Islamic media (i.e., conservative, traditional, and Ottoman) and secular media (i.e., civilized, modern, rationalist, urban, and European) have some features in common.

First, as proposed by Kristensen and From (2012), fashion is seen as a representation of lifestyles and a symbolic indicator of taste and personal style. The editorial policy of both conservative *Aysha* and *Âlâ* magazines, as well as the secular *Hürryet*, *Milliyet,* and *Sabah* newspaper's lifestyle articles, can be characterized as providing readers with suggestions about fashion, beauty, and style. A significant portion of the outfits featured in these articles consist of haute couture products by famous local or foreign fashion designers. This positioning simultaneously presents the reader as a stylish individual capable of affording upper-class consumption. Lifestyle articles, thus, serve as cultural artefacts; they construct a unique female image and embody a form of conspicuous consumption. Both secular and conservative lifestyle articles establish a sense of homogeneous identity among their readers, promoting shared consumption patterns and beauty ideals (Dinç, 2014; Sayan-Cengiz, 2019). However, these lifestyle articles also serve as a reflection of social, cultural, and economic changes in Turkey.

Second, in analysing commonly used words in the texts, terms such as being a style icon, being classy, beauty secrets, elegance, chic, passion, charm, keeping up with fashion, feeling like a star, shining, pushing the boundaries of luxury, being trendy, knowing the golden rules of shopping, gaining a sophisticated look, and feeling on top of the world are consistently used in *Âlâ* and *Aysha* magazines (Sayan-Cengiz, 2018; Erkilet, 2012). A similar terminology is employed by secular lifestyle media. When it comes to food, *Istanbul Life* magazine, for example, uses the following terminology: "The Most Classic", "The Most Bohemian", "The Coolest", "The Most Authentic", "The Most Metropolitan", and "The Most Nostalgic" (Ülken, 2015). Venues are described with labels such as noble, trendy, cool, favourite, and Parisian spirit, and are used as a means to gain prestige and status (Ülken, 2015). These phenomena are inherently global.

Third, cosmetic advertisements constitute a significant portion of Islamic lifestyle media and commercial media. Advertisements feature hundreds of make-up products, anti-aging skincare products, and haircare items produced by multinational companies. Their articles are full of ads for serums, powders, foundations, moisturizers, and perfumes. The only difference remains in the introduction of new cosmetics certified as world of luxury, comfort, and prestige, their primary target audience "consists of individuals who either belong to the upper class or carefully follow the lifestyles of the upper classes with admiration" (Pınar & Dağtaş, 2023, p. 60). Turkish lifestyle journalists, therefore, also aim to engage readers who may not currently belong to these classes but aspire to do so.

Future directions

In considering the broader implications of the Turkish context on a global understanding of lifestyle journalism, particularly in a de-Westernized framework, this chapter offers several areas that might be worth expanding upon: firstly, the visibility of Islamic values in the Islamic lifestyle media might lead researchers to question: how can cultural values, religious beliefs, and practices influence lifestyle journalism? This aspect can significantly contribute to de-Westernizing the study of lifestyle journalism by incorporating how different cultural and religious contexts affect media representation and consumption.

Secondly, future research on lifestyle journalism and its interplay with consumer culture could consider studying the relationship between lifestyle journalism and the construction of global identities. In other words, given this chapter outlines that Turkish lifestyle media and lifestyle journalism play a role in shaping and reflecting identities that are predominantly influenced by both local norms/Eastern traditions and global consumer trends/Western modernity, this dual influence can be explored to understand how lifestyle journalism contributes to the formation of hybrid identities within a complex global culture. Researchers could conduct comparative studies into how lifestyle media across different cultures – whether Muslim or Christian – integrate diverse cultural elements. Relevant questions might include: How do different cultural contexts adapt the global narrative of lifestyle and luxury to fit local social structures? What role does lifestyle journalism play in promoting global consumerist values among diverse populations, such as those in the Middle East, African, and non-European regions? Finally, it would be valuable to explore how the consumption-focused narratives of lifestyle journalism in Turkey impact readers' perceptions of their roles as citizens versus consumers. Researchers may ask: does engagement with lifestyle media match with political engagement or activism? In sum, these studies would contribute significantly to our understanding of lifestyle media's role in the evolving narrative of what it means to be a global citizen in a consumer-driven world.

Note

The author is responsible for all translations from Turkish to English.

Further reading

Bali, R.N. (2013). *Tarz-ı Hayat'tan Life Style'a Yeni Seçkinler, Yeni Mekanlar, Yeni Yaşamlar [From Stylish Life to Lifestyle: New Elites, New Places, New Lives]*. 8th Edition. Istanbul: İletişim Publishing.

Gökarıksel, B., & Secor, A.J. (2009). New transnational geographies of Islamism, capitalism and subjectivity: The veiling-fashion industry in Turkey. *Area*, 41(1), 6–18.

Meşe, İ. (2015). İslami bir moda dergisi örneğinde moda ve tesettür: Ne türden bir birliktelik? [A case of an Islamic fashion magazine, fashion, and modesty: What kind of partnership?]. *Fe Dergi: Feminist Eleştiri*, 7(1), 146–158.

Yel, A.M., & Nas, A. (2014). Insight Islamophobia: Governing the public visibility of Islamic lifestyle in Turkey. *European Journal of Cultural Studies*, 17(5), 567–584.

"halal" (permissible or lawful in Islamic law), which takes place only in Islamic lifestyle media (Erkilet, 2012). Advertisements emphasizing beauty salons, furniture stores, plastic surgery hospitals, hotels and resorts, airlines, and jewellers, which do not differ from those in secular lifestyle articles, are prominently featured in Islamic lifestyle media as important complements to public visibility (Erkilet, 2012; Dinç, 2014). In terms of travel and tourism, commercial media introduce Eurocentric destinations, highlighting touristic icons familiar to Western travellers. In contrast, Islamic lifestyle media provide information about Umrah, Mecca, and Madinah, along with Saudi Arabian tour operators, among the vacation options. Another distinction in Islamic lifestyle media is the emphasis on religion and family, a feature not commonly found in secular lifestyle media. Similar to all other secular lifestyle magazines, it is crucial to understand that *Âlâ* magazine and its successor *Aysha* operate within the capitalist framework of a fashion magazine and a commodity product, with its primary objective being profit-making (Sayan-Cengiz, 2018). Both magazines "produce much content that is in fact very similar to the content found in secular fashion magazines" (Sayan-Cengiz, 2018, p. 169). To address this issue, Dinç (2014, p. 661) maintains that "like other fashion magazine in Turkey, *Âlâ Dergisi* follows a distinct capitalistic logic". The ideal portrayal of women depicted in *Âlâ* and *Aysha* magazines closely aligns with that of 'modern' women. However, they are also religiously active and, at the very least, veiled (Dinç, 2014).

Despite my focus on a specific cultural, political, and socioeconomic context, I have shown that lifestyle journalism practices in Turkey, contents, themes, and narratives are not significantly different from the conventional/traditional lifestyle journalism practiced in the Global North. When comparing Turkish commercial media with Islamic media in terms of lifestyle journalism practices, I argue that they share more commonalities than differences. Similar to commercial lifestyle media covering the Western style of dressing, the practice of veiling in Islamic lifestyle media is also intricately linked to consumption, commodities, and patterns of pleasure and is influenced by both global and local trends within the market economy (Sayan-Cengiz, 2019; Kılıçbay & Binark, 2002).

Where commercial lifestyle media permits us to scrutinize the propagation of a modern and Western image through consumption, Islamic lifestyle media provides a parallel opportunity to explore the dissemination of images and narratives that shape emerging Muslim subjectivism. It crafts a commercial version of Muslim lifestyle culture, guiding Muslim consumers in a global discourse of Islamic identity articulated through consumerism. It creates a commercial portrayal of Muslim lifestyle culture, directing Muslim consumers into a global conversation about Islamic identity expressed through consumerism. The shared features observed in both secular and Islamic lifestyle media raise concerns about the increasing overlap between the Islamic and secular upper–middle classes, facilitated by consumerism and converging consumption patterns (Sayan-Cengiz, 2018). The perception of the Islamic way of life, once associated with backwardness, lack of education, and resistance to urbanization, experienced a transformation through consumption. It evolved into a lifestyle symbolizing urbanity, modernity, sophistication, and high social status (Navaro-Yashin, 2002).

In the context of Turkey, lifestyle journalism practice reflects the cultural values, social norms, and evolving lifestyle choices within Turkish society. I find that lifestyle media often package a world with rose-coloured glasses, a finding that aligns with those of Hanusch and Hanitzsch (2013). Additionally, I note that Turkish lifestyle journalists certainly do not target disadvantaged or working-class people, who only have a "taste of necessity" (Bourdieu, 1984), but rather focus on the rich or the crème de la crème class in Turkey. By mediating a positive

References

Algan, E. (2003). Privatization of radio and media hegemony in Turkey. In L. Artz and Y.R. Kamalipour (Eds.), *The Globalization of Corporate Media Hegemony*, pp. 169–193. Albany: State University of New York Press.

Arık, E. (2008). *Yaşam Tarzı Haberciliğinin Gelişimi ve Ardındaki Temel Dinamikler [The Development of Lifestyle Journalism and the Fundamental Dynamics Behind It]*. Selçuk University Social Sciences Institute, unpublished Master Thesis, Konya.

Banjac, S., & Hanusch, F. (2022). Aspirational lifestyle journalism: The impact of social class on producers' and audiences' views in the context of socio-economic inequality. *Journalism*, 23(8), 1607–1625.

Baş, M.N. (2022). Lifestyles presented in weekend supplements in the context of consumption culture. *International Journal of Media and Communication Research-MEDIAJ*, 5(2), 327–354.

Bayazit, H.K. (2016). Media ownership and concentration in Turkey. In E.M. Noam (Ed.), *Who Owns the World's Media? Media Concentration and Ownership Around the World*, pp. 387–424. New York: Oxford University Press.

Bourdieu, P. (1984[1979]). *Distinction: A Social Critique of the Judgement of Taste*. London: Routledge.

Brennen, B. (2009). The future of journalism. *Journalism*, 10(3), 300–302.

Campbell, V. (2004). *Information Age Journalism: Journalism in an International Context*. London: Arnold.

Cocking, B. (2009). Travel journalism: Europe imagining the Middle East. *Journalism Studies*, 10(1), 54–68.

Dağtaş, B. (2009). *Reklam Kültür Toplum [Advertising Culture Society]*. Ankara: Ütopya Publishing House.

Dağtaş, B., & Dağtaş, E. (2009). Tüketim kültürü, yaşam tarzları, boş zamanlar ve medya üzerine bir literatür taraması [Literature review on consumer culture, lifestyles, leisure time, and media]. In B. Dağtaş and E. Dağtaş (Eds.), *Medya, Tüketim Kültürü ve Yaşam Tarzları [Media, Consumer Culture and Life Styles]*, pp. 27–75. Ankara: Ütopya Publishing House.

Dağtaş, B., & Erol, D.D. (2009). Yaygın medyanın haftasonu eklerinde tüketime dayalı yaşam tarzı sunumları [The weekend supplements of the mainstream media and the presentations of lifestyles]. In B. Dağtaş and E. Dağtaş (Eds.), *Medya, Tüketim Kültürü ve Yaşam Tarzları*, pp. 167–201. Ankara: Ütopya Publishing House.

Demir, Ö., Acar, M., & Toprak, M. (2004). Anatolian tigers or Islamic capital: Prospects and challenges. *Middle Eastern Studies*, 40(6), 166–188.

Dinç, C. (2014). Veiling and (fashion-) Magazines – 'Âlâ Dergisi' Magazine as a case for a new consumer image of a new devout middle class in Turkey. *The Journal of International Social Sciences*, 7(34), 650–665.

Duffy, A., & Ashley, Y.Y. (2012). Bread and circuses: Food meets politics in the Singapore media. *Journalism Practice*, 6(1), 59–74.

Ergul, I.N., & Cakir, B. (2019). Inequality in Turkey: Looking beyond growth. Retrieved online from https://arxiv.org/pdf/1910.11780.pdf on 18 April 2024.

Erkilet, A. (2012). Mahremiyetin dönüşümü: Değer, taklit ve gösteriş tüketimi bağlamında "İslami" moda dergileri [Transformation of privacy: "Islamic" fashion magazines in the context value, imitation and conspicuous consumption]. *Birey ve Toplum*, 2(4), 27–39.

Featherstone, M. (1991). *Consumer Culture and Postmodernism*. London: Sage.

Fürsich, E. (2012). Lifestyle journalism as popular journalism: Strategies for evaluating its public role. *Journalism Practice*, 6(1), 12–25.

Fusté-Forné, F., & Masip, P. (2019). Food and journalism: Storytelling about gastronomy in newspapers from the U.S. and Spain. In L. Vodanovic (Ed.), *Lifestyle Journalism: Social Media, Consumption and Experience*, pp. 129–140. London: Routledge.

Gencel Bek, M. (2004). Tabloidization of news media: An analysis of television news in Turkey. *European Journal of Communication*, 19(3), 371–386.

Günenç, E.B. (2022). The conservative woman body and modernization practices in the context of consumption culture: The example of Âlâ and Aysha magazines. *KILAD-Kocaeli Üniversitesi İletişim Fakültesi Araştırma Dergisi*, 19, 38–69.

Gürgen, V.S. (2022). Why is income inequality rigid in Turkey? Some evidence and a theoretical framework. *Ekonomik Yaklaşım, 33*(122), 21–44.

Haller, M. (2013). The image of Turkey in Europe today. *European Review, 21*(3), 327–335.

Hamid-Turksoy, N., Kuipers, G., & Van Zoonen, L. (2014). "Try a taste of Turkey": An analysis of Turkey's representation in British newspapers' travel sections. *Journalism Studies, 15*(6), 743–758.

Hanitzsch, T. (2007). Deconstructing journalism culture: Towards a universal theory. *Communication Theory, 17*, 367–385.

Hanitzsch, T., Hanusch, F., Ramaprasad, J., & de Beer, A. (2019). *Worlds of Journalism: Journalistic Cultures Around the Globe*. New York: Columbia University Press.

Hanitzsch, T., & Vos, T.P. (2018). Journalism beyond democracy: A new look into journalistic roles in political and everyday life. *Journalism, 19*(2), 146–164.

Hanitzsch, T., & Vos, T.P. (2017). Journalistic roles and the struggle over institutional identity: The discursive constitution of journalism. *Communication Theory, 27*, 115–135.

Hanusch, F. (2012). Broadening the focus: The case for lifestyle journalism as a field of scholarly inquiry. *Journalism Practice, 6*(1), 2–11.

Hanusch, F., Hanitzsch, T., & Lauerer, C. (2017). 'How much love are you going to give this brand?' Lifestyle journalists on commercial influences in their work. *Journalism, 18*(2), 141–158.

Hanusch, F., & Hanitzsch, T. (2013). Mediating orientation and self-expression in the world of consumption: Australian and German lifestyle journalists' professional views. *Media, Culture & Society, 35*(8), 943–959.

Hanusch, T. (2019). Journalistic roles and everyday life: An empirical account of lifestyle journalists' professional views. *Journalism Studies, 2*(2), 193–211.

Harcup, T., & O'Neill, D. (2001). What is news? Galtung and Ruge revisited. *Journalism Studies, 2*(2), 261–280.

Jansson, A. (2002). The mediatization of consumption: Towards an analytical framework of image culture. *Journal of Consumer Culture, 2*(1), 5–31.

Kaya, A. (2020). Right-wing populism and Islamophobism in Europe and their impact on Turkey–EU relations. *Turkish Studies, 21*(1), 1–28.

Kaya, R., & Çakmur, B. (2010). Politics and the mass media in Turkey. *Turkish Studies, 11*(4), 521–537.

Keeley, B. (2015). *Income Inequality: The Gap between Rich and Poor*. OECD Insights, Paris: OECD Publishing.

Kejanlıoğlu, D.B. (2001). The media in Turkey since 1970. In D. Lovatt (Ed.), *Turkey Since 1970: Politics, Economics and Society*, pp. 111–135. London: Palgrave Macmillan.

Kılıçbay, B., & Binark, M. (2002). Consumer culture, Islam and the politics of lifestyle: Fashion for veiling in contemporary Turkey. *European Journal of Communication, 17*(4), 495–511.

Kristensen, N.N., & From, U. (2012). Lifestyle journalism: Blurring boundaries. *Journalism Practice, 6*(1), 26–41.

Li, S. (2012). A new generation of lifestyle magazine journalism in China: The professional approach. *Journalism Practice, 6*(1), 122–137.

McQuail, D. (2000). *McQuail's Mass Communication Theory*. London: SAGE.

Morris, C. (2006). *The New Turkey: The Quiet Revolution on the Edge of Europe*. London: Granta Books.

Muchtar, N., Hamada, B.I., Hanitzsch, T., Masduki, A.G., & Ullah, M.S. (2017). Journalism and the Islamic worldview: Journalistic roles in Muslim-majority countries. *Journalism Studies, 18*(5), 555–575.

Mumyakmaz, A. (2014). Elitlerin yeni yüzü, İslami burjuvazi [The new face of the elites: Islamic bourgeoisie]. *Mustafa Kemal University Journal of Graduate School of Social Sciences, 11*(27), 367–382.

Navaro-Yashin, Y. (2002). *Faces of the State: Secularism and Public Life in Turkey*. Princeton: Princeton University Press.

Öncü, A. (1995). Packaging Islam: Cultural politics on the landscape of Turkish commercial television. *Public Culture: Society for Transnational Cultural Studies, 8*, 51–71.

Öztürkmen, A. 2005. Turkish tourism at the door of Europe: Perceptions of image in historical and contemporary perspectives. *Middle East Studies, 41*(4), 605–621.

Pınar, L., & Dağtaş, E. (2023). Tüketim kültürü ve yaşam biçimleri çerçevesinde cemiyet dergilerinin eleştirel ekonomi politik çözümlemesi [Critical ecopolitical analysis of society magazines within the framework of consumer culture and lifestyle]. *Akdeniz İletişim*, *40*, 46–73.

Poole, E., & Richardson, J.E. 2006. *Muslims and the News Media*. London: I.B. Tauris.

Rodrigues-Blanco, S., & Cardenas-Hernandez, D. (2019). The impact of social media in lifestyle journalism in Mexico: Serving citizens versus creating consumers. In L. Vodanovic (Ed.), *Lifestyle Journalism: Social Media, Consumption and Experience*, pp. 77–88. London: Routledge.

Roy, O. (Ed.) (2005). *Turkey Today: A European Country?* London: Anthem Press.

Saeed, A. (2007). Media, racism and Islamophobia: The representation of Islam and Muslims in the media. *Sociology Compass*, *1*(2), 443–462.

Sandikci, Ö., & Ger, G. (2010). Veiling in style: How does a stigmatized practice become fashionable? *Journal of Consumer Research*, *37*, 15–36.

Sandikci, Ö., & Ger, G. (2002). In-between modernities and postmodenities: Theorizing Turkish consumptionscape. *Advances in Consumer Research*, *29*, 465–470.

Sayan-Cengiz, F. (2019). Reconciling religion and consumerism: Islamic lifestyle media in Turkey. In L. Vodanovic (Ed.), *Lifestyle Journalism: Social Media, Consumption and Experience* (pp. 53–65). London: Routledge.

Sayan-Cengiz, F. (2018). Eroding the symbolic significance of veiling? The Islamic fashion magazine Âlâ, consumerism, and the challenged boundaries of the "Islamic neighborhood". *New Perspectives on Turkey*, *58*, 155–178.

Schudson, M. (2003). *The Sociology of News*. New York: W.W.Norton

Silsüpür, Ö. (2016). Popüler ve tüketim kültürü bağlamında gazetelerin hafta sonu eklerinde sundukları yaşam tarzları [Lifestyles that newspapers present in their weekend supplements within the context of popular and consuming culture]. *İnönü Üniversitesi İletişim Fakültesi Elektronik Dergisi*, *1*(1), 122–138.

Sine, R. (2017). Tüketim kültürü bağlamında yazılı basında hafta sonu ekleri [Weekend supplements in the print media: From the context of consumer culture]. *Abant Kültürel Araştırmalar Dergisi*, *2*(4), 94–113.

Stone, M.J. (2018). Eat there! Shop here! Visit that! Presenting the city in mass media travel writing. *Current Issues in Tourism*, *21*(9), 998–1013.

Strasser, S. (2008). Europe's other: Nationalism, transnationals and contested images of Turkey in Austria. *European Societies*, *10*(2), 177–195.Tekin, B.Ç. (2010). *Representations and Othering in Discourse: The Construction of Turkey in the EU Context*. Amsterdam: John Benjamins Publishing Company.

Torlak, Ö. (2010). Gündelik hayatta tüketime yön veren değerlerdeki değişim [The change in values shaping everyday consumption]. In R. Şentürk (Ed.), *Tüketim ve Değerler*, pp. 203–214. İstanbul Ticaret Odası Publications.

Trentmann, F. (2016). *Empire of Things: How We Became a World of Consumers, from the Fifteenth Century to the Twenty-First*. New York: Harper Collins.

Utkan, O. (2015). Magazin eklerinde tüketimin özendirilmesi: Köşe yazıları üzerine bir inceleme [Encourage consumption in magazine supplements: A study on column articles]. *Gümüşhane Üniversitesi İletişim Fakültesi Elektronik Dergisi*, *3*(2), 96–111.

Ülken, F.B. (2015). İstanbul Life Dergisi'nde yaşam tarzı sunumu [Lifestyle representation in Istanbul Life Magazine]. *Karadeniz Teknik Üniversitesi İletişim Fakültesi İletişim Araştırmaları Dergisi*, *9*, 39–57.

Ülken, F.B. (2012). Hafta sonu eklerinde mekân tasarımları [Place design in weekend supplements of newspapers]. *Selçuk İletişim Dergisi*, *7*(2), 156–167.

Veblen, T. (2006). *Conspicuous Consumption: Unproduction Consumption of Goods Is Honourable*. 58, 335th Edition. New York: Penguin Books.

Veblen, T. ([1899] 1994). *The Theory of the Leisure Class*. New York: Penguin Books.

Vodanovic, L. (2019). *Lifestyle Journalism: Social Media, Consumption and Experience*. London: Routledge.

Wimmel, A. (2009). Beyond the Bosporus? Comparing public discourse in the German, French and British quality press. *Journal of Language and Politics*, *8*(2), 223–243.

PART III

Lifestyle journalism, emotion and identity

12
ASPIRATIONAL LIFESTYLE JOURNALISM

Sandra Banjac

Introduction

To aspire is to have the capacity to imagine a future in which you possess or are able to achieve something not yet realized or present in your life. It is something people may experience throughout their life to different degrees and across varying contexts. As a concept, aspiration, therefore, refers to cognitive aspects of goal-setting and goal-directed motivations and behaviour such as gaining access to higher education, cultivating stronger relationships, volunteering at local organizations, owning a home, becoming well regarded within the workplace, or being healthy. However, not all have equal ability and power to aspire. The capacity to aspire may be found more readily in people who have a bigger archive of experiments with "the good life" or concrete experiences with success that equip them with the "navigational capacity" to form aspirations (Appadurai 2004: 69). In other words, the extent to which people can aspire and go on to realize those aspirations can depend on their access to lived experiences that have exposed them to examples of possibilities. Rooted in a rich body of scholarship in (social) psychology and sociology, the concept of aspiration allows us to highlight inequalities across societal fields (Baillergeau and Duyvendak 2022; Baker 2017; Gale 2015), and as this chapter shows, also within journalism.

Among journalists, to aspire towards enacting certain behaviour, such as providing audiences with timely information and news, is to have a role. Journalist aspire to perform certain roles and functions within society as a way of fulfilling what they believe is their duty to the public. Lifestyle journalists seek to provide audiences with an orientation for how to manage their lives, perform their lifestyles, and articulate their identity (Hanusch and Hanitzsch 2013). They offer audiences journalistic content that speaks to three key dimensions of everyday life: emotion or facilitating affective experiences and mood management, identity or providing orientation for management of the self and developing a sense of belonging, and consumption or exposure to products and services that allow audiences to enact lifestyles (Hanitzsch and Vos 2018). To reach audiences within these realms of everyday life, lifestyle journalists provide entertainment and relaxation, news-you-can-use and advice, introduce audiences to products and services, foster a positive attitude towards life, and show audiences exemplars of desired lifestyles (Hanusch and Hanitzsch 2013). It is in showing audiences these exemplars of desired lifestyles that we begin to see traces of aspiration as journalists invite audiences to imagine alternative ways of living and being. Indeed, in a study of journalists and audiences in South Africa, one of the most dominant role orientations articulated by lifestyle journalists was to *provide aspiration* to audiences; and in turn, for audiences, receiving aspiration was among the most dominant expectations that they had of lifestyle journalists (Banjac and Hanusch 2022). To provide aspiration was to expose audiences to products and service that they could imagine at some point having themselves and to share with audiences success stories of ordinary people that they could look up to and imagine a future in which they too achieve such success.

In post-apartheid South Africa, lifestyle journalism has empowered previously oppressed communities to express their identities through conspicuous consumption rather than identity categories imposed on them by the apartheid regime (Wasserman 2010). Conspicuous consumption refers to accessing goods that visibly signal status or class position, while inconspicuous consumption is understood as an understated form of status-making through subtle but equally luxury goods and services (Currid-Halkett et al. 2019). In that way, lifestyle journalism potentially acts as a tool for audiences to nurture their capacity to aspire towards desirable future selves, albeit within the realm of social class. Whereas glossy magazines tend to appeal to the aspirations of the elite, tabloids do so for audiences with a lower economic capital (Wasserman 2010). Conscious of class stratification, for lifestyle journalists, providing aspiration involved having an attuned awareness of gradations of affordability across their audiences (Banjac and Hanusch 2022). As such, journalists saw themselves as mindful marketers, tasked with both manipulating the economy of wants and needs and discouraging explicit conspicuous consumption. For audiences, to aspire was to be equally cautious of conspicuous consumption and to fashion alternative ways of meeting aspirational goals through more accessible and affordable means (I elaborate on this later on in the chapter).

While social class mediated aspiration in this study of lifestyle journalists and audiences and is a key structuring principle of the social space in Bourdieusean work, other forms of power such as gender and race tend to be discussed in passing, although these intersect to dictate cultural distinctions within society (Veenstra 2005). To that end, this chapter reengages the concepts of *doxa* and *habitus* (Bourdieu 1984) to account not only for classed predispositions and tastes for cultural products and lifestyles but also gendered and racialized ideals found within society and reflected in lifestyle journalism and how these interact with aspiration. This approach echoes a growing focus within journalism scholarship on exposing power inequities and injustices in journalism. This chapter expands on previous iterations on aspiration in relation to lifestyle journalism (Banjac and Hanusch 2022) by offering new cross-disciplinary insights into conceptualizations of 'aspiration' and how they may help us highlight more critically the societal contribution of lifestyle journalism. This chapter is structured around Zipin et al.'s (2013) conceptualizations of three forms of aspiration, *doxic aspirations* (that reflect dominant ideals), *habituated aspirations* (based on one's individual situated experience), and *emerging aspirations* (those imagined beyond the constraints of *doxa* and *habitus*). Inspired by this work, I discuss how these aspirations may be present and explored within lifestyle journalism as a site where journalists and audiences construct and challenge aspirations and experience inclusion and exclusion.

Aspiration

Aspiration captures one's hope, ambition, or plan for achieving or gaining access to something, material or otherwise. Conceptually, aspiration can be traced to self-determination theory, which argues that all individuals have an innate motivation towards psychological growth and development and the fulfilment of basic needs (Ryan and Deci 2000). Here, aspirational goals can be both extrinsic or intrinsic and can influence an individual's psychological and physical wellbeing (Kasser and Ryan 1996). While extrinsic aspirational goals gain value through external validation and include financial success, social recognition, and an appealing appearance, intrinsic aspirational goals carry inherent value and include achieving affiliation and meaningful relationships, community feeling through helpfulness and contributions, and self-acceptance or personal growth (Kasser and Ryan 1996).

Useful conceptualizations of aspirations have been developed within sociology, and in particular education, where the connection between social class and education has been examined. Here, Bourdieu's concept of (cultural) capital and access to education is seen to reproduce (dis)advantage (Bourdieu and Passeron 1990). Within this focus, a number of studies have shown how social class shapes young people's aspirations and identified ways in which classed aspirations are embedded in educational policies. Among 12- and 13-year-old school-going children in the United Kingdom, Archer et al. (2014) found that although all children showed high aspirations for diverse occupations, their *habitus* and access to capital (especially cultural and social) influenced what occupations they aspired towards and what they felt was 'for them' and what cultivated these aspirations (family social network or hobbies, among others). Television was a key source for young people across social classes to form occupational aspirations (Archer et al. 2014), which parallels findings that lifestyle journalism as a medium was also a source of aspiration for adults across the social class spectrum (Banjac and Hanusch 2022). Applying the social class lens to understand the formation or withering of aspirations, however, does not always account for how people from similar classed life trajectories show diverse processes in aspiring. Developing the 'capacity to aspire,' (Appadurai 2004) or the ability to imagine a desirable future and realize it, depends on a number of factors in one's life that may or may not facilitate experiences from which to draw inspiration and form aspirations. These may include a young person's migrant descent and networks with diasporic communities, as well as school-based career education initiatives and mentorship programmes to discover occupational possibilities and interests that they may not be exposed to in their immediate social networks (Baillergeau and Duyvendak 2002). While these settings broaden the options to image a future, young people's capacity to aspire can be mired in contradictions between their own aspirations and the aspirations others (e.g., parents) have for them—contradictions that could render the person powerless to plan their future.

Beyond classed analysis, aspirations are shaped by "moral meanings" or normative beliefs and attitudes, including what young people think they should become and who they think they should be. Aspiring to higher education is informed not only by the normative value of credentials and succeeding in the labour market but also by how it contributes to young people's self-development and values central to their identity (Baker 2017). Education is perceived as affording status and respect and a moral superiority over peers who show less commitment to gaining education—an idea that highlights the normative power of certain societal and cultural beliefs in shaping aspirations. We see similar symbolic distinction-making among audiences' classed perceptions of their own consumption of culturally 'superior' forms of news (quality journalism) and those of the 'Other' who consumes tabloids and lifestyle journalism (Lindell 2020; Banjac 2021). What people aspire towards can thus be shaped by what is socially ideal and normalized by dominant beliefs and assumptions, even when those aspirations do not reflect people's lived experiences and conditions—a disconnect that has been problematized (Gale 2015). To explore what this disconnect might look like and how it can inform studies of lifestyle journalism, the rest of the chapter is organized around what Zipin and colleagues (2013) refer to as *doxic aspirations* (socially desirable), *habituated aspirations* (personal experience), and *emergent aspirations* (imagined futures).

Doxa *and aspirations*

The hierarchy of what is socially desirable or worthy of aspiring towards, in Bourdieusian terms, is maintained by the *illusio* or the belief that some forms of cultural production are more legitimate than others and that participating in this legitimacy game (or *doxa*) is worth playing (Bourdieu 1984). *Doxa*, as conceptualized by Bourdieu, refers to the unspoken rules and presuppositions that define and organize action within a specific field. Within the journalistic field, such rules and presuppositions refer to the dominant norms and practices that define what journalism is (Benson and Neveu 2005). These go on to shape journalists' imagined selves, their motivations for the work they want to do and are able to do, and the journalistic content they go on to produce. News reproduces dominant doxic ideals for social reality and arguably what one aspires to become or how one aspires to (not) be seen. Patterns of "class disgust'" are found in British news media's reporting on White working-class women who appropriate African American popular culture (Tyler 2008: 19). Killers in US school shootings are framed either as children or as 'one of us' (normalized and invisible) or as the criminal 'other' depending on their race and social class (Leavy and Maloney 2009). Media rely on classed, racialized, and gendered narratives to diminish the talents and belonging of athletes within different sports (Foote 2003; Buffington and Fraley 2008). In their coverage of Indigenous and White women, news media reproduce stereotypes through insidious racist, sexist, and classist belief systems (Gilchrist 2010).

Within lifestyle journalism across genres—fashion and beauty, health and fitness, gardening, food, travel, music and arts, and parenting, among others—we see similar dominant gendered, classed, and racialized ideals of what life could look like. Aspiring towards culturally legitimate or socially desirable forms of being is what we might understand as a *doxic* logic for aspiring. Zipin et al. (2013) define *doxic aspirations* as aspirations founded on taken-for-granted beliefs and assumptions defined by those with power about what is normatively desirable in everyday life. They argue these are often grounded in individualist neoliberal ideologies and meritocratic principles of hard work and self-responsibility over one's success, mediated in populist discourses such as news and popular culture. This raises the question: What types of doxic aspirations for lifestyles might be embedded in journalists' articulations of their work and what they are aiming to achieve and in the content that audiences encounter within the online and offline pages of lifestyle journalism? What follows is a discussion of lifestyle journalism as a space within which doxic ideals might be reproduced, constructing an archive of possible socially desirable lifestyles and ways of being—and thus aspirations.

Lifestyle journalism and doxic aspirations

Semiotic, content, and discourse analyses of lifestyle magazines have found a variety of gendered and racialized norms reinforced within its glossy pages. Yoga magazines in the United States and the United Kingdom feature on their covers models that are primarily White, in their 20s and 30s, and embodying a thin and lean body shape and aesthetic (Webb et al. 2017). Analysing advertisements placed in the magazines *Playboy* and *Men's Health* and *Cosmopolitan* in Croatia, Lončar et al. (2016: 3124-5) found that the men depicted tend to be young, White, attractive and muscular, fully dressed in formal clothing, and are most frequently found in fashion advertisements. They are portrayed primarily as "consumer bodies" promoting the consumption of products and services; as "instrumental bodies" that are emblematic of success and achievement; and as "objectified bodies" with a focus on the "erotic male" often gazing directly at the reader (otherwise commonly found among depictions of female bodies). *Men's Health* and *Women's Health* in the United States reinforce similar gendered body stereotypes on their covers, with both magazines objectifying men's and women's bodies equally; the women's magazine by promoting stereotypical ideals of feminine beauty and thin bodies and the men's magazine by promoting muscular body ideals (Bazzini et al. 2015). Investigating beauty ideals in the editorial content and cover pages of fashion magazines *Cosmopolitan*, *Glamour*, and *Marie Claire* and health magazines *Shape*, *Fitness*, and *Women's Health*, Conlin and Bissell (2014) found that although the women in the fashion magazines were more often depicted as glamorous, appearance and thinness as a body ideal was emphasized across both types of magazines.

Travel magazine content and advertising also engage in cataloguing behaviour, distinguishing between legitimate and illegitimate travellers and destinations. In-flight magazine advertisements produce, mediate, and reproduce the norms and values associated with socially and culturally acceptable types of travellers who are rich in mobility, money, and time to pursue luxury travel products and services (Small et al. 2008). A discourse analysis of travel magazines in Australia, the United Kingdom, and the United States revealed travel writers' imaginations of their readers reinforce the tourist–traveller opposition. Rather than constructing their imagined readers as tourists seeking homogenous mass experiences, journalists wrote for autonomous travellers seeking authentic experiences—an imagined readership that was an extension of the journalist's own anti-tourist self-identity (McWha et al. 2016). Travel journalists have demonstrated in their articulation of roles a commitment to being cultural mediators and critics, with an ethical concern for reporting on foreign places and cultures in ways that do not reinforce stereotypes and criticize harmful aspects of tourism (Hanusch 2011).

Within food journalism, which spans the provision of recipes and meal ideas to structural issues affecting food security and access, literature highlights nationalist, classed, and gendered ideals. In Singapore, food journalism has played a key social and political function in constructing a national identity and positioning the country as a global cultural destination (Duffy and Ashley 2012). Across newspapers in Canada and the United States, Oleschuk (2019) found that news on food recognized the structural challenges affecting low-income families or working parents in their efforts to afford and prepare healthy meals in a market saturated with cheap processed and ready-made ones. However, in the solutions the articles proposed, responsibility was individualized and gendered and placed in the hands of mothers. Gale (2015: 258) problematizes such individualization to argue that the fulfilment of aspiration is often understood as "private troubles" with cultural or psychological origins and solutions (i.e., lack of motivation), rather than a public problem rooted in structural inequalities that requires structural solutions. In other words, for the disadvantaged, aspiration needs to be understood as something that is mediated by possibility. Intersecting with issues of public health, recipes in food magazines have been found not to comply with standard nutritional recommendations, potentially exposing readers to an unhealthy diet (Muharemovic et al. 2016).

There is no shortage of gendered discourses within parenting magazines. Content, advertising, and images in parenting magazines reinforce gendered stereotypes about parents and children by implicitly targeting mothers and drawing distinctions between male children as athletic and stronger and appearance as more important for girls (Greve Spees and Zimmerman 2003). Mothers are constructed around contested and contradictory roles that reinforce experiences of motherhood as a double bind; mothers as selfish or selfless, fostering in their children independence or dependence, succeeding or failing in either the private or public sphere of life, and mothers as intuitive or needing expert help (Johnston and Swanson 2003). The portrayal of fathers in parenting magazines is equally gendered. Among US magazines, Schmitz (2016) found evidence of hegemonic ideals of masculinity, with fathers portrayed more often as breadwinners and resilient figures of authority fearful of emasculation than as parents.

Across these examples and genres of lifestyle journalism, we see doxic—normatively dominant—distinctions drawn around ideal forms of appearance, health, travel, food, and parenting, among others not reviewed here. While this discussion offers a bleak view into lifestyle journalism as projecting harmful ideals, lifestyle journalists in their articulations of their roles seek to enable audiences to experience essential aspects of everyday life, including entertainment and inspiration, access to useful information and advice on products and services, see examples of different lifestyles, and also to be aware of ethical and moral dimensions of certain lifestyles and lifestyle industries (albeit to a lesser extent) (Hanusch 2019). In a similar critical vein, lifestyle journalists also aim to celebrate Black culture, local and national identities, and food, as well as empower women by dismantling patriarchal ideas, problematize the fashion industry, and offer emotional guidance and support (Banjac and Hanusch 2022), among many other roles. This prompts the question: to what extent do journalists' role aspirations end up reflected in content.

Lifestyle journalists produce this content within broader doxic principles structuring the journalistic field, within which soft-versus-hard-news hierarchies are reproduced. Distinctions are drawn by journalists and audiences who produce and have a taste for consuming lowbrow (tabloid, popular media) and highbrow (quality, broadsheet) cultural products (i.e., news). Whereas highbrow cultural products are perceived to include quality journalism that reports on the economy and politics, that is, issues of legitimate concern for the functioning of a public sphere, lowbrow cultural products refer to popular forms of journalism, such as tabloids and lifestyle journalism whose concerns are seen to lie with the less legitimate private domain of everyday life. The latter refers to symbolic products associated with the poor, uneducated, working, "uncultured classes," while the former is associated with "high culture" and refers to the consumption of products preferred by the educated elite (Grabe 1996).

Who has the authority and legitimacy to decide which forms of journalism and knowledge are most valuable and relevant for society? Journalists across genres engage in discursive struggles to claim their belonging within the field and define its contours. Political journalism or 'hard' news is perceived as contributing to an informed citizenry, while popular forms of journalism or 'soft' news "frivolously focus on individual pleasures and consumption" (Fürsich 2012: 17). Indeed, political journalists draw on gendered discourses to delegitimize lifestyle journalism as 'fluffy', and lifestyle journalists have to some extent internalized such gendered characterizations, perceiving themselves and their work as trivial (Banjac & Hanusch 2023; Hanusch & Hanitzsch 2013). Cultural journalists, as highlighted by scholars as increasingly indistinguishable from lifestyle journalists (Kristensen & From 2012), also occupy a space of precarious cultural legitimacy. Perceived as neither cultural critics nor fully journalists, cultural journalists are 'doubly dominated'—holding subordinate positions in both the journalistic and cultural fields. They are critiqued by journalists as lacking autonomy from cultural sources and by cultural producers as lacking the legitimate cultural taste to truly enrich the public (Hovden and Knapskog 2015). We see such distinctions drawn by audiences as well. White middle- and upper-class audiences disparage cultural products such as tabloid and lifestyle journalism, seeing them as 'mindless' content consumed by working-class Black audiences, thus symbolically distancing themselves from those they perceive as the 'Other' (Banjac 2021). This despite the fact that tabloids provide a vital service to audiences marginalized at the intersection of class and race, whose lived experiences and the politics of everyday are neglected by mainstream journalism (Wasserman 2010; Ndlovu 2021). Such discourses around doxic ideals among journalists and audiences are symbolic acts of distinction that position them within power and define for those outside of that domain of power what they should aspire towards.

The above discussion on lifestyle journalism is not exhaustive, but it begins to illustrate how doxic societal norms and structures of power define that which is desirable and potentially invites audiences of lifestyle journalism to develop doxic aspirations about legitimate and illegitimate forms of health and beauty, travel and leisure, food and nutrition, and being a parent, among other realms of life. Although lifestyle journalism serves a valuable societal function of prioritizing the private sphere of life and offering audiences fodder for aspiration about living their best life, we also need to problematize dominant portrayals of the good or ideal life and the types of aspirations it might be promoting. In other words, what do such doxic aspirations do for those who do not possess the means to enact them? Zipin et al. (2013) argue doxic aspirations are ideas of "desirable futures" that are achievable for those rich in capital and power, but fall into the realm of fantasy for the socio-economically marginalized. As such, futures that are normatively desirable or worthy of aspiring towards, the authors argue, "function to reproduce inequality by inducing many to affirm out-of-reach aspirations, disappoint themselves in pursuing them, and come to conclusions that their supposed deficits make them incapable of achieving the aspirations that doxic logic valorizes" (Zipin et al. 2013: 233). The following section unpacks this disconnect between aspirational ideals and the predisposed resources one has to realize them.

Habitus and aspirations

Journalistic content is produced by journalistic actors who are not neutral actors but themselves embody predispositions and beliefs about what is socially and culturally worthy (Hovden 2008). Often, that which is consecrated as valuable by journalism stands in stark contrast to that which audience communities and journalists with diverse lived experiences and funds of knowledge deem valuable and worthy of public attention. Herein lies the disconnect between doxic aspirations and what Zipin and colleagues call *habituated aspirations*. Where doxic aspirations are articulations of normatively desirable goals, habituated aspirations exist within the limits of one's own *habitus* or socially constituted and deeply internalized dispositions (ways of knowing and being) and structures of power relations (Zipin et al. 2013). A person's *habitus* is shaped by socialization, exposure to diverse experiences, opportunities, and struggles that shape their sense of self (Bourdieu 1984). The nature of these experiences and thus predispositions is shaped by diverse factors and structures of power, including a person's access to various forms and volumes of capital, such as cultural (education, embodied knowledge), economic (money, assets), social (networks, relationships), and symbolic (recognition, prestige) (Bourdieu 1986). While access to capital positions one within the classed social space, that position is maintained or contested through oppositional 'tastes' for distinct cultural products and practices, which shape a person's lifestyle (Bourdieu 1984). Taste is a system of "cultivated dispositions"—a set of internalized preferences for specific cultural practices and goods that are structured by and structure class distinctions (Bourdieu 1984: 13). Our taste or distaste for art, music, and food, among other things, is formed through early childhood and lifelong socialization and interaction with cultural products and institutions. As such, taste shapes both how lifestyle journalists think about the journalism they produce and audiences' consumption and interpretation of said journalism (Banjac and Hanusch 2022). Markers of "taste" can present themselves in non-material ways through "embodied" capital (how people think, speak, or behave) and as "objectified" or "materialized" capital (house or car owned, social recognition) (Bourdieu 1986).

Fashion, a key aspect of lifestyle journalism, is one such materialized symbol of class inclusion and exclusion. Upper classes engage in "symbolic struggle" for the exclusive appropriation of unique cultural products and practices and abandon them as soon as these have been absorbed and popularized by the masses (Blumer 1969). Classes wealthier in capital volume are said to possess a "taste of luxury" associated with rarity, which they enact to signal class belonging and to distinguish themselves from the lower classes who are relegated to a "taste of necessity" associated with 'vulgar' and 'modest' practices and goods that fulfil functional needs and aspire towards higher-class belonging (Bourdieu 1984: 175-6). Speaking in extremes, such symbolic contests play out between those who eat high-end cuisine in restaurants and shop exclusive brands and those who eat fast food and seek out highstreet fashion. By participating in this ongoing game of exclusive appropriation and mass imitation of cultural products, the upper classes maintain and legitimize the "natural" hierarchy and distinction between legitimate and popular culture (Bourdieu 1984: 250). Having said that, how taste has been interpreted in past scholarship against specific forms of cultural capital and highbrow versus lowbrow cultural products has been critiqued as reflecting taken-for-granted and outdated classification regimes, that have been problematised—a discussion that is outside the scope of this chapter, but requires further attention (for overview, see Nault et al. 2021). Drawing on critical race theory, Yosso (2005) has argued that cultural capital among communities of colour is researched through the lens of deficit (absence of traditionally revered forms of culture) and repositions it to highlight the often-unrecognized forms of cultural knowledge and skills necessary for marginalized groups to navigate social and racial injustice. People in possession of such knowledge and skills are enriched with aspirational capital (a resilience to lived conditions by hoping for and imagining a different future) and resistant capital (ways of resisting oppression).

Lifestyle journalism and habituated aspirations

For Bourdieu, taste was primarily conceptualized within the context of social class, although predispositions for specific cultural products and experiences (lifestyles) are formed at its intersection with other domains of power, such as gender and race (among many others). To that end, what journalists produce is shaped by their unique intersectional lived experiences and knowledge-worlds. Likewise, what audiences aspire to may or may not correspond to the doxic aspirations they encounter within lifestyle journalism.

Journalism is a field of cultural production, and journalists as tastemakers—often composed of those with origins in the social elite—are in a position to deem as worthy certain cultural products over others, and in doing so, reproduce cultural hierarchies within society (Hovden 2008). Beyond social class, however, race plays a role in journalists' ability to imagine their possible selves and be an active agent in shaping the focus of their work. Black journalists experience being pigeonholed into covering Black stories where their racial identity needs to be foregrounded, while at the same time, media organizations and newsroom cultures demand of Black journalists to suspend their racial identity in order to fit a (White) professional ideal (Slay and Smith 2011). Long before journalists are socialized within newsrooms and organisations, such classed, but also gendered and racialized inclusion and exclusion, begins with journalism education, which fosters in emerging journalists a mentality that lacks appreciation for diverse worldviews (Hoffmann 1991). Journalists are taught to evaluate newsworthiness not only on values found within journalism textbooks but also on what they "know" (familiar lived experiences) and what they "love" (passions, interests, and tastes): pedagogical strategies that promote a homogenous journalism (Alemán 2014: 79). Indeed, lifestyle journalists are often motivated to enter the field because it offers them the "opportunity to do what they love", a passion cultivated early in life, which is negotiated vis-à-vis institutional and newsroom expectations (Perreault and Bélair-Gagnon 2024).

Who journalists are and the audiences they are able to speak to is further complicated by journalism's institutional ideology, which smooths over journalists' unique intersectional identities, lived experiences, and knowledge systems and socializes them to do journalism in a way that speaks to the needs and wants of dominant social groups. Journalists write for audiences that they imagine to be extensions of themselves, reinforcing a homophily between journalists and audiences who share similar *habitus* (Coddington et al. 2021). Audiences, as well, mobilize their diverse news consumption practices and preference and the value they ascribe to a specific quality or popular news formats to reinforce their class belonging (Lindell 2020; Hartley 2018). Scholarship of cultural omnivorousness has challenged ideas of homophily to argue that people across social classes appreciate and consume both high- and low-brow culture. While this appeared at first to be an equalizing force flattening taste hierarchies, the power to signal cultural open-mindedness remains with the elite (Peterson and Kern 1996; Nault et al. 2021).

Even in the way journalists imagine their work and their audiences and how audiences imagine themselves and the journalism they consume, suggests a disconnect between dominant (doxic) norms and personal or occupational (habituated) aspirations of journalists and audiences. Journalists cannot mobilize their unique standpoints and lived realities when producing lifestyle content and the ideals embedded in them, as these are socialized out of them to reflect broader societal norms and ideals. The effects of these processes have been captured within journalism broadly, but it is not as clear how they shape lifestyle journalists' experiences of disconnect between habituated and doxic aspirations. Do female journalists who happen to be mothers find it jarring to purport in their work contradictory gendered and parental roles? Do health writers whose own bodies do not resemble those they display in lifestyle magazines experience dissonance? Are travel journalists aware of gradations of affordability when writing for their audiences? Do food journalists who themselves may be exhausted parents or have origins in working class experiences realize they are reinforcing individualist rather than structural solutions to issues of public health and food security? In that sense, habituated aspirations are a person's estimation of the probability of achieving imagined futures within the realm of possibilities and resources available to them (Zipin et al. 2015). Put differently, a parent may aspire to feed their children healthy food but may not have the economic resources to do so or structural support to offset economic struggles. Looking back to some of the literature discussed in the previous section on doxic aspirations within lifestyle journalism, we see that intersecting with social class, journalists may experience a disconnect between doxic and habituated aspirations that are racialized and gendered, too.

In turn, we may ask how audiences negotiate doxic lifestyle aspirations against their more realistic habituated aspirations. Does a woman who happens to be a working-class mother experience guilt for serving affordable processed meals or challenge the individualist solutions proposed by food journalism? Are men and women cautious in their aspirations to emulate the health and beauty standards found within health journalism? Aesthetic doxic aspirations imposed on the body are gendered and racialized in the different ways that primarily White men and women are portrayed to ought to look like in health magazines (Webb et al. 2017; Lončar et al. 2016), although people draw on their intersectional lived experiences and lifestyles to form habituated aspirations that render achieving such aesthetic ideals impossible. For those consuming parenting magazines, doxic aspirations are found within contradictory gendered and classed tropes as to what it means to be a good mother or father (Johnston and Swanson 2003; Schmitz 2016), while the reality of parenthood for many looks vastly different, reflected in their habituated aspirations. Someone who consumes travel journalism may aspire to be a traveller setting off on authentic adventures immersed in local culture (McWha et al. 2016), but their situated *habitus* and available capital may curtail the possibilities of realizing such a doxic aspiration, ultimately to be replaced by a more realistic habituated aspiration of engaging in affordable mass tourism. What kind of life does lifestyle journalism tell us is worth aspiring to and to what extent can these be achieved within the possibilities of one's lived realities and the structural limitations that surround it. Such contradictions between doxic and habituated aspirations are what Zipin et al. (2013: 234) describe as "mood swings between habituated sobriety and doxic fantasy in aspiring".

While the disconnect between doxic and habituated aspirations is palpable and points us towards acknowledging structural inequality, when people are presented with opportunities to imagine alternative futures, these experiences can empower them to engage in envisioning emergent expectations (Zipin et al. 2013). Despite lifestyle journalism's potential contribution to aspirational tensions, the following section also argues that lifestyle journalism can offer exemplars of lifestyles to audiences who may have little concrete experiences of such lifestyles and as such could act as a capacitating tool for them to envision desired futures while transcending dominant ideals and the limitations of their *habitus*.

Imagined futures and aspirations

Emergent aspirations refer to a person's capacity to be an active agent in desiring, imagining, articulating, and pursuing alternative futures that exceed or reimagine rather than reproduce the limits of their *habitus*. Enabling the expression of emergent aspirations requires both resourcing and capacitating; the former refers to individuals drawing on their "lifeworld-based funds for knowledge" or their past lived experiences to reimagine their futures, while the latter refers to providing people with opportunities to cultivate and voice such aspirations (Zipin et al. 2013: 239). The resources people have at their disposal to reimagine their futures may be vastly unequal; however, they also enrich people with unique archives of experiences that, capacitated by aspirational lifestyle journalism as a tool, audiences can use to challenge hegemonic ideals and envision possible futures. For example, popular TV programmes with positive depictions of Black characters in various situations and contexts equip audiences with both aspirational and resistant capital to imagine ways of engaging and connecting with others, deal with life's dilemmas, and resist stereotypical portrayals of their communities (Stamps 2020). In post-apartheid South Africa, soap operas similarly have been sites of resistance, cultivating among audiences what Jacobs (2019: 63) calls "aspirational politics" or new ways of making sense of changing racial attitudes within the country. What these studies suggest is that for lifestyle journalism to challenge existing gendered, racialized, and classed doxic aspirations, it would need to consciously portray the good life as more inclusive of diverse ways of living and being. To some extent, lifestyle journalists in South Africa, aware of racial and class diversity, attempt to represent in their work products and services across gradations of affordability and depict diverse people and realities (Banjac and Hanusch 2022).

Somewhere between negotiating dominant institutional ideals of journalism, their professional and personal *habitus*, and their imaginations of their audiences, lifestyle journalists have been found (as noted at the start of this chapter) to want to provide their audiences with aspiration. Providing aspiration was a vital aspect of not only what lifestyle journalists sought to offer their audiences but also what audiences expected to receive from lifestyle journalists and content (Banjac and Hanusch 2022). On the one hand, many of the lifestyle journalists, having adopted dominant doxic aspirations about what good lifestyles are, targeted aspirational lifestyle products and service to audiences that they perceived to have sufficient cultural and economic capital to appreciate and afford it (*aspiration through consumption*). On the other hand, they sought to offer audiences, especially those they perceived as economically marginalized, *aspiration through motivation and hope*, by sharing with them stories of success achieved by people like them. The latter of these types of aspirations, Zipin et al. (2013) argue, represent "subcultural doxic aspirations" or a "model of actually achieved aspiration from a marginalized locale" that seems innocuous but presents audiences with a fantasy that very few will achieve. Such aspirations encourage audiences to "leap at doxic straws" in their efforts to "emulate the aspirations of 'the haves'" (Zipin et al. 2013: 235).

At the same time, looking at audiences' expectations for aspiration and how they interpret lifestyle content makes me somewhat optimistic that lifestyle journalism can also act as a tool for audiences to navigate the limits of their own *habitus* while articulating and enacting their aspirations. Across the social class spectrum, indeed, audiences aspired to what might be seen as doxic aspirations for decorating their homes as those seen in magazines, buying trending fashion and recommended beauty products or stating that 'one day…' they too will succeed as did others like them depicted in the stories they consumed (Banjac and Hanusch 2022). However, the same audiences across the class spectrum also critiqued the economic risks of pursuing doxic aspirations and negotiated ways around their *habitus*, by creating their own clothes or buying more affordable versions. In some cases, audiences even rejected doxic aspirations that lean towards consumption, arguing their sense of community and the values they derive from that were far more important. Challenging the deficit-driven argument that working-class people have merely a "taste of necessity" (Bourdieu 1984: 175), the study by Banjac and Hanusch (2022) showed that socioeconomically disadvantaged audiences of lifestyle journalism have a 'taste of aspiration' with a relative choice over how they pursue and realize such aspirations with limited economic capital. While these examples of audiences' interpretations of lifestyle journalism may not suggest concrete evidence of emergent aspirations, they begin to suggest their potential to emerge with lifestyle journalism as a capacitating tool. Such counter-cultures to dominant doxic aspirations is a fascinating avenue of future research within lifestyle journalism scholarship.

Conclusion

This chapter sought to illustrate that aspiration, to greater or lesser extent, is a vital component of every person's life and, by extension, is an aspect of lifestyle journalism's key function of providing people with an orientation for everyday life. Aspiration is embedded not only in lifestyle journalism's content in the way of presenting audiences with ideas for how to live their best lives but is also found in what journalists as their unique selves (are able to) portray to their audiences as desirable or worthy and what audiences as their unique selves expect from journalists and the content they consume. As the scholarship reviewed in this chapter shows, however, not all lifestyles are treated equal. The way we as scholars go on to investigate aspirational thinking and behaviour within lifestyle journalism, therefore, requires a critical lens that exposes dominant normative ideals for the good life and the model person. Inspired by the works of Zipin, Sellar, Brennan, and Gale (2015) and many others, this chapter lays out a potential framework for examining doxic, habituated, and emergent aspirations, as found in lifestyle journalism content and among its producers and consumers.

Drawing on methods such a critical and multimodal discourse analysis, future studies could examine different types of doxic aspirations present not only in traditional lifestyle journalism commonly found in magazines and sections of newspapers but also in diverse social media platforms, such as Instagram or TikTok, increasingly fulfilling similar functions (see, e.g., Maares and Hanusch 2020). Beyond the studies discussed in this chapter, such a project would offer journalism studies a more comprehensive and systematic insight into how popular forms of journalism shape dominant ideals of the good life and person.

Behind lifestyle journalism as a product are journalists with a unique personal and occupational *habitus*, confronted by institutional norms, values, and hard-soft genre hierarchies and economic considerations—all of which are orchestrating doxic decisions about what constitutes the ideal life and to whom such content should appeal. Future studies could, therefore, investigate the *habitus* of lifestyle journalists, editors, and content producers, vis-à-vis the doxic content they produce to understand where their ideals stem from (themselves, the institution of journalism, and commercial imperatives) and how they navigate and negotiate any dissonance that emerges.

Ultimately, journalism exists because of its audiences. How consumers of lifestyle journalism interpret its doxic aspirations vis-à-vis their habituated aspirations, whether they see themselves represented or excluded, and how they process these aspirations to potentially envision emergent aspirations are questions that warrant further research. As the scholarship reviewed in this chapter begins to show, audiences not only expect from lifestyle journalism aspiration but also reject certain aspirational ideals (Banjac and Hanusch 2022), which invites further inquiry into what happens after this rejection. If lifestyle journalism, even when it aims to speak to diverse audiences, fails to reach them, it ultimately fails to fulfil its mandate of offering diverse people diverse guidance on the private sphere of everyday life—a service as important as any other that claims to speak to the public (or political) sphere of life.

Further reading

Appadurai, A. (2004). The capacity to aspire: Culture and the terms of recognition. In V. Rao & M. Walton (Eds.), *Culture and public action* (pp. 59–84). Stanford: Stanford University Press.

Bourdieu, P. (1984). *Distinction: A social critique of the judgement of taste*. Harvard University Press.

Yosso, T. J. (2005). Whose culture has capital? A critical race theory discussion of community cultural wealth. *Race Ethnicity and Education*, 8(1), 69–91.

Zipin, L., Sellar, S., Brennan, M., & Gale, T. (2015). Educating for futures in marginalized regions: A sociological framework for rethinking and researching aspirations. *Educational Philosophy and Theory*, 47(3), 227–246.

References

Alemán, S. M. (2014). Locating whiteness in journalism pedagogy. *Critical Studies in Media Communication*, 31(1), 72–88.

Appadurai, A. (2004). The capacity to aspire: Culture and the terms of recognition. In V. Rao & M. Walton (Eds.), *Culture and public action* (pp. 59–84). Stanford: Stanford University Press.

Archer, L., DeWitt, J., & Wong, B. (2014). Spheres of influence: What shapes young people's aspirations at age 12/13 and what are the implications for education policy? *Journal of Education Policy*, 29(1), 58–85.

Baillergeau, E., & Duyvendak, J. W. (2022). Dreamless futures: A micro-sociological framework for studying how aspirations develop and wither. *Critical Studies in Education*, 63(2), 196–211.

Baker, W. (2017). Aspirations: The moral of the story. *British Journal of Sociology of Education*, 38(8), 1203–1216.

Banjac, S. (2021). An intersectional approach to exploring audience expectations of journalism. *Digital Journalism*, 1–20, 128–147.

Banjac, S., & Hanusch, F. (2022). Aspirational lifestyle journalism: The impact of social class on producers' and audiences' views in the context of socio-economic inequality. *Journalism*, 23(8), 1607–1625.

Banjac, S., & Hanusch, F. (2023). The struggle for authority and legitimacy: Lifestyle and political journalists' discursive boundary work. *Journalism*, 24(10), 2155–2173.

Bazzini, D. G., Pepper, A., Swofford, R., & Cochran, K. (2015). How healthy are health magazines? A comparative content analysis of cover captions and images of women's and men's health magazine. *Sex Roles*, 72, 198–210.

Benson, R., & Neveu, E. (2005). Introduction: Field theory as a work in progress. In R. Benson & E. Neveu (Eds.), *Bourdieu and the Journalistic Field* (pp. 1–25). Cambridge: Polity.

Blumer, H. (1969). Fashion: From class differentiation to collective selection. *The Sociological Quarterly*, 10(3), 275–291.

Bourdieu, P. (1986). The forms of capital. In J. Richardson (Ed.), *Handbook of theory and research for the sociology of education* (pp. 241–258). Greenwood.

Bourdieu, P. (1984). *Distinction: A social critique of the judgement of taste*. Harvard University Press.

Bourdieu, P., & Passeron, J.-C. (1990). *Reproduction in education, society and culture* (2nd ed.). London: Sage.

Buffington, D., & Fraley, T. (2008). Skill in Black and White: Negotiating media images of race in a sporting context. *Journal of Communication Inquiry*, 32(3), 292–310.

Coddington, M., Lewis, S. C., & Belair-Gagnon, V. (2021). The imagined audience for news: Where does a journalist's perception of the audience come from? *Journalism Studies*, 22(8), 1028–1046.

Conlin, L., & Bissell, K. (2014). Beauty ideals in the checkout aisle: Health-related messages in women's fashion and fitness magazines. *Journal of Magazine Media*, 15(2).

Currid-Halkett, E., Lee, H., & Painter, G. D. (2019). Veblen goods and urban distinction: The economic geography of conspicuous consumption. *Journal of Regional Science*, 59(1), 83–117.

Duffy, A., & Ashley, Y. Y. (2012). Bread and circuses: Food meets politics in the Singapore media. *Journalism Practice*, 6(1), 59–74.

Fürsich, E. (2012). Lifestyle journalism as popular journalism. *Journalism Practice*, 6(1), 12–25.

Foote, S. (2003). Making sport of Tonya: Class performance and social punishment. *Journal of Sport and Social Issues*, 27(1), 3–17.

Gale, T. (2015). Widening and expanding participation in Australian higher education: In the absence of sociological imagination. *The Australian Educational Researcher*, 42(2), 257–271.

Gilchrist, K. (2010). "Newsworthy" victims? Exploring differences in Canadian local press coverage of missing/murdered Aboriginal and White women. *Feminist Media Studies*, 10(4), 373–390.

Grabe, M. E. (1996). Tabloid and traditional television news magazine crime stories: Crime lessons and reaffirmation of social class distinctions. *Journalism & Mass Communication Quarterly*, 73(4), 926–946.

Greve Spees, J. M., & Zimmerman, T. S. (2003). Gender messages in parenting magazines. *Journal of Feminist Family Therapy*, 14(3–4), 73–100.

Hanitzsch, T., & Vos, T. P. (2018). Journalism beyond democracy: A new look into journalistic roles in political and everyday life. *Journalism*, 19(2), 146–164.

Hanusch, F. (2019). Journalistic Roles and Everyday Life. *Journalism Studies*, 20(2), 193–211.

Hanusch, F. (2012). Broadening the focus. *Journalism Practice*, 6(1), 2–11.

Hanusch, F. (2011). A profile of Australian travel journalists' professional views and ethical standards. *Journalism*, 13(5), 668–686.

Hanusch, F., & Hanitzsch, T. (2013). Mediating orientation and self-expression in the world of consumption: Australian and German lifestyle journalists' professional views. *Media, Culture & Society*, 35(8), 943–959.

Hartley, J. (2018). 'It's something Posh people do': Digital distinction in young people's cross-media news engagement. *Media and Communication*, 6(2), 46–55.

Hoffmann, G. (1991). Racial stereotyping in the news: Some general semantics alternatives. *ETC: A Review of General Semantics*, 48(1), 22–30.

Hovden, J. F. (2008). *Profane and Sacred: A study of the Norwegian journalistic field*. University of Bergen.

Hovden, J. F., & Knapskog, K. (2015). Doubly dominated. *Journalism Practice*, 9(6), 791–810.

Jacobs, S. (2019). *Media in postapartheid South Africa: Postcolonial politics in the age of globalization*. Indiana University Press.

Johnston, D. D., & Swanson, D. H. (2003). Undermining mothers: A content analysis of the representation of mothers in magazines. *Mass Communication and Society*, 6(3), 243–265.

Kasser, T., & Ryan, R. M. (1996). Further examining the American dream: Differential correlates of intrinsic and extrinsic goals. *Personality and Social Psychology Bulletin*, 22(3), 280–287.

Kristensen, N. N., & From, U. (2012). Lifestyle journalism: Blurring boundaries. *Journalism Practice*, 6(1), 26–41.

Leavy, P., & Maloney, K. P. (2009). American reporting of school violence and 'people like us' A comparison of newspaper coverage of the Columbine and Red Lake school shootings. *Critical Sociology*, 35(2), 273–292.

Lindell, J. (2020). Battle of the classes: News consumption inequalities and symbolic boundary work. *Critical Studies in Media Communication*, 37(5), 480–496.

Lončar, M., Vučica, Z. Š., & Nigoević, M. (2016). Constructing masculinity through images: Content analysis of lifestyle magazines in Croatia. *International Journal of Humanities and Social Sciences*, 10(10), 3447–3450.

Maares, P., & Hanusch, F. (2020). Exploring the boundaries of journalism: Instagram micro-bloggers in the twilight zone of lifestyle journalism. *Journalism*, 21(2), 262–278.

McWha, M. R., Frost, W., Laing, J., & Best, G. (2016). Writing for the anti-tourist? Imagining the contemporary travel magazine reader as an authentic experience seeker. *Current Issues in Tourism*, 19(1), 85–99.

Muharemovic, K., Taboul, N., & Håkansson, A. (2016). Home cooking trends and dietary illness: nutritional compliance of recipes in a Swedish food magazine 1970–2010. *Scandinavian Journal of Public Health*, 44(2), 195–201.

Nault, J.-F., Baumann, S., Childress, C., & Rawlings, C. M. (2021). The social positions of taste between and within music genres: From omnivore to snob. *European Journal of Cultural Studies*, 24(3), 717–740.

Ndlovu, K. (2021). Tabloids in Zimbabwe: A moral-ethical research agenda. In Martin Conboy and Scott Eldridge II (Eds.), *Global Tabloid: Culture and technology* (pp. 75–92). Routledge.

Oleschuk, M. (2019). "In today's market, your food chooses you": News media constructions of responsibility for health through home cooking. *Social Problems*, 67(1), 1–19.

Perreault, G. P., & Bélair-Gagnon, V. (2024). The lifestyle of lifestyle journalism: How reporters discursively manage their aspirations in their daily work. *Journalism Practice*, 18(7), 1641–1659.

Peterson, R. A., & Kern, R. M. (1996). Changing highbrow taste: From Snob to Omnivore. *American Sociological Review*, 61(5), 900–907.

Ryan, R. M., & Deci, E. L. (2000). Self-determination theory and the facilitation of intrinsic motivation, social development, and well-being. *American Psychologist*, 55(1), 68.

Schmitz, R. M. (2016). Constructing men as fathers: A content analysis of formulations of fatherhood in parenting magazines. *The Journal of Men's Studies*, 24(1), 3–23.

Slay, H. S., & Smith, D. A. (2011). Professional identity construction: Using narrative to understand the negotiation of professional and stigmatized cultural identities. *Human Relations*, 64(1), 85–107.

Small, J., Harris, C., & Wilson, E. (2008). A critical discourse analysis of in-flight magazine advertisements: The 'social sorting' of airline travellers? *Journal of Tourism and Cultural Change*, 6(1), 17–38.

Stamps, D. L. (2020). B(l)ack by popular demand: An analysis of positive black male characters in television and audiences' community cultural wealth. *Journal of Communication Inquiry*, 45(2), 97–118.

Tyler, I. (2008). "Chav mum chav scum": Class disgust in contemporary Britain. *Feminist Media Studies*, 8(1), 17–34.

Veenstra, G. (2005). Can taste illumine class? Cultural knowledge and forms of inequality. *The Canadian Journal of Sociology*, 30(3), 247–279.

Wasserman, H. (2010). *Tabloid Journalism in South Africa: True Story!* Indiana University Press.

Webb, J. B., Vinoski, E. R., Warren-Findlow, J., Padro, M. P., Burris, E. N., & Suddreth, E. M. (2017). Is the "Yoga Bod" the new skinny?: A comparative content analysis of mainstream yoga lifestyle magazine covers. *Body Image*, 20, 87–98.

Yosso, T. J. (2005). Whose culture has capital? A critical race theory discussion of community cultural wealth. *Race Ethnicity and Education*, 8(1), 69–91.

Zipin, L., Sellar, S., Brennan, M., & Gale, T. (2015). Educating for futures in marginalized regions: A sociological framework for rethinking and researching aspirations. *Educational Philosophy and Theory*, 47(3), 227–246.

13
PASSION AS PROFESSION? LIFESTYLE JOURNALISTS BETWEEN EXCEPTIONALISM AND CRUEL OPTIMISM

Johana Kotišová

Introduction: The emotional exceptionalism of lifestyle journalism

Journalism and media researchers are increasingly interested in emotions. English-language research on the role and place of emotions, subjectivity, and affect in media content, journalists' work, and relationships between journalists and audiences started flourishing around the turn of the millennium (e.g., van Zoonen, 1998; Tumber, 2004), marking the "emotional turn" in journalism studies (Wahl-Jorgensen, 2016, 2020). As this chapter illustrates, researchers' sensitivity to emotions and subjectivity in journalism partly responds to the prominence of emotional ties and discourses in the current networked and digitalized versions of journalism (Wahl-Jorgensen, 2016; Beckett & Deuze, 2016).

Within the emotional turn, journalism researchers have adopted or adapted a variety of – typically sociological or anthropological – definitions of emotions, such as the "experience of involvement" (Peters, 2011, p. 297) or "biologically preconditioned, but to a large extent culturally determined, defined and shaped practices of feeling and thinking" (Kotišová, 2019a, p. 93). Some authors also distinguish emotion from affect, the latter often being understood as an individual bodily experience and the former as its public, articulated, named, circulated, and inherently relational interpretation (e.g., Wahl-Jorgensen, 2020).

Few journalistic beats, forms, and styles have passed the emotional turn unnoticed (see e.g., Harbers & Broersma, 2014; Kukkakorpi & Pantti, 2021). However, there are journalistic subfields where emotions have been studied more traditionally because of their potentially detrimental effect on journalists' emotional and mental wellbeing and health, such as crisis or conflict journalism (see Flannery, 2022; Posetti, Bell & Brown, 2020), or because of their centrality to journalists' epistemological practices – such as lifestyle and cultural journalism. The importance of examining emotions in lifestyle and cultural journalism stems from their "emotional exceptionalism" (Kotisova, 2022), meaning that lifestyle and cultural journalists are openly and legitimately driven by their passion for the subjects they write about (Harries & Wahl-Jorgensen, 2007; Jaakkola, 2012; G. P. Perreault & Bélair-Gagnon, 2024) and that all beats falling under lifestyle and cultural journalism share a strong appeal on aesthetic or moral emotions "because that is what arts and culture do—stimulate emotions" (Kristensen, 2021, p. 1594). The journalists are expected to provide guidance, advice, and entertainment in the realms of consumerism and culture (Hanusch, 2019; Jaakkola, 2012), which ties together journalists' subjectivity with emotionality and the identity formation of their audiences.

The chapter brings together the most frequently discussed emotion-related aspects of lifestyle and cultural journalism. It treats lifestyle and cultural journalism as synonyms, while also respecting the definitions and vocabulary of cited authors. The chapter draws from research revolving around (1) the multifaceted role of lifestyle and cultural journalists' subjectivity, joy, and passion; (2) their emotional labor and (3) emotional work and affective links between journalists and audiences; and (4) lifestyle journalists' strategies to reconcile passion with precarity, namely, "cruel optimism."

This chapter provides an illustrative review of the body of research on emotions in lifestyle journalism that takes these four themes as nodes that help understand the complexity of emotions in lifestyle journalism. The review is based on thematic analysis (Braun & Clarke, 2006) of 25 papers and book chapters addressing emotions, affect, or subjectivity in lifestyle and cultural journalism, facilitated by MAXQDA, and their subsequent thematic synthesis (Xiao & Watson, 2019). Since lifestyle journalism is sometimes understood as a subset of cultural journalism (Kristensen & Riegert, 2021) and vice versa (Hanusch & Hanitzsch, 2013), this review connects research on both the beats. The remainder of the chapter is organized around four themes corresponding to four categories of topics and tallying codes:

a *Journalists' involvement in their work*: subjectivity, joy, passion, exceptionalism, authenticity, aesthetic bias, and persona-driven approach;
b *The management of journalists' own emotions* in particular beats: emotional labor, lifestyle as political, blurring beat boundaries, and the strategic ritual of objectivization of emotions;
c *The management of audience emotions and its role in the digital era*: emotional work, roles, empathy, the digital, engaging audiences, moral emotions, and therapeutic culture;
d *Precarity and its reconciliation with passion*: precarity, cruel optimism, and ambivalence.

In what follows, I summarize and illustrate research on the four themes, some of which epitomize pressing issues and tensions of journalism (research) more broadly. In particular, the role of emotions in journalists' epistemological practices, the question of how to navigate precarity and emotional wellbeing, and the challenges in digital audience engagement resonate with current research on other journalistic beats (e.g., Istek, 2017; Kukkakorpi & Pantti, 2021; Wahl-Jorgensen, 2022). Therefore, lifestyle journalism and the solutions to its inner tensions developed by its practitioners might serve as sources of inspiration for non-lifestyle areas of journalism (research).

Subjectivity, joy, passion, and authenticity

Lifestyle journalists, more legitimately and openly than journalists writing about "hard" beats, use subjectivity – including emotions and personal engagement, aesthetic bias, interpretation, individual voice, in-depth reflection, and self-interest – as their motivational force, epistemological tool, and stylistic principle (Chong, 2019; Jaakkola, 2012; Jaakkola & Skulte, 2023; Kristensen, 2022; Kristensen & Riegert, 2021; Riegert & Widholm, 2019). Lifestyle journalists are believed to select topics, products, events, and even whole beats to cover based on their aesthetic bias and passion. For example, Chong (2019) describes how aesthetic bias, or taste, positively and negatively prejudices a reviewer toward a book. Perreault and Bélair-Gagnon (2024) show how important passion for sports is for getting involved in sports journalism in the first place. Emotional exceptionalism also manifests itself in lifestyle and cultural journalists' style, which tends to be more emotional, subjective, and individualized (Kristensen, 2021). Emotional exceptionalism does *not* mean that lifestyle journalists are exceptionally emotionally invested in their work; rather, the usual journalistic emotional management (Hochschild, 2012; Hopper & Huxford, 2015) and strategic rituals of objectivity and emotionality (Tuchman, 1972; Wahl-Jorgensen, 2013) are legitimately replaced with other mechanisms (see below).

Several recent studies brought up the topics of joy, passion, and love as news values and/or motivating forces in journalism. Parks, drawing on the Dalai Lama's dialogues with Desmond Tutu, seeks to locate journalism "along joyful dimensions of perspective, humility, humor, acceptance, forgiveness, gratitude, compassion, and generosity" (Parks, 2021, p. 820). In a reaction to Parks' work, Perreault (2023) sees journalists as motivated by three key dimensions of joy: gratitude for their past, the opportunity to provide a different perspective, and compassion for their readers. Similarly, Perreault and Bélair-Gagnon link journalists' joy to their love and passion for their work and investigate how, and with what consequences, lifestyle journalists are grateful for their ability to "enact professionally what they loved personally: travel, gaming, sport" (Perreault & Bélair-Gagnon, 2024, p. 10). They argue that lifestyle journalists are often motivated to enter the profession by their personal connection to the topic/genre or the people involved – such as traveling or sport: "It's that passion that drives them to enter the niche, drives them to work to—and, at times, work beyond—their capabilities" (Perreault & Bélair-Gagnon, 2024, p. 13). The lifestyle and cultural topics "bring joy and allow journalists to experience such joy in their reporting" (G. Perreault & Miller, 2022, p. 1986). However, as Stupart (2023) suggests, even work in other journalistic beats can be deeply emotionally fulfilling.

Personal joy, passion, and love for a particular object motivate both involvement in journalism *and* particular roles and practices. For example, Maares and Hanusch cite a micro-blogger – an Instagrammer – who, being a passionate traveler and mountaineer, described:

> I want to ensure that people see what beautiful landscapes we have, and I want to motivate them to go outside; to not just sit at home in front of the television, but to go outside climbing mountains and experience great things out in nature.
>
> *(2020, p. 272)*

The Instagrammer's passion motivated them not only to *inspire* others (Hanitzsch & Vos, 2018) and provide incentives to travel and experience nature but also to do so in a visually aesthetic and "authentic" – and thus efficient – way.

Work and passion, professional and personal, reason, and emotion are, indeed, intimately interconnected in lifestyle journalism. While some lifestyle journalists seem to use "passionate" as a synonym for "ambitious" (Soronen, 2018) and thus locate their passion within the professional/organizational context, Perreault and Bélair-Gagnon (2024) suggest that lifestyle journalists position themselves within journalism through their personal identity. These arguments are not conflicting; rather, they show the faded boundary between personal and professional. Lifestyle journalism is, thus, an evident example of the blurring of personal and professional that we see across news beats (Deuze & Witschge, 2018). Stupart observes the same trend in conflict and investigative reporting. He argues that journalists' joy is located not only in journalism as a profession but also in the extent to which a journalist is able to integrate the profession with their personality. The good feelings, particularly positive moral feelings, "may depend on the extent to which one is being both a good journalist and a good person" (Stupart, 2023, p. 22).

The love and passion for work participate in the infamous illusion that the work you love is not real work, which, together with feelings of gratitude and privilege, can potentially lead to self-exploitation. Therefore, how passion and love are used and abused must be studied critically. Later in this chapter, I further discuss Perreault and Bélair-Gagnon's (2024) conclusion that being passionate about one's work is potentially mentally taxing and link it to wider discussions of self-exploitation in creative industries. An excellent example of the critical approach is Lindén et al.'s (2021) analysis of journalism online job advertisements. The authors show that, across 11 years (2002–2013), advertisements seeking "passionate" journalists increased by 12 percent; passion has become institutionalized as a marketable journalistic skill. Thus, not only in lifestyle journalism, feelings have become a commodity within the attention economy (Illouz, 2007; Nixon, 2020).

Besides passion, love, and joy, an aspect of subjectivity that seems to stand out in micro-blogging and increasingly in professional lifestyle and cultural journalism – and helps conceptualize the blurring boundary between journalists and influencers and yet remains understudied – is authenticity (see also Chapter 10). Moestrup, studying the novelist, cultural journalist, and food critic Martin Kongstad, develops the notion of "persona-driven journalism" and criticism where the journalist's persona is the message and "the performance of the journalist's or critic's personality is a fundamental part of the media text" (Moestrup, 2022, p. 54). The persona-driven approach works with the critic's authenticity and originality since it involves "staging of the journalist's persona across media, platforms, and time" (Moestrup, 2022, p. 54) and developing a particular literary style and strategy. In Kongstad's case, the style and strategy include constructing an alter ego, dramatizing written text, using multiple voices, and blending fictional characters with real-life sources. Moestrup shows how Kongstad's body and bodily practices – ways of dressing, gestures, manners, body language, verbal utterances, emotions, attitudes and opinions, thoughts, beliefs, and worldview – become consciously and strategically deployed in his work. While Kongstad is perhaps an extreme case of the persona-driven approach, the readers might think of many lifestyle and cultural journalists and critics who use elements of their authenticity in their work.

Heřmanová (2024) observes yet more developed and strategic use of authenticity among social media influencers. Based on qualitative content analysis of ten Instagram profiles of prominent influencers and culture sections of ten legacy media, she argues that the Instagram influencers use authenticity to make cultural artifacts – "be it a book, vinyl record, brutalist building, clothing outfit, or a vegan bistro in a small Czech town" (Heřmanová, 2024, p. 10) – seem interesting, cool, and worthy as objects of consumption. By comparison, legacy media make things consumption-worthy by labeling them as a "cult" or "cultish." The performance of authenticity, Heřmanová argues, takes a variety of forms – from writing and speaking of "genuine" liking of a recommended everyday product or a "life-changing" book to posting intimate everyday moments, such as personal/family pictures and images of consumed food in a (reviewed) bistro. Authenticity works as a strategy to appear relatable and sincere and thus shapes influencers' social and economic capital:

> Cultural consumption and products recommended by influencers – such as Erik's recommendation of political essays, Vladimir's interest in brutalist architecture or Teri's minimalist fashion choices – are thus presented as aspirational lifestyle choices, interesting for their audiences because they are based on authentic taste.
>
> *(Heřmanová, 2024, p. 9)*

Heřmanová implies that authenticity and displaying raw experiences and emotions are the influencers' mechanism of boundary work, delimiting them from journalists and critics working in legacy media (see also Chong, 2019; Kotisova, 2022; Kristensen, 2021). However, others' work on lifestyle journalists indicates that these boundaries are, indeed, very porous, not least when it comes to authenticity (Madsen & Ytre-Arne, 2012; Moestrup, 2022; Soronen, 2018), which has become a buzzword in professional lifestyle journalism, too.

Emotional labor as a boundary-construction ritual

Thus, on the one hand, the emotional exceptionalism and inherent subjectivity of lifestyle/cultural journalism allow us to distinguish it from some other journalisms (cf. Kristensen, 2022). On the other hand, emotional authenticity, if not managed, policed, disciplined, and strategically dosed, threatens to blur the boundary between journalists and "amateur" bloggers and influencers (Heřmanová, 2024; Kotisova, 2022; Riegert & Widholm, 2019) and let the former vanish into the void of irrelevance. The concept of emotional labor offers a fruitful way to understand this tension and how it is reconciled.

(Lifestyle) journalists' management of their own emotions in line with the requirements of their job, matching their feelings with situations at work – i.e., their emotional labor – has been increasingly studied (Hochschild, 2012; Hopper & Huxford, 2015; Kotisova, 2022; Soronen, 2018). Lifestyle and cultural journalists' emotional labor often resides in what can be called a "strategic ritual of objectivization of emotions" (Kotisova, 2022; cf. Tuchman, 1972; Wahl-Jorgensen, 2013). Chong was among the first to identify this complex mechanism. In her study based on interviews with 40 book reviewers, she cites a reviewer as saying: "When a book is good, a book is good. And I'll identify it usually in a very sort of visceral, maybe even primitive emotional manner" (in Chong, 2019, p. 435).

Yet, while the immediate reactions may be primitive, private, and personalized, these emotional responses triggered by reading books operate as "tools for gauging the success of the writing. For example, feelings of being 'swept away' or 'engaged' by a narrative were common indicators that a book was working" (Chong, 2019, p. 435). Chong further investigates how reviewers utilize and represent these emotional experiences and explains that they seek "to articulate emotion in a rational format" (Chong, 2019, p. 435). Importantly, the process of rationalization or externalization of inner emotional reactions is facilitated by review section editors:

> The 'ritual' of working with an editor, then, is not to help authors figure out what they think (which is informed by their emotional reaction while reading the book) but to help them articulate why the readers might reach the same conclusion.
>
> *(Chong, 2019, p. 435)*

There are specific narrative and stylistic devices – plot, tone, and voice – helping evoke the same emotional responses in readers.

I identify a very similar mechanism in my study on food and film critics, some of whom articulated thought-through strategies of emotional management:

> I use to say that I watch films in my stomach. It means that rather than watching the films themselves, I observe what they do to me.
>
> *(Richard, a film critic)*

> When the food is exceptional, there is an element that … awakens some emotion, … that engages your attention. When it engages you, then it starts to be, logically, interesting.
>
> *(Paul, a food critic; in Kotisova, 2022, p. 799)*

Another film critic, Alice, explained that their bodies – their tastes, experiences, fatigue, and anger – are their primary tool. She lets the film – the combination of its aesthetic and technical elements – move her to tears or trigger other strong emotions. Only after that does she look into the feelings and start analyzing why they emerged at specific moments.

Particularly the food critics, writing or speaking about tangible objects of bodily consumption, vividly talked about the place and role of their feelings and memories in the evaluation practice. Food critics such as Paul or Iris explained that food consumption can be emotionally surprising, sophisticated, or comforting. Food has the potential to make people happy or not – and this is where its critical assessment starts. The (un)happiness can also follow from memories and nostalgia, for example, when writing about a dish that "no one can cook better than my grandmother" (Paul, a food critic; in Kotisova, 2022, p. 798). Furthermore, journalism about film and food is permeated by moral feelings linked to political opinions and ethical values. In turn, these values – confronted with how the film depicts minorities, gendered violence, etc. – implicitly shape critics' perspectives and writing, colored by a moral tone. Likewise, some of the food critics equated "tasty" with "ethically produced" (see also Jenkins, 2017).

While the critics cherish these emotional cues and clues, they cannot allow their emotions to take the reins. This is why they perform the "objectivization of emotionality": "making the emotions conscious, analysing them and their sources/causes, questioning and challenging them, and, eventually, making them intelligible for their readers" (Kotisova, 2022, p. 802).

Kristensen (2021) argues that this rationalization or objectivization of emotions – that manifest themselves as a discourse through the "externalization of judgemental practice" (Jaakkola, 2012, p. 488) – is grounded in key professional elements of criticism, namely, description, classification, contextualization, elucidation, interpretation, and analysis. And while Hartley (2000, p. 40) believes that lifestyle journalists belong to "the smiling professions," the emotional labor based on rationalization, objectivization, and externalization can be rather demanding. Kristensen cites the film critic Christian Monggaard's column "The Self Interview" from 2012:

> It is hard work watching so many movies and reflecting critically and skilfully upon them. And I also often write quite long pieces … Damn, I spend a long time thinking about the movies and writing about them. Film criticism, like we do it here at

Information, is a craft, one has to learn, yes, it is an art form that one has to have a sense for.

(Kristensen, 2021, p. 1604)

Can this strategy be professional lifestyle journalists' "unique selling point"? Heřmanová's above work draws a clear line between legacy journalists' discursive repression and social media influencers' open utilization of genuine feelings (Heřmanová, 2024). Where the influencers strategically show their authentic feelings, legacy journalists speak of a "cult" or simply denote the qualities of their objects. Similarly, Chong's above research, also including prominent bloggers, shows how they feature their emotional reactions as a part of publicizing themselves and foregrounding their personas as a form of branding:

The tone of traditional reviews is formal and can be described as a 'voice from nowhere' perspective insomuch as reviewers efface their personal emotions while still communicating their personal judgment about a book. In contrast, it is the voice from a very particular someone that is a defining feature of many book blogs.

(Chong, 2019, pp. 436–437)

In the digital era, which gives rise to a multiplicity of lifestyle voices and threatens the legitimacy of lifestyle journalists' professional existence (Elkins & Newman, 2008; McDonald, 2007), emotional labor can be one of the boundary-construction tactics.

Thus, paradoxically enough, while emotions are seen as an aspect of lifestyle journalism that makes it distinct, emotional labor can be understood as a mechanism of "journalistification" of lifestyle and cultural journalism that brings them closer to political journalism and other beats considered more "serious." The role it plays in the increasing blurring of boundaries between news beats, between the lifestyle and the political, is not yet fully understood. However, there is enough evidence to suggest that lifestyle journalists' emotional labor – as well as their emotional work – might productively inform the reconceptualization of their roles and moving beyond the politics vs. lifestyle binary (Banjac & Hanusch, 2022; Jaakkola & Skulte, 2023; Kristensen, 2022; Kristensen & Riegert, 2021; Riegert & Widholm, 2019). Furthermore, emotional labor and the below-discussed emotional work are also analytically fruitful illustrations of the feminist slogan "the personal is political" and show how politics is reconfigured at the level of the self (Banjac & Hanusch, 2022; Madsen & Ytre-Arne, 2012).

Emotional work: Engaging audiences in the digital age

Some authors distinguish emotional labor from emotional work. While emotional labor conceptualizes emotional management oriented to oneself and one's feelings, emotional work usually refers to the management of other people's emotions – such as those of audiences, colleagues, and subjects (Pantti & Wahl-Jorgensen, 2021; Perreault & Bélair-Gagnon, 2024). Journalism is, of course, a strong player shaping the emotional public sphere – its power is probably why media researchers became interested in emotions in the first place (see, e.g., Papacharissi, 2016; Richards, 2007). Lifestyle journalism is no exception.

In her research on magazine work, Soronen illustrates how the logic of emotional work starts from the effect the produced content should have on audiences. All the levels of emotional management – that of sources', colleagues', and audiences' emotions – follow from this desired state and from one another. More precisely, journalists manage the emotional atmosphere in the workplace during teamwork and try to induce pleasant feelings in their sources, with the aim of evoking the same emotions in audiences. Soronen explains:

> A desired emotional tone is included in the brief. The photographer is typically informed through the inspirational page. Hence, the starting point in content production is a shared understanding of the desired emotional state that the journalist, the art director and the photographer aspire.
>
> Art directors feed energy into the members of the editorial photography team and they must reflect on the potential of the photos to engender emotional reactions. In a broader sense, this relates to the organization's practices for managing meaning aesthetically by stimulating the consumers' emotional reactions.
>
> *(Soronen, 2018, pp. 297–298)*

Soronen's research shows very well how emotions in magazine work, content, and audiences are inseparable from one another, from the economic imperatives and digital production technologies: the emotion on the face of the photographed subject is mirrored in a reader's reaction, and the whole production process follows a carefully considered plan to achieve a certain intensity of affect. Readers' desired emotional reactions are "operationalized" through particular photographic choices, colors, gaze directions, angles, mise-en-scène, cropping, etc.

The emotional work has its roots in the relationship between journalists and audiences – namely, the "empathy" of journalists for audiences – and its changed dynamics in the digital era. This empathy, understanding audiences' feelings and desires, has a profit-seeking and increasingly important digital/algorithmic side. At the same time, researchers have observed that journalists try to approach their audiences with compassion and emotional imagination – particularly those from lower classes (Banjac & Hanusch, 2022). These two sides of empathy – empathy as compassion stemming from the shared human condition and empathy as the calculated, technologically outsourced strategy – appear inseparable in lifestyle journalism. For instance, Soronen (2018) found out that in women's magazines, the editorial staff together define a model, fictive reader, and their lifestyle: the place where they live, age, gender, hobbies, and socio-economic position. This reader is then used as a tool in planning and content production: the journalists try to think about content production from the perspective of the model reader. The habitual identification of journalists with their readers and journalist-source intimacy forms a part of what Abrahamson calls "magazine exceptionalism" (Abrahamson, 2007; Jenkins, 2017). However, Heřmanová (2024) shows that the same practice exists in cultural sections of legacy media when she discusses how journalists' language is based on their projections to audiences, and the quality and success of these projections are measured based on the relationship between readers and the products that journalists write about. Thus, the authority of journalists as cultural intermediaries stems from their ability to tune to the audience's expectations. The important takeaway from the research is the dual side of empathy: the profoundly human imagination and sharing that becomes an institutionalized methodological-epistemological tool, a structured practice of getting to know the audiences and, based on this knowledge, tailoring the content to them.

The whole exercise in empathy and infusing journalistic narratives with emotions to engage audiences (Chong, 2019; Kristensen, 2022; Kristensen & Riegert, 2021; Riegert et al., 2015) has gained new dynamics in the digital era. On the one hand, digitally augmented forms of storytelling and the affordances of digital technologies carry the potential to create emotional immediacy and affectively absorb the audiences (Kukkakorpi & Pantti, 2021). On the other hand, they open the door for new competing actors who change the rules of the journalistic game, raising the stakes. As discussed above, digital 'newcomers' to journalism or actors at the edge of the profession, such as (micro-)bloggers and social media influencers, are probably still more unrestrained to connect to their audiences by embracing subjectivity and authenticity (Heřmanová, 2024; Maares & Hanusch, 2020). While exchanging their affective connections with audiences/consumers for direct profit, they bring into play marketing agencies and diverse industries. Journalists are trying to catch up by code-switching to more subjective, emotional styles for the sake of audience engagement and profit (see above; Chong, 2019; Kristensen, 2021; Kristensen & Riegert, 2021). Furthermore, as will be discussed in the next section, digital technologies are also an important factor in (poor) well-being among journalists more broadly. Lifestyle journalists are caught between the implicit imperative of constant availability and incessant digital connectedness to their work and audiences and the desire to disconnect, turn off all distractions, and delete social media apps from their phones (Perreault & Bélair-Gagnon, 2024).

The professional–ideological context of lifestyle journalists' emotional work is formed by their perceived roles. Indeed, in lifestyle journalism, the perceived roles are often defined in emotional language. Lifestyle journalists, but to a large extent also the (micro-)bloggers and Instagram influencers, perceive themselves as service providers, life coaches, community advocates, and inspiring entertainers (Hanusch, 2019; Maares & Hanusch, 2020). A finer perspective reveals that they see themselves as mood managers, friends, therapists, marketers, guides, and curators (Banjac & Hanusch, 2022; Hanusch, 2019; Heřmanová, 2024). As such, lifestyle journalists link consumption to positive feelings, allow audiences to escape the outside world into pleasant emotional experiences, offer psychological and emotional support, and provide tips and advice on consumption. Hanusch (2019, p. 195) summarizes: "issues of guidance, advice, review, consumerism and entertainment appear to be key aspects" for any definition of lifestyle journalists and their roles. Some of the roles thus fit into Hanitzsch and Vos's (2018) informational–instructive, advocative-radical, and developmental-educative dimensions. Banjac and Hanusch (2022, p. 1609) point out that the roles differ based on the audiences' class: "the elite consume lifestyle journalism for pure pleasure, the economic middle classes to find aspiration (and imitation), and the working classes to feel excluded." For example, providing aspiration is achieved through psychological and emotional motivation and hope in achieving the same as famous and successful people with equally mediocre background (Banjac & Hanusch, 2022, p. 1609).

A broader perspective to look at the emotional work and its mechanisms is through the lens of the all-encompassing therapeutic culture as the context of lifestyle journalism. The performance of emotional and wellbeing management often happens through the circulation of therapeutic discourse and persuasive accounts of audiences' self-efficacy permeated with pop psychology. Madsen and Ytre-Arne (2012) summarize the three underlying ideas of therapeutical culture: liberation through self-esteem (the self needs to be liberated from society and be esteemed and affirmed rather than surrendered to society), emotive ethics (searching for true feelings and turning them into the criteria for decision-making), and the therapeutic vessel (therapeutic language turns the self into a cultural resource). In their study of Norwegian women's magazines, they show how the content of these magazines is pervaded by the notion of continuous self-improvement, self-care, and a never-ending inner revolution. There are, of course, articles dedicated to therapy, psychology, mental wellbeing, and mental health. However, these are not only topics for special features. "'The therapeutic' simply becomes an easily transferable and flexible metaphor or a language which permeates other domains" (Madsen & Ytre-Arne, 2012, p. 35). "The therapeutic" is, thus, everywhere: all everyday consumption, activities, and objects – food, sport, TV shows, theatre, kittens, hobbies, gardening, and house-cleaning – are interpreted through their therapeutic potential. A literal expression of the merging of everyday consumption with the therapeutical is a *'Recipe for a positive inner milieu,' which requires:*

'1/3 cup of self-respect; 1/2 cup of positive thinking; 1 tsp gratitude; 100 g laughter; 2 tsp of time for yourself; 2 tsp smile; 1 pinch of self-irony; and for extra taste, add friends and family as required'

(Madsen & Ytre-Arne, 2012, p. 35)

Being "the best possible version" of oneself, being "at one's best," is clearly articulated in the genre of makeovers. Makeovers, the authors show, are based on the practice of providing expert-assisted instructions for self-governance. They promise and document improvement in distinct categories, of which many are explicitly therapeutic/psychological: style, make-up, training, nutrition, interior, personal economy and budget, self-development, self-confidence, self-management, chaos control, relations, and consciousness-raising (Madsen & Ytre-Arne, 2012). The ideal outcome of the makeover and other lifestyle content is an empowered woman who is able to take care of herself by making substantial changes in her life.

The underlying ethos of the therapeutic discourses is the neoliberal ideal of self-governance through technologies of the self that also blur the boundaries between work and consumption: all consumption is work on one's self, constructing subjectivities, capacities, and predispositions required of employees (Du Gay, 1996; Foucault, 1988; Illouz, 2007; Thorpe, 2008).

Find a job you love – you will never stop working and lose a hobby

Another contextual lens through which we can see the emotional management and emotion-based attempts to attract audiences is the overall precarity of journalism practice (Deuze & Witschge, 2018) reflecting the general crisis in the news industry (e.g., Reinardy, 2011; Zelizer et al., 2022). Jaakkola (2017) illustrates the precarity–crisis nexus by suggesting that the "crisis" in cultural journalism is publicly discussed with the aim of showing how cultural journalism is relevant to democracy, improving its reputation, and achieving better working conditions.

Cultural and lifestyle journalism is precarious in many respects: it is affected by downsizing and (fear of) job loss, fragmentation of work, multiskilling, increased workload, growing pressure on efficiency, increasing prevalence of freelancers and newsroom collaborators on a single-assignment basis, journalists with non-permanent and part-time positions, overall uncertainty, harassment, and stress. Many journalists and critics need a side job to make a living or, vice versa, perform journalism only as a secondary activity. Journalists are indirectly forced to promote themselves as a brand and to be constantly available and adaptable to emerging digital trends – while at the same time often feeling the need to disconnect. (Kristensen, 2021; Kristensen & Riegert, 2021; Perreault & Miller,

2022; Perreault & Bélair-Gagnon, 2024; Soronen, 2018). While this may be said about all news workers, lifestyle journalists, cultural journalists, and critics, with their traditionally volatile connections to newsrooms and competition with more "authentic" influencers and other content creators, are particularly exposed (Kristensen, 2021; Soronen, 2018). Moreover, Perreault and Miller (2022), in their analysis of harassment in lifestyle journalism, illustrate that the lack of organizational identities, policies, and support from managers can be tricky when dealing with harassment: there is no "higher up" that the reporters can report to, and the journalists feel they need to deal with it on their own. This can lead them to normalize the harassment. On the other hand, despite all the institutional decoupling of lifestyle journalists and newsrooms, some journalists still see newsroom expectations as a burden preventing them from having enough freedom/autonomy and work-life balance (Perreault & Bélair-Gagnon, 2024).

This tension illustrates that speaking of precarity or bad work without taking into account joy and good work (Hesmondhalgh & Baker, 2011) can be simplistic. Lifestyle and cultural journalism is not only full of misery, uncertainty, stress, and exploitation. As discussed earlier, it is also driven by passion and joy, offers rewards, and (sometimes) autonomy. It is profoundly ambivalent, in that most good aspects of the work have their dark side, and vice versa, thus forming inherently ambivalent professional identities (Deuze et al., 2020; Kotišová, 2019b; Soronen, 2018). However, Conor warns that the seductive/destructive duality of creative work and the narratives about inherently pleasurable and painful work also mythicize and romanticize creative professions (Conor, 2014). Applied to lifestyle and cultural journalism, we should not let the ambivalence naturalize cultural and lifestyle journalists' hardships and normalize the decline of their working conditions.

The core ambivalence of lifestyle and cultural journalism lies in the very passion–profession tension. Perreault and Bélair-Gagnon describe it as lifestyle journalists' "cognitive dissonance":

> While drawn to the idea they would never actually work, since they were embedded in their passion—in reality what many journalists described reflected that they had difficulty leaving work, given that even their passion had become work.
> *(2022, p. 14)*

The authors show how passion for work can become a starting point and a mechanism of self-exploitation. A similar tension can be found in Soronen's research (2018), who narrates how magazine staff experience stress and uncertainty, while eagerly voicing their passion for work. Eventually, "doing what you love" turns bitter, as the work does not fulfil the journalists' aspirations and expectations and does not allow them to live the personal life they imagined:

> It's that passion that drives them to enter the niche, drives them to work to—and, at times, work beyond—their capabilities. It is also that passion that can cause disillusionment with lifestyle journalism and cause them to reconsider … their commitment.
> *(Perreault & Bélair-Gagnon, 2024, p. 1654)*

For instance, attending sports games for work can be initially exciting and addictive, but it also feels like working more than enjoying the game experience: the pleasure wears off.

Based on this logic, the popular phrase "find a job you love, and you will never have to work a day in your life" could be rephrased as "find a job you love, and you will never stop working" or "find a job you love, and you will lose a hobby." Perhaps both.

A personal strategy to deal with the precarity, workload, and uncertainty has been discussed as "cruel optimism:" suppressing the feelings of anxiety and maintaining attachment to a problematic or compromised object/scene of desire or a hardly attainable goal (Berlant, 2011). Soronen (2018, p. 290) explains that cruel optimism among magazine journalists is a form of emotional labor within which journalists are "invoking in themselves feelings of enjoyment and suppressing feelings of strain." For example, they try to push away stressful to-do lists and focus on the actual tasks that bring about joy.

The magazine work – but also other sites of lifestyle journalism – is a fragile scene of desire precisely because of its uncertain outlook and related forms of precarity. Since the attachment to a problematic object implies sustaining hopes (that at some point, the work will secure a desired lifestyle), in practice, the cruel optimism is performed as hope/aspirational labor, promising a good life and sometimes stimulating to work harder (Perreault & Bélair-Gagnon, 2024; Soronen, 2018).

The solution is, of course, not to leave journalism and find a job one dislikes or to which one is indifferent. A more productive way to approach these tensions – that make journalists trade lack of interest for financial struggles and rigid working hours for job insecurity – is to disentangle the ambivalence and mitigate its precarious pole. A part of the solution can be collective organizing, which, however, is traditionally weaker among freelance creative professionals (at least in Europe).

Conclusion: Ways ahead

This chapter, based on an illustrative review, showcases previous research on the most noticeable emotion-related questions in lifestyle and cultural journalism, linked to the peculiar position of subjectivity and emotions in journalists' practice, journalists' emotional management of their feelings, audience engagement in the digital age, and the psychosocial aspects of precarity. I believe the tensions in lifestyle journalism epitomize emotion-related problems and potential solutions relevant and inspiring for journalism (studies) more broadly, such as the role of emotions in journalists' epistemologies, precarity and emotional wellbeing, and digital audience engagement. This is only one of the many reasons why lifestyle journalism is worth studying.

The research to date considers lifestyle journalists' emotional involvement in their professional practice exceptional: their work is legitimately driven by their passion for the chosen beat as well as by their unique taste or aesthetic bias, full of joy, and strategically uses authenticity. The research also looks into journalists' management of their emotions, suggesting that the emotional labor serves as a boundary-construction ritual that draws a line between amateur critics or social media lifestyle influencers and professional journalists, thus justifying the latter's existence. Where non-journalists tend to monetize their emotional authenticity, journalists scrutinize their emotional reactions and turn them into methodological or epistemological tools. However, as the boundaries between the lifestyle and the political, as well as between lifestyle journalists and influencers, are fading, the emotional exceptionalism may be changing. Another question that we still need to understand better is the emotional labor of "interlopers" such as social media influencers. Moreover, future research on emotional labor should also focus on non-artistic beats such as travel journalism or sex journalism, i.e., beats that involve intense bodily experiences and risks (Francoeur, 2021; Middleweek, 2022).

The extant research also shows the importance and the double face of empathy, which is both profoundly humane and strategically deployed to engage audiences. With the ever-growing affordances of digital journalism tools, there will be many opportunities to study new mechanisms of emotional work, technologies of the self, and the overall proliferation of the emotional public sphere. Lifestyle journalism is very promising in this respect as it often concerns the body, everyday consumption, and everyday manifestations of power and agency.

Finally, research should more seriously look into the emotional aspects of precarity, self-exploitation, and the overall crisis in the (lifestyle/cultural) journalism industry. There is only scarce research on the passion-precarity nexus, the ambivalence of the work, and the cruel optimism the news workers tend to adopt; future research can also focus on the "aspirational" and "hope" in aspirational/hope labor and, most importantly, the possibilities of (collective) resilience and change.

Further reading

Chong, P. (2019). Valuing subjectivity in journalism: Bias, emotions, and self-interest as tools in arts reporting. *Journalism*, 20(3), 427–443.

Kristensen, N. N. (2021). Critical emotions: Cultural criticism as an intrinsically emotional type of journalism. *Journalism Studies*, 22(12), 1590–1607.

Madsen, O. J., & Ytre-Arne, B. (2012). Me at my best: Therapeutic ideals in Norwegian women's magazines. *Communication, Culture & Critique*, 5(1), 20–37.

Perreault, G. P., & Bélair-Gagnon, V. (2024). The lifestyle of lifestyle journalism: How reporters discursively manage their aspirations in their daily work. *Journalism Practice*, 18(7), 1641–1659.

Soronen, A. (2018). Emotional labour in magazine work: Suppressing and evoking emotions as part of project-based teamwork. *Journalism Practice*, 12(3), 290–307.

References

Abrahamson, D. (2007). Magazine exceptionalism: The concept, the criteria, the challenge. *Journalism Studies*, 8(4), 667–670. https://doi.org/10.1080/14616700701412225

Banjac, S., & Hanusch, F. (2022). Aspirational lifestyle journalism: The impact of social class on producers' and audiences' views in the context of socio-economic inequality. *Journalism*, 23(8), 1607–1625. https://doi.org/10.1177/1464884920956823

Beckett, C., & Deuze, M. (2016). On the role of emotion in the future of journalism. *Social Media + Society*, 2(3), 1–6. https://journals.sagepub.com/doi/full/10.1177/2056305116662395

Berlant, L. G. (2011). *Cruel Optimism*. Durham: Duke University Press.

Braun, V., & Clarke, V. (2006). Using thematic analysis in psychology. *Qualitative Research in Psychology*, 3(2), 77–101. https://doi.org/10.1191/1478088706qp063oa

Chong, P. (2019). Valuing subjectivity in journalism: Bias, emotions, and self-interest as tools in arts reporting. *Journalism*, 20(3), 427–443. https://doi.org/10.1177/1464884917722453

Conor, B. (2014). *Screenwriting: Creative Labor and Professional Practice*. London: Routledge.

Deuze, M., Kotišová, J., Newlands, G., & Van't Hof, E. (2020). Toward a theory of atypical media work and social hope. *Artha Journal of Social Sciences*, 19(3), 1–20. https://doi.org/10.12724/ajss.54.1

Deuze, M., & Witschge, T. (2018). Beyond journalism: Theorizing the transformation of journalism. *Journalism*, 19(2), 165–181. https://doi.org/10.1177/1464884916688550

Du Gay, P. (1996). *Consumption and Identity at Work*. London: SAGE. https://doi.org/10.4135/9781446221945

Elkins, J., & Newman, M. (Eds.) (2008). *The State of Art Criticism*. New York: Routledge.

Flannery, R. B. (2022). News journalists and postruamatic stress disorder: A review of literature, 2011–2020. *Psychiatric Quarterly, 93*(1), 151–159. https://link.springer.com/article/10.1007/s11126-021-09920-z

Foucault, M. (1988). Technologies of the self. In L. H. Martin, H. Gutman, & P. H. Hutton (Eds.), *Technologies of the Self: A Seminar with Michel Foucault* (pp. 16–49). London: Tavistock Publications.

Francoeur, C. (2021). Bodying the journalist. *Brazilian Journalism Research, 17*(1), 202–227. https://doi.org/10.25200/BJR.v17n1.2021.1354

Hanitzsch, T., & Vos, T. P. (2018). Journalism beyond democracy: A new look into journalistic roles in political and everyday life. *Journalism, 19*(2), 146–164. https://doi.org/10.1177/1464884916673386

Hanusch, F. (2019). Journalistic roles and everyday life: An empirical account of lifestyle journalists' professional views. *Journalism Studies, 20*(2), 193–211. https://doi.org/10.1080/1461670X.2017.1370977

Hanusch, F., & Hanitzsch, T. (2013). Mediating orientation and self-expression in the world of consumption: Australian and German lifestyle journalists' professional views. *Media, Culture & Society, 35*(8), 943–959. https://doi.org/10.1177/0163443713501931

Harbers, F., & Broersma, M. (2014). Between engagement and ironic ambiguity: Mediating subjectivity in narrative journalism. *Journalism, 15*(5), 639–654. https://journals.sagepub.com/doi/10.1177/1464884914523236

Harries, G., & Wahl-Jorgensen, K. (2007). The culture of arts journalists: Elitists, saviors or manic depressives? *Journalism, 8*(6), 619–639. https://doi.org/10.1177/1464884907083115

Hartley, J. (2000). Communicative democracy in a redactional society: The future of journalism studies. *Journalism, 1*(1), 39–48. https://doi.org/10.1177/146488490000100107

Heřmanová, M. (2024). Authentic cult: Media representations of cultural consumption and legitimization of cultural hierarchies. *Media, Culture & Society, 46*(3), 518–533. https://doi.org/10.1177/01634437231203880

Hesmondhalgh, D., & Baker, S. (2011). *Creative Labour: Media Work in Three Cultural Industries*. London: Routledge.

Hochschild, A. R. (2012). *The Managed Heart: Commercialization of Human Feeling*. Berkeley: University of California Press.

Hopper, K. M., & Huxford, J. E. (2015). Gathering emotion: Examining newspaper journalists' engagement in emotional labor. *Journal of Media Practice, 16*(1), 25–41. https://doi.org/10.1080/14682753.2015.1015799

Illouz, E. (2007). *Cold Intimacies: The Making of Emotional Capitalism*. Cambridge: Polity Press.

Istek, P. (2017). On their own: Freelance photojournalists in conflict zones. *Visual Communication Quarterly, 24*(1), 32–39. https://doi.org/10.1080/15551393.2016.1272419

Jaakkola, M. (2012). Promoting aesthetic tourism: Transgressions between generalist and specialist subfields in cultural journalism. *Journalism Practice, 6*(4), 482–496. https://doi.org/10.1080/17512786.2012.667284

Jaakkola, M. (2017). Producing a drama for the common good: The theatricalization of the crisis discourse on cultural journalism. *Open Journal for Sociological Studies, 1*(2), 51–64. https://doi.org/10.32591/coas.ojss.0102.03051j

Jaakkola, M., & Skulte, I. (2023). Reporting like there was no pandemic: Cultural journalism during the COVID-19 pandemic in Finland, Sweden, and Latvia. *MedieKultur: Journal of Media and Communication Research, 38*(73), 028–049. https://doi.org/10.7146/mk.v38i73.128154

Jenkins, J. (2017). Low-stakes decisions and high-stakes dilemmas: Considering the ethics decision-making of freelance magazine journalists. *Journal of Media Ethics, 32*(4), 188–201. https://doi.org/10.1080/23736992.2017.1359609

Kotišová, J. (2019a). *Crisis Reporters, Emotions, and Technology: An Ethnography*. Basingstoke: Palgrave Macmillan.

Kotišová, J. (2019b). Devastating dreamjobs: Ambivalence, emotions, and creative labor in a post-socialist audiovisual industry. *Iluminace, 31*(4), 27–45. https://www.iluminace.cz/artkey/ilu-201904-0002_devastating-dreamjobs-ambivalence-emotions-and-creative-labor-in-a-post-socialist-audiovisual-industry.php

Kotišová, J. (2022). An elixir of life? Emotional labour in cultural journalism. *Journalism, 23*(4), 789–805. https://doi.org/10.1177/1464884920917289

Kristensen, N. N. (2021). Critical emotions: Cultural criticism as an intrinsically emotional type of journalism. *Journalism Studies*, 22(12), 1590–1607. https://doi.org/10.1080/1461670X.2021.1910544

Kristensen, N. N. (2022). The kinship of literary journalism and cultural journalism: Everyday life, interpretation, and emotionality. *Literary Journalism Studies*, 14(1), 10–31. https://ialjs.org/june-2022-vol-14-no-1/

Kristensen, N. N., & Riegert, K. (2021). The tensions of the cultural news beat. *Journalism Practice*, 15(9), 1329–1343. https://doi.org/10.1080/17512786.2021.1971547

Kukkakorpi, M., & Pantti, M. (2021). A sense of place: VR journalism and emotional engagement. *Journalism Practice*, 15(6), 785–802. https://doi.org/10.1080/17512786.2020.1799237

Lindén, C.-G., Lehtisaari, K., Grönlund, M., & Villi, M. (2021). Journalistic passion as commodity: A managerial perspective. *Journalism Studies*, 22(12), 1701–1719. https://doi.org/10.1080/1461670X.2021.1911672

Maares, P., & Hanusch, F. (2020). Exploring the boundaries of journalism: Instagram microbloggers in the twilight zone of lifestyle journalism. *Journalism*, 21(2), 262–278. https://doi.org/10.1177/1464884918801400

Madsen, O. J., & Ytre-Arne, B. (2012). Me at my best: Therapeutic ideals in Norwegian women's magazines. *Communication, Culture & Critique*, 5(1), 20–37. https://doi.org/10.1111/j.1753-9137.2011.01118.x

McDonald, R. (2007). *The Death of the Critic*. London: Continuum.

Middleweek, B. (2022). What is sex journalism or, rather, how does it become? Interviews with news workers on the risk and precarity of a gendered news niche. *Journalism*, 23(5), 1114–1131. https://doi.org/10.1177/1464884920952267

Moestrup, S. (2022). Theatricality, body, voice, spatiality: Applying performance analysis to persona-driven literary journalism. *Literary Journalism Studies*, 14(1), 52–73. https://ialjs.org/june-2022-vol-14-no-1/

Nixon, B. (2020). The business of news in the attention economy: Audience labor and MediaNews Group's efforts to capitalize on news consumption. *Journalism*, 21(1), 73–94. https://doi.org/10.1177/1464884917719145

Pantti, M., & Wahl-Jorgensen, K. (2021). Journalism and emotional work. *Journalism Studies*, 22(12), 1567–1573. https://doi.org/10.1080/1461670X.2021.1977168

Papacharissi, Z. (2016). Affective publics and structures of storytelling: Sentiment, events and mediality. *Information, Communication & Society*, 19(3), 307–324. https://doi.org/10.1080/1369118X.2015.1109697

Parks, P. (2021). Joy is a news value. *Journalism Studies*, 22(6), 820–838. https://doi.org/10.1080/1461670X.2020.1807395

Perreault, G. P. (2023). Finding joy as journalists. In V. Bélair-Gagnon, A. E. Holton, M. Deuze, & C. Mellado (Eds.), *Happiness in Journalism* (1st ed., pp. 25–32). London: Routledge. https://doi.org/10.4324/9781003364597-5

Perreault, G. P., & Bélair-Gagnon, V. (2024). The lifestyle of lifestyle journalism: How reporters discursively manage their spirations in their daily work. *Journalism Practice*, 18(7), 1641–1659. https://doi.org/10.1080/17512786.2022.2111697

Perreault, G., & Miller, K. (2022). When journalists are voiceless: How lifestyle journalists cover hate and mitigate harassment. *Journalism Studies*, 23(15), 1977–1993. https://doi.org/10.1080/1461670X.2022.2135583

Peters, C. (2011). Emotion aside or emotional side? Crafting an 'experience of involvement' in the news. *Journalism*, 12(3), 297–316. https://journals.sagepub.com/doi/abs/10.1177/1464884910388224

Posetti, J., Bell, M., & Brown, P. (2020). *Journalism & the Pandemic: A Global Snapshot of Impacts*. ICFJ and Tow Center for Digital Journalism. https://www.icfj.org/our-work/journalism-and-pandemic-survey

Reinardy, S. (2011). Newspaper journalism in crisis: Burnout on the rise, eroding young journalists' career commitment. *Journalism*, 12(1), 33–50. https://doi.org/10.1177/1464884910385188

Richards, B. (2007). *Emotional Governance: Politics, Media and Terror*. Basingstoke: Palgrave Macmillan. https://doi.org/10.1057/9780230592346

Riegert, K., Roosvall, A., & Widholm, A. (2015). The political in cultural journalism: Fragmented interpretative communities in the digital age. *Journalism Practice*, 9(6), 773–790. https://doi.org/10.1080/17512786.2015.1051358

Riegert, K., & Widholm, A. (2019). The difference culture makes: Comparing Swedish news and cultural journalism on the 2015 terrorist attacks in Paris. *Nordicom Review, 40*(2), 3–18. https://doi.org/10.2478/nor-2019-0009

Soronen, A. (2018). Emotional labour in magazine work: Suppressing and evoking emotions as part of project-based teamwork. *Journalism Practice, 12*(3), 290–307. https://doi.org/10.1080/17512786.2017.1297685

Stupart, R. (2023). The joy in journalism. In V. Bélair-Gagnon, A. E. Holton, M. Deuze, & C. Mellado (Eds.), *Happiness in Journalism* (1st ed., pp. 19–24). London: Routledge. https://doi.org/10.4324/9781003364597-4

Thorpe, H. (2008). Foucault, technologies of self, and the media: Discourses of femininity in snowboarding culture. *Journal of Sport and Social Issues, 32*(2), 199–229. https://doi.org/10.1177/0193723508315206

Tuchman, G. (1972). Objectivity as strategic ritual: An examination of newsmen's notions of objectivity. *American Journal of Sociology, 77*(4), 660–679. https://www.jstor.org/stable/2776752

Tumber, H. (2004). Prisoners of news values? Journalists, professionalism, and identification in times of war. In S. Allan & B. Zelizer (Eds.), *Reporting War: Journalism in Wartime* (pp. 190–205). London: Routledge.

Van Zoonen, L. (1998). A professional, unreliable, heroic marionette (M/F): Structure, agency and subjectivity in contemporary journalisms. *European Journal of Cultural Studies, 1*(1), 123–143. https://journals.sagepub.com/doi/10.1177/136754949800100108?icid=int.sj-abstract.citing-articles.19

Wahl-Jorgensen, K. (2013). The strategic ritual of emotionality: A case study of Pulitzer Prize-winning articles. *Journalism, 14*(1), 129–145. https://doi.org/10.1177/1464884912448918

Wahl-Jorgensen, K. (2016). Emotion and journalism. In T. Witschge, C. W. Anderson, D. Domingo & A. Hermida (Eds.), *The SAGE Handbook of Digital Journalism* (pp. 128–143). London: SAGE. Pre-print version. https://orca.cf.ac.uk/87552/

Wahl-Jorgensen, K. (2020). An emotional turn in journalism studies? *Digital Journalism, 8*(2), 175–194. https://www.tandfonline.com/doi/full/10.1080/21670811.2019.1697626

Wahl-Jorgensen, K. (2022). Local knowledge and epistemic authority in entrepreneurial journalism. *Digital Journalism, 12*(1), 48–62. https://doi.org/10.1080/21670811.2022.2128388

Xiao, Y., & Watson, M. (2019). Guidance on conducting a systematic literature review. *Journal of Planning Education and Research, 39*(1), 93–112. https://doi.org/10.1177/0739456X17723971

Zelizer, B., Boczkowski, P. J., & Anderson, C. W. (2022). *The Journalism Manifesto*. Cambridge: Polity Press.

14
WELLNESS INFLUENCING IN INDIA

Ayurveda and identity on social media

Anuja Premika and Sumana Kasturi

Introduction

The significance of the wellness industry in modern life is hard to deny. The Global Wellness Institute, a non-profit research and education organisation, defines wellness as "the active pursuit of activities, choices, and lifestyles that lead to a state of holistic health" (Global Wellness Institute, 2023, p. i). The modern global wellness economy has come to include a range of health- and lifestyle-related markets, including personal care and beauty; healthy eating, nutrition, and weight loss; physical activity; wellness tourism; traditional and complementary medicine; public health, prevention, and personalised medicine; wellness real estate; and mental wellness, putting the market's size at an estimated $5.6 trillion in 2022 (Global Wellness Institute, 2023, p. 1). More conservative estimates placed it at over $1.5 trillion, albeit with a less precise definition of wellness as including health, fitness, nutrition, appearance, sleep, and mindfulness (McKinsey, 2021). Industry sources assert that spending in wellness is at an all-time high (McKinsey, 2021), and by all estimates, wellness is a category on the rise.

The wellness nexus also includes wellness media—as individual and institutional sources populate pages, soundwaves, and screens in response to the widespread appetite for wellness information. The prevalence of experts—self-styled or otherwise—has in some ways been a mainstay of wellness culture, from the religious practitioners associated with ancient Eastern wellness cultures to modern day self-styled "wellness gurus" (Baker, 2022).

Wellness gurus of some sort have always existed—evangelical healers, yoga teachers, other kinds of wellness practitioners, charismatic individuals, and those with the ability to effectively market and advertise their products and services have often been successful. Where traditional media such as radio and television allowed a level of gatekeeping, social media has amplified these teachings and allowed for a greater reach, with everyone from doctors, healthcare professionals, and hobbyists turning influencers to offer their unique take on health. While there is no doubt that genuine and scientific content is available on social media, economic and algorithmic imperatives mean that certain kinds of content—weight loss, beauty, diets, and exercise routines—dominate the platforms.

DOI: 10.4324/9781003396727-17

Hund (2023) charts how the early influencer industry was built of traditional media professionals who sought ways to continue to create culture, even as journalism became a less viable career path following the global financial crisis in the 2000s. The productive labor carried out by these influencers is often no different than that of traditional media producers (Duffy, 2022, p. 8), and they in fact become "miniature media empires in their own right" (Hund, 2023, p. 26), occupying a "professional class of their own…in the vein of advertising, film, or journalism" (Hund, 2023, p. 152). As such, influencers, particularly in lifestyle areas, have come to perform the functions that traditional lifestyle journalists have and do, often challenging or even upending traditional hierarchies of tastemaking (Duffy, 2022).

In this chapter, we examine a slice of the lifestyle journalism landscape in India by focusing on wellness influencers on YouTube. We study a selection of videos from a sample set of YouTube channels to observe how traditional wellness is framed and constructed in the diverse but fluid areas of health, nutrition, exercise, and beauty. In three different languages—Hindi, Tamil, and English—these content creators, from professional healthcare providers to self-styled experts and hobbyists, offer advice, tutorials, and reviews on Ayurvedic and/or natural/traditional practices and products. We explore their discourse around wellness in general and Ayurveda in particular to examine how social media influencers such as those in our sample survey contribute to the larger construction of Ayurveda as an indigenous knowledge system within the Indian sociopolitical landscape.

Wellness culture and the global wellness industry

Baker (2022) traces the beginnings of what we now know as wellness culture to the counter-culture movements of the 60s and 70s in the United States. Encompassing the wave of anti-war protests, the hippie and human potential movements, and the fight for civil rights and women's rights, the period involved a large-scale questioning of mainstream ideas about society, economics, education, and healthcare. Rejecting the tenets of capitalism and materialism that seemed to define American life at that time, there was a widespread interest in wellness practices based on nature and a holistic lifestyle. Many of those in these movements looked East for inspiration, adapting ideas from Buddhism and Hinduism and adopting practices such as yoga, meditation, Chinese medicine, and Ayurveda. Thus, the concept of holistic wellness grew as an alternative to mainstream medicine and as part of a larger rejection of the capitalist imperatives of many institutions including healthcare. Over time, the concept of wellness has undergone a transformation, maintaining its counter-culture roots, and its interest in ancient wellness practices, but coalescing into an amalgamation of consumer goods and services to be sold in the marketplace. This is concurrent with the blurring boundaries between lifestyle, culture, and consumption in journalistic coverage and the popular imagination (Kristensen & From, 2012).

Ostensibly, wellness is a nebulous category, and the leakiness between health and wellness has allowed for a plurality of framings to populate the market, as well as the popular imagination—ranging from the health and para-health categories of nutrition and mental health, to recreational spas and resorts, and to everyday consumables such as soaps and toothpastes. This ambiguity allows for a range of practitioners from the well-qualified medical/health professional to the self-taught influencer to all clamour for our attention in the crowded and extremely lucrative wellness market.

Wellness, or the practice of it, has always been surrounded by misinformation. The old snake-oil salesmen and the patented tonics and tinctures claiming cures for all kinds of ailments have always been part and parcel of the healthcare and wellness arena. Questionable science and doctors and self-styled experts with shaky credentials have always existed. But social media has escalated that connection, and the entrance of celebrity culture into the wellness space has not helped. The example of Hollywood actress Gwyneth Paltrow selling questionable products based on pseudo-science and pop-spirituality via her lifestyle brand Goop is a commonly cited one (Baker, 2022).

Over the years, as social media platforms have grown in scale, usage, and influence, calls to regulate these for-profit platforms have only grown. For the most part, these influential tech companies have resisted those efforts, making small gestures of appeasement by creating guidelines and promising to self-regulate. Knee-jerk responses in the wake of upheavals—such as the COVID-19 pandemic or the January 6 insurrection at the US Capitol in 2021—have resulted in punitive measures after the fact such as de-platforming key figures, cracking down on users who promote misinformation, and creating a body of social media experts as advisers—have been half-hearted and largely ineffective in addressing the serious concerns that social media scholars and policy experts continue to have (Cusumano et al., 2021; Mirchandani, 2020; Stockmann, 2023). With regard to health and wellness, social media platforms have made some efforts to curb disinformation and promote greater transparency and accuracy by establishing formal partnerships with credible partners such as the Cleveland Clinic, The American Association for Public Health, and the New England Journal of Medicine, as can be seen from their respective public websites. Similarly, YouTube community guidelines also lay down specific rules to prevent medical misinformation.

Much of the writing and critique of wellness culture comes out of the Global North and situates their arguments within the sociopolitical terrain of those countries. The literature on this new and emerging phenomenon in the South Asian context is sparse, and we believe that it is vital to rectify this gap. Media studies scholars have noted that the Global South continues to be viewed, understood, and analysed in comparison to or juxtaposed against the vantage point of the Global North. With more than a quarter of the world's population living in South Asia, this becomes especially important in the context of digital cultures: a perspective that does not account for the sheer numbers of media creators and consumers is an incomplete one. Such an approach renders the experiences of ordinary people in the Global South invisible and denies them agency (Willems, 2014; Iqani & Resende, 2019). As part of the larger goal of decolonising the field of media studies, we seek to offer perspectives and theory grounded in the everyday life experiences of the average Indian media consumer/influencer but set against the sociopolitical backdrop of larger global trends. For our study of the construction of how Ayurveda is framed and constructed within Indian social media, we have, therefore, sought to situate our analysis within the specific historical, social, and political contexts of the Indian experience.

The Indian wellness industry

The wellness industry in India has shown a steady increase over the past several years, and market watchers have identified a few different factors for this growth, including an increase in disposable incomes among middle-class consumers, and the entry of private-sector investors into the wellness space. Other factors include greater awareness of the value of health and wellbeing especially since the COVID-19 pandemic and a Government of India initiative that has renewed the focus on alternative medicine and general wellness issues (Bakhtiani, 2021). Market research statistics show that the Indian wellness market was valued at nearly 78 billion in 2020, ranking 12th among the top 20 wellness markets for that year. In that same period, the Asia Pacific region, of which India is a part, had the world's largest wellness economy at an estimated 1.5 trillion USD (Global Wellness Institute, 2023).

The Government of India has sought to highlight traditional systems of medicine and wellness with the establishment of the Ministry of AYUSH (an acronym for Ayurveda, Yoga, Unani, Siddha, and Homeopathy, which as a word also means 'Age' or 'Long-life' in Hindi) in order to boost awareness and visibility both within the country and abroad. Despite the name, the ministry's focus has been largely concentrated on Ayurveda and yoga, both associated with Hindu tradition. Ayurveda, an indigenous medicine system native to the Indian subcontinent, has emerged as a key focus both institutionally and in the cultural landscape. Described by some as part of the Indian government's attempt at "restoring India's past glory" (Doshi, 2018), Ayurveda has often been tied to the rhetoric of "Indian culture" (Langford, 2002) and has been seen as a token of "national belonging and biomoral consumerism" (Khalikova, 2017).

The Indian sociopolitical context with regard to health and wellness follows a different trajectory from that identified in the United States and other Western countries. Where the idea of wellness culture emerged as a factor of the counter-culture movement of the 60s and 70s in the United States, India's initial imperative to focus on wellness traditions like Ayurveda, Unani, yoga, and meditation was part of the larger postcolonial project to reclaim and reinvigorate indigenous knowledge systems after Indian Independence in 1947. In recent years, a renewed sense of nationalism has emerged, involving a push to regain India's past glory in the 21st century. This new motivation results in a heady mix of nationalistic fervour and market imperatives, where reclaiming wellness practices and knowledge systems derided by Western medicine and colonial administrators on the one hand and appropriated by neo-liberal wellness culture on the other act as a reassertion of ethnic and religious identity and a potent tool of soft power.

National identity and homegrown traditions

Drawing on Foucault's idea of biopolitics and biopower, Berger (2013) argues that the framing of Ayurveda in contemporary discourse needs to be seen within the scope of the biopolitical. Similarly, Khalikova describes how the policy of promoting traditional (alternative) medicine in India is inextricably linked with the "cultural politics of nationalism" (2017, p. 105) and notes that scholarship has shown how strategically framed health practices like yoga, Indian wrestling, and blood donations (Alter, 2021 as cited in Khalikova, 2017) are capable of "generating experiences of embodied nationalism" (2017, p. 117). The concept of swadeshi or homegrown (a concept developed during the Indian independence movement as a call to boycott British-made goods and become self-sufficient) is strategically deployed here to build pride, ownership, and a sense of patriotic duty to not just follow certain traditional practices but also to consume the products sold within that framework of understanding. India has a few striking examples of self-styled (mostly male) lifestyle/wellness gurus and spiritual teachers who have successfully combined the rhetoric of ancient, authentic, homegrown pride and savvy marketing and media skills to spread their message and build their business empires both in India and abroad (Choudhury, 2019).

Perhaps the biggest example of this phenomenon is the rise of yoga guru and Ayurvedic businessman, Baba Ramdev, and his homegrown brand Patanjali (Chakraborty, 2006; Khalikova, 2017). We observe here a form of "biomoral consumerism" (Khalikova, 2017, p. 115) deftly intermingled with a nationalist rhetoric that imbues both the traditions and the products and services with an uninterrogated credibility and legitimacy that encourages greater and greater consumption keeping people coming back for more and more. Thus, the growth and visibility of carefully chosen Indian wellness traditions has been fuelled by the combination of media-savvy "gurus", a supportive administration, and an eager citizenry as a point of nationalist pride on the domestic front and tool of soft power on the global stage, all facilitated by the strategic deployment of traditional mass media and social media.

Wellness influencing in India

From licensed healthcare providers to self-styled experts to the casual enthusiast, wellness influencing in the Indian content space today comes from a range of sources. Accurate information does exist, but as in other countries, misinformation abounds, and, following social media platform policies, the Government of India has also issued specific guidelines for content creators and influencers in the wellness space regarding disclosure and disclaimers based on one's qualifications or the lack of them (Department of Consumer Affairs, Government of India).

In this chapter, we chose to focus on lifestyle and wellness influencers on YouTube who consistently focus on the practice of Ayurveda to examine how it is framed within a popular wellness discourse, given Ayurveda's dominant position (along with yoga) in the Indian wellness space, as well as its success as a global cultural export. Our understanding and analysis is drawn from studying a large number of videos from within this wellness space and also by close reading of a sample set of videos drawn from five popular influencers who create content in three languages—English, Hindi, and Tamil. We chose these channels for their robust content catalogue, the diverse domains of interest and content formats they represent, as well as their reach.

- FitTuber (English, 7.48 million subscribers): a fitness enthusiast who creates videos about health and nutrition. He regularly makes videos about natural, herbal, and Ayurvedic living.
- Gunjan Shouts (Hindi, 1.71 million subscribers) also runs a fitness company. She makes videos primarily around weight loss, diet, and exercise and frequently makes videos about Ayurvedic food and wellness principles.
- Ayurveda for Everyone (Hindi, 1.05 million subscribers) is run by a licensed Ayurvedic practitioner with a Bachelors and Masters in Ayurvedic Medicine and Surgery. She creates videos about various aspects of health and disease, while also talking about mental wellness, lifestyle, and personal care.
- Akshara Rao's (Tamil, 745,000 subscribers) eponymous channel features videos centred around beauty. She frequently engages with Ayurvedic beauty practices in the form of home remedies, reviews of herbal products, and skin and hair care routines.
- SugarSpiceNice India (English, 304,000 subscribers) makes videos about food, lifestyle, and travel primarily in the form of vlogs. She regularly visits Ayurvedic resorts and spas across India and documents her experiences.

Genres of wellness influencing

While the arena of wellness spans a wide range of topics, we identified four broad categories of content and recurring tropes that seemed most popular:

Lifestyle: Everyday wellness: Amply justifying their place within the larger arena of lifestyle journalism, these videos often emphasise Ayurveda as a lifestyle choice. Returning to nature, rejecting the tenets of the West, practicing mindfulness, and slow living—the influencers call on shared culture, a sense of nostalgia, and a resistance from external influence to promote everyday Ayurvedic wellness.

Health: The medicalisation of wellness: Perhaps most closely associated with the notion of wellness, health discourse seeped into much of the content we surveyed. Emphasising Ayurveda's holistic approach to health and its focus on preventative rather than curative care, the vocabulary of health and medicine permeated many conversations, from offering solutions to ailments like acidity and rhinitis to framing a scalp massage as a form of hair treatment.

Beauty: External proof of wellness within: Indian women have always grappled with the cultural expectations that are embedded in the health and beauty discourse. In these videos, the focus on health easily transitions into references to beauty and essentialising around what bodies are considered healthy and thus beautiful.

Food: Where wellness begins: What to eat? When to eat it? What is the right way to prepare it? And how do you optimally pair foods? The influencers in our sample spoke a great deal about how food was Ayurveda's first line of defence against a host of maladies and offered highly prescriptive rules around eating natural and local to restore balance to one's body.

Performing an Ayurvedic identity: Culture, religion, and the nation

While some practices associated with Ayurveda are deeply embedded in Indian living, its specific deployment in the public sphere can be traced to the years during and following India's independence movement. Practitioners conceived Ayurveda as a "sign of the nation" and sought with urgency to construct Ayurveda as an indelible part of Indian culture and yoke its growth and inclusion in India's health frameworks as the healing of national culture itself, a potent sentiment in postcolonial India (Langford, 2002). Other scholars have noted how everyday practices are consciously linked to Ayurvedic tradition, with practitioners prescribing home remedies and diets that were already a part of the Indian cultural framework (Tirodkar, 2008, p. 239), thus "constructing Ayurveda as a symbol of Indian civilisation" (Khalikova, 2017, p. 107).

These linkages were clearly displayed in our sample. Gunjan Shouts describes researching and looking for remedies to treat hair loss and finding that everyone, including her mother, suggests Ayurvedic remedies. Shweta of SugarSpiceNice compares a high-end hair treatment at an Ayurvedic spa to the home remedies that "our grandmothers used," calling on shared cultural memory and connecting them to Ayurvedic tradition. Such linkages abound in the universe of videos we examined and show how these juxtapositions serve to imbue everyday household practises with the weight of tradition, culture, and civilisation.

But who decides what constitutes tradition and culture is a matter of social and political expediency, and both "culture" and "Indian" are far from stable categories. Plural imaginations around who and what counts as Indian have always existed—predominantly along territorial, cultural, and religious lines (Varshney, 1993, p. 234). Baba Ramdev—yoga guru and Ayurveda businessman—has perhaps most successfully reinforced the link between Ayurveda and India and codified who the Ayurvedic Indian is. The markers he deploys—language, clothing, and religious references—all signify Hindu tradition.

> By mobilising people at yoga camps and other gatherings where he promotes yoga and Ayurveda as evidence of India's glorious past, Ramdev engages in a biopolitical project, not only seeking to discipline Indian bodies, but also implicitly determining whose bodies count as Indian.
>
> *(Khalikova, 2017, p. 117)*

The privileging of these particular knowledge systems as constituting Indianness over other state-sanctioned health traditions such as Unani or Siddha coincides with the disproportionate and unprecedented state support offered to yoga and Ayurveda over the other systems under AYUSH, which Khalikova attributes to their association with Hinduism, and "rival conceptualisations of the Indian nation, situated within the neo-liberal discourses on health, morality and consumption" (2017, p. 106).

Flowing from this notion of Indianness, we begin to see how an "Ayurvedic identity" begins to emerge in this particular wellness universe. A sense of belonging and ownership of the Ayurvedic system was apparent as the influencers appealed to a sense of shared identity and culture with their audiences. Marwick (2013) notes that the construction and performance of identity on social media is a deliberate, reflexive, and self-conscious process. The influencers in our sample all performed some version of this—the espousal of Ayurvedic living as essential to wellness and the stylised performance of this Ayurvedic living. When the influencers engage in this performative exercise, they do so while embedded within a culture where this framing has been strategically employed. We note that even as they draw from these cultural constructions, as highly followed creators holding some cultural capital (Bourdieu, 1986), they are also producers of this culture, reinforcing understandings around what constitutes the "Indian."

Situated within this cultural framework, the influencers' performances of Indian identity range from the mundane to the overtly religious. In one video, Shweta exhorts her audience not to "come at" her for not eating with her hand—an ostensibly "Indian" way to eat; other visuals show her lighting a lamp at a Hindu altar and saying that she loves that the treatment begins with prayer. Another video features an Ayurvedic doctor narrating an origin story for Ayurveda that includes the divine gifting of this knowledge to a group of upper caste families. FitTuber shares videos of herbal drinks and other dietary recommendations and underscores them by citing the Gita, a Hindu sacred text, as endorsing some of these food practices. His videos are often delivered in a didactic style, with opening visuals for his videos showing him reading from books, emphasising his apparent expertise of the ancient texts. The Ayurvedic identity emerging in this sphere draws on a religious- and caste-coded legacy and involves performative practices that are conspicuously Hindu.

As such, we do not intend to interrogate or speculate about the religious identity of the creators in our sample. Rather, we aim to explicate the dominant framework within which this Ayurvedic identity is constructed. As Tirodkar points out, Ayurvedic practitioners often "draw on patients' spiritual beliefs—even the patients who are not practicing Hindus will listen and accept this advice, because they are raised in a Hindu cultural framework" (2008, p. 238). Against the sociopolitical landscape of India today, where increasingly hegemonic narratives of national identity are constructed in religio-cultural terms, the deliberate, and as we go on to demonstrate, sometimes uncritical championing of Ayurveda to online audiences today (re)produces this dominant cultural framework.

Modern Ayurveda and biomedicine: Continuities and tensions

Over the years, Ayurveda has gone through periods of revival and resignification, and contemporary scholars understand "modern Ayurveda" largely as a product of its 19th-century revivalism (see Wujastyk & Smith, 2008). Modern Ayurveda is understood as having undergone a degree of secularisation (Wujastyk & Smith, 2008) and standardisation (Langford, 2002). Central to this project was the institutionalisation of the field, through the introduction of medical curricula, colleges, and hospitals (see Langford, 2002). In doing so, the mysticism of Ayurvedic texts was largely replaced by forms of scientific knowledge associated with coloniality, offering "closure to the open-endedness" of Ayurvedic texts:

> Contemporary urban practitioners, at least those working in hospitals, are largely committed to a representation of Ayurveda as a tidy system satisfying even the most structuralist desire for a narrative in which diseased oppositions are (re)solved through synthesizing cures.
>
> *(Langford, 2002, p. 15)*

This adoption of the vocabulary and sometimes even the philosophies of biomedicine—an orientation towards curative rather than preventative medicine (Banerjee, 2020)—are part of the broader picture of how Ayurveda was made legible within the frame of modern/Western biomedicine. This legibility also renders Ayurveda palatable—allowing general audiences on social media to consume and assimilate content without having to challenge the dominant episteme of modern biomedicine. Tirodkar (2008) points out that modern Ayurvedic practitioners use biomedical tools such as stethoscopes and blood pressure gauges and often wear white coats—"a symbol associated with Western medical knowledge" (see Kleinman, 1988). These symbols serve as "performing objects," communicating meaning, and standing in for aspects of the influencers' identity (Raman & Premika, 2024, p. 123).

The influencers in our sample often used the vocabulary and visuality associated with biomedicine in their explications of Ayurvedic practice. Many of the doctors featured in the videos wear white lab coats (which is, in fact, uncommon when visiting a traditional Ayurvedic practitioner) and often have stethoscopes and other paraphernalia prominently displayed. One doctor mentions the World Health Organization's (WHO) definition of health as the absence of disease, showing how Ayurveda aligns with this definition, and others mention that modern medicine agrees with a key Ayurvedic tenet—prevention is better than cure. We see how the doctors featured in these videos are themselves products of the institutionalisation project.

While the doctors' positionality as authority figures is in part strengthened by the veneer of biomedicality, this authority is employed to bolster the validity of a range of practices—from the "resident doctor consultations" offered to visitors of an Ayurvedic spa to "medical authorities" quality testing oils and mixes produced for in-house treatments. The presence of licensed doctors and their self-conscious deployment of recognisable motifs allow viewers to read Ayurveda without the dissonance associated with comprehending an alternative medical system.

The creators adopted a degree of medical pluralism as well, where "Ayurvedic patients and practitioners strike a balance between accepting elements of competing medical systems and maintaining the distinctiveness of Ayurvedic insights and methods" (Langford, 2002, p. 12). One influencer shares his research process for suggesting Ayurvedic alternatives to common allopathic medicines, by explaining that he consulted classical texts and both Ayurvedic practitioners and modern medical doctors. This balancing between ancient wisdom and modern science is a recurring theme in the videos we examined. Interestingly, where the creators adopted identifiable themes from biomedicine or invoked biomedical perspectives, they only did so insofar as it helped build their case for Ayurveda. Indeed, they invoked Western medicine with still greater force when criticising it helped achieve the same end. While the systematisation of Ayurveda served to offer a viable alternative to Western medicine, it was also meant to "offer a corrective for it" (Langford, 2002, p. 10) and the poor health that resulted from the "imitation of European lifestyles" (p. 20).

This sentiment, a driving force of the 20th-century efforts to reinvent Ayurveda, continues to find resonance today:

> [Ramdev] argues that India has been deprived of respect and recognition due to the hundreds of years of foreign colonisation and weak post-colonial politics. Because of their lack of self-respect and pride in Indian culture, Ramdev says, Indians erroneously aspire to be like Westerners, wear Western clothes and use Western medicine
> *(Khalikova, 2017, p. 111)*

Even as the practitioners in our video sample sought to use markers of biomedicality to boost credibility, there was a performative rejection of the West by several of the influencers themselves. For instance, FitTuber describes the ideal Ayurvedic diet and advocates for maintaining an eating window that aligns with the Sun, but he is careful to differentiate it from intermittent fasting—its modern (and Western) equivalent—saying that only that which is aligned with the laws of nature will work in the long term. In another video, he criticises modern medicines including antibiotics as merely suppressing but not healing the problem. This performative rejection of Western living includes creators bemoaning the malady of modernity and a culture of globalisation where people eat and use foods and products that aren't local to them and hence are inherently worse.

Ayurveda in the public imagining and as evidenced in our study as well is presented as a natural, safe, and non-toxic alternative to modern Western medicine. This theme was reiterated across the Ayurvedic wellness influencer universe and was offered as a justification for many different things. The theme of food as medicine was a recurring one in the videos, an emphasis on local, natural foods and remedies and particular ways of eating including combinations of food, eating times, and freshness. Dr Rupali of Ayurveda for Everyone, for instance, recommends eating local varieties of rice to combat obesity and diabetes but offers no supporting material for this recommendation. Other influencers similarly suggest eating local fruits and vegetables over "foreign" foods, for example, coconuts rather than avocados. There is little explanation for why this may be so; instead, we are offered a categorical dismissal of all foreign foods and a didactic recommendation to eat local. The videos also frequently recommend vegetarianism, which is framed as pure and most desirable. Notably, while vegetarianism in the West is associated with animal rights and ethical eating and considered a liberal cause, in India, it is usually a marker of upper caste identity and a key component of Indian gastro-politics (Sathyamala, 2019;

Kasturi, 2023). These and other endorsements are often justified by the rationale that they are Ayurvedic. Merely adding the word "Ayurvedic" or even "herbal" before a product or treatment seems to legitimise its safety and efficacy. Gunjan and Shweta both recommend "Ayurvedic khichdi," but their recipes are no different from standard preparations of the rice and lentil dish.

By extension, there is a belief that everything related to Ayurveda is natural and in alignment with nature and therefore safe. Influencers frequently mention that Ayurveda takes them "back to the roots" or "back to basics." Tirodkar notes that "many patients are willing to give Ayurvedic medicines a try because they do not believe it will harm them. It can either work in a positive way or not have any side effects (adverse effects) at all." He points out that products labelled as "natural" are not automatically without adverse effects, and modern Ayurvedic medicines are often not even fully natural as consumers understand the word (2008, p. 234). Through candid personal accounts or the persuasive rhetoric of "all-natural" living, the appeal of which is rising globally (Callaghan et al., 2021), the influencers endorse sometimes suspect products or practices. By reinforcing Ayurveda as self-evidently powerful, they also become actors in a broader politics of knowledge and the institutional and historical project to construct Ayurveda as a legible medical system.

Selling the Ayurvedic lifestyle: Commerce, consumption, and class

Several of the influencers in our sample focus on describing their experiences and feelings. For example, Shweta frequently mentions treatments having a calming or cooling effect, feeling relaxed, and even experiencing "sheer bliss." She confesses to not knowing how to pronounce the Ayurvedic terms, and while she invokes the science behind the treatments, she rarely shares in-depth information about the methods or treatments she is undergoing. She focuses instead on vivid, sincere, and affective descriptions of her firsthand experiences. Similarly, Akshara shares her process and experience in using a product without delving into any details. This casual approach conveys immediacy, authenticity, and a personal connection with their audiences and is part of their appeal. Commenters for both influencers laud the sharing of these personal experiences, rendered authentic by their casual approach.

The perception of authenticity is key to the life of a social media influencer. Performing authenticity entails conveying one's "real self," but this self is presented for and validated by the "consumption" of others—through views and engagement (Gaden & Dumitrica, 2014). Further, authenticity, or at least the appearance of it, is central to creating a personal brand, one that is appealing to potential sponsors and advertisers, making authenticity the "axis on which the influencer industry" spins (Hund, 2023, p. 56). As Hund points out, "to reconcile the competing demands to 'be true' with the needs of advertisers for predictable, reliable, and measurable media channels, participants in the influencer industry began to differentiate between authenticity and accuracy" (p. 59). This distinction between authenticity and accuracy is further complicated in today's information environment:

> [I]n this era of fake news, deepfakes, and the wide circulation of misinformation, where particular concepts of the "truth" are questioned, authenticity means both more and less: the mandate to present as "authentic" has become more urgent, even as we increasingly no longer believe in the concept of the authentic
>
> *(Banet-Weiser, 2021, p. 142)*

This is still more precarious in the wellness sphere, where health and health-related information is routinely circulated and online discourse affords the production and reinforcing of counterknowledge and misinformation (Numerato et al., 2019). Privileging the experiential over the informational conveys authenticity, but one has to examine whether accuracy is sacrificed in the interest of "speaking one's truth."

In our sample, experience usually trumped information, and when information was offered, it was often built on shaky foundations. In Akshara's video about a hair oil product, the clickbait thumbnail shows side-by-side images of hair growing progressively longer, with the hashtag #hairgrowth. Yet the video itself contains no information about this supposed feature of the product. Similarly, Shweta tours a Patanjali Ayurved store, showing her viewers various products that are ostensibly unique and potent, but shares little information on why this may be so. The mere fact that this was a branded product of Patanjali Ayurved seems to be enough reason to endorse its efficacy. She raves about a "herbal cleaner" from the brand, but a quick check of the ingredients list reveals standard industry surfactants. Similarly, FitTuber makes bold claims about the superiority of certain Ayurvedic medicines as compared to standard OTC medications without corroborating these claims in any way. Several of the creators appeared to uncritically buy into product or treatment claims, even when they seemed exaggerated—such as a dry massage powder that could get rid of excess fat or that cold-pressed coconut oil (a highly comedogenic substance) could cure acne simply because they were labelled Ayurvedic.

Despite the popular rhetoric of influencers creating content for the "passion" of it, scholars of digital cultures have pointed out that influencers engage in a great deal of "aspirational labour"—a "mode of (mostly) uncompensated, independent work that is propelled by the much-venerated ideal of *getting paid to do what you love*," with the implicit expectation that "they will *one day* be compensated for their productivity" (Duffy, 2022, p. 4, emphasis in original). This economic insecurity is not without precedent in traditional media industries, where freelance and contract models are prevalent (Hesmondhalgh & Baker, 2013; Duffy, 2022; Bishop, 2022). In the context of lifestyle journalism, this economic precarity forms the backdrop for and further complicates the inherent consumerism of the field and the commercial influences on journalists in the form of free products and experiences (Fürsich, 2012). For influencers to get paid by or receive giveaways from brands and other sponsors, they first need to construct identities that are perceived as authentic, but are nonetheless balanced with commerciality—influencers need to "[commodify] different aspects of their everyday lives" (Arriagada & Bishop, 2021) and live "shoppable lives" (Hund & McGuigan, 2019). Influencers engage in modes of self-presentation that embody the qualities of brands they (hope to) work with (Carah & Shaul, 2016) and make the constituent elements of their lives purchasable by their viewers (Hund & McGuigan, 2019). Therefore, conspicuous consumption—sponsored or otherwise—needs to be brand-appropriate and brand-friendly.

In the case of the influencers in our sample, this means that they consistently engage with degrees of Ayurvedic consumption and embody the principles that guide that consumption—an unwavering belief in the Ayurvedic system, the promotion of Ayurveda over its alternatives, and the apologetic reconciliation of the inherent dissonance between what is supposed to be natural and local, with the regime of mass production and standardisation necessary to build an Ayurvedic brand.

Concurrent with the 19th-century revivalism of Ayurveda, Ayurvedic medicine manufacturing companies and non-governmental organisations rallied against "stereotypes, distortions and the maligning of an ancient medical knowledge system of India" and ultimately, along with the state, produced modern Ayurveda in line with a "pharmaceutic episteme," which focused on Ayurveda as a new source of pharmaceuticals and deemphasised its underlying philosophies about health and disease (Banerjee, 2002, p. 1136). Ayurveda itself adopted a consumerist ethos in the 20th century, as is evident from the establishment and growth of large-scale Indian Ayurvedic consumer goods brands such as Dabur in 1884, Himalaya Wellness Company in 1930, and most recently, Patanjali Ayurved in 2006.

The influencers in our sample have branded engagements to differing degrees—FitTuber's and Gunjan's videos featured sponsored segments for products such as herb-infused protein powders; Dr. Rupali's and Akshara's videos included affiliate links to herbal supplements and cosmetics, respectively; and Shweta makes videos about sponsored visits to Ayurveda resorts. At whatever level of collaboration, the influencers' brand engagements showed how they sold (and bought into) the commercialised logic of modern Ayurveda and how the class of the imagined viewer played into how content was conceived.

The way the influencers spoke of Ayurvedic consumption offers a means to understand how this dissonance is reconciled in the popular imagination. "If you want fast results," shares FitTuber in a video about Ayurvedic remedies for acne, "please avoid cosmetic products as much as possible," calling them "toxic and chemical-laden" products that will worsen the condition. In a video about hair care, Gunjan instructs her viewers that their use of modern hair care products that are "merely called safe" but "filled with chemicals" can cause hair breakage and loss. By contrast, she promotes a herbal hair oil by describing it as "not just a normal hair oil" but an Ayurvedic medicine. Akshara's video on Ayurvedic skincare and beauty tips that "will change your life" features an Ayurvedic brand's "toxic-free" face cream and moisturiser. Over and over again, the influencers promoted Ayurvedic consumption by insisting that the products were still "natural," as opposed to the "chemical" or "toxin-filled" products synthesised in labs. The demand for "natural" and "clean" products is hardly a uniquely Indian phenomenon, but Ayurveda's image as a nontoxic alternative to modern consumer goods and products is strengthened by its association with national identity and thus seems to offer a greater sense of satisfaction to its consumers.

Scholars have examined how Baba Ramdev's Patanjali effectively harnesses the "neoliberal discourses that weave together people's desires for health, consumption and national belonging, through the concept of Swadeshi (homegrown)" (Khalikova, 2017, p. 106). Further, Khalikova points out, by building on the rhetoric that Ayurveda embodies India's glory, Ramdev frames Ayurvedic consumption as a matter of national duty and moral obligation to revive this lost glory—a form of "biomoral consumerism," where consumption of his host of mass-produced products "is not just tolerated, but deemed ethical" (p. 115).

The influencers in our sample not only engage in and promote this kind of consumerism but also either turn a blind eye or justify the logic of the wide range of processed products sold as Ayurvedic, under the banner of various commercial brands such as Patanjali. The inherent contradictions in these stances require some disingenuous positioning, as when on the one hand, Shweta platforms doctors who insist that an Ayurvedic regimen requires that one must cut out all refrigerated food from one's diet, but on the other, showcases the various processed products—including frozen foods—during her tour of a Patanjali megastore. This contradiction surfaces frequently as influencers emphasise local and freshly prepared foods as a key aspect of Ayurvedic diets and then go on to unironically endorse an array of Ayurvedic-branded packaged foods, salt-laden snacks, and perhaps most egregiously, instant noodles. Patanjali noodles, in fact, are a notable case in point, having been launched at the time when Nestle's widely popular instant noodles brand Maggi was facing a ban in India. Christened "Ayurvedic Maggi" in popular discourse, the product became a subject of great debate—criticised for being an inferior replica or lauded for being a "wholesome domestic product" (Khalikova, 2017, p. 113). While trying the Patanjali instant noodles at the in-store cafeteria, Shweta points out that "they actually make it with a little bit of veggies here," as if trying to justify that the noodles are not completely devoid of natural nutrition. In another instance, Shweta shares her surprise on finding a wasabi-flavoured packaged food product, not because it is neither local nor fresh, but perhaps because it brings an element of international cuisine to the product. The construct of natural and local is then just that—a construct—one that the influencers either unhesitatingly buy into or simply do not care to question, even as they contribute to generating greater visibility and interest in Ayurvedic consumption.

While wellness is understood globally as a largely "feminised" space (O'Neill, 2020), wellness in India seems to indicate a different landscape. Ranging from the hyper-masculinised to the stereotypically feminine, imaginations around natural/Ayurvedic living in these spaces (and beyond) exhibit various modes of gendered subjectivity, which are entangled explicitly or otherwise with religion, class, and caste positions, as well as cultural practices and identities. The larger wellness landscape is dominated by strong male icons like Baba Ramdev and Sadhguru, while the social media space also features both male and female content creators. Some of the topics apply to both men and women, but a range of topics especially those about female health, beauty, make-up, food, and body issues seem to directly address women. Our survey of the larger landscape of such videos showed that male influencers—such as FitTuber—unabashedly provide advice on these issues, including what to eat during menstruation and what makeup/hygiene products to use and to avoid.

The modes of Ayurvedic consumption on display in the videos we analysed ranged from the affordable (items in your kitchen) to the luxurious (specialised oil massages performed by trained experts). Ayurveda is not the privilege of a particular class, as Tirodkar points out, but the question of "who uses which type of Ayurveda" is deeply classed (p. 230). Patanjali's consumer goods, for instance, often framed as local and affordable, are actually most commonly purchased by the wealthier classes of Indians, "who are familiar with the global discourses on organic, local, sustainable and natural produce," but his "more direct nationalism of authentic traditionalism and Vedic purity," Khalikova points out, appeals to a much broader range of class groups (2017, p. 116).

In several of his videos, FitTuber highlights the low prices of different items he mentions, even calculating the cost of his recommended skincare and diet routines to underscore the affordability of an Ayurvedic lifestyle and emphasising that modern alternatives are far more expensive. Dr. Rupali—a trained Ayurvedic professional cum influencer—also advocates for Ayurvedic solutions that offer relief that "expensive treatments cannot give you." Even as some of the influencers highlight affordability and hyper-locality as positive factors, others, such as Shweta, endorse luxury experiences at high-end Ayurvedic spas and resorts, a phenomenon that has become an integral part of international wellness tourism, catering mainly to foreign tourists and the urban middle and upper classes in India (Wujastyk & Smith, 2008, pp. 1–2).

This wide spectrum of Ayurvedic consumption, and the modes in which the influencers appropriate, represent, and promote it, demonstrates how popular rhetoric has captured the public imagination, offering a window into the complex market that has emerged for Ayurvedic products and experiences and the ways in which contradictions between the philosophy and market of modern Ayurveda become rationalised, still wearing the guise of naturalness and Indianness.

Discussion

The story of the modernisation and revival of Ayurveda, whose thread runs through any commentary one can make about the state of the system in today's context, is a compelling one. The brand of nationalism this project appropriated perhaps resonated in postcolonial India: nation and national identity building, cultural reclamation, and challenges to the hegemony of knowledge, science, and practices that smacked of colonialism. The rhetoric around Ayurveda today, and the form of nationalism it engenders, however, is far removed from the early postcolonial context. In a nation grappling with issues of religious fundamentalism, threats of disenfranchisement, and the rewriting of the nation's history to promote a majoritarian narrative, one must scrutinise any tool employed in the building of a nationalistic agenda.

Khalikova argues that "Ayurveda and yoga in contemporary India emerge as political projects that structure human conduct" (2017, p. 117). The culture around Ayurveda could indeed be thought of as disciplining bodies to be more Indian. We use discipline here in the way feminist materialist scholar Susan Bordo (1993) invokes Foucault's notion of discipline in relation to self-transformation and the body: "Pointing to practices that do not merely transform but normalize the subject" (p. 254).

If Ayurveda is a disciplining tool, it's hard to argue that the content creators studied here are either the disciplinarians or the disciplined. Their authentic self-narratives, candid performances, and their stated intention to "empower" their audiences with information are both entertaining and compelling to audiences. It is, however, important to interrogate the positions they occupy and the discourse they are contributing to—their own agendas notwithstanding. The influencers are all placed in relative positions of privilege within the extant frameworks of power—with access to tools of digital production, the cultural capital to engage and draw large audiences, and the commercial connections with brands to monetise their creative labour. Within these frameworks of power, they are at once being socialised into powerful state (or state-endorsed) narratives of health and heritage, while also producing their own narratives for consumption by audiences and employment by brands and other commercial entities. Straddling the authentic and the commercial, the modern and the traditional, and the local and the global, the influencers' performances tell us much about how wellness in India is constructed, imagined, and lived today. The story of wellness in India today is as much about nation, identity, and belonging, as it is about health and vitality.

Conclusion

The dominant framing of wellness as a feminised space and the privilege of certain classes is largely based on scholarship from the Global North. The landscape in India indicates that wellness may be constructed as a gender-neutral, or sometimes masculinised space, that gains at least part of its cachet from being accessible, everyday, and an alternative to the classed consumption associated with modernity and the West. The roots of several modern wellness cultures may be traced to ancient Eastern traditions, and the benefit of studying wellness not only in the forms they exist today but also against the backdrop of the contexts from which they've emerged cannot be overstated. There is a need to not only study wellness from plural contexts and understand how wellness is constructed and practiced in various regions but also historicise how modern, even Western wellness practices may have evolved from their Global South roots over the years.

Further reading

Baker, S. A. (2022). *Wellness Culture: How the Wellness Movement Has Been Used to Empower, Profit and Misinform*. Emerald Publishing Limited.

Duffy, B. E. (2022). *(Not) Getting Paid to Do What You Love: Gender and Aspirational Labor in the Social Media Economy*. Yale University Press.

Hund, E. (2023). *The Influencer Industry: The Quest for Authenticity on Social Media*. Princeton University Press. https://doi.org/10.2307/j.ctv2v6pczn

Iqani, M., & Resende, F. (2019). Theorizing Media in and Across the Global South: Narrative as territory, culture as flow. In M. Iqani & F. Resende (Eds.), *Media and the Global South:Narrative Territorialities, Cross-Cultural Currents* (pp. 1–16). Routledge.

Khalikova, V. R. (2017). The Ayurveda of Baba Ramdev: Biomoral Consumerism, National Duty and the Biopolitics of 'Homegrown' Medicine in India. *South Asia: Journal of South Asian Studies*, 40(1), 105–122. https://doi.org/10.1080/00856401.2017.1266987

References

Alter, J. S. (2021). Pahalwan Baba Ramdev: Wrestling with Yoga and Middle-Class Masculinity in India. *Modern Asian Studies*, 55(4), 1359–1381. https://doi.org/10.1017/S0026749X20000219

Arriagada, A., & Bishop, S. (2021). Between Commerciality and Authenticity: The Imaginary of Social Media Influencers in the Platform Economy. *Communication, Culture and Critique*, 14(4), 568–586. https://doi.org/10.1093/ccc/tcab050

Baker, S. A. (2022). *Wellness Culture: How the Wellness Movement Has Been Used to Empower, Profit and Misinform*. Emerald Publishing Limited.

Banerjee, M. (2020). Ayurveda and Covid-19: The Politics of Knowledge Systems, Yet Again. *Fieldsights*. https://culanth.org/fieldsights/ayurveda-and-covid-19-the-politics-of-knowledge-systems-yet-again

Banerjee, M. (2002). Public Policy and Ayurveda: Modernising a Great Tradition. *Economic and Political Weekly*, 37(12), 1136–1146. https://www.jstor.org/stable/4411901

Bakhtiani, G. (2021). How the Wellness Market in India Is Witnessing a Meteoric Rise. *Financial Express*. https://www.financialexpress.com/business/brandwagon-how-the-wellness-market-in-india-is-witnessing-a-meteoric-rise-2189156/

Banet-Weiser, S. (2021). Gender, Social Media, and the Labor of Authenticity. *American Quarterly*, 73(1), 141–144. https://doi.org/10.1353/aq.2021.0008

Berger, R. (2013). *Ayurveda Made Modern: Political Histories of Indigenous Medicine in North India, 1900-1955*. Palgrave Macmillan. https://doi.org/10.1057/9781137315908

Bishop, S. (2022). Influencer Creep. *Real Life*. https://reallifemag.com/influencer-creep/

Bordo, S. (1993). *Unbearable Weight: Feminism, Western Culture, and the Body*. University of California Press.

Bourdieu, P. (1986). The Forms of Capital. In J. Richardson (Ed.), *Handbook of Theory and Research for the Sociology of Education* (pp. 241–258). Bloomsbury Academic.

Callaghan, H., Lösch, M., Pione, A., & Teichner, W. (2021). *Feeling Good: The Future of the $1.5 Trillion Wellness Market*. McKinsey & Company. https://www.mckinsey.com/industries/consumer-packaged-goods/our-insights/feeling-good-the-future-of-the-1-5-trillion-wellness-market

Carah, N., & Shaul, M. (2016). Brands and Instagram: Point, Tap, Swipe, Glance. *Mobile Media & Communication*, 4(1), 69–84. https://doi.org/10.1177/2050157915598180

Chakraborty, C. (2006). Ramdev and Somatic Nationalism: Embodying the Nation, Desiring the Global. *Economic and Political Weekly*, 41(5), 387–390.

Choudhury, A. (2019). Why Hindutva nationalists need a Sadhguru. *The Wire*. https://thewire.in/politics/why-hindutva-nationalists-need-a-sadhguru

Cusumano, M. A., Gawer, A., & Yoffie, D. B. (2021). Social Media Companies Should Self-Regulate. Now. *Harvard Business Review*, 15. https://hbr.org/2021/01/social-media-companies-should-self-regulate-now

Department of Consumer Affairs, Government of India. *Additional Influencer Guidelines for Health and Wellness Celebrities, Influencers and Virtual Influencers*. https://consumeraffairs.nic.in/sites/default/files/file-uploads/latestnews/Additional%20Influencer%20Guidelines%20for%20Health%20and%20Wellness%20Celebrities%2C%20Influencers%20and%20Virtual%20Influencers.pdf

Doshi, V. (2018). How Ghee, Turmeric and Aloe Vera Became India's New Instruments of Soft Power. *The Washington Post*. https://www.washingtonpost.com/world/asia_pacific/how-ghee-turmeric-and-aloe-vera-became-indias-newinstruments-of-soft-power/2018/01/28/5eb8d836-f4ce-11e7-9af7-a50bc3300042_story.html

Duffy, B. E. (2022). *(Not) Getting Paid to Do What You Love: Gender and Aspirational Labor in the Social Media Economy*. Yale University Press.

Fürsich, E. (2012). Lifestyle Journalism as Popular Journalism: Strategies for Evaluating its Public Role. *Journalism Practice*, 6(1), 12–25. https://doi.org/10.1080/17512786.2011.622894

Gaden, G., & Dumitrica, D. (2014). The 'Real Deal': Strategic Authenticity, Politics and Social Media. *First Monday*. https://doi.org/10.5210/fm.v20i1.4985

Global Wellness Institute (2023). *Global Wellness Economy Monitor 2023*. https://globalwellnessinstitute.org/the-2023-global-wellness-economy-monitor/

Hesmondhalgh, D., & Baker, S. (2013). *Creative Labour: Media Work in Three Cultural Industries*. Routledge. https://doi.org/10.4324/9780203855881

Hund, E. (2023). *The Influencer Industry: The Quest for Authenticity on Social Media*. Princeton University Press. https://doi.org/10.2307/j.ctv2v6pczn

Hund, E., & McGuigan, L. (2019). A Shoppable Life: Performance, Selfhood, and Influence in the Social Media Storefront. *Communication, Culture and Critique*, 12(1), 18–35. https://doi.org/10.1093/ccc/tcz004

Iqani, M., & Resende, F. (2019). Theorizing Media in and Across the Global South: Narrative as territory, culture as flow. In M. Iqani & F. Resende (Eds.), *Media and the Global South: Narrative Territorialities, Cross-Cultural Currents* (pp. 1–16). Routledge.

Kasturi, S. (2023). Of Clay Stoves and Cooking Pots: "Village Food" Videos and Gastro-Politics in Contemporary India. In E. Fakazis & E. Fürsich (Eds.), *The Political Relevance of Food Media and Journalism: Beyond Reviews and Recipes* (pp. 135–152). Routledge.

Khalikova, V. R. (2017). The Ayurveda of Baba Ramdev: Biomoral Consumerism, National Duty and the Biopolitics of 'Homegrown' Medicine in India. *South Asia: Journal of South Asian Studies*, 40(1), 105–122. https://doi.org/10.1080/00856401.2017.1266967

Kleinman, A. (1988). *The Illness Narratives: Suffering, Healing, and the Human Condition*. Basic Books.

Kristensen, N. N., & From, U. (2012). Lifestyle Journalism: Blurring Boundaries. *Journalism Practice*, 6(1), 26–41. https://doi.org/10.1080/17512786.2011.622898

Langford, J. (2002). *Fluent Bodies: Ayurvedic Remedies for Postcolonial Imbalance*. Duke University Press.

Marwick, A. E. (2013). *Status Update: Celebrity, Publicity, and Branding in the Social Media Age*. Yale University Press. https://www.jstor.org/stable/j.ctt5vkzxr

Mirchandani, M. (Ed.) (2020). *Tackling Insurgent Ideologies in a Pandemic World*. ORF and Global Policy Journal. https://www.orfonline.org/public/uploads/posts/pdf/20230501120009.pdf

Numerato, D., Vochocová, L., Štětka, V., & Macková, A. (2019). The Vaccination Debate in the "Post-Truth" Era: Social Media as Sites of Multi-Layered Reflexivity. *Sociology of Health & Illness*, 41(S1), 82–97. https://doi.org/10.1111/1467-9566.12873

O'Neill, R. (2020). Pursuing "Wellness": Considerations for Media Studies. *Television & New Media*, 21(6), 628–634. https://doi.org/10.1177/1527476420919703

Raman, U., & Premika, A. (2024). Creating and Curating the Performing Object: Self-Making on #Bookstagram and #Inktober. In A. Ray, E. G. Dattatreyan, U. Raman, & M. Web (Eds.), *Digital Expressions of the Self(ie): The Social Life of Selfies in India* (pp. 97–128). Routledge.

Sathyamala, C. (2019). Meat-Eating in India: Whose Food, Whose Politics, and Whose Rights? *Policy Futures in Education*, 17(7), 878–891. https://doi.org/10.1177/1478210318780553

Stockmann, D. (2023). Tech Companies and the Public Interest: The Role of the State in Governing Social Media Platforms. *Information, Communication & Society*, 26(1), 1–15.

The future of wellness: Connected and customized. (2021). https://www.mckinsey.com/~/media/McKinsey/Featured Insights/The Next Normal/The-Next-Normal-The-future-of-wellness

Tirodkar, M. (2008). Cultural Loss and Remembrance in Contemporary Ayurvedic Medical Practice. In D. Wujastyk & F. M. Smith (Eds.), *Modern and Global Ayurveda: Pluralism and Paradigms* (pp. 227–241). State University of New York Press.

Varshney, A. (1993). Contested Meanings: India's National Identity, Hindu Nationalism, and the Politics of Anxiety. *Daedalus*, 122(3), 227–261. https://www.jstor.org/stable/20027190

Willems, W. (2014). Beyond Normative Dewesternization: Examining Media Culture from the Vantage Point of the Global South. *The Global South*, 8(1), 7–23.

Wujastyk, D., & Smith, F. M. (2008). Introduction. In D. Wujastyk & F. M. Smith (Eds.), *Modern and Global Ayurveda: Pluralism and Paradigms* (pp. 1–28). State University of New York Press.

15
BRINGING THE WORLD TO US
Travel journalism and the mediation of others

Ben Cocking

Introduction

A window on the world, a mediator of different cultures, a commentator on a seemingly never-ending array of leisure experiences and a form of journalism derided as frivolous and less serious than 'proper' news journalism, travel journalism is a rich, fast-evolving and contested genre fraught with contradiction and dissonance. Like most areas of lifestyle journalism, the massive technological transformation of the media landscape has meant that more traditional print-based forms of travel journalism now compete with professional and user-generated content across a range of media platforms.

Closely linked to the tourism industry, travel journalism is a highly commercial form of journalism, premised on promoting the consumption of tourism-related activities, experiences and products. Travel journalism trades in the representation of destinations, cultural mores and practices (Santos, 2006; Duffy, 2019). Academic interest in the topic is relatively new and emerging and has tended to centre on understanding the genre as a significant source of cultural mediation, where the representations of different cultures and cultural differences are constantly contested and refigured (Fürsich and Kavoori, 2001).

This chapter seeks to examine how the ways in which travel journalism mediates culture have become further complicated by the breadth of travel content we now encounter across media platforms. Drawing on a critical discourse analysis approach, it focuses on a sample of travel journalism content including print journalism and social media sites such as Instagram and TikTok. It considers the extent to which these different media platforms, built as they are on very different economic models, facilitate different forms of cultural mediation. The case study finds that whilst travel journalism's historical 'stock in trade' use of stereotypical cultural discourse and the exoticization of 'others' still proliferate, the breadth of travel content across platforms has impacted on the mediation of cultural difference in some surprising and unexpected ways.

Historical perspectives

Along with fashion journalism, travel journalism is one of the oldest and most well-established forms of lifestyle journalism (Mee, 2009, pp. 206–208) and has been a core part of the newspaper content 'package' for well over a hundred years. The origins of travel journalism can be traced back to the mid-1800s, a period in which travel became more accessible and affordable with the aristocratic grand tour seguing into middle-class, more mass-orientated tourism (Sezgin and Yolal, 2012). Modern tourism began to develop in Britain, Western Europe and North America as a form of leisure time – a by-product of the Industrial Revolution (Coltman, 1989). Newspapers quickly began to attune to the cultural phenomenon of mass tourism. From the 1830s and 1840s onwards, newspapers started to include travel features (Haugen, 2018). Such features emerged from a broader travel literature which included monographs, ethnographies, maritime narratives, published diaries, road and aviation writings and memoirs (Youngs, 2013, p. 3). In Britain, the repealing of stamp duty on newspapers in 1855 led to a rapid expansion in the numbers of daily papers and periodicals. Steward notes this enabled, "many would-be professional writers to make the bulk of their living by writing for the weekly and daily papers. Many took advantage of the fluidity of the boundaries between literature and journalism making it easy to move between them" (2005, p. 41). This literary heritage mixed with the genre's intrinsically commercial drive to represent other parts of the world through the use of "extravagant vocabulary and details in order to seduce readers" (Santos, 2006, p. 624). Travel journalism played a fundamental role in contributing to the rapid growth of mass tourism and shaping modern leisure activities of the late 19th and early 20th centuries:

> The world was presented as something to be consumed and it was here that the search for novelty, authenticity and difference was at its most frenetic. The new breed of travel journalists not only constructed their images of their own social and cultural identities but also contributed to the formation of those available to others.
>
> *(Steward, 2005, p. 52)*

Critical issues in travel journalism

Whilst it is clear travel journalism has made a significant contribution to the development of mass tourism, it is also the case that defining what it precisely is and what its relationship to other forms of journalism is remains contested and contradictory. Historically, news journalism has played an important function in Western democracies, holding power to account, challenging authority and ultimately enable us to participate as "citizens" in democratic processes (Humphreys, 2023). In some senses today, this may not be much more than an ideal, given the highly charged commercial environment in which journalism now exists. Nonetheless, this conception of journalism as a watchdog which checks and balances political power still lies very much at the heart of the industry's professional identity (Canella, 2023). Travel journalism speaks to its audience differently. In the context of travel journalism, we are not addressed as "citizens" with political agency but as "consumers" with economic and cultural capital (Brett, 2023).

There is a further interrelated problem. In the main, journalism content purports to be 'true'. It purports to cover and report things that have happened in the real world. The public, journalists themselves and academics who study journalism commonly understand journalistic content as portrayals of real-world events (McNair, 1998; Lau, 2012). Professional journalists are commonly understood to be our witnesses on the world. Is travel journalism content derived from real experiences of touristic activities? Arguably, in many respects, the answer is yes. However, it should also be acknowledged that the extent to which travel journalism is true is far less clear-cut than other forms of journalism. It is quite common for travel journalists to be given free holidays or free flights or free stays in hotels as part of them reporting upon touristic experiences. This compromises the journalistic integrity of the genre (Hanusch, 2012). Consequently, the industry has often perceived travel journalism as frivolous, advertorial copy, lower in status and of less importance than news and current affairs journalism. (Ashe, 2023).

Compounding these issues, travel journalism content can now be found on all media platforms, many of which actively facilitate users producing their own content. Nowadays, it is not always immediately apparent whether we are consuming user-generated or professionally produced content. Should we include this sort of content in trying to define travel journalism? I want to suggest that we should. After all, we can acknowledge that news content on X/Twitter may or may not be true or produced to the same ethical standards as, for example, television news, there is no doubt that it plays an important role in modern political communication (Wells et al., 2020). That travel content is produced by social media users alongside professional journalists is not a point of delineation for the genre but rather needs to be understood as part of the fast-evolving and multifaceted nature of the political economy of travel journalism (Blaer, Frost and Laing, 2020). Travel journalism can be most productively understood as travel-related content produced by both professional journalists and 'produsers', that is, in the public domain presented in written, visual and audio forms – typically, the narrative style is first person with the readers/audience being directly appealed to (Cocking, 2020, p. 14; Hanusch and Fürsich, 2014, pp. 6–8). Focused on touristic activities and experiences, it is a highly commercial form of journalism, stratified by socioeconomic indicators. Travel journalism is fast-changing and alive to the new developments in the tourism industry as well as commercial imperatives and stresses. It also influences and is influenced by other media and literary genres.

Current contributions and research: Why study travel journalism?

As a relatively emergent area of academic enquiry, a number of justifications for the study of travel journalism have been made. Opening the field of study, Fürsich and Kavoori outline five key aspects of the genre that warrant academic consideration (2001, pp. 150–154). They point to the huge growth of the tourism industry in the 1980s and 1990s as well as social and cultural roles of tourism and leisure time in society as three important contextual factors in understanding the significance of travel journalism. As one of the biggest and most prolific industries in the world, tourism continues to be a primary driver of travel content. The industry has been severely impacted by the pandemic, particularly during 2020–2022, and tourism still accounts for 7.6 percent of the global GDP in 2023, an increase of 22 percent from 2021 (World Travel and Tourism Council, n.d.). Additionally, the World Travel and Tourism Council's research indicates that 22 million new jobs in the tourism industry were created in 2022 (World Travel and Tourism Council, n.d.).

The potential of travel journalism to shape and influence our ideas about tourism is revealing of what Fürsich and Kavoori describe as "the ideological dimensions of tourism and transcultural encounters" (2001, p. 150). In the context of social media and user-generated reviews, Pirolli (2018) has written about the ways in which sites like AirBnB use journalistic techniques as a means of creating a travelling lifestyle aura around their products. Further, Fürsich and Kavoori also identify the genre as being inherently involved in the mediation of other cultures and as having its own 'special contingencies', in terms of its relationship with advertising and the tourism industry. They note the following:

> ...Free trips and other inducements for travel journalists are common – only a few publishers are willing to finance the trips of the journalists. This places man travel journalists in a difficult position between major interest groups.
>
> *(2001, p. 154)*

In taking stock of the academic study of travel journalism in 2014, Hanusch and Fürsich point to four 'dimensions' or developing lines of enquiry, which resonate with and build on Fürsich and Kavoori's (2001) earlier work. They too emphasize the significance of travel journalism's symbiotic relationship with the tourism industry, pointing to the consumer-driven market orientation of travel journalism as garnering academic attention (Mansfield, 2017; Rosenkranz, 2016).

A further dimension Hanusch and Fürsich propose relates to the ways in which travel journalism plays a role in shaping how tourism is experienced and practiced. Termed the "motivational aspects of travel journalism" (2014, p. 11), this line of enquiry has emerged from the sociological study of tourism. Influenced by seminal works such as those by Boorstin (1961), MacCannell (1973), Cohen (1978, 1988) and Urry (1990), consideration has been given to how travel journalism influences the social and cultural practices of tourism. Santos (2004, p. 394), for example, explores the ways in which readers interpret and "socially justify meanings" in American travel journalism on Portugal.

By far, the most dominant and productive area of academic research on travel journalism relates to its representation of foreign countries, destinations and cultural practices (see, for example, Fürsich, 2002; Daye, 2005, Santos, 2006 Cocking, 2009; Good, 2013; Pirolli, 2018, Cocking, 2020). This builds on the perception that travel journalism is an important "site where meaning is created and where a collective version of the 'Other/We' is negotiated, contested and constantly redefined" (Fürsich and Kavoori, 2001, p. 167). In step with the consumer-focused and advertorial aspects of the genre, representations of foreign countries, regions and cultural practices tend to be enthusiastic, entertaining and affirmatory. This is often predicated on an "exoticizing and stereotypical discourse of the Other" (Hanusch and Fürsich, 2014, p. 9). Often framed as light-hearted, such representations are nonetheless important discursive indicators of our collective cultural imagination and, arguably, bear a trace of influence on how we practice tourism. Work in this area has addressed the circulation of cultural stereotypes in relation to specific destinations as well as tracing the lineage of such representations discursively, in relation to older, often colonialist discourses. One example includes the echoes of older Orientalist referents from "nineteenth-century European travel writing on the Middle East" in contemporary British travel journalism (Cocking, 2009, p. 65). In playing on the cultural preconceptions of its audience, travel journalism often draws on cultural stereotypes and commonly held assumptions. For example, in examining the representation of Turkey in the travel sections of British broadsheet and tabloid newspapers, Hamid-Turksoy, Kuipers and Van Zoonen (2014) found that representations of Turkish culture and heritage tended to draw on orientalist imagery. As a tourist destination, Turkey was

> Commodified by repacking orientalism, including harmless, aestheticized references to Islam: "beautiful mosques", "minarets" and "calling to prayer" enter the texts and allow readers to imagine an oriental place with an Ottoman and Arabic flavour.
> *(Hamid-Turksoy et al., 2014, p. 756)*

Scholars see travel journalism as a dynamic receptor of new and historic discourses and in its representations of interactions with locals, often imbalanced and often problematic power relations (Fowler, 2007). The travel journalist is in effect "on the lookout for scenes that carry an already established interest for a Western audience, thus investing perception itself with the mediating power of cultural difference" (Spurr, 1993, p. 21).

Analysing travel journalism

In examining differences in representations of cultural mediation, this chapter develops a small case study based on travel content drawn from print, blogs and social media sources. This comprises articles from the *The Independent* and *The Sun*, a travel blog, *Nomad Revelations*, and a TikTok travel vlog, *#wilderness_addict*. This selection was motivated by several considerations. The content comes from media platforms that are significant producers of travel content – both in terms of quantity and the fact that this content attracts high numbers of viewers. Politically right-wing and tabloid in format, 31.1 million people per month read *The Sun* across its print and online platforms (Tobitt, 2023). Centre–left, broadsheet and online only, *The Independent* presents itself as the 'UK's largest quality digital news brand' with a readership of 24.5 million per month (Broughton, 2019). Similarly, several academic studies have sought to draw attention to the significant role travel blogs play in shaping our perceptions of other cultures and places (Gholamhosseinzadeh, Chapuis, and Lehu, 2023; Mainolfi, Lo Presti, Marino and Filieri, 2022). Lastly, TikTok, has become well known for its use of a powerful AI-based algorithm system to determine "users' tailored information distributions based on analysing the content of each video and watching the preference of users to perform an endless and highly attractive video stream" (Ma and Hu, 2021, p. 384). Travel content has quickly grown to be a very popular sub-category with #budgettravel and #luxurytravel attracting 2.8 billion and 2.5 billion views, respectively (MarketingWeek, 2024). No attempt has been made at focusing on a specific region or destination or specific characteristics of travel content on a particular medium or platform. Rather, the aim is to explore the underlying textual and visual characteristics that shape the representations of different places and other cultures *across* different media forms.

In so doing, this chapter makes use of a critical discourse analysis approach. 'Discourse' is understood as

> Language use in speech and writing – as a form of 'social practice… a dialectical relationship between a particular discursive event and the situation(s), institution(s) and social structure(s)…That is, discourse is socially constitutive as well as socially

conditioned – it constitutes situations, objects of knowledge, and the social identities of and relationships between people and groups of people.

(Wodak, 2002, p. 7)

In the context of media communication, the analytical practice of CDA aims to "demystify (problematic) power relations and representations in the content and manner of language and communication practices in their contexts of use" and explore how "boundaries of difference, uniqueness, and distinctiveness are marked and represente" (KhosraviNik, 2014, p. 283). This is particularly pertinent to the focus on the mediation of culture in travel journalism here.

Whilst the origins of critical discourse analysis can be traced to the study of language and linguistics (Wodak and Meyer, 2009), amongst the broad range of analytical practices associated with CDA, a more recent strand of enquiry has sought to adopt a 'multimodal' approach. A 'multimodal' approach seeks to take in the contribution to meaning made by visual imagery, the ways in which visual imagery can support, contradict and create interplays with text. As Okado-Gough notes, this involves consideration of "'ideas, absences, and taken-for-granted assumptions' in both the images and texts in order to reveal the kinds of power interests buried in them" (2017, p. 62). In this way, the adoption of a multimodal CDA approach helps facilitate consideration of the ways in which cultural mediation is represented in and via the interplay between visual images, captions, layout and positioning in travel journalism content. This enables us to ask how are different cultures represented in travel journalism? To what extent do different content platforms facilitate different modes of cultural representation? How do representations of different peoples and places function as forms of identity signalling, helping to construct and promote travel identities such as 'digital nomad' or discursive practices such as presenting destinations as embodying 'middle class' aspirations and values?

Tabloid travels

Titled 'Go Sea it: European city where Santa's buried has shorts weather in December and 90p beers', *The Sun*'s feature on Bari in Italy centres on a city break style holiday which brings together season aspects of travel with a typically cheeky reference to beer – an appeal to the leisure time interests and activities the paper presumably associates with its readership. Beyond the opening headline, the most immediately apparent features of this article are the ways in which it brings together very short, typically tabloid-esque sentences with quite contrasting very traditionally Italian images. What is also quite striking and rather unusual is that the text is not written in the first person – this is relatively unusual for the genre of travel journalism where content tends to take the form of a first-person account (Hannigan, 2013). The opening lines of this feature draw us in with a seasonal reference – the cold winter months of the United Kingdom are contrasted with the possibilities of being somewhere warm abroad, and there is an immediate attempt to position the readers' day-to-day experiences of winter in the United Kingdom against the possibilities of spending time in abroad. Bari is presented as an appealingly mild destination for a winter city break, with temperatures in December reaching as high as 17 degrees. A further seasonal reference is made in the form of a link to Christmas: Saint Nicholas (Father Christmas) is buried at the Basilica di San Nicola. The novelty of this connection leads into a broader account of some of the historical, cultural and architectural aspects of the city. We learn of Bari's historical centre "Bari Vecchia is a maze of narrow alleyways, open piazzas, and cobbled side streets" and the 'pasta nonnas' "who make pasta from scratch on a series of wooden tables on Strada Arco Basso" (Brotherton, 2023).

Whilst this text is presented in short paragraphs, it feels somewhat at odds with the headline's claims about cheap beer. It seems the tabloid values of the paper clash with more traditional aspects of travel journalism which draw on the genre's literary heritage (travel writing) in order to convey a 'cultural frame' – a frame of reference in which to contextualize the destination for the reader (Pan and Ryan, 2009). The emphasis in the text on the cultural attributes of the city fits well with the images used in the feature, which also focus on its architecture, market squares and traditional aspects of Italian life. In this way, Bari is established as an unchanged and very traditional destination – very few references to globally connected modern life are present. That said, whilst this might meet readers' expectations of Bari and Italy, the city is not portrayed in an overly stereotyped or jingoistic way. This, in combination with the opening references to weather, accentuates the contrast with 'home'. Not only does Bari offer respite from the winter in the United Kingdom but also as a destination which "remains largely untouched by Brit holidaymakers" (Brotherton, 2023).

Beyond addressing the appeal and points of interest in Bari, the article turns to the practicalities of accommodation, food and drink and getting there. Bari is presented as a cheap, relatively low-cost city destination that offers great value. It is interesting to read this against the backdrop of a cost of living crisis in the United Kingdom, particularly in terms of how the feature emphasizes the good value of food, drink and accommodation in Bari. In many respects, such as the reference to 90 pence beers, Bari is presented as better value than being at home. *The Sun*'s feature on Bari resonates with broader discourses about the cost of living and value for money in the United Kingdom. It seeks to appeal to *The Sun*'s readers by bringing together several different semantic elements: the winter in the United Kingdom is contrasted with Bari's warm and sunny climate; its authenticity and value is played off against the expense of home. The fact that Father Christmas (St Nicolas) is buried there serves as a further point of novelty, interest and intrigue, serving as a means of drawing the reader's attention to Bari over other 'winter sun' destinations.

Broadsheet meanderings

Like *The Sun*'s feature on Bari, *The Independent*'s article on Lake Ohrid in North Macedonia – "Why you should swap Lake Como for North Macedonia" – makes use of lots of large images that position us in a point of view perspective. The highly stylized images of Lake Ohrid in *The Independent*'s travel feature focus on traditional and historic scenes, such as churches and farm houses convey the impression that this destination has remained unchanged over time. In contrast to *The Sun,* the text is much denser, more literary and written in the first person. The emphasis is on the experiential. From the opening line, there is a strong appeal to the middle-class values of its readership. We are brought into a first-hand account of the journalist's experience:

Glasses clink and cutlery scrapes the plates at a pavement café by the side of the lake. People drink Aperol and espresso and take bites of pizza, their heads turned towards the peacock-green water and the villa-dappled hills that frame it. The scene wouldn't be out of place in Lake Como – but I'm 1,300 miles away from northern Italy, in a pocket of southwest North Macedonia called Ohrid (pronounced och-rid).

(Holt, 2023)

In this way, we are lulled into some recognizably familiar cultural stereotypes about Italy: drinking Aperol and espresso, eating pizza and taking in "villa-dappled hills". The language used is poetic and metaphysical. Here, the familiarity of one established holiday destination – Lake Como, Italy – is played on in order to establish a cultural frame of reference in which to understand North Macedonia. Put simply – as the title of the article indeed does – the appeal here is that culturally, geographically and visually, this place is like the Lombardy region of Italy, an area well known as an upmarket holiday destination and one readers are – directly in the title of the article – exhorted to consider swapping for Lake Ohrid and North Macedonia. The implication, indeed an explicit statement, is that we are, of course, familiar with Lake Como, what it has to offer and what it represents in terms of holiday cultural value.

Once this cultural frame of reference has been established, the article focuses on a series of cultural reference points – ones that are very much in keeping with the narrative broadsheet travel journalism might typically use to promote Lake Como and the Lombardy region to its readers. The theme of being more Italian than the Lombardy region or, more precisely, more Lake Como than Lake Como continues throughout the article. We learn that Lake Ohrid is more than twice the size of Lake Como and older too, with Ohrid town being acknowledged as one of the oldest human settlements in Europe.

In this way, Lake Ohrid is presented as a destination steeped in authenticity, one that allows the visitor to come into contact with the unchanged past. We learn that Ohrid old town has been on the UNESCO World Heritage Site list since 1997. It is also renowned for its jewellery and precious gem shops. The cultural values of the readership are further appealed to by the accounts of sampling local wine and food. The article ends with a description of eating al fresco and Holt's sense that they could indeed be in Lake Como, concluding though that on reflection, Lake Ohrid is so much more than a "Como lookalike. It's a history-rich, nuance-filled destination in its own right" (Holt, 2023).

The use of Lake Como and Italian culture works as frame of reference in order to establish a familiar context in which to situate Lake Ohrid and North Macedonia. Once this has been established, the destination is presented as being imbued with all the cultural elements of Lake Como only more so. This helps present Lake Ohrid as appealingly exclusive, a little known-known, an off-the-beaten track yet ostensibly mass tourism destination which is very typical of the ways in which destinations are marketed to middle-class consumers via what Voase refers to as a "discourse of the undiscovered" (2006, p. 288).

Travel blogging – it's a lifestyle thing

Nomadic Revelations is an 'adventure'-focused travel blog, run by João Leitão. Originally from Portugal, Leitão has been travelling since 1999 and has visited over 145 countries. Leitão's blog is aimed at the aspirant 'digital nomad', a subcultural trend that has brought out the possibilities facilitated by internet technology and changes in "employment patterns, particularly in the creative industries where 'the idea of a location-independent style of working and living' is increasingly widely desired and commonly practiced" (Müller, 2016, p. 344; Azariah, 2012). *Nomadic Revelations* claims to offer insights and advice on travelling off the beaten track "to encourage and motivate other travelers to discover exciting and unknown places around the world… Are you ready to think outside the box for your next adventure?" (Leitão, n.d.).

Unlike newspaper- and other print-based travel journalism where advertising revenue, hardcopy sales and subscriptions fund the salaries of professional journalists, typically bloggers are not paid to produce content but rather hope their content will generate income from "advertising, sponsorship, endorsements, products, subscription, affiliate commission and donations" (Cocking, 2020, p. 60). *Nomadic Revelations* also serves as a means of promoting Leitão's own adventure travel agency, containing many blog posts on countries across the continents. This chapter focuses on three blog posts on Morocco – 'Nomads of Morocco – Sahara Desert nomadic life', 'Nomads of Morocco – High Atlas Mountains nomadic life' and 'Sahara Motorcycle Adventure – Morocco'. These were selected not because of the destination but because they are indicative of the content on *Nomadic Revelations*. Following a well-established blog format, *Nomadic Revelations* uses a combination of large photographs accompanied by short paragraphs and, in some places, lists.

In contrast to newspaper-based travel journalism where photographs are often drawn from tourism marketing and publicity content, the photographs included here are taken by Leitão, cementing the notion that these are real journeys personally undertaken by him. We gain an impression of what nomadic Berber life is like living in the Sahara desert and the High Atlas mountains via photos of, for example, typical meals, the sleeping quarters of a Berber tent, Kasbah architecture and traditional cultural scenes such as the Imilchil camel market. The photographs take centre-stage with the text providing supplementary information. Taken in isolation, some of these images could be seen as stylistically consistent with the British and European 'orientalist' representational frame, romanticising traditional cultural practices and the nomadic way of life. However, viewed holistically, these photographs convey a rather different impression. In the photograph of the sleeping quarters, we see, for example, a rucksack and a plastic bag, and in another photograph, a solar panel sits on the desert floor next to a traditional Berber tent. Elements of Western capitalist modernity mingle in a seemingly unaffected way. The overall impression is that these blog posts do not (re)produce the clichéd and stereotypical cultural motifs often found in professional travel journalism on desert travel and nomadic ways of life (Cocking, 2009; Fowler, 2007). Rather, there is an attempt here to show life as it is lived or perhaps more accurately to document the experience of visiting/staying with nomadic groups in the Sahara and High Atlas mountains. In this way, the content seeks to appeal to the aspirant 'digital nomad'. Newspaper travel journalism often encourages the reader to travel in the footsteps of the journalist, providing an experiential experience Ashe, 2023). Here, the framing of content is more candid and 'fly on the wall', lacking the glossy veneer of tourism marketing content often found in professionally produced travel journalism.

The visual depiction of digital nomad lifestyle is supported by light-hearted and entertaining advice on how to undertake similar journeys. There is an emphasis on fun and madcap adventure in Leitão's posts. For example, a journey across the Sahara opens with: 'What is then peculiar about this trip? Well, *the motorcycle was not really an authentic motorcycle… It has pedals… and it is called: "Moped".*' (emphasis in the original, Leitão, no date). Perhaps, there were financial considerations that played a part in choosing mopeds over other more appropriate and reliable forms of transport. Such considerations are not made apparent, though, in Leitão's post. Whilst the risks associated with using mopeds are acknowledged, this is very much presented as adding a further degree of excitement to the journey. This sense of risk-taking and embracing the unexpected characterizes much of the content on *Nomadic Revelations*. For example, in a list of fun aspects of the journey, Leitão writes: "Getting lost – THE FUNNIEST OF IT ALL'… 'Motorcycle malfunction – AFTER PROBLEM FIXED, YES, FUNNY" (Leitão, no date).

Newspaper-based travel journalism stories often exoticize and 'other' locations like Morocco, for example, framing the architecture and/or cultural practices in ways that resonate with the colonialist modes of representation of 18th- and 19th-century European travel writing (Pratt, 2007; Cocking, 2009). Nonchalant but not arrogant, Leitão's emphasis on fun and – at times rash – adventure adds the kind of 'spice' that typifies the digital nomad travel experience. Consequently, the representation of nomadic desert life as it is lived is ultimately a vehicle for encouraging and – such are the economic imperatives of blogs – creating 'buy in' to the consumption of digital nomad-inspired travel experiences.

TikTok travel vlogs: Image is everything

Tiktok is fast becoming a significant influencer of consumers' inspiration for tourism activities and destinations (Wengel et al., 2022). As with the other travel content under discussion here, *#wilderness_addict* was not selected by destination but for the extent to which it is broadly indicative of TikTok's travel vlog content. *#wilderness_addict* focuses primarily on outdoors adventure, particularly mountainous destinations in winter in Europe, North America and New Zealand. Each vlog posted includes viewing statistics, and most also have active chat threads. None of the vlogs have voice-over, and all are around 10 seconds long and accompanied by atmospheric music. For these reasons, it seems more productive not to focus on one individual vlog post but rather to examine a small range of posts on the site. This includes: "Train through Whoville #Switzerland #imobsessed" (2.6 million views), "Missing this place #fyp #newzealand #wanderlust #boat #foryou #home" (29.3 million views) and "Probably my new favourite country #greenland #bucketlist #tiktoktravel #iceburgs #adventurevibes" (16.3k views). The viewing statistics of the vlogs at *#wilderness_addict* tend to be in the 10–20 k range with some such as ones on New Zealand and Switzerland attracting significantly higher viewing figures. Destination choice, video footage used, background sounds/music and choice of hashtag are all important factors in the popularity of specific vlogs (Sachs, Wise and Karell, 2021).

What is striking about these vlogs in comparison with other forms of travel content is the fleeting, almost ephemeral nature of them. The 10-second duration passes very quickly and, for those less familiar with TikTok content (such as this author!), some acclimatization is required in order to tune into this format and its semantic constitution. Whilst with travel blogs images tend to dominate with the text performing a more supplementary role, with these TikTok vlogs, the moving images entirely dominate. Here, the presence of the text is limited to the comment threads. Its principle function is social network building through largely affirmatory comments that symbiotically promote the social networks of both the vlogger and the users leaving the comments (Darvin, 2022). For example, in the comments thread on New Zealand, one user comments "lets go now flights should be cheap", whilst the vlogger, Caroline Foster replies, "I wish, doesn't look like I'll be making it home for a while" (Foster, 2020). Foster's reply, given that it was posted in 2020 at the height of the COVID-19 pandemic, perhaps refers to the fact that New Zealand was in 'lock down', not reopening its borders to citizens until February 2022. It is also indicative of the ways in which TikTok facilitates the building of 'travelling' social networks. Representationally and stylistically, the tone is very different to travel blogs like *Nomadic Revelations*. Whereas *Nomadic Revelations* sought to document aspects of nomadic life from a digital nomad perspective, here the focus is on conveying the beauty of the natural world, one enhanced by filters, background music and in which the vlogger is front and centre.

In contrast to the established representational tropes of newspaper travel journalism such as generating appeal and engagement through encouraging the reader to 'walk in the footsteps of the journalist' or tropes of travel blogging where advice is mixed with documenting the digital nomad life, there are few, if any, depictions of cultural practices in these TikTok vlogs. Rather than representations of how other lives are lived, the emphasis is very much on presenting the vlogger in dramatic, aesthetically beautiful locations. As the hashtag *#wilderness_addict* suggests, the aesthetic of this vlog site centres on 'big nature'. We see dramatic mountain-scapes, snow and ice and wave-crested seas. This is nature writ large, and with the application of dark, monochrome filters (sometimes contrasting with brightly coloured items of clothing warm by the vlogger), it is reminiscent of Ansel Adam's photographs, particularly those of American national parks in the 1930s and 1940s.

Very much present in this visual aesthetic is the vlogger. Most of the footage is either point of view (POV) shot or features the vlogger against dramatic natural backdrops. We see, for example, her bright orange hat as she looks out of the train window at the 'Whoville'-sque village in Switzerland, before the camera pans across its snow-covered roof tops to the jagged peaks of the mountains beyond. Similarly, in the video on Greenland, amongst the footage of husky puppies, icebergs and whales, we see the Foster paddle boarding, floating in an icy pool and sitting on rocks looking out to sea. In each image, the Foster's brightly coloured clothing contrasts with the icy blues and greys of Greenland's shoreline. The music accompanying each vlog is listed next to the video for other users to engage with. Along with filters, music enables vloggers to develop their own unique style: "extra edits could improve the quality of videos and allow an expression of a positive self" (Du, Liechty, Santos and Park, 2022, p. 3418).

In contrast to newspaper and travel blog content, we are not afforded an insight into different cultural practices; rather we encounter a series of fast-delivered snapshots of aesthetically stunning nature. The day-to-day aspects of travelling life do not feature, and we are left to be inspired, wondering what it would be like to visit these locations and perhaps, in the context of the identity signalling combination of the vlogger in dramatic locations, aspiring to live the travel vlogger life, "gaining social recognition and building social identity" (Du, Liechty, Santos and Park, 2022, p. 3417).

Conclusion

This chapter illustrates how, as a relatively new and emerging field of study, academic interest in travel journalism has mainly focused on four broad lines of enquiry. Travel journalism is founded on and formed by its close reliance on the tourism industry and associated advertising and marketing (Hanusch and Fürsich, 2014, p. 9). Related to its characteristically highly commercial nature is its problematic status as a form of 'non-news' journalism which positions us as 'consumers' rather than 'citizens' (Cocking, 2018, p. 1349). Emerging from the sociological study of tourism, another strand of research centres on the role of travel journalism in influencing and shaping the practices of tourism; where tourists go and the activities they engage in (Creech, 2018). By far, the largest area of research centres on the role of travel journalism as a significant media source of cultural mediation (Good,

2013). Here, the focus has tended to be on the mediation of specific cultures and the representation of specific destinations or regions.

This chapter has sought to draw attention to the ways in which the proliferation of travel journalism across media platforms affords potential for different forms of cultural mediation. For example, in the article from *The Sun*, the Italian city of Bari and representations of Italian culture serve as an appealing foreground for a characteristically tabloid championing of the needs and desires of its readers/consumers. Bari is represented as a seasonal destination offering great value for money – better than being at home. By contrast, *The Independent* feature on North Macedonia calls on the reader's cultural capital and through the well-established literary technique of exhorting the reader to walk in the footsteps of the journalist constructs North Macedonia as a more culturally rich version of Lake Como and the Lombardy region. The *Nomadic Revelations* blog presented a sense of life as it is lived by Berber nomads in Morocco – through a lens filtered by the subcultural signifiers of the 'digital nomad' lifestyle. Here, the representation of an 'other' culture serves as an adventurous, real and somewhat gritty foundation on which to promote the digital nomad as a travel practice and, ultimately, a lifestyle choice. The format of TikTok's travel vlogs facilitates a strong sense of identity signalling. Here, other landscapes are curated in digitally enhanced (filtered) ways in order for vloggers to establish their own unique travel aesthetic. Central to this is the vlogger whose presence in footage constructs a sense of 'vlog life' identity – identities that TikTok users are, through the building of social networks, encouraged to affirm or navigate away from.

Whilst this chapter provides a small snapshot of how different media forms with their different technological and economic infrastructure facilitate different forms of cultural mediation, much remains unexplored. Travel journalism is fast-evolving and now well-established on social media platforms, and the cultural and sociological significance of this content is worthy of further academic consideration. This relates specifically to the significance and potential of travel journalism on sites like TikTok in terms of cultural mediation and in terms of its motivational capacity to shape and influence tourism practices.

Further readings

Ashe, I. (2023) Time to go: Aspirational framing and place-making in domestic travel journalism. *Journalism Practice*, 1–18. https://doi.org/10.1080/17512786.2023.2244931

Cocking, B. (2020) *Travel Journalism and Travel Media: Identities, Places and Imaginings*. Springer Nature.

Du, X., Liechty, T., Santos, C. A., & Park, J. (2022) "I want to record and share my wonderful journey": Chinese Millennials' production and sharing of short-form travel videos on TikTok or Douyin. *Current Issues in Tourism*, 25(21), 3412–3424.

Gholamhosseinzadeh, M. S., Chapuis, J. M., & Lehu, J. M. (2023) Tourism netnography: How travel bloggers influence destination image. *Tourism Recreation Research*, 48(2), 188–204.

Lekant, M., & Palau-Sampio, D. (2022) Reinventing travel journalism in the digital age: Quality, specialization, technology, and a unique perspective. *Comunicación y Sociedad*, 19, 1–21.

References

Ashe, I. (2023) Time to go: Aspirational framing and place-making in domestic travel journalism. *Journalism Practice*, 1–18. https://doi.org/10.1080/17512786.2023.2244931

Azariah, D. R. (2012) *Mapping the Travel Blog: A Study of the Online Travel Narrative* (Doctoral dissertation, Curtin University).

Blaer, M., Frost, W., & Laing, J. (2020). The future of travel writing: Interactivity, personal branding and power. *Tourism Management*, 77, 104009.

Boorstin, D. J (1961) *The Image: A Guide to Pseudo-Events in America*. New York: Harper & Row.

Brett, D. F. (2023) Is travel journalism more similar to newspaper language or the language of tourism? A corpus-based study. *Studies in Travel Writing*, 26(2), 152–167. https://doi.org/10.1080/13645145.2023.2261635

Brotherton, H. (2023, Winter) Go Sea it The short-haul winter sun destination where Santa Claus is buried – you can wear shorts in December and drink 90p beers. *The Sun*. Available at: https://www.thesun.co.uk/travel/

Broughton, C. (2019, Winter). The Independent overtakes Guardian to become UK's largest quality digital news brand. *The Independent*. Available at: https://www.independent.co.uk/news/media/comscore-november-uk-figures-largest-quality-website-a9255676.html

Canella, G. (2023). Journalistic power: Constructing the "truth" and the economics of objectivity. *Journalism Practice*, 17(2), 209–225.

Cocking, B. (2020) *Travel Journalism and Travel Media: Identities, Places and Imaginings*. Springer Nature.

Cocking, B. (2018) News values go on holiday: The ideological values of travel journalism. *Journalism Studies*, 19(9), 1349–1365.

Cocking, B. (2009) Travel journalism: Europe imagining the Middle East. *Journalism Studies*, 10(1), 54–68. https://doi.org/10.1080/14616700802560500

Cohen, E. (1988) Traditions in the qualitative sociology of tourism. *Annals of Tourism Research*, 15(1), 29–46.

Cohen, E. (1978) The impact of tourism on the physical environment. *Annals of Tourism Research*, 5(2), 215–237.

Coltman, M. M. (1989) *Introduction to Travel and Tourism. An International Approach*. New York: Van Nostrand Reinhold.

Creech, B. (2018) Postcolonial travel journalism and the new media. In Clarke R., (Ed.), *The Cambridge Companion to Postcolonial Travel Writing* (pp. 157–172). Cambridge University Press.

Darvin, R. (2022) Design, resistance and the performance of identity on TikTok. *Discourse, Context and Media*, 46, 1–11.

Daye, M. (2005) Mediating tourism: An analysis of the Caribbean holiday experience in the UK national press. In Crouch, David, Jackson, Rhona and Thompson, Felix (eds.) *The Media and the Tourist Imagination Converging Cultures* (pp. 14–26). London and New York: Routledge.

Du, X., Liechty, T., Santos, C. A., & Park, J. (2022) "I want to record and share my wonderful journey": Chinese Millennials' production and sharing of short-form travel videos on TikTok or Douyin. *Current Issues in Tourism*, 25(21), 3412–3424.

Duffy, A. (2019) If I say you're authentic, then you're authentic: Power and privilege revealed in travel blogs. *Tourist Studies*, 19(4), 569–584.

Foster, C. (2020) 19th March, Missing this place #fyp #newzealand #wanderlust #boat #foryou #home. Available at: https://www.tiktok.com/@wilderness_addict/ (Accessed: 14th November, 2023).

Foster, C. (no date) 11th November, *Probably My New Favourite Country #Greenland #Bucketlist #Tiktoktravel #Icebergs #Adventurevibes*. Available at: https://www.tiktok.com/@wilderness_addict/ (Accessed: 14th November, 2023).

Fowler, C. (2007) *Chasing Tales: Travel Writing, Journalism and the History of British Ideas about Afghanistan*. Amsterdam and New York: Rodopi.

Fürsich, E. (2002) How can global journalists represent the 'other'?: A critical assessment of the cultural studies concept for media practice. *Journalism*, 3(1), 57–84. https://doi.org/10.1177/146488490200300102

Fürsich, E., & Kavoori, A. P. (2001) Mapping a critical framework for the study of travel journalism. *International Journal of Cultural Studies*, 4(2), 149–171.

Gholamhosseinzadeh, M. S., Chapuis, J. M., & Lehu, J. M. (2023) Tourism netography: How travel bloggers influence destination image. *Tourism Recreation Research*, 48(2), 188–204.

Good, K. D. (2013) Why we travel: Picturing global mobility in user-generated travel journalism. *Media, Culture & Society*, 35(3), 295–313.

Hamid-Turksoy, N., Kuipers, G., & Van Zoonen, L. (2014) "Try A Taste of Turkey" An analysis of Turkey's representation in British newspapers' travel sections. *Journalism Studies*, 15(6), 743–758.

Hannigan, T. (2013) Travel journalism. In Turner, B. and Orange, R. (eds.) *Specialist Journalism* (pp. 171–180). London: Routledge.

Hanusch, F. (2014) On the relevance of travel journalism. In Hanusch, F. and Fürsich, E. (eds.) *Travel Journalism Exploring Production Impact and Culture* (pp. 1–17). London: Palgrave MacMillan.

Hanusch, F. (2012) A profile of Australian travel journalists' professional views and ethical standards. *Journalism*, 13(5), 668–686.

Haugen, M. W. (2018) News of travels, travelling news: The Mediation of travel and exploration in the gazette de France and the journal de l'Empire. In Brandtzaeg, S. G., Goring, P. and Watson, C. (eds.) *Travelling Chronicles: News and Newspapers from the Early Modern Period to the Eighteenth Century* (pp. 159–180). Leiden: Brill.

Holt, S. (2023) Why you should swap Lake Como for North Macedonia. *The Independent*, 12th July. Available at: https://www.independent.co.uk/travel/

How brands can inspire wanderlust on TikTok. (n.d.) *MarketingWeek*. Retrieved March 24, 2024. from https://www.marketingweek.com/how-travel-brands-can-inspire-wanderlust-on-tiktok/

Humphreys, A. (2023) Journalism. *Victorian Literature and Culture*, 51(3), 439–442.

KhosraviNik, M. (2014) Critical discourse analysis, power and new media discourse. In Kalyango, Y. and Kopytowska, M. W. (eds.) *Why Discourse Matters: Negotiating Identity in the Mediatized World* (pp. 283–301). Bristol: Peter Lang.

Lau, R. W. (2012) Re-theorizing news' construction of reality: A realist-discourse-theoretic approach. *Journalism*, 13(7), 886–902.

Leitão, J. (no date) Nomads of Morocco – Sahara Desert nomadic life. *Nomadic Revelations*. Available at: https://www.joaoleitao.com/

Leitão, J. (no date) Nomads of Morocco – High Atlas Mountains nomadic life. *Nomadic Revelations*. Available at: https://www.joaoleitao.com/

Leitão, J. (no date) Sahara Motorcycle Adventure – Morocco. *Nomadic Revelations*. Available at: https://www.joaoleitao.com/

Ma, Y., & Hu, Y. (2021). Business model innovation and experimentation in transforming economies: ByteDance and TikTok. *Management and Organization Review*, 17(2), 382–388.

MacCannell, D. (1973) Staged authenticity: Arrangements of social space in tourist settings. *American Journal of Sociology*, 79(3), 589–603.

Mainolfi, G., Lo Presti, L., Marino, V., & Filieri, R. (2022). "YOU POST, I TRAVEL." Bloggers' credibility, digital engagement, and travelers' behavioral intention: The mediating role of hedonic and utilitarian motivations. *Psychology and Marketing*, 39(5), 1022–1034.

Mansfield, C. (2017) Travel writing in place branding - A case study on nantes. *Journal of Tourism, Heritage & Services Marketing*, 3(2), 1–7.

McNair, B. (1998) *The Sociology of Journalism*. London: Arnold.

Mee, C. (2009). Journalism and travel writing: From grands reporters to global tourism. *Studies in Travel Writing*, 13(4), 305–315.

Müller, A. (2016) The digital nomad: Buzzword or research category? *Transnational Social Review*, 6(3), 344–348.

Okado-Gough, D. (2017) Critical discourse analysis: Current approaches and the advent of multimodality. *Mulberry*, 67, 51–65.

Pan, S., & Ryan, C. (2009). Tourism sense-making: The role of the senses and travel journalism. *Journal of Travel & Tourism Marketing*, 26(7), 625–639.

Pirolli, B. (2018) *Travel Journalism: Informing Tourists in the Digital Age*. Abingdon, Oxon and New York: Routledge.

Pratt, M. L. (2007) *Imperial Eyes: Travel Writing and Transculturation*. London: Routledge.

Rosenkranz, T. (2016) Becoming entrepreneurial: Crisis, ethics and marketization in the field of travel journalism. *Poetics*, 54, 54–65.

Sachs, J., Wise, R., & Karell, D. (2021, April 7). The TikTok Self: Music, Signaling, and identity on social media. https://doi.org/10.31235/osf.io/2rx46

Santos, C. A. (2004) Perception and interpretation of leisure travel articles. *Leisure Sciences*, 26(4), 393–410. https://doi.org/10.1080/01490400490502462

Santos, A. C. (2006) Cultural politics in contemporary travel writing. *Annals of Tourism Research*, 33(3), 624–644.

Sezgin, E., & Yolal, M. (2012) Golden age of mass tourism: Its history and development. In Kasimoglu, M. (ed.) *Visions for Global Tourism Industry-Creating and Sustaining Competitive Strategies* (pp. 73–90). London: Intech. Spurr, S. (1993) *The Rhetoric of Empire: Colonial Discourse in Journalism, Travel Writing, and Imperial Administration.* Durham and London: Duke University Press.

Steward, J. (2005) "How and where to go": The role of travel journalism in Britain and the evolution of foreign tourism, 1840–1914. In Walton, J. K. (ed.) *Histories of Tourism: Representation, Identity and Conflict* (pp. 39–40). Clevedon, Buffalo and Toronto: Channel View Publications.

Tobitt, C. (2023, Summer). Who reads The Sun? Circulation and reader demographic breakdown for The Sun. *The Press Gazette.* Available at: https://pressgazette.co.uk/media-audience-and-business-data/media_metrics/who-reads-the-sun-circulation-demographic/

Urry, J. (1990) *The Tourist Gaze.* London: Sage.

Voase, R. (2006) Creating the tourist destination: narrating the 'undiscovered' and the paradox of consumption. In Meethan, K., Anderson, A., Miles S., (Eds.), *Tourism Consumption and Representation. Narratives of Place and Self* (pp. 284–299). CABI.

Wells, C., Shah, D., Lukito, J., Pelled, A., Pevehouse, J. C., & Yang, J. (2020). Trump, Twitter, and news media responsiveness: A media systems approach. *New Media & Society*, 22(4), 659–682. https://doi.org/10.1177/1461444819893987

Wengel, Y., Ma, L., Ma, Y., Apollo, M., Maciuk, K., & Ashton, A. S. (2022) The TikTok effect on destination development: Famous overnight, now what? *Journal of Outdoor Recreation and Tourism, 37,* 100458.

Wodak, R. (2002). Aspects of critical discourse analysis. *Zeitschrift für angewandte Linguistik*, 36(10), 5–31.

Wodak, R., & Meyer, M. (2009) Critical discourse analysis: History, agenda, theory and methodology. *Methods of Critical Discourse Analysis, 2,* 1–33.

Youngs, T. (2013) *The Cambridge Introduction to Travel Writing.* Cambridge and New York: Cambridge University Press.

16
ROLE PERCEPTIONS IN LIFESTYLE JOURNALISM

Folker Hanusch

Introduction

The question of what journalists aim to achieve in their work has been a key focus of journalism scholarship for at least 60 or so years. In an attempt to better understand news production processes, researchers have studied journalistic roles, which express a range of things that journalists deem important to do in their daily work. This line of scholarship, as Hanitzsch & Vos (2018, p. 115) have argued, has become "central to our understanding of journalism's identity and place in society". As a result, there exists a plethora of studies that have explored the concept, leading to a diverse and quite sophisticated understanding of journalists' role perceptions in a variety of national and international contexts. At the same time, there are still some important blind spots in the field. One of these relates to the relatively undertheorized and under-researched area of specifically lifestyle journalists' role perceptions. While scholars have explored a range of specialized journalistic beats, the focus of research has typically been on journalism's relationship with political life. Matters of everyday life, which include lifestyle journalism, have only begun to receive attention from scholars for the past 15 years or so.

This chapter provides an overview of the study of journalistic roles in general, including some conceptual concerns that affect studying these, before discussing in more detail the research that already exists in relation to lifestyle journalistic roles. Importantly, this chapter identifies continued blind spots in the study of these roles and argues for more comprehensive approaches. These include a more sophisticated understanding of the factors that impinge not only on roles in a cross-national context but also across sub-beats within the broader lifestyle journalism field. Gaps also still exist in terms of lifestyle journalism's relationship with its audiences, with other, so-called peripheral actors, as well as how roles are enacted in practice. Finally, this chapter argues for a more integrated approach to studying lifestyle journalistic roles that addresses what is identified as an artificial gap between the political and private (or everyday life) realms of journalism.

Role orientations in journalism

The study of journalists' role perceptions has been a central concern for scholars of journalism since at least the middle of the 20th century. Following the experience of World

War 2, which demonstrated the power that a quickly growing mass media could have, particularly when misused for propaganda purposes, scholars in the United States, in particular, began to invest effort into better understanding how news was produced. This time period led to the establishment of important theoretical concepts in what was then more likely to be referred to as mass communication than specifically journalism, including key journalism study paradigms like gatekeeping, news values and role perceptions.

Early studies, such as Cohen's (1963) seminal account of foreign correspondents and Janowitz's (1975) study of US journalists, differentiated between essentially two kinds of journalists. Cohen (1963) identified one group as neutral observers, who placed emphasis on uninvolved reporting of events, while the other group, referred to as participants, saw it as their role to intervene in political processes by taking a stance. Janowitz (1975) similarly argued there was a group of "gatekeepers", who focused on objective reporting and non-involvement in the news process, and a group of "advocates", who saw it as their role to be partisan and actively advocate for certain values. To this day, these two roles are considered essential parts of how journalists view their role and how societies view journalists in normative terms.

Yet, scholarship of journalistic roles has evolved considerably in the 60 or so years since, developing into one of the most popular areas of what from around the year 2000 became known as the field of journalism studies. The vast majority of the work over the course of the second half of the 20th century focused primarily on measuring how journalists perceived their roles, typically through interviews and surveys, with the implicit assertion that how journalists saw their roles in society also impacted on the content they produced. Some of the most seminal studies in the field developed in this way, including the much-cited American Journalist studies. Conducted roughly every ten years since the mid-1970s (Johnstone et al., 1972; Weaver & Wilhoit, 1986, 1996; Weaver et al., 2007; Weaver & Willnat, 2016), these studies firmly entrenched the journalistic roles of "disseminators", "interpreters", "adversaries", and "populist mobilizers". These studies quickly became a hallmark of the field, inspiring countless other, similar efforts around the world.

The burgeoning and widespread growth of studies into journalistic roles resulted in very diverse findings and insights into how journalists around the world viewed their role, prompting a need for more comparative, global views. US scholar David Weaver's (1998) edited collection thus presented the first comprehensive overview of journalistic roles in 21 countries and territories across the globe, providing an integrated analysis of similarities and differences. Advancing this approach further, Hanitzsch et al. (2011) – based on a theoretical framework developed by Hanitzsch (2007) that identified interventionism, market orientation and power distance as key dimensions of roles – conducted surveys in 19 diverse countries. This was the first study to use the same questionnaire in each country and strict methodological guidelines to ensure the comparability of findings. The project, known as the Worlds of Journalism Study, has become perhaps the most central global study of journalistic roles, most recently providing an analysis of journalists' professional views in 67 countries, covering all inhabited continents through representative surveys (Hanitzsch et al., 2019).

While there has undoubtedly been enormous growth in the study of journalistic roles, scholars have also identified a number of blind spots, which are particularly relevant to consider here, before we move into studying the kinds of role perceptions that lifestyle journalists may have. Notably, many of these desiderata have recently been articulated by Hanitzsch and Vos (2017, 2018) in their assessment of the state of the field.

These concerns, which will be discussed in turn in the remainder of this section, include (a) an undertheorization of the concept of roles, (b) the conflation of the "attitudinal and performative" dimensions of journalistic roles (Hanitzsch & Vos, 2017, p. 118), and (c) the unproportionate focus on journalism's relationship with political life, at the expense of its role in everyday life.

Theorizing journalistic roles

When reading many of the existing studies of journalistic roles, the absence of in-depth theorizing or conceptualizing what exactly are journalistic roles is extremely apparent. As Hanitzsch & Vos (2017, p. 117) point out, "most work on journalists' roles is remarkably thin on theory. The majority of studies still take an inductive and descriptive perspective". Even though the authors are at pains to point out important exceptions to this (see, for example, Christians et al., 2009; Donsbach & Patterson, 2004; Hanitzsch, 2007), there has been little "feed back into conceptual work" (Hanitzsch & Vos, 2018, p. 148). In fact, studies have used different terms almost interchangeably when referring to roles, including terms such "press functions", "media roles", "role perceptions", "role conceptions" or "journalistic paradigms" (see Hanitzsch & Vos, 2017, p. 117).

One particularly useful concept for thinking about journalistic roles is role theory, developed by Biddle (1979). Originating from the dramaturgical perspective (Simmel, 1920; Goffman, 1959), which views people as following scripts in their interactions with others, this conceptual approach has in recent years found its way into the scholarship on journalistic roles (Banjac, Juarez Miro & Hanusch, 2024; Hanusch & Banjac, 2018; Tandoc & Duffy, 2016; Hellmueller & Mellado, 2015; Vos, 2005). As Hanusch and Banjac (2018) argue, role theory offers multiple perspectives through which role conceptions can be studied. One way that a role can be understood is as a "collection of patterns of behavior which are thought to constitute a meaningful unit and deemed appropriate to a person occupying a particular status in society" (Turner, 1956, p. 316). While role theory also suffers from conceptual blurriness, most studies agree on one key point. Roles are deemed to exist in response to expectations. Thus, actors have an expectation of how to behave themselves, how others should behave and what they themselves believe others expect of them (Turner, 1956; Merton, 1957). Like actors on a stage, journalists in this view shape their beliefs of the roles they are supposed to play in society on the basis of what they believe that society expects of them (Banjac et al., 2024).

Expectations, therefore, become "generators of roles" (Biddle, 1986, p. 69) and can be understood as responses to patterned behaviours (Turner, 1956), interaction between individuals (Blumer, 1962) and relationship conduct (Merton, 1957). Particularly important here is to include the analysis of roles at the systemic level, including structural, functional or organizational considerations, as well as at the individual level (Stryker, 1980). Hanusch and Banjac (2018, p. 30) argue that focusing on only one instead of both levels

> Would dismiss the idea that journalistic roles are on the one hand discursively and symbolically constructed and their relationship to audiences is one increasingly built on interaction and, on the other hand, that journalists operate within an institution that is organized and hierarchical in nature (albeit increasingly less so), where roles

are generated in response to expectations directed at their journalistic position and status in society.

Attitudinal and performative dimensions

One key point of criticism of much research on journalistic role conceptions in recent years has been directed at the fact that typically such studies have examined journalists' self-conceptions of their role, which was then implicitly equated with what they actually do in their work. Yet, scholars have long known that phenomena like social desirability bias mean that what people tell us they do is not always what they actually do. Yet, only over the past 10 years or so have journalism scholars paid more attention to this gap between role perception and role enactment or role performance. Tandoc, Hellmueller and Vos (2013) were the first to theorize this phenomenon, while Mellado and colleagues (see, for example, Mellado, Hellmueller & Donsbach, 2016; Mellado et al., 2024; Hallin et al., 2023) have in recent years begun to apply those considerations by comprehensively examining the gap in various countries across the globe, combining surveys with content analyses. Not surprisingly, studies have often found a disconnect between how journalists perceive and how they perform their roles, prompting Hanitzsch and Vos (2018) to theorize about the ways in which the attitudinal and performative dimensions of journalistic roles can be conceptualized.

To do so, Hanitzsch & Vos combine two of the dominant perspectives in existing work on journalistic roles. They argue that while empirical studies have focused on individuals and their role perceptions, theoretical approaches have tended to focus on journalism's institutional identity. They believe that "implicitly, journalism's identity is then often understood as an aggregate of journalists' role perceptions, construing the relationship between the two as a black box" (Hanitzsch & Vos, 2018, p. 118). In order to resolve this tension, the authors propose what they call a "discursive turn", which views "journalism and journalistic roles as ontological objects that are discursively created" (Hanitzsch & Vos, 2018, p. 118). Thus, "journalistic roles are the discursive articulation and enactment of journalism's identity as a social institution" (Hanitzsch & Vos, 2018, p. 121). They guide the right behaviour in a given context, and the approach can explain points of tension, for example, when organizations expect behaviour from journalists that go against their own preferences.

Following from this approach, Hanitzsch and Vos (2018) develop a process model to explain how journalistic roles come into being and how they are enacted in journalists' work, thus resolving a fundamental tension that had existed in much of the scholarship on journalistic roles. The model combines the normative, cognitive, practiced and narrated aspects of journalists' roles, with the first two identified as role orientations, while the latter two refer to role performance. Starting from institutional norms of journalists, roles can be understood as journalists' discourses about what they ought to do, which is often learned behaviour and instilled in journalists through societal discourse about journalism, but also concrete things like journalism education (normative roles). These norms are internalized and articulated as cognitive values, i.e., what journalists want to do (cognitive roles). These values are subsequently enacted in journalists' work, allowing us to analyse what journalists actually do (practiced roles). When journalists talk about their work, they reflect on their actual performance, providing us with information from journalists about what they say they do (narrated roles). This image of their own practice ultimately feeds back into normative and cognitive roles. Through this circular approach based on discursive institutionalism, we are, therefore, better able to conceptualize, assess and understand how journalistic roles come into being and how they are perceived and enacted by journalists (Hanitzsch & Vos, 2018).

Political and everyday life

A final conceptual shortcoming of the literature on journalistic roles, which is particularly relevant to this chapter, relates to the overwhelming focus on journalism's relationship with political life. Journalism studies as a field has since its inception focused predominantly on the role that news work plays in political processes. For decades, this focus was largely unquestioned, but in recent years, scholars have begun paying more attention to journalism's role beyond its involvement in political life. As Zelizer (2011) has argued, the preoccupation with normative expectations of journalism's role in society has privileged certain kinds of journalism at the expense of others. Indeed, these other fields of journalism – such as service, lifestyle, entertainment or sports journalism, have "become denigrated, relativized, and reduced in value alongside aspirations for something better" (Zelizer, 2011, p. 9).

In fact, when we explore the rich scholarship on journalistic roles, we find a dazzling array of roles concerned with how journalism functions against the background of particularly democratic societies. One example includes Christians et al.'s (2009) account of normative roles of journalism in society. These include roles such as observing events, participating in public life, advocacy, surveillance, setting the agenda or being a watchdog. Classified as four basic media roles – monitorial, facilitative, collaborative and radical – we can see the clear focus on matters that relate to civic or political life. In a similar way, Hanitzsch and Vos (2018) summarize the scholarship on roles that relate to political life by identifying six dimensions. These are referred to as (1) informational-instructive (including roles such as being a disseminator, curator or storyteller); (2) analytical-deliberative (analyst, access provider and mobilizer); (3) critical-monitorial (monitor, detective and watchdog); (4) advocative-radical (missionary, advocate and adversary); (5) developmental-educative (mediator, educator and change agent); and (6) collaborative-facilitative (facilitator, collaborator and mouthpiece). These roles are primarily aimed at providing a comprehensive, theoretically informed overview of roles that relate to civic life and which capture contexts of countries in the Global South as well as the North.

More importantly, however, Hanitzsch and Vos (2018) respond to calls from scholars like Zelizer (2011) or Hanusch and Hanitzsch (2013) to incorporate into our thinking about roles the relationship that journalism has with everyday life. With this term, they refer to a broad array of non-political news, i.e., roles which include

> Realities such as securing daily provisions, self-maintenance, and entertainment. Through it, all persons must manage their emotional state and negotiate their identity. These everyday activities are not without implications for politics and public life, but also not reducible to the political.
> *(Hanitzsch & Vos, 2018, p. 151)*

These roles will be discussed in more detail in the following section.

Theorising role orientations in lifestyle journalism

Subsumed under the broader umbrella of journalism and everyday life, lifestyle journalism plays a particularly important role in modern societies – as, indeed, the broad array of chapters in this collection demonstrates. This is because lifestyle journalism provides help, advice, guidance and information about the management of self and everyday life through consumer news and 'news-you-can-use' items (Eide & Knight, 1999; Underwood, 2000). These are typically seen as distinct from what is often deemed as the more pressing, normatively desirable task of journalism: providing news that audiences need to fulfil their role as active participants in public life. Hence, scholars have tended to either ignore lifestyle journalistic roles, or they have differentiated between political and private roles – as evidenced in Hanitzsch and Vos's (2018) already discussed separation of journalism's relationship with political life on one hand and with everyday life on the other. As the overview of the existing scholarship on lifestyle journalistic roles in this chapter demonstrates, however, it is important to not see these as distinct from one another.

A useful way to begin thinking about the kinds of roles that lifestyle journalism may want to pursue is with Hanusch and Hanitzsch's (2013, p. 947) definition of lifestyle journalism as "the journalistic coverage of the expressive values and practices that help create and signify a specific identity within the realm of consumption and everyday life". This definition forces us to think of lifestyle journalism as primarily aimed at audiences in their role as consumers, who seek advice on how to live their lives. It emanates from the consideration that in modern societies, people require orientation in an increasingly multioptional environment (Hanusch & Hanitzsch, 2013). Broader processes of individualization (Beck, 1992) have meant that traditional institutions are losing their grip on people's lives, resulting in individuals needing to choose their own identities (Bauman, 2000). Accompanying this, increased disposable income and social value changes have led to more options and flexibility to shape one's lifestyle, including through consumption of products and leisure-time activities (Taylor, 2002; Chaney, 1997). Finally, mediatization – "the process whereby society to an increasing degree is submitted to, or becomes dependent on, the media and their logic" (Hjarvard, 2008, p. 13) – has resulted in the already-discussed aspects like identity work and expression of lifestyles no longer being possible without the media. Thus, "not only do the media shape people's lifestyles through news coverage, advertising and other kinds of content, they also provide a platform to express one's personal lifestyle through means of social media" (Hanusch & Hanitzsch, 2013, p. 946).

In their interviews with 89 lifestyle journalists in Australia and Germany about the professional views these journalists had, Hanusch and Hanitzsch (2013) subsequently identified a number of dimensions which relate to these theoretical considerations. The first role was to provide *entertainment and relaxation*, i.e., journalists wanted to produce entertaining content aimed at audiences, by making them laugh or by captivating their attention, with the goal of allowing them to relax. Second, lifestyle journalists aimed to provide a *service* or give advice and news-you-can-use to their audience, for example, by giving consumer advice to help audiences when making purchasing decisions. Another role Hanusch and Hanitzsch (2013) found was the desire to provide *orientation in daily life*. This relates to the notion of self-expression "in that it provides basic ideas and content to allow audiences to use them as orientation for their own life" (Hanusch & Hanitzsch, 2013, p. 953). Providing *inspiration and a positive attitude toward life* was also considered important, in that journalists wanted to give their audiences a generally positive feeling and new ideas for how they could live their lives. Finally, *exemplars of desired lifestyle* related to the signification of identity, with journalists wanting to show audiences or consumer goods that they believed their audiences aspired to. While these findings were based on qualitative interviews with non-representative samples, Hanusch and Hanitzsch (2013) noted it appeared from the interviews that providing entertainment as well as service and advice were the two dominant roles. All of the five roles together fulfiled lifestyle journalism's function of self-expression, signification of identity and consumption.

In their conceptual work on journalistic roles, Hanitzsch and Vos (2018) built in part on this work and examined roles of journalism in what they referred to as everyday life. These roles were mapped onto three interrelated spaces: consumption, identity and emotion. Across the three spaces, they argue, we can identify seven ideal-typical roles: The first relates to the role of *marketer*, who is central in the realm of consumption and who aims to promote lifestyles and consumable goods to audiences, serving advertisers in the process. Second, the *service provider* wants to give practical information and advice about services and products, but in contrast to the marketer is more independent and more likely to serve audiences instead of advertisers. The third role is that of the *friend*, who acts as a companion who helps audiences navigate their identity work. Fourth, the *connector* is located at the intersection of emotion and identity and provides audiences with "a sense of belonging, and by contributing to shared consciousness and identity" (Hanitzsch & Vos, 2018, p. 159). Fifth, the *mood manager* relates to journalists' aims to provide entertainment and provide positive experiences. Sixth, the *inspirator* is a role in which journalists address both consumption and emotion by providing inspiration for new lifestyles and products. Finally, the *guide* is the most generic role as it addresses consumption, identity and emotion, through providing orientation more broadly, for example, on desired lifestyles. While Hanitzsch and Vos (2018) conceptualized these roles in relation to everyday life more generally, it is, nevertheless, obvious how they relate to many of the already discussed facets of lifestyle journalism specifically.

Empirical studies of roles in lifestyle journalism

Aside from Hanusch & Hanitzsch's exploration of role perceptions in lifestyle journalism, recent years have also seen an increasing range of attempts to better understand what lifestyle journalists aim to achieve with their work. Many of these studies have been conducted in relation to particular lifestyle beats, such as travel journalism. For example, a small exploratory study interviewed 13 German travel journalists, identifying two dimensions along which role perceptions could be examined (Lischke, 2006). The first related to where these journalists placed themselves on a continuum between providing practical information or merely entertainment for audiences, while the second related to travel journalists' motivations. These could be located ranging from traditional journalistic motivations also found in political journalists to a more basic motivation of wanting to travel. Informed by this early work, a survey of Australian travel journalists identified five dimensions of role perceptions (Hanusch, 2012). The *cultural mediator* role relates to how travel journalists perceive their role in reporting on foreign cultures, such as raising an interest in other cultures among audiences, playing a role in intercultural understanding and actively working against stereotypes. The role of *critic* was also present, which relates to journalists' role as critical observers of the tourism industry. This role perception was perhaps the closest to established role perception known in relation to political life and saw travel journalists also aiming to highlight social or political problems at destinations. Travel journalists also saw themselves as *information providers* who played a more basic role of informing prospective travellers about travel options or what to do at a destination. The role dimension of *entertainer* saw travel journalists wanting to provide enjoyable accounts of travel experiences, through entertaining and interesting information. Finally, the role of the traveller meant respondents viewed their role as one of motivating readers and viewers to experience the joys of travel, seeing it as their job to encourage audiences in this way. These roles were not considered as equally important, however. In fact, the entertainer and traveller dimensions were the most popular among the sample of travel journalists who were surveyed, followed by the cultural mediator and information provider roles. The role of the critic was, perhaps unsurprisingly, supported much less than the other roles. Yet, it is worth pointing out that at least this role perception existed and some journalists did value it.

A number of studies have examined, in particular, the market orientation of lifestyle journalists. Perreault, Ferrucci and Ficara (2024), on the basis of interviews with US lifestyle journalists, have reported that while this group perceives commercial pressures, they also do not feel that it is starkly different from the commercial pressures experienced by hard news journalists. In Germany, lifestyle editors reported that they not only aimed to primarily provide entertainment, spread positivity, inspire their readers and offer a service and advice but also placed importance on autonomy and objectivity (Viererbl, 2023). While these journalists felt that their perceptions well matched those of their audiences, they experienced considerable role conflict when it came to commercial pressures from PR and marketing departments. Such role conflict could lead to a sense of resignation among lifestyle journalists, explaining less critical reporting on products and services (Viererbl, 2023). A study of consumer magazine journalists in China demonstrated that in their attempt to avoid pressure from both political and commercial influences, consumer journalists "reorient the multiple functions of journalism as an 'information vehicle' in the 'service of the rising class', 'independent from media ownership and commercial forces', and 'contributing consumerism to culture and traditional society'" (Li, 2012, p. 134).

In relation to the broader field of lifestyle journalism, Hanusch's (2019) large-scale survey of 616 Australian lifestyle journalists provides an opportunity not only to empirically validate some of the theorized role dimensions but also to dig deeper into differences within the field, based on aspects such as sub-beats. Broadly, the study found very similar role dimensions as have already been discussed. These included the service provider, life coach, community advocate and inspiring entertainer roles. *Service providers* want to inform audiences, provide reviews of new products and services, report on new trends and ideas, promote the lifestyle industries and provide more general advice to audiences. *Life coaches* want to motivate people to change their lifestyle, offering examples of how people can live their lives, as well as help people navigate through their lives and focus on content audiences can use in their daily lives. *Community advocates* want to provide a forum for readers to ask questions; help to create communities of audiences; provide a service to audiences, but – in a more critical tradition – also advocate for audiences' interests; tell audiences about ethical and moral dimensions of certain lifestyles and experiences; and monitor and scrutinize businesses involved in the lifestyle industries. Inspiring entertainers focus on content that entertains and inspires audiences, that is fun to consume, lets audiences relax and which provides ideas on how audiences can spend their leisure time (Hanusch, 2019, p. 201). Similar to prior research, the inspiring entertainer role was considered the most important by respondents, followed by the role of the service provider. The life coach and community advocate roles were considered the least important. In substantial ways, then, the study found empirical evidence to support the range of roles that had been conceptualized previously (e.g., Hanitzsch & Vos, 2018; Hanusch & Hanitzsch, 2013).

Crucially, however, it also identified important differences within the sample, particularly in terms of the individual, organization and specialization levels. Individual-level factors played only a minor role, with women slightly more likely than men to support the life coach role. But on the organizational and beat levels, more pronounced differences were identified. These point to the importance of particularly commercial aspects, such as the level of competition experienced in a newsroom, where higher competition resulted in higher support for all roles, except the life coach role. In terms of beats, travel journalists were the strongest supporters of the inspiring entertainer role, followed by fashion and beauty journalists, who were also more likely than others to support the service provider role. This indicates that entertainment is a hallmark for particularly these two beats. On the other hand, health and wellness as well as personal technology journalists were more likely to support the role of being a life coach, indicating that these two beats place more emphasis on providing more concrete advice on how to change or live their lives to audiences. Overall, these results show that "it would be a mistake to tar all lifestyle journalists with the same brush" (Hanusch, 2019, p. 207).

Scholarship on the differences among the various beats that make up lifestyle journalism, and also journalism in everyday life more broadly, is still in its infancy. The existing research discussed in this chapter points to some interesting departure points from which to explore these. Above all, it is important to recognize that there are substantial differences within lifestyle journalism, pointing to the fact that it is not a cohesive field, despite its overall focus on matters related to consumption, emotion and identity. Compared with the wide range of evidence that exists on journalism and political life, it is clear that we are only at the beginning of a better understanding of the dynamics in the field. Another key consideration going forward in the scholarship of lifestyle journalism is the need to overcome the artificial dichotomy – which still underlies much of journalism research – between soft and hard news journalism or political and everyday life. Often, the literature has regarded these as polar opposites or as mutually exclusive (Reinemann et al., 2012), with journalists either producing news aimed at citizens or consumers, but not both. But evidence from role perception studies in lifestyle journalism – and increasingly from such studies into political journalism as well (see, for example, Baym, 2005; Mellado & van Dalen, 2017) – points to the fact that these journalists do not distinguish as strictly as some scholars do. While scholars, therefore, typically talk about journalists wanting to address their audiences as "citizens or consumers" (Deuze, 2005, p. 447), it may be just as likely that they actually see them as "citizens and consumers", particularly in a world increasingly affected by consumption cultures more generally (Hanusch & Hanitzsch, 2013). This point is reinforced by studies from Global South contexts, where, for example, South African political and lifestyle journalists alike have "been engaging in 'acts of lifestyle' and 'acts of politics'" (Banjac & Hanusch, 2023, p. 2169). Similarly, Elgesem, Knudsen and Fløttum (2024) found much congruence in terms of the role orientations between reporting on serious topics like climate change on one hand and lifestyle journalism on the other (see also Chapter 20).

Future directions

The overview of scholarship on lifestyle journalistic role conceptions presented in this chapter has already pointed to a range of blind spots that still need to be addressed. Without claiming to be exhaustive in determining these gaps, there appear to be four areas in particular that may be worth exploring in more detail in future studies. These include the need to study the impact of peripheral actors on lifestyle journalists' role perceptions; how lifestyle journalistic roles are actually enacted in the content they produce; how audience expectations may influence lifestyle journalists' role perceptions; and how lifestyle journalists outside the Global North perceive their roles. This section discusses each of these one by one.

One important consideration for scholarship going forward is the dynamic development of what can be considered lifestyle journalism, as other chapters in this book also point out (see Part V). In particular, the emergence of a range of so-called peripheral actors, who may in some audiences' views be conducting work that is at least somewhat similar to journalism, is an important phenomenon to study in relation to role perceptions. Existing evidence has already pointed out that there may be pronounced similarities between lifestyle influencers' perceived role perceptions and those of professional lifestyle journalists (Maares & Hanusch, 2020). Interviews with 19 German and Austrian lifestyle influencers on Instagram revealed they wanted to provide exemplars of lifestyle; provide inspiration; educate followers and providing orientation; provide a service and giving advice; and provide entertainment and relaxation – all of which were highly similar to those that Hanusch and Hanitzsch (2013) found among lifestyle journalists (Maares & Hanusch, 2020). Given that role perceptions can be considered important boundary markers as established and new actors struggle over authority in the journalistic field (see Chapter 24), how these varying actors' conceptions of their role in society develop and are used will be an important area for future research. This is particularly because the arrival of a wider range of producers in the field of lifestyle has been hailed as potentially leading to more diversity in representation, and a more democratic view of, for example, fashion (Boyd, 2015). Thus, there may emerge a wider array of roles or perhaps also a more balanced representation of roles as peripheral actors aim to plug the holes that traditional lifestyle journalism leaves. On the other hand, established lifestyle journalists have been shown to more strongly identify with traditional roles of journalism, such as the critical observer, in the light of the arrival of lifestyle influencers (see Cheng & Chew, 2024; Perreault & Hanusch, 2024).

As already discussed briefly, increased scrutiny of how journalistic roles are studied has in recent years led to a considerable upsurge in exploring not only journalists' role perceptions but also how these roles are actually enacted (Tandoc et al., 2013) or performed (Hellmueller & Mellado, 2015). These studies have substantially advanced our understanding of the "real-world behaviour of journalists" (Mellado & Hallin, 2024, p. 1), and some of this work has even touched on lifestyle journalism, albeit not always directly. Still, evidence from the Journalistic Role Performance project demonstrates that lifestyle roles subsumed in what it defines as infotainment and service dimensions are particularly prevalent in lifestyle beats. Results from the project's most recent analysis of news-making in 37 countries show that the service role is more associated with economic and lifestyle news, while the infotainment role is more present in celebrity and sports news (Mellado et al., 2024). It is worth pointing out, of course, that studies such as these are still typically conducted within a wider framework, rather than a specific focus on lifestyle journalistic role performance, given they use broader conceptualizations of these roles. Therefore, while pointing to some preliminary and important evidence about how specifically lifestyle journalists perform their roles, more focused studies are necessary. In addition, it is also important to engage in more ethnographic research to better understand how roles come to be performed (Mellado et al., 2024, p. 118). Such work could include the very promising method of reconstructive interviews, which has shown to yield important insights into production processes (Reich & Barnoy, 2020). But there are also opportunities to observe lifestyle journalists in their newsrooms or out in the field, building on the rich tradition of newsroom observation in journalism studies (e.g., Gans, 1979; Tuchman, 1978), which has in recent years experienced a resurgence (see Willig, 2013). In fact, Usher's (2012) analysis of personal technology and personal finance journalists at the *New York Times* is one of the rare occasions where journalists on the lifestyle beats have been observed at work. It is curious that not more work has been conducted in this area. Perhaps one explanation might be that it would still be considered frivolous if, for example, scholars tagged along with travel journalists on an all-expense paid travel familiarization, given the enduring normative assumptions of the field of journalism studies. Yet, to truly understand the range of influences and pressures on lifestyle journalists in their work, exactly such initiatives might be fruitful in better approximating the real contexts within which lifestyle journalists work.

We also still know relatively little about the roles that audiences expect lifestyle journalists to fulfil. Yet, this is increasingly important, as the recent substantial growth in research on audience expectations of journalism more generally has shown (see, e.g. Banjac et al., 2024). As scholars have argued, switching the perspective on roles away from journalists toward what audiences actually expect enables us to better "assess the changing functions which journalism fulfils in society and the roles it enables the public to play in social life" (Mellado & Van Dalen, 2017, p. 214). Whereas journalists (and scholars of journalism) had previously for the most part ignored audiences, the so-called 'audience turn' has led to substantial focus on this aspect (Costera Meijer 2020). Audiences are increasingly challenging established journalistic practices, requiring a re-think on the part of journalists, including those working in the area of lifestyle, in order to better meet audience expectations (Hanitzsch & Vos, 2018). Some evidence has already suggested that journalists' role perceptions may be affected by the extent to which they read online comments, for example (Hanusch & Tandoc, 2019). An important consideration in relation to how audience expectations may affect journalists' role perceptions is that the prominence of certain audience communities and their expectations will likely differ across countries depending on their specific geographical, political, cultural and historical contexts (Hanusch & Banjac, 2018, p. 36). In fact, as evidence from South Africa shows, audiences expect different things from lifestyle journalists depending on the class these audiences belong to. For example, more affluent audiences preferred advice for do-it-yourself projects, whereas working class audiences requested more serious guidance such as financial advice or information about HIV or mental health (Banjac & Hanusch, 2022).

In line with this consideration is the inescapable fact that the vast majority of our understanding of lifestyle journalistic roles is based on studies that have originated in the Global North. While there are some notable studies that have explored these roles in the context of Singapore (Cheng, 2020; Cheng & Chew, 2024) and also South Africa (Banjac & Hanusch, 2022, 2023), the field is still very much Western in terms of its paradigms. This may not be too surprising given the overall Western bias in journalism studies, as well as the fact that the consumption cultures so central to much of lifestyle journalism are more prevalent in the rather wealthy Global North. The value changes discussed earlier in this chapter are perhaps more pronounced there, and audiences tend to have larger amounts of leisure time and disposable income that appear to be so central to lifestyle journalism. Traditional institutions may also still be more powerful in many parts of the Global South. Yet, this does not mean that lifestyle journalism does not exist or may not be consumed in the Global South per se.

In fact, as Banjac and Hanusch's (2022) study has shown, even those 'poorer' communities access lifestyle journalism, albeit perhaps for different reasons. Interviews with 22 South African lifestyle journalists and focus groups with audiences demonstrated the conceptual benefit that scholars can gain from studying lifestyle journalistic roles outside the Global North. The study showed that class disparity and the country's history of racial segregation and oppression shapes the role perceptions lifestyle journalists hold and the expectations audiences have of them. In particular, lifestyle journalists were – perhaps more so than their counterparts in the Global North – more supportive of traditional political roles, but they also more heavily connected them with the 'softer' mission of lifestyle journalism. In addition, lifestyle journalists "acted as 'responsible' cultural intermediaries, mediating the worlds of luxury and inequality" (Banjac & Hanusch, 2022, p. 1607). Finally, the study discovered a particular relevance of the role to "provide aspiration through stories and consumer goods that audiences could aspire toward" (Banjac & Hanusch, 2022, p. 1618; see also Chapter 12). While aspects of this role had also been conceptualized elsewhere (Hanusch & Hanitzsch, 2013), the South African context demonstrated important nuances and differences in its relevance, both for journalists and audiences, demonstrating the need for studies to branch out beyond established Global North contexts to more fully understand universal and particular aspects of lifestyle journalistic roles.

Conclusion

The aim of this chapter was to provide an overview of the current state of scholarship on lifestyle journalistic roles and particularly the blind spots that still exist in our understanding of these. In tracing the history of studies of journalists' role perceptions, we could see that the heavy emphasis in journalism studies on normative roles led to a lack of recognition of journalistic roles beyond political life for most of the 20th century. Recently, however, scholarship has realized the relevance of lifestyle journalism more broadly and begun to conceptualize and empirically study the roles that practitioners in this field have. These relate to the areas of consumption, emotion and identity (Hanitzsch & Vos, 2018), with both studies of specific lifestyle beats and of lifestyle journalism identifying a range of specific roles that can nevertheless be grouped within the larger dimensions. However, some more recent work exploring contexts beyond the Global North suggests that we still do not have a full understanding of the variety of contexts in which lifestyle roles come to exist.

For this reason, this chapter has outlined a range of blind spots that still require focused attention by scholars. These include the need to study the arrival of peripheral actors in journalism, which may be prompting a rethink of journalistic roles, or at the very least a broadening and diversification. Further, the relative lack of observational and content analytical work in this space means we know very little about whether what lifestyle journalists tell us about their roles is what they actually do. Clearly, this is an important area for future studies. Similarly, research on the role expectations that audiences have of lifestyle journalists is also still scarce. Given the increased focus on audiences in journalism studies, future studies should provide us with a better understanding of whether lifestyle journalists are actually meeting audiences' expectations. Finally, the vast majority of empirical studies have so far been conducted in the Global North, leading to a lack of knowledge about whether the dimensions that have so far been examined actually constitute all possible dimensions, as well as about the relative importance of various dimensions in a global context. Clearly, more comparative work is needed in this regard. As the chapter has shown, then, there are still important desiderata in the study of lifestyle journalistic roles.

Further reading

Hanusch, F., & Hanitzsch, T. (2013). Mediating Orientation and Self-Expression in the World of Consumption: Australian and German Lifestyle Journalists' Professional Views. *Media, Culture & Society*, 35(8), 943–959.

Hanitzsch, T., & Vos, T. P. (2018). Journalism beyond democracy: A new look into journalistic roles in political and everyday life. *Journalism*, 19(2), 146–164.

Hanitzsch, T., & Vos, T. P. (2017). Journalistic roles and the struggle over institutional identity: The discursive constitution of journalism. *Communication Theory*, 27(2), 115–135.

Tandoc Jr., E. C., Hellmueller, L., & Vos, T. P. (2013). Mind the gap: Between journalistic role conception and role enactment. *Journalism Practice*, 7(5), 539–554

Viererbl, B. (2023). Writing for the audience or for public relations? How lifestyle editors perceive expectations about their professional role and manage potential for conflict. *Journalism*, 24(7), 1593–1609.

References

Banjac, S., & Hanusch, F. (2023). The struggle for authority and legitimacy: Lifestyle and political journalists' discursive boundary work. *Journalism*, 24(10), 2155–2173. https://doi.org/10.1177/14648849221125702

Banjac, S., & Hanusch, F. (2022). Aspirational lifestyle journalism: The impact of social class on producers' and audiences' views in the context of socio-economic inequality. *Journalism*, 23(8), 1607–1625. https://doi.org/10.1177/1464884920956823

Banjac, S., Juarez Miro, C., & Hanusch, F. (2024). Expectations of journalistic actors in the digital age: A conceptual framework. *Communication Theory*, 34(2), 60–70. https://doi.org/10.1093/ct/qtae002

Bauman, Z. (2000). *Liquid modernity*. Polity Press.

Baym, G. (2005). The daily show: Discursive integration and the reinvention of political journalism. *Political Communication*, 22(3), 259–276. https://doi.org/10.1080/10584600591006492

Beck, U. (1992). *Risk society: Towards a new modernity*. Sage.

Biddle, B. J. (1979). *Role theory: Expectations, identities, and behaviors*. Academic Press.

Biddle, B. J. (1986). Recent developments in role theory. *Annual Review of Sociology*, 12(1), 67-92.

Blumer, H. (1962). Society as symbolic interaction. In A. M. Rose (Ed.), *Human Behavior and Social Processes* (pp. 179–192). Houghton Mifflin.

Boyd, K. C. (2015). Democratizing fashion: The effects of the evolution of fashion journalism from print to online media. *McNair Scholars Research Journal*, 8(1), 17–34.

Chaney, D. C. (1997). *Lifestyles*. Routledge.

Cheng, L. (2020). *Print vs digital: The changing production of Singaporean women's magazines* [Master's Thesis, Nanyang Technological University]. https://doi.org/10.32657/10356/143190

Cheng, L., & Chew, M. (2024). Functional interlopers: Lifestyle journalists' discursive construction of boundaries against digital lifestyle influencers. *Journalism*, 25(2), 372–390. https://doi.org/10.1177/14648849221143875

Christians, C. G., Glasser, T. L., McQuail, D., Nordenstreng, K., & White, R. A. (2009). *Normative theories of the media: Journalism in democratic societies*. University of Illinois Press.

Cohen, B. C. (1963). *The press and foreign policy*. Princeton University Press.

Costera Meijer, I. (2020). Understanding the audience turn in journalism: From quality discourse to innovation discourse as anchoring practices 1995–2020. *Journalism Studies*, *21*(16), 2326–2342. https://doi.org/10.1080/1461670X.2020.1847681

Deuze, M. (2005). What is journalism?: Professional identity and ideology of journalists reconsidered. *Journalism*, *6*(4), 442–464. https://doi.org/10.1177/1464884905056815

Donsbach, W., & Patterson, T. E. (2004). Political news journalists: Partisanship, professionalism, and political roles in five countries. In F. Esser & B. Pfetsch (Eds.), *Comparing political communication* (pp. 251–270). Cambridge University Press. https://doi.org/10.1017/CBO9780511606991.012

Eide, M., & Knight, G. (1999). Public/private service: Service journalism and the problems of everyday life. *European Journal of Communication*, *14*(4), 525–547. https://doi.org/10.1177/0267323199014004004

Elgesem, D., Knudsen, E., & Fløttum, K. (2024). The impact of climate change on lifestyle journalism. *Journalism Studies*, *25*(4), 337–357. https://doi.org/10.1080/1461670X.2023.2299463

Gans, H. J. (1979). *Deciding what's news: A study of CBS evening news, NBC nightly news, newsweek, and time*. Pantheon Books.

Goffman, E. (1959). *The presentation of self in everyday life*. Doubleday.

Hallin, D. C., Mellado, C., Cohen, A., Hubé, N., Nolan, D., Szabó, G., Abuali, Y., Arcila, C., Attia, M., Blanchett, N., Chen, K., Davydov, S., De Maio, M., Garcés, M., Himma-Kadakas, M., Humanes, M. L., I- Hsuan Lin, C., Lecheler, S., Lee, M., … Ybáñez, N. (2023). Journalistic role performance in times of COVID. *Journalism Studies*, *24*(16), 1977–1998. https://doi.org/10.1080/1461670X.2023.2274584

Hanitzsch, T. (2007). Deconstructing journalism culture: Toward a universal theory. *Communication Theory*, *17*(4), 367–385. https://doi.org/10.1111/j.1468-2885.2007.00303.x

Hanitzsch, T., Hanusch, F., Mellado, C., Anikina, M., Berganza, R., Cangoz, I., Coman, M., Hamada, B., Elena Hernández, M., Karadjov, C. D., Virginia Moreira, S., Mwesige, P. G., Plaisance, P. L., Reich, Z., Seethaler, J., Skewes, E. A., Vardiansyah Noor, D., & Kee Wang Yuen, E. (2011). Mapping journalism cultures across nations: A comparative study of 18 countries. *Journalism Studies*, *12*(3), 273–293. https://doi.org/10.1080/1461670X.2010.512502

Hanitzsch, T., Hanusch, F., Ramaprasad, J., & de Beer, A. S. (Eds.) (2019). *Worlds of journalism: Journalistic cultures around the globe*. Columbia University Press.

Hanitzsch, T., & Vos, T. P. (2018). Journalism beyond democracy: A new look into journalistic roles in political and everyday life. *Journalism*, *19*(2), 146–164. https://doi.org/10.1177/1464884916673386

Hanitzsch, T., & Vos, T. P. (2017). Journalistic roles and the struggle over institutional identity: The discursive constitution of journalism: Journalistic roles and institutional identity. *Communication Theory*, *27*(2), 115–135. https://doi.org/10.1111/comt.12112

Hanusch, F. (2019). Journalistic roles and everyday life: An empirical account of lifestyle journalists' professional views. *Journalism Studies*, *20*(2), 193–211. https://doi.org/10.1080/1461670X.2017.1370977

Hanusch, F. (2012). A profile of Australian travel journalists' professional views and ethical standards. *Journalism*, *13*(5), 668–686. https://doi.org/10.1177/1464884911398338

Hanusch, F., & Banjac, S. (2018). Studying role conceptions in the digital age. A critical appraisal. In S. A. Eldridge & B. Franklin (Eds.), *The Routledge Handbook of developments in digital journalism studies* (pp. 28–39). Routledge.

Hanusch, F., & Hanitzsch, T. (2013). Mediating orientation and self-expression in the world of consumption: Australian and German lifestyle journalists' professional views. *Media, Culture & Society*, *35*(8), 943–959. https://doi.org/10.1177/0163443713501931

Hanusch, F., & Tandoc, E. C. (2019). Comments, analytics, and social media: The impact of audience feedback on journalists' market orientation. *Journalism*, *20*(6), 695–713. https://doi.org/10.1177/1464884917720305

Hellmueller, L., & Mellado, C. (2015). Professional roles and news construction: A media sociology conceptualization of journalists' role conception and performance. *Communication & Society*, *28*(3), 1–12. https://doi.org/10.15581/003.28.35948

Hjarvard, S. (2008). The mediatization of religion: A theory of the media as agents of religious change. *Northern Lights: Film & Media Studies Yearbook*, *6*(1), 9–26. https://doi.org/10.1386/nl.6.1.9_1

Janowitz, M. (1975). Professional models in journalism: The gatekeeper and the advocate. *Journalism Quarterly*, 52(4), 618–626. https://doi.org/10.1177/107769907505200402

Johnstone, J. W. C., Slawski, E. J., & Bowman, W. W. (1972). The professional values of American newsmen. *Public Opinion Quarterly*, 36(4), 522. https://doi.org/10.1086/268036

Li, S. (2012). A new generation of lifestyle magazine journalism in China: The professional approach. *Journalism Practice*, 6(1), 122–137. https://doi.org/10.1080/17512786.2011.622901

Lischke, J. (2006). *Reisejournalisten: Akteure im Spannungsfeld [Travel journalists: Actors in a field of tension]* [Unpublished master's thesis]. University of Munich.

Maares, P., & Hanusch, F. (2020). Exploring the boundaries of journalism: Instagram microbloggers in the twilight zone of lifestyle journalism. *Journalism*, 21(2), 262–278. https://doi.org/10.1177/1464884918801400

Mellado, C., & Hallin, D. (2024). Introduction: Journalistic role performance in times of change. *Journalism Practice*, 18(9), 2167–2171. https://doi.org/10.1080/17512786.2024.2393669

Mellado, C., Hellmueller, L., & Donsbach, W. (Eds.) (2016). *Journalistic role performance: Concepts, contexts, and methods*. Routledge.

Mellado, C., Márquez-Ramírez, M., Van Leuven, S., Jackson, D., Mothes, C., Arcila-Calderón, C., Berthaut, J., Blanchett, N., Boudana, S., Chen, K. Y. N., Davydov, S., De Maio, M., Fahmy, N., Ferrero, M., Garcés, M., Hagen, L., Hallin, D. C., Humanes, M. L., Himma-Kadakas, M., … Viveros Aguilar, D. (2024). Comparing journalistic role performance across thematic beats: A 37-country study. *Journalism & Mass Communication Quarterly*, 101(1), 97–126. https://doi.org/10.1177/10776990231173890

Mellado, C., & Van Dalen, A. (2017). Challenging the citizen–consumer cournalistic dichotomy: A news content analysis of audience approaches in Chile. *Journalism & Mass Communication Quarterly*, 94(1), 213–237. https://doi.org/10.1177/1077699016629373

Merton, R. K. (1957). The role-set: Problems in sociological theory. *The British Journal of Sociology*, 8(2), 106. https://doi.org/10.2307/587363

Perreault, G. P., Ferrucci, P., & Ficara, G. (2024). No more market-driven than hard news: Lifestyle journalists' market drive and perceived audience obligations. *Journalism Studies*, 25(7), 723–737. https://doi.org/10.1080/1461670X.2024.2333819

Perreault, G., & Hanusch, F. (2024). Field insurgency in lifestyle journalism: How lifestyle journalists marginalize Instagram influencers and protect their autonomy. *New Media & Society*, 26(7), 3767–3785. https://doi.org/10.1177/14614448221104233

Reich, Z., & Barnoy, A. (2020). How news become "news" in increasingly complex ecosystems: Summarizing almost two decades of newsmaking reconstructions. *Journalism Studies*, 21(7), 966–983. https://doi.org/10.1080/1461670X.2020.1716830

Reinemann, C., Stanyer, J., Scherr, S., & Legnante, G. (2012). Hard and soft news: A review of concepts, operationalizations and key findings. *Journalism*, 13(2), 221–239. https://doi.org/10.1177/1464884911427803

Simmel, G. (1920). Zur Philosophie des Schauspielers [Toward the philosophy of the actor]. *Logos: Internationale Zeitung Für Die Philosophie Der Kultur*, 9, 339–362.

Stryker, S. (1980). *Symbolic interactionism: A social structural version*. Benjamin/Cummings Pub. Co.

Tandoc Jr., E. C., & Duffy, A. (2016). Keeping up with the audiences: Journalistic role expectations in Singapore. *International Journal of Communication*, 10(21). https://ijoc.org/index.php/ijoc/article/view/4565

Tandoc, E. C., Hellmueller, L., & Vos, T. P. (2013). Mind the gap: Between journalistic role conception and role enactment. *Journalism Practice*, 7(5), 539–554. https://doi.org/10.1080/17512786.2012.726503

Taylor, L. (2002). From ways of life to lifestyle: The 'ordinari-ization' of British gardening lifestyle television. *European Journal of Communication*, 17(4), 479–493. https://doi.org/10.1177/02673231020170040501

Tuchman, G. (1978). *Making news: A study in the construction of reality*. The Free Press.

Turner, R. H. (1956). Role-taking, role standpoint, and reference-group behavior. *American Journal of Sociology*, 61(4), 316–328. https://doi.org/10.1086/221763

Underwood, D. (2000). Reporting and the push for market-oriented journalism: Media organizations as businesses. In W. L. Bennett & R. M. Entman (Eds.), *Mediated politics: Communication in the future of democracy* (pp. 99–116). Cambridge University Press. https://doi.org/10.1017/CBO9780511613852.006

Usher, N. (2012). Service journalism as community experience: Personal technology and personal finance at the New York Times. *Journalism Practice*, 6(1), 107–121. https://doi.org/10.1080/17512786.2011.628782

Viererbl, B. (2023). Writing for the audience or for public relations? How lifestyle editors perceive expectations about their professional role and manage potential for conflict. *Journalism*, 24(7), 1593–1609. https://doi.org/10.1177/14648849211067586

Vos, T. P. (2005, May 29). *Journalistic role conception: A bridge between the reporter and the press* [Paper presentation]. International Communication Association (ICA) Conference, New York, NY, United States.

Weaver, D. H. (Ed.) (1998). *The global journalist: News people around the world*. Hampton Press.

Weaver, D. H., Beam, R. A., Brownlee, B. J., Voakes, P. S., & Wilhoit, G. C. (Eds.) (2007). *The American journalist in the 21st century: U.S. news people at the dawn of a new millennium*. Routledge.

Weaver, D. H., Weaver, D. H., Wilhoit, G. C., & Wilhoit, G. C. (1996). *The American journalist in the 1990s: U.S. news people at the end of an era*. Routledge.

Weaver, D. H., & Wilhoit, G. C. (1986). *The American journalist: A portrait of U.S. news people and their work*. Indiana University Press.

Weaver, D. H., & Willnat, L. (2016). Changes in U.S. journalism: How do journalists think about social media? *Journalism Practice*, 10(7), 844–855. https://doi.org/10.1080/17512786.2016.1171162

Willig, I. (2013). Newsroom ethnography in a field perspective. *Journalism*, 14(3), 372–387. https://doi.org/10.1177/1464884912442638

Zelizer, B. (2011). Journalism in the service of communication. *Journal of Communication*, 61(1), 1–21. https://doi.org/10.1111/j.1460-2466.2010.01524.x

17
THE ROLE OF EXPERTS IN LIFESTYLE JOURNALISM

Daniel Nölleke

Introduction

Today's societies are experiencing an unprecedented increase in the volume of knowledge (Stehr & Grundmann, 2011, p. 1). At the same time that its production is accelerating, the demand for and dependence on knowledge is increasing throughout society. This is both an opportunity and a challenge for journalism: Because of their central position in the flow of information and their skills in researching, selecting, and disseminating complex issues, journalists can act as knowledge brokers (Gesualdo et al., 2020) and share much-needed knowledge with the public. In this respect, journalism is considered the "new knowledge profession" (Donsbach, 2014). However, because journalists typically cannot provide this expertise themselves (and are even less able to do so the more specialized these areas become; Nichols, 2017), they rely on expert sources (Reich & Lahav, 2021). These sources are not only used to provide expertise but also serve strategic purposes by reflecting the journalistic ideology of presenting unbiased and reliable information (Albaek, 2011). Therefore, relying on expert sources has become a hallmark of credible reporting in various fields: Former military personnel serve as popular TV pundits in war coverage (Steele, 1995), former athletes explain the results of sporting events (Nölleke, 2024), former politicians analyze the rationale behind election campaigns (Cross, 2010), and scientists provide expertise on topics such as the COVID-19 pandemic (Leidecker-Sandmann et al., 2022; Nölleke et al., 2023) or climate change (Takahashi et al., 2017). In addition, popular chefs like Jamie Oliver demonstrate how to prepare delicious meals quickly and inexpensively. This latter example shows that the need for expertise is not limited to the fields of abstract (academic) knowledge, but that it also extends to areas of the ordinary, including lifestyle journalism.

In the course of the recent knowledge explosion, everyday life has become increasingly complicated: Once mundane questions such as what to cook, who to date, and how to decorate the living room have become areas of uncertainty. Questions that in the past could – against a backdrop of limited options – be addressed through intuition, individual experience, and common sense suddenly call for authoritative expert knowledge in order to make informed decisions. In that regard, Stehr and Grundmann (2011, p. 11) claim that "[…] nowadays every individual – sometimes willingly, sometimes not – must seek expertise, not only in order to make serious consequential decisions, but also often to deal with smaller, everyday problems". The media portrayal of diverse lifestyle topics such as travel, health, food, and fitness is, therefore, increasingly characterized by the involvement of experts on the ordinary (Lewis, 2010), often in the form of celebrities such as Jamie Oliver. In this respect, lifestyle journalism serves as an apt indicator of larger trends in contemporary expert societies. It exemplifies the expanded understanding of expertise and illustrates what is meant by the seemingly paradoxical assertion that "we believe less and less in experts, yet we use them more and more" (Limoges, 1993, p. 424).

At the same time that academic knowledge is coming under increasing criticism, we are witnessing a democratization of expertise (Lunt & Lewis, 2008, p. 10) and a revaluation of practical experience as a guarantor of expertise. We are not only expanding the circle of people we consider to have relevant expertise but also the areas in which this expertise is needed to include ordinary topics such as lifestyle and everyday life. At the same time, the functions these experts perform are evolving: Whereas in the past they were mainly concerned with imparting abstract knowledge, today they are increasingly called upon to convey practical knowledge for solving very specific problems. They are becoming service providers for everyday life and are increasingly taking on advisory roles.

In this chapter, I will examine what characterizes the presentation of expertise in lifestyle journalism. I will discuss why authoritative knowledge is increasingly in demand even when reporting on softer topics. Against the backdrop of changes in the digital knowledge and risk society, I will argue that trends in lifestyle journalism reflect larger developments that influence social status and our understanding of expertise. While lifestyle journalists' approaches to utilizing and portraying expertise may be unique, I will show that the general mechanisms in the use of expert sources are prevalent in all journalistic beats. Ultimately, it is always the journalist who decides which sources to ascribe expert status to. Accordingly, expertise is conceptualized as the result of a social construction process that reflects journalistic norms, routines, and constraints. Since empirical evidence on the role of experts in lifestyle journalism is largely lacking, this claim is illustrated by studies on the use of experts in general news reporting. In the concluding section, I will also discuss the extent to which lifestyle influencers take on functions that were previously reserved for expert sources in (lifestyle) journalism. Thus, this chapter aims to not only provide insights into the role, nature, and function of expert sources in (lifestyle) journalism, but it also uses the case of lifestyle journalism to highlight larger trends in the social role and media representation of expertise.

Lifestyle journalism and the democratization of expertise

Lunt and Lewis (2008) vividly argue that the figure of the expert can be seen as one of the main characters in lifestyle journalism; more than that, according to them, it is precisely "the rise and mainstreaming of lifestyle journalism" that has triggered an "explosion of expertise" (Lunt & Lewis, 2008, p. 13). At first glance, this strong assertion may seem paradoxical: Why should reporting on seemingly mundane topics, in particular, require the use of expert sources? And how could this even lead to a renaissance of the role of experts when we are simultaneously witnessing increasing skepticism toward expert knowledge (Collins, 2014; Nichols, 2017) and experiencing a "crisis of scientific expertise" (Stehr & Grundmann, 2011, p. 104)? However, what appears contradictory at first glance becomes less so when one considers the explosion of knowledge in knowledge societies on the supply side (Reich & Lahav, 2021), the growing demand for knowledge in the course of individualization processes in risk societies (Beck, 1992; Giddens, 1990; Lupton, 2024), and the associated expanded understanding of expertise, which is no longer based solely on scientific knowledge but is increasingly tied to "the ordinary, the domestic and the everyday" (Lewis, 2010, p. 580).

Stehr and Grundmann (2011) describe the expert as a key figure in knowledge societies. The term "knowledge society" refers to a society in which the production, dissemination, and use of knowledge play a central role in promoting social, economic, and cultural development (Kastberg, 2018). In a knowledge society, the creation and accumulation of knowledge occur at an increasingly rapid pace. Knowledge has become a key resource for all sectors of society, and its effective use shapes economic innovation, (political) decision-making, and the overall progress of individuals. Importantly, knowledge societies are not characterized by fixed barriers between knowledge producers and consumers, but rather by increasingly blurred boundaries (Kastberg, 2018).

In that regard, trends in knowledge societies have facilitated a "growing democratization of knowledge and expertise" (Lunt & Lewis, 2008, p. 10), in the course of which the traditional hierarchies between experts and laypeople have shrunk. Remarkably, it is precisely the realization that traditional (often scientific) experts are not always able to provide meaningful knowledge that has led to an increasing appreciation of other sources of knowledge (beyond science) and thus to the alleged explosion of expertise. In this sense, the example of lifestyle journalism makes it particularly clear that contemporary knowledge societies are "pluralized" (Heinrichs, 2005, p. 42), and we are experiencing a "multiplication of expertise" (Stehr & Grundmann, 2011, p. ix) that is no longer limited to scientific elites but also includes the practical experience of experts for everyday life.

The growing supply of and demand for specialized expert knowledge

The increasing emergence of and reliance on authority figures who impart expertise can be explained by the exponential growth of knowledge in knowledge societies (Stehr, 1994). This growth is based both on technical innovations, which make it possible to store and process huge amounts of data, and on social developments. In particular, the development of social subsystems (like politics, science, judiciary, and economics) in the course of functional differentiation processes, accompanied by the professionalization of ever-new niche areas, has led to a high degree of specialization of knowledge within society. Such an increase in knowledge production goes hand in hand with a growing dependence on knowledge. It was primarily the demand side that Lane had in mind with his concept of the "knowledgeable society" (Lane, 1966, p. 650), which he characterized by the fact that its members are dependent on scientific knowledge and use this knowledge to achieve their goals and values. Accordingly, scientific knowledge spreads into all areas of society, making its members dependent on the possession of this knowledge and thus willing to devote resources to its production.

Similarly, Stehr and colleagues argue that the degree of our dependence on professions that trade in knowledge is becoming ever more extensive (Stehr et al., 2006). It follows that the knowledge society is reflected in the growth of knowledge-based occupations and their diffusion into ever-new areas of society. Accordingly, socially differentiated societies are characterized by a high degree of specialization (Reich & Lahav, 2021). Specialized professions act self-referentially, thereby increasing their efficiency and thus also the potential to generate ever more specific knowledge. This increase in complexity leads to further differentiation, which in turn accelerates the growth of specialized knowledge. As a result of the progressive division of labor, then, the proportions of general knowledge and specialized knowledge shift in favor of the latter. This is the fundamental difference between contemporary and archaic societies. Whereas members of archaic societies had to be able to do everything and "knowledge" was equated with "general knowledge", functionally differentiated societies are characterized by a high degree of specialization that allows for an exponential increase in knowledge. As access to such specialized information has become increasingly convenient in digital media landscapes, people are not only aware that such expertise exists, but they may also misinterpret their access to information as actually possessing expert knowledge (Collins, 2014), which fosters an effect referred to as "knowledge illusion" (Sloman & Fernbach, 2017).

What applies to the production of knowledge also holds true for its employment. As knowledge increases, so does the dependence on it. Again, the comparison with archaic societies is revealing: In societies with a simple social distribution of knowledge, most adults are in full possession of the available general knowledge, which allows them to competently solve the most pressing everyday problems themselves. In functionally differentiated societies, however, individuals are so heavily burdened with dealing with their specific field of expertise that they can hardly accumulate any knowledge beyond this specialization. This puts them in a difficult position: Although people know that there is specialist knowledge for all areas of daily life, they are also aware that they precisely lack such knowledge. However, in order to be able to act confidently and competently in everyday situations, they feel dependent on such expertise and therefore demand it. It is precisely this discrepancy between the awareness of the general availability of specialist knowledge and the limited ability to possess this knowledge oneself that explains the (growing) demand for expert knowledge in modern societies (Stehr & Grundmann, 2011, p. 101). Whereas people used to be able to act intuitively and without reference to knowledge in certain areas (especially in everyday life), the realization that expertise exists for precisely these areas (even the most private, intimate, and mundane ones) means that people feel dependent on this knowledge. As the possibilities grow, so do the demands.

This growing need for experts on the ordinary is further fostered by the fact that people increasingly lack competent resources in their immediate environment and that any everyday situation is experienced as being fraught with a certain degree of uncertainty: In his individualization thesis, Beck (1992) describes the detachment of the individual from traditional social structures. While people have long relied on advice from their immediate environment (e.g., on their ancestors in matters of nutrition) and on stable institutions (such as the church), individualization explains the increasing dependence of the individual on external specialists (Giddens, 1990). As traditional forms of coping with uncertainty fail, individuals are increasingly dependent on other sources of knowledge. And this, in turn, is driven by another apparent paradox of today's societies, namely, that increasing (scientific) knowledge does not necessarily lead to more security, but rather the opposite. As the COVID-19 pandemic has vividly demonstrated, scientists tend to disagree with one another; one of the defining characteristics of scientific knowledge is its ambiguity and uncertainty (e.g., Peters & Dunwoody, 2016; Ratcliff et al., 2022). While this is in the nature of scientific progress, it also shows that science does not provide definitive solutions to everyday problems (which it may have caused itself). This not only makes people skeptical of the superiority of scientific knowledge (as opposed to other forms of knowledge) but also leads to a feeling of constant uncertainty and insecurity (Lupton, 2024). In this situation, people increasingly demand experts to guide them through these uncertainties and help them navigate the various options.

While knowledge in modern societies is, therefore, inexorably increasing on an abstract level, people are simultaneously confronted with uncertainties in their everyday lives. Even though they are aware of different knowledge options, they often lack the specialized knowledge to act competently and are, therefore, dependent on experts. This relates not only to abstract topics from the scientific field but also to more everyday areas that have become increasingly professionalized (and thus knowledge-based) and in which the detachment from traditional networks and institutions has further contributed to the experience of uncertainty. As Lupton (2024, p. 84) has argued, "because traditions have lost their power and there is more 'openness' about how to live, the concept of lifestyle has become increasingly important to selfhood, forcing people to negotiate between a range of options". Yet, while today's societies are characterized by an increasing diffusion of knowledge, people have *not* gained more security as a result. Instead, they are even more dependent on others to provide them with the knowledge they need to navigate the decisions they have to make. Hence, in modern societies, the areas where experts are needed are expanding and the knowledge that is valued as expert knowledge is evolving.

The reconfiguration of expertise in pluralistic knowledge societies

The discussion so far has argued that people increasingly need expert knowledge in most areas of their lives, including more mundane lifestyle issues. This inevitably leads to the question of who is authorized to provide knowledge or – more simply – who can be considered an expert. In scholarly debates, expert status has traditionally been ascribed to those with academic qualifications; interestingly, this applies both to research on the role of experts in contemporary societies in general (Ericsson et al., 2006) and to most studies on the use of expert sources in journalism in particular (Albæk, 2011; Leidecker-Sandmann et al., 2022; Wien, 2014). However, as scholars are increasingly beginning to argue, expert knowledge is not limited to academics. Since expertise is attributed by those who require knowledge for their ability to act, it is not sufficient to assign expert knowledge only to those who have acquired academic qualifications. Instead, those who have experience in applying this knowledge in practical contexts may even be seen as the more legitimate sources of expertise. In this regard, Stehr and Grundmann (2011, p. x) argue that experts "are persons of whom it is assumed that, based on their routine contact with specific topics, they have accumulated experience in contexts relevant for taking action". This definition, therefore, includes farmers with "experience in cultivating plants" and travel agents with "experience in the tourist trade" or – applied to lifestyle topics – chefs with experience in preparing dishes and interior designers with experience in designing home furnishings. Such understanding, which focuses on both (1) experience in action and (2) expertise as a result of attributions, makes it clear that although scientific qualifications can still be an asset for experts, they do not automatically give people expert status.

In fact, it seems that scientists in today's societies experience less public trust and less social respect, which can both be seen as further important pillars for gaining expert status (Stehr & Grundmann, 2011). While science was long able to claim a monopoly on relevant, 'correct' knowledge, this monopoly is dissolving because of disappointed expectations toward the certainty of science. Not least in the wake of the COVID-19 pandemic, scientists have increasingly lost their authority and instead been confronted with skepticism and even hatred (Nogrady, 2021; Nölleke et al., 2023; Rutjens et al., 2021). At the same time as science's ability to conclusively solve concrete problems is being questioned, we are experiencing a renaissance of practical knowledge (Zhao & Bouvier, 2022), which was the only basis for action in pre-modern societies and had been increasingly marginalized in the course of the scientification of society (Weingart, 1999). Today, the practical relevance of scientific solutions for concrete everyday problems is doubted, and scientific expertise is accused of being unsuitable for everyday use. Scientific knowledge, so the argument goes, loses its connection to the everyday lives of members of society: "[S]cientific and other forms of expert knowledge become so separated from ordinary thinking [...]." (Livingstone & Lunt, 1994, p. 92) Due to its high level of abstraction, science cannot provide problem-related and action-relevant knowledge. With the obvious distance between scientific knowledge and everyday experience, trust in scientific expertise is dwindling. However, this does not mean that experts would no longer have currency today. Rather – as Lewis (2010, p. 583) argues particularly with regard to lifestyle media – "it has translated into a radical reconfiguration of expertise along more popular (and putatively 'democratized') lines".

As the understanding of experts has expanded, everyday experts are increasingly in demand. This ultimately leads to a tendency to equalize the rationality gap between experts and laypeople (Beck, 1992), in the course of which, for example, those affected question medical diagnoses and thus traditional claims to authority (Giddens, 1991). In this flat hierarchy of knowledge, scientific knowledge is, therefore, not per se superior to practical knowledge (Wynne, 1996). In fact, in media reporting, it is often the other way around: when problem-relevant everyday knowledge competes with scientific knowledge, scientists run the risk of either being ignored by the media or occasionally being labeled as unrealistic theorists who do not properly understand the practical problem (Peters, 2008). Here, it is precisely the laypeople who are portrayed as the authentic, the true experts: "For some, lay accounts are valid because they are grounded in experience" (Livingstone & Lunt, 1994, p. 99).

Lifestyle experts

The developments described above imply two things: first, people are increasingly reliant on expert knowledge, even in areas of life that can be described as softer, such as private relationships, food, health, and travel – which can be summarized under the term lifestyle. And second, those whose expertise is in demand are ultimately characterized by the fact that they have acquired practical experience in relation to precisely these issues. Thus, the general development in the so-called knowledge societies has favored the emergence of the figure of the lifestyle expert, who gives advice on topics that relate to the private sphere. In this sense, experts are asked "by private individuals to aid decisions in everyday life" (Stehr & Grundmann, 2011, p. 80). According to Lewis (2010, p. 580), such lifestyle experts have recently developed into an "important cultural authority". What is special about them compared to the previously advocated understanding of experts as elite figures is their ordinariness both in terms of the content of their expertise and their style of presentation (Lunt & Lewis, 2008). Rather than embodying abstract forms of knowledge and authority – as intellectuals would do – lifestyle experts are characterized by providing simple how-to knowledge that can be adopted by anyone (Lunt & Lewis, 2008). This is important considering that much of lifestyle journalism also relates to providing advice, orientation, and guidance for everyday life (Hanusch & Hanitzsch, 2013). Consequently, these experts tend to engage in life coaching and counseling in their work with individuals, rather than disseminating analysis and background knowledge. In this way, they strive to build empathy with clients "by lowering their differences in knowledge, personality and outlook between themselves and audiences" (Taylor, 2002, p. 487) (see also Chapter 26).

Despite (or because of) their expertise being rooted in the ordinary and despite/because they build such a close relationship with the audience, some lifestyle experts have achieved high popularity and even celebrity status. This is particularly due to their high visibility in the media. In this respect, lifestyle journalism plays a crucial role in communicating the everyday knowledge of experts on the ordinary to the average person.

The construction of expertise in lifestyle journalism

In today's societies, people are largely dependent on the media to impart specialized knowledge (Cottle, 1998; Walter, 2004). In this respect, journalists act as knowledge brokers (Gesualdo et al., 2020) for their audiences. To efficiently fulfill this function, journalists have developed a special expertise, which is institutionalized in beat reporting and refers to thematic specializations in journalism (Magin & Maurer, 2019). Beat journalists have specific experience reporting on topics from areas such as politics, business, sports, and lifestyle. However, they cannot possibly keep up with the specialization in these areas and the exponential growth of knowledge associated with it. This has long led to debates about how journalists can fulfill their role as knowledge brokers and what kind of knowledge their specific expertise should include. In this context, Reich and Lahav (2021, p. 76) argue that specialized journalists build on a "complex interplay between journalistic knowledge and subject-matter knowledge" and that they avoid "an entirely insider and an entirely outsider position" while maintaining "access to insider knowledge". In short, even specialist journalists cannot possibly have all the expertise, and from a normative point of view, they should not. Nevertheless, the perceived lack of expertise serves as a gateway for new players from the periphery of the journalistic field. Fan-bloggers in sports journalism (McEnnis, 2017) and science bloggers in science journalism (Walejko & Ksiazek, 2010) have entered the scene, promising to fill the very void left by established media organizations (even beat reporters) due to a lack of expertise. Similarly, lifestyle influencers can be conceptualized as peripheral actors in journalism who claim legitimacy and authority through their authentic insights into lifestyle topics (Maares & Hanusch, 2020) (see also Chapter 10). In this context, Hanusch and Löhmann (2023) show that expertise is an important element through which new entrants claim their membership to the journalistic field.

Since traditional (specialized) journalists cannot possibly keep up with the ever-growing specialized knowledge, they are increasingly dependent on the knowledge of external experts. Therefore, the search and selection of expert sources can be seen as a crucial professional journalistic skill. Indeed, research has identified a great (and increasing) importance of expert sources in the media (Albaek et al., 2003; Merkley, 2020; Nölleke, 2013; Wien, 2014). However, this can only be partially explained by the aforementioned decline in journalists' ability to possess relevant expert knowledge (especially due to economic constraints in the media industry). The employment of experts is also encouraged by a shift from descriptive to interpretative journalism, which requires expert analysis (Albaek, 2011). Obviously, journalists are not only neutrally turning to experts to obtain the knowledge they lack but are strategically using these experts for their own purposes. This suggests that journalists have developed a unique approach to expertise; and in line with the arguments outlined above, research shows that their understanding does not grant expert status exclusively to scientists but also others. Furthermore, the role of experts in journalism is not limited to providing superior knowledge.

In that connection, the same is true for journalists as it is for everyone else: "First of all, it is the clients of expertise who are [...] in the position to choose among various (types of) experts" (Stehr & Grundmann, 2011, p. 33). So while people can certainly stage themselves as experts by trying to "convince customers of the utility and correctness of their advice" (Stehr & Grundmann, 2011, p. 117), and while it is the requested expert who ultimately decides whether or not they are willing to provide expertise, it is the customer who has the upper hand in who they choose and how they process this expertise. Applied to journalism, this means that since it is the "journalists who ultimately write the stories, and decide what to include and what not to include" (Strömbäck & Nord, 2006, p. 156), journalists act as gatekeepers for expert sources. In most cases, it is the journalists who take the initiative to contact experts (Albaek, 2011, p. 335) – and not the other way around. Journalists, therefore, do not simply passively pass on expert knowledge in their reporting but actively construct expert knowledge according to certain requirements and routines (Huber, 2014; Nölleke, 2013). In this sense, experts are used as dramaturgical elements in reporting (Väliverronen, 2001): they are often routinely used simply to have an expert voice that gives the reporting weight and a "flavor of objectivity" (Wien, 2014, p. 427) (regardless of whether the expertise was actually needed), used as opportune witnesses to support the intended framing of the coverage by an authoritative source (Anter, 2021, p. 408), or juxtaposed as expert and counter-expert to signal diversity and balance (Dixon & Clarke, 2013). Especially in audiovisual media and for topics with a lot of airtime, experts can also simply serve as "sparring partners" (Albæk, 2011, p. 343) for journalists to prepare topics in dialogue. It is, therefore, clear that experts fulfill other functions in journalism, in addition to the specific task of contributing specialist knowledge. In this context, they can also serve as a tool for brand-building strategies. Using the example of pundits in political journalism, research has shown that media outlets tend to frequently employ the same experts (Hopmann & Strömbäck, 2010; Soley, 1994) and use them as a competitive element "to increase audience ratings and to stand out in the news media market" (Figueiras, 2017, p. 313). This not only applies to political journalism but can also be observed in sports journalism (Nölleke, 2024) and is a key feature of expert presentation in lifestyle journalism. Regardless of whether they actually have relevant specialist knowledge, this repeated presentation as an expert source in media reporting serves as an indicator of reliable expertise (Stehr & Grundmann, 2011) for audiences and other journalists.

Knowing that audiences are familiar with certain experts is, therefore, a crucial criterion for journalistic practices of sourcing experts. As indicated above, journalists select experts not only on the basis of their superior expertise, but they also apply other criteria that are closely related to those they use to define newsworthiness (Steele, 1995). Here, previous research has shown that journalists prefer experts who have a strong opinion, who can articulate themselves precisely, and who respond reliably to media inquiries (Conrad, 1999; Peters, 2008; Nölleke, 2013).

So far, we do not know how exactly lifestyle journalists select their experts; however, anecdotal evidence clearly suggests that superior knowledge is also accompanied by other – softer – factors. What we can say with great certainty is that expertise in lifestyle journalism is not only attributed to academics. Rather, academic qualifications seem to play a negligible role here. While some studies on the use of expert sources in news media have focused primarily on academic experts, other studies clearly show that the understanding of journalists is far broader. In addition to scientists, it also includes fellow journalists, former politicians, and athletes but also craftsmen and even people who pursue a niche topic as a hobby (Cross, 2010; Horsbøl, 2010; Nölleke, 2013; Soley, 1994). Again, there is a lack of empirical evidence for the range of expert sources in lifestyle journalism; however, popular examples clearly show that it favors people with practical experience in relevant professions (such as DIY, cooking, and gardening).

With a few notable exceptions, empirical research on lifestyle journalism has largely neglected the role of experts in this context. To list some examples, Livingstone and Lunt (1994) examined televised debates; Lunt and Lewis (2008) analyzed the role of lifestyle experts on Oprah Winfrey's website Oprah.com; Taylor (2002) investigated modes of presentation in garden lifestyle shows; and Verriet (2022) explored the role of celebrity athletes as sources of lifestyle advice. The findings of these studies suggest that lifestyle journalism celebrates the practical knowledge of ordinary people and stages it as superior to that of credentialed experts. In this context, Livingstone and Lunt (1994, p. 128) show that TV talk show hosts introduce high-status experts but ask the ordinary person, the laity, for their knowledge. The situation is similar with gardening programs on British television: Rather than presenting experts as authoritative figures delivering hard facts, these shows rely on the expertise of "friendly, well-researched consumers, interpreting the latest lifestyle shopping ideas for the would-be gardener" (Taylor, 2002, p. 487). In this way, the differences between experts and laypeople are reduced and empathy is created. It is crucial that not just a single solution without alternatives is offered, but that various ideas for makeovers are presented. In this respect, lifestyle expertise tends to present options for action and allows laypeople to decide how these fit in with their individual lifestyle and possibilities. This is also the key to the makeover expertise presented on Oprah.com. Although the experts here are not ordinary people, but "charismatic lifestyle gurus" (Lunt & Lewis, 2008, p. 14), they are not used purely as advisors, but rather to accompany people on their individual makeover journey. Here too, instead of imparting distanced, abstract specialist knowledge, the experts on Oprah.com are characterized by the fact that they put themselves in their clients' shoes and give practical advice tailored to this situation. This empathy is additionally staged by deliberately showing emotional life stories of the experts that relate to the lives of their clients. Experts are presented as ordinary people who can empathize with the needs of their clients and in this way "enhance the capacity of individuals to improve and thereby empower themselves" (Lunt & Lewis, 2008, p. 22). Verriet (2022) focuses on a different type of expert, namely, celebrities, who have become popular sources of lifestyle advice, often based on their pre-fame occupations. Using the example of a former top Dutch cyclist, Verriet shows how athletes embody expertise, namely, expertise about a healthy lifestyle through their physical appearance. In this way, expertise is not legitimized by credentials, but by visual cues that demonstrate the ability to convey expertise. However, because the Dutch cyclist struggled with an eating disorder, there may be tensions between actual experience and expertise that need to be resolved in order to be recognized as a legitimate expert. But again, this example shows that lifestyle journalism favors practical advice that is justified by real-life experience and presented by evoking empathy with ordinary people.

In summary, it can be said that (lifestyle) journalism's approach to specialist knowledge reflects general trends in expert societies. The increasing specialization of knowledge makes them increasingly dependent on external expertise to ensure accurate reporting. As clients, however, they actively construct expertise according to journalistic needs. In doing so, their understanding of legitimate experts is not limited to scientists; the role of experts is not limited to imparting superior knowledge, and journalists' demand for experts also includes more mundane reporting topics such as lifestyle. Lifestyle journalism is, therefore, a suitable indicator for identifying typical mechanisms in the journalistic use of expert sources, in particular their use as consultants in everyday contexts and the celebritization of expert sources (Lewis, 2010), as can be seen in examples such as Jamie Oliver.

Conclusion and future directions

Research into the professional views of lifestyle journalists has repeatedly shown that providing advice and news-to-use is at the forefront of their work (Fürsich, 2012; Hanusch, 2019; Hanusch & Hanitzsch, 2013). Lifestyle journalists offer "exemplars of lifestyles" (Hanusch & Hanitzsch, 2013, p. 956) by aligning themselves with the specific needs of their audiences, thus creating a potential for identification. This is crucially based on the perception of authenticity. In this chapter, I have suggested that the aforementioned goals of lifestyle journalism can be achieved particularly well with the help of experts. Rather than relying on academic credentials, these everyday experts draw on practical experience to offer advice, signaling an understanding of and identification with the needs of the lay audience. The repeated use of the same experts leads to their celebritization, which further strengthens their perceived legitimacy and audience trust in them.

In the digital era, however, such experts in lifestyle journalism are facing competition. It is doubtful whether these actors can still be considered the ideal agents to give advice on everyday topics. In fact, it seems likely that lifestyle influencers, who present their 'expertise' on social media channels such as Instagram and YouTube, are better suited to meeting the needs of people who are overwhelmed by the multitude of options on how to organize their life(style). Fueled by neoliberalism and tendencies of anti-intellectualism, lifestyle influencers harness social media affordances to impart information in a way that is relatable to lay individuals (Maddox, 2022). They claim expertise not through referring to professional or formal qualifications but rather by creating discourses of authenticity, presenting themselves as real people with real problems and on-site experience (Zhao & Bouvier, 2022) (see also Chapter 10).

Against the backdrop of broader trends in journalism in which journalists are competing with new entrants for authority and legitimacy (Banjac & Hanusch, 2023; Carlson, 2017; Tong, 2018), research has studied the impact of such influencers on lifestyle journalism. It was found that influencers are reluctant to describe themselves as journalists, despite having similar goals, such as providing exemplars of lifestyle, guidance, and advice (Maares & Hanusch, 2020). Lifestyle journalists, on the other hand, recognize the similarities of the work but deny influencers to pursue journalistic norms and values (Perreault & Hanusch, 2024). While these studies do not relate to the role of experts, they are, nonetheless, revealing in that regard and raise questions that future research should address. Influencers may not see themselves as journalists, but they undoubtedly embody the elements that lifestyle journalists turn to experts for – giving practical advice on everyday topics while being relatable and authentic, which creates trust between the 'expert' and the layperson. So while influencers don't necessarily do lifestyle journalism, they (seemingly) represent all the aspects that lifestyle journalists expect from 'good' experts.

Given the "soft boundaries" (Perreault & Hanusch, 2024) that lifestyle journalists draw vis-à-vis influencers, it would be a promising endeavor for future research to investigate how journalists legitimize their experts as opposed to lifestyle influencers and whether they push the boundaries by inviting lifestyle influencers, of all people, to act as expert sources in lifestyle journalism. While I have referred in this chapter to general trends in (digital) knowledge societies to explain the emergence of experts on the ordinary, it is notable that there still exists very limited empirical evidence in journalism scholarship on the precise relevance of expert sources in lifestyle journalism, the contexts in which they are predominantly deployed, the basis of their knowledge claims, and the discursive construction of their legitimacy. So far, we also do not know what value popular experts have for building media brands and how exactly trust in experts is built and maintained. Therefore, it is an urgent concern for future research to finally pay more attention to these protagonists in lifestyle journalism. This is not only valuable for understanding practices in lifestyle journalism as compared to other journalistic fields but will also help provide empirical evidence for the reconfiguration of expertise in wider society.

Further reading

Albæk, E. (2011). The interaction between experts and journalists in news journalism. *Journalism*, 12(3), 335–348.

Lunt, P., & Lewis, T. (2008). Oprah.com: Lifestyle expertise and the politics of recognition. *Women & Performance: A Journal of Feminist Theory*, 18(1), 9–24.

Nichols, T. M. (2017). *The Death of Expertise: The Campaign against Established Knowledge and Why it Matters*. New York: Oxford University Press.

Reich, Z., & Lahav, H. (2021). What on Earth do journalists know? A new model of knowledge brokers' expertise. *Communication Theory*, 31(1), 62–81.

Stehr, N., & Grundmann, R. (2011). *Experts: The Knowledge and Power of Expertise*. Routledge.

References

Albæk, E. (2011). The interaction between experts and journalists in news journalism. *Journalism*, 12(3), 335–348.

Albaek, E., Christiansen, P. M., & Togeby, L. (2003). Experts in the mass media: Researchers as sources in Danish daily newspapers, 1961–2001. *Journalism & Mass Communication Quarterly*, 80(4), 937–948.

Anter, L. (2021). Mein text, meine Meinung, meine Wissenschaftlerin? *Medien & Kommunikationswissenschaft*, 69(3), 397–415.

Banjac, S., & Hanusch, F. (2023). The struggle for authority and legitimacy: Lifestyle and political journalists' discursive boundary work. *Journalism*, 24(10), 2155–2173.

Beck, U. (1992) *Risk Society: Towards a New Modernity*. London: Sage.

Carlson, M. (2017). *Journalistic Authority: Legitimating News in the Digital Era*. New York: Columbia University Press.

Collins, H. (2014). *Are We All Scientific Experts Now?* Cambridge: Polity Press.

Conrad, P. (1999). Uses of expertise: Sources, quotes, and voice in the reporting of genetics in the news. *Public Understanding of Science*, 8(4), 285–302.

Cottle, S. (1998). Ulrich Beck,Risk Society'and the Media: A Catastrophic View? *European journal of communication*, 13(1), 5–32.

Cross, K. A. (2010). Experts in the news: The differential use of sources in election television news. *Canadian Journal of Communication*, 35(3), 413–429.

Dixon, G. N., & Clarke, C. E. (2013). Heightening uncertainty around certain science: Media coverage, false balance, and the autism-vaccine controversy. *Science Communication*, 35(3), 358–382.

Donsbach, W. (2014). Journalism as the new knowledge profession and consequences for journalism education. *Journalism*, 15(6), 661–677.
Ericsson, K. A., Charness, N., Feltovich, P. J., & Hoffman, R. R. (eds.) (2006). *The Cambridge Handbook of Expertise and Expert Performance*. Cambridge: Cambridge University Press.
Figueiras, R. (2017). Primetime consociation: Portuguese punditry in between media independence and political patronage. *European Journal of Communication*, 32(4), 312–332.
Fürsich, E. (2012). Lifestyle journalism as popular journalism: Strategies for evaluating its public role. *Journalism Practice*, 6(1), 12–25.
Gesualdo, N., Weber, M. S., & Yanovitzky, I. (2020). Journalists as knowledge brokers. *Journalism Studies*, 21(1), 127–143.
Giddens, A. (1991). *Modernity and Self-Identity*. Cambridge: Polity Press.
Giddens, A. (1990). *The Consequences of Modernity*. Cambridge: Polity Press.
Hanusch, F. (2019). Journalistic roles and everyday life: An empirical account of lifestyle journalists' professional views. *Journalism Studies*, 20(2), 193–211.
Hanusch, F., & Hanitzsch, T. (2013). Mediating orientation and self-expression in the world of consumption: Australian and German lifestyle journalists' professional views. *Media, Culture & Society*, 35(8), 943–959.
Hanusch, F., & Löhmann, K. (2023). Dimensions of peripherality in journalism: A typology for studying new actors in the journalistic field. *Digital Journalism*, 11(7), 1292–1310.
Heinrichs, H. (2005). Advisory systems in pluralized knowledge societies: A criteria-based typology to assess and optimize environmental policy advice. In S. Maasen & P. Weingart (eds.), *Democratization of Expertise? Exploring Novel Forms pf Scientific Advice in Political Decision Making* (pp. 41–62). Dordrecht: Springer.
Hopmann, D. N., & Strömbäck, J. (2010). The rise of the media punditocracy? Journalists and media pundits in Danish election news 1994–2007. *Media, Culture & Society*, 32(6), 943–960.
Horsbøl, A. (2010). Experts in political communication: The construal of communication expertise in prime time television news. *Journal of Language and Politics*, 9(1), 29–49.
Huber, B. (2014). *Öffentliche Experten: Über die Medienpräsenz von* Fachleuten [Public experts: On the media presence of experts]. Wiesbaden: Springer VS.
Kastberg, P. (2018). Knowledge Society. In R. L. Heath & W. Johansen (eds.), *The International Encyclopedia of Strategic Communication*. Hoboken: Wiley Blackwell.
Lane, R. E. (1966). The decline of politics and ideology in a knowledgeable society. *American Sociological Review*, 31(5), 649–662.
Leidecker-Sandmann, M., Attar, P., Schütz, A., & Lehmkuhl, M. (2022). Selected by expertise? Scientific experts in German news coverage of COVID-19 compared to other pandemics. *Public Understanding of Science*, 31(7), 847–866.
Lewis, T. (2010). Branding, celebritization and the lifestyle expert. *Cultural Studies*, 24(4), 580–598.
Limoges, C. (1993). Expert knowledge and decision-making in controversy contexts. *Public Understanding of Science*, 2(4), 417–426.
Livingstone, S. M., & Lunt, P. K. (1994). *Talk on Television. Audience Participation and Public Debate*. London: Routledge.
Lunt, P., & Lewis, T. (2008). Oprah.com: Lifestyle expertise and the politics of recognition. *Women & Performance: A Journal of Feminist Theory*, 18(1), 9–24.
Lupton, D. (2024). *Risk*. London: Routledge.
Maares, P., & Hanusch, F. (2020). Exploring the boundaries of journalism: Instagram micro-bloggers in the twilight zone of lifestyle journalism. *Journalism*, 21(2), 262–278.
Maddox, J. (2023). Micro-celebrities of information: Mapping calibrated expertise and knowledge influencers among social media veterinarians. *Information, Communication & Society*, 26(14), 2726–2752.
Magin, M., & Maurer, P. (2019). Beat Journalism and Reporting. *Oxford Research Encyclopedia of Communication*. Retrieved 14 September 2024, from https://oxfordre.com/communication/view/10.1093/acrefore/9780190228613.001.0001/acrefore-9780190228613-e-905.
McEnnis, S. (2017). Playing on the same pitch. *Digital Journalism*, 5(5), 549–566.
Merkley, E. (2020). Are experts (news) worthy? Balance, conflict, and mass media coverage of expert consensus. *Political Communication*, 37(4), 530–549.

Nichols, T. M. (2017). *The Death of Expertise: The Campaign against Established Knowledge and Why it Matters*. New York: Oxford University Press.

Nogrady, B. (2021). "I hope you die": How the COVID pandemic unleashed attacks on scientists. *Nature*, 598(7880), 250–253.

Nölleke, D. (2024). Expertainment im Fernsehsport: Zur Rolle von ehemaligen Sportler_innen als TV-Expert_innen. In S. Rehbach (ed.), *Sport in audiovisuellen Medien. Entwicklungen, Strategien, Inszenierungsformen* (pp. 143–162). Wiesbaden: Springer VS.

Nölleke, D. (2013). *Experten im Journalismus. Systemtheoretischer Entwurf und empirische Bestandsaufnahme*. Baden-Baden: Nomos.

Nölleke, D., Leonhardt, B. M., & Hanusch, F. (2023). "The chilling effect": Medical scientists' responses to audience feedback on their media appearances during the COVID-19 pandemic. *Public Understanding of Science*, 32(5), 546–560.

Perreault, G., & Hanusch, F. (2024). Field insurgency in lifestyle journalism: How lifestyle journalists marginalize Instagram influencers and protect their autonomy. *New Media & Society*, 26(7), 3767–3785.

Peters, H.-P. (2008). Scientists as public experts. In M. Bucchi & B. Trench (eds.), *Handbook of Public Communication of Science and Technology* (pp. 131–146). London: Routledge.

Peters, H. P., & Dunwoody, S. (2016). Scientific uncertainty in media content: Introduction to this special issue. *Public Understanding of Science*, 25(8), 893–908.

Ratcliff, C. L., Wicke, R., & Harvill, B. (2022). Communicating uncertainty to the public during the COVID-19 pandemic: A scoping review of the literature. *Annals of the International Communication Association*, 46(4), 260–289. https://doi.org/10.1080/23808985.2022.2085136

Reich, Z., & Lahav, H. (2021). What on Earth do journalists know? A new model of knowledge Brokers' expertise. *Communication Theory*, 31(1), 62–81.

Rutjens, B. T., van der Linden, S., & van der Lee, R. (2021). Science skepticism in times of COVID-19. *Group Processes & Intergroup Relations*, 24(2), 276–283.

Sloman, S., & Fernbach, P. (2017). *The Knowledge Illusion*. New York: Penguin.

Soley, L. C. (1994). Pundits in print: "Experts" and their use in newspaper stories. *Newspaper Research Journal*, 15(2), 65–75.

Steele, J. E. (1995). Experts and the operational bias of television news: The case of the Persian Gulf War. *Journalism & Mass Communication Quarterly*, 72(4), 799–812.

Stehr, N. (1994). *Knowledge Societies*. London: Sage.

Stehr, N., & Grundmann, R. (2011). *Experts: The Knowledge and Power of Expertise*. London: Routledge.

Stehr, N., Henning, C., & Weiler, B. (2006). Die Entzauberung der Eliten. Wissen, Ungleichheit und Kontingenz. In H. Münkler, G. Straßenberger, & M. Bohlender (eds.), *Deutschlands Eliten im Wandel* (pp. 239–254). Frankfurt am Main: Campus Verlag.

Strömbäck, J., & Nord, L. W. (2006). Do politicians lead the tango? A study of the relationship between Swedish journalists and their political sources in the context of election campaigns. *European Journal of Communication*, 21(2), 147–164.

Takahashi, B., Huang, K., Fico, F., & Poulson, D. (2017). Climate change reporting in Great Lakes Region newspapers: A comparative study of the use of expert sources. *Environmental Communication*, 11(1), 106–121.

Taylor, L. (2002). From ways of life to lifestyle: The 'Ordinari-ization' of British gardening lifestyle television. *European Journal of Communication*, 17(4), 479–493.

Tong, J. (2018). Journalistic legitimacy revisited. *Digital Journalism*, 6(2), 256–273.

Väliverronen, E. (2001). Popularisers, interpreters, advocates, managers and critics. Framing science and scientists in the media. *Nordicom Review*, 22(2), 39–47.

Verriet, J. (2022). Representing embodied expertise: Anorexia and the celebrity athlete's lifestyle advice. *Celebrity Studies*, 13(3), 448–466.

Walejko, G., & Ksiazek, T. (2010). Blogging from the Niches. *Journalism Studies*, 11(3), 412–427.

Walter, W. (2004). Experts' discourses as judicial drama or bureaucratic coordination: Family debate in the United States and Germany. In E. Kurz-Milcke & G. Gigerenzer (eds.), *Experts in Science and Society* (pp. 27–46). Boston, MA: Springer US.

Weingart, P. (1999). Scientific expertise and political accountability: Paradoxes of science in politics. *Science and Public Policy*, 26(3), 151–161.

Wien, C. (2014). Commentators on daily news or communicators of scholarly achievements? The role of researchers in Danish news media. *Journalism*, 15(4), 427–445.

Wynne, B. (1996). May the sheep safely graze? A reflexive view of the expert-lay knowledge divide. In S. Lash, B. Szersynski, & B. Wynne (eds.), *Risk, Environment & Modernity: Towards a New Ecology* (pp. 44–83). London: Sage.

Zhao, W., & Bouvier, G. (2022). Where neoliberalism shapes Confucian notions of child rearing: Influencers, experts and discourses of intensive parenting on Chinese Weibo. *Discourse, Context & Media*, 45, 100561.

PART IV

The public utility of lifestyle journalism

18
POPULAR AND POLITICAL
The radical origins of lifestyle journalism

Bethany Usher

Introduction

In the 19th century, politically, socially and commercially minded journalists developed popular cultures and constructs that shaped the national psyche and linked "individual to individual in [a] massive agglomeration of power" (McLuhan, 1964, p. 188). The press became the "context in which people lived and worked and from which they derived their sense of the outside world" (Shattock and Wolff, 1982, p. xv). That world was rapidly changing. A larger and increasingly literate population wanted to read about diverse people, different models for organised societies and to reconsider "life" and "being". A range of publications were launched that forged new alliances between working and reformist middle-class readers to epistemologically shape their sense of self and society through journalism written for consumption during leisure time. They entertained, offered models for moral(ised) education relating to taste and opinion and some linked this to radical political reform. But the "political myth" invented by the bourgeois daily press at this time of their unique "place in the sun" as arbitrators of democracy (Boyce, 1978, p. 21) led to many blind spots and even, at times, wilful misunderstandings of the social and political significance of softer, slower forms of journalism in press history (Usher, 2020, 2023). Folker Hanusch (2013, p. 3) argues that lifestyle journalism is too often considered by scholars as "a frivolous pursuit or guilty pleasure, barely worthy of the term journalism". In contrast, this chapter argues its fundamental significance to fights for social and political equality as modern capitalist democracies developed. Lifestyle journalism shaped our sense of self and worth in relation to active citizenry, self-improvement, cultural taste and consumer habits and in origin was a genre of revolution.

Enlightenment debates and Romantic literary cultures in the 18th century influenced journalistic development to shape public spheres and the "expressive conception of man", which together "made us who we are" through circulating self-identities based on balances between public opinion and private lives and interests (Taylor, 1989, p. 393; see also Usher, 2020, p. 23). Now through the "dominant principle" of "language", the press brought "individual-to-individual" together in relation to issues of national identity and cultural citizenship (Taylor, 1989, p. 415). Democratic and capitalist "modern societies…have been information societies from their inception" (Giddens, 1985, pp. 177–178) and seminal 20th-century research focused largely on how constructs of daily news shaped our realities, our understanding of political and cultural institutions that govern our lives and our understanding of others and ourselves (e.g., Schudson, 1978; Tuchman, 1978). Amidst booms in daily news which reconstructed understandings of time and space and made "SPEED" the "most salient characteristic" of news and society (Greg, 1875, pp. 264–268, original emphasis), a range of publications looked to bring together different social groups as audience and community and then *slow them down* to critically consider their lives, wants and needs. In longer forms, they explored issues of inclusion, exclusion, reconciliation, media and political literacy and shaped cultural citizenship through symbolic representations and displays.

While the term "lifestyle journalism" did not exist at this time, "lifestyles", for example, of gentlemen and ladies or people in other countries were generally discussed, such as in the earliest surviving British Newspaper Archive reference in the *General Evening Post* in 1809. Across establishment bourgeois dailies, radical weeklies and early periodicals, there was debate about the moral obligations of the press in relation to the "idea of universal benevolence"; the "imperative to reduce suffering"; the continued significance of "ordinary life"; and, above all, principles of "universal justice" (Taylor, 1989, pp. 394–395). As Raymond Williams (1958 [1989], p. 4) described, parts of the popular press also considered "a whole way of life – the common meanings, to mean arts and learning – the special process of discovery and creative effort". These things were often linked directly to politics, and the response from bourgeois establishment newspapers and Parliament alike demonstrates that was considered a significant risk to the social order. Some questioned whether social improvement might lead to "cunning and trickery" amongst the "lower orders" and linked this to thefts of consumer items, riot and revolt (*Morning Post*, 23 November 1805; *The Times*, 6 January 1837; *Chronicle*, 7 January 1837). Amidst such conflicts emerged rhetorical and thematic parameters that forever shaped the sociocultural and political power-of-press.

This chapter demonstrates that lifestyle journalism offered models for "being" that shaped the temporal and geographic dimensions of capitalist democracies by linking cultural self-fulfilment to political and economic emancipation. Three chronological shifts linked universal justice to self-worth and agency through education, recreational leisure-times and media literacy and reimagined audiences as cultural and political communities. Together, these offered new models for commercialisation of press as well as other cultural events and consumer goods. Firstly, weekly publications expanded longer-form lifestyle features that shaped knowledge, taste and opinion, with some journalists directly communicating with audiences as an imagined community. Secondly, Victorian "weekender" publications expanded content to be read for pleasure at leisure, which explored personalised interests, sociopolitical morality and self and societal worth. Finally, New Journalists modernised the press and solidified how parasocial bonds of intimacy could reimagine cultural citizenship and irrevocably made celebrity culture part of lifestyle-as-genre. In short, this chapter highlights how British lifestyle journalism shaped the "politics of being" and argues why this matters.

Lifestyle and the radical weekly press (1810–1840)

Between 1810 and the 1830s, a range of publications launched by the most infamous radical journalists of the 19th century reimagined Britain and its people on a more equal basis.

They argued the rights of working people to vote, education, leisure-time, healthcare and many amassed relatively large audiences. At a time where social upheaval made direct action for democratic and working rights a background beat to life and mob violence a constant topic of news (Usher, 2023, pp. 98–121), many amongst the bourgeois establishment and their press were deeply concerned that "notorious demagogues" threatened their commercial and political dominance, declared they fed the worst tendencies of the "lower orders" and demanded their imprisonment (e.g., *The Morning Post*, 30 November 1819; *The Times*, 24 December 1830).

There were many booms and busts, often because of prosecutions or new laws such as the infamous "Six Acts" (1819), which increased stamp duty and broadened the definition of treason, and some journalists mentioned here were gaoled several times. Form and shape shifted between newspaper and longer periodical or pamphlet forms in attempts to bypass legislation or escape prosecution, but from the outset, they were usually printed towards the end of the week or weekends to differentiate from daily newspapers. While the bourgeois establishment press often dismissed them as "trash" (Conboy, 2004, p. 94), they also feared how they reimagined audiences as cultural and political communities across traditional class boundaries. These were usually monetised by subscription rather than advertising, and diversification of revenue streams – and cultural engagement – was achieved by public lectures and learning clubs that looked to educate, inform and entertain and were attended and sponsored by both working men and women organisations and middle-class reformers. Martin Conboy (2004, p. 102) dismisses those who argue their editors were political "publicists" rather than journalists because they overtly rejected the active mythologies of objectivity and balance circulated by bourgeois establishment newspapers to maintain their power. Certainly, these drew from other, equally significant, journalistic traditions including the linguistically direct and personalised longer-form pamphleteering of Thomas Paine (many republished or referenced his work and travels as influences) and the grubs of Grub Street, the London base for popular print culture from the mid-17th century. In its print shops and pubs was produced a range of cultural content, from theatre and concert reviews, biographies of the famous and infamous, fashion features, romantic ballads or short stories as well as general and political news (Usher, 2023, p. 107). As the bourgeois establishment press became ever more professionalised and determined that their heavily rationalised model of journalism was the only one that counts, the radical press often turned to content produced by working-class penny-a-liners.

Content included longer-form features often, in the early days at least, written as letters directly to the audience, sometimes with illustrations. There were personalised accounts of political cuts and thrusts and the injustices faced by those with the least social and economic power at the hands of those with the most. Although there were many differences in approach, there was a broad emphasis on cultural citizenship linked to greater understanding of the world, the diverse ways people lived and social and political exploration. William *Cobbett's Weekly Political Register* (hereafter *Register*, 1802–1836), for example, highlighted the expansion of mind and political understanding through becoming a "well-informed…traveller" both at home and abroad (23 February 1811), how through this you might view "mankind under…a diversity of social and political aspects" to form one's own view of the world (21 October 1820) and often commented on "brilliancy of arts, science and letters" in expanding one's own horizons (6 January 1810). His popular *Two-Penny Trash* (1812–1817, 1830–1835), named as a two-fingered salute at critics, offered long-form features addressed directly to his audience, sometimes generally or in specific geographical locations. These considered, for example, local histories and their social, cultural and/or political significance (e.g., 1 July 1830), or the realities and difficulties of emigration to America (8 July 1830). Thomas J. Wooler's *The Black Dwarf* (1817–1824) sometimes included theatre reviews, building from his own foray into theatrical criticism, *The Stage* (1814–1816) and commented widely on arts, science and rights to education. Richard Carlile's *The Republican* (1819–1825) and *The Prompter* (1830–1831) were print arms of educational clubs and his Rotunda lecture theatre in Blackfriars Road, launched in 1830. The public lectures and educational classes offered here, as reported in colourful detail in his daughter Theophila's affectionate account of her father's *Battle of the Press* (Carlile Campbell, 1899), aimed to create "birth-place of the mind", where the "the focus of virtue's public excitement" was advertised as the "most rational and cheapest way of spending an evening". *The Prompter* contained many satirical illustrations and comment pieces on religion and clergy and lavish lifestyles of the rich. *The Republican* discussed the significance of "science and the liberal arts" and advocated that it is "necessary to cast our eyes amongst all the arts, the professions, or even among the common and daily intercourse of social transactions" to understand "the power of excited interest…of education" and that such "activity of rich motives" could have great influence on self-identity (22 August 1823).

The Times dismissed both Carlile's written works and the lecturers at the Rotunda (which included many of the other journalists and writers such as Samuel Taylor Coleridge and William Hazlitt) as "absurd trash" and added for good measure that "pickpockets and prostitutes, by whom the streets have been somewhat disturbed, are proper executors of the political systems recommended in the speeches and writings of the persons above named" (11 November 1830). Fellow "Rotunda Radicals" Leigh and John Hunt's *The Examiner* (1808–1881) passed out of their hands from 1828 and became more commercial but was from the outset advertised as a "Sunday paper, on politics, domestic economy, and theatricals". It contained literary notices (e.g., 23 February 1820), poetry or articles from fellow romantics, including Byron, and a "courts and fashionables" section which considered the private lives and lifestyles of the aristocracy and famous. This was balanced with regular arguments against inherited privilege and criticism of how the establishment bourgeois press shrouded the corrupt lifestyle habits of the monarchy (22 March 1812). Discussions of "theatricals" also often included details of consumer habits, for example, of "prima donnas" and how achievement in the arts offered pathways from poverty (27 February 1820).

Martin Conboy (2004, p. 104) and James Curran (Curran and Seaton, 2018, pp. 10–14) highlight how the "new radical" resurgence of the 1830s and 1840s focused on liberty and paved the way for more print products that spoke directly to and for the working classes. These publications extended and began to refine the parameters of features, including balances between present-day witnessing and retrospective storytelling. Left-wing weeklies such as *The Working Man's Friend* (1832–1833) and Henry Hetherington's *The Poor Man's Guardian* (1830–1835) proved popular and included pieces on working-class artisanship but quickly folded because of governmental prosecution. While planning and launching his publications, Hetherington was a regular at the Rotunda and an ally of the Hunt brothers and used his newspaper to plough the ground for better political organisation with the foundation of the London Working Man's Association. His editor, Chartist[1] and anti-capitalist James Bronterre O' Brien linked the struggles of the poor to the "wickedness" of the propertied and created new linguistic strategies to consider how best to fight back. Chartist publications simplified language and helped to form the model of a "free press" that could be both popular and a public good (Curran, 1978, pp. 67–70). Many placed popular crime news at the forefront of content, as highlighted in titles such as the *People's Weekly Police Gazette* (1835–1836), (John) *Cleave's Weekly Police Gazette* (1834–1836, hereafter *Cleave's*) and *Hetherington's Twopenny Dispatch and People's Police Register (Twopenny Dispatch*, 1834–1836). *Cleave's* also offered readers tips for travel with adverts for more expanded travel guides such as for emigrants to America (18 April 1836), detailed descriptions of food from around the world such as "a Chinese dinner" (26 December 1835), accounts of public lectures on the arts and science or "readings and recitations for mutual improvement" (9 July 1836). These sat alongside expanding advertising sections focusing on self-improvement including travel guides, lectures, exhibitions, theatre and concerts. *Twopenny Dispatch* sat somewhere between a newspaper and periodical and offered details of "Rapes, Murders" and "Police Intelligence" alongside theatre news, reviews, political opinion pieces and discussions of self-improvement. Hetherington switched the emphasis towards science, theatre, travel and the "liberal arts" and linked these to politics in the *Halfpenny Magazine of Entertainment and Knowledge* (1840–1841), but amidst the vast competition of the mid-century weekender boom (considered next), it was relatively short-lived.

By the 1840s, radical weekend newspapers such as *The Northern Star and Leeds General Advertiser* (hereafter *The Star*, 1837–1852) and the *Weekly Dispatch* (1801–1961) adopted elements of "moral education" and the idea of Fourth Estate popularised in the bourgeois establishment press to speak not just to but for their readers. They offered positive representations of working-class achievement, with content, as stressed by the editor in the fifth anniversary issue, chosen "to reflect" the minds and lives of readers (19 November 1842). *The Star* overtly rejected bourgeois rationalisation for what made for a "better" society. The working class were not a "'mob'…guilty of murder" as the "daily press terms them", but a "moral force" and "virtuous people" standing up to "Bloody Whigs[2] and their physical force" (9 July 1838). Longer form features explored working-people class histories and cultures and the advancement of media and political literacy including the place of the bourgeois establishment press in facilitating governmental control and limiting meaningful emancipation. For example, on 8 October 1842, an anonymous writer looked back at all the moments of direct action:

The Press was therefore set to work. Conspiracies to turn the destitution of the people to their own destruction were formed. "IT WAS THE CHARTISTS THAT DID IT ALL" was the instant cry!" "The Chartists have inflamed the passions and excited the feelings of the ignorant mob". "Property is insecure"! "The strong arm of the law must be exerted to put down those who create tumult and cause disorder".

This first wave of the "weekender press" burned brightly and cast long shadows for a new wave of weekender publications that were perfectly pitched to provide recreational reading material fit for the sensibilities of a new generation of readers with a growing sense of self-agency.

The "weekenders": Lifestyle, leisure and Victorian states of mind (1830s–1870s)

While the earlier 19th-century radical weekly press was primarily concerned with the state of society and the building of community, the mid-century popular weekenders focused ever more on readers' state(s) of mind and the individual. During a time "still in pangs of travail with the New" (Carlyle, 1831, p. 32), where people searched for "some clear light and sure stay" amongst the "breakup of [the] traditional and conventional" (Arnold, 1877, p. 287), a wave of publications embraced positive changes, looked towards greater emancipations and generally became less overt about class dimensions of social inequality. They responded to increased leisure time at weekends first for professionals and then working-class people, as reflected in the growth of reading as parlour culture, Saturday sports, Sunday Park promenades, concerts on bandstands and circuses (see Flanders, 2007). While the amount of time to play varied vastly across gender and class boundaries, the weekenders universally circulated the *right to* leisure time as a social norm, something that hitherto was considered by many amongst the propertied classes as radical and revolutionary.

Pioneering journalists and literary writers developed representations, narrative themes, plays with time and linguistic constructs that slowed down the reader and left space for self-reflection. They had two main influences – the popular rhetoric and themes of the early radical weekenders and educational magazines such as *The Penny Magazine* (1832–1845) set up by the moderate reformist Society for the Diffusion of Useful Knowledge (1826–1846). It offered longer-form features about travel, arts and science, infographics, illustrations and comment pieces that looked to social inclusion via education rather than systemic societal change. These were, in essence, easier to digest versions of monthly, quarterly and later weekly essay sheets, such as *The Edinburgh Review* (1802–1929) and *The Nineteenth Century* (1801–1930), which offered highbrow cultural and political content for those with social power and argued opportunities to improve society on their terms. In *The Victorian Frame of Mind*, Walter E. Houghton (1957) brought together varied arguments of "major… writers and minor prophets" who wrote for such periodical reviews, penny educational magazines, cultural and philosophical pamphlets or periodicals and newspapers, to highlight how cultural critics responded to social change including increased leisure time, clockwatching and speed, train travel for both leisure and the working day and increased demands for political freedom and working and social rights. "Though Victorians never ceased to look forward to a new period of firm convictions and established beliefs", Houghton declared, "they had to live in the meantime between two worlds, one dead or dying, one struggling to be born" (1957, pp. 9–10). Features on travel, fashion, self-improvement, social manners and sport, for example, captured the dominant Victorian mind-frame of "optimism" through self-improvement (Houghton, 1957, pp. 27–89). Weekenders, including magazines and newspapers, brimmed with individualised celebration of achievement. They also often included large amounts of crime news and highlighted exploitation of workers, political corruption and accounts of direct political action, which allowed means to explore the other major state-of-mind identified by Houghton (1957) – "anxiety". Readers could consider root causes and potential solutions in more relaxed and leisurely ways than enabled by daily news often produced for working weeks and commutes.

Histories of the press often divide Saturday and Sunday publications that launched during this period according to whether they were radical or not (Conboy, 2004, pp. 67–75), quality or not (Hollis, 1970) or "working class" or not (e.g., Berridge, 1978; Rowbotham et al., 2013). But many were produced by working and middle-class writers working together, and the political dimensions at play were often complex and nuanced. While the radical weekend press of the 1810s to 1830s screamed their politics, the second and third waves of weekender publications brought working-class and middle-class audiences together through softer more generalised discussions of social and moral responsibility. Many explored both the potentials and risks of modernity, capitalism and democracy and what it meant to "be" in these new societies through exploration of education as a pathway to social cohesion, rather than revolution. But their unwavering and unquestioned acceptance of the place of working people in society was in itself radical, and many publications continued to highlight exploitations that limited their meaningful emancipation. Publishers realised the commercial and political potentials of cultural communities formed around common social interests, and more than 20 Sunday newspapers launched the 1840s and 1850s primarily focused on crime, lifestyle and leisure activities such as the theatre and racing, consumer habits, travel, history, celebrity culture and sport. Virginia Berridge (1978, p. 247) claimed these "marked a synthesis" between the political radicalism of the unstamped and the Chartist papers" as a "half-way stage in the development of the modern popular press". Older weekender publications soon followed suit. The once radical *Weekly Dispatch* (1801–1928) included longer-form pieces and popular content that argued that financially secure "happy holms" were the key to success of the Commonwealth (5 October 1851), educational features about arts and science, theatre reviews as well as campaigns to combat crime and discussions of political corruption (5 December 1852; 17 April 1853; 21 August 1853). *The Era* (1838–1939), a liberal weekender newspaper, not only focused on sport, the theatre and crime but also included long-form feature style accounts of "what becomes" of convicts and the need for prison reform (8 January 1850) and celebratory reviews of literature that exposed these things (24 February 1850). *The Illustrated London News* (1842–2003) – which declared itself the world's first illustrated news magazine – constantly addressed the exploitation of working people, union activities and legislation to prevent it and celebrated reform, for example, to "provide for the effectual cleansing and ventilation of factories and to regulate the labour of children" (13 August 1864). Many of the weekender illustrated press articles discussed and depicted the abhorrent working conditions in factory and mill towns (e.g., *The Illustrated Times,* 8 March 1862), particularly after preventable disasters (e.g., "Boiler Explosion-Large Loss of Life", *The Illustrated London News*, 22 March 1851). Description of everyday lives juxtaposed with sensational events was common, as were editorial asides to underlying social reasons.

The most commercially successful were launched by Chartist George W.M. Reynolds and former sheet printer Edward Lloyd. Each used melodrama, illustrations and general popular interest and culture and saw how commercial power might link to political power (see Humpherys, 1983; Usher, 2023). Some press historians have argued that these Sunday newspapers (and we might extend their arguments to the Saturday press too) only had a "veneer of radicalism", which concealed "an adherence to commercial interests" with a presumption that by nature such things act in binary opposition, despite much evidence that popularity was understood as both commercial and politically useful (Boyce et al., 1978, p. 223; Berridge, 1978). In *Reynolds's Weekly Newspaper* (1850–1967, hereafter *Reynolds'*) and *Lloyd's Weekly* (1842–1931, *Lloyd's*), the working classes were a respectable community with much in common with the professional middle class, looking to improve their own lifestyles through education, social activities and consumer purchases. Their achievements, artisanship and the ongoing inequalities that governed their lives were all on display. They were more political than many of the weekenders but also more subtle in their approach than the earlier radical weekenders. George W.M. Reynolds was more overt in his attacks on injustice and corruption in the legal and political systems than Edward Lloyd. But he also saw the political and commercial benefits of "generalized social radicalism" and not being too overt as to attract the distemper of the authorities

(Williams, 1978, pp. 44–45). He included both factual and literary stories focusing on exploited working people at the hands of the corrupt elite. L. Perry Curtis (2001, p.59) argues that it "appealed to a slightly more plebeian readership interested in radical social reforms as well as sensational fiction and new" and still exuded some of "the spirit of aggressive insubordination...while championing trade unionism and workers' rights". *Reynolds'* became the first newspaper to "break through" the 100,000 circulation barrier in the mid-1850s (Curran and Seaton, 2018, pp. 11–12), and this was largely because of how it forged new alliances between working class and working middle-class audiences, Reynolds' own entertaining, melodramatic and gripping literary style and the variety of popular content. *Reynolds'* and *Lloyd's* each took both popularity and politics seriously, and their editors and owners hoped to shift attitudes to the poor through an emotional and entertaining display of their everyday life and hardships. This set the scene for a new wave of popular and political journalists who, for good and ill, are hailed as the pioneers of the modern tabloid press.

New journalism, lifestyle and press parasociality (1870–1900)

By the last quarter of the 19th century, recreational Saturday afternoons and Sundays were commonplace, and New Journalism emerged as a fully commercialised press model, where human interest, lifestyle and celebrity stories "differentiate[d]...from the dull routine of news agencies" which made popular products that attracted advertisers (Conboy, 2004, p. 174). Journalists on both sides of the Atlantic invented new journalistic cultures, constructs and commercial powers across both fast-paced daily newspapers and slower periodical forms. They brought together traditions from bourgeois establishment, radical and popular weekenders and among their many inventions was the first text with image representations of the famous to shape citizenship, taste and consumer habits across class boundaries and, of course, promote their cultural products. This built from celebrity news which actively circulated new notions of self-identity relating to consumers and citizens from the early 18th century. Now, New Journalists forged elements of lifestyle journalism that uses representational discourses, photographs, description of leisure activities and contemplation of their meaning to both private and public self as pathways to self-fulfilment (Usher, 2020).

"The New Journalism" was initially an ambivalent term coined by poet and cultural critic Matthew Arnold (1822–1888), who, in a long-form feature for *The Nineteenth Century* (1887), criticised it as "feather-brained" despite it being full of "ability, novelty, variety, sensation, sympathy and generous instincts" (pp. 689–689). This has similarities to Guy Debord's (1967) criticism of 20th-century mass media as distracting us from what really matters because it is governed by the priorities of capitalist production, as well as many contemporary condemnations of popular lifestyle, human interest, entertainment or consumer journalism. New Journalists were certainly unashamedly populist, commercial and saw their work as illustrating the rich tapestry of society. But the earliest pioneers also had radical visions for social liberalism, inclusion and the tearing down of systems of privilege, universal suffrage and greater protections for the poorest and saw lifestyle journalism a means to achieve these things. In Britain, the work of Liberal reformists, school friends and erstwhile business partners W.T. Stead (1849–1912) and George Newnes (1851–1910) stands out, despite vastly different approaches. This was succinctly captured by Newnes in a letter to his friend in 1890 when he ended their partnership because of Stead's increasingly radical attempts at "governance through journalism":

> There is one kind of journalism that directs the affair of nations; it makes and unmakes cabinets; it upsets governments...and does many great things. It is magnificent. This is your journalism. There is another kind of journalism, which has no great ambitions. It is content to...give wholesome and harmless entertainments to crowds of hard working people craving a little fun and amusement. It is quite humble and unpretentious. This is my journalism.
> *George Newnes to W.T Stead (1890) in Friederichs (1911, pp. 116–117)*

In *Tit-Bits* (1881–1984), *The Strand Magazine* (1891–1949) and *The Million* (1892–1895), George Newnes adapted "popular American styles...to the British market" (Conboy, 2002, p. 167) with quite extraordinary success. His publications created two- and three-way interactions between himself and his journalists, celebrities and readers and then channelled them towards the promotion of magazine brands and later associated products. He acted as an editor, a publisher, a proprietor and a writer and as Kate Jackson (2001, p. 87) describes in her detailed analysis of his life and work, each periodical talked to its different target audiences with its own individual tone to create intimacy with the audience. Regardless of their social position, Newnes viewed his audiences as aspirational and seeking models of self-improvement. He developed a *press parasociality*, which became a key to how journalists shape cultural citizenship through displays of celebrity and lifestyle (Usher, 2020, pp. 66–72). While this had similarities to the parasocial relationships identified by Horton and Wohl (1956) 50 years later in relation to broadcast personalities, it was not a by-product of media consumption, but a means to build audiences and support their social and cultural development. In this, it was a forerunner to the way contemporary lifestyle television show hosts or social media influencers might deliberately speak to their audiences to develop bonds of intimacy, often with the aim of selling consumer or cultural goods. Parasociality, in a way that became commonplace in the 20th century, became a means to offer models for audiences to "enhance the presentation of personality, refine lifestyle skills and expand social appeal" (Rojek, 2012, p. 139).

Despite his protestations that he only wished to amuse, there was a radical edge in how Newnes encouraged working people to want more and to self-improve that was more than a little reminiscent of early radical journalist William Cobbett, and both also became Liberal MPs. *Tit-Bits* was produced for the aspirational literate working classes and acted as a "familiar companion" to their life and included gossip, sport, crime, recipes, weather and cultural commentary. Readers were encouraged to join in with the production and promotion of the news brand through sending "lines of inquiry", entering competitions and purchasing *"Tit-Bitites"* insurance policies and branded merchandise. The magazine "offered connection, interaction and creative potential to a community of readers" (Jackson, 2001, p. 54), with intimacy between celebrities, audiences and journalists at the centre of structure and narratives. This included strategic use of the banal, particularly in relation to celebrities and described "Favourite Dishes" (19 November 1881) or which celebrities had taken the new fashion of wearing "wedding rings" (4 March 1882). Sister publication *The Million* (1892–1895) pitched for a different social group – the new semi-professional commuter class. "Millionaires" – the collective name for the readership – were of the weekend variety, who worked hard six days a week and enjoyed leisure activities on Sundays. Carefully crafted personal bonds between Newnes, the celebrities featured in his magazines, and readers used the illusion of face-to-face intimacy as part of discourse that looked to influence their lifestyle choices around education and consumption. Technical and linguistic developments of journalistic production allowed for "personal connection with the otherwise impersonal capitalistic structure of the developing press" (Jackson, 2001, p. 64). Millionaires were a "democratic mass" to whom the editor had to "account himself", and Newnes' editorial voice rang out as "innovator and preacher, patriarch and pioneer, democratic representative, business partner, adviser and friend" (p. 63). Like other celebrities, and arguably most notably lifestyle TV hosts today, he created "sympathetic intimacy" and presented as an "everyday man" through "fraternisation…the impression of friendship, shared understanding, common ground and other features of reciprocity" (Rojek, 2012, p. 133). Newnes acted as a conduit and gatekeeper, fan and celebrity, and opportunities for direct interaction with him were ever-present, but rarely fulfiled.

If *Tit-Bits* and *The Million* established Newnes' "place in the world of journalism", then "*The Strand* represented his consolidation and celebration" of it (Jackson, 2001, p. 87). When it closed in 1949, *Time Magazine* described its importance to British culture and American understanding of it, "from the drawing room to below stairs", and how it influenced a generation of magazines on both sides of the Atlantic (Pound, 1966, p. 192). Pitched at the affluent upper middle classes – but with an aspirational lower-middle and working-class audience too – *The Strand* balanced artistic quality and journalistic innovation and included short stories and serials, including the first publication of Sherlock Holmes. It offered "unification of literary tradition and journalistic innovation, of commercialism and professionalism and of inclusivity and exclusivity" and was "comforting to a middle-class audience who, beset by anxiety change and uncertainty, sought reassurance" in its models for lifestyle (Jackson, 2001. p. 92). For the educated, affluent middle class, it reflected and reinforced their position and importance. For members of the aristocratic establishment, it offered reassurance of a place in the new social order, by including them, for example, as part of the celebrity class featured in its pages. For working-class readers, it offered aspirational windows into lifestyles and methods of cultural, social and educational improvement. Newnes also developed his most influential ritual for celebrification – "Portraits of Celebrities" – devised when he flicked through a photo album at the home of his friend Sir Richard Webster. In the first 18 months of *The Strand*, he published 126 "Portraits" and during this time invested heavily in technology to improve the quality of image reproduction and page layout, and these were then reproduced in biannual anthologies. Each "portrait" featured three or four pictures, alongside brief descriptions of appearance, private lives and anecdotes from childhood. For example, readers learned that Thomas Hardy was born in "a Dorsetshire Village" and "trained as an architect" (July–December 1891, p. 475) and that journalist George Manville Fenn enjoyed "experimental gardening" (January–June 1892, p. 170). The Lord Mayor of London, David Evans, had "a family of eight children" (January–June 1892, p. 44), and Madame Arabella Goddard played concerts from just "four years old", standing "on an improvised board", because she was so small (p. 172). Pieces also included insights into production processes, such as "Tennyson himself had the kindness to assist us" (January–June 1891, p. 22) or Henry Irving "placed at our disposal" pictures from age 3 to 34 (January–June 1891, p. 45). Newnes brought the voice of the journalist and the celebrity together and pointed them towards social, political and commercial change through revelations of true self behind public face.

W.T. Stead saw representation of the lifestyles of others across class bounds as part of his wider mission of "governmentality through journalism" and press modernisation. This included transformations to newsgathering, such as on scene pack reporting and interviewing, campaigns for social and political change and a reimagining of how audiences might understand "other" and "us", through greater use of direct speech and nuanced balances between displays of private life, public work and self-identity. His mission began at *The Northern Echo* (1870–present) in northeast England, where he was appointed editor in 1871 at the age of just 22. He transformed it from a small-scale publication to a modern popular newspaper with on-scene crime reporting, newsgathering interviews written in direct speech, longer-form travel features and a housewives' corner with tips and hints for easier home-keeping. Stead's work made ordinary people visible with the specific aim to show the "semiotic furniture" of life in a similar way described by John Hartley (1996, p. 188) in his optimistic argument that through increased visibility of ordinary people in media and the "performances of domestic discourses", audiences may be aided to reconsider and construct their own "cultural identities", "citizenry" and "knowledge". Stead's works offered opportunities for readers to consider radically different self-determination. This included the development of a new type of behind-the-scenes interview with a range of public figures often at home with descriptions of professional work, life and lifestyle and helped establish the discourses of stardom and its place in lifestyle journalism. His 18-month series of interviews for *The Pall Mall Gazette* (1883–1885, hereafter *Gazette*) were a display of private lifestyles, public work and the potentials of equality and inclusivity (Usher, 2020, pp. 57–61).

Stead balanced the voices of celebrities (46 percent of interviews), experts (28 percent) and ordinary people (26 percent), with his own commentary and witty interjections, relating to culture, society and politics. His narrative was broadly one of tolerance, benevolence and personal fulfilment through endeavour, and interviews included military leaders, explorers and merchants, foreign visitors to Britain and a range of people involved in the arts and were usually conducted in described domestic, private realms. He asked Japanese ambassador Mori Arinori about similarities between the nations, which the ambassador responded to with discussions of geography and nationalism (26 February 1884). When interviewing freed slave Oko Jumbo of Bonny, Stead described him as "genial and gentleman-like" and discussed his son – an "agreeable gentleman...educated in Liverpool" (29 June 1885). Such emphasis on similarities reflected his own radical social liberalism also evident in interviews with "Socialists" (10 September 1885; 8 October 1885); former prisoners who discussed the horrific conditions in British gaols (9 October 1885); and the celebrity leaders of new religions, such as "modern prophetess" Madame Blavatsky (24 April 1884) and "well-known" evangelist Dwight Moody (4 July 1884). There was no difference in how he approached dialogues with prison inmates than celebrities such as William Morris (23 September 1885), Ford Maddox Brown (24 September 1885) or the America actress "Lotta" (22 December 1883). Stead's *purpose* was to use journalism to *include* ordinary people in public spheres via processes of celebrification to make social liberalism and popular culture part of citizenship. It is not just that these people were visible in the *Gazette* that was significant but that Stead showed equal civility and valued their voice and way-of-life, regardless of the social position or nationality.

Stead's choice of interviewees emphasised talent, endeavour and achievement and, like contemporary celebrity interviews, offered "the general community [...] an avenue through which to discuss issues of morality – family neighbourhood, of production and consumption" (Marshall, 1997, p. 16). More than 10 percent of *Gazette* interviews were with entertainers, and fame was described as the counterpart of endeavour and artistic self. It is in the interviews with actors of the London stage particularly that he helped establish languages and performances associated with stardom, long before Hollywood magazines would affirm its cultural significance for the 20th century (Usher, 2020, pp. 68–73, see also Dyer, 1979; deCordova, 1990). These interviews were the forerunner of those with stars in glossy magazines and were set in domestic realms. They began usually with an account of the journalist arriving at the actor's home and describing intimate settings and private contemplations. Stead described fashion-trends, home décors and how taste reflected the artistic prowess. Questions focused on stage success, consumer and leisure habits and linked public adoration to private contemplation and understanding of self and others. Only one person was interviewed by Stead twice – the now largely forgotten American actor Mary Anderson (1859–1940) – who also featured in *The Strand's* "Portraits of Celebrities" (July-December 1883). Anderson and Stead's interaction displayed many constitutive elements of later Hollywood magazines including displays of consumerism and fashion; description of "extraordinary" talent balanced against glimpses of the "private" person behind the glamorous public image; romantic artistry as the true reflection of authentic self; and the adoration by audiences, peers and/or journalists. In their second exchange (5 December 1883), Anderson and Stead engaged in dialogic persona construction, which linked her fame directly to that of British 18th-century Romantic-era actresses and created a narrative of proto-stardom. Stead – with one eyebrow firmly raised – described how Anderson swept "into the room with that ease and grace which are remarkable among [...] many qualifications for the stage" and the gifts sent as a "tribute to her art", including from the author Henry Irving and the famous English actors "Mr and Mrs Kendal". She described how she had watched the sunset while leaning on the railings at Sarah Siddons' grave, in deep contemplation of their shared craft, and showed him "stacks of letters" from "the perfect sea of faces" of her "audience", before casting "them into the fire" and declaring, "[...] unmeasured praise...has no value". They both name-dropped Longfellow and his advice when she was "just a girl of fifteen" to "never pass a day without seeing a beautiful picture, reading a beautiful poem or hearing beautiful music". Lifestyle became a representational means of demonstrating how through leisure activities, art and contemplation of their meaning, one might achieve meaningful self-emancipation.

George Newnes would later incorporate this style of interviewing with his celebrity picture biographies in *The Strand's* "Illustrated Interviews" which focused entirely on the famous and in pieces about actors particularly, echoed the emerging narratives of stardom, with text focusing on elements of beauty, unique, remarkable talent on and beyond the stage and popularity. Pictures displayed celebrities both on stage and behind the scenes at home in opulent dress and with expensive furnishings on display. The dominant theme of portraits was also achievement, but once again, those who were included were from far beyond the realms of entertainment such as those from political, religious and scientific spheres. There was also a comment about the significance of the growing power of celebrities. In a long-form feature article titled "Celebrities at Play" (July 1891, pp. 145–149), an anonymous journalist (probably Newnes given its writing style) opened with an account of how dynamics between journalists, celebrities and audiences were shifting print production. As a source of "infinite amusement to the populace", it pondered a "special journalism exists mainly to chronicle the small-doings of the great" and "every newspaper now has its gossip column". "Celebrities at Play" was not simply a fluff piece. It also analysed how celebrity culture challenged reverence shown to monarchy, with the "gossipy par" (paragraph), highlighted as impossible during absolute rule and as a reflection of greater democratic and press freedoms. It discussed how revelations about the private lives of politicians are often "political spite" and "partisan animosity", but how it also functioned to satisfy an "insatiable ... demand for such information". The impact of "competition in the journalistic world [was] so keen that the demand supplied with as much detail as possible". Accounts of Gladstone's hobby of "tree felling" or how author Richard Doddridge Blackmore "adopted market gardening and fruit growing" were framed as giving readers the content they demanded but were also an opportunity for a political and social commentary about why journalism and celebrity cultures were so intertwined. Such extensions to long-form features, with details of everyday life of celebrities in their private realms, cultural taste and the political dimensions of everyday life, were established as part of lifestyle journalism.

The "politics of being" and the power of lifestyle journalism in capitalist democracies

There is a persistent myth that dominates the understanding of the political histories of the press. It is that the separation of politics from popular, or news from lifestyle, was fundamental to its development as arbitrators of democracy. This myth was deliberately forged by the 19th-century bourgeois establishment press to affirm their own place and limit engagement with working class and radical journalists who understood that building a better way-of-life was fundamental to fights for universal justice, suffrage and equality. This myth permeated early histories of journalism, with some still blindly following the narrative, at times by ignoring or belittling popular journalism as "trash". There is far too little discussion of how the invention of lifestyle journalism for working-classes and lower middle-classes was itself a politically radical act.

At worst, this damages the critical understanding needed to facilitate the democratic opportunities of lifestyle-as-genre and particularly how it has, and can, holistically re-imagined audiences as social, cultural and political communities. Dismissing lifestyle journalism in binary to politics proper leaves little room to highlight and support models that focus more on the development of cultural citizenship and social education than the perpetuation of consumerism. Indeed, such labelling, from the outset, was a politicised attack aimed at eradicating radical and working-class journalists who claimed working people had equal rights from public spheres. The balances between "politics" in relation to democratic systems, governance and electioneering and "the political" aspects that permeate our "being" in democratic societies are fundamental, and if we want to encourage journalism that could reimagine audiences-as-publics, we need to better understand them. There's much to learn from the approach of liberal radical journalists and their power and place during its advancement to help steer lifestyle journalism towards better ethical paths.

The shifts between terminologies of "public" and "audience" and "citizen" and "consumer" here are deliberate. These terms, like the maddening binaries between histories of lifestyle and political journalism, often perpetuate class-based bias that values narrow and exclusive models for the production and consumption of "worthy" content over popular content. We might reconsider what journalists and broader lifestyle creators have taken from how the genre first formed and look to readdress imbalances between content that focuses on consumerism rather than cultural citizenship. From its earliest origins, bonds of intimacy – described here as *press parasociality* – between journalists and audience became part of the genre. This began with the earliest radical journalists who spoke directly to their readers as an imagined political and cultural community across class boundaries, to the branded and named communities of New Journalists, who looked to emancipation through self-improvement by providing knowledge and models of others. It is still evident in how prominent lifestyle presenters and journalists approach their magazine and news style shows. But while such parasociality is more evident than ever as an affirmed part of lifestyle influencing culture, this is without the link to meaningful self-agency and instead too often perpetuates "repressive ambiences of consumerism" (see Usher, 2018). If we look at most lifestyle magazine television shows or food, or beauty or travel journalists and the innumerable lifestyle influencers, there is an imbalance in the hard sell and gaps in encouragement of cultural citizenship, consideration of the politics of everyday life or what it means to "be" in capitalist democracies. The critical mass of lifestyle-as-genre too often appears to equate self-worth and agency with the ability to purchase. Editorial strategies need more rounded understandings of place, worth, inclusion, exclusion and ethical and political responsibilities. Lifestyle journalism was once a genre of revolution that supported people through tumultuous change and linked self-agency and fulfilment to meaningful political emancipation and the fundamental right to a place in society. Amidst current crises of capitalism and democracy, the question becomes: could it reclaim this place and what scholarly work is needed to help steer it in that direction? Too little research focuses on the fundamental questions of *why* we have the journalism we do. What are the underpinning historical, social and cultural factors? How can we help establish better ethical paths in local, national and global contexts? As we approach research, we need to ask ourselves a simple question – how does this help to better explain and guide the production and practices of lifestyle journalism?

Notes

1 Chartism was a working-class political movement of the 1830s–1850s, named for "The People's Charter" (1838) which called for six reforms to make the political system more democratic and inclusive.
2 The Whigs (1680s–1850s) were a political party that leaned more towards political reform than rivals the Tories. They merged with the Liberal Party in the 1850s.

Further reading

Boyce, G., Curran, J. and Wingate, P. (Eds.) *Newspaper History from the 17th Century to the Present Day*. Sage.
Houghton, W.E. (1957) *The Victorian Frame of Mind 1830–1870*. Oxford University Press.
Hollis, P. (1970) *The Pauper Press*. Oxford University Press.
Usher, B. (2020) *Journalism and Celebrity*. Routledge.
Usher, B. (2023) *Journalism and Crime*. Routledge.

References

Berridge, V. (1978) "Popular Sunday Papers and Mid-Victorian Society". In G. Boyce, J. Curran and P. Wingate (Eds.) *Newspaper History from the 17th Century to the Present Day.* Sage, pp. 247–264.

Boyce, G. (1978) 'The Fourth Estate: A Reappraisal of a Concept'. In G. Boyce, J. Curran and P. Wingate (Eds.) *Newspaper History from the 17th Century to the Present Day.* Sage, pp. 19–40.

Boyce, G., Curran, J. and Wingate, P. (1978) "Preface to Second Section". In G. Boyce, J. Curran and P. Wingate (Eds.) *Newspaper History from the 17th Century to the Present Day.* Sage, pp. 51–57.

Conboy, M. (2002) *The Press and Popular Culture.* Sage.

Conboy, M. (2004) *Journalism: A Critical History.* Sage.

Curran, J. (1978) "The Press As an Agency of Social Control: A Historical Perspective". In G. Boyce, J. Curran and P. Wingate (Eds.) *Newspaper History from the 17th Century to the Present Day.* Sage, pp. 51–75.

Curran, J. and Seaton, J. (2018) *Power without Responsibility.* 8th edn. Routledge.

Curtis, L.P. (2001) *Jack the Ripper and the London Press.* Yale University Press.

Debord, G. (1967) *The Society of the Spectacle.* 1st edn. Zone Books.

deCordova, R. (1990) *Picture Personalities: The Emergence of the Star System in America.* University of Illinois Press.

Dyer, R. (1979) *Stars* (1998 Edition). BFI.

Flanders, J. (2007) *Consuming Passions: Leisure and Pleasure in Victorian Britain.* Harper Collins.

Friederichs, H. (1911) *The Life of Sir George Newnes.* Hodder and Stroughton.

Giddens, A. (1985) *The Nation State and Violence: Volume Two of a Contemporary Critique of Historical Materialism.* Polity.

Hanusch, F. (2013) "Broadening the Focus: The Case for Lifestyle Journalism as a Field of Scholarly Activity". In F. Hanusch (Ed). *Lifestyle Journalism.* Routledge, pp. 2–11.

Hartley, J. (1996) *Popular Reality: Journalism, Modernity, Popular Culture.* Arnold.

Hollis, P. (1970) *The Pauper Press.* Oxford University Press.

Horton, D. and Wohl, R. (1956) "Mass Communication and Para-social Interaction: Observations on Intimacy at a Distance". *Psychiatry*, 19, pp. 213–229.

Houghton, W.E. (1957) *The Victorian Frame of Mind 1830–1870.* Oxford University Press.

Humpherys, A. (1983) "G.W.M. Reynolds: Popular Literature and Popular Politics". *Victorian Periodicals Review*, 16, pp. 78–89.

Jackson, K. (2001) *George Newnes and the New Journalism in Britain, 1890–1910.* Ashgate Publishing.

Marshall, P.D. (1997) *Celebrity and Power: Fame in Contemporary Culture.* University of Minnesota Press.

McLuhan, M. (1964) *Understanding Media.* Sphere Publishing.

Pound, R. (1966) *Mirror of the Century: The Strand Magazine 1891–1950.* Heinemann.

Rojek, C. (2012) *Fame Attack: The Inflation of Celebrity and its Consequences.* Bloomsbury Academic.

Rowbotham, J., Stevenson, K. and Pegg, S. (2013) *Crime News in Modern Britain: Press Reporting and Responsibility 1820–2010.* Palgrave Macmillan.

Schudson, M. (1978) *Discovering the News: A Social History of American Newspapers.* Basic Books.

Shattock, J. and Wolff, M. (1982) *The Victorian Periodical Press: Samplings and Soundings.* Leicester University Press.

Taylor, C. (1989) *Sources of the Self: The Making of the Modern Identity.* Cambridge University Press.

Tuchman, G. (1978) *Making News: A Study on the Construction of Reality.* Simon and Schuster.

Williams, R. (1978) "The Press and Popular Culture: A Historical Perspective". In G. Boyce, J. Curran and P. Wingate (Eds.) *Newspaper History from the 17th Century to the Present Day.* London: Sage, pp. 41–50.

Williams, R (1989 [1958]) *Resources of Hope.* London: Verso.

Usher, B. (2018) "Rethinking Microcelebrity: Key Points in Practice, Performance and Purpose". *Celebrity Studies*, 11 (2), pp. 171–188.

Usher, B. (2020) *Journalism and Celebrity.* Routledge.

Usher, B. (2023) *Journalism and Crime.* Routledge.

Cited 19th century commentary and analysis

Arnold, M. (1877) "Bishop Butler and the Zeit-Geist". *Last Essays on Church and Religion.* Smith Elder.
Arnold, M. (1887) Up to Easter". *Nineteenth Century.* May 1887. pp. 629–643.
Carlile Campbell, T. (1899) *The Battle of the Press: Life of Richard Carlile.* Bonner. E-book Gutenberg Press Project.
Carlyle, T. (1831) "Characteristics". In H.D. Trail (Ed.) (1838) *Critical and Miscellaneous Essays.* C. Scribner's Sons.
Greg, W.R. (1875) "Life at High Pressure". *Literary and Social Judgements,* 2.

Cited 19th century newspaper and periodical press

Cleave's Weekly Police Gazette (1834–1836)
Cobbett's Weekly Political Register (1802–1836)
Halfpenny Magazine of Entertainment and Knowledge (1840–1841),
Hetherington's Twopenny Dispatch and People's Police Register (1834–1836)
*Illustrated New*s (1832–2003)
Lloyd's Weekly (1842–1931)
Pall Mall Gazette (1883–1921)
Reynolds's Weekly Newspaper (1850–1967)
The Black Dwarf (1817–1824)
The Edinburgh Review (1902–1929)
The Examiner (1808–1881)
General Evening Post (1801–1822)
The Graphic (1869–1932)
The Illustrated Police News (1864–1938)
The Illustrated Times (1855–1872)
The Million (1892–1895)
The Morning Chronicle (1769–1865)
The Morning Post (1772–1932)
The Nineteenth Century (1801–1930)
The Northern Echo (1870–current)
The Northern Star and Leeds General Advertiser (1837–1852)
The Penny Magazine (1832–1845)
The People's Weekly Police Register (1835-1836)
The Poor Man's Guardian (1831–1835)
The Prompter (1830–1831)
The Republican (1819–1825)
The Saturday Review (1855–1938)
The Stage (1814-1816)
The Strand (1891–1949)
The Times (1785–present)
The Working Man's Friend (1832–1833)
Tit-Bits (1881–1984)
Two-Penny Trash (1812–1817, 1830–1835)
Weekly Dispatch (1801–1961)

19
THE POLITICAL RELEVANCE OF FOOD JOURNALISM

Elizabeth Fakazis

Introduction

Food journalism provides important stories about food and its complex relationship to our health and wellbeing, as well as to our identity and social status, and to other aspects of our private, social, and civic lives through a variety of multimedia, multiplatform narrative forms. Most journalism about food follows the practices and conventions of lifestyle journalism, which "addresses audiences as consumers, providing them with factual information and advice, often in entertaining ways, about goods and services they can use in their everyday lives" (Hanusch, 2012, p. 5). Yet food journalists also cover food-as-news, investigating food safety and nutrition, regulatory agencies, agricultural and labor policies and practices, and the impact of both individual food choices and the broader food system on public concerns such as sex- and-gender-based violence and racism in restaurants and other food industries, ethical treatment of animals and, increasingly, climate change.

Food journalists are also increasingly writing about the cultural politics of identity and social justice, posing "critical questions of how media select, frame, and tell stories about food, which journalists get assignments, whose perspectives are routinely privileged, and which audiences' interests and needs are taken into account in editorial decision making" (Fakazis & Fürsich, 2023, p. 9). They are also finding new markets for their work and gaining support from editors to create hybrid forms that infuse politics into the conversational, consumer-oriented, entertainment-and-advice tenor of lifestyle. In fact, it is the enduring popularity, ability to attract advertising and build brand loyalty, and increasing engagement with the intersections of private/domestic and public/political life, especially with regards to identity politics and climate change, which has inspired journalism scholars, educators, and professionals to predict that food journalism will becoming increasingly relevant, providing us with many of our most politically significant stories in coming years (Food Sustainability Index, 2021).

I begin this chapter by reviewing significant studies that have illuminated the political relevance of food journalism as a multifaceted field with a history of providing advice grounded in ideologies of gender, family, socioeconomic distinction, and self-actualization, and of covering the political aspects of food, especially in times of war, migration, and political change. Many of these studies have examined food journalism as lifestyle media, although some analyze the production, representation, and framing of food-as-news. I then turn to opportunities and challenges that food journalists have faced, especially in the past 10 years, and that they will continue to face in years to come. These include the imperative to stay relevant by providing cultural critiques not only of food but also of food media itself, finding ways to produce more insightful, inclusive, and meaningful stories capable of engaging a wide range of audiences by making systemic changes to how food media are structured and how they operate; and examining how the stories that food journalists choose to tell and how they produce and frame those stories can shape individual and collective responses to food accessibility, sustainability, and climate change – issues that need to be addressed on multiple levels, from the private household to national and international corporations and institutions. I end by suggesting paths for future research that can deepen and specify our understanding of food journalism and that can support journalism structures, practices, and pedagogies that help individuals feel pleasure and empowerment not only in their everyday private lives but also in their social and civic lives as well.

Roots of food journalism

While food journalism has long included hard news about the business and politics of food, mid-to-late 19th-century forms in the United States were produced by and for women-as-housewives, offering advice and instruction centered around the metaphorical heart of the home – the fireside hearth and later the modern kitchen – on how to manage a white, middle-class Protestant household; how to raise morally, spiritually, and physically strong families; and, for immigrant families, how to assimilate into American values and practices by cooking hearty American meals and eschewing "ethnic" ingredients (Shapiro, 1986). This advice literature was published in home management manuals, women's magazines, and the women's pages of newspapers and included articles on how to become judicious and guilt-free consumers of an increasing array of mass-produced goods, from canned fruits and vegetables to kitchen appliances that falsely promised to relieve them of the drudgery of daily housework (Cowan, 1985), a theme that gained relevance throughout the 20th century as more women entered the workforce and aspired to participate in the burgeoning consumer-leisure culture and as the acquisition and ability to use such goods began to signal social and cultural capital (Shapiro, 2005).

Food journalism remained largely the province of women throughout the 1940s. Yet, it didn't take long for the economic potential hidden in the untapped market of men to be recognized and exploited. In the prosperity that followed WWII, more people began to eat out and take an expanded interest in food that included reading recipes integrated with memoir, travel, culture, and advice on how to participate in an emerging modern, urban, masculine, and cosmopolitan society that was represented as both aspirational and achievable. Food journalism and soon food television began to encourage women to think of cooking not only as a duty but also as entertainment and (for both men and women) as a marker of social distinction (see Johnston & Baumann, 2015; Mapes, 2019). They also addressed male audiences directly, encouraging them to hone their gourmet cooking skills to seduce romantic partners or, if they were married, to master outdoor grilling of hearty steaks and hamburgers, allowing them to cook without compromising their masculinity (Contois, 2020).

Food journalism thus began to redefine cooking as an appropriate masculine pastime delineating what "real men" cooked (steaks, burgers, and gourmet meals), where they cooked (campfires, BBQs, and professionalized home kitchens), how they cooked (competitively, publicly), and why they cooked (for entertainment, artistic expression, sexual conquest, and breadwinning) (Hollows, 2002, 2003). For example, *Esquire* magazine, the first U.S. national lifestyle magazine for men launched in 1939 ran a food column by Iles Brody titled "Man the Kitchenette," which combined food with travel and tales of seduction (Fakazis, 2011); *Gourmet* magazine, one of the earliest and longest-running food, wine, and "good living" magazines, followed in 1941, signaling the demise of food journalism that championed Victorian ideologies and defined food as solely women's domestic concern, and embracing instead a cosmopolitan, aspirational food-as-"lifestyle" for men and women that celebrated leisure, consumption, and the expression of identity and values through consumer "choices."

In this way, food journalists participated in discourses of race, class, and gender, thereby also participating in the politics of everyday life and in the labor of women within and outside the home. Food journalists also fortified links between the politics of the private and public spheres, especially during times of war, immigration, and political change by connecting the health of the family to the moral, spiritual, and physical health and identity of the nation. For example, journalists in the United States and the United Kingdom encouraged women to "do their part" in the two world wars by growing "Victory gardens" to feed their families economical and nutritious meals so that rationed resources could be sent to the front to feed the soldiers and to raise strong sons who would be ready to defend the nation in the future (Lonsdale, 2023; Yang, 2005). Food became central not just for the defense of the nation but also for fostering national pride and constructing a national identity both at home and abroad. Food was and continues to be deployed rhetorically to identify who belongs, who is marginalized, and who is excluded from the imagined community of the nation (Duffy & Ashley, 2011; Gabaccia, 1998; Kasturi, 2023), and this political project began with women, their families, and their homes (see also Chapter 4).

Food journalists also contributed directly to the politics of food, especially in the 1960s and 1970s when they began covering counter-cultural critiques of the way food was produced, distributed, and consumed and began framing individual decisions about where to shop, what ingredients to buy, how to cook, and how to eat as overt political acts (Belasco, 2006). Alice Waters, owner of the iconic California restaurant Chez Panisse, which opened in 1971, was an early advocate of ethical, social, and pleasurable eating, supporting local, seasonal, organic, humane, and environmentally responsible food, all of which became hallmarks of the global Slow Food organization, founded in 1986 in Italy by Carlo Petrini. Waters later became an advocate for school lunch reform through her Edible Schoolyard initiatives and her collaboration on the 2009 planting of U.S. First Lady Michelle Obama's organic garden at the White House as part of a broader campaign to promote healthy eating for children. Like other celebrity chefs who rose to prominence, Waters leveraged her economic and cultural capital to advocate for political and social reforms while simultaneously promoting her professional brand (Bell, Hollows, & Jones, 2015; Naccarato & Lebesco, 2012). Other prominent examples include Rachael Ray, who partnered with the Alliance for a Healthier Generation, an organization formed by the William J. Clinton Foundation and the American Heart Association to combat child obesity. Ray introduced her campaign on her food television program in April 2007 with former U.S. President Bill Clinton as her guest. Similarly, celebrity chef Jamie Oliver initiated "Feed Me Better," a school meal reform campaign in the United States associated with his television show "Jamie's School Dinners." The campaign led to the government pledging $500 million to improve school lunches (see Hollows & Jones, 2010). But the celebrity chef with the most profound global influence is Jose Andres, whose NGO World Central Kitchen provides emergency food relief and humanitarian aid to people devastated by natural and human-caused disasters, as well as developing long-term strategies for alleviating poverty and hunger around the world. In covering these chefs and their advocacy work, food journalists engage with local, national, and global politics, blurring the boundaries between hard news and lifestyle journalism, information, and entertainment.

It is clear that food journalism has long engaged with politics and has provided pathways and models for civic engagement. Scholars have argued for the "democratic and even empowering potential of journalism that is produced outside the traditional hard news discourse" (Fürsich, 2012, p. 13) because it reflects how audiences experience consumer culture and civic engagement as "interconnected and co-creative rather than opposing value systems" (Deuze, 2009, p. 21), and it provides audiences with resources to manage a complex "hybrid social identity – part citizen, part consumer, part client" that is "oriented to resolving the problems of everyday life in ways that can combine individualistic and collective, political forms of response" (Eide & Knight, 1999, p. 527). These "lifestyle politics" are deeply social "collectivities in which participants advocate lifestyle change as a primary means to social change, politicizing daily life while pursuing morally coherent 'authentic' identities" (Haenfler, Johnson & Jones, 2012, p. 14). Such lifestyle politics are intensifying as the effects of problems rooted in the global food system – including those related to labor, migration, food safety, access and sovereignty, and climate change – are impacting daily life in ways that are becoming increasingly difficult to ignore.

Food journalism's continued political relevance lies in its potential to name these problems, identify causes, attribute responsibility, and recommend solutions that audiences believe are achievable and meaningful (Brüggemann, Kunert & Sprengelmeyer, 2024, pp. 2713–2714). At the same time, scholars have not lost sight of the limitations of most food journalism's grounding in a neoliberal ideology that privileges a "model of citizenship that puts more emphasis on private institutions, individual choice and self-empowerment" (Ouellette, 2016, p. 75) and forecloses the desirability or possibility of effective collective action and corporate and government solutions to systemic problems. As food journalist Michael Pollan has argued, "It's important to vote with your fork. It's not trivial. It's necessary but not sufficient. We also have to vote with our votes" (Fassler, 2016, para. 14). Food journalism seems to be heeding Pollan's words, moving toward more "holistic" narratives that are engaging with politics of diversity, equity and inclusion, and climate change and finding ways to highlight the interplay between personal, individual food choices, and collective action and systemic solutions.

Food journalism as cultural critique

In October 2021, the Food Sustainability Index, developed by the *Economist* and the Barilla Center for Food and Nutrition, predicted that food journalism would become increasingly relevant by grounding stories about food in local and global contexts; addressing inequities in labor, supply chains, and sustainability; and revivifying ethics enacted through individual choices and practices of consumption with civic engagement aimed at collective action and systemic change (Food Sustainability Index, 2021). Their prediction echoed writer Mayukh Sen's belief that "in its finest form, food writing can function as both vivid storytelling and bracing cultural critique" and his exhortation to the field to expand inroads made in response to *BlackLivesMatter*, *MeToo*, climate change activism, and other social justice movements by continuing to diversify its labor force and structure in meaningful ways and by expanding its narratives to regularly include deeply reported stories that "brush up against the politics of identity and inequality" (Sen, 2018, para. 6). For Sen and other writers, the continued relevance of food journalism depends on a willingness to engage directly, intentionally, and unapologetically with not only the economic and regulatory politics of food narrowly defined but also with the cultural politics of food in all its complexity and contradictions.

The "hard news" politics of food has long been covered by investigative and beat reporters and distributed through newspapers and news magazines, programming, and social media accounts. But what Sen and others are advocating for is sustained engagement with the cultural politics of food in *lifestyle* journalism: glossy food magazines, high-production value food-and-travel documentaries, YouTube cooking videos and reality television celebrity cooking programs, Instagram recipes and recipe blogs, stand-alone newspaper digital and print cooking sections, culinary memoirs, restaurant reviews, and even food-centered "live journalism" events organized to promote community engagement with local news agencies and concerns (e.g., Andreasen & Asmusse, 2023). Yet, such engagement breaches traditional boundaries of professional practice and audience expectations of what food lifestyle journalism should be – a celebration of food and flavors; a vicarious escape to exotic, welcoming and peaceful cultures (Heldke, 2003); a well-spring of entertainment and self-actualization; a resource for acquiring and performing social status and distinction (Johnston & Baumann, 2015). As *New York Times* writer Ligaya Mishan recently noted that food writers and audiences alike often resist food narratives that engage with politics, cultural, or otherwise. Mishan writes, "food should not be political, they insist. Food is universal. Food unites us. Let us have our cake in peace" (Mishan, 2022, para. 4).

One of the most prominent examples of food-as-lifestyle programming engaging with politics – and in the process invigorating the debate over the role and boundaries of food journalism – was produced by Anthony Bourdain (1956–2018), a graduate of the Culinary Institute of America who worked his way up the ranks of the restaurant business before becoming a best-selling writer and celebrity chef. His media career began in 1999 when *The New Yorker* published "Don't Eat Before Reading This," in which Bourdain described the dark side of the restaurant business in provocative detail:

> Good food, good eating, is all about blood and organs, cruelty and decay. It's about sodium-loaded pork fat, stinky triple-cream cheeses, the tender thymus glands and distended livers of young animals. It's about danger—risking the dark, bacterial forces of beef, chicken, cheese, and shellfish...Gastronomy is the science of pain.
> *(Bourdain, 1999, para. 1–2)*

This essay led to Bourdain's first bestselling book, *Kitchen Confidential: Adventures in the Culinary Underbelly* (2000), which revealed his ability to write incisively about conflicts at the heart of food. Three years later, Bourdain hosted his first food-and-travel program, *A Cook's Tour* (Food Network 2002–2003), followed by *Anthony Bourdain: No Reservations* (Travel Channel 2005–2012), *The Layover* (Travel Channel 2011–2013), and finally *Anthony-Bourdain: Parts Unknown* (CNN 2013–2018). It was while filming an episode for *No Reservations* in Beirut in 2006 during the Israel-Lebanon war that Bourdain brought military conflict into what was supposed to be an entertaining food-centered adventure program. Seven years later, while filming a *Parts Unknown* episode in Gaza, the West Bank, and Jerusalem, Bourdain brought what John Nichols, a national affairs correspondent for *The Nation*, described as "his most powerful assessment of the challenges and the possibilities of the work he did" (Nichols, 2018, para. 3) rejected by including in his stories lived experiences marked by joy and celebration as well as suffering and pain. Bourdain made the most of the dramatic conflict necessary for good storytelling while avoiding reducing people's lives to melodrama and entertainment. Bourdain's willingness to breach expected boundaries of food and entertainment media earned him several Emmy nominations and awards, praise from the American Constitution Society and the Muslim Public Affairs Council, and acknowledgement from seasoned political reporters like Nichols who wrote that "Bourdain was invariably a clearer commentator on geopolitics than the pundits who seem always to be conspiring against that deeper understanding of our shared humanity that might someday yield a safer and saner world" (Nichols, 2018, para. 2), and Kim Ghattas who wrote in *The Atlantic*:

> Growing up in Beirut during Lebanon's 15–year civil war, I wished for someone like Anthony Bourdain to tell the story of my country: a place ripped apart by violence, yes, but also a country where people still drove through militia checkpoints just to gather for big Sunday family lunches, or dodged sniper fire to get to their favorite butcher across town to sample some fresh, raw liver for breakfast… Coming of age during conflict made me want to become a journalist. I hoped to tell the story of my country and the Middle East—a place rife with conflicts, sure, but also layered with complexities, a place of diverse peoples full of humanity.
>
> *(Ghattas, 2018, para. 1)*

As Bourdain extended his political engagement to his social media posts and interviews, commenting especially on the exploitation of immigrant labor and widespread sexual violence in the restaurant and media industries, assessments of his "auxiliary role as a political journalist" were mixed (The Quint, 2018). In an interview for *Food & Wine* (Kanani, 2017, subheading On Politics), Bourdain said that he was often told to stick to food and stop talking about politics, but that was an impossible task. "There's nothing more political than food," he said. "Who eats? Who doesn't? Why do people cook what they cook? It's always the end or part of a long story, often a painful one."

Bourdain was just one, albeit one of the most visible, of the many food writers, editors, film-makers, and producers working to expand and deepen the coverage of the hard news politics of food or to weave politics into food-as-lifestyle journalism or both. Examples proliferate – from the food news web sites like *Civil Eats*, the *Food and Environment Reporting Network*, and *the Earth Journalism Network* – to journalists such as Serena Maria Daniels (*The Tostada* magazine), Soleil Ho (*The Racist Sandwich* podcast and food editor for the *San Fransisco Chronicle*), Andi Murphy (*Toasted Sister* podcast), Jamila Robinson (editor-in-chief *Bon Appetit*), Tom Philpott (food and agriculture correspondent for *Mother Jones*), and programs such as *What's Eating America* hosted by Andrew Zimmern and produced by the news television channel MSNBC – among many others. This recent growth gives credence to the Food Sustainability Index's prediction that food journalism's political relevance will increase in coming years, and it suggests that food journalists are increasingly taking up Sen's challenge to produce narratives that provide both

Diversifying food journalism

"vivid storytelling and bracing cultural critique" and that "brush up against the politics of identity and inequality" (Sen, 2018, para. 6) – narratives centered on the communities and industries of food that regularly make up their beat and, increasingly, on their profession and the media that employ them.

In 2003, food journalist Molly O'Neill wrote a widely cited history of food journalism in the United States for the *Columbia Journalism Review*, arguing, 15 years before Sen, that food journalism was uniquely suited to engaging audiences with important issues of politics and culture, but that the field had largely abrogated journalistic responsibility in favor of feel-good, product-oriented pieces that advertisers loved. O'Neill wrote: "some of the most significant stories today are about food. But you won't find them in the food section, where journalism has been supplanted by fantasy" (O'Neill, 2003, para. 7). O'Neill argued that this fantasy was pornographic, offering "prose and recipes so removed from real life that they cannot be used except as vicarious experience" (O'Neill, 2003, para. 14). And while she acknowledged that "there is a place in newspaper food sections, and food magazines for cheery, revisionist, nostalgic waxings, for songs of dew-kissed baby lettuces, for Proustian glances back, and for personal opinion," she argued that food fantasy had gone too far, supplanting rigorous food journalism to a lamentable degree. "There is a line," O'Neill wrote, "between soothing readers' anxieties and becoming the Victoria's Secret of the Fourth Estate" (O'Neill, 2003, subsection Regeneration).

Twenty years later, O'Neill's critique continues to remind us how easy and lucrative it can be to write "food fantasy"; at the same time, it reminds us that food journalists have long been quietly producing stories that are meaningful for both writers and audiences because of their engagement with and relevance to the politics of everyday life. Yet, in recent years, O'Neill's criticism of food media has been extensively broadened and refined, focusing attention specifically on inequities in food journalism as a business, a set of practices, and a canon of narratives. Journalists have been harnessing the momentum of *MeToo* and *Black Lives Matter* and using their influence and media access to advocate for lasting industry changes in leadership, hiring practices, pay scales, and editorial policies and decisions. A pivotal moment came in June 2020 when *Bon Appetit* published a pledge to change that reflected many of the criticisms leveled at food media:

> Our mastheads have been far too white for far too long. As a result, the recipes, stories, and people we've highlighted have too often come from a white-centric viewpoint. At times we have treated non-white stories as "not newsworthy" or "trendy." Other times we have appropriated, co-opted, and Columbused them. While we've hired more people of color, we have continued to tokenize many BIPOC [Black, Indigenous, people of color] staffers and contributors in our videos and on our pages. Many new BIPOC hires have been in entry-level positions with little power, and we will be looking to accelerate their career advancement and pay. Black staffers have been saddled with contributing racial education to our staffs and appearing in editorial and promotional photo shoots to make our brands seem more diverse. We haven't properly learned from or taken ownership of our mistakes. But things are going to change.
>
> (Bon Appetit, *2020, June 10, para. 2*)

Other publications followed suit, and food journalists began airing their own experiences of discrimination and advocating for change. Culinary historian Michael Twitty (2017), for example, recommended practices that food media could implement to make their workplaces and stories more inclusive and equitable (Twitty, 2017, para. 1). These included recruiting journalists from under-represented and under-served communities; assigning stories to writers based on their expertise rather than their ethnicity, race, or other demographic characteristics; drawing on expert voices from within a community being written about; going beyond Black, Indigenous, people of color (BIPOC), and immigrant "boat narratives" that reduce people to archetypes by focusing repeatedly on deprivation and struggle; documenting not only conflict but also culinary justice and partnership initiatives that empower communities; and resisting "authenticity" as a staged performance and body of expert knowledge delivered by an outsider "discovering" an ingredient, dish, or technique that has been around for centuries (Twitty, 2017).

While Twitty's article coalesced the grievances and remedies identified by many working in food media, *The Objective*, a nonprofit newsroom launched in 2020, institutionalized these efforts. Under the direction of Gabe Schneider and Janelle Salanga, the organization set out to critically examine "systems of power and inequity in journalism" and to work through possible remedies. Its mission statement asserts,

> We believe in journalism's ability to be both representative of communities around the U.S. and thoughtful of how coverage is written for (not just about) them. We believe in building collective and narrative power for communities that have been misrepresented or dismissed in order to change the way journalism is practiced in the U.S. We believe there's a better way to practice journalism—and we're exploring how to make it happen.
>
> (The Objective, *2023, para. 5*)

In April 2023, *The Objective* turned its attention specifically to food journalism, inviting contributions to a special series "The Reckoning in Food Media." Articles included "Where the Hell is Africa in Food Coverage?" (Omnia Saed), "Noodles are Tasty: The Economic Implications Behind Race and Cultural Appropriation in Food Media" (Frankie Huang), "I Was a Millennial Diversity Hire" (Izzy Johnson), and an interview with Stephen Satterfield discussing Black-owned food publications and alternatives to formulaic food journalism (Gabe Schneider). That same year, *Serious Eats* published a "2023 Anti-Racism Pledge" that continued in this vein. The pledge acknowledged that the "underrepresentation of BIPOC voices in food media is well-known and often remarked and reported upon, yet it remains endemic to our industry," and promised to work toward the creation of a "sustainable editorial strategy that prioritizes and centers the need for better representation among our full-time and among our full-time and freelance team members, as well as the types of stories they tell" (*Serious Eats*, 2023). Diversifying food media staff and stories beyond tokenism and typecasting was increasingly recognized as both a sound ethical and business practice, capable of attracting new talent and audiences.

One prominent entrepreneur who has leveraged these trends is Stephen Satterfield, founder of Whetstone Media, which includes two magazines (*Whetstone* and *Rasa*) and a podcast that cover global foodways, as well as a talent agency providing support to those working in various food industries who wish to use "food and beverage as means to organize, activate and educate," especially through "more inclusive storytelling" (Satterfield, (n.d)).

Yet, for all his success, Satterfield and other journalists worry that the recent diversification of stories and staff will prove to be a flash in the pan, a momentary leveraging of political and cultural events rather than lasting structural change in food journalism and media industries. "I need to be convinced," Satterfield writes, "that this isn't just reflective of a business opportunity through the lens of contemporary conversation – this moment that can be capitalized on" (Sen, 2018, para. 14). Sen shares Satterfield's concerns. "As we look forward to where food writing can go, I am skeptical about whether publications can expand their editorial purviews rapidly enough to reach the same audiences they may have once alienated" (Sen, 2018, para. 18).

Of course, the kind of systemic changes in the practice and business of food journalism that are increasingly being called for require sustained efforts, and they continue to face powerful resistance especially in the wake of U.S. legislation banning Diversity, Equity, and Inclusion (DEI) initiatives designed to diversify recruiting and hiring practices and to provide equal access and opportunities to underrepresented people in schools, government, and workplaces and as corporations dismantle their own DEI programs (Vivian, 2023). Still, food journalism, in order to continue engaging new and existing audiences, and attracting – and keeping – the best talent, can't afford to shun critical self-scrutiny, default on pledges so recently made, or limit themselves to stories told from narrow perspectives using familiar frames, all of which could deny food journalism the increasing relevance to private and political life that journalism scholars and professionals, including but not limited to the ones mentioned above, have predicted for the field.

Food, journalism, sustainability

The 2023 UN Climate Convention (COP28) emphasized the effects that global food systems and farming are having on climate change as we struggle to adequately feed 8 billion people – a global population predicted to grow by nearly 2 billion in the next 30 years. These effects include contributing 30 percent to the world's greenhouse gas emissions, using 70 percent of the world's freshwater, and being responsible for 80 percent of the deforestation and habitat loss in tropical areas, according to Mariam Almheiri, Minister of Climate Change and Environment of the UAE. Almheiri argues that "countries must put food systems and agriculture at the heart of their climate ambitions, addressing both global emissions and protecting the lives and livelihoods of farmers living on the front line of climate change" (Birch, 2023, para. 8). Specifically, agreements were forged during COP28 to fund and otherwise support programs to increase food-and-climate research; stimulate demand for sustainable, low-emission agricultural products; decrease methane produced by livestock; grow new varieties of crops that are more resilient to stress caused by climate change, among others (Birch, 2023).

Given the centrality of food to the climate crisis (Springmann et al., 2018), the need for food-centered sustainability journalism that can inform, engage, and motivate individual and collective action will only continue to grow, as will obstacles presented by a phenomenon whose complexity is impossible to overstate, by the widespread societal transitions that climate change is forcing on us, and by the disorienting disruptions to media in general and journalism in particular (Russell, 2023; Hackett et al., 2017).

Despite decades of worldwide scientific studies, deliberations of international bodies and conventions and news and public affairs books, articles, documentaries, and social media campaigns addressing climate change, we have yet to see the kind or degree of action needed to avert its worst realized, impending, and long-term effects (Weder et al., 2021). Not surprisingly, scholars have turned critical attention to communication, asking how climate-change denial as well as the failure to motivate individuals and institutions who believe the crisis is real but have yet to take recommended actions is a failure in communication and, if so, what persuasive communication strategies might include. Such inquiry is broad, analyzing diverse forms of communication, including political, scientific, risk-management, medical, and other discourses and, of course, journalism, which plays a crucial role in communicating sustainability issues by shaping public awareness and political agendas.

A robust body of literature exists that examines how news is shaping climate change discourse and, more fundamentally, the appropriate role of journalism in the face of unprecedented global transitions (Russell, 2023; Berglez et al., 2017; Hackett et al., 2017). However, there isn't much research that specifically investigates food news-and-lifestyle journalism's engagement with issues of climate change and sustainability (Craig, 2016, p. 125). The studies that do exist often underestimate food journalism's constructive contributions, finding that food journalists still tend "towards apolitical food coverage that does not problematize the ecological or social down-sides of food production and consumption" (Brüggemann et al., 2024, p. 2717). Yet, these findings may be the result of a focus on news sections of major newspapers, including *The New York Times* and *The Washington Post*, rather than on these newspapers' food sections; on the growing number of digital media that have dedicated resources for environmental coverage, such as the *Food and Environmental Reporting Network*, *Food Tank*, *Context*, *Civil Eats*, and myriad others that produce regular critical coverage of global food systems and enjoy a wide readership and financial success (Russell, 2023, p. 18); or on food lifestyle journalism, which has growing potential to "raise awareness with regard to the ecological dimensions of food choices" (Brüggemann et al., 2024, p. 30).

Even with the establishment of such food journalism outlets staffed by well-trained and experienced investigative reporters, writing effectively about food in connection with broader societal problems, especially climate change, remains difficult. Critics often blame journalism for failing to cover sustainability in ways that drive home the urgency and scope of the topic, engage audiences, and motivate them to take appropriate actions. These criticisms are "based on the assumption that public ignorance, apathy, and denial are evidence of news-media shortcomings" (Russell, 2023, p. 14). Alan Rusbridger, former editor of *The Guardian*, described climate change as "journalism's great failure" and "called for a reinvigorated conversation about how to sustain journalism that contributes to the public interest" (Painter, 2019, p. 424). Similarly, *Washington Post* columnist Margaret Sullivan admonished journalists with the reminder that "the best minds in the media should be giving sustained attention to how to tell this most important story in a way that will create change" (Painter, 2019, p. 425).

The challenges and constraints facing sustainability/climate-change journalism are profound, beginning with the fact that the phenomenon of climate change "involves science that is difficult to understand and seems distant and abstract to those who have not yet experienced the climate crisis firsthand –although they are a rapidly dwindling portion of the population" (Russell, 2023, p. 14). Climate change is also integrally linked with racism and inequity on local, national, and global levels, and covering it effectively requires addressing "the racist structures that undergird it, including, of course, the structure of our media environment" (Russell, 2023, p. 4). Climate change journalism is also challenged by political polarization and well-funded campaigns of climate change denial that thrive as public trust in the press erodes, as "publics are fractured by receding shared standards for truth," and as misinformation and conspiracy theories proliferate (Russell, 2023, p. 9).

Additionally, journalists are faced with challenges specific to their profession and practice, such as the financial instability of news outlets and related lack of funding for local and in-depth reporting of complex issues, including fewer specialist beats such as science and environment (Boykoff & Yulsman, 2013); the limited audience reach and inability to cross political divides of niche media(Painter, 2019, p. 428); and a persistent yet faulty assumption that the way to build public engagement is to provide ever more facts, ever more clearly. Professional experience and research have demonstrated, however, that persuasive sustainability communication is more complex than translating scientific facts into language that the public understands (Laininen, 2019; Godemann, 2011) because information and data are not always seen as trustworthy especially when they don't align with people's existing values and beliefs; because exposure to information, even information that is believed to be credible, does not necessarily alter people's values, attitudes, or behavior (Weder et al., 2021, p. 21); and because stories are more persuasive than data (Russell, 2023; Guber, Bohr & Dunlap, 2021), making *how* information is communicated as important as the information itself.

In light of this, journalists are organizing climate change data into narratives employing a variety of interpretive frames (Entman, 1993) that they hope will resonate more effectively with audiences and will offer avenues for individual and collective action, unlike apocalypse frames that are commonly used in news but are also contested by those who fear their alienating impact (Hulme, 2009). Apocalypse frames "tend to paint a picture of a climate crisis so alarmingly advanced that either there is nothing we can do, or only extreme measures will do" (Russell, 2023, p. 24). More effective frames are those that promote "agency, hope and efficacy" by "telling local stories, inspiring community-level resistance and transformations, and amplifying counternarratives for people who are becoming active citizens" (Painter, 2019, p. 427).

Such frames also help make visible connections between structural problems that require systemic change and collective action and personal responsibility and individual solutions. This

> tension between personal and structural framing of problems points back to the fact that although the changing climate is a scientific phenomenon, how to respond is a question of values, and understanding people's values is a key component to effective climate communication.
>
> *(Russell, 2023, p. 27)*

Linking stories to audience's "existing ethics and understanding of the world and their communities plays a central role in public engagement with scientific issues" (Russell, 2023, p. 28), as does emphasizing how climate change affects their everyday lives (Boykoff, 2019) and how sustainable living can be ethical, successful, and pleasurable (Craig, 2016, p. 137). Craig argues that this "does not ignore the extraordinary political, economic, and structural dilemmas that we face in responding to climate change," but instead recognizes that "climate change is a complex phenomenon that requires multifaceted responses and actions across different levels of society" (Craig, 2016, p. 137). In other words, climate change as well as environmental stewardship occur across and undermine traditional distinctions between private and public spheres, demanding "not only a public politics but also an individual ethics that has both a public and a private orientation" (Craig, 2016, p. 126).

And herein may lie the strength and increasing political relevance of not only food news but also and especially food-as-lifestyle journalism. Many lifestyle stories are focused "on the domestic arrangements of families but they cannot be characterized as a form of 'cocooning'" (Cullens, 1999) where "individuals retreat from the outside world. Instead, they represent lifestyle practices where private and public coalesce in ways that defy easy categorization" (Craig, 2016, p. 134). Lifestyle journalism, though often understood as relating almost exclusively to individual, aesthetic, and consumption-oriented concerns, also speaks to and helps guide a "life politics" (Giddens, 1991) that is "distinguished from, but still articulated with, conventional emancipatory politics, though its primary task is the development of an ethics of 'how we should live now'" (Craig, 2016, p. 127). Changes in lifestyle become inextricably linked to social change as people meet the environment on "an intimate level, not as part of universal and generalized abstractions, but as connected to their daily practices, leisure pursuits and identities" (Macnaghten, 2006, p. 137), and as the environment is made meaningful through engagement with social life, "inhibiting or facilitating the development of ongoing human relationships, whether in the context of the family, friends, or communities of interest" (Macnaghten, 2006, p. 141). These "communities of interest" are constituted around shared food ethics and practices, including practices of political engagement and activism played out in both domestic and public spaces. And, contrary to common laments, people are increasingly engaging in food-related politics and civic actions, empowered by digital media, and often driven by growing cynicism in traditional politics and policymakers "regarding the level of political will toward environmental issues at state and federal level" (Lewis, 2020, pp. 151–152). Engagement is taking many forms, including establishing community gardens and food-sharing initiatives, building backyard chicken coops and beehives, and sharing information and expertise. Such intensely local practices are transformational even as they are embedded in household sites and routines (Lewis, 2020, pp. 151–152). Food journalism, as both news and lifestyle, can inform and amplify such individual, connective, and collective civic practices, helping "organize and 'scale up' the activities of households and domestically located civic food politics" (Lewis, 2020, p. 150) as well as supporting more conventional forms of political engagement.

Future directions

The pace of technological, economic, political, and social changes that have been dogging journalism for the past 25 years promises only to accelerate, and the challenges and opportunities that arise in their wake only to intensify. The impact of these changes – and appropriate responses to them – must necessarily reflect the complexity of journalism as a field that includes a multiplicity of forms, practices, functions, audiences, and ideologies (Deuze, 2005; Zelizer, 2009, 2013). As Deuze & Witschge have noted, the "amplification and acceleration of new news genres, forms, products and services today point towards the fact that the occupational ideology of journalism allows for many different 'journalisms' to flourish'" (Deuze & Witschge, 2017).

Food journalism itself mirrors this multiplicity, encompassing news, lifestyle, and hybrid forms across media and distribution platforms. Taken together, food 'journalisms' articulate the "politics of ordinariness" (Ryan, 2018, p. 102) or of everyday life with the politics of civic life and collective action; and, given the nature of their subject – food – they are ideally positioned to investigate the intersections of personal and social identity and sustainability/climate issues on scales from the intensely local to the global. In so doing, food journalism has the potential to move away from the neoliberal ideology that governs much of lifestyle media and that reduces systemic problems to personal ones that are best managed through individual creativity, resilience, choice, and strategic consumption toward a more "holistic position" that acknowledges that such problems are collective and require government and corporate solutions (Fürsich, 2023, p. 109). This move accelerated in the wake of the COVID-19 global pandemic, with social movements such as #metoo, #blacklivesmatter, and global protests against climate change inaction, all of which provoked "a re-evaluation of the core tenets of the food and media industries. Suddenly, experimentation and innovation became not only possible but necessary" (Fürsich, 2023, p. 109). Innovations have included contextualizing stories in global foodways, environments, and economies; framing solutions to systemic problems as political, collective, and achievable; and creating opportunities for individuals traditionally marginalized in food media to find work in the field, including as decision-makers, and to be quoted extensively as experts with authority and valuable knowledge and experience (Fürsich, 2023, p. 109).

These practices have recently been analyzed, evaluated, and advocated for by journalism professionals, educators, and researchers, and their work offers a solid foundation and direction for future studies. First, studies of emerging, hybrid forms of journalism can help us better understand how and to what extent such experiments are attracting new audiences and increasing engagement with civic life and with journalism itself. The Constructive Institute based at Aarhus University, for example, offers support for conceptualizing, producing, and studying journalism that works with community members to identify problems and work toward possible solutions, to support rather than undermine democracy by finding ways to make journalism relevant and capable of inspiring engagement rather than apathy, and to facilitate collective action and community building rather than isolated and isolating individual actions (constructiveinstitute.org). Several studies have examined constructive journalism and its ability to implement and realize its ambitious goals (Mast, Coesemans & Temmerman, 2019; Bro, 2019; From & Kristensen, 2018), and one in particular has specifically examined how food covered as constructive journalism and presented through innovative practices such as live journalism events "can serve as a relevant and insightful combination to facilitate engagement and community" (From & Asmusse, 2023, p. 168). More research on the potential and practices of constructive journalism, specifically in relation to food, can help us better understand this emerging form, and especially how audiences are actually engaging with it (Meier, 2018).

Second, more research is needed on how food journalism gets produced, the daily conditions facing journalists that facilitate and hinder their work, and how journalists navigate these through alliances formed with government, non-profit, and corporate entities that shape food journalism content and modes of distribution (Duffy & Ashley, 2011; McGaurr, 2023; Hanusch, 2017, 2019). Such studies can help us better understand the work of journalism and its complex and often intractable demands and limitations, and they can help ground academic analyses of food journalism content and representations in the realities of the field.

Third, studies on food journalism's contributions to (in)effective communication about climate change are much needed. The difficulties of reporting on such a widespread, systemic, and complex problem that is still regarded by many as remote in both time and place, as abstract rather than experiential, and as politically divisive have been well documented (Appelgren & Jonsson, 2021; Bodker & Morris, 2022; Russell, 2023; Schafer & Painter, 2020). The link between food and climate change has also garnered more media attention, especially after COP28, the United Nation's 2023 Climate Change Conference held in Dubai, made it a focus of its agenda. A few studies have critically examined food journalism's contributions to climate change discourse, and much of it focused on factory farming, animal agriculture, and meat consumption (Almiron, 2020; Kristiansen, Painter & Shea, 2021; Lahsen, 2018), but there is opportunity and need for much more research especially as the profound disruptions of climate change begin to be increasingly felt and to be felt in concrete ways closer to home.

Finally, much more research needs to be done on food journalism's contributions to discourses of diversity, equity, and inclusion, especially in terms of removing barriers and creating opportunities for individuals from traditionally marginalized communities to find work in the field, including in decision-making positions; permitting such voices to be heard, recognized, and compensated as valuable and deeply knowledgeable; and scrutinizing how food journalism covers, reproduces, and potentially challenges inequities in the food system, including in food media (Kahn, 2020; Mann, 2023).

Further readings

Durrschmidt, J., & Kautt, Y. (Eds.) (2019). *Globalized Eating Cultures: Mediation and Mediatization*. Palgrave MacMillan.

Lam, L. T. (2020). Diversity *in Food Media New Voices on Food: Anthology No.1*. SomeKind Press.

Phillipov, M. (2017). *Media and Food Industries: The New Politics of Food*. Palgrave Macmillan.

Phillipov, M., & Kirkwood, K. (2018). *Alternative Food Politics: From the Margins to the Mainstream*. Routledge.

References

Almiron, N. (2020). The 'Animal-Based Food Taboo': Climate change denial and deontological codes in journalism. *Frontiers in Communication*, 5, 512956. https://doi.org/10.3389/fcomm.2020.512956

Andreasen, U. F., & Asmusse, A. B. (2023). Heritage, belonging and promotion: Food journalism reconsidered. In E. Fakazis & E. Fürsich (Eds.), *The Political Relevance of Food Media and Journalism: Beyond Reviews and Recipes* (pp. 167–180). Routledge.

Appelgren, E., & Jonsson, A. M. (2021). Engaging citizens for climate change—Challenges for journalism. *Digital Journalism*, 9(10), 755–772. https://doi.org/10.1080/21670811.2020.1827965

Belasco, W. (2006). *Appetite for Change: How the Counterculture Took on the Food Industry*. Cornell University Press.

Bell, D., Hollows, J., & Jones, S. (2015). Campaigning culinary documentaries and the responsibilization of food crises. *Geoforum*, 84, 179–187. https://doi.org/10.1016/j.geoforum.2015.03.014

Berglez, P., Olausson, U., & Ots, M. (Eds.) (2017). *What Is Sustainable Journalism? Integrating the Environmental, Social and Economic Challenges of Journalism*. Peter Lang.

Birch, K. (2023, December 11). COP28: The biggest sustainable food and farming commitments. *Sustainability*. https://sustainabilitymag.com/sustainability/the-biggest-sustainable-food-and-farming-commitments-at-cop

Bødker, H., & Morris, H. E. (Eds.) (2022). *Climate Change and Journalism: Negotiating Rifts of Time*. Routledge. https://doi.org/10.4324/9781003090304

Bon Appetit. (2020, June 10). *A Long-Overdue Apology, and Where We Go From Here*. https://www.bonappetit.com/story/where-we-go-from-here

Bourdain, A. (1999, April 12). Don't eat before reading this: A New York chef spills some trade secrets. *The New Yorker*. https://www.newyorker.com/magazine/1999/04/19/dont-eat-before-reading-this

Bourdain, A. (2000). *Kitchen Confidential: Adventures in the Culinary Underbelly*. Bloomsbury.
Boykoff, M. T. (2019). *Creative (Climate) Communications: Productive Pathways for Science, Policy and Society*. Cambridge University Press. https://doi.org/10.1017/9781108164047
Boykoff, M. T., & Yulsman, T. (2013). Political economy, media, and climate change: Sinews of modern life. *WIRES: Climatic Change*, 4(5), 359–371. https://doi.org/10.1002/wcc.233
Bro, P. (2019). Constructive journalism: Proponents, precedents, and principles. *Journalism*, 20(4), 504–519.
Brüggemann, M., Kunert, J., & Sprengelmeyer, L. (2024). Framing food in the news: Still keeping the politics out of the broccoli. *Journalism Practice*, 18(10), 2712–2734. https://doi.org/10.1080/17512786.2022.2153074
Contois, E. (2020). *Diners, Dudes, and Diets: How Gender and Power Collide in Food Media and Culture*. University of North Carolina Press.
Cowan, R. S. (1985). *More Work for Mother: The Ironies of household Technology from the Open Hearth to the Microwave*. Basic Books.
Craig, G. (2016). Political Participation and Pleasure in Green Lifestyle Journalism. *Environmental Communication*, 10(3), 122–141. https://doi.org/10.1080/17524032.2014.991412
Cullens, C. (1999). Gimme Shelter: At home with the millennium. *Differences*, 11(2), 204–227.
Deuze, M. (2005). What is journalism? Professional identity and ideology of journalists reconsidered. *Journalism*, 6(4), 442–464.
Deuze, M. (2009). Journalism, Citizenship and Digital Culture. In Z. Papacharissi (Ed.), *Journalism and Citizenship: New Agendas in Communication* (pp. 18–28). Routledge.
Deuze, M., & Witschge, T. (2017). What journalism becomes. In C. Peters & M. Broersma (Eds.), *Rethinking Journalism Again: Societal role and Public Relevance in a Digital Age* (pp. 115–130). Routledge.
Duffy, A., & Ashley, Y. Y. (2011). Bread and circuses: Food meets politics in the Singapore Media. *Journalism Practice*, 6(1), 59–74. https://doi.org/10.1080/17512786.2011.622892
Eide, M., & Knight, G. (1999). Public/private service: Service journalism and the problems of everyday life. *European Journal of Communication*, 14(4), 525–547.
Entman, R. M. (1993). Framing: Toward clarification of a fractured paradigm. *Journal of Communication*, 43(4), 51–58.
Fakazis, E. (2011). Esquire Mans the Kitchenette. *Gastronomica*, 11(3), 29–39. https://doi.org/10.1525/gfc.2011.11.3.29
Fakazis, E., & Fürsich, E. (Eds.) (2023). *The Political Relevance of Food Media and Journalism: Beyond Reviews and Recipes*. Routledge.
Fassler, J. (2016 June, 7). Michael Pollan's New Dilemma. *The Counter*. https://thecounter.org/michael-pollans-new-dilemma/
Food Sustainability Index. (2021). https://impact.economist.com/projects/foodsustainability/
From, U., & Asmusse, A. (2023). Heritage, belonging, and promotion: Food journalism reconsidered. In E. Fakazis & E. Fürsich (Eds.), *The Political Relevance of Food Media & Journalism* (pp. 167–180). Routledge.
From, U., & Kristensen, N. N. (2018). Rethinking constructive journalism by means of service journalism. *Journalism Practice*, 12(6), 714–729. https://doi.org/10.1080/17512786.2018.1470475
Fürsich, E. (2012). Lifestyle Journalism as popular Journalism: Strategies for Evaluating its Public Role. *Journalism Practice* 6(1), 12–25.
Fürsich, E. (2023). Cooking in the time of corona: The politicized domesticity of food journalism in *The New York Times*. In E. Fakazis & E. Fürsich (Eds.), *The Political Relevance of Food Media and Journalism* (pp. 101–114). Routledge. https://doi.org/10.4324/9781003283942-9
Gabaccia, D. R. (1998). *We Are What We Eat: Ethnic Food and the Making of Americans*. Harvard University Press.
Ghattas, K. (2018, June 9). How Lebanon transformed Anthony Bourdain. *The Atlantic*. https://www.theatlantic.com/international/archive/2018/06/how-lebanon-transformed-anthony-bourdain/562484/
Giddens, A. (1991). *Modernity and Self-Identity: Self and Society in the Late Modern Age*. Stanford University Press.
Godemann, J., & Michelsen, G. (Eds.) (2011). *Sustainability Communication: Interdisciplinary Perspectives and Theoretical Foundations*. Springer.

Guber, D. L., Bohr, J., & Dunlap, R. E. (2021). Time to wake up: Climate change advocacy in a polarized Congress, 1996–2015. *Environmental Politics*, 30(4), 538–358. https://doi.org/10.1080/09644016.2020.1786333

Hackett, R., Forde, S., Gunster, S., & Foxwell-Norton, K. (2017). *Journalism and Climate Crisis: Public Engagement, Media Alternatives*. Routledge.

Haenfler, R., Johnson, B., & Jones, E. (2012). Lifestyle movements: Exploring the intersection of lifestyle and social movements. *Social Movement Studies*, 11(1), 1–20. https://doi.org/10.1080/14742837.2012.640535

Hanusch, F. (2012). Broadening the focus: The case for lifestyle journalism as scholarly inquiry. *Journalism Practice*, 6(1), 2–11. https://doi.org/10.1080/17512786.2011.622895

Hanusch, F. (2017). 'How much love are you going to give this brand?' Lifestyle journalists on commercial influences in their work. *Journalism*, 18(2), 141–158. https://doi.org/10.1177/1464884915608818

Hanusch, F. (2019). Journalistic Roles and Everyday Life: An Empirical Account of Lifestyle Journalists' Professional Views. *Journalism Studies* 20(2), 193–211. https://doi.org/10.1080/1461670X.2017.1370977

Heldke, L. M. (2003). *Exotic Appetites: Ruminations of a Food Adventurer*. Routledge.

Hollows, J. (2002). The Bachelor Dinner: Masculinity, class and cooking in *Playboy*, 1953-1921. *Continuum: Journal of Media & Cultural Studies*, 16(2), 143–155.

Hollows, J. (2003). Oliver's Twist: Leisure, labor and domestic masculinity in The Naked Chef. *International Journal of Cultural Studies*, 6(2), 229–247. https://doi.org/10.1177/13678779030062005

Hollows, J., & Jones, S. (2010). 'At least he's doing something': Moral entrepreneurship and individual responsibility in Jamie's Ministry of Food. *European Journal of Cultural Studies*, 13(3), 307–322.

Hulme, M. (2009). Mediating the messages about climate change: reporting the IPCC Fourth Assessment in the UK print media. In T. Boyce, & J. Lewis (Eds.), *Climate Change and the Media* (pp. 117–128). Peter Lang.

Johnston, J., & Baumann, S. (2015). *Foodies: Democracy and Distinction in the Gourmet Foodscape*. Routledge.

Kahn, S. A. (2020). Mediating food sovereign voices in documentary media. *Frontiers in Communication*, 5. https://doi.org/10.3389/fcomm.2020.553466

Kanani, R. (2017, May 24). The world according to Anthony Bourdain. *Food & Wine*. https://www.foodandwine.com/news/world-according-anthony-bourdain

Kasturi, S. (2003). Of Clay Stoves and Cooking Pots: "Village Food" Videos and Gastro-Politics in Contemporary India. In E. Fakazis & E. Fürsich (Eds.) *The Political Relevance of Food Media and Journalism* (pp. 135–152). Routledge.

Kristiansen, S., Painter, J., & Shea, M. (2021). Animal agriculture and climate change in the US and UK Elite Media. *Environmental Communication*, 15(2), 153–172.

Lahsen, M. (2018). Buffers against inconvenient knowledge: Brazilian newsapeper representations of the climate-meat link. *P2P & INOVACAO, Rio de Janeiro*, 4(1), 59–84.

Laininen, E. (2019). Transforming Our worldview towards a sustainable future. In J. W. Cook (Ed.), *Sustainability, Human Well-Being, and the Future of Education* (pp. 161–200). Springer.

Lewis, T. (2020). *Digital Food: From Paddock to Platform*. Bloomsbury Academic. https://doi.org/10.1080/22041451.2018.1476795

Lonsdale, S. (2023). Patriotic Hens, Tomato Turbans, and Mock Fish: The Daily Mail Food Bureau and national identity during the First World War. In E. Fakazis & E. Fürsich (Eds.), *The Political Relevance of Food Media and Journalism: Beyond Reviews and Recipes* (pp. 183–198). Routledge.

Mann, A. (2023). Who Speaks and Are We Listening? Food Sovereign Voices in a Changing Climate. In E. Fakazis & E. Fürsich (Eds.), *The Political Relevance of Food Media and Journalism*. Routledge.

Mapes, G. (2019). Marketing elite authenticity: Tradition and terroir in artisanal food discourse. *Discourse, Context & Media*, 34(3), 1–9. https://doi.org/10.1016/j.dcm.2019.100328

Mast, J., Coesemans, R., & Temmerman, M. (2019). Constructive journalism: Concepts, practices, and discourses. *Journalism*, 20(4), 492–503.

McGaurr, L. (2023). Agribusiness, environmental conflict, and food in travel journalism: Image work for the Bay of Fundy in New Brunswick. In E. Fakazis & E. Fürsich (Eds.), *The Political Relevance of Food and Media and Journalism* (pp. 48–65). Routledge. https://doi.org/ 10.4324/9781003283942-5

MacNaghten, P. (2006). Environment and Risk. In G. Mythen & S. Walklate (Eds.), *Beyond the Risk Society: Critical reflections on risk and human security* (pp. 132–146). Open University Press.

Meier, K. (2018). How does the audience respond to constructive journalism? *Journalism Practice* 12(6), 764–780. https://doi.org/10.1080/17512786.2018.1470472

Mishan, L. (2022, February 18). What we write about when we write about food. *New York Times*. https://www.nytimes.com/2022/02/18/t-magazine/food-writing-journalism-criticism.html

Naccarato, P., & Lebesco, K. (2012). *Culinary Capital*. Berg.

Nichols, J. (2018, June 8). Anthony Bourdain Knew there was nothing more political than food. *The Nation*. https://www.thenation.com/article/archive/anthony-bourdain-knew-nothing-political-food/

O'Neill, M. (2003, September 1). *Food Porn*. Columbia Journalism Review. https://www.cjr.org/from_the_archives/food-writing-cookbook.php

Ouellette, L. (2016). *Lifestyle TV*. Routledge.

Painter, J. (2019). Climate change journalism: Time to adapt. *Environmental Communication*, 13(3), 424–429. https://doi.org/10.1080/17524032.2019.1573561

Russell, A. (2023). *The Mediated Climate: How Journalists, Big Tech, and Activists Are Vying for Our Future*. Columbia University Press.

Ryan, M. E. (2018). *Lifestyle Media in American Culture: Gender, Class and the Politics of Ordinariness*. Routledge. https://doi.org/10.4324/9781315464978

Satterfield, S. (n.d.) *Hone*. https://www.hone-talent.com/about

Schafer, M. S., & Painter, J. (2020). Climate journalism in a changing media ecosystem: Assessing the production of climate change-related news around the world. *Wiley Interdisciplinary Reviews: Climate Change*, 12(1), e675. https://doi.org/10.1002/wcc.675

Sen, M. (2018, November 15). Where food writing leads. *Columbia Journalism Review*. https://www.cjr.org/special_report/food-writing-race-identity.phpq

Serious Eats. (2023). *A 2023 Anti-Racism Pledge*. https://www.seriouseats.com/our-anti-racism-pledge-5186466

Shapiro, L. (1986). *Perfection Salad: Women and Cooking at the Turn of the Century*. North Point Press.

Shapiro, L. (2005). *Something from the Oven: Reinventing Dinner in 1950s America*. Penguin Publishing.

Springmann, M., Clark, M., Mason-D'Croz, D., et al. (2018). Options for keeping the food system within environmental limits. *Nature* (562), 519–552. https://doi.org/10.1038/s41586-018-0594-0

The Objective. (2023). *About*. https://objectivejournalism.org/about/

The Quint. (2018, June 9). *Anthony Bourdain's Colleagues Pay Tributes* https://www.thequint.com/hotwire-text/anthony-bourdain-s-colleagues-pay-tributes

Twitty, M. (2017, Spring). *Rules of Engagement: Food Journalism in a Multicultural America*. Gravy. https://www.southernfoodways.org/rules-of-engagement-food-journalism-in-a-multicultural-america/

Vivian, B. (2023, June 13). DEI education in America actually dates back to the 18th century. *Washington Post*. https://www.washingtonpost.com/made-by-history/2023/06/13/dei-education-diversity-founders-antislavery/

Weder, F., Krainer, L., & Karmasin, K. (Eds.) (2021). *The Sustainability Communication Reader: A Reflective Compendium*. Springer VS.

Yang, M. (2005). Creating the Kitchen Patriot: Media promotion of food rationing and nutrition campaigns on the American home front during World War II. *American Journalism*, 22(3), 55–75.

Zelizer, B. (2009). *The Changing Faces of Journalism*. Routledge.

Zelizer, B. (2013). On the shelf life of democracy in journalism scholarship. *Journalism*, 14(4), 459–473.

20
GREEN LIFESTYLE JOURNALISM

Geoffrey Craig

Introduction

Green lifestyle journalism is a complex form of media: it has a marginal status within journalism and a problematic identity within lifestyle media, and yet it explores important environmental issues and responses to the climate emergency, although often within a commercialised framework that foregrounds consumption and cultural capital. Green lifestyle journalism is also complex because it manifests in different ways across forms of media: as news, and sometimes as entertainment, although it is unified through an address to audiences about the environmental impacts of their everyday lives. Green lifestyle journalism has not attracted much academic research attention within journalism studies, or other areas, such as environmental communication, and this chapter suggests that the climate emergency demands greater thought and advocacy around forms of public communication that investigate the sustainability of the everyday lives of citizens. Evaluations of green lifestyle journalism, as such, are informed by substantive considerations of issues such as ethical consumption, lifestyles, sustainability, the political economy of journalism, and the generic constitution of news.

This chapter begins with a consideration of the three key terms of 'green,' 'lifestyle,' and 'journalism' as a means of understanding the breadth of meaning of each of these terms and their relationship to each other. This will be followed by a discussion of various types of green lifestyle journalism, noting that representations of everyday sustainability span different types of news and media formats. This chapter will then consider how we can evaluate green lifestyle journalism and associated environmental issues, including ethical consumption and commercialisation. Subsequently, this chapter provides a brief overview of research on green lifestyle journalism and media, along with comments on its possible future developments.

Key terms – Green, lifestyle, and journalism

We can derive a greater understanding of green lifestyle journalism if we unpack each of the three terms – green, lifestyle, and journalism – and explore the relationships between those terms. *Green* lifestyle journalism simply refers to forms of lifestyle journalism where environmentalism and sustainability are foregrounded. The term 'green' has, of course, long been associated with the environmental movement, most particularly through the environmental activist organisation, Greenpeace, and also through Green political parties around the world who have advocated for environmental welfare and justice. These parties distinguished themselves from those political parties on both the right and left of the political spectrum, who are located within the contexts of industrial modernity, where there have been primary goals of wealth creation and distribution, often without due regard for the environment. 'Green,' though, is also a complex and contested term (Leach, 2015). Within popular culture, it can be used as a quick and sometimes superficial association with environmental welfare, as we see with all sorts of 'green' consumer products. More substantively, different green philosophical positions can either value nature for its own sake or, from a more anthropocentric position, value the environment for its ability to facilitate human purposes and wellbeing (Soper, 1995). Equally, there are questions about how the environmentalism of a green political position intersects with issues of social justice, indigeneity, feminism, democratic reform, and community empowerment. Within the context of a climate emergency, what it means to be green these days is

> Powerfully associated with respect for environmental limits: whether in relation to climate change, biodiversity, water, land, oceans or their 'nexus' interactions... [and the knowledge that] growth and progress ... must keep within limits or else founder amid dangerous resource scarcities, crisis and turbulence.
>
> *(Leach, 2015, p. 27)*

The term 'green' then not only refers to the simple colour connotations associated with the 'greenness' of nature, and an associated general support for nature, but it is also a short-hand description of a political orientation that critiques the way that industrial modernity has wrought environmental destruction and alienated people from the environment. It is this breadth of meaning, or variability of understandings of the term, that is often the basis for critiques of individual uses of the term, particularly with regard to its commercial usage (Peattie & Crane, 2005). It is argued here that the polysemic character of the concept is not problematic, but rather, as with any other highly important concept, the meaning of what it is to be 'green' will always be subject to political contestation.

Equally, the term 'lifestyle' is laden with cultural connotations, a concept that often evokes images of a bourgeois, consumer-oriented mode of existence but also a concept that can point to more substantive and constructive engagements with the dilemmas of everyday life. While it can be argued ostensibly that every person has always adopted a particular style of living, the concept of 'lifestyles' can be traced broadly to the 18th and 19th centuries where the burgeoning bourgeois class obtained sufficient leisure time to be able to cultivate an identity and engage in everyday practices that expressed their wealth and status (Chaney, 1996). More recently though, our understandings of lifestyles derive from the ways that individuals create a sense of self through their negotiations with the products, practices, and uses of time and space which are afforded by consumer culture (Featherstone, 1991). In particular, it has been theorised that from the 1970s, we entered a 'post-Fordist' era when standardised mass production gave way to more differentiated and ephemeral forms of production, giving individuals greater choice about how they expressed their everyday identity through patterns of consumption. As Featherstone (1991, p. 86) previously wrote, such individuals are

> The new heroes of consumer culture [who] make lifestyle a life project and display their individuality and sense of style in the particularity of the assemblage of goods, clothes, practices, experiences, appearance and bodily dispositions they design together into a lifestyle.

Such a description continues to resonate strongly with us in the contemporary era of social influencers, Instagram, and TikTok, but equally such an account does not fully capture the breadth of possible understandings of lifestyles. Modernity, more generally, has also involved the erosion of traditional institutions and accompanying value systems that previously provided greater shape and certainty to individual life trajectories. In previous generations, people were born into familial contexts of class, religion, ethnicity, and geography, that tended to define who they were, but increasingly, we live in more 'individualised' social contexts where people must formulate their own 'lifestyles.' Such a task is facilitated in some ways by greater freedoms and opportunities for more people, but equally there are challenges and risks of failure, particularly when faced with greater economic and social contexts of austerity, precarity, and imminent environmental collapse. The task of living a meaningful, ethical, and pleasurable life, then, is increasingly a fraught exercise involving complex engagements with, and critiques of, the available resources of modern societies. Lifestyles, as such, include but are also much more than simple manifestations of identity formation through consumption practices and extend to the normative and political question of how we should and can live now.

The *journalism* of green lifestyle journalism is also a complex phenomenon which, in turn, compels us to consider the boundaries, functions, and evaluations of contemporary journalism. Green lifestyle journalism is a marginalised form of journalism in two different ways: it is marginalised as a form of *environmental* journalism, and it is marginalised as a form of *lifestyle* journalism. *Environmental* journalism has the crucial task of reporting on the climate emergency – 'the biggest news story of the twentieth first century' – and the accompanying scientific, political, and economic infrastructures that give meaning to the existential crisis currently facing humanity. In comparison, news stories that discuss the energy efficiencies of dishwashers or the sustainability of a fashion brand can seem trivial and superficial. *Lifestyle* journalism conventionally embraces the products and experiences that give substance and positive value to everyday life (Fürsich, 2012). Green lifestyle journalism can replicate this orientation, and there can be a lifestyle cachet associated with sustainability, but often, there is also an underlying critical engagement with the commercial and commodity contexts of modern life that are the cause of environmental damage. Such distinctions are more broadly based upon traditional evaluative frameworks for journalism that privilege and separate the public sphere over the private sphere and the 'rationality' of public affairs over the emotion and pleasures of domestic life (Craig, 2016). Such frameworks, however, are problematic, and this is strongly apparent in green lifestyle journalism, where the political character of everyday life is highlighted, where consumers consider the ethical and civic dimensions of their everyday practices, and where the pleasures and aesthetics of quotidian existence co-exist with a global environmental consciousness. While conventional forms of journalism may sometimes struggle with where and how to report on the sustainable character of everyday life, they are, nonetheless, the sites where the meanings of green lifestyles are represented and contested, bearing witness to Hartley's (1996, p. 33, original emphasis) claim that "journalism is *the* sense-making practice of modernity."

Types of green lifestyle journalism

Green lifestyle journalism operates at the fault-lines of journalistic structural organisation of the news, and the personal environmental concerns of green lifestyle journalism are also manifested across a range of media genres and texts, sometimes extending beyond familiar forms of journalism. In terms of content, green lifestyle journalism more readily replicates the content of lifestyle journalism more generally, except that it has an environmental and sustainability focus. As such, green lifestyle journalism can cover issues relating to gardening, food and cooking, domestic energy and waste, household appliances and technology, shopping, transport and travel, fashion, leisure activities and house-building and renovation.

As a form of lifestyle journalism, green lifestyle journalism is usually assigned as a form of 'soft news,' a broad classificatory term that also incorporates human interest stories, celebrity and entertainment news, and other forms of information relating to the private sphere (Reinemann, Stanyer, Scherr & Legnante, 2012). The contrast between 'soft news' and the 'hard news' of politics, international relations, business, and public affairs carries with it the kind of evaluative framework of the news that has already been identified. It suggests how a perceived lack of significance of everyday environmentalism is coded in the very structure and presentation of the news, even though there has been growing recognition in recent decades of the public and political significance of issues relating to other topics such as domestic relationships and parenting, fitness and diet, and forms of personal identity (Lehman-Wilzig & Seletzky, 2010). While green lifestyle journalism battles against the noted structural organisation of the news, it is also the case that green lifestyle journalism can benefit from the news value of 'composition,' where its distinctive and personal story type can provide greater diversity and balance in daily news schedules. The perceived relevance of green lifestyle journalism to a general audience does also, to some degree, render such stories newsworthy, particularly as the effects of the climate emergency increasingly impinge on citizens. After cyclone Gabrielle damaged the city of Auckland, New Zealand, in early 2023, there have been news stories about a range of lifestyle topics, such as changing daily transport practices and food production and consumption (see, for example, Mathias, 2024). The concerns of green lifestyle journalism in this sense are not singularly contained in particular news sections. In an analysis of environmental lifestyle reportage in U.K. newspapers, I have previously (Craig, 2019) identified the ways in which environmental stories relating to the politics and public policy contexts of climate change and sustainability often embed discussion within the stories about the ramifications such issues will have for individual lifestyles.

Green lifestyle journalism can appear across a range of journalistic forms. While the 'hard news' relevance of green lifestyle stories occasionally surfaces in response to changing circumstances for citizens, green lifestyle stories more conventionally appear in other sections of the news. In print and online news publications, such stories are located in newspaper supplements or online sections relating to consumer living. Such supplements contain different kinds of textual components, including reviews, feature stories, and regular columns, and the stories in these supplements derive value from their timely relevance – the latest trend or product range release. The consumer-oriented character of supplements is an important way for news companies to attract advertising, and the green lifestyle journalism in supplements often 'co-exists' with such commercialised contexts. Columns have been prominent means by which green lifestyle issues are discussed in supplements. The foregrounded and regular presentation of the individual character of a columnist can be a useful and effective means to initiate parasocial relationships with readers, and the multitudinous 'dilemmas' of everyday sustainability are a plentiful source of regular copy ideas. Green lifestyle journalism can also be found in magazines that cover the subjects relevant to everyday sustainability, such as gardening, food, fashion, and housing. There are also magazines that focus exclusively on green living, addressing the concerns of those people who have substantively adopted green lifestyles and providing more detailed and specialist advice and information. Such magazines include *New Zealand Lifestyle Block* and in Australia, *ReNew: Technology for a Sustainable Future* and *Sanctuary: Modern Green Homes* and in the United States, *Green Living*. Such a spectrum of print and online publications attests to the breadth and complexity of green lifestyle journalism, in turn reflecting the differing investments that people are making in adopting forms of sustainable living.

In one sense, broadcast news and current affairs treat green lifestyle journalism in a similar manner to print and online journalism, with the novelty of everyday sustainability surfacing occasionally in reports relating to the climate emergency, while they are also largely excluded from serious and regular coverage in bulletins. Recent interviews I conducted with broadcast environmental journalists in Aotearoa New Zealand revealed a commitment by the journalists to highlight climate and sustainability issues and their manifestations in changing lifestyles, but there remained ongoing struggles in newsrooms to recognise the significance of such stories (Craig, 2024). That is, different types of journalism still largely fail to appreciate that the climate crisis necessitates profound and radical changes, not only to national economies but also to the ways in which people live their everyday lives. Of course, this failure can be partly attributed to indexing (Bennett, 1990), where low levels of reportage align with a lack of important public figures, notably politicians, articulating such concerns. Green lifestyle issues do, however, sometimes feature in broadcast media beyond news journalism in forms of lifestyle television formats. Generically, such programmes are entertainment, 'eco-reality' style programmes (Craig, 2010), but they do, nonetheless, provide information and advice about sustainable lifestyles. These programmes can focus on a range of issues, such as house-building and renovation, fashion, and food. Bell, Hollows, and Jones (2017) identify a genre of programmes they call "campaigning culinary documentaries" where celebrity food activists highlight issues of food sustainability. Craig (2019, p. 145), for example, notes how Hugh Fearnley–Whittingstall in *Hugh's War on Waste* replicates journalistic behaviour, researching subjects, interviewing people, and holding them to account, while also reproducing current affairs investigative journalism conventions, with direct addresses to camera before 'taking on' subjects in interviews.

Evaluating green lifestyle journalism

The outlined problematic identity of green lifestyle journalism means, not surprisingly, that any evaluation of its merits and deficiencies will be equally complex and not contained in any singular judgement. Any evaluations of green lifestyle *journalism* are also informed to some degree by assessments of the merits or otherwise of *green lifestyles*, and we need to more broadly discuss associated issues such as ethical consumption, and its ability to facilitate political agency and change, as well as issues such as commodification, class, and status.

It follows from the final discussion of the previous section that we can begin to evaluate green lifestyle journalism, and green lifestyle media more generally, by unpacking its status as a form of both information and entertainment. Green lifestyle journalism is always informative, providing details about sustainable living and assessing how effective and pleasurable are such forms and features of sustainable living. As Craig (2019, pp. 49–53) has previously discussed, a core function of green lifestyle journalism is not only the provision of information but also the subsequent governance of media consumers, with the promotion of appropriate value systems and patterns of behaviour. While green lifestyle journalism can sometimes critique features of sustainability, it is fundamentally informed by the task of conveying the desirability and positive necessity of living in ways that ameliorate environmental damage. Green lifestyle journalism, as with lifestyle journalism more generally, is, however, also often presented as a form of entertainment to the extent that it is designed to be 'appealing' to media consumers, manifested across a variety of forms of media, and usually differentiated from conventional hard news sections. The assignation of 'entertainment' journalism and media carries with it negative connotations (Ekström, 2000, p. 46) because it is deemed to be composed of 'superficial' content and to provide audiences with what they 'want' rather than what they 'need,' driven by the economic interests of media producers. Such views, however, need to be countered with acknowledgments that entertainment media are also sites where social values, identities, and issues are presented, offering contexts of public understanding and evolving evaluative negotiations of such values, identities, and issues (Curran, 2011). Nonetheless, we again find that green lifestyle journalism can suffer from such evaluative frameworks, with perceptions that it is a lesser form of entertainment because it is deemed to be 'worthy' content and less significant as a source of information because of its 'popular' orientation.

Green lifestyle journalism covers the full range of sustainability and can consider forms of production and distribution, such as electricity generation, fruit and vegetable growing, and food miles, but it is predominantly associated with reportage on the practices of everyday *consumption*. As Binkley and Littler (2011, p. 7) have noted, there is a distinction between consuming less in anti-consumption and consuming differently in anti-consumerism, but regardless of our critical orientation towards the consumer society, consumption is a necessary feature of everyday existence. Green lifestyles are associated with types of *ethical* consumption to the extent that contemporary lifestyles, as already noted, are largely defined by, and generate meaning through, engagements with the consumer society. Ethical consumption can occur through a variety of ways: through the purchase of Fair Trade and other environmentally certified products, the patronage of farmers' markets, and the buying of organic produce and 'eco-friendly' products. Of course, many such forms of ethical consumption are predicated not only on an awareness of the product's environmental benefits but also on the labour that has gone into the making of the product. Ethical consumption recognises that every individual purchasing choice we make has an ethical basis and collectively that consumption patterns can influence levels and trends of market production.

The increased popularity of ethical consumption over recent decades derives from knowledge about both the *unethical* basis of capitalist production and the *unsustainability* of consumption levels across the modern Western world. The growth of different types of ethical consumption has meant it has become less socially marginalised, and it should also be recognised that political agency can be expressed through consumption patterns, and the more general exercise of a particular lifestyle. In this sense, consumption can be understood not as a passive phenomenon but as an active practice of engaging with the 'stuff' of the world, through which we embody and express our values and identities. This understanding of ethical consumption informs much green lifestyle journalism with appeals to the ways such practices not only contribute to healthier, happier, and more fulfilled selves, but they are also the 'right' thing to do, and they are a small part of social change.

Green lifestyle journalism, and the ethical consumption it promotes, can be critiqued, nonetheless, on several different grounds, including (a) its commercial character, (b) its individual orientation, (c) its reproduction of class distinctions, and (d) its emphasis on consumption over production.

a While green lifestyle journalism can interrogate the commercial culture which plays such an important role in animating contemporary capitalism, it is undeniable that it often supports the commercial interests of both the news organisations that produce the journalism and the companies that produce the products that are deemed to be environmentally friendly. It has already been noted that green lifestyle journalism is often an advertiser-friendly type of journalism, and its frequent placement in media outputs and sections where commodities and commodification are highlighted means that it plays a role in reproducing and 'naturalising' commercial culture. Equally, green lifestyle journalism can contribute to processes of 'greenwashing' by inadvertently promoting the false, inaccurate, or incomplete claims of companies about the environmental merits of their products (Nemes et al., 2022).

b Green lifestyle journalism, and ethical consumption more generally, can be criticised because its primary tendency to address consumers *individualises* what is a *structural* problem for society. As has been discussed, individual lifestyles have significance as a form of identity production that facilitates the circulation of cultural values, yet it is also the case that such contemporary lifestyles exist within *neoliberal* societies that shift the responsibility of political, social, and corporate problems onto individual citizens and consumers. In neoliberalism, there is a belief in limiting the role of the State and promoting market mechanisms and, as such, there is a prioritisation of the individual as an economic agent to bear social costs (Hay, 2004). Addressing the climate emergency and greater levels of sustainability are said to be sourced, then, from market mechanisms, such as emission trading schemes, and the individual actions of corporate actors and consumers.

c Another critique that is levelled against green lifestyle journalism, and ethical consumption more generally, is that it reproduces middle-class values (Guthman, 2003). 'Ethical' products usually cost more precisely because they are sourced from materials that are less environmentally damaging and they seek to address labour and production inequities, and so they are usually more expensive, and thus patronised by people who are more able to pay a premium for a product. 'Cost,' and an accompanying cultural cachet, thus becomes aligned with the ethics of sustainable consumption, and subsequently a source of class division. The ideological outcome is that a just and sustainable cost of a product becomes a means to perpetuate class inequalities in capitalistic societies and undermine broader uptakes of environmentally friendly products.

d Finally, green lifestyle journalism can be said to primarily locate the site of political agency in acts of *consumption* rather than the forces of *production*. While ethical consumption legitimately and importantly emphasises the political status of acts of consumption, complicating the subject binary of citizens and consumers, this can also be at the expense of the political capacities of individuals in other spheres, such as the workplace and the community (Humphery, 2010).

Green lifestyle media research and the future of green lifestyle journalism

As this volume attests, there is now a burgeoning research profile for lifestyle journalism, building on important work that has been conducted over the past decade or so (From, 2018; Fürsich, 2012; Hanusch, 2012). Such research has given us an appreciation of this often-overlooked form of journalism as well as the political and cultural significance of lifestyles as vehicles of change and as instruments in the political economy of the media. It is difficult though to provide an overview of specific research on green lifestyle journalism because there is not yet a sustained and coherent body of work. Nonetheless, we can note the range of research that has been conducted more broadly on media and everyday sustainability, and this, in turn, provides insights into the diverse ways green lifestyles are presented across media, and the fundamental difficulty journalism has with the task of considering green lifestyles as a critical and newsworthy subject. Such discussion is necessary because, as already stated, the climate emergency is clearly demonstrating that there is an urgent need to not only reorientate our economies and societies but also our everyday lives.

While green lifestyle journalism has an uncertain and variable presence in news media, it is the case that everyday responses to environmental challenges are manifested across different types of media. We have seen, for example, increases in the 'green' profiles of consumer products, with resulting growth in forms of green advertising, and this has attracted research interest (Banerjee, Gulas & Iyer, 1995; Sheehan & Atkinson, 2012). Green advertising can accompany green lifestyle journalism within a media text, and sometimes the advertised products can *themselves* be subject to green lifestyle journalism stories. It has been previously noted how some green lifestyle supplements retain their presence because of their ability to attract particular forms of advertising (Craig, 2019, pp. 41–42). These general commercial contexts, including processes of greenwashing, highlight the ways in which green lifestyle journalism can be implicated in the consumer society, and sometimes substantially compromised by business imperatives.

Another manifestation of the concerns of green lifestyle journalism can be found in 'green blogging.' Blogging as a type of media lends itself to individual reflections on a given topic, and Joosse and Brydges (2018) found a concentration on the individual as "the location of change for the environment" (2018, p. 697) in the green blogs they analysed, replicating the individual focus of much green lifestyle journalism. While Joose and Brydges discuss the dangers of such an individual focus distracting from more substantive structural causes of environmental damage, their study "demonstrates that while blogs may promote sustainability as consumerism, … they also cater to individual practices that can fundamentally redefine consumption" (2018, p. 697). As such, the research supports arguments that such forms of green media can implement a critical reflexivity towards consumerism.

Green lifestyles have perhaps been chiefly subject to media representation through forms of lifestyle television, and this has corresponded with a body of research over the past decade or so (Bell & Hollows, 2011; Hollows & Jones, 2010; Bell, Hollows & Jones, 2017; Craig, 2010, 2019, 2020; Lewis, 2008; Thomas, 2011), and this research followed earlier work on lifestyle television (Bonner, 2003; Brunsdon, 2003; Taylor, 2002). These forms of green lifestyle television programmes have taken on a variety of formats, including variations on the 'makeover' genre of more general forms of lifestyle television (Craig, 2010), and, as Bell, Hollows, and Jones (2017) have noted, in more recent years, more explicitly 'political,' eco-style documentaries have emerged that often feature prominent celebrity chefs who have assumed food activist profiles. This body of research has explored issues such as the class politics of green consumption (Bell & Hollows, 2011), the affect and agency informing alternative food communities and cultures (Parkins & Craig, 2009), the 'individualisation' of ethical consumption and forms of cultural governance (Hollows & Jones, 2010), the cultural power of celebrities (Craig, 2019), and the political economy of global food production, distribution, and consumption, including the roles of supermarket chains (Lewis & Huber, 2015). Such a list of issues attests to the complexity and comprehensiveness of these types of programmes, and their frequency and popularity suggests they are a televisual genre that blends entertainment and issues relating to environmentally friendly lifestyles in a relatively successful manner.

In contrast, forms of green lifestyle journalism have been less prominent across different types of news media with correspondingly more muted research investigation. The climate emergency has resulted in an impressive growth in research that explores how climate change and the environment is reported by journalists (see, for example, Boykoff, 2011; Hammond, 2018; Hansen, 2019; Painter, 2013), but such studies usually focus on politics and public policy contexts, and not on everyday responses. The contrast between green lifestyle television and forms of green lifestyle journalism is highlighted by a recent study that examines news media coverage across three different nations. It demonstrates how food, for all its cultural significance and relevance to climate change, "rarely becomes the focus of news coverage" and also that it is "not framed as a social problem" (Brüggemann, Kunert, & Sprengelmeyer, 2022, p. 18). Craig's (2019) discussion of green lifestyle journalism focuses on the roles of such journalism in the lifestyle supplements of British newspapers, and he also attempts to broaden the recognition of green lifestyle journalism, drawing attention to the ways that news stories "about emergent climate change issues are increasingly linked with the need for lifestyle change" (2019, p. 64). The research revealed that the politically conservative newspapers contained the greatest amounts of green lifestyle reportage, but this was explained by the negative framing of the stories, promoting "perceived hypocrisies associated with sustainability or difficulties associated with the implementation of policies and practices associated with greater sustainability" (Craig, 2019, p. 67). As such, it can be noted that not only is there a general journalistic difficulty in thematising green lifestyles in conventional news discourse, but also green lifestyles are frequently treated critically when they are reported, often due to the ideological leanings of the publication. Craig's research of environmental lifestyle reportage in the British weekend supplements reveals a more positive orientation towards green lifestyles, although often such articles involve "the posing of everyday environmental dilemmas that posits a reader who, while motivated to live in a sustainable manner, is positioned as lacking in knowledge about how to do so, and possessing emotions of anxiety, uncertainty, and fear" (2019, p. 76).

This discussion suggests that green lifestyles are represented at different levels and in different ways across various types of media, and that they receive more attention in media texts that are more entertainment-oriented, while conventional news journalism struggles with reportage of everyday sustainability. It can be speculated that green lifestyles have assumed a greater presence in television programmes because the genre of lifestyle television facilitates both an individual and domestic context and an emotional and dramatic landscape where the pleasures and struggles of sustainable living can be effectively represented. The discussion suggests that green lifestyles have an explicit presence in news journalism to the extent to which they can attract advertising, and this commercial context challenges how effective green lifestyle journalism can be in direct challenges to the consumer society. It is also difficult for green lifestyles to have a prominent place in news discourse when the climate emergency is framed primarily as a macro-political, scientific, and technological phenomenon and when everyday sustainability is not articulated in the discourse of primary political actors (Hammond, 2018).

At the same time, the increasingly evident impacts that the climate emergency is having on the everyday lives of people around the world suggest that green lifestyle journalism may well have a greater presence in future journalism formats, and such a scenario prompts questions about what is required for this form of journalism to flourish. Parham identifies the need for both broader cultural conduciveness to environmentalism and strategies to intervene in the culture of more general environmental reportage (2015, pp. 106–107). While there may be an already-growing mainstream awareness and acceptance of the need for everyday sustainability and that a 'conduciveness to environmentalism' will be eventually forced on cultures by climatic circumstances, it is also the case that green lifestyles suffer primarily from their negative framing in news media, always defined against a 'normal' consumer existence, and characterised primarily in terms of obligation, sacrifice, and cost. In response, Craig (2016) has previously argued for the need to reframe quotidian pleasures in accordance with an environmental consciousness. More generally, it has been noted (see Parham, 2015, p. 20) that contemporary Western culture is informed by 'contradictory desires,' with love for nature co-existing with a rampant consumerism. Journalism, through its categorisation of news, and popular media more generally, allows for that contradiction not to be interrogated sufficiently. We do see, though, in the noted successes of green lifestyle television the dramatic potential that resides from individuals wrestling with the dilemmas and rewards of everyday sustainability, and perhaps this could be incorporated more into other journalistic formats. Journalists, too, can exercise their agency in the promotion of green lifestyles. Recent research has noted the ways that lifestyle journalists can enhance and enrich their reportage, moving beyond simple recognitions of trends, experiences, and products to more contextual, 'sense-making' journalism within a more positive orientation (Faramarzi, 2019; Viererbl, 2022).

Conclusion

This chapter has outlined the main features of green lifestyle journalism, highlighting its complex character and its often-problematic status within news organisations. This identity makes it an interesting subject of study, revealing structural divisions across society and newsrooms that reproduce fundamental contradictions or tensions that are only becoming increasingly apparent as the climate emergency intensifies. The discussion has noted that the complexity of green lifestyle journalism derives partly from the discursive multi-accentuality circulating around 'green' and 'lifestyle' identity, values, and behaviour. Another complexity of green lifestyle journalism is its different manifestations in different sections of the news and also across various forms of media, serving both informational and entertainment functions. It has been illustrated how green lifestyle journalism prompts consideration of issues such as the political efficacy of consumption, the class status of lifestyles, and the commercial nature of news media.

This chapter has provided discussion of some of the research that has been conducted around the broad terrain of green lifestyle media, but it has also noted that more research is required, and it is suggested that our future understandings of green lifestyle journalism would benefit from a greater input from scholars across a broad range of academic disciplines, such as journalism, media and communications, sociology, environmental humanities, and relevant lifestyle-related subjects, such as food, travel and tourism, transport, fashion, and energy. As suggested in this chapter, future research could explore in more detail the ways in which green lifestyles are invoked and represented across different news genres, including hard news stories about climate change. Equally, more research could be conducted on specific green living magazines and the discourses of expertise that are articulated in such publications. More substantively, the issues that have been discussed in this chapter suggest the need to investigate restructurings of the categories of news and the practices of journalism in ways that foreground the climate crisis and sustainability across domains of public and private life (Berglez, Olausson & Ots, 2017). Green lifestyle journalism highlights the way that individual lifestyle activities have – and have always had – social and environmental consequences, and it reflects poorly on journalism that it has largely been structurally incapable of interrogating this phenomenon of everyday existence. It is hoped that this chapter, and associated research, prompts realisations that such an incapacity is no longer 'sustainable' as societies wrestle with how we should live our everyday lives in a rapidly changing world.

Further reading

Berglez, P., Olausson, U., & Ots, M. (Eds.) (2017). *What is sustainable journalism? Integrating the environmental, social, and economic challenges of journalism.* Peter Lang.
Craig, G. (2019). *Media, sustainability and everyday life.* Palgrave Macmillan.
Parham, J. (2015). *Green media and popular culture: An introduction.* Bloomsbury Academic.

References

Banerjee, S., Gulas, C. S., & Iyer, E. (1995). Shades of green: A multidimensional analysis of environmental advertising. *Journal of Advertising*, 24(2), 21–31.
Bell, D., & Hollows, J. (2011). From *River Cottage* to *Chicken Run*: Hugh Fearnley-Whittingstall and the class politics of ethical consumption. *Celebrity Studies*, 2, 178–191.
Bell, D., Hollows, J., & Jones, S. (2017). Campaigning culinary documentaries and the responsibilization of food crises. *Geoforum*, 84, 179–187.
Bennett, W. L. (1990). Toward a theory of press-state relations in the United States. *Journal of Communication*, 40(2), 103–125.
Berglez, P., Olausson, U., & Ots, M. (Eds.) (2017). *What is sustainable journalism? Integrating the environmental, social, and economic challenges of journalism.* Peter Lang.
Binkley, S., & Littler, J. (2011). Introduction: Cultural studies and anti-consumerism: A critical encounter. In S. Binkley & J. Littler (Eds.), *Cultural studies and anti-consumerism: A critical encounter*, (pp. 1–12). Routledge.
Bonner, F. (2003). *Ordinary television: Analysing popular* TV. Sage.
Boykoff, M. T. (2011). *Who speaks for the climate? Making sense of media reporting on climate change*. Cambridge University Press.
Brüggemann, M., Kunert, J., & Sprengelmeyer, L. (2022). Framing food in the news: Still keeping the politics out of the broccoli. *Journalism Practice*, 18(10), 2712–2734. https://doi.org/10.1080/17512786.2022.2153074
Brunsdon, C. (2003). Lifestyling Britain: The 8–9 slot on British television. *International Journal of Cultural Studies*, 6(1), 5–23.

Chaney, D. (1996). *Lifestyles*. Routledge.
Craig, G. (2010). Everyday epiphanies: Environmental networks in eco-makeover lifestyle television." *Environmental Communication*, 4, 172–189.
Craig, G. (2016). Political participation and pleasure in green lifestyle journalism. *Environmental Communication*, 10(1), 122–141. https://doi.org/10.1080/17524032.2014.991412
Craig, G. (2019). *Media, sustainability and everyday life*. Palgrave Macmillan.
Craig, G. (2020). Representations of sustainability and environmental welfare in *Country Calendar*. *Communication Research and Practice*, 6(3), 176–190. https://doi.org/10.1080/22041451.2020.1785191
Craig, G. (2024). Aotearoa New Zealand climate and environmental journalists: Profiles, practices, and perspectives. *Journalism and Media*, 5(1), 108–122. https://doi.org/10.3390/journalmedia5010008
Curran, J. (2011). *Media and democracy*. Routledge.
Ekström, M. (2000). Information, storytelling and attractions: TV journalism in three modes of communication. *Media, Culture & Society*, 22, 465–492.
Faramarzi, S. (2019). Agents of change. The parallel roles of trend forecasters and lifestyle journalists as mediators and tastemakers of consumer culture. In L. Vodanovic (Ed.), *Lifestyle journalism. Social media, consumption and experience* (pp. 38–50). Routledge.
Featherstone, M. (1991). *Consumer culture and postmodernism*. Sage.
From, U. (2018). Lifestyle journalism. In M. Powers (Ed.), *Oxford research encyclopedia of communication*. Oxford University Press. https://doi.org/10.1093/acrefore/9780190228613.013.835.
Fürsich, E. (2012). Lifestyle journalism as popular journalism. *Journalism Practice*, 6(1), 12–25. https://doi.org/10.1080/17512786.2011.622894
Guthman, J. (2003). Fast food/organic food: Reflexive tastes and the making of 'yuppie chow'. *Social and Cultural Geography*, 4(1), 45–58.
Hammond, P. (2018). *Climate change and post-political communication: Media, emotion and environmental advocacy*. Routledge.
Hansen, A. (2019). *Environment, media and communication*. 2nd Edition. Routledge.
Hanusch, F. (2012). Broadening the focus: The case for lifestyle journalism as a field of scholarly inquiry. *Journalism Practice*, 6(1), 2–11. https://doi.org/10.1080/17512786.2011.622895
Hartley, J. (1996). *Popular reality: Journalism, modernity, popular culture*. Arnold.
Hay, C. (2004). The normalizing role of rationalist assumptions in the institutional embedding of neoliberalism. *Economy & Society*, 33(4), 500–527.
Hollows, J., & Jones, S. (2010). 'At least he's doing something': Moral entrepreneurship and individual responsibility in Jamie's *Ministry of Food*. *European Journal of Cultural Studies*, 13, 307–322.
Humphery, K. (2010). *Excess: Anti-consumerism in the West*. Polity.
Joosse, S., & Brydges, T. (2018). Blogging for sustainability: The intermediary role of personal green blogs in promoting sustainability. *Environmental Communication*, 12(5), 686–700.
Leach, M. (2015). What is Green? Transformation imperatives and knowledge politics. In I. Scoones, M. Leach & P. Newell (Eds.), *The politics of green transformations* (pp. 25–38). Routledge.
Lehman-Wilzig, S. N., & Seletzky, M. (2010). Hard news, soft news, 'general' news: The necessity and utility of an intermediate classification. *Journalism*, 11, 37–56.
Lewis, T. (2008). Transforming citizens? Green politics and ethical consumption on lifestyle television. *Continuum*, 22, 227–240.
Lewis, T., & Huber, A. (2015). A revolution in an Eggcup? Supermarket wars, celebrity chefs and ethical consumption. *Food, Culture & Society*, 18(2), 289–307.
Mathias, S. (2024, March 20). If there was a disaster next week, where would you go for food? *The Spinoff*. Retrieved from https://thespinoff.co.nz/kai/20-03-2024/if-there-was-a-disaster-next-week-where-would-you-go-for-food.
Nemes, N., Scanlan, S., Smith, P., Smith, T., Aronczyk, M., Hill, S., Lewis, S.L., Montgomery, A.W., Tubiello, F.N., & Stabinsky, D. (2022). An integrated framework to assess greenwashing. *Sustainability*, 14(8), 4431. https://doi.org/10.3390/su14084431.
Painter, J. (2013). *Climate change in the media: Reporting risk and uncertainty*. I. B. Tauris.
Parham, J. (2015). *Green media and popular culture: An introduction*. Bloomsbury Academic.
Parkins, W., & Craig, G. (2009). Culture and the politics of alternative food networks. *Food, Culture & Society*, 12(1), 77–103.

Peattie, K., & Crane, A. (2005). Green marketing: legend, myth, farce or prophesy? *Qualitative Market Research: An International Journal, 8*(4), 357–370.

Reinemann, C., Stanyer, J., Scherr, S., & Legnante, G. (2012). Hard and soft news: A review of concepts, operationalizations and key findings. *Journalism, 13*(2), 221–239.

Sheehan, K., & Atkinson, L. (2012). Special Issue on Green Advertising. *Journal of Advertising 41*(4), 5–7.

Soper, K. (1995). *What is nature? Culture, politics, and the non-human.* Blackwell.

Taylor, L. (2002). From ways of life to lifestyle: The 'ordinari-ization' of British gardening lifestyle television. *European Journal of Communication, 17*(4), 479–493.

Thomas, L. (2011). 'Ecoreality': The politics and aesthetics of 'green' television. In G. Palmer (Ed.), *Exposing lifestyle television: The big reveal* (pp. 177–188). Routledge.

Viererbl, B. (2022). Writing for the audience or for public relations? How lifestyle editors perceive expectations about their professional role and manage potential for conflict. *Journalism, 24*(7), 1593–1609. https://doi:10.1177/14648849211067586

21
LIFESTYLE JOURNALISM PRACTICES IN HARD NEWS

Dismantling the hard news versus soft news binary

Gregory P. Perreault and Ella Hackett

Introduction

When Hadley Freedmen took her first job on *The Guardian's* fashion desk, she thought she'd found a dream position. It was only after she moved to reporting on other niches in the newsroom that she gained an appreciation for how lifestyle journalism was perceived. In a commentary, Freedman (2016) described reading the negative comments on her job applications, which routinely would focus on her first job – overlooking so much of her other work – as evidence that her work in journalism wasn't "serious." Comments often tended to be harsh, with commenters wondering if she had simply been inspired by the *Spotlight* movie or whether she might rather spend her days looking at shoes. She found the negativity both unexpected and unwarranted. As she put it:

> When, earlier this month, *The Guardian* looked at which kinds of journalism attract the most blocked comments, fashion was number one – more than world news – proving definitively that readers find dresses more upsetting than, say, the Israeli-Palestinian conflict...One of the reasons I loved writing about fashion is that there was always something new to write about. There were its flaws, for sure...But there was also the way it bled into so many other things: photography, music, art. Most of all, I loved to write about the way people–from teenagers on a Saturday afternoon to politicians–use fashion to send a message about themselves.
> *(Freedman, 2016, n.p.)*

Freedman (2016) isn't alone in seeing the significant reporting being done in 'soft news' areas such as fashion. Often described in scholarship as part of *lifestyle journalism*, fashion journalism is regularly grouped in with other lifestyle areas such as travel (Hanusch, 2010), gaming (Perreault & Vos, 2018), and sport (Perreault & Nölleke, 2022). The research in lifestyle journalism has centered around four key themes: commercial and consumerist aspects, representations and notions of identity, democratizing elements of lifestyle journalism, and the political and critical dimensions of the subfield (Hanusch, 2018). Studies show that lifestyle journalists aim to entertain, inspire, provide advice, act as service providers, community advocates, friends, or connectors (Hanusch, 2019; Hanusch & Hanitzsch, 2013; Hanitzsch & Vos, 2018). But in a similar way, and to the point of this chapter, it is also worth considering the "soft" work conducted in hard news: work which would naturally trouble existing dichotomy and which, for understandable reasons, hard news journalists would in many cases consciously object to (Reinemann et al., 2012).

After all, lifestyle journalism is often viewed as less substantial than hard news specialties, such as political journalism (Fürsich, 2012). Due to its association with commercial interests, lifestyle journalism is considered a specialty with a "soft boundary". This soft boundary raises questions about journalistic independence, while simultaneously allowing adaptability to navigate the challenges posed by the digital turn in journalism (Perreault & Hanusch, 2024a p. 3769).

This chapter aims to explore the *lifestyle* work of hard news and to trouble the – at times – almost binary distinction between *hard news* and *soft news*. In particular, we highlight two areas that are at the core of lifestyle journalism work and reflect on the ways in which they also appear in hard news specialties: practices aimed at social cohesion and a commitment to the audience. In this way, the chapter aims to push for a reconsideration of the democratic contributions of lifestyle and the valuable lifestyle practices in hard news.

Theoretical perspectives: Lifestyle journalism as soft news

Boundary work and lifestyle

The binaries between lifestyle journalism and hard news specialties are rooted in a core discussion within journalism studies theory that is related to journalistic boundaries. Boundary work in journalism refers to the efforts made by journalists to differentiate between appropriate and inappropriate practices, as well as valid and invalid sources – this discourse highlights how professionals within the field consistently define and redefine the acceptable norms through their interpretive efforts (Carlson, 2015; Gieryn, 1983). Hence, within journalism, boundary work often involves debates among journalists to determine the appropriate classification of certain activities, whether they fit within journalism, and then, additionally, where these activities fit within journalism. Certain activities, such as verification, exist at the core of the profession, while others, such as personal branding, exist further from the core of the profession (Molyneux, 2019). This occurs through three different mechanisms of boundary work: expansion (i.e., extending boundaries of the acceptable beyond the previously demarcated), expulsion (i.e., repositioning a problematic element outside of the boundaries of journalism), or protection of autonomy (i.e., a negotiated position which would defend core journalism norms from ill-fitted actors or boundaries) (Gieryn, 1983). These play out in research on the gray areas between hard news and soft news, in relation to debates regarding distinctions such as professional versus amateur, producer versus user, and journalist versus non-journalist. These distinctions are continuously evolving. These delineations influence both the production and consumption of news, underscoring that boundaries are not fixed but are constructed through discourse (Carlson & Berkowitz, 2014).

To this end, Banjac and Hanusch found that lifestyle journalists often feel "self-othered and self-expelled" from the boundaries of journalism (Banjac & Hanusch, 2022, p. 8). Placement of specialties and activities are often drawn in relation to perceived pressure and influence from actors outside of journalism's boundaries. In this way, lifestyle journalism is often criticized for being excessively uncritical and heavily influenced by external pressures, particularly those originating from public relations and advertising (Perreault & Vos, 2018). Some journalists have demonstrated that lifestyle journalism has a *soft* boundary, which allows lifestyle journalism to be adaptable and to draw from innovation in other fields (Perreault & Hanusch, 2022), but this also means that lifestyle has frequently been critiqued for allowing such an influence. Hence, through the lens of boundary work, lifestyle journalism could be perceived as existing close to the field's boundaries, where there is some possibility of having certain activities perceived as "outside" of the norms of the profession. Such activities would include the acceptance of free items or perks, such as gifts or promotional materials, by lifestyle journalists, which can compromise their objectivity and independence (Perreault & Vos, 2020) (see also Chapter 23). Lifestyle journalists also typically reflect emotional investment in their topic and often personally engage or advocate on the part of a specific issue (Perreault & Bélair-Gagnon, 2024). Hence, lifestyle journalists unsurprisingly also believe that political journalists view lifestyle reporting as less serious, unimportant, having an insignificant influence, and being done by people who are not real journalists (Banjac & Hanusch, 2022).

This points toward boundary work as a theoretical lens that would largely premise on placing lifestyle reporting on the boundaries of journalism and hard news safely within it. This theoretical lens allows for generative work considering the tensions that could occur in using practices more accustomed to the margins, when a specialty is at the core.

Field theory in lifestyle journalism

Conversant with boundary work, field theory is a framework developed by French sociologist Pierre Bourdieu that aimed at envisioning professional landscapes as a field. Within the field, orthodox perspectives on the journalistic profession are often favored, which would place dominant hard news actors at the core of the field (Perreault, Kananovich & Hackett, 2023) with privileged access to resources of the field or *capital*. These forms of capital include economic capital (e.g., financial resources), social capital (e.g., audience), cultural capital (e.g., awards), and symbolic capital (e.g., newsroom recognition).

Field theory research in lifestyle journalism has found that lifestyle journalists discursively center the work of political journalism by attributing to it the role of safeguarding human lives, while asserting that political journalists also encountered more substantial safety risks (Broussard, 2020).

Lifestyle was seen as a broad term encompassing various genres, which – in a similar vein to boundary work – pushes the specialty from the core to the *periphery* of the field (Banjac & Hanusch, 2022). That said, lifestyle journalism has historically had strong access to economic capital within the field (Perreault et al., 2024), which perhaps explains why hard news journalists have at times leaned on the norms and processes of lifestyle journalism (Perreault & Stanfield, 2019). Conversely, some lifestyle journalists have worked to obtain other forms of capital by taking a *hard news approach* to covering soft news. In doing this, they felt they had reasserted their influence and participated in the process of 'capitalization' by incorporating value into their work, as well as fulfilling their entertainer role while making sure that the content is informative (Banjac & Hanusch, 2022). Through the lens of field theory, lifestyle journalists would seem to have an *illusio* centered on the expectation of passion within their work (Perreault & Bélair-Gagnon, 2024). The passion for their work is a centralizing trait of lifestyle journalists, and it allows them to work beyond their capabilities within their niche. While their personal identity is a driving force in their placement within the field, they are also driven by institutional expectations such as the need to be available and adaptable. In other words, although lifestyle journalists see institutional expectations as drivers for producing higher-quality work, they also see them as a hindrance in pursuing work–life balance (Perreault & Bélair-Gagnon, 2024).

Lifestyle journalism's access to economic capital and social capital – reflected in lifestyle's strong economic position and strong access to audiences (Hanusch & Hanitzsch, 2013; Hanusch, 2019; Perreault et al., 2023) – has proven valuable for the journalistic field as a whole, with lifestyle specialties sharing access to economic capital in return for recognition for the symbolic capital reflected in newsroom recognition. They also think it is important to focus on positive stories and delivering content that is enjoyable, giving the audience a break from the negative news often disseminated by political journalists, ultimately working to engage audiences, who typically avoid news all together, with political issues in an entertaining way (Banjac & Hanusch, 2022).

From the standpoint of *doxa*, or the knowledge of how to play on the field, lifestyle would seem to also have generative opportunities in regards to its expressive principles and customs that contribute to the formation and representation of a distinct identity in the context of consumerism and daily life (Hanusch & Hanitzsch, 2013). Covering topics like travel, gaming, fashion, and sport would seem to offer a doxa that privileges particular modes of reporting compared to traditional reporting. Scholarly perspectives vary when it comes to defining the distinctions between these categories; however, Reinemann et al. (2016) identified topic, production process, news focus, news presentation, and audience effect as the key dimensions of the hard and soft news distinction. With these distinctions in mind, soft news has been defined as slow, personalized, and visually orienting and places more emphasis on giving advice, entertainment, inspiration, and guidance (Banjac & Hanusch, 2022; Perreault & Bélair-Gagnon, 2024).

Scholars generally view the proliferation of soft news in hard news spaces as unfavorable, given that it would run against traditional *doxa* for the field (Nguyen, 2015; Plasser, 2005; Zhu & Fu, 2024). Political journalists, for example, do not tend to accept or approve of individuals who combine the roles of socialite and journalist (Banjac & Hanusch, 2022) and in general tend to disapprove of such *mixed* practices in lifestyle, which they see as mere attempts to boost readership or audience numbers through sensational or attention-grabbing tactics (Whipple, 2025). All of this together reflects the degree to which field theory – as a part of conceptualizing journalism as an overall field – offers generative potential for lifestyle journalism as a subfield.

Feminist theories of lifestyle

Feminist theories serve as critical tools in understanding and addressing gender inequalities across various spheres. These theories delve into the origins and ongoing manifestations of women's systematic undervaluation in society (Steeves, 1987). Since the gender system is socially constructed, media concerns hold significant importance within feminism, with a considerable portion of feminist discourse revolving around media-related controversies (Steiner, 2014). Steiner (2014) argues that feminist media theory "applies philosophies, concepts, and logics articulating feminist principles and concepts to media processes such as hiring, production, and distribution; to patterns of representation in news and entertainment across platforms; and to reception" (Steiner, 2014, p. 359). Such feminist media studies apply regardless of whether the media content itself aligns with feminist beliefs, and when applied to the realm of news media, feminist perspectives shed light on how gender biases permeate coverage (Steeves, 1987), especially in topics that are gendered in nature. In this way, feminist media theory considers gender as a fundamental element shaping identity and experiences (Steiner, 2014).

A gendered hierarchy persists within this hard-soft news binary: hard news is often defined as factual and significant reporting of newsworthy events that usually focus on topics such as matters of public concern (Baum, 2003), politics, economics, and crimes; necessitates prompt dissemination (North, 2016); and is linked to concepts of democracy and citizenship (Banjac & Hanusch, 2022). Political journalists in Banjac and Hanusch's (2022) study addressed a similar gendered discourse when voicing their perception of the role of lifestyle journalism, noting that their work was lightweight, they "have it easy," and that they weren't "changing people's lives" (p. 9). Political journalists' perceptions further relied on gendered discourse reflecting the private-public, emotionality–rationality, and soft–hard news differences.

Political journalism is thus considered the more prestigious type of journalism. Soft news, or lifestyle journalism, leans toward a private sphere and, hence, tends to be viewed as less prestigious (Meijer, 2001). It is typically associated with terminology such as human interest (van Zoonen, 1998), trends (North, 2016), opinion, emotion, intuition, nurturing, and reproduction, which are all elements indicative of a more feminine domain (Banjac & Hanusch, 2022). Gender-based assumptions about what defines 'authentic' journalism underlie the division between quality (hard news) and popular (lifestyle) journalism. Expressions of emotion are viewed as unsuitable for democratic discourse, which is expected to be rational (Kotišová & van der Velden, 2023). This in part causes "soft news" stories, or lifestyle topics, to take on a less prominent role in the news hierarchy (North, 2016). Because these topics are deemed feminine, they are often covered by female journalists, partially defining their role and ultimately invalidating the importance of female work (Ross & Carter, 2001; North, 2016; Banjac & Hanusch, 2022). Cultural feminism's explanation for the gendered binary in media roles suggests that women possess innate qualities such as communication skills, empathy, and compassion that make them well-suited for certain positions, particularly in lifestyle reporting. However, the emphasis on these inherent traits may perpetuate gender stereotypes and limit women's opportunities (Steiner, 2014). The sexual implications of the two are fairly clear as the work typically done by men sits at the top of the news hierarchy and is considered *important* work, while work typically done by women sits underneath and is considered less important (North, 2016).

To strengthen the hierarchical divisions between individuals who are part of the journalistic field and those who are not, it is necessary to employ the process of 'othering.' This term involves the degradation of "us" versus "them," where those in positions of power symbolically create and subjugate "the other" by using interconnected systems of oppression. For example, political journalists, who consider themselves the superior group (Perreault, Kananovich & Hackett, 2023), use language or symbolic markers to create distinctions that set them apart from lifestyle journalists. In response, lifestyle journalists, who are considered the marginalized or excluded group, might employ strategies of capitalization (making the most of their situation) and refusal (rejecting or resisting these hierarchical distinctions) as a way to assert themselves and challenge the dominance of the political journalists. Such traditional gender roles and perceptions influence the way the public, by extension, categorizes and understands soft and hard news, with important implications for the roles and expectations of journalists in these fields. This further demonstrates how rooted gendered stereotypes are in perceptions of lifestyle journalism's societal value.

The binary reflected here, of course, fails to acknowledge the significant contribution made by softer forms of journalism, or lifestyle journalism.

Pressures shared by hard news and lifestyle journalism

While the audience-focused, "lighter" elements of lifestyle journalism have been much discussed, it is also nevertheless true that lifestyle journalism faces many of the same cultural challenges as those faced, but not always acknowledged, by hard news journalists. These include issues of hostility, labor and market pressures.

Hostility. Much has been made in recent years of the issues of hostility that journalists face (Miller & Lewis, 2022; Miller, 2023), and while one might expect that lifestyle journalists – with their emphasis on the joyful, enriching aspects of human existence – might be able to eschew such hostility, research suggests this is not the case. Lifestyle journalists frequently experience hate and harassment, responding by disengaging from such negativity when they can (Perreault & Miller, 2022). Perreault and Miller (2022) describe journalists witnessing race and gender-based hate, aimed at the audience, and at times similar forms of hate received digitally by the journalist. Less common among Perreault and Miller's (2022) journalists were experiences of physical harassment of journalists, which in particular are received in broadcast specialties (Miller & Lewis, 2022). The normalization of abuse in journalistic work is evident, with journalists setting boundaries to manage the routine occurrence of hate. Despite the lack of organizational support, journalists develop their own rules and policies to cope with the emotional toll of hate. Lifestyle journalists report having a lack of supervisors to report incidents to, which then resulted in lifestyle journalists needing to manage the hostility alone (Perreault & Miller, 2022). In this way, lifestyle journalism and hard news would seem to have much in common: devastatingly consistent in journalism research is the finding that journalists tend to have to face hostility alone (Ivask et al., 2024; Mesmer, 2022; Miller, 2023).

But even while lifestyle journalists might be driven to disengage from hostility directed at them, they actively report on hate affecting their audience and thus fulfil their normative responsibility to inform and provide context. In Perreault and Miller (2022), for example, a reporter described covering a basketball game and, when confronted with racist signs, needing to cover the race-based hate as opposed to their original, planned story. This dichotomy reflects the hidden emotional labor of lifestyle journalists, who, while drawn to the field for its aspirational labor – the opportunity to "do what you love" (Duffy, 2017, p. 4) – must also navigate and mitigate hate, a challenge potentially more acute than in traditional hard news subfields. Lifestyle journalists, often covering topics with less experience in handling hate, may feel compelled to conceal instances of harassment to align with audience expectations that they love their work (Perreault & Miller, 2022). In Perreault and Miller's (2022) study, the authors described participants who routinely received gender- and race-based insults, but felt the need to, nevertheless, emphasize the joyful aspects in their reporting. As one participant put it:

> I think a lot of people think about lifestyle journalism as super like 'fluffy' or whatever. It can be…But that's not always the case, like for example…you're literally

writing about things like race and, you know, like, violence and like all these things happening, but you're just doing it through a more human lens so I think there's that aspect of it.

(Perreault & Miller, 2022, p. 1985)

Labor. Lifestyle journalists also manage similar labor conditions as the rest of the newsroom and, similarly, may face a labor experience potentially *more* challenging than in hard news, in that they are unable to disconnect from the work. Lifestyle journalism is often perceived as a "labor of love," reflecting the passion of journalists for soft news topics and the individuals associated with those topics (Perreault & Bélair-Gagnon, 2024, p. 5), but also – conversant with hard news – lifestyle journalists operate with the strong conviction that their work is worth doing (Powers & Vera-Zambrano, 2023). This normative commitment in lifestyle reporting would still uphold the ethical value of independence, but its manifestation differs given the subfield's stronger emphasis on audience orientation (Fürsich, 2012). It's important to recognize that journalists experience significant joy in their work, ranging from the practice of it – producing, editing, writing, and reporting on interesting people – but also in the topics they cover – lifestyle journalists, for example, would seem to spend their days embedded in topics that others would covet (Parks, 2021). Many journalists find it challenging to separate their passion from work, blurring the lines between the two (Perreault & Bélair-Gagnon, 2024, p. 14). Lifestyle journalists prefer a direct connection with their audiences, adopting the recipients' perspective and offering clear value judgments (Fürsich, 2013, p. 14). This approach is part of their conceptualization of giving *voice to the voiceless.* Journalists perceive audiences not only as citizens and consumers but also as clients actively participating in the reporting process (Skovsgaard & Bro, 2016). Despite their commitment to the audience, research suggests that journalists may not fully know their audience, potentially overlooking the potential for hate and harassment within that audience (Nelson, 2021).

Lifestyle journalists are motivated by their passion for the lifestyle niche, driving them to work beyond their capabilities at times. However, despite the myth that "doing what you love" means "you won't have to work," the reality is often different. Institutional expectations, such as constant availability and adaptability to digital trends, clash with journalists' initial motivations. Lifestyle journalists find themselves caught in a situation where their love for the topic and people in the genre leads to a challenging work–life balance. The journalists in Perreault and Bélair-Gagnon's (2024) study struggle with the demands of their work, especially in adapting to digital technologies. This difficulty contrasts with the perception that lifestyle journalism is less demanding than hard news areas, challenging the notion that they may be working harder to meet institutional expectations. Additionally, Perreault and Bélair-Gagnon (2024) prompt consideration of how journalists' personal love for lifestyles has been commodified in the U.S. journalism market context.

This emphasis reflects the consumerist ideals within the subfield (Hanusch, 2018; Perreault & Vos, 2018). Lifestyle journalists address critiques regarding their independence through transparency, for example, by explaining the sources of their free products and services (Hanusch, 2012). Despite receiving "freebies" and experiences, journalists, nevertheless, privilege editorial independence in their work. Recent research indicates that lifestyle journalists are embracing digitalization to some extent, providing more participatory opportunities for bloggers in their content (Cheng & Tandoc Jr., 2022). However, the openness of lifestyle journalists fosters a "culture of radical sharing," with potential dangers, as regular engagement with audiences can impact sources and challenge perceptions of journalistic authority over editorial judgment (Usher, 2016, p. 191).

Indeed, lifestyle journalists often find themselves on the cutting edge of new technologies in part as a reflection of this close tie with audiences and markets. Games journalism, for example, reflects a niche that was among the first on the internet and proved able to employ interactivity with audiences even early on in web publishing (Perreault & Vos, 2020). And as new technologies have been employed, lifestyle journalists have leveraged the expertise of external actors such as podcasters (Maares & Perreault, 2023) in order to work toward normalizing them (Perreault & Hanusch, 2024b). However, as was the case with labor in lifestyle journalism, integration of new technologies – perhaps in contrast with hard news colleagues – often needs be undertaken with very little support from their organizational environment (Perreault & Hanusch, 2024b).

Market Pressures. Finally, it remains the case that lifestyle journalists often find themselves faced with market pressures felt acutely throughout journalism. Historically, lifestyle journalists have often been considered *more* market-driven than hard news journalists given the consumerist ideals mentioned above. Yet lifestyle journalists perceive the influence of market forces on their work to be quite similar to those experienced by hard news journalists (Perreault et al., 2024). In particular, lifestyle journalists experience market pressure in newsrooms with a range of specialties given the need to engage audiences and potentially attract more viewers for hard news (Perreault et al., 2024). While there's no clear evidence that lifestyle journalism is more market-driven, journalists in Perreault et al.'s (2024) study feel a heavier burden to attract audiences in multispecialty newsrooms, navigating forces they actively avoid. Any variation in market orientation among journalists by beat seems to be minimal (Perreault et al., 2024), yet this does raise the question of why a market-driven mindset matters to journalists, especially if the normative mission of serving the public is fulfilled.

The examination of the shared pressures faced by lifestyle journalists alongside their hard news counterparts reveals the multifaceted nature of challenges within the journalism profession. Despite the perception of lifestyle journalism as a realm of lighter reporting, it becomes evident that journalists in this domain confront similar cultural obstacles. Just as we see a crossover between pressures, lifestyle journalism practices themselves are not exclusive to soft news but are also prevalent in hard news reporting. The nature of hard news is increasingly incorporating elements traditionally associated with lifestyle journalism.

Current contributions & research

Lifestyle practices in hard news: Social cohesion

Lifestyle journalism scholarship reflects the value for *bringing a community together*. In sports journalism, for example, this social cohesion is what allows teams and clubs to develop dedicated fan bases and to bring a local community together despite a range of disciplines. In this way, lifestyle journalists ascribe to "a normative role that contributes to a more general public good and conveys a sense of solidarity" (Perreault & Nölleke, 2022, p. 1862), and they "instill a sense of common experience and a basis for social cohesion by not excluding systematically the experiences of particular social groups" (Costera Meijer, 2001, p. 201). Gaming and travel would seem to offer similar opportunities by reflecting lesser known aspects of the gaming community (Perreault & Vos, 2020), or less explored travel locations (Maares & Hanusch, 2022), but increasing their familiarity, and thereby uniting a readership behind their love of a hobby. Yet, this is a practice that is equally well-established within hard news.

Social cohesion, far from being a fringe practice of journalism, would seem to be at the very core of the journalistic mission: bringing people together is after all what allows the democratic process to work. Luhmann (1996) argued that journalism provides an essential means for developing social cohesion, in that it is the primary means through which people learn about the world around them. Social cohesion is a part of communicating the buy-in that allows the democratic process to work successfully, and it grants journalists the means with which to help a public deliberate the difficult discussions within a society. The concept of social cohesion is drawn from the work of Emile Durkheim and, as he articulated it, social cohesion works at a group level. Durkheim (1893/1983) argued that societies depend on providing a "collective way of life…shared values and beliefs" (p. xvii) even amid "ever-increasing" differentiation and individual complexity within them (p. xxx). He argued that through *social discourse*, as in journalism, individuals are forced to follow their different interests, and capabilities, gaining a better understanding of how they need to depend on one another since their different roles and activities are complementary. Social cohesion not only "keeps individuals together" (Bottoni, 2018, p. 836) but also maintains their commitment to each other through the community (Kim et al., 2021). Kim et al. (2021) explored whether diversity in a community made social cohesion more difficult to achieve and – a heartening finding – it did not.

Social cohesion has been a key way of reflecting on public media in particular (Leupold et al., 2018; Gutsche & Hess, 2018). Leupold et al. (2018) argue that local journalism plays an essential role in the development of social cohesion, and it is developed through

1 Social relations – trust and acceptance of diversity
2 Connectedness – identification and perception
3 Focus on the common good – solidarity and acceptance of social rules

Steensen (2011) argued that social cohesion has become increasingly central to online journalism where people skills are more important than ever, yet this norm would seem to be in tension with "traditional" ideologies of journalism.

> This ideal comes into conflict with the traditional ideal of independent reporting, which implies keeping a critical distance from sources rather than cozying up with them. It might also come into conflict with the traditional ideal of providing relevant information to the audience as quickly as possible, as the ideal of social cohesion is directed towards pleasing mainly the participating part of the audience.
> *(Steensen, 2011, p. 700)*

Yet, the ways in which social cohesion appears naturally differ according to the journalistic environment (Reimer et al., 2025). As Reimer et al. (2025) argue, social cohesion would, in particular, be different across countries, given that people's capabilities and complementary skills would differ. Kim et al.'s (2021) study of local and national newspapers' social cohesion efforts noted several areas of hard news in which social cohesion occurs, including immigration, reporting on poverty, and reporting on housing. In other words, these are arenas of reporting that have a pro-social element to them and in which hard news reporting is often seen as having a "perspective" even in tension with the nods toward objectivity within these domains of hard news. Noteworthy is that the ways local and national news in Kim et al.'s (2021) approach on social cohesion differ: small town news coverage tended to project local unity, whereas national news tended to report more conflict and division. But equally noteworthy is that the shared tenor of cohesion was shared in coverage of immigration, poverty, and housing.

News coverage of divisive problems can connect community members and organizations with those who have resources to help (Hickman et al., 2012) – in this way, hard news coverage accomplishes the at-times perceived "soft" task of bringing a community together.

Lifestyle practices in hard news: Advocacy

Lifestyle journalism has a strong rooting in the role of advocacy on behalf of consumers (Hanusch et al., 2017), particularly "in a world where ads make choosing the best product increasingly difficult" (Usher, 2012, p. 113). Yet this rooting in advocacy runs counter to what centers a subfield in journalism.

Considered to be the *central* norm within the journalistic field, objectivity (Schudson, 2001) is a norm that reflects journalistic impartiality, fairness, and verification practices. Both hard news and lifestyle journalists subscribe to the overall notions of objectivity, even as objectivity is often deemed to have "less relevance" in lifestyle reporting (Harries & Wahl-Jorgensen, 2007, p. 635). Yet, even as hard news has often ascribed to strong notions of objectivity, it has historically always created spaces for advocacy – often deemed to be the binary opposite of objectivity. For example, newspapers have long had a history of "editorial endorsements" – which, while never produced by hard news journalists, are nevertheless often published in the same section as hard news and continually cause confusion among news readers (Perreault, Kananovich & Hackett, 2023). Defenders of the editorial endorsement practice often point out that these pieces are labeled as *opinion*, yet this does not negate the fact they are often published in a hard news section that has ascribed to notions of objectivity, notions seemingly in stark contrast with the endorsement.

And yet there would seem to be numerous areas of hard news that would seem to be more akin to *advocacy* than objectivity. For example, political journalism has normalized a form of writing known as the *news analysis* that aims to not only provide the news but also to explain what it means and how readers should think about it (Esser, 1999). Advocacy is often conceptualized as existing apart from journalism, more in line with public relations, and hence not a central component of hard news (Fisher, 2016). Yet increasingly, advocacy has been conceived as an essential component of hard news in order to best promote the public good. For example, during the peak of the COVID-19 pandemic, medical journalists aimed at offering pro-vaccine, pro-masking coverage for pro-social reasons; while outlier cases in vaccine reactions did occur, journalists were encouraged to contextualize such coverage in order to encourage readers to act in the best interests of the global community (e.g., by masking and obtaining vaccination) (Perreault, Hackett & Handler, 2024). Similarly, a coverage of climate change has increasingly reflected that *fair* and *neutral* coverage, far from propelling the public good, actually diminishes it (Bodker & Neverla, 2014). Finally, research on mass shootings in the United States has reflected that objective reporting – far from diminishing their pervasiveness – actually can encourage more mass shootings. Widespread reporting on an individual mass shooting tragedy can then often be followed by several mass shootings within a several day period. As a result, many news organizations have taken to reshaping their coverage of mass shooting events in ways that are more akin to advocacy reporting (Alaimo, 2022).

Indeed, hard news has often framed the pro-social advocacy turn in hard news as *solutions journalism* (McIntyre & Lough, 2021) – that is hard news that is aimed toward solutions. All of this together should reflect a few things (1) that advocacy is not solely the domain of lifestyle journalism but has a well-established history in hard news topics *even when not specifically flagged as advocacy*; (2) that such advocacy is firmly in line with journalism's normative mission; hence, arguing for advocacy occurring in hard news is not to diminish such reporting but to rather elevate its pro-social work; and also that (3) lifestyle journalism is firmly in line with journalism's normative mission in advocacy. While the scale of advocacy across the journalistic field can vary wildly (e.g., ranging from guidance on holiday meals with in-laws and makeup purchases to solutions reporting on how combat school mass shootings), this does not change the fact that the overall norm and purpose remain the same: to advocate on behalf of the audience.

Lifestyle practices in hard news: Audience commitment

Lifestyle journalism views the audience as central to its overall function and, indeed, the Hanusch (2012) definition of lifestyle journalism foregrounds the importance of the audience: "a distinct journalistic field that primarily addresses its audiences as consumers..." (p. 2). And, indeed, Hanusch and Hanitzsch (2013) reflect that this commitment to the audience is an essential professional feature in how they conceptualize their professional roles.

A commitment to relationality necessitates the inclusion of audiences within journalism as not merely consumers of news content but rather as active and intrinsic components of journalism as a cultural practice. The audience is more than recipients of information; they are considered potential co-creators of news. This collaboration involves both back-end interactions, such as feedback and criticism, and front-end contributions, including first-hand accounts of events (Carlson et al., 2018).

With respect to this point, most reporting is crafted with a specific audience in mind (Schramm, 1949) as the significance of relationality has increased with the proliferation of mediated voices through digital technologies (Carlson et al., 2018). The idea goes beyond involving the audience in the production of news; it extends to a holistic approach where the audience is integrated into the entire process of journalism. This idea draws inspiration from Carey's (1992) view of communication, which sees news not only as a source of information but also as a tool for community-building. Instead of presenting information in a generic or one-size-fits-all manner, the news content is customized to appeal to the interests, preferences, or information needs of a particular group of people. A considerable portion of audience research indicates that organizational and societal factors play a crucial role in molding news media content (Ngomba, 2011). Furthermore, correlated studies have demonstrated that journalists' professional behavior is shaped by their attitudes, adherence to professional norms, and their perception of the audience (Ngomba, 2011).

Lifestyle reporting is strongly tied to the identity of its audience (Perreault et al., 2024), given that lifestyle reporters "prefer a direct connection to their audiences by taking on the recipients' perspective and by giving clear value judgments" (Fürsich, 2012, p. 14). In this way, hard news can be emblematic of lifestyle when the news coverage is both informative and targeted to meet the expectations or engage the particular demographic of the audience. This approach recognizes the diversity of news consumers and the needs of consumers for guidance and aims to make the information more relevant and compelling for a specific group. After journalists conceptualize their audiences, their objectives shift from simply producing news to crafting news in a manner that will connect with the individuals they aim to engage. Essentially, once audiences are envisioned, they can develop a distinct identity and influence (Nelson, 2021). For example, Ngomba's (2011) research on the professional role conceptions of political journalists in Cameroon finds that the teacher/educator/informant roles emerged as particularly prominent among journalists. Within their articulations about serving as teachers/educators/informants, the image of the audience was most deeply ingrained.

Additionally, the legitimacy of journalism as a cultural activity cannot be solely determined by journalists; it necessitates the establishment of a specific authority relationship with the audience; hence, this is why audience orientation is essential in both hard and soft news (Carlson, 2017). While the commitment to an audience may be representative of lifestyle journalism characteristics, hard news journalists have taken on a more collaborative and inclusive approach to journalism that recognizes the active role of the audience in order to shape and legitimize the practice (Carlson et al., 2018).

Whether one identifies as a soft news or hard news journalist, the perception that a news organization holds regarding its particular audience profoundly influences the manner in which it molds its coverage (Nelson, 2021). In recent times, a growing number of individuals in the field of journalism have adopted the idea that news consumers tend to favor political information that aligns exclusively with their own ideologies, rather than content that presents opposing viewpoints (Nelson, 2021). In order to best reach consumers, journalists, thus, tend to report on political ideas through emotionalization, which is recognized as crucial for capturing audience attention and likely to influence audience perceptions (Varma, 2020).

Apart from deciding the extent to which they should heed their audiences, journalists' perceptions of their imagined audiences also influence the shaping of their news content (Nelson, 2021; Ngomba, 2011). Journalists rely on their conceptualizations of their audiences to assess the newsworthiness of potential stories and to decide how these stories should be presented and communicated (Nelson, 2021). Emotional news stories employ verbal, visual, or auditory techniques that have the potential to evoke or intensify emotions in the audience. This can be achieved through various means, such as (a) dramatizing events, portraying them as extraordinary, captivating, or suspenseful; (b) using emotive language and speech, including superlatives, powerful adjectives, and employing the present tense when describing past events, along with pronounced emphasis; (c) covering or visually displaying explicit manifestations of emotions, such as hurt, anger, fear, distress, or joy (Reinmann, 2011).

Vos and Craft (2017) examine how transparency is discursively constructed to build cultural capital. It is argued that an ethic of transparency, coupled with audience inclusion in digital content production, has the potential to challenge and undermine traditional journalistic values. On the other hand, emerging norms are not necessarily adopted to enhance practices and relationships but are strategically employed to safeguard the authority of the journalism profession (Carlson, 2017). As an example, the majority of journalists operate under the assumption that the audience is more inclined to trust news when it is presented in an objective and transparent manner. The quest for objectivity involves journalists making a concerted effort to maintain an appearance of impartiality, irrespective of the nature of the news they are covering (Nelson, 2021): a tall order in many arenas of hard news reporting.

Future directions: Breaking down the binary

Robin Givhan serves as the *Washington Post*'s senior critic-at-large in the United States, and her specialty raised more than a few eyebrows: the fashion of politics. Writing piece after piece about the political messages written into Sarah Palin's star-spangled cardigan, Bernie Sanders' too-big sports coats and off-sized button-up shirts, and Hillary Clinton's makeup-free diplomatic visit to Bangladesh, Givhan generated a sizable following dedicated to understanding the political implications of fashion. Givhan is in a position that troubles the neat binaries of the journalistic field: she is in a seemingly *lifestyle* position, where she primarily operates at the political desk. Is she a lifestyle journalist? A political journalist?

These debates are not merely conceptual but have practical implications for journalists in newsrooms. For example, mobile journalists in US newsrooms reflected in numerous ways about the affordances of mobile phones, which lent themselves to lifestyle reporting; yet, mobile journalists often found themselves assigned to specialties that were certainly not anticipating lifestyle content (Perreault & Stanfield, 2019). Hence, mobile journalists who were often hired because of their ability to produce mobile journalism frequently found themselves discursively marginalized in the newsroom for doing the exact journalism they'd been hired to do. In this way, mobile journalists felt in some ways like they didn't fit anywhere: using technology that was most treasured in hard news, but with affordances that lent themselves to soft news.

What all of this chapter should indicate is that the work they were doing, as with the rest of lifestyle journalism, speaks to the very core of journalism's normative mission. It is impossible to paint with a broad brush about different forms of journalism with such an enormous range in quality, focus, and democratic import. But it is precisely for this reason that historic hierarchies within the journalistic field prove so problematic. Lifestyle journalism's lower standing within the field has often been rationalized as being a result of (1) producing reporting of a lesser democratic import and (2) producing reporting with practices deemed unacceptable (Perreault & Vos, 2020). Yet as this chapter reflects, neither of these rationales prove entirely persuasive given that hard news would seem to engage in many of lifestyle journalism's practices.

Future research ought to explore a few different avenues regarding the hard news/soft news binary. These include:

- Lifestyle journalism's coverage of critical topics: Oftentimes, lifestyle journalism has been seen as *soft* given that it has been characterized as centrally focused on relatively joyful topics: the hobbies and passions of individuals. Yet research has shown that lifestyle journalism has, in individual specialties, reported on concerns and fears as well. What does this look like overall within the lifestyle journalism subfield?
- Lifestyle journalism's humanizing coverage and inclusion efforts: Hard news has often been tasked with coverage aimed at increasing the scope of the *us* within a society – a task with which research reflects that hard news has proven rather unsuccessful: creating conflict as opposed to consensus. The development of social cohesion, however, has been

prescribed as a goal in hard news, yet would seem to have more grounding in lifestyle journalism.
- Interrogating the journalistic hierarchy: this chapter reflects that rationales for hard news' preferential standing within the field no longer seem adequately persuasive. It is worth questioning whether there may be alternative rationales that could explain the historically disadvantaged standings of lifestyle journalism's presence in newsrooms: (1) a higher emphasis on the voices of women in lifestyle journalism would reflect and perhaps (2) an advantaged position in attracting advertising revenue, which has proven evasive in areas of hard news.

Lifestyle journalism offers an engaging avenue for future research within the journalistic field – research that reflects contributions at the very core of the field's mission.

Further reading

Hanusch, F. (Ed.) (2014). *Lifestyle journalism*. Routledge.
Hanusch, F., & Fürsich, E. (Eds.) (2014). *Travel journalism: exploring production, impact and culture*. Springer.
Perreault, G., & Stanfield, K. (2019). Mobile Journalism as Lifestyle Journalism? Field Theory in the integration of mobile in the newsroom and mobile journalist role conception. *Journalism Practice*, 13(3), 331–348.
Rogstad, I. D. (2014). Political news journalists in social media: Transforming political reporters into political pundits? *Journalism Practice*, 8(6), 688–703. https://doi.org/10.1080/17512786.2013.865965
Widholm, A., & Appelgren, E. (2022). A softer kind of hard news? Data journalism and the digital renewal of public service news in Sweden. *New Media & Society*, 24(6), 1363–1381. https://doi.org/10.1177/1461444820975411

References

Alaimo, K. I. (2022). Finishing the story: Narrative ritual in news coverage of the Umpqua Community College shooting. *Journalism*, 23(11), 2417–2433.
Banjac, S., & Hanusch, F. (2022). A question of perspective: Exploring audiences' views of journalistic boundaries. *New Media & Society*, 24(3), 705–723.
Baum, M. A. (2003). Soft news and political knowledge: Evidence of absence or Absence of evidence? *Political Communication*, 20(2), 173–190. https://doi.org/10.1080/10584600390211181
Bodker, H., & Neverla, I. (2014). *Environmental journalism*. Routledge.
Bottoni, G. (2018). A multilevel measurement model of social cohesion. *Social Indicators Research*, 136(3), 835–857.
Broussard, R. (2020). "Stick to sports" is gone: A field theory analysis of sports journalists' coverage of socio-political issues. *Journalism Studies*, 21(12), 1627–1643.
Carey, J. W. (1992). *Communication as culture: Essays on media and society*. New York: Routledge.
Carlson, M. (2015). Introduction: The many boundaries of journalism. In M. Carlson & S. C. Lewis (Eds.), *Boundaries of journalism* (pp. 1–18). Routledge.
Carlson, M. (2017). *Journalistic authority: Legitimating news in the digital era*. Columbia University Press.
Carlson, M., & Berkowitz, D. (2014). 'The emperor lost his clothes': Rupert Murdoch, News of the World and journalistic boundary work in the UK and USA. *Journalism*, 15(4), 389–406.
Carlson, M., Robinson, S., Lewis, S. C., & Berkowitz, D. A. (2018). Journalism studies and its core commitments: The making of a communication field. *Journal of Communication*, 68(1), 6–25.
Cheng, L., & Tandoc Jr, E. C. (2022). From magazines to blogs: The shifting boundaries of fashion journalism. *Journalism*, 23(6), 1213–1232.Duffy, B. E. (2017). *(Not) getting paid to do what you love: Gender, social media, and aspirational work*. Yale University Press.

Durkheim, E. (1983). *The division of labor in society* (pp. 37–66). Blackwell. (Original work published 1893)
Esser, F. (1999). Tabloidization' of news: A comparative analysis of Anglo-American and German press journalism. *European Journal of Communication, 14*(3), 291–324.
Fisher, C. (2016). The advocacy continuum: Towards a theory of advocacy in journalism. *Journalism, 17*(6), 711–726.
Freedman, H. (2016) Hadley Freeman: is writing about fashion really such a crime? *The Guardian*. https://www.theguardian.com/fashion/2016/apr/30/hadley-freeman-the-problem-with-fashion-journalism
Fürsich, E. (2012). Lifestyle journalism as popular journalism: Strategies for evaluating its public role. *Journalism Practice, 6*(1), 12–25.
Gieryn, T. F. (1983). Boundary-work and the demarcation of science from non-science: Strains and interests in professional ideologies of scientists. *American Sociological Review, 28*(6), 781–795.
Gutsche Jr, R. E., & Hess, K. (2018). Contesting communities: The problem of journalism and social order. *Journalism Studies, 19*(4), 473–482.
Hanitzsch, T., & Vos, T. P. (2018). Journalism beyond democracy: A new look into journalistic roles in political and everyday life. *Journalism, 19*(2), 146–164.
Hanusch, F. (2010). *Representing death in the news: Journalism, media and mortality*. Springer.
Hanusch, F. (2012). A profile of Australian travel journalists' professional views and ethical standards. *Journalism, 13*(5), 668-686.
Hanusch, F. (2018). Political journalists' corporate and personal identities on Twitter profile pages: A comparative analysis in four Westminster democracies. *New Media & Society, 20*(4), 1488–1505.
Hanusch, F. (2019). Journalistic roles and everyday life: An empirical account of lifestyle journalists' professional views. *Journalism Studies, 20*(2), 193–211.
Hanusch, F., & Hanitzsch, T. (2013). Mediating orientation and self-expression in the world of consumption: Australian and German lifestyle journalists' professional views. *Media, Culture & Society, 35*(8), 943–959.
Hanusch, F., Hanitzsch, T., & Lauerer, C. (2017). 'How much love are you going to give this brand?' Lifestyle journalists on commercial influences in their work. *Journalism, 18*(2), 141–158.
Harries, G., & Wahl-Jorgensen, K. (2007). The culture of arts journalists: Elitists, saviors or manic depressives? *Journalism, 8*(6), 619–639.
Hickman, M. J., Mai, N., & Crowley, H. (2012). *Migration and social cohesion in the UK*. Palgrave Macmillan.
Ivask, S., Waschková Císařová, L., & Lon, A. (2024). "When can I get angry?" Journalists' coping strategies and emotional management in hostile situations. *Journalism,25*(10), 2099–2116.
Kim, B., Lowrey, W., Buzzelli, N., & Heath, W. (2021). News organizations and social cohesion in small, large, and global-local communities. *Mass Communication and Society, 24*(3), 418–440.
Kotišová, J., & van der Velden, L. (2023). The affective epistemology of digital journalism: Emotions as knowledge among on-the-ground and OSINT media practitioners covering the Russo-Ukrainian War. *Digital Journalism*, 1–20. https://doi.org/10.1080/21670811.2023.2273531
Leupold, A., Klinger, U., & Jarren, O. (2018). Imagining the city: How local journalism depicts social cohesion. *Journalism Studies, 19*(7), 960–982.
Luhmann, N. (1996). *Die Realität der Massenmedien [The reality of the mass media]*. Westdeutscher Verlag.
Maares, P., & Hanusch, F. (2022). Challenging the tourist gaze?: Exploring majority world countries' Instagram influencer practices and the link to citizen travel journalism. In B. Korte & A. K. Sennefelder (Eds.), *Travel, writing and the media* (pp. 226–246). Routledge.
Maares, P., & Perreault, G. P. (2023). True crime podcasting: Journalistic epistemology and boundary marking. *Association for Education in Journalism & Mass Communication Conference*. Washington, DC.
McIntyre, K. E., & Lough, K. (2021). Toward a clearer conceptualization and operationalization of solutions journalism. *Journalism, 22*(6), 1558–1573.
Meijer, I. C. (2001). The public quality of popular journalism: Developing a normative framework. *Journalism Studies, 2*(2), 189–205. https://doi.org/10.1080/14616700120042079
Mesmer, K. (2022). An intersectional analysis of US journalists' experiences with hostile sources. *Journalism & Communication Monographs, 24*(3), 156–216.

Miller, K. C. (2023). Hostility toward the press: A synthesis of terms, research, and future directions in examining harassment of journalists. *Digital Journalism, 11*(7), 1230–1249.

Miller, K. C., & Lewis, S. C. (2022). Journalists, harassment, and emotional labor: The case of women in on-air roles at US local television stations. *Journalism, 23*(1), 79–97.

Molyneux, L. (2019). A personalized self-image: Gender and branding practices among journalists. *Social Media+ Society, 5*(3), 2056305119872950.

Nelson, J. L. (2021). *Imagined audiences: How journalists perceive and pursue the public*. Oxford University Press.

Ngomba, T. (2011). Journalists' perceptions of 'the audience' and the logics of participatory development/communication: A contributory note. *Ecquid Novi: African Journalism Studies, 32*(1), 4–24.

Nguyen, A. (2015). The effect of soft news on public attachment to the news: Is 'infotainment' good for democracy? In B. Franking (Ed.), *The Future of Journalism: Developments and Debates* (pp. 44–55). Routledge.

North, L. (2016). The gender of "soft" and "hard" news: Female journalists' views on gendered story allocations. *Journalism Studies, 17*(3), 356–373. https://doi.org/10.1080/1461670X.2014.987551

Parks, P. (2021). Joy is a news value. *Journalism Studies, 22*(6), 820–838.

Perreault, G. P., & Bélair-Gagnon, V. (2024). The lifestyle of lifestyle journalism: How reporters discursively manage their aspirations in their daily work. *Journalism Practice, 18*(7), 1641–1659.

Perreault, G. P., Caberlon, L., & Stuart, C. (2023). Audience repair as paradigm repair: Fixing the 'gamer' in games journalism. *Journalism History, 49*(2), 95–109.

Perreault, G. P., Ferrucci, P., & Ficara, G. (2024). No more market-driven than hard news: Lifestyle journalists' market drive and perceived audience obligations. *Journalism Studies, 25*(7), 723–737.

Perreault, G. P., Hackett, E., & Handler, A. (2024). Coronavirus and Journalism: A Meta-analysis of Early Research on Journalism in the COVID-19 pandemic. In M. Perreault & S. Smith-Frigerio (Eds.), *Crisis Communication Case Studies on COVID-19*. Peter Lang.

Perreault, G., & Hanusch, F. (2024a). Field insurgency in lifestyle journalism: How lifestyle journalists marginalize Instagram influencers and protect their autonomy. *New Media & Society, 26*(7), 3767–3785.

Perreault, G. P., & Hanusch, F. (2024b). Normalizing Instagram. *Digital Journalism, 12*(4), 413–430.

Perreault, G., Kananovich, V., & Hackett, E. (2023). Guarding the firewall: How political journalists distance themselves from the editorial endorsement process. *Journalism & Mass Communication Quarterly, 100*(2), 354–372.

Perreault, G., & Miller, K. (2022). When journalists are voiceless: How lifestyle journalists cover hate and mitigate harassment. *Journalism Studies, 23*(15), 1977–1993.

Perreault, G., & Nölleke, D. (2022). What is sports journalism? How COVID-19 accelerated a redefining of US sports reporting. *Journalism Studies, 23*(14), 1860–1879.

Perreault, G. P., & Vos, T. P. (2018). The GamerGate controversy and journalistic paradigm maintenance. *Journalism, 19*(4), 553–569.

Perreault, G., & Vos, T. (2020). Metajournalistic discourse on the rise of gaming journalism. *New Media & Society, 22*(1), 159–176.

Plasser, F. (2005). From hard to soft news standards? How political journalists in different media systems evaluate the shifting quality of news. *Harvard International Journal of Press/Politics, 10*(2), 47–68.

Powers, M., & Vera-Zambrano, S. (2023). *The journalist's predicament: Difficult choices in a declining profession*. Columbia University Press.

Reimer, J., Albert, V., & Loosen, W. (2025). On society's reachability, representativity, and ability for dialogue: Exploring the interrelation between journalism and social cohesion. *Journalism, 26*(1), 89–107.

Reinemann, C., Stanyer, J., Scherr, S., & Legnante, G. (2012). Hard and soft news: A review of concepts, operationalizations and key findings. *Journalism, 13*(2), 221–239.

Reinemann, C., Stanyer, J., & Scherr, S. (2016). Hard and soft news. In C. de Vreese, F. Esser & D.N. Hopmann (Eds.), *Comparing political journalism* (pp. 131–149). Routledge.

Ross, K., & Carter, C. (2001). Women and news: A long winding journey. *Media, Culture & Society, 33*(8), 1148–1165. https://doi.org/10.1177/0163443711418272

Schudson, M. (2001). The objectivity norm in American journalism. *Journalism, 2*(2), 149–170.

Schramm, W. (1949). The nature of news. *Journalism Quarterly, 26*(3), 259–269. https://doi.org/10.1177/107769904902600301

Skovsgaard, M., & Bro, P. (2016). Journalistic roles in the mediated public sphere. In C. Mellado, L. Hellmueller & W. Donsbach (Eds.) *Journalistic role performance* (pp. 78–92). Routledge.

Steensen, S. (2011). Cozy journalism: The rise of social cohesion as an ideal in online, participatory journalism. *Journalism Practice, 5*(6), 687–703.

Steiner, L. (2014). Feminist media theory. In R.S. Fortner & P.M. Fackler (Eds.), *The handbook of media and mass communication theory* (pp. 359–379). Wiley.

Usher, N. (2012). Service journalism as community experience: Personal technology and personal finance at the New York Times. *Journalism Practice, 6*(1), 107–121.

Usher, N. (2016). *Interactive journalism: Hackers, data, and code.* University of Illinois Press.

van Zoonen, L. (1998). One of the girls? The changing gender of journalism. In S. Allan, G. Branston & C. Carter (Eds.), *News, gender and power* (pp. 33–46). Routledge.

Varma, A. (2020). Evoking empathy or enacting solidarity with marginalized communities? A case study of journalistic humanizing techniques in the San Francisco Homeless Project. *Journalism Studies, 21*(12), 1705–1723.

Vos, T. P., & Craft, S. (2017). The discursive construction of journalistic transparency. *Journalism Studies, 18*(12), 1505–1522.

Whipple, K. (2025). Contextualizing the art and the artist: How US arts and culture journalists perceive the impact of cancel culture practices and discourses. *Journalism Practice, 19*(1), 203–221.

Zhu, Y., & Fu, K. W. (2024). How propaganda works in the digital era: soft news as a gateway. *Digital Journalism, 12*(6), 753–772.

22
HOW TO BE HUMAN
Turns in health, lifestyle, and wellness journalism

Mariah L. Wellman, Aly Hill and Avery E. Holton

Introduction

More than a decade ago, journalism studies scholars produced a special issue in the peer-reviewed journal, *Journalism Practice*, outlining the case for an increased focus on studying lifestyle journalism. In that special issue, lifestyle journalism is defined as a "distinct journalistic field that primarily addresses its audiences as consumers, providing them with factual information and advice, often in entertaining ways, about goods and services they can use in their daily lives" (Hanusch, 2012, p. 5). Lifestyle journalists' increased focus on consumption has resulted in criticism, primarily from hard news journalists, arguing the goals of lifestyle journalism align too closely with commercial demand and the public relations industry.

Therefore, many professionals and also journalism and communication scholars have discounted this type of journalism altogether, resulting in limited work on the subject. Yet, since the publishing of the 2012 special issue, lifestyle journalism has rapidly expanded, especially in the areas of health and well-being, where coverage has increasingly aligned within trends in the wellness industry. Health and wellness journalism grew significantly during the COVID-19 pandemic when journalists and influencers alike contributed to an influx of digital wellness content emphasizing holistic health, personal development, and self-care practices. However, this interdependence has drawn criticism from traditional health and science journalists, consumers, and advertisers who have raised concerns surrounding the influence of commercial interests on content and the accuracy of information provided to consumers.

Moreover, the meteoric rise of entertainment-minded social media platforms such as TikTok and Instagram, coupled with the growing accessibility of digital media globally, has forced wellness journalists to compete for audience attention in a saturated global marketplace. The result is an evolving relationship between lifestyle, wellness, and health journalism, which presents new challenges and considerations for journalists navigating this evolving industry. Scholars, too, are beginning to engage with these changing dynamics.

This chapter offers a historical review of health journalism and wellness lifestyle journalism, discusses current trends and critical issues, and makes predictions about the future

DOI: 10.4324/9781003396727-26

of this type of soft news. We thread together histories of health journalism with emerging forms of entertainment journalism focused on individual wellness and wellbeing, exploring the roles that wellness influencers and health journalists play in shaping the health information landscape.

The history of health journalism

For decades, journalists have played a pivotal role in delivering essential health information to the public. But before contemporary health journalism was established, writers were first assigned to cover science topics such as physics. According to Jon Franklin (2008), when science journalism first emerged in the 1960s, scientists were quite separate from journalists who considered themselves to be humanists and therefore, were hardly ever in conversation with one another. This posed a problem for those assigned to write about science as the cultural barricades were high and the vernacular utilized by scientists of the time was not easily understood by the public.

When the second generation of science journalists emerged in the 1970s, however, they began focusing on the body and medicine – topics the public had a vested interest in understanding. This required writers to work with scientists more closely and bridge the divide between the two groups to serve their readers more fully. Decades later, this issue persists. The media often does not have enough space to cover all nuanced points brought forth by scientists, while scientists and journalists still speak in terms the other doesn't understand (Van Eperen, Marincola, & Strohm, 2010).

These complications have only increased as science journalism has expanded to include health journalism under its umbrella. A subset of science journalism, health journalism involves the "…dissemination of medical and health information and related subjects in the media" (Paul et al., 2021, p. 1). Originating from the wave of science popularization and growing interest in scientific discoveries related to the body and medicine during the mid-20th century, health reporting has long served as a vital bridge between specialized health research and the broader public, capable of influencing individual health behaviors (Dunwoody, 2008).

Recognized for delivering crucial public health information and shaping health policies, health journalism was placed under the 'hard news' umbrella. Characterized by headline-grabbing pieces culled from academic journals, health-reporting features stories that address critical health issues such as heart disease, obesity, cancer, and diabetes. It, too, has focused on disseminating public health information during health crises and relaying news related to health policies. However, the 'hard news' character of health journalism faced a reckoning in the 1980s and 1990s when news coverage of the HIV/AIDS epidemic raised questions about the politicization of health news (Hallin et al., 2013).

Faced with conflicting scientific viewpoints and social stigma surrounding the disease, the crisis and the initial scientific uncertainties surrounding it marked a watershed moment for reporters navigating the challenges of scientific popularization and their own biases in health coverage (Williams, 1999). While journalists played a crucial role in raising awareness about the disease and its prevention, the early stages of reporting on the crisis were marred by inaccuracies, prompting scrutiny into how journalists selected and interpreted health information that had previously been regarded as objective.

Who covered health came to matter, too. Public attention to the crisis saw a growing number of journalists assigned to cover the health beat, distinguishing health journalists from general reporters for their ability to sift through a deluge of competing medical opinions circulating at the time. This shift sedimented health journalism as a distinct category of reporting that transcended its early science journalism roots. This normalization went beyond the HIV/AIDS epidemic, with a growing number of broadcasters dedicating airtime to segments featuring medical doctors and newspapers developing dedicated health and science sections, including a wide range of health contributors (Williams, 1999).

Scientific popularization and polarization contributed to shifting boundaries between journalism and health, which Briggs and Hallin (2016) refer to as biomediatization. This perspective, which came to characterize health journalism in the 1980s and 1990s, situates health journalism not as a top–down translation of science and medicine by health practitioners but as a collaborative form of knowledge shaped by journalists, medical practitioners, public relations practices, normative biases, and commercial interests (McKeever, 2021; Stroobant et al., 2019). Indeed, this view acknowledges the complex web of institutional pressures and competing interests that have long influenced the dynamics of health journalism.

The emergence of new technologies in the 1990s and 2000s brought these tensions into sharper focus. The widespread adoption of broadband in the 1990s paved the way for the rise of social media in the 2000s, reshaping how health information was accessed and interpreted by the public, journalists, and medical experts alike. While these advancements democratized access to health information and fostered a collaboration between journalists and healthcare professionals, they also presented challenges. Health journalists found themselves grappling with new economic models, reductions in newsroom staff, and the move toward news personalization, which challenged traditional journalistic practices and raised concerns about the quality and credibility of health reporting.

In 2009, a report examining the state of health journalism in the United States shed light on the myriad challenges confronting both local and national newsrooms, revealing a decline in complex health policy stories and an increase in hyper-local and lifestyle-oriented content (Schwitzer, 2009). This transformation stemmed from dwindling editorial space and resources allocated to health journalists as media outlets moved to meet their financial objectives. Consequently, journalists found themselves under mounting pressure to deliver news rapidly in limited space.

At the same time, commercial incentives from advertisers and PR professionals created additional pressures for journalists and editors who were incentivized to promote the efficacy of pharmaceutical drugs vaccinations, medical devices, and medical centers. Local television stations saw a dramatic rise in sponsored health news segments, while newspapers increasingly relied on short, syndicated wire reporting to cover health research and policies, contributing to a decline in the criticality of health information and diminishing the boundary between health and lifestyle journalism (Schwitzer, 2009; Hanusch et al., 2020).

This convergence amplified critiques of health journalists, whose reporting had long faced scrutiny for inaccuracies and a lack of critical analysis, contributing to a widening "…gulf between detail-obsessed academics and time-poor, space-hungry, national newspaper journalists" (Coombes, 2009, p. 1; Dentzer, 2009). Concerns over the accuracy of information and the obscuring of journalistic principles compounded longstanding concerns surrounding journalists shoehorning health stories into boxes reflecting journalistic tropes like novelty and timeliness (Dunwoody, 2008). Consequently, health-related news often took an episodic presentation, lacking broader contextualization and amassing a cycle of trendy stories related to the consumption of wine and heart health, the efficacy of low-fat diets, and the effects of sugar consumption, among others (Dentzer, 2009; Maksimainen, 2017).

In response to these criticisms, there were appeals for health journalists to adopt contextual reporting approaches, improve their communication with clinicians, delve deeper into the scientific processes behind relevant findings, and embrace more critical approaches to reporting (Nisbet & Fahy, 2015; Maksimainen, 2017). These measures, however, did little to slow the growing overlap between traditional health reporting and lifestyle journalism, particularly in online spaces, resulting in what is now known as wellness journalism.

The emergence of wellness journalism

In recent years, health reporting has expanded in scope to include a focus on 'wellness'. This shift emerged from the convergence of health and lifestyle journalism, driven by technological advancements in the 1950s that allowed newspapers to produce more pages in each issue (Cole, 2005). This surplus of space was filled with specialized reporting on fitness, food, fashion, travel, home and garden, relationships, and health, which came to be known as lifestyle journalism.

Characterized by a focus on public trends, human-interest stories, and a 'news-you-can-use' approach, lifestyle journalism covers what many consider 'soft news' topics, including in the areas of health and fitness. Part of the humanistic turn in journalism, lifestyle content centers on "the expressive values and practices that help create and signify a specific identity within the realm of consumption and everyday life" (Hanusch & Hanitzsch, 2013, p. 947).

As lifestyle journalism grew in popularity during the late 20th century, it challenged conventional journalistic principles (e.g., truth, objectivity, and verification) and reshaped journalists' personal relationship to their work. The growth of consumer culture and self-expression was reflected in consumer interest in journalism that provided guidance to this end (Hanusch, 2012). As the line between journalism and entertainment blurred, lifestyle journalists were forced to navigate their unique position as citizens, consumers, and clients (Hanitzsch & Vos, 2018). Online journalism intensified these trends.

The emergence of new media platforms in the early 2000s drove a shift toward personalized and commercialized content, reflecting the progression of lifestyle journalism within a Western economic framework that prioritized consumption and identity expression (Hanusch, 2019). Moreover, the blogging style prevalent in the early internet era complemented the soft news format synonymous with lifestyle reporting. The heightened commercialization of content facilitated the proliferation of 'advertorials,' spotlighting lifestyle journalism for its perceived role in promoting products (From, 2018).

The impact of lifestyle journalism, particularly in health and fitness domains, paved the way for the emergence of wellness journalism. Wellness journalism represents a genre and cultural movement that goes beyond the limits of traditional science reporting to envision health holistically as a physical, mental, emotional, and spiritual process. Before wellness journalism, the wellness movement began taking shape in the 1950s, "driven by people's unmet medical needs and their dissatisfaction with traditional forms of medical care at the time" (Baker, 2022, p. 22).

Citizens pursued wellness as a means of balance and well-being in all aspects of their lives. They sought alternative medical practices that promoted self-care, prevention, and personal empowerment (Baker, 2022). Unlike conventional approaches centered on established medical paradigms, the early wellness movement was led by alternative medical practitioners who viewed health as intertwined with one's social environment and lifestyle choices (Baker, 2022). In the 1980s, the popularization of fitness culture brought about the commercialization of wellness, as advertisers capitalized on people's physical insecurities. During this period,

> Consumers internalised the physical representations of beauty, sexuality, masculinity and femininity displayed by celebrities, television personalities, models, magazines and advertising, which were simultaneously normalised and aspirational, fusing together ideas about fitness, beauty, diet and nutrition that would come to form much of the wellness industry in the late twentieth century.
>
> *(Baker, 2022, p. 70)*

By the 1990s, the wellness movement entered the mainstream, drawing further attention from advertisers who drew on 'wellness' to promote products aimed at improving health, nutrition, and spirituality. This expansion positioned wellness not only as a movement interested in genuine wellbeing but also as a lucrative commercial enterprise now known as the wellness industry (Baker, 2022). This shift was pivotal in the emergence of wellness lifestyle journalism.

The rise of the wellness industry online bolstered the popularity of lifestyle wellness journalism centered on health and wellbeing, often through the endorsement of products and services. Journalists were central to this expansion, navigating the intersection of public interest, authenticity, health, and financial incentives within the wellness landscape. This is evident in news combining details about popular diets with mindfulness techniques, fitness advice with meditation practices, and medical research with its personal implications.

Such reporting has revitalized and challenged the conventional role of health and lifestyle journalism as they have evolved over several decades. While wellness content has not supplanted traditional health journalism, which maintains its 'hard-news' roots in science reporting, the frequent intertwining of health and lifestyle journalism, often in sections titled 'Health & Wellbeing' and 'Health and Lifestyle', has raised concerns about the impact of this convergence on journalists' duty of care to the public.

Apprehensions over the commercial focus and soft news format of lifestyle journalism have merged with questions over the veracity and depth of more traditional health coverage increasingly troubled by the threat of health misinformation and consumer safety (Nguyen & Catalan, 2020). In recent years, these concerns have been compounded by the influence of wellness industry influencers who have challenged the authority of journalists and play a significant role in shaping the online wellness discourse, sometimes in problematic ways.

Furthermore, the tendency for lifestyle content to center on human-interest stories – those that focus on the personal experiences and struggles of individuals – may ignore "…structural and social conditions and focusing on episodic, singular events, tend to attribute agency and responsibility to the individual" (Figenschou et al., 2023, p. 4). This highlights a broader criticism of the contemporary wellness movement for its tendency to ignore the broader environmental factors and role of institutions in affecting consumer wellbeing.

Still, the benefits of wellness journalism cannot be overlooked. By accommodating health information into the folds of lifestyle coverage, wellness reporting has made health information more accessible to consumers who otherwise wouldn't have engaged with it. As consumers turn more frequently to the internet for health information, the role of wellness lifestyle journalism is significant. Therefore, health journalism stands at a crossroads, occupying a unique space between hard and soft news that envisions audiences both as consumers and citizens and grapples with the broader function of journalism.

Critical issues and current contributions

Today's health and wellness lifestyle journalism industry has not escaped many of its initial critiques, especially with the attention to how this type of knowledge, typically considered entertainment bolstered by fact (see Hanusch, 2012), is actively growing online and becoming increasingly participatory in nature. As hard news health journalists face scrutiny for their reliability, reliance on particular sources, and political affiliations (Maksimainen, 2017), soft news journalists covering wellness topics continue to pump out articles at audience demand. For example, as journalists covering emergent health topics such as genetic testing or COVID treatments attempt to demystify complex health issues for the public, they have encountered an onslaught of counter-information, misinformation, and accusations of bias from audiences who find their coverage to be asymmetrical with their own beliefs or values. Amid these tensions, soft news journalists and other content creators (see Lorenz, 2023) swoop in to provide content that more closely aligns with audience cues, often with minimal organizational oversight and increasingly enticing revenue streams.

Given their specialty, health journalists are responsible for disseminating medical and health information to the public through reporting health news and trending medical research, as well as health policies and programs, and their critics. Since the beginning of the COVID-19 pandemic, research has explored the role of hard news health journalists as they navigate their professional responsibility of educating the public and combatting misinformation alongside their personal experience of living through a pandemic (Luengo & Garcia-Marin, 2020; Nguyen & Catalan, 2020; Parker et al., 2021).

In an interview study with health journalists working in the United States during the pandemic, researchers found these journalists were particularly concerned by a vulnerable news ecosystem (Perreault & Perreault, 2021). Not only did health journalists express a sense of responsibility for educating the public, but they also felt tasked with analyzing and disseminating government reports, navigating their own well-being, and adapting within a system that consistently devalued their work, questioned their credibility, and silenced their expertise.

Through the pandemic, news organizations remained committed to improving the quality of health journalism to increase audience trust. Part of that commitment is their desire to fact check and filter misinformation. During the pandemic, though, many people reported no longer trusting the journalistic sources they had in the past (Perreault & Perreault, 2021). Due, in part, to the pandemic and the 2020 U.S. presidential election, journalists were forced to sift through (mis)information from various sources. They were also challenged by audiences who wanted answers but did not always trust journalists to provide them (Perreault & Perreault, 2021). This led to journalists having to work that much harder at reporting accurate news while having to follow-up on rumors and misinformation related to the virus and eventual vaccines.

Challenging misinformation and legitimizing the role of health journalists has been made even more difficult by the increasing number of people utilizing digital and social media for the sharing and consuming of health and wellness information (Chen & Wang, 2021). It has been made more arduous by the soft news lifestyle journalists who are tasked with publishing work that may be perceived as hard news. For some news audiences, there seems to be a misunderstanding of what constitutes hard health news and what may be considered soft, wellness lifestyle journalism.

Lifestyle journalists have grappled with their position within the field long before the COVID-19 pandemic began (Hanusch, 2019; Maares & Hanusch, 2020), due, in part, to the surge of digital creators, micro-celebrities, and social media influencers online. These actors are progressively carving out space within the journalistic field challenging journalists' role and authority.

For example, Maares and Hanusch (2020) found that while professional influencers on Instagram did not immediately link their work to journalism, over two-thirds of the participants in the study perceived themselves as doing something online that resembles journalism. The study ultimately found social media influencers see their role online as deeply connected to conceptions of lifestyle journalism. This aligns with studies that have demonstrated the impact of journalistic interlopers – those actors performing acts of journalism outside of news organizations and beyond their organizational and institutional norms – on the broader field of journalism (Eldridge, 2018; Holton & Bélair-Gagnon, 2018; Kim & Shin, 2021). Guided less by traditional tenets and more by audience feedback, these actors at once provide a more comfortable source of news and information for audiences while dismantling the gates to news that held up for decades (see also Chapter 24).

Furthermore, the number of social media influencers whose work mirrors that of lifestyle journalists is increasing, especially within health and wellness (see also Chapters 14 and 26). Wellness influencers, lifestyle gurus (Baker & Rojek, 2020), and others who consider themselves to be educators and motivators of individual wellbeing are actively growing audiences to which they promote products, services, and ideologies, while also spreading health information (Wellman, 2023). Additionally, the wellness industry has long been tied to misinformation and conspiracy theories, especially in recent years.

Baker (2022) has argued that wellness itself is a gateway to misinformation, disinformation, and conspiracy, and Beres et al. (2023) explore the connections between spirituality, a common topic among wellness influencers, and conspiracy theories. As conversations and coverage of conspirituality (Ward & Voas, 2011) – the collision between spirituality and conspiracy theories – trend within the influencer and journalistic fields, both parties will be charged with the responsibility to educate the public, whether they do or do not see themselves as allies in the digital space.

Wellness influencers are sometimes seen as threats to lifestyle journalists, especially on platforms like Instagram and TikTok (Perreault & Hanusch, 2024). Theoretical research on boundary work has begun to tackle this present threat and to explain how lifestyle journalists are responding to wellness and lifestyle influencers. For example, one study found journalists engaged in boundary work through a protection of autonomy. They believe influencers within the wellness and lifestyle niche have a relationship with audiences that is deemed too close and that influencers are not as professional as is necessary for journalists (Perreault & Hanusch, 2024). Lifestyle journalists see themselves as dominant within the journalistic field, while influencers remain on the periphery. They also view influencers as a sort of competition, but not professionally, and utilize core tenets of hard news journalism to set themselves apart. This is a unique finding as historically, lifestyle journalists have struggled to connect with hard news values and are often perceived by hard news journalists as outsiders (Perreault & Hanusch, 2024).

The boundaries between wellness influencers and wellness lifestyle journalists are blurred on both sides, partly due to actions taken by influencers and journalists alike. The journalism industry, and especially those within lifestyle genres, is particularly vulnerable to what is known as influencer creep (Bishop, 2023). While the primary study on influencer creep examined artists who felt pressured to utilize influencer tactics to gain legitimacy and attention from online audiences, this can also apply to lifestyle journalists. When influencer tactics bleed into other industries that utilize digital and social media spaces, those professionals have no choice but to ascribe to those behaviors (Bishop, 2023).

Influencer creep often occurs in tandem with other critical issues facing lifestyle journalists today, including the commitment to performing aspirational labor to continue finding success in online spaces (Perreault & Bélair-Gagnon, 2024). Originally coined by influencer scholar Brooke Erin Duffy (2017), aspirational labor is understood as the labor done by someone for free with the hope of one day making a sustainable career out of that labor. Both influencer creep and aspirational labor are ongoing critical issues present within the lifestyle journalistic field and will continue to permeate this industry as wellness influencers expand their reach.

Collectively, this chapter offers perspectives symmetric to those of lifestyle journalism, while also hinting at challenges and opportunities unique to health journalism, wellness journalism, and the engagement of non-traditional actors (i.e., interlopers) in the health and wellness journalism environment that is, we argue, still in early stages.

Future directions

The COVID-19 pandemic marked a turning point for health and lifestyle journalism. The convergence of these journalistic subfields intensified as the public increasingly turned to journalists for crucial public health information and guidance on navigating life in an unprecedented era (Lewis, 2022). Stuck at home, people were thrust into a vast online information landscape where the distinctions between journalists and influencers blurred, and the credibility of content was threatened. Simultaneously, longstanding challenges within the journalism profession reached a tipping point.

As health journalists navigated a deluge of critical public health information, they grappled with their own health struggles: burnout, anxiety, and depression stemming from extended hours, online harassment, isolation, and a lack of institutional support (Bossio & Holton, 2021; Osmann et al., 2021). While newsrooms were replaced with home offices, the boundary between work and life was further blurred for lifestyle journalists who, already stretched thin before the pandemic, found themselves reporting on their own lives. Stories about at-home haircuts, bread recipes, and loungewear became necessary respite from the severity of the pandemic reality. In a world where health became a way of life, we relied on health and lifestyle journalists to make sense of our new reality. Years later, we continue to grapple with the pandemic's impact on the industry and its implications for these journalists.

Today, journalists continue to face challenges including mistrust, harassment, competition, and newsroom pressures (see Bélair-Gagnon et al., 2023). At the same time, the advent of new technologies is raising questions about the trajectory of lifestyle health journalism. In the era of generative AI, concerns reflect those seen in the early days of the internet. While platforms like Google are developing AI platforms to help journalists more efficiently write and edit articles, concerns over quality and transparency harken back to early uncertainties surrounding online news syndication (Schwitzer, 2009). Copyright lawsuits, like the one involving *OpenAI* and *The New York Times*, add another layer of complexity, revealing that the very models used to train AI may rely on copyrighted material taken without attribution from journalists. This is compounded by the ever-present threat of misinformation in AI-generated content, providing opportunities for bad actors to craft articles that undermine legitimate news information.

Still, progress is not out of reach. Advocacy for enhanced support of journalists' mental wellbeing and the preservation of journalistic autonomy presents a new opportunity for journalistic resilience that serves to strengthen the profession and ensure its vital public role (Bélair-Gagnon et al., 2023). Additionally, a growing emphasis on ethical journalism (Galikova Tolnaiova & Galik, 2022) compels journalists to be more deliberate in disclosing PR relationships and actively combat the proliferation of misinformation by enhancing the rigor and transparency of their reporting. Such shifts may ultimately apply to a broader spectrum of content creators, drawing together hard and soft news journalists in ways that amplify common goals rather than diminish the informative power of journalism.

Further reading

Bélair-Gagnon, C, Holton, A. E., Deuze, M., & Mellado, C. (2023). *Happiness in journalism*. London: Routledge. https://doi.org/10.4324/9781003364597.

Keshvari, M., Yamani, N., Adibi, P., & Shahnazi, H. (2018). Health journalism: Health reporting status and challenges. *Iranian Journal of Nursing and Midwifery Research*, 23(1), 14–17. https://www.ncbi.nlm.nih.gov/pmc/articles/PMC5769179/.

Maksimainen, H. (2017). Improving the quality of health journalism: When reliability meets engagement. *Reuters Institute for the Study of Journalism*. https://reutersinstitute.politics.ox.ac.uk/our-research/improving-quality-health-journalism-when-reliability-meets-engagement.

Perreault, G. P., & Bélair-Gagnon, V. (2024). The lifestyle of lifestyle journalism: How reporters discursively manage their aspirations in the daily work. *Journalism Practice*, 18(7), 1641–1659. https://doi.org/10.1080/17512786.2022.2111697.

References

Baker, S. A. (2022). *Wellness Culture: How the wellness movement has been used to empower, profit, and misinform*. Emerald Publishing Limited.

Baker, S. A., & Rojek, C. (2020). *Lifestyle Gurus: Constructing authority and influence online*. Polity Press.

Bélair-Gagnon, V., Holton, A. E., Deuze, M., & Mellado, C. (2023). Fostering a culture of well-being in journalism. In C. Bélair-Gagnon, A. E., Holton, M., Deuze, and C. Mellado (Eds.), *Happiness in journalism* (pp. 1–10) Routledge. https://doi.org/10.4324/9781003364597.

Beres, D., Remski, M., & Walker, J. (2023). *Conspirituality: How new age conspiracy theories became a health threat*. Public Affairs. [include DOI if available]

Bishop, S. (2023). Influencer creep: How artists strategically navigate the platformisation of art worlds. *New Media & Society*, 1–18. https://doi.org/10.1177/14614448231206090.

Bossio, D., & Holton, A. E. (2021). Burning out and turning off: Journalists' disconnection strategies on social media. *Journalism*, 22(10), 2475–2492. https://doi.org/10.1177/1464884919872076

Briggs, C. L., & Hallin, D. C. (2016). *Making health public: How news coverage is remaking media, medicine, and contemporary life*. Routledge. https://doi.org/10.4324/9781315658049

Chen, J., & Wang, Y. (2021). Social media use for health purposes: Systemic review. *Journal of Medical Internet Research*, 23(5), 1–16. https://doi.org/10.2196/17917

Cole, P. (2005). The structure of the print industry. In R. Keeble (Ed.), *Print journalism: A critical introduction* (pp. 21–38) Routledge. https://doi.org/10.4324/9780203006764.

Coombes, R. (2009). Health journalism: Two clicks away from Britney Spears? *British Medical Journal*, 338, 1–4. https://doi.org/10.1136/bmj.b570.

Dentzer, S. (2009). Communicating medical news--pitfalls of health care journalism. *New England Journal of Medicine*, 360(1), 1–3. https://doi.org/10.1056/NEJMp0805753.

Duffy, B. E. (2017). *(Not) getting paid to do what you love: Gender, social media, and aspirational work*. Yale University Press.

Dunwoody, S. (2008). Science journalism. In M. Bucchi and B. Trench (Eds.), *Handbook of public communication of science and technology* (pp. 15–26). Routledge. https://doi.org/10.4324/9780203928240.

Eldridge, S. A. (2018). *Online journalism from the periphery interloper media and the journalistic field*. Routledge

Figenschou, T. U., Thorbjørnsrud, K., & Hallin, D. C. (2023). Whose stories are told and who is made responsible? Human-interest framing in health journalism in Norway, Spain, the U.K. and the U.S. *Journalism*, 24(1), 3–21. https://doi.org/10.1177/14648849211041516.

Franklin, J. (2008). The end of science journalism. In M. W. Bauer & M. Bucchi (Eds.), *Journalism, Science, and Society* (pp. 143–156) Routledge. https://doi.org/10.4324/9780203942314.

Galikova Tolnaiova, S., & Galik, S. (2022). Epistemic and ethical risks of media reporting in the context of the Covid-19 pandemic, as challenges for the development of journalistic practice. *Media Literacy and Academic Research*, 5(1), 76–94.

Hallin, D. C., Brandt, M., & Briggs, C. L. (2013). Biomedicalization and the public sphere: newspaper coverage of health and medicine, 1960s-2000s. *Social Science & Medicine*, 96, 121–8. https://doi.org/10.1016/j.socscimed.2013.07.030

Hanitzsch, T., & Vos, T. P. (2018). Journalism beyond democracy: A new look into journalistic roles in political and everyday life. *Journalism*, 19(2), 146–164. https://doi.org/10.1177/1464884916673386.

Hanusch, F. (2018). Lifestyle journalism. In T. P. Vos (Ed.), *Journalism: Handbooks of communication science* (Vol. 19, pp. 433–450) De Gruyter Mouton. https://doi.org/10.1515/9781501500084.

Hanusch, F. (2012). Broadening the focus: The case for lifestyle journalism as a field of scholarly inquiry. *Journalism Practice*, 6(1), 2–11. https://doi.org/10.1080/17512786.2011.622895

Hanusch, F., Banjac, S., & Maares, P. (2020). The power of commercial influences: How lifestyle journalists experience pressure from advertising and public relations. *Journalism Practice*, 14(9), 1029–1046. https://doi.org/10.1080/17512786.2019.1682942

Hanusch, F., & Hanitzsch, T. (2013). Mediating orientation and self-expression in the world of consumption: Australian and German journalists' professional views. *Media, Culture, & Society*, 35(8), 943–959. https://doi.org/10.1177/0163443713501931.

Holton, A. E., & Bélair-Gagnon, V. (2018). Strangers to the game? Interlopers, intralopers, and shifting news production. *Media and Communication*, 6(4), 70–78. https://doi.org/10.17645/mac.v6i4.1490

Kim, C., & Shin, W. (2021). Unbound journalism: Interloper media and the emergence of fortune-telling journalism. *International Journal of Communication*, 15, 3519–3536.

Lewis, T. (2022). How the pandemic remade science journalism. *Scientific American*. https://www.scientificamerican.com/article/how-the-pandemic-remade-science-journalism/.

Lorenz, T. (2023). Content creators surge past legacy media as news hits a tipping point. *Washington Post*. https://www.washingtonpost.com/technology/2023/10/31/creator-economy-news-outlets-influencers/

Luengo, M., & Garcia-Marin, D. (2020). The performance of truth: Politicians, fact-checking journalism, and the struggle to tackle COVID-19 misinformation. *American Journal of Cultural Sociology*, 8, 405–427. https://doi.org/10.1057/s41290-020-00115-w

Maares, P., & Hanusch, F. (2020) Exploring the boundaries of journalism: Instagram microbloggers in the twilight zone of lifestyle journalism. *Journalism*, 21(2), 262–278. https://doi.org/10.1177/1464884920959552

Maksimainen, H. (2017). Improving the quality of health journalism: When reliability meets engagement. *Reuters Institute for the Study of Journalism*. https://reutersinstitute.politics.ox.ac.uk/our-research/improving-quality-health-journalism-when-reliability-meets-engagement.

McKeever, B. (2021). Public relations and public health: The importance of leadership and other lessons learned from "Understanding AIDS" in the 1980s. *Public Relations Review*, 47(1), 1–9. https://doi.org/10.1016/j.pubrev.2020.102007

Nisbet, M. C., & Fahy, D. (2015). The need for knowledge-based journalism in politicized science debates. *The Annals of the American Academy of Political and Social Science*, 658(1), 223–234. https://doi.org/10.1177/0002716214559887.

Nguyen, A., & Catalan, D. (2020). Digital mis/disinformation and public engagement with health and science controversies: Fresh perspectives from Covid-19. *Media and Communication, 8*(323), 323–328. https://doi.org/10.17645/mac.v8i2.3352.

Osmann, J., Selva, M., & Feinstein, A. (2021). How have journalists been affected psychologically by their coverage of the COVID-19 pandemic? A descriptive study of two international news organisations. *SMJ Open, 11*(7), 1–9. https://doi.org/10.1136/bmjopen-2020-045675

Paul, B., Jha, S., Dasgupta, A., Bandyopadhyay, L., & Mandal, S. (2021). Health journalism: A challenging paradigm. *Medical Journal of Dr. D.Y. Patil Vidyapeeth, 14*(3), 357. https://link.gale.com/apps/doc/A660468401/HRCA?u=anon~2a5ac2c7&sid=googleScholar&xid=9a3ca7a1

Parker, L., Byrne, J. A., Goldwater, M., & Enfield, N. (2021). Misinformation: An empirical study with scientists and communicators during the COVID-19 pandemic. *BMJ Open Science, 5*(1), 1–11. https://doi.org/10.1136/bmjos-2021-100188.

Perreault, G. P., & Bélair-Gagnon, V. (2024). The lifestyle of lifestyle journalism: How reporters discursively manage their aspirations in the daily work. *Journalism Practice, 18*(7), 1641–1659. https://doi.org/10.1080/17512786.2022.2111697.

Perreault, G. & Hanusch, F. (2024). Field insurgency in lifestyle journalism: How lifestyle journalists marginalize Instagram influencers and protect their autonomy. *New Media & Society, 26*(7), 3767–3785. https://doi.org/10.1177/14614448221104233.

Perreault, M. F., & Perreault, G. P. (2021). Journalists on COVID-19 journalism: Communication ecology of pandemic reporting. *American Behavioral Scientist, 65*(7), 976–991. https://doi.org/10.1177/0002764221992813.

Schwitzer, G. (2009). The state of health journalism in the U.S. *Kaiser Family Foundation*. https://www.kff.org/wp-content/uploads/2013/01/7858.pdf.

Stroobant, J., & Bogaert, S., & Raeymaeckers, K. (2019). When medicine meets media: How health news is co-produced between health and media professionals. *Journalism Studies, 20*(13), 1828–1845. https://doi.org/10.1080/1461670X.2018.1539344

Van Eperen, L., Marincola, F. M., & Strohm, J. (2010). Bridging the divide between science and journalism. *Journal of Translational Medicine, 8*(25), 1–3. https://doi.org/10.1186/1479-5876-8-25

Ward, C., & Voas, D. (2011). The emergence of conspirituality. *Journal of Contemporary Religion, 26*(1), 103–121. https://doi.org/10.1080/13537903.2011.539846.

Wellman, M. L. (2023). "A friend who knows what they're talking about": Extending source credibility theory to analyze the wellness influencer industry on Instagram. *New Media & Society, 26*(12), 7020–7036. https://doi.org/10.1177/14614448231162064.

Williams, K. (1999). Dying of ignorance? Journalists, news sources, and the media reporting of HIV/AIDS. In B. Franklin (Ed.), *Social policy, the media and misrepresentation* (pp. 79–96). Routledge. https://doi.org/10.4324/9780203031322-11

23
ETHICAL CONSIDERATIONS IN LIFESTYLE JOURNALISM

Renita Coleman

Introduction

Not two weeks after the end of a recent semester, a student in my Lifestyle Journalism class sent me an email asking for advice. She had just started an internship with a news outlet writing lifestyle stories. An editor approached her with a press release about a woman who owned a small business and who was also a mom and asked her to write a "feel good" piece for Mother's Day. Her question to me – could she say "no" to the story? She didn't see a compelling angle – after all there are lots of business-owning moms out there. This would just be free advertising for one. And, as she found out later, the public relations person who pitched the story was married to someone in the newsroom.

There, summed up in one 150-word email, was an example of *the* major ethical issue of lifestyle journalism – pressure from commercial influences. The reporter was conflicted about promoting a business when she saw no benefit to readers. Furthermore, she worried that one business would receive favorable coverage and possible financial gain because of a PR person's insider connection.

While this is only one dilemma, there is no shortage of similar examples of commercial influences in lifestyle journalism: Travel journalists are offered free or subsidized trips that readers want to know about, but newsrooms couldn't afford otherwise. Fashion journalists are routinely given expensive make-up and clothing. Movie critics are flown *gratis* to Hollywood to preview a movie before it is released. Do lifestyle journalists soften negative criticism knowing that advertisers expect positive coverage in return for financing lifestyle news, especially considering how increasingly unwilling audiences are to pay for it? Facing pressure to be more productive, lifestyle journalists depend on PR people for story ideas, making them feel pressured to return the favor when less newsworthy stories are pitched.

While these and other commercial pressures are not unique to lifestyle journalism, research has shown that they are "disproportionately more important in lifestyle journalism" than in other, hard news areas (Hanusch et al., 2017, p. 142). To date, research in lifestyle journalism has revolved around four major themes (Perreault & Miller, 2022). Of those, the one with an ethical angle is the one related to commercial and consumer aspects.

"Commercial" is defined as that which addresses its audiences not as citizens but as consumers (Hanusch et al., 2017). For example, travel stories that focus on shops, restaurants, and other experiences where one can spend money on individual pleasure are commercial. This is in line with the definition of lifestyle journalism as a field that "primarily addresses its audiences as consumers...about goods and services" (Hanusch, 2012, p. 2). And therein lies the difficulty in conceiving of lifestyle journalism as ethical. The "gold standard" of journalism ethics is political and hard-news journalism, which prizes objectivity and detachment. It is also a gendered view of journalism ethics (Costera Meijer, 2001). Perhaps, as Costera Meijer (2001) suggests, subjectivity and attachment are more suitable values for lifestyle journalism, considering that we live interdependently, not independent of others. Furthermore, people's personal lives are not insignificant to them and not divorced from their performance as good citizens.

We begin this chapter by discussing the theoretical foundations of our understandings of lifestyle ethics. While some research expands on the ethics of care and utilitarianism, most of them do not rely on classical ethical theory. Some hints of lifestyle ethics are found in research using theories of role conceptions and boundary work. Most of what we know is normative. The last half of this chapter focuses on our knowledge of commercial influences, including advertising, public relations, and taking freebies.

Ethics and commercial influences

We should first dispense with the idea that any kind of journalism is free from commercial pressures; clearly it is not (McManus, 1995; Weber, 2006). All newsrooms are financed by advertising and work with public relations representatives. These bring pressures, although different from those in lifestyle journalism, for example, the pressure to downplay stories about airplane crashes or the safety of mobile homes under threat of major advertisers pulling their support.

Rather, ethical lifestyle journalism should not deny or minimize its commercial purpose but acknowledge the tensions and deliver useful information and advice so that audiences can make informed choices, including about how to spend their money. Scholars have called for lifestyle to include more economic, social, and cultural contexts to reach its civic and political potential (Fürsich, 2012). The expansion of music journalism to include more global artists is one example of fulfilling this ethical role. The solution is not to strive for traditional journalism's definition of objectivity as neutrality, or to refuse all paid trips, but to substitute definitions of ethics that are more appropriate to lifestyle journalism, such as disclosing who paid and including multiple viewpoints, especially from those normally excluded as a way of achieving the goal of objectivity, conceived of as fairness. An ethic for the lifestyle journalism profession would be to acknowledge the importance of people's personal worlds (Costera Meijer, 2001, 2003, 2005) and give audiences insights on social issues, helping them envision a better world (Costera Meijer, 2005).

Another part of the definition of lifestyle journalism includes entertaining (Hanusch, 2012), that is, to provide amusement or diversion that is pleasurable. Studies of how lifestyle journalists conceive of their roles have borne out these purposes, showing that these professionals consider it their function to provide reviews of new products and services – the commercial aspect – and to provide fun, entertainment, and ideas on how to spend one's leisure time (Hanusch, 2019). Slowly, we are coming to realize that audiences for all types of journalism are both citizens *and* consumers, especially in a more consumption-driven world (Hanusch & Hanitzsch, 2013).

Ethical theory

Despite a large and growing body of work on lifestyle journalism, including its ethical practices, studies rarely address lifestyle ethics at the theoretical and conceptual levels. Instead, they tend to focus on "right" choices rather than the reasoning that makes those choices right, which is the concern of ethical theory. Jones (2023) is one of the few scholars to explicitly link lifestyle journalism with any ethical theory, in this case, the ethics of care. This normative theory was created by Carol Gilligan (1982) and subsequently developed by feminist scholars. Both its creation and principles make it uniquely appropriate for lifestyle journalism, given its foundations in journalism by and for women. While Jones only applies the ethics of care to food journalism, this essay offers a good basis to understand the ethics of other lifestyle journalism domains as well.

Care ethics, as it is now called, is different from other ethical theories such as Kantian ethics or Utilitarian ethics because it values relationships and caring for others over justice, reason, and logic. It is primarily a theory that considers ethics in terms of people's relationships and interdependence, as opposed to one of independent individuals. Care ethics came about when Gilligan, a student of psychologist Lawrence Kohlberg, perceived his theory of moral development to have a masculine perspective, focused on justice and rights at the expense of what she saw as more feminine concerns such as empathy and compassion (Gilligan, 1982). It was no small matter that studies of moral development using Kohlberg's theory (Kohlberg, 1981, 1984) consistently showed men as more morally advanced than women. In her book *In a Different Voice*, Gilligan (1982) interviewed women contemplating abortions to show how they incorporated considerations for individuals who would be affected when the woman was making an ethical decision, making the point that this had been left out of Kohlberg's theory. Gilligan (1982) theorized three stages comparable to those proposed by Kohlberg but incorporating these women's concerns such as considering one's own needs, responsibility for others, and power imbalances. Her stages progress from selfishness or prioritizing the self, to sacrificing oneself and prioritizing the needs of others, and to the highest level that recognizes a balance must be achieved, equally valuing oneself and others. Eventually, the instrument that measures moral development as well as the theory itself incorporated Gilligan's ideas, and now women and men score about the same. Interestingly, when there are significant differences, it is women who outperform men (Thoma, 1986).

Jones' (2023) essay is intriguing because it incorporates a specific ethical theory, showing how historically and contemporarily food journalism has, perhaps unwittingly, incorporated the ethic of care as its moral mascot. This feminist ethical orientation is fitting for a field that grew out of the "women's pages." It contrasts with the more justice-oriented subjects of objectivity and conflict of interest found in hard news journalism. It essentially offers a different yardstick by which to measure the ethics of lifestyle journalism than one that compares it to traditional journalism, always leaving lifestyle journalism as a less-ethical stepchild the way women were once considered inferior to men. It is a yardstick grounded in ethical theory, which most of the research on lifestyle ethics to date is not. This essay on food journalism offers a roadmap for how other specialty areas within lifestyle journalism could conceive of their own domains using an ethical lens.

To apply this theory to other aspects of lifestyle journalism, Jones first points out that the fundamental ethical duty arising from care ethics is that journalism should be able to "identify its service to citizens" (Jones, 2023, p. 132). Extending his argument from food journalists, all lifestyle journalists should adopt a care ethic to address readers as citizens who must consider relationships necessary for collectively living well. As examples of this function in the food realm, he cites a story from *Civil Eats* about monopolies in the food industry, which offers solutions that prioritize the needs of ranchers and farmers. This approach serves a public interest, in that it approaches readers as fellow citizens and cultivates awareness, empathy, and caring, in line with care ethics. He points out how these types of stories make links from private issues such as personal food choices, to public issues including the needs of others. This essay outlines the general principles that food journalists should use to ground their routines in care ethics so that lifestyle journalists should be able to apply these to their specialty whether it is travel, fashion, music, or any other category. For example, travel stories that explain culture and address audiences as interested in the living conditions of others would be fulfilling their ethical duties under the care model.

In applying care ethics to lifestyle journalism, Jones says that journalists should understand themselves "not as detached observers, but as fellow citizens who care with the public" (Jones, 2023, p. 134). Lifestyle journalists operating from a perspective of care ethics would "notice who is left out ... in whose specific interest the watchdog operates, and how the apparent marketplace fails to provide for everyone's needs" (p. 134).

Jones' framework does not apply just to serious, investigative, or long-form stories in the lifestyle domain. Recipes from different cultures can be contextualized with historic and political information about the culture. Sources should be sought from within the culture and locally owned restaurants included alongside expensive ones with renowned chefs. Reviewers can evaluate without being discouraging and maybe even acknowledge that livelihoods are affected by reviews. This way, small businesses are on an even playing field with those who hire large PR firms, satisfying the power balance imperative in care ethics. This "encourages care for the vulnerable and connects private and public worlds" (Jones, 2023, p. 140). All lifestyle journalists can pursue their work while asking, "who has what level of power and influence in any given situation... who benefits in a particular relationship; who is expected to do what work; and who is left with what specific needs?" (Jones, 2023, p. 140). Care-based journalism considers those who are vulnerable and invites audiences to care. Information is not value-neutral.

To my mind, this is a good model, grounded in a time-tested theoretical approach, one that is generalizable and thus appropriate for all lifestyle journalists. It offers a theoretical foundation for lifestyle journalism ethics research and guidance for practice, going beyond the best practices approach normally used.

While care ethics is growing in popularity, the most common type of ethical philosophy seen in traditional journalism under democratic societies is utilitarianism (Christians, 2011). Elliott calls it a "staple" in journalism (Elliott, 2007, p. 100). Much ethical work on traditional journalism (i.e., hard news) has adopted a utilitarian or Kantian ethics perspective (Steiner & Okrusch, 2006). Deuze (2005) identifies latent signs of utilitarianism when analyzing the perceptions and values of popular culture tabloid journalists in the Netherlands. Utilitarianism (Mill, 1859) is a normative ethical theory that prescribes maximizing happiness, most often reduced to the phrase "the greatest good for the greatest number." While it considers the interests of everyone equally, as also prescribed by care ethics, the definition of good or right in utilitarianism depends on the consequences or results. In

Deuze's (2005) study, one of the categories that arises out of interviews with journalists who cover gossip and celebrities is ethics. They talk about finding truth, minimizing harm, editorial autonomy, and serving the public – echoes of traditional, hard news journalism ethics. Deuze (2005) concludes that the ethical reasoning of these journalists reflects the core principles of utilitarianism. These journalists emphasized the need to serve the public, but this ideal was strongly connected to commercial interests in terms of sales figures; that is, the public was being well-served if they were buying the tabloids. These journalists' discussions about minimizing harm revolved around not harming celebrities to get their cooperation as sources, hardly the ideals that utilitarianism aspires to.

While this study shows how some lifestyle journalists think about their ethical obligations, Jones' essay maps a better route. It may be a stretch to suggest that celebrity journalists, who have been virtually excommunicated from the lifestyle realm following the death of princess Diana (Hindman, 2003), could adopt care ethics in their work; however, other lifestyle domains may do so the way food journalists have. Scholars have yet to address the paucity of ethical theory applied to lifestyle areas the way they have to traditional hard news. Jones' essay offers a model for that kind of theorizing with practical applications.

Current contributions and research

As already noted, very little research has examined lifestyle journalism ethics through the lens of ethical theory such as the care ethics essay (Jones, 2023) or Deuze's (2005) utilitarianism study. Instead, most conceive of ethics as questions of good versus bad practices. However, research using different theoretical perspectives such as role conceptions and boundary work frequently contains ethical concerns.

Role conceptions

Research into the professionalization of journalism is grounded in early studies of how journalists conceive of their roles in society (Cohen, 1963; Johnstone, 1976; Weaver et al., 2019; Weaver & Wilhoit, 1996; Weaver & Wilhoit, 1986; Weaver & Willnat, 2012). While these roles mainly describe the functions journalists' saw themselves as providing, a strong foundation of these studies was the influence of ethical ideologies. Theoretically, roles say something about ethics. In some cases, which role journalists saw themselves in was predicted by their ethical stances. For example, approving of the use of unauthorized documents aligned with the adversarial or watchdog role. A sense of ethics was the most salient influence on those who subscribed to the interpreter role, while disseminators were the most ethically cautious (Weaver et al., 2006).

Researchers eventually began adapting theories of role conceptions to lifestyle journalists (see also Chapter 16). The common ethical thread throughout this work is how these lifestyle journalists saw themselves as committed to the basic tenets of journalism, pointing to core journalistic values (Hanusch & Hanitzsch, 2013, p. 950). There are hints of the ethical and moral dimensions found within these roles, most notably the Community Advocate, which was the most centrally focused on the ethical and moral aspects of certain lifestyles, such as healthy cooking techniques or food practices that exploit vulnerable people, such as highly processed foods sold door-to-door in areas without grocery stores. The Life Coach role was similar, with these journalists expressing desires to help people – always a worthy ethical goal. The most strongly supported role, however, was the least ethical – the

Inspiring Entertainer, described as having "little consideration of providing critical voices" (Hanusch, 2019, p. 206).

One study also examined ethical perceptions separately and found that "an overwhelming majority of travel journalists subscribe to high ethical ideals" (Hanusch, 2011, p. 679) – a seeming contrast to a later study that found travel journalists identifying with the "softest" role of Inspiring Entertainer (Hanusch, 2019, p. 207). The study of only travel journalists measured ethical standards using travel journalists' self-reported agreement with practices such as disclosing if trips were sponsored and telling the truth even if it upset sponsors. However, few said they should not accept such trips even while agreeing it did affect their reporting (Hanusch, 2011).

Boundary work

Similar to studies of role conceptions, which is defined as how journalists view their work (Hanusch, 2019), is the area of boundary work, defined as "identifying who is and who is not a journalist" (Cheng & Tandoc, 2022, p. 1215). Within this framework is an area that discusses practices that are considered appropriate. Boundary work uses these practices to enact "expulsion," whereby someone or something is considered "non-journalistic" (Cheng & Tandoc, 2022, p. 1215). Studies from this theoretical perspective have also been conducted with lifestyle subfields, including fashion (Cheng & Tandoc, 2022) and lifestyle bloggers (Maares & Hanusch, 2020). The connection to ethics was more tenuous in these works, mainly comparing how these journalists define their own professionalism with respect to the values of traditional, hard news journalism of public service and immediacy to determine if they are legitimate journalists (Banjac & Hanusch, 2023; Cheng & Tandoc, 2022). One study comparing the "About" pages of fashion magazine websites with those of fashion bloggers found that the magazine journalists believe they are legitimate journalists, but there was little to show that bloggers subscribed to the same values (Cheng & Tandoc, 2022).

A study of general lifestyle bloggers on Instagram, however, found that these bloggers did hold ideologies that were like those of lifestyle journalists (Maares & Hanusch, 2020). However, the bloggers also acknowledged that as individual journalists, they were unable to follow journalistic ethical guidelines as well as journalists in larger organizations because of commercial pressures. They echoed the ethics of journalism in their responsibility to protect under-age audiences by acting as good role models, being transparent about sponsorships, and referencing their sources.

While role conceptions and boundary work studies secondarily describe lifestyle journalists' approach to journalism ethics as norms, there is a larger body of work that deals directly with the nature of practices as good and right and moral rules for lifestyle journalists. Commercial influences are a predominant theme in these descriptive studies.

Commercial influences

Even as the hallmark ethical issues in hard news journalism are truth and objectivity, research on lifestyle journalism ethics has focused on its commercial influences. Interviews with lifestyle journalists in Germany and Australia showed they constantly struggled to maintain control of editorial content (Hanusch et al., 2017). Even in China, where media are controlled by the government, lifestyle journalists found it hard to resist advertising demands (Li, 2012).

However, not all studies show lifestyle journalists hard-pressed to resist commercial influences; personal technology journalists saw no connection between the products they reviewed and the same products advertised in their sections (Usher, 2012). Instead, they claimed to be advocates for audiences bombarded by ads. Australian travel journalists likewise believed public relations did not influence their work (Hanusch et al., 2015). In another study in Australia, the journalists said there was little outside influence (Hanusch et al., 2020). The authors expressed skepticism, suggesting socially desirable answers were being given, especially in the face of the lifestyle journalists reporting they receive many press releases and contacts from public relations and advertising representatives. The authors say that journalists deny these pressures in accordance with the ideology that journalism should operate independently of economic and political interests (Hanusch et al., 2020). Hanusch et al. (2020) found that journalists who were younger; at magazines; or in travel, fashion, or beauty journalism experienced the most pressure.

Not all these studies view commercial influences through an ethical lens. For example, Hanusch and colleagues (2020) looked at the commercial influences using the hierarchy of influences approach (Shoemaker & Reese, 1996). Within this realm of commercial pressures, research has found the most dominant ethical pressures on lifestyle journalists come from advertising, public relations, and free products and services (Hanusch et al., 2017, p. 142), reviewed below.

Advertising

The cost of producing news is simply too great for the price of a newspaper, magazine, or subscription to a website to support. Additionally, advertising revenue accrues journalistic benefits in the form of larger staff, more independence, and better quality in addition to profits (Poutanen et al., 2016). Thus, media organizations rely on selling advertising as their primary business model. This is true whether the news is about politics, sports, or lifestyle. The problem arises because of the closer connection between lifestyle news and the products and services advertised alongside the editorial content – grocery stores, restaurants, and food brands advertise their products and services in the food sections and on food TV; travel destinations, agencies, airlines, and hotels purchase advertising in the corresponding travel media; corporations that produce makeup, perfume, and clothing are supporting the beauty and fashion media with their advertising dollars. Rarely do local TV news shows or metro sections of newspapers feature advertising from those they cover – school boards, city hall, or the local police department. Thus, there is pressure, whether actual or implied, to provide positive editorial coverage for those advertisers who pay for lifestyle media (Hanusch et al., 2017).

Research has primarily examined lifestyle journalists' perceptions about the influence of advertising and the conflict with duties to their audience. In studies using self-reports, lifestyle journalists admit to feeling pressure from advertising but claim not to bend to it. For example, in one study, only 20 percent of lifestyle journalists said advertising interests outweighed audience interests (Hanusch et al., 2020). Around 30 percent said they look for stories that will attract advertising, consider advertiser interests, or are dictated what to cover by advertisers (Hanusch et al., 2020). Even in China, with its state-controlled media system, advertising exerts more pressure than competition from colleagues and other media (Li, 2012). There is very little research that compares editorial content with advertising, but what there is shows a close connection between travel editorial content about certain destinations and advertising for them (Fürsich, 2012; Hanusch, 2012).

Lifestyle journalists are adamant that they are not mouthpieces of advertisers but have standards and strategies to resist such pressure (Hanusch et al., 2017). They do, however, admit that the walls between advertising and editorial departments are weakening (Hanusch et al., 2017). One way this has manifested is in the advent of so-called "advertorial" stories – a story written to look like an objective editorial that promotes a particular product or service but which an advertiser has paid for. Most discussion of the ethics of this revolves around transparency or disclosure in labeling, with most news organizations eventually settling on identifying it as "advertorial" or "sponsored content." Denisova (2021) even suggests the "paid advertising" label be added to clothes celebrities in photographs receive for free. Research is silent on whether audiences recognize what this means, but at least one study has found that audiences do want information about products that advertisers sell (Finnish Magazine Media Association, 2014).

More recently, discussion has come to include adjacent areas of native advertising and brand collaboration (Poutanen et al., 2016). Native advertisements are the online spinoff of advertorials. Embedded within the content of a story online rather than appearing as a separate banner or ad, using the same style as the news content, they are designed to appear as if they are news. For example, a video embedded within a story on a news outlet's site that is paid for rather than posted by a journalist is native advertising. The primary ethical concern is how to make sure audiences can distinguish paid advertising from the non-paid content. In some countries where media are regulated, disclosure is mandated in specific ways and places; in the United States and other countries, various organizations have established guidelines, although following them is voluntary (Poutanen et al., 2016). Clear labels such as "advertisement" are recommended over more ambiguous terms such as "produced by" or "in collaboration with," although "sponsored content" is still common (Poutanen et al., 2016).

Brand collaboration is when two or more brands or products work together to produce something that will appeal to both of their customers, for example, when an ice cream company and Kraft teamed up to produce a mac 'n cheese-flavored ice cream (Beer, 2021). In the media space, brand collaboration has been most common in lifestyle magazines (Poutanen et al., 2016). Special theme sections, about cars or weddings, for example, are produced by the news organizations in collaboration with businesses and advertisers. Sometimes, advertisers create the content and provide it; other times, the content is created by the media's sales department. Eventually, "hybrid editors" (Poutanen et al., 2016, p. 108) who had experience in both marketing and journalism were employed.

Poutanen et al. (2016) surveyed editors in Finland to identify the ethical dilemmas that arise and to understand how they handle and/or rationalize the ethical decisions. They identified four dilemmas, with some overlap. In most of these dilemmas, editors took on the role of explaining journalism's ethical principles and upholding them. The first dilemma was described as editors getting involved by promoting their media outlet to advertisers so that they will choose to advertise with it (Poutanen et al., 2016). The second dilemma involved making sure the ads were distinguishable from the editorial content. Editors relied on journalists' codes of ethics to achieve this. The third dilemma was the problem of journalists who had to take time away from creating news to produce advertorials. The fourth category was the problem of clearly disclosing the sponsorship of the content, i.e., transparency. In Finland, laws against media deception made it easier to turn down some collaborations; however, in countries without such laws and where codes of ethics are not binding, it may be trickier. Overall, Poutanen and colleagues (2016) were surprised to see how positive editors were toward sponsored content. They argued this could signal a possible industry shift in attitudes.

Rosenkranz (2016) takes up these same issues in travel journalism in the United States, pointing out that when travel sections were cut, freelancing for less pay became the rule rather than the exception, and audiences expected everything to be free on the Internet. With that came financial incentives to override ethical norms. The author shows how this market transformation has also transformed journalistic ethics. In interviews with travel journalists and bloggers, Rosenkranz (2016) explains how they justify these entrepreneurial endeavors while creating new meanings for journalistic practices. Ethics are not abandoned but reinterpreted. Mainly, the narrative is one of declining ethics in travel journalism. Economic crises precipitated the rise in what the author calls "the entrepreneurial spirit," (Rosenkranz, 2016, p. 59) or learning new skills that take advantage of technology. This manifests as creating websites, finding sponsors, using social media, and integrating business with journalism. Some travel journalists also have TV shows and guidebooks and turn themselves into a brand.

As with every domain, fashion journalism has its unique concerns. Much of the ethical discussion now revolves around sustainability or how cheap clothes that are thrown away quickly pollute the environment. While presenting evidence of how little fashion journalism covers sustainability, Denisova (2021) also offers practical advice such as writing stories that reduce the pressure to have the latest look, giving advice on "restyling" old clothes, and filling ones' psychological needs without shopping. Denisova (2021) also problematized the issue of "affiliated links" to stores that sell fashion items in the stories. In the United Kingdom, fully 100 percent of the fashion stories in the *Daily Mirror* had such links, 90 percent in *The Sun*, and more than half in *The Times*.

Public relations

Another aspect of commercialism that is separate from but tied to advertising is the public relations industry. Public relations (PR) is not tasked with directly selling products and services, but with creating goodwill between an entity and others. For example, governments want to create goodwill with citizens and businesses in their jurisdictions. Businesses want to create goodwill with customers and other companies they do business with. And everyone wants to create goodwill with the news media that cover them. PR is more media-connected than advertising because advertisers simply pay for the messages they want to convey via ads; PR professionals primarily aim to get media coverage for clients for free. This close connection to PR is not a one-way street with PR beholden to journalists; the relationship is also valuable to journalists in terms of ideas and access. They may feel obligated to consider the commercial interests of PR representatives in their work (Viererbl, 2022). PR people are sources of story ideas and information to journalists, saving them valuable time (Hanusch et al., 2017).

While lifestyle journalists say they are aware of PR attempts to garner favorable coverage and are skeptical of PR material, a content analysis showed nearly 20 percent of newspaper stories in the United Kingdom overall were derived from PR material (Lewis et al., 2008).

"Churnalism" is the name for using information in press releases with little to no independent reporting or even verification (Perreault & Vos, 2020). US journalists estimate 44 percent of news is influenced by PR (Sallot & Avery, 2006), although there are no estimates on the rate in lifestyle news alone. Despite these pressures, one study showed some travel journalists found ways to discuss controversial issues and not just provide positive coverage (McGaurr, 2012). PR is also a potential future career for journalists; in Germany, nearly half of freelance journalists work in PR (Koch & Obermaier, 2014), and it is also common for journalists in the United States to transition to PR.

Perceptions that PR practitioners and journalists have of one another can be another line of research with ethical implications. The relationship is not oppositional or adversarial (Koch & Obermaier, 2014). Generally, PR practitioners see their influences on journalists as more powerful than journalists do and think their work makes journalists' jobs easier, while journalists discounted this (Koch & Obermaier, 2014). Journalists think their ethics are superior to those of PR practitioners (Lee & Coleman, 2018), but still want to have good relationships with them (Sallot & Avery, 2006).

The relationship between PR and fashion journalism is especially symbiotic and is evolving to include social media influencers as well as journalists (Watson, 2019). Influencers and journalists need PR people to provide them with clothes, makeup, and accessories before they are available in stores to photograph and review. They need PR people to gain access to designers and celebrities and to get entrance to fashion shows and events.

Likewise, journalists who are critics are influenced in different ways by PR – pressure to write favorable reviews or review certain restaurants, for example (Titz et al., 2004). These critics have also developed ways of resisting, for example, restaurant reviewers are known for paying for their own meals and commonly do not let the establishments know they are coming, even refusing to publish photographs of themselves to keep waitstaff from recognizing them and altering their service. The influence of PR is especially strong for consumer-feedback sites, blogs, and social media influencers who review (English & Fleischman, 2019). In addition to the self-reports of lifestyle journalists who resist the influence of PR, there is anecdotal evidence in one study of an Australian food critic who gave a restaurant a rating of zero. He also admitted to not writing about the bad experiences – a more common work-around for reviewers of all domains, including travel journalists (Rosenkranz, 2016; Sallot & Avery, 2006).

Freebies

Receiving free products or services is another common practice in lifestyle journalism, with travel, fashion, and personal technology among the most affected (Hanusch et al., 2017). Few areas of lifestyle journalism are adamant about not taking freebies the way restaurant reviewers are (English & Fleischman, 2019). Taking free products or services is considered a softer form of pressure, in that it may lead journalists to be purely positive in their coverage (Hanusch, 2010). Despite how it sounds, some of this is understandable; journalists who review personal technology and games could not do so unless they were provided with the products before they are available for sale, for example (Perreault & Vos, 2018). Movie critics may be flown to Hollywood or New York to see the latest blockbuster before it is released locally. Fashion writers need to be ahead of the curve, with access to clothing before it is in the stores. In these cases, it serves the public to know about the movie or product as soon as possible. Where the line is drawn is more questionable in other situations.

Visitor boards, hotels, and airlines frequently host travel journalists, who typically justify this based on the high cost of such travel. Some even call this a "necessity" (Hanusch et al., 2017, p. 145). Among Australian travel journalists, about two-thirds say 75 percent of their travel is free (Hanusch, 2011). But what about music writers who are generally given free tickets to music festivals, even though the news organization could have purchased those tickets? How expensive should it be to cross the line into acceptability? What a journalist should do with the free products after photographing and writing about them is another area of concern; do free books and clothes get donated to a library or women's shelter or taken home to one's personal collection and closet? One area especially known for egregious freebies is fashion and beauty media. Clothing, perfume, and makeup are routinely sent to bloggers and traditional media fashion writers in hopes that the writers will promote the brand by wearing it. While some of these are billed as samples for review, others are not, such as flowers and meals. In the PR industry, this is known as "gifting" (Brooke, 2017).

While some media organizations have internal rules against taking freebies, others, including bloggers, do not. Some bloggers, in fact, view these items as part of their compensation (Bana, 2023). In the United States, the Federal Trade Commission has guidelines that require bloggers online and in social media to disclose when items they write about or pictures have been provided free or they have been paid to write about them (Darwin, 2015). As part of its consumer protection laws, the FTC guidelines say this is, "To ensure that products and services are described truthfully online and that consumers get what they pay for" Federal Trade (Commission, 2013, p. i). However, it is rarely enforced, and there are no penalties for failing to comply.

In the United States, the industry's broadest organization, The Society of Professional Journalists, has a code of ethics that states journalists should "refuse gifts, favors, fees, free travel and special treatment…that may compromise integrity or impartiality" (Society of Professional Journalists, 2018). Yet other domain-specific organizations are more equivocal; for example, the North American Travel Journalists Association says, "A member shall personally pay for all expenses incurred by that member *that are personal or beyond the services voluntarily provided by the host*" (italics mine) (Association, 2021). Similarly, the British Guild of Travel Writers' code of conduct says members will

> Accept facilities necessary for work offered to the press only on the understanding that they are in no way obliged to publicise any or all of the operation concerned and that the provision of such facilities will not influence their judgement.
> *(British Guild of Travel Writers, 2023)*

In other words, take freebies but not more than necessary, and don't let it influence your work.

One study textually analyzed the "About" pages of travel media websites including Conde Nast's *Traveler* to gauge the changes in ethics statements (Rosenkranz, 2016). It found a sea change – in 2013, ethics statements were removed, and condemnation of accepting free trips disappeared from the award-winning magazine published since 1987. Others, such as *Travel + Leisure* and *The New York Times*' travel section still retain these classic ethics guidelines. And there are also accounts of media outlets' use of a "don't-ask-don't-tell" (Rosenkranz, 2016, p. 61) policy, where their journalists actually do take free trips.

The common wisdom is that when free trips, products, or services have been provided, acknowledging this will satisfy a journalist's responsibility to the audience (Hanusch et al.,

2017). Sometimes, this is effective, with funded stories providing critical perspectives (McGaurr, 2012), and sometimes not. One study of Australian travel stories found that when a disclosure was provided, the coverage was even more overtly positive than when it was not (Hill-James, 2006).

Some countries lack laws or even codes of ethics proscribing the acceptance of gifts and freebies. This was the case in Spain, where researchers conducted interviews and surveys to understand journalists' perceptions of accepting gifts (Damas & Barber, 2009). They found, unsurprisingly, that journalists in lifestyle areas were more accepting of the practice than those in hard news, even calling the acceptance of free tickets and passes "a habitual practice" (84). Also more accepting were young reporters, women, those without college degrees, and journalists with online, magazine, and TV outlets. Low-value gifts caused the least concerns.

Conclusion

While this picture painted by research into lifestyle ethics is somewhat dreary, there are lessons and food for thought. First, it is no longer helpful to continue comparing lifestyle journalism ethics to political and other hard news journalism ethics. This view of ethics rests on the role of the press as informing citizens so that they can govern themselves in a democracy. Yet, there are aspects of good citizenship relevant to lifestyle journalism that are not adequately conveyed in traditional news, including creating awareness of social issues in entertaining ways and encouraging empathy for others. Without empathy, quality moral reasoning is impossible (Hoffman, 2000). Compassion and altruism are other worthy goals for lifestyle journalism to strive for. If reality TV that shows humanitarian and philanthropic efforts, such as *The Nanny* and *Undercover Boss*, can promote altruism in viewers (Tsay-Vogel & Krakowiak, 2016), how can that be bad for democracy? Other worthy ethical goals of lifestyle journalism can be to normalize gender identity and sexual practices once deemed deviant; to help create a sense of belonging for marginalized people, giving the feeling that they are represented and normalized; and recognizing and respecting differences (Costera Meijer, 2005). Quality ethical lifestyle journalism can help form people's moral competence (Nussbaum, 1997). These all lead to a more democratic culture. The yardstick by which ethics is measured must be expanded to encompass all forms of journalism.

Care ethics is an excellent grounding for this new view of ethical lifestyle journalism, as Jones (2023) shows in his essay on food journalism. This should be expanded to other areas of lifestyle journalism, providing a roadmap for areas including travel, fashion, beauty, gaming, and even celebrity journalism. Furthermore, it fills a gaping hole in lifestyle ethics research, which is that it is not grounded in ethical theory. Descriptive studies can take us only so far. Theory guides us to think more abstractly, applying insights in more generalizable ways.

And finally, it should be recognized that not every story in lifestyle media needs to fulfill ethical goals. It is fine to run listicles of the most popular songs or roundups of the best burgers. Fun and breezy "feel good" pieces with no major social issue at the center are also fine. However, if that is all that lifestyle media do, then they are not fulfilling their obligations to their audiences or society at large. Major investigative pieces on food corporations putting profits before people do not need to be a frequent occurrence. Ethical goals can be accomplished with smaller, but regular efforts. It isn't hard to incorporate a little background on the culture that invented the recipe being featured or some economic and historical information about the place in the travel story. Turning these inclusions into habit will make the job easier.

Some grounding in ethical thinking is helpful in solving practical dilemmas such as the student's at the opening of this chapter. She had been asked by an editor to write a "feel good" piece about a business owned by a woman, also a mom, for Mother's Day. The story idea came from a PR representative, who also happened to be married to someone in the newsroom. Rather than outright refusing to do the story, as was her first reaction, the student approached the editor with her concerns, and they were able to find another angle that sidestepped the ethical issues. In this case, the business-owner mom volunteered with a charity that helped minority women secure small-business loans. That angle solved the commercial pressure problem of promoting one person's business. As for the PR person being married to another employee, once the story evolved into something of benefit to readers, that issue was also eliminated.

Future directions

The body of evidence on lifestyle ethics is growing. One notably positive point is the globalization of this topic. The United States is not the dominant country as it is in so much journalism research. Instead, there are pictures of lifestyle ethics from China, Finland, Germany, Spain, Australia, Great Britain, South Africa, Singapore, and others. There is evidence from the fields of travel, food, fashion, celebrity, gaming, esports and more.

In addition to incorporating ethical theory into research about lifestyle ethics, the moral psychology perspectives of moral judgment (Coleman & Wilkins, 2020) and moral foundations (Haidt, 2003; Maxwell & Narvaez, 2013) could tell us much about how and why lifestyle journalists make ethical decisions and put it into context within the profession and among others. Also missing are audience perspectives on the ethics of lifestyle journalism. How do readers perceive a story that discloses free goods and services compared to one that doesn't? The body of knowledge contains many self-reports from the perspective of journalists, especially from interviews. A next step would be to examine the content these journalists create. How often does disclosure of freebies occur? How is it related to the positive tone of coverage?

That many of the findings reported conflict with those of other studies points to the need for more research using different techniques; for example, rather than assessing journalists' ethical standards with self-reports or even by comparing their self-reports to the content they produce, instruments that unobtrusively measure moral judgment such as the Defining Issues Test (Rest et al., 1997; Rest et al., 1999) could help shed light on these questions. Absent from the literature are experiments that test cause and effect, for example, whether journalists who were offered freebies respond differently compared to those who were not. More unobtrusive methods can help us better understand the actual effects of commercial pressures, rather than the effects lifestyle journalists think they have. There is potential here to help journalists do their work in more ethical ways.

Further reading

Costera Meijer, I. (2001). The public quality of popular journalism: Developing a normative framework. *Journalism Studies*, 2(2), 189–205. https://doi.org/10.1080/14616700120042079

Jones, J. P. (2023). If it feeds, it leads: Food journalism, care ethics, and nourishing democracy. *Journal of Media Ethics* 38(3), 132–145.

Plaisance, Patrick Lee. (2018). *Journalism ethics*. In Tim P. Vos (Ed.), *Journalism* (Chapter 5, pp. 83–102). DeGruyter Inc.

Steiner, L., & Okrusch, C. M. (2006). Care as a virtue for journalists. *Journal of Mass Media Ethics*, 21(2/3), 102–122. https://doi.org/10.1207/s15327728jmme2102&3_2

References

Bana, A. (2023). Why should fashion bloggers disclose freebies, when magazine editors rarely do? *Untouchable*, May 18. Retrieved from https://www.untouchableblog.com/blog/fashion-bloggers-ftc-paid-posts.

Banjac, S., & Hanusch, F. (2023). The struggle for authority and legitimacy: Lifestyle and political journalists' discursive boundary work. *Journalism*, 24(10), 2155–2173. https://doi.org/10.1177/14648849221125702

Beer, J. (2021, July 16). Why marketers love mashups, from mac 'n' cheese ice cream to baked bean smoothies. *Fast Company*. Retrieved from https://www.fastcompany.com/90655417/why-marketers-love-mashups-from-mac-n-cheese-ice-cream-to-baked-bean-smoothies. Accessed March 1, 2024.

British Guild of Travel Writers. (2023). *Code of conduct*. Retrieved from https://bgtw.org/about/. Accessed December 28, 2023.

Brooke, E. (2017). But what do publicists think of swag? *Racked*, November 13. Retrieved from https://www.racked.com/2017/11/13/16615380/editor-gifting. Accessed December 28, 2023.

Cheng, L., & Tandoc, E. C. (2022). From magazines to blogs: The shifting boundaries of fashion journalism. *Journalism*, 23(6), 1213–1232. https://doi.org/10.1177/1464884920988183

Christians, C. G. (2011). Journalism ethics in theory and practice. In G. Cheney, S. May, & D. Munshi (Eds.), *The handbook of communication ethics* (pp. 190–203). Routledge.

Cohen, B. (1963). *The press and foreign policy*. Princeton University Press.

Coleman, R., & Wilkins, L. (2020). *Moral development: A psychological approach to understanding moral decision making*. Routledge.

Costera Meijer, I. (2001). The public quality of popular journalism: Developing a normative framework. *Journalism Studies*, 2(2), 189–205. https://doi.org/10.1080/14616700120042079

Costera Meijer, I. (2003). What is quality television news? A plea for extending the professional repertoires of newsmakers. *Journalism Studies*, 4(1), 15–29. https://doi.org/10.1080/14616700306496

Costera Meijer, I. (2005). Impact or content? Ratings vs quality in public broadcasting. *European Journal of Communication*, 20(1), 27–53. https://doi.org/10.1177/0267323105049632

Damas, S. H., & Barber, C. M. (2009). Journalism ethics and acceptance of gifts: A view from Madrid journalists. *Brazilian Journalism Research*, 5(2), 64–92. https://doi.org/10.25200/BJR.v5n2.2009.212

Darwin, L. (2015). Why those FTC blogger requirements aren't working. *Refinery29*, April 7. Retrieved from https://www.refinery29.com/en-us/2015/04/85144/ftc-blogger-requirements. Accessed Dec. 28, 2023.

Denisova, A. (2021). *Fashion media and Sustainability: Encouraging ethical consumption via journalism and influencers*. University of Westminster Press.

Deuze, M. (2005). Popular and professional ideology: Tabloid reporters and editors speak out. *Media, Culture & Society*, 27(6), 861–882. https://doi.org/10.1177/0163443705057674

Elliott, D. (2007). Getting Mill right. *Journal of Mass Media Ethics*, 22(2–3), 100–112. https://doi.org/10.1080/08900520701315806

English, P., & Fleischman, D. (2019). Food for thought in restaurant reviews. *Journalism Practice*, 13(1), 90–104. https://doi.org/10.1080/17512786.2017.1397530

Federal Trade Commission. (2013). comDisclosures. chrome-extension: Retrieved from //efaidnbmnnnibpcajpcglclefindmkaj/https://www.ftc.gov/sites/default/files/attachments/press-releases/ftc-staff-revises-online-advertising-disclosure-guidelines/130312dotcomdisclosures.pdf. Accessed December 28, 2023.

Finnish Magazine Media Association. (2014). The effects of magazine advertising: Survey statements concerning magazine advertising. *Aikakausmedia*. Retrieved from https://www.aikakausmedia.fi/en/research/. Accessed December 27, 2023.

Fürsich, E. (2012). Lifestyle journalism as popular journalism. *Journalism Practice*, 6(1), 12–25. https://doi.org/10.1080/17512786.2011.622894

Gilligan, C. (1982). *In a different voice: Psychological theory and women's development*. Harvard University Press.

Haidt, J. (2003). The moral emotions. In R. J. Davidson, K. R. Scherer, & H. H. Goldsmith (Eds.), *Handbook of affective sciences* (pp. 852–870). Oxford University Press.

Hanusch, F. (2010). The dimensions of travel journalism: Exploring new fields for journalism research beyond the news. *Journalism Studies*, 11(1), 68–82. https://doi.org/10.1080/14616700903290569

Hanusch, F. (2011). A profile of Australian travel journalists' professional views and ethical standards. *Journalism: Theory, Practice & Criticism*, 13(5), 668–686. https://doi.org/10.1177/1464884911398338

Hanusch, F. (2012). Broadening the focus: The case for lifestyle journalism as a field of scholarly inquiry. *Journalism Practice*, 6(1), 2–11. https://doi.org/10.1080/17512786.2011.622895

Hanusch, F. (2019). Journalistic roles and everyday life: An empirical account of lifestyle journalists' professional views. *Journalism Studies*, 20(2), 193–211. https://doi.org/10.1080/1461670X.2017.1370977

Hanusch, F., Banjac, S., & Maares, P. (2020). The power of commercial influences: How lifestyle journalists experience pressure from advertising and public relations. *Journalism Practice*, 14(9), 1029–1046. https://doi.org/10.1080/17512786.2019.1682942

Hanusch, F., & Hanitzsch, T. (2013). Mediating orientation and self-expression in the world of consumption: Australian and German lifestyle journalits' professional views. *Media, Culture & Society*, 35(8), 943–959. https://doi.org/10.1177/0163443713501931

Hanusch, F., Hanitzsch, T., & Lauerer, C. (2017). "How much love are you going to give this brand?" Lifestyle journalists on commercial influences in their work. *Journalism*, 18(2), 141–158. https://doi.org/10.1177/1464884915608818

Hanusch, F., Mellado, C., Boshoff, P., Humanes, M. L., de Leon, S., Pereira, F., Ramirez, M. M., Roses, S., Subveri, F., Wyss, V., & Yez, L. (2015). Journalism students' motivations and expectations of their work in comparative perspective. *Journalism and Mass Communication Educator*, 70(2), 141–160. https://doi.org/10.1177/1077695814554295

Hill-James, C. R. (2006). *Citizen tourist: Newspaper travel journalism's responsibility to its audience*. Unpublished PhD dissertation, Queensland University of Technology. Brisbane, QLD, Australia.

Hindman, E. B. (2003). The princess and the paparazzi: Blame, responsibility, and the media's role in the death of Diana. *Journalism and Mass Communication Quarterly*, 80(3), 666–688. https://doi.org/10.1177/107769900308000311

Hoffman, M. L. (2000). *Empathy and moral development: Implications for caring and justice*. Cambridge University Press.

Johnstone, J. W. S., Edward, J., & Bowman, William W. (1976). *The news people: A sociological portrait of American journalists and their work*. University of Illinois Press.

Jones, J. P. (2023). If it feeds, it leads: Food journalism, care ethics, and nourishing democracy. *Journal of Media Ethics*, 38(3), 132–145. https://doi.org/10.1080/23736992.2023.2228294

Koch, T., & Obermaier, M. (2014). Blurred lines: German freelance journalists with secondary employment in public relations. *Public Relations Review*, 40(3), 473–482. https://doi.org/10.1016/j.pubrev.2014.02.006

Kohlberg, L. (1981). *The philosophy of moral development: Moral stages and the idea of justice*. Cambridge, MA: Harper & Row.

Kohlberg, L. (1984). *The psychology of moral development: The nature and validity of moral stages*. San Francisco: Harper & Row.

Lee, A. M., & Coleman, R. (2018). "We're more ethical than they are:" Third-person and first-person perceptions in the ethical climate of American journalists. *Journalism*, OnlineFirst (May 30, 2018). https://doi.org/10.1177/1464884918778249.

Lewis, J., Williams, A., & Franklin, B. (2008). A compromised fourth estate? UK news, journalism, public relations and news sources. *Journalism Studies*, 9(1), 1–20. https://doi.org/10.1080/14616700701767974

Li, S. (2012). A new generation of lifestyle magazine journalism in China. *Journalism Practice*, 6(1), 122–137. https://doi.org/10.1080/17512786.2011.622901

Maares, P., & Hanusch, F. (2020). Exploring the boundaries of journalism: Instagram micro-bloggers in the twilight zone of lifestyle journalism. *Journalism*, 21(2), 262–278. https://doi.org/10.1177/1464884918801400

Maxwell, B., & Narvaez, D. (2013). Moral foundations theory and moral development and education. *Journal of Moral Education*, 42(3), 271–280. https://doi.org/10.1080/03057240.2013.825582

McGaurr, L. (2012). Travel journalism and environmental conflict: A cosmopolitan perspective. *Journalism Studies*, 11(1), 122–137. https://doi.org/10.1080/14616700903068924

McManus, J. H. (1995). A market-based model of news production. *Communication Theory*, 5(4), 301–338. https://doi.org/10.1111/j.1468-2885.1995.tb00113.x

Mill, J. S. (1859). *On liberty*. J. W. Parker.

North American Travel Journalists Association. (2021). *Code of ethics*. Retrieved from https://www.natja.org/about-us/code-of-ethics/#:~:text=Honesty%20and%20integrity%20should%20be,be%20clearly%20stated%20as%20such. January 1. Accessed December 28, 2023.

Nussbaum, M. (1997). *Cultivating humanity*. Harvard University Press.

Perreault, G., & Miller, K. (2022). When journalists are voiceless: How lifestyle journalists cover hate and mitigate harassment. *Journalism Studies*, 23(15), 1977–1993. https://doi.org/10.1080/1461670X.2022.2135583

Perreault, G. P., & Vos, T. P. (2018). The GamerGate controversy and journalistic paradigm maintenance. *Journalism*, 19(4), 553–569. https://doi.org/10.1177/1464884916670932

Perreault, G., & Vos, T. P. (2020). Metajournalistic discourse on the rise of gaming journalism. *New Media & Society*, 22(1), 159–176. https://doi.org/10.1177/1461444819858695

Poutanen, P., Luoma-Aho, V., & Suhanko, E. (2016). Ethical challenges of hybrid editors. *International Journal of Media Management*, 18(2), 99–116. https://doi.org/10.1080/14241277.2016.1157805

Rest, J. R., Edwards, L., & Thoma, S. J. (1997). Designing and validating a measure of moral judgment: Stage preference and stage consistency approaches *Journal of Educational Psychology*, 89(1), 5–28.

Rest, J. R., Narvaez, D., Thoma, S., & Bebeau, M. J. (1999). DIT2: Devising and testing a revised instrument of moral judgment. *Journal of Educational Psychology*, 91(4), 644–659.

Rosenkranz, T. (2016). Becoming entrepreneurial: Crisis, ethics and marketization in the field of travel journalism. *Poetics*, 54, 54–65. https://doi.org/10.1016/j.poetic.2015.09.003

Sallot, L. M., & Avery, E. J. (2006). Investigating relationships between journalists and public relations practitioners: Working together to set, frame and build the public agenda, 1991–2004. *Public Relations Review*, 32(2), 151–159. https://doi.org/10.1016/j.pubrev.2006.02.008

Shoemaker, P., & Reese, S. (1996). *Mediating the message: Theories of influences on mass media content*. Longman.

Society of Professional Journalists. (2018). *SPJ code of ethics*. Retrieved from https://www.spj.org/ethicscode.asp Accessed December 11, 2023.

Steiner, L., & Okrusch, C. M. (2006). Care as a virtue for journalists. *Journal of Mass Media Ethics*, 21(2/3), 102–122. https://doi.org/10.1207/s15327728jmme2102&3_2

Thoma, S. (1986). Estimating gender differences in the comprehension and preference of moral issues. *Developmental Review*, 6(2), 165–180.

Titz, K., Lanza-Abbott, J. A., & Cordua y Crus, G. (2004). The anatomy of restaurant reviews. *International Journal of Hospitality & Tourism Administration*, 5(1), 49–65. https://doi.org/doi:10.1300/J149v05n01_03

Tsay-Vogel, M., & Krakowiak, K. M. (2016). Inspirational reality TV: The prosocial effects of lifestyle transforming reality programs on elevation and altruism. *Journal of Broadcasting & Electronic Media*, 60(4), 567–586. https://doi.org/10.1080/08838151.2016.1234474

Usher, N. (2012). Service journalism as community experience. *Journalism Practice*, 6(1), 107–121. https://doi.org/10.1080/17512786.2011.628782

Viererbl, B. (2022). Writing for the audience or for public relations? How lifestyle editors perceive expectations about their professional role and manage potential for conflict. *Journalism*, 24(7), 1593–1609. https://doi.org/10.1177/14648849211067586

Watson, C. (2019). Fashion journalism and PR. In J. Bradford (Ed.), *Fashion Journalism* (pp. 283–298). New York: Routledge.

Weaver, D. H., & Wilhoit, G. C. (1986). *The American journalist: A portrait of U.S. news people and their work*. Indiana University Press.

Weaver, D. H., & Wilhoit, C. G. (1996). *The American journalist in the 1990s: U.S. news people at the end of an era*. Lawrence Erlbaum Associates.

Weaver, D., Beam, R., Brownlee, B., Voakes, P., & Wilhoit, G. C. (2006). *The American journalist in the 21st Century: U.S. newspeople at the dawn of a new millenium*. Lawrence Erlbaum Associates.

Weaver, D., & Willnat, L. (2012). *The global journalist in the 21st century*. Routledge.

Weaver, D., Willnat, L., & Wilhoit, C. G. (2019). The American journalist in the digital age. *Journalism Studies*, *20*(3), 423–441.

Weber, J. (2006). Strassburg, 1605: The origins of the newspaper in Europe. *German History*, *24*(3), 387–412. https://doi.org/10.1191/0266355406gh380oa

PART V

New horizons in lifestyle journalism studies

24
TASTEMAKERS OR THOUGHT LEADERS? LIFESTYLE INFLUENCERS AND BOUNDARIES OF LIFESTYLE JOURNALISM

Phoebe Maares

Introduction

Lifestyle influencers and (micro-)bloggers are often accused of being vain, materialistic, and primarily sharing content with (overt) sponsorship. Many vocal critics in this regard tend to be lifestyle journalists. In 2016, senior editors at *US Vogue* reaped backlash in a perfect storm when they criticised bloggers and influencers as they wrote: "Note to bloggers who change head-to-toe paid-to-wear outfits every hour: please stop. Find another business. You are heralding the death of style" (Topping, 2016). Similarly, German weekly lifestyle magazine *Iconist* argued that a better term for bloggers and influencers would be "Digital Native Sales Agent", as they – just like women selling Tupperware – would primarily sell "pretty but superfluous nonsense" (Hackober, 2017 own translation). Vogues' blog post was met with criticism from long-established bloggers like Susanna Lau, who pointed out that *Vogue* and other lifestyle journalists were also "beholden to brands in one way or another, getting salaries at publications that are stuffed full of credits that are tied to paid advertising" (Hall, 2016). Others claimed that influencers and bloggers would finally bring fashion out of the "ivory tower" (Kemp, 2016), and some journalists even argue digital journalists "are really just creators by a different name" (Stenberg, 2021). These examples illustrate the immense difficulty of defining the boundaries around lifestyle journalism in digital spaces.

What makes someone a journalist? In many countries, journalism is not a restricted occupation, which means that journalism can be practised without educational credentials, and anyone can call themselves a journalist. While this approach is rooted in the historical evolution of democracies and the role freedom of speech and information plays in them, it has also always been open to debate. In the early days of journalism, teachers, physicians, and civil servants would write for newspapers and magazines, but soon, emerging trade unions marked their territory and pushed to exclude these writers from the field (Ruellan, 1993). Likewise, women, especially noble and upper-class women, have long been writing for periodicals as "writing jobs could be completed in the privacy of one's home" (Duffy,

2013, p. 25) and were thus viewed as an acceptable occupation. However, they were rarely perceived as journalists.

In recent decades, digitisation has led to a surge of new, digital actors like (micro-) bloggers and influencers that scholarship subsumes under the umbrella term of 'peripheral journalistic actors' (see Hanusch & Löhmann, 2023). These peripheral actors encompass a heterogeneous group of individual and collective actors who produce and distribute content that sometimes has similarities with journalistic content. At the same time, they often differ from what is considered the 'core' of journalism, most profoundly regarding their education, practices, professionality, and motives. With such actors on the rise, both the journalistic community and scholarship grapple again with the question of whether journalism can be understood as a profession. The problem with such an approach is that the (legal) barriers to calling oneself a 'journalist' and to 'do journalism' are relatively low compared to other prototypical professions, such as medicine, law, or education (Lewis, 2015). Abbott (1988, p. 255), thus, also argues for thinking of journalism as a "permeable occupation" instead as it shares many tasks and practices with other occupations like communication work (see also Deuze, 2007). Such a view shifts the question around whether journalism is a profession to an interest in the professional struggles that journalists engage in to discursively demarcate what they are doing from similar work, emphasising the legitimacy of their work (Carlson, 2017).

This chapter provides an overview of the literature on the contested boundaries between lifestyle journalism and influencers, discussing research on journalists' and influencers' motivations and perceptions of each other as well as studies on the audience's perspective of these boundaries. By exploring boundary discourses from the perspective of (a) traditional journalists, (b) bloggers and influencers, and (c) audiences, this chapter contributes to a more nuanced understanding of issues of complementation or competition and, ultimately, the blurring boundaries of the lifestyle journalistic field.

Definitions and historical perspectives

Journalism as an occupation with permeable boundaries

We can think of journalism as a social space in which actors share a common understanding of what they want to achieve with their work and how it can be distinguished from other social fields. From a research perspective, this notion has been addressed through the idea of journalism as an interpretive community (Zelizer, 1993), institution (Vos, 2019), or field (Neveu, 2007). These approaches think of journalism as bounded in some way. We can distinguish between social and symbolic boundaries; while the former refers to differences based on unequal access to resources and social opportunities, the second describes "conceptual distinctions made by social actors to categorise objects, people, practices, and even space and time" (Lamont & Molnár, 2002, p. 168). As such, social and symbolic boundaries are often linked, as the dominant social groups have power in defining symbolic value and tend to legitimise their own culture and group identity as superior (Bourdieu, 1984).

Likewise, we can distinguish between actors at the core of a social field, who define what the field is about, and those at the periphery, who enter from the outside and claim to be part of the field (Eldridge, 2018; Hanusch & Löhmann, 2023). When it comes to professions or occupations with more permeable boundaries, like journalism, peripheral actors can more easily claim membership. As a consequence, the core of the field competes over the legitimacy of their jurisdictional claims, that is, that their claimed expertise and control of an issue are accepted as legitimate by the state, the public, and the members of their field (Abbott, 1988). For journalists, this issue could be to inform the public factually, to provide citizens with everything of relevance for them to make informed decisions, or to inspire audiences and provide them exemplars for living their lives (Hanitzsch & Vos, 2018). At the same time, external and peripheral actors can claim that they fulfil similar roles for society and, as such, challenge existing boundaries of the field.

These examples illustrate that the struggle over jurisdiction can exist within the bounds of the journalistic field as well as at its boundaries. Such struggles over jurisdiction and claims of legitimacy can also be understood as boundary work, a concept that describes how different actors challenge, maintain, protect, or expand existing boundaries (Gieryn, 1999). In examining how scientists distinguish themselves from other forms of knowledge producers, Gieryn (1999) conceptualises three discursive responses to challenges attacking their authority: expansion, expulsion, and protection of autonomy. Transferred to the journalistic field, journalistic discourse can react to challenges by including or rejecting new actors, practices, or issues of professionalism or by protecting the field's autonomy (Carlson, 2015). Journalistic boundary work can, therefore, include the normalisation or incorporation of non-traditional journalistic actors, practices, or new norms; the dismissal of deviant actors, practices, or norms; and the protection of any attack on the field's autonomy (Carlson, 2017). At the same time, new actors can claim access to the journalistic field with different intentions, such as financial gain or the distribution of a specific ideology. A systematic review of scholarship on peripheral actors develops ten dimensions relating to *journalistic identities*, *practices*, and *structures* along which they can be positioned (Hanusch & Löhmann, 2023). Subsumed under the realm of *journalistic identities*, Hanusch & Löhmann (2023) identify the dimensions of (1) values, (2) journalistic experience, and (3) claimed membership to the field; relating to the area of *practices*, they include actors' (4) professionality, (5) specific expertise, and (6) formats; and combined under *structures*, they consider actors' (7) transformativity, (8) autonomy, (9) audience-centricity, and (10) organisation. These dimensions allow a more nuanced understanding of different peripheral actors. For example, relating to the dimension of transformativity, some actors have been found to pursue antagonistic, i.e., destructive, or agonistic, i.e., constructive, intentions (Eldridge, 2019; Maares & Hanusch, 2023). Likewise, peripheral actors can be described as either highly autonomous or dependent on external influences. As such, peripheral and outside actors challenge the fields' authority as well as threaten access to resources that journalism depends on, like sources, audience reach, and advertising funds.

Importantly, boundary work and, subsequently, the definition of what constitutes legitimate journalism is contextual and highly relational (Banjac & Hanusch, 2022; Hanusch & Löhmann, 2023; Maares & Hanusch, 2023). For example, Buzzfeed was long rejected as a legitimate journalistic format until the company invested in well-known reporters, journalists in other media adapted some of its key reporting techniques, and journalistic discourse included it through the process of expansion (Tandoc, 2018). Likewise, research illustrates that journalists emphasise different boundary markers, i.e., indicators that best describe their journalistic legitimacy in comparison to other actors, depending on the reference group they compare themselves with (Ferrucci & Vos, 2017). Discourses surrounding the boundaries of lifestyle journalism illustrate these different strategies very well.

Boundaries of lifestyle journalism

Throughout this book, we find references to the relationship between lifestyle journalism and political journalism and between 'soft' and 'hard' news, that is, news that is more entertaining and focuses on personal strokes of fate (Reinemann et al., 2011; see also Chapters 2, 3, 26, and 27). Traditionally, journalistic discourse and journalism research have focused on journalists working on political or breaking news beats (Hanitzsch & Wahl-Jorgensen, 2020). Consequently, the dominant boundary discourses relating to lifestyle journalism revolved around the question of whether soft and lifestyle topics could be considered legitimate journalism (Carlson, 2017, p. 39). On the one hand, these discourses concern key values of the journalistic field; on the other hand, they reflect the gendered division of the journalistic field (Banjac & Hanusch, 2023). Moreover, lifestyle journalism is viewed as highly market-dependent, violating journalism's core ideal of autonomy and, as such, sitting in the "margins of traditional areas of journalism" (Viererbl, 2022, p. 1596). Its close relationship to consumer culture, reporting on products and services, as well as the latest trends, has positioned lifestyle journalism in greater dependency on commercial influences (Hanusch et al., 2017, 2020). Travel, fashion, beauty, and personal technology journalism, in particular, are areas in which journalists are dependent on public relations material as well as so-called freebies, free services, or products to test (Hanusch, 2012; Hanusch et al., 2020; Rosenkranz, 2016).

Moreover, research on lifestyle journalists' perception of their position in the journalistic field has long illustrated that lifestyle journalists believe their work to be completely different from that of traditional news journalists (Hanusch & Hanitzsch, 2013). Some of the respondents in an interview study comparing Australian and German lifestyle journalists even preferred to refer to themselves as "classical journalists who work in a lifestyle area", as the term 'lifestyle' carried a negative reputation linking it primarily to promotion and marketing work (Hanusch & Hanitzsch, 2013, p. 955). Similarly, Banjac and Hanusch (2023) illustrate that political journalists have the power to define what counts as 'good' journalism more so than lifestyle journalists: Both political and lifestyle journalists view political journalism as the journalistic core against which lifestyle journalism is compared. Boundary discourses show that lifestyle journalism is viewed as private, emotional, soft, and trivial, whereas political journalism is perceived as public, societally relevant, rational, and hard. However, the boundaries between lifestyle and political journalism have been blurring for some time, among others, with the increase of infotainment (Otto et al., 2017), but also with political and lifestyle journalists increasingly "engaging in 'acts of lifestyle' and 'acts of politics' respectively" (Banjac & Hanusch, 2023, p. 2169).

With the emergence of new media, boundary discourses have shifted from claiming journalistic legitimacy within the field to fending off outside actors, like audiences or public relations actors, at the border of lifestyle journalism. Similar to other areas of journalism, lifestyle journalism is deeply affected by the emergence of new actors on social media who produce and disseminate content on lifestyle topics to growing audiences. While audiences have always produced their own media and a large part of left-wing alternative and counterhegemonic media, like fanzines and pirate or free radio stations, have traditionally been produced by interested laypeople (Rauch, 2016; Triggs, 2006), digitalisation and the advent of the World Wide Web provided audiences with much more opportunities to produce content and distribute it to a potentially large audience (Bruns, 2018). While such actors like (micro-)bloggers and -vloggers are generally subsumed into the category of peripheral or alternative media actors, in lifestyle journalism today, they are often referred to as influencers (Abidin, 2016; Maares & Hanusch, 2020).

Early forms of publishing activities were personal web pages, forums, email lists, and blogs (Findlay, 2015). Tracing the genealogy of blogs, Siles (2011) showcases how different online communities emerged, creating various self-publishing formats in the late 1990s: (1) online diarists, who shared their personal thoughts about their everyday lives and interacted with their community; (2) personal publishers who focused on producing more sophisticated websites and content; and (3) weblog users whose sites shared a similar interface with the earliest entries on top and a sidebar linking to other weblogs, emphasising the community character. In the beginning, media coverage focused more on blogs covering politics or current affairs, again ignoring developments in lifestyle areas (Findlay, 2015; Gregg, 2006). However, blogging was used as early as 2001 by users to communicate about their interests, also in lifestyle areas like fashion (Rocamora & Bartlett, 2009) or travel (van Nuenen, 2015), even though early lifestyle blogs "bear little resemblance to the personal style blogs" we know today (Findlay, 2015, p. 160). Many of these initial blogs were mostly text-based as digital cameras were not as widespread, uploading photos required specific skills and bandwidth, and early blogging platforms like Blogger and LiveJournal did not enable easy integration of photos (Findlay, 2015). Moreover, early lifestyle bloggers' motivations aimed at discussing their interests and experiences with like-minded people and less on monetising their blogs.

The commodification of lifestyle blogs started with the fashion industry inviting bloggers like Tavi Gevinson to their fashion shows (Wiseman, 2009) and legacy media inviting bloggers to write for them (Duffy, 2017; Rocamora, 2017). This recognition of amateur bloggers shifted the focus and aim in the lifestyle blogging community, contributing to what Findlay (2015, p. 170) calls the "second wave" of bloggers in the late 2000s, which ultimately culminated in influencers (Abidin, 2016). This second wave of bloggers started their blogs with a sense of aspirational labour and perceived the blog as "an opportunity to generate income, as an 'online curriculum vitae,' or to establish a professional platform as an authority on style" (Findlay, 2015, p. 170). As such, lifestyle bloggers, vloggers, and other content creators started to invest more time and resources in their content, as well as in the curation of content across different blogs and social media (Abidin, 2016; Duffy & Hund, 2015). In the field of fashion, this meant that content producers shifted from simple 'what I wore' blog posts to glamour shoots mimicking traditional lifestyle magazines (Pedroni, 2023). Furthermore, through the commodification and branding of their content, creators lose their amateur status and the appeal of being 'ordinary' like their readers (McRae, 2017). Yet, as they cannot rely on the credibility of a news brand, content creators have turned to branding themselves as authentic and relatable members of their community (Duffy & Hund, 2015; Maares et al., 2021).

Critical issues and topics

Why is it relevant for journalism scholarship to engage with the boundaries of lifestyle journalism and, in particular, with (micro)bloggers and influencers? When we look at discourses surrounding the new digital actors in lifestyle content production discussed so far, we can identify two critical issues: (1) (Micro)bloggers and influencers compete with lifestyle journalism over specific resources, and (2) they challenge specific perceptions about what reporting on lifestyle issues should be about.

(1) First, research indicates that (micro)bloggers and influencers have become serious competitors for lifestyle journalists in terms of the audiences' attention, access to resources, and access to sources and content. A steady increase in news offerings from various actors also increases audiences' choice of selection, while audiences' time does not increase in the same way (Örnebring & Hellekant Rowe, 2022). This leads to an increasing audience fragmentation (Fletcher & Nielsen, 2017). In such a competitive environment, audiences' attention is the key commodity for journalists and peripheral actors alike (Myllylahti, 2020). In platform publics, peripheral actors are often described as more savvy in attracting and retaining audience attention than journalists (Pirolli, 2018). Here, working *with* influencers has been brought up as a strategy for lifestyle journalists to remain relevant to audiences, complicating journalists' claims to authority (Cheng & Chew, 2024).

In line with this, the lifestyle industry increasingly spreads its advertising budgets across legacy lifestyle media and lifestyle influencers to maximise its reach. Brands increasingly invest in sponsored posts with Instagram, YouTube, or other social media content producers to attract very specific consumer segments with personalised statements (Duffy, 2017). Printed magazines receive less funding and need to adapt to survive (Sinclair, 2020). While advertising sales used to be the main source of income for lifestyle media, they have drastically shrunk since the 2000s, starting with the introduction of Google (Sinclair, 2012). At the same time, shrinking budgets add to economic pressure and influence on newsrooms, especially in more costly areas like travel journalism, where many news companies have stopped funding journalists' trips and rely on tourism authorities, travel companies, or airlines to cover the travel costs (Hanusch, 2012; Rosenkranz, 2016). In turn, lifestyle media adapt by including native advertising (Ferrer-Conill et al., 2020) or affiliate links in their reporting (Vodanovic, 2019), blurring the boundary between journalistic and advertorial content.

(2) Second, the lifestyle industry increasingly caters its events to formats on social media, having much more impact in communicating their services and products. For example, not only are bloggers and influencers invited to sit in front rows of fashion shows, but also fashion labels are increasingly conceiving their shows with Instagram or TikTok in mind. This includes catering to these social media publishing affordances, like creating aesthetics on the runway that will look particularly good in vertical short videos (Rocamora, 2017). Similarly, travel campaigns put considerable effort into creating opportunities for ideal images of tourism destinations and are planned with dissemination on social media in mind (Canavan, 2020). Here, both scholarship and journalism warn of negative effects like over-consumption in fast fashion or over-tourism, criticising peripheral actors like bloggers and influencers as amplifiers (Holson, 2018; Pirolli, 2018).

At the same time, (micro-)bloggers and influencers are often criticised as lacking autonomy and being mere mouthpieces for the industry (Cheng & Chew, 2024; Perreault & Hanusch, 2024). Here, peripheral actors in lifestyle journalism, like influencers and other (micro)bloggers, challenge some of the professional norms and ideas of lifestyle journalism as they are much more overtly collaborating with brands and engaging in sponsorship (Carter, 2016; Maares et al., 2021). However, peripheral actors can also challenge existing ideas about lifestyle journalism. For instance, (micro-)bloggers have been found to emphasise activist approaches when informing audiences about different ways of living, like sustainability (Maares & Hanusch, 2020). They also employ more personal and 'authentic' forms of reporting and consider under-served communities and topics, like plus-size fashion (Peters, 2014). As such, peripheral actors in lifestyle journalism can not only be considered "gatekeepers of taste" (Pedroni, 2015, p. 190) but also thought leaders for societally relevant issues.

Current contributions and research

Current research on the boundaries of journalism can be divided into boundary work that is conducted by traditional lifestyle journalists, boundary work conducted by new peripheral lifestyle content creators, and the perceptions of the audience about the boundaries between the two. This body of work is relatively new, in contrast to research on boundary discourses in political journalism, which can be traced back to the mid-2000s. This indicates that issues around the blurring boundaries of lifestyle journalism have only recently been acknowledged in scholarship. While most studies have focused on the perspective of lifestyle journalists, we can still discuss the state of scholarship along these three groups.

Boundary work as practised by lifestyle journalists

Most research exploring lifestyle journalists' perspectives finds that they discursively draw and maintain a boundary that distinguishes their work from that of peripheral actors like bloggers and influencers. These distinctions mostly occur in aspects that highlight their professionalism but also in their relationship with the audience and their knowledge and experience. For instance, journalists engage in the expulsion of (micro)bloggers and influencers based on their deviant norms and a lack of a shared journalistic ideology (Pirolli, 2018, p. 32). They highlight that influencers violate journalistic ethics by collaborating with brands and publishing sponsored posts.

Furthermore, journalists reject influencers as journalistic on the basis that they arguably lack journalistic professionality. In this view, to be a journalist, one must work in an organisation with a newsroom, where occupational roles are divided among a set of groups; but also one needs to have a specific education and in-depth knowledge about their beat (Cheng & Tandoc, 2022; Pirolli, 2018). Journalists argue that influencers are subjective, focus on themselves, and lack legitimate knowledge (Cheng & Chew, 2024; Perreault & Hanusch, 2024). Lastly, journalists reject influencers as part of journalism based on how they approach their audience. While they admire the closeness that influencers have established to their audience, they believe journalism ought to provide a more general audience with the information that it needs (Perreault & Hanusch, 2024). Here, lifestyle journalists draw on boundary markers that journalists often employ to demarcate political journalism from more 'soft' news reporting.

Lifestyle journalists do see similarities between their work and that of (micro)bloggers and influencers (Perreault & Hanusch, 2024). Still, only a few studies focus on aspects of expanding the boundaries of journalism, although newsrooms and journalists adopt influencer practices, especially to reach young audiences (Negreira-Rey et al., 2022). Cheng and Chew (2024) find that even though influencers are sometimes invited to contribute content for lifestyle magazines, lifestyle journalists are more willing to adapt new practices from influencers to lifestyle journalism than accept influencers as actors in the field. This includes more visuals, a personal voice, and building closer, seemingly personal relationships with audiences online. Likewise, and similar to other areas of journalism, travel journalists try to adapt to self-branding strategies to remain relevant in digital spaces (Pirolli, 2018, p. 129; Molyneux et al., 2019).

However, journalists also describe their relationship with influencers and bloggers as more complicated. Cheng and Chew (2024) summarise journalists' perception of influencers as 'frenemies', that is, people they are friendly with despite a rivalry. On the one hand, this is rooted in influencers' status as competitors over audience attention and financial resources (Perreault & Hanusch, 2024). At the same time, influencers also act as sources for lifestyle reporting (Pirolli, 2018). For example, magazines position bloggers explicitly as outsiders to the journalistic field by reporting on bloggers as objects of interest similar to celebrities or other public figures (Cheng & Tandoc, 2022). In contrast, interviews with lifestyle journalists from the US and Austria indicate that they protect their autonomy by sourcing original stories instead of re-using influencers' content or amplifying their stories (Perreault & Hanusch, 2024). Consequently, lifestyle journalists primarily engage in boundary work through the protection of autonomy (Cheng & Chew, 2024; Perreault & Hanusch, 2024). Interestingly, they do so by focusing on journalism's core values of neutrality and independence – two values that are "difficult to apply in lifestyle journalism given its close connection to commercial interests, which has been the focus of much criticism of the field" (Perreault & Hanusch, 2024, p. 10).

Boundary work from peripheral actors

Only little research has so far examined the role that bloggers and other lifestyle content creators play in the struggles over jurisdiction as providers of lifestyle news. Early studies conceptualise them as an "extension" (Pedroni, 2015, p. 181) of the journalistic field as they provide similar content but are still distinct from traditional lifestyle journalism. The research investigating lifestyle content creators' motivations and membership claims finds that they view their work as similar or in proximity to lifestyle journalism.

Peripheral lifestyle content creators might not see themselves as journalists, but they resemble lifestyle journalists through their discourses on journalistic ideology. A study examining lifestyle Instagrammers' perception of membership found that while they are more likely to call themselves bloggers, content creators, role model, or influencers, they saw their work as something that was similar to journalism, located in a "subcategory" or a "twilight zone" of journalism (Maares & Hanusch, 2020, p. 269, see also Cheng & Tandoc, 2022). Another study found fashion bloggers saw themselves as something other than journalists because blogging "lacks a deontological code and a specific training course" of journalism (Pedroni, 2015, p. 193). As such, influencers reproduce normative ideas of journalism as objective hard news and, by doing so, emphasise the difficult standing of lifestyle journalism in general (Banjac & Hanusch, 2023). On the other hand, some peripheral actors might claim membership more explicitly to be able to access resources reserved for journalists. For example, Pirolli (2018, p. 70) argues travel bloggers and influencers need the authority of a (semi-)journalistic status to gain financial support for their trips. For some, their work as bloggers is also a form of aspirational labour to enter more traditional areas of (lifestyle) journalism (Duffy, 2017), and they leverage the recognition they receive from legacy media as symbolic capital (Cheng & Tandoc, 2022).

Moreover, research finds that peripheral lifestyle actors locate themselves more inside the journalistic field than outside with their discursive boundary-drawing and narrations of what they perceive as their role. For example, Maares and Hanusch (2020) find that lifestyle Instagrammers across various niche topics exhibit similar role perceptions to lifestyle journalists in general, like showcasing a specific lifestyle, offering inspiration, educating followers and providing information, offering service and advice, and providing entertainment and relaxation. Furthermore, while they thought their work sometimes followed journalistic practices, like researching, fact-checking, writing, and publishing, they only perceived their work as journalistic when it covered more serious issues, like sustainability, and was less personal. This also illustrates that peripheral actors recognise institutional borders and acknowledge that they adhere to slightly different norms compared to journalism (Maares & Hanusch, 2020; Pedroni, 2015). For instance, they acknowledge that they lack objectivity and especially economic autonomy when they receive their income through collaborations with companies. However, they also recognise that they have an ethical responsibility towards their audiences.

Instead, peripheral actors claim authority by sharing their personal experiences and being "intensely personal" (Cheng & Tandoc, 2022, p. 1221). They cultivate their own brand by covering niche topics that are relevant to their audiences, while at the same time remaining authentic and relatable (Maares et al., 2021). This enables them to build and manage seemingly intimate relationships with their audience, introducing new ways of engaging with the audience in the field of lifestyle reporting. In that sense, they might be disruptive to lifestyle journalism as they have an advantage in these skill sets over traditional journalists and do not negotiate tensions between the objectivity norm and relationship-building (Pirolli, 2018). Moreover, similar to peripheral actors focusing on political issues, lifestyle actors can explicitly pursue transformational and counter-hegemonic aims when they draw on embodied or niche knowledge and cover topics that they believe are ignored or missed by legacy lifestyle journalism (Maares & Hanusch, 2022; Pedroni, 2015; Titton, 2015).

Boundary-drawing by audience members

While more and more research investigates what audiences define and understand as 'news' (Edgerly & Vraga, 2020; Schneiders, 2023; Swart et al., 2017; Wunderlich et al., 2022), less research has focused on audiences' boundary-drawing in lifestyle journalism. One key study by Banjac and Hanusch (2022) examines audience discourses through focus groups with young audience members to disentangle who they believe is allowed to do journalism, what they consider journalistic, and to what extent they think peripheral actors can be viewed as legitimate professionals. The study reiterates findings on peripheral actors' and lifestyle journalists' definitions of journalism (Banjac & Hanusch, 2023; Maares & Hanusch, 2020): Audiences' initial ideas of journalism are highly normative, linking it to objective political, watchdog, and investigative reporting (Banjac & Hanusch, 2022). However, they also struggle to define clear boundaries and are contradictory in their boundary discourses, indicating that the boundaries are indeed blurring in everyday media use.

Audiences draw the boundaries of journalism along dimensions of autonomy, professionality, and experience, as well as the motivation and intention behind different forms of content. For example, when comparing journalism to peripheral content creators, audiences broadly view journalists as "selfless, autonomous and detached, fact- and research-driven, educated professionals providing in-depth analysis" (Banjac & Hanusch, 2022, p. 714). Peripheral actors are instead viewed as amateurs who are dependent on commercial influences, highly subjective, and emotional. However, audiences also believe that some influencers and (micro-)bloggers employ practices similar to those of journalists, like researching, while journalists also produce journalism that doesn't meet their expectations, e.g., clickbait news (Banjac & Hanusch, 2022). Likewise, audiences draw on the form of content to decide whether it is journalistic or not. Here, audiences connect journalism with written, and often long, texts instead of short videos or visuals (Wunderlich et al., 2022). As such, blogs, "and in particular travel blogs, were more likely to 'qualify as journalism'" than Instagram posts (Banjac & Hanusch, 2022, p. 714). For some audiences, no information on social media can be considered news as they only view television evening news and newspapers as legitimate sources (Swart & Broersma, 2024).

Yet, audiences still consume peripheral actors' content because it is more relevant and authentic to them, and they trust influencers and bloggers due to the affective element of a seemingly personal connection (Swart & Broersma, 2024; Wunderlich et al., 2022). Thus, while "traditional journalism remains recognisable as a cultural form" (Swart & Broersma, 2024, p. 1626), digital platforms complicate distinctions for audiences. While some audiences value the content they receive on social media platforms, blogs, and in podcasts as journalism – or news-like, they also have high expectations for quality content. They expect content creators to be authentic, transparent, consistent in their content creation, and interested in engaging with their audience (Banjac & Hanusch, 2022). At the same time, they feel that peripheral lifestyle actors are too dependent on commercial influences. Audiences generally criticise the lack of commercial autonomy in lifestyle journalism and (micro-)blogger communities, lowering their trust in lifestyle content in general. Following Banjac and Hanusch's (2022, p. 718) argument, peripheral actors can be understood as "implicitly journalistic" as the expectations their audiences have of them are largely reminiscent of the ones audiences have of lifestyle journalism. Accordingly, audiences' expectations of peripheral actors' authenticity are related to the expectation that journalism is credible, and their expectations that peripheral actors interact with them are related to the expectation that journalists should consider their audience and provide them with original and relevant information (see also Swart & Broersma, 2024).

Summarising scholarship on the boundaries of lifestyle journalism, we find that the most dominant dimensions of distinction relate to peripheral actors' autonomy and how well – and authentic – they navigate these issues. Similarly, peripheral actors' lack or command of professional expertise and how well they overcome this with thematic experience and embodied knowledge appear relevant markers of distinction. As such, perceived authenticity, as well as the deep knowledge these peripheral actors derive by being embedded in a niche community (Vos & Hanusch, 2024), might balance out shortcomings in financial autonomy. At the same time, this chapter also highlights that the discourses around the boundaries of lifestyle journalism are complicated by lifestyle journalism's position in the hierarchy of the journalistic field in general. Traditional lifestyle journalists, peripheral actors, and audiences all draw on folk theories (Nielsen, 2016) of journalism that primarily relate to hard news factual reporting, discriminating more soft news reporting as less or not journalistic.

Future directions

As this handbook illustrates, lifestyle journalism encompasses a wide range of different actors who are also diverse in terms of their role perceptions, motivations, and practices. The periphery of lifestyle journalism is likewise not a monolith and encompasses actors pursuing both journalistic and commercial objectives. As such, future boundary research should (a) dedicate more explicit focus on areas of lifestyle journalism and (b) approach the boundaries of lifestyle journalism in a holistic way, comparing perspectives from traditional journalists, peripheral actors, and audiences. One perspective on the boundaries of journalism that has been largely ignored in scholarship is that of protagonists, sources, and objects of reporting (Juarez Miro et al., 2024). However, as some research points out, implicitly, these protagonists are involved in boundary discourses when they privilege one journalistic actor over another (Canavan, 2020; Rocamora, 2017). Future research should, thus, investigate how, for example, fashion brands, artists, or ordinary people, who are at the core of lifestyle news, distinguish between different actors in lifestyle journalism.

Furthermore, much of public discourse argues peripheral lifestyle journalistic actors engage in covert advertising and are dependent on sponsorship. Lifestyle journalists themselves draw on values of autonomy when distinguishing themselves from influencers or other peripheral lifestyle journalistic actors (Perreault & Hanusch, 2024), despite working in an area that regularly experiences similar commercial influences (Hanusch et al., 2020). Here, future research should on the one hand investigate journalists', peripheral actors', and audiences' perceptions of commercial autonomy in lifestyle reporting more closely to understand the different layers of claimed and ascribed autonomy. On the other hand, scholarship should explore in what ways peripheral actors introduce new norms and institutionalise routines to enhance their perceived credibility and to what extent these are adopted among traditional lifestyle journalists. Here, practices like disclosing sponsored content have been mandated by law in some regions of the world (European Commission, n.d.) or established through discourse within the industry (Wellman et al., 2020). By examining discourses around autonomy, scholarship could trace this professionalisation at the periphery and distinguish between different peripheral actors and niche topics.

Lastly, we also see that boundary markers that are commonly referred to in political journalism might not be as dominant when it comes to reporting on lifestyle topics. Instead, we should investigate the applicability of authenticity, credibility, and embeddedness in a (niche) topic and community as markers of distinction (Juarez Miro et al., 2024). These aspects can be especially relevant when it comes to the ostensibly blurring of lifestyle and political realms, where more authentic voices might be viewed as more credible and having more impact on their audience. This is especially relevant in areas concerning the intersection of lifestyle journalism and the climate crisis (Dekoninck & Schmuck, 2024; Haastrup & Marshall, 2024), as well as lifestyle journalism and health communication (Baker & Rojek, 2020), or lifestyle journalism and anti-democratic radicalisation (Bauer, 2024).

Further reading

Banjac, S., & Hanusch, F. (2022). A question of perspective: Exploring audiences' views of journalistic boundaries. *New Media & Society*, 24(3), 705–723. https://doi.org/10.1177/1461444820963795

Carlson, M. (2017). *Journalistic authority: Legitimating news in the digital era*. Columbia University Press.

Duffy, B. E. (2017). *(Not) getting paid to do what you love: Gender, social media, and aspirational work*. Yale University Press.

Hanusch, F., & Löhmann, K. (2023). Dimensions of Peripherality in Journalism: A Typology for Studying New Actors in the Journalistic Field. *Digital Journalism*, 11(7), 1292–1310. https://doi.org/10.1080/21670811.2022.2148549

Perreault, G., & Hanusch, F. (2024). Field insurgency in lifestyle journalism: How lifestyle journalists marginalize Instagram influencers and protect their autonomy. *New Media & Society*, 26(7), 3767–3785. https://doi.org/10.1177/14614448221104233

References

Abbott, A. (1988). *The system of professions: An essay on the division of expert labor*. University of Chicago Press.

Abidin, C. (2016). "Aren't these just young, rich women doing vain things online?": Influencer Selfies as Subversive Frivolity. *Social Media + Society*, 2(2), 2056305116641342. https://doi.org/10.1177/2056305116641342

Baker, S. A., & Rojek, C. (2020). The Belle Gibson Scandal: The rise of lifestyle gurus as micro-celebrities in low-trust societies. *Journal of Sociology*, 56(3), 388–404. https://doi.org/10.1177/1440783319846188

Banjac, S., & Hanusch, F. (2022). A question of perspective: Exploring audiences' views of journalistic boundaries. *New Media & Society*, 24(3), 705–723. https://doi.org/10.1177/1461444820963795

Banjac, S., & Hanusch, F. (2023). The struggle for authority and legitimacy: Lifestyle and political journalists' discursive boundary work. *Journalism*, 24(10), 2155–2173. https://doi.org/10.1177/14648849221125702

Bauer, M. F. (2024). Beauty, baby and backlash? Anti-feminist influencers on TikTok. *Feminist Media Studies*, 24(5), 1023–1041. https://doi.org/10.1080/14680777.2023.2263820

Bourdieu, P. (1984). *Distinction. A Social Critique of the Judgement of Taste*. Harvard University Press.

Bruns, A. (2018). *Gatewatching and news curation: Journalism, social media, and the public sphere*. Peter Lang. https://doi.org/10.3726/b13293

Canavan, B. (2020). Let's get this show on the road! Introducing the tourist celebrity gaze. *Annals of Tourism Research*, 82(March), 102898. https://doi.org/10.1016/j.annals.2020.102898

Carlson, M. (2015). Introduction: The Many Boundaries of Journalism. In M. Carlson & S. C. Lewis (Eds.), *Boundaries of journalism: Professionalism, practices and participation* (pp. 1–17). Routledge.

Carlson, M. (2017). *Journalistic authority: Legitimating news in the digital era*. Columbia University Press.

Carter, D. (2016). Hustle and brand: The sociotechnical shaping of influence. *Social Media + Society*, 2(3), 2056305116666305. https://doi.org/10.1177/2056305116666305

Cheng, L., & Chew, M. (2024). Functional interlopers: Lifestyle journalists' discursive construction of boundaries against digital lifestyle influencers. *Journalism*, 25(2), 372–390. https://doi.org/10.1177/14648849221143875

Cheng, L., & Tandoc, E. C. (2022). From magazines to blogs: The shifting boundaries of fashion journalism. *Journalism*, 23(6), 1213–1232. https://doi.org/10.1177/1464884920988183

Dekoninck, H., & Schmuck, D. (2024). The "greenfluence": Following environmental influencers, parasocial relationships, and youth's participation behavior. *New Media & Society*, 26(11), 6615–6635. https://doi.org/10.1177/14614448231156131

Deuze, M. (2007). *Media Work*. Polity.

Duffy, B. E. (2013). *Remake, Remodel: Women's magazines in the digital age*. University of Illinois Press.

Duffy, B. E. (2017). *(Not) getting paid to do what you love: Gender, social media, and aspirational work*. Yale University Press.

Duffy, B. E., & Hund, E. (2015). "Having it all" on social media: Entrepreneurial femininity and self-branding among fashion bloggers. *Social Media + Society*, 1(2), 2056305115604337. https://doi.org/10.1177/2056305115604337

Edgerly, S., & Vraga, E. K. (2020). That's not news: Audience perceptions of "news-ness" and why it matters. *Mass Communication and Society*, 23(5), 730–754. https://doi.org/10.1080/15205436.2020.1729383

Eldridge, S. (2018). *Online journalism from the periphery: Interloper media and the journalistic field*. Routledge.

Eldridge, S. (2019). Where do we draw the line? Interlopers, (ant)agonists, and an unbounded journalistic field. *Media and Communication*, 7(4), 8–18. https://doi.org/10.17645/mac.v7i4.2295

European Commission. (n.d.). *Influencer legal hub*. Retrieved July 31, 2024, from https://commission.europa.eu/live-work-travel-eu/consumer-rights-and-complaints/influencer-legal-hub_en

Ferrer-Conill, R., Knudsen, E., Laurer, C., & Barnoy, A. (2020). The visual boundaries of journalism: Native advertising and the convergence of editorial and commercial content. *Digital Journalism*, 9(7), 929–951. https://doi.org/10.1080/21670811.2020.1836980

Ferrucci, P., & Vos, T. P. (2017). Who's in, who's out? *Digital Journalism*, 5(7), 868–883. https://doi.org/10.1080/21670811.2016.1208054

Findlay, R. (2015). The short, passionate, and close-knit history of personal style blogs. *Fashion Theory*, 19(2), 157–178. https://doi.org/10.2752/175174115X14168357992319

Fletcher, R., & Nielsen, R. K. (2017). Are news audiences increasingly fragmented? A cross-national comparative analysis of cross-platform news audience fragmentation and duplication. *Journal of Communication*, 67(4), 476–498. https://doi.org/10.1111/jcom.12315

Gieryn, T. F. (1999). *Cultural boundaries of science: Credibility on the line*. University of Chicago Press.
Gregg, M. (2006). Posting with passion: Blogs and the politics of gender. In A. Bruns & J. Jacobs (Eds.), *Uses of blogs* (pp. 151–160). Peter Lang.
Haastrup, H. K., & Marshall, P. D. (2024). The influencer in the age of climate change: The authentic role model for sustainability. *Celebrity Studies*, 0(0), 1–17. https://doi.org/10.1080/19392397.2024.2341596
Hackober, J. (2017, August 1). "Influencer"—Warum das Wort problematisch ist. *Iconist - Welt*. https://www.welt.de/iconist/mode/article160963232/Allein-das-Wort-Influencer-ist-schon-gefaehrlich.html
Hall, E. (2016, June 10). "Vogue" versus the blogger…and how are Irish influencers involved? | Irish Independent. *Irish Independent*. https://www.independent.ie/style/fashion/style-talk/vogue-versus-the-bloggerand-how-are-irish-influencers-involved/35107218.html
Hanitzsch, T., & Vos, T. P. (2018). Journalism beyond democracy: A new look into journalistic roles in political and everyday life. *Journalism*, 19(2), 146–164. https://doi.org/10.1177/1464884916673386
Hanitzsch, T., & Wahl-Jorgensen, K. (2020). Journalism studies: Developments, challenges, and future directions. In K. Wahl-Jorgensen & T. Hanitzsch (Eds.), *The handbook of journalism studies* (pp. 3–20). Routledge, Taylor & Francis Group.
Hanusch, F. (2012). Travel journalists' attitudes toward public relations: Findings from a representative survey. *Public Relations Review*, 38(1), 69–75. https://doi.org/10.1016/j.pubrev.2011.10.001
Hanusch, F., Banjac, S., & Maares, P. (2020). The power of commercial influences: How lifestyle journalists experience pressure from advertising and public relations. *Journalism Practice*, 14(9), 1029–1046. https://doi.org/10.1080/17512786.2019.1682942
Hanusch, F., & Hanitzsch, T. (2013). Mediating orientation and self-expression in the world of consumption: Australian and German lifestyle journalists' professional views. *Media, Culture & Society*, 35(8), 943–959. https://doi.org/10.1177/0163443713501931
Hanusch, F., Hanitzsch, T., & Lauerer, C. (2017). 'How much love are you going to give this brand?' Lifestyle journalists on commercial influences in their work. *Journalism*, 18(2), 141–158. https://doi.org/10.1177/1464884915608818
Hanusch, F., & Löhmann, K. (2023). Dimensions of peripherality in journalism: A typology for studying new actors in the journalistic field. *Digital Journalism*, 11(7), 1292–1310. https://doi.org/10.1080/21670811.2022.2148549
Holson, L. M. (2018). Is geotagging on instagram ruining natural wonders? Some say yes. *The New York Times*. https://www.nytimes.com/2018/11/29/travel/instagram-geotagging-environment.html?searchResultPosition=33
Juarez Miro, C., Maares, P., Hendrickx, J., & Hanusch, F. (2024, June). *Understanding the role of community membership in journalistic authority claims: A framework informed by fan journalistic actors*. 74th conference of the International Communication Association (ICA), Gold Coast, Australia.
Kemp, N. (2016, April 10). Vogue blogger backlash underlines disconnect between media owners and influencers. *Campaign*. https://www.campaignlive.co.uk/article/vogue-blogger-backlash-underlines-disconnect-media-owners-influencers/1411073?utm_source=website&utm_medium=social
Lamont, M., & Molnár, V. (2002). The study of boundaries in the social sciences. *Annual Review of Sociology*, 28(1965), 167–195. https://doi.org/10.1146/annurev.soc.28.110601.141107
Lewis, S. C. (2015). Epilogue. Studying the boundaries of journalism: Where do we go from here? In M. Carlson & S. C. Lewis (Eds.), *Boundaries of journalism: Professionalism, practices and participation* (pp. 218–228). Routledge.
Maares, P., Banjac, S., & Hanusch, F. (2021). The labour of visual authenticity on social media: Exploring producers' and audiences' perceptions on Instagram. *Poetics*, 84, 1–10. https://doi.org/10.1016/j.poetic.2020.101502
Maares, P., & Hanusch, F. (2020). Exploring the boundaries of journalism: Instagram micro-bloggers in the twilight zone of lifestyle journalism. *Journalism*, 21(2), 262–278. https://doi.org/10.1177/1464884918801400
Maares, P., & Hanusch, F. (2022). Challenging the tourist gaze?: Exploring majority world countries' instagram influencer practices and the link to citizen travel journalism. In B. Korte & A. K. Sennefelder (Eds.), *Travel, writing and the media* (pp. 226–246). Routledge.
Maares, P., & Hanusch, F. (2023). Understanding peripheral journalism from the boundary: A Conceptual framework. *Digital Journalism*, 11(7), 1270–1291. https://doi.org/10.1080/21670811.2022.2134045

McRae, S. (2017). "Get off my internets": How anti-fans deconstruct lifestyle bloggers' authenticity work. *Persona Studies*, *3*(1), 13–27. https://doi.org/10.21153/ps2017vol3no1art640

Molyneux, L., Lewis, S. C., & Holton, A. E. (2019). Media work, identity, and the motivations that shape branding practices among journalists: An explanatory framework. *New Media and Society*, *21*(4), 836–855. https://doi.org/10.1177/1461444818809392

Myllylahti, M. (2020). Paying attention to attention: A conceptual framework for studying news reader revenue models related to platforms. *Digital Journalism*, *8*(5), 567–575. https://doi.org/10.1080/21670811.2019.1691926

Negreira-Rey, M.-C., Vázquez-Herrero, J., & López-García, X. (2022). Blurring boundaries between journalists and tiktokers: Journalistic role performance on TikTok. *Media and Communication*, *10*(1), 146–156.

Neveu, E. (2007). Pierre Bourdieu—Sociologist of media, or sociologist for media scholars? *Journalism Studies*, *8*(2), 335–347. https://doi.org/10.1080/14616700601149026

Nielsen, R. K. (2016). Folk theories of journalism. *Journalism Studies*, *17*(7), 840–848. https://doi.org/10.1080/1461670X.2016.1165140

Örnebring, H., & Hellekant Rowe, E. (2022). The media day, revisited: Rhythm, place and hyperlocal information environments. *Digital Journalism*, *10*(1), 23–42. https://doi.org/10.1080/21670811.2021.1884988

Otto, L., Glogger, I., & Boukes, M. (2017). The softening of journalistic political communication: A comprehensive framework model of sensationalism, Soft news, infotainment, and tabloidization. *Communication Theory*, *27*(2), 136–155. https://doi.org/10.1111/comt.12102

Pedroni, M. (2015). "Stumbling on the heels of my blog": Career, forms of capital, and strategies in the (sub)field of fashion blogging. *Fashion Theory*, *19*(2), 179–199. https://doi.org/10.2752/175174115X14168357992355

Pedroni, M. (2023). Two decades of fashion blogging and influencing: A critical overview. *Fashion Theory*, *27*(2), 237–268. https://doi.org/10.1080/1362704X.2021.2017213

Perreault, G., & Hanusch, F. (2024). Field insurgency in lifestyle journalism: How lifestyle journalists marginalize Instagram influencers and protect their autonomy. *New Media & Society*, *26*(7), 3767–3785. https://doi.org/10.1177/14614448221104233

Peters, L. D. (2014). You are what you wear: How plus-size fashion figures in fat identity formation. *Fashion Theory*, *18*(1), 45–71. https://doi.org/10.2752/175174114X13788163471668

Pirolli, B. (2018). *Travel journalism: Informing tourists in the digital age*. Routledge/Taylor & Francis Group.

Rauch, J. (2016). Are there still alternatives? Relationships between alternative media and mainstream media in a converged environment. *Sociology Compass*, *10*(9), 756–767. https://doi.org/10.1111/soc4.12403

Reinemann, C., Stanyer, J., Scherr, S., & Legnante, G. (2011). Hard and soft news: A review of concepts, operationalizations and key findings. *Journalism*, *13*(2), 221–239. https://doi.org/10.1177/1464884911427803

Rocamora, A. (2017). Mediatization and digital media in the field of fashion. *Fashion Theory*, *21*(5), 505–522. https://doi.org/10.1080/1362704X.2016.1173349

Rocamora, A., & Bartlett, D. (2009). Blogs de mode: Les nouveaux espaces du discours de mode. *Sociétés*, *104*(2), 105–114. https://doi.org/10.3917/soc.104.0105

Rosenkranz, T. (2016). Becoming entrepreneurial: Crisis, ethics and marketization in the field of travel journalism. *Poetics*, *54*, 54–65. https://doi.org/10.1016/j.poetic.2015.09.003

Ruellan, D. (1993). An undefined profession. The issue of professionalism in the journalistic milieu (L. Libbrecht, Trans.). *Réseaux. Communication - Technologie - Société*, *1*(2), 231–243. https://doi.org/10.3406/reso.1993.3252

Schneiders, P. (2023). News from the user's perspective: With naivety to validity. *Digital Journalism*, *0*(0), 1–22. https://doi.org/10.1080/21670811.2023.2182804

Siles, I. (2011). From online filter to web format: Articulating materiality and meaning in the early history of blogs. *Social Studies of Science*, *41*(5), 737–758. https://doi.org/10.1177/0306312711420190

Sinclair, J. (2012). *Advertising, the media and globalisation: A world in motion*. Routledge.

Sinclair, J. (2020). Magazines and advertising in the digital age. In M. Sternadori & T. Holmes (Eds.), *The handbook of magazine studies* (pp. 105–119). Wiley. https://doi.org/10.1002/9781119168102.ch8

Stenberg, M. (2021). The rise of the journalist-influencer. *Nieman Lab*. https://www.niemanlab.org/2020/12/the-rise-of-the-journalist-influencer/

Swart, J., & Broersma, M. (2024). What feels like news? Young people's perceptions of news on Instagram. *Journalism*, 25(8), 1620–1637. https://doi.org/10.1177/14648849231212737

Swart, J., Peters, C., & Broersma, M. (2017). Navigating cross-media news use. *Journalism Studies*, 18(11), 1343–1362. https://doi.org/10.1080/1461670X.2015.1129285

Tandoc, E. C., Jr. (2018). Five ways BuzzFeed is preserving (or transforming) the journalistic field. *Journalism*, 19(2), 200–216. https://doi.org/10.1177/1464884917691785

Titton, M. (2015). Fashionable personae: Self-identity and enactments of fashion narratives in fashion blogs. *Fashion Theory*, 19(2), 201–220. https://doi.org/10.2752/175174115X14168357992391

Topping, A. (2016, September 29). Vogue editors accused of hypocrisy after declaring war on fashion bloggers. *The Guardian*. https://www.theguardian.com/media/2016/sep/29/vogue-editors-declare-war-fashion-bloggers

Triggs, T. (2006). Scissors and glue: Punk fanzines and the creation of a DIY aesthetic. *Journal of Design History*, 19(1), 69–83. https://doi.org/10.1093/jdh/epk006

van Nuenen, T. (2015). Here I am: Authenticity and self-branding on travel blogs. *Tourist Studies*, 16(2), 192–212. https://doi.org/10.1177/1468797615594748

Viererbl, B. (2022). Writing for the audience or for public relations? How lifestyle editors perceive expectations about their professional role and manage potential for conflict. *Journalism*. https://journals.sagepub.com/doi/full/10.1177/14648849211067586

Vodanovic, L. (2019). Journalism "without news". In L. Vodanovic (Ed.), *Lifestyle journalism. Social Media, consumption, experience* (pp. 38–50). Routledge.

Vos, T. P. (2019). Journalism as institution. In T. P. Vos (Ed.), *Oxford research encyclopedia of communication*. Oxford University Press. https://doi.org/10.1093/acrefore/9780190228613.013.825

Vos, T. P., & Hanusch, F. (2024). Conceptualizing embeddedness as a key dimension for analyzing journalistic cultures. *Communication Theory*, 34(1), 39–48. https://doi.org/10.1093/ct/qtad018

Wellman, M. L., Stoldt, R., Tully, M., & Ekdale, B. (2020). Ethics of authenticity: Social media influencers and the production of sponsored content. *Journal of Media Ethics*, 35(2), 68–82. https://doi.org/10.1080/23736992.2020.1736078

Wiseman, E. (2009, September 20). Tavi Gevinson: The 13-year-old blogger with the fashion world at her feet. *The Guardian*. https://www.theguardian.com/lifeandstyle/2009/sep/20/tavi-gevinson-new-york-fashion

Wunderlich, L., Hölig, S., & Hasebrink, U. (2022). Does journalism still matter? The role of journalistic and non-journalistic sources in young peoples' news related practices. *The International Journal of Press/Politics*, 27(3), 569–588. https://doi.org/10.1177/19401612211072547

Zelizer, B. (1993). Journalists as interpretive communities. *Critical Studies in Media Communication*, 10(3), 219–237.

25
DIGITAL TECHNOLOGIES AND CHANGE IN THE FIELD OF FASHION JOURNALISM

Agnès Rocamora

Introduction

In this chapter, I draw on Bourdieu's field theory to argue for its relevance for interrogating the contemporary space of fashion journalism, and, particularly, recent changes related to digital media. Although many scholars have drawn on Bourdieu's work to conceptualise journalism as a field (see, e.g., Chalaby 1998; Benson and Neveu 2005; Eldridge 2018; Wu et al. 2019; Perreault and Stanfield 2018; Vos 2016), they have tended to focus on news journalism at the expense of other forms of journalism, such as fashion journalism. This reflects the lack of attention that has been given to soft news in journalism studies more generally.

In the first section, I introduce Bourdieu's field theory. I apply it to the case of contemporary fashion journalism to begin mapping some of its key dimensions and drawing attention to the value of field theory to discuss dynamics at play in this space of cultural production. The section also provides a conceptual and contextual ground for the focus of subsequent sections on the topics of field change and digital technologies. I concentrate on the United Kingdom although, as in the rest of this chapter, I will often engage with a wider geographical space, since, as I will argue, the field of fashion journalism and fashion media is transnational. In the second section, I look at the way Bourdieu theorises field change through the notions of morphological, technological, social and economic factors of change. His framework offers useful analytical tools for making sense of the emergence of a new range of players that have entered the field of the fashion media in recent years – namely, bloggers, TikTokers, fashion brands and tech companies. I draw on this theoretical discussion in the third section to continue mapping the contemporary field of fashion journalism and to explore recent changes in this field.

In this chapter, I approach fashion journalism as lifestyle journalism, that is, a type of journalism that covers topics related to consumer goods and provides news, information, and advice in a factual and/or entertaining way (From and Kristensen 2020; Hanusch 2013, see also Findlay and Reponen 2023). I also include fashion industry-related commentary and information and, as with journalism more generally, 'reporting, criticism, editorializing and the conferral of judgment on the shape of things' (Adam, cited in Zelizer 2017: 230).

This is a working definition only and a purposely broad and 'soft' (Deuze and Witschge 2017) one since what constitutes fashion journalism – and journalism more generally – is itself an object of struggle in both the field of fashion and that of academia, an idea I return to in this chapter. As many journalism scholars have argued, 'journalism' is a moving target, an ever-shifting set of practices, definitions and boundaries. It is 'in a permanent process of becoming' and 'a dynamic object of study' (Deuze and Witschge 2017: 13). Bourdieu's field theory gives us conceptual tools for mapping and interrogating this process of becoming.

The field of fashion journalism

Bourdieu's concept of field lies at the centre of this work. It is 'a way of thinking'[1] that allows one to explore the social mechanisms at play in a particular space (2015: 532). A field is a relational space of positions and position-taking, which through a historical process of differentiation and division of labour has become relatively independent from other social spaces (see, e.g., Bourdieu 1995). The fashion media are not a contemporary invention and date back to the 17th century with the launch in France in 1677 of what is often seen as the first fashion magazine, *Le Mercure Galant*, whilst the first UK title was the *Lady's Mercury* (1693) (see Nelson Best 2017 for a history of fashion journalism). A social historian may locate the birth of this field in past centuries. However, this chapter does not aim to present a genesis of the field of fashion journalism in the manner Bourdieu (1993) does, for instance, with the French field of literature. Rather, it offers, as Bourdieu says of his analysis of the French academic field, 'a structural history of recent developments' (1996b: 33), in the space of fashion journalism and the fashion media.

A field is a space made up of what Bourdieu, using the metaphor of the football game, calls players. There are collective as well as individual players. In the United Kingdom, collective players include a broad constituency of media genres such as legacy consumer magazines (*Elle UK*, *Vogue UK*, *GQ*, for instance), business titles (e.g., *Business of Fashion* (hereafter BOF), *Drapers*), independent magazines (e.g., *Tank*, *Huck*), fashion websites (e.g., SHOWstudio) or newspapers with their style sections as in *The Times* or *The Telegraph*. Individual players include the many fashion journalists who work for such titles. Some of them are what Bourdieu calls 'established players', such as Tim Banks for the BOF or Jess Cartney-Morley for *The Guardian*, in contrast with 'newcomers' such as TikTok fashion critics.

Fields are hierarchical spaces of position, with some players in a dominant position. In the United Kingdom, these include Penny Martin, the editor of *The Gentlewoman*, for example, or Alex Fury, Fashion Features Director of *Another Magazine* and menswear critic for the *Financial Times*. Others are in a subordinated position: newcomer fashion journalists working for less prestigious titles, for instance. In the field of fashion journalism, hierarchies are 'materialised' in the sitting arrangements at fashion shows, with the front row being the famously coveted space that makes visible one's dominant position in the field, that is, one's amount of 'field specific capital' (Bourdieu 2015: 73; Entwistle and Rocamora 2006). Here, Bourdieu makes a distinction between four types of capital, which can be converted into one another: Economic (financial resources); cultural (one's command of the knowledge needed to make it in a field); social (the strength of one's social network) and symbolic (a capital of prestige). In the field of fashion journalism, they are, for instance, respectively, a journalist's possession of branded high-end goods; their command of fashion history; the size of their PR network; the authority attached to working for a prestigious title or the wearing of designer fashion (Entwistle and Rocamora 2006).

Players are caught not only in the internal hierarchies of the field they are part of but also in a broader network of hierarchies. In the field of fashion journalism, they include the hierarchies pertaining to the wider 'field of cultural production' (Bourdieu 1993), which both the field of journalism and the field of fashion belong to. The field of cultural production is divided between the subfield of restricted production and the subfield of large-scale production, which are situated at polar ends, and in between which all cultural goods and players are in a relation of hierarchy (Bourdieu 1993). The subfield of restricted production, the autonomous pole, is governed by the ideal of 'art for art's sake', whilst that of large-scale production, the heteronomous pole, is governed by the forces of commerce. Cultural goods and producers located at the autonomous end of the field have a high symbolic capital, although they might have a low economic capital compared to players situated at the heteronomous end of the field (Bourdieu 1993).

In the field of cultural production, fashion is still placed low in the symbolic hierarchy of culture, not least due to its association with commerce (Rocamora 2009). This is not just by virtue of the fashion media reporting on what are essentially commercial products and practices but because of the often-incestuous relationship between brands and media. As fashion writer Colin McDowell (2020) puts it: 'the large fashion houses have such total control over the major media outlets that they can close down gossip by threatening to withhold the ever-scarcer advertising revenue'.

Although the journalistic field more generally is increasingly dependent on the forces of commerce and so 'increasingly heteronomous', as Bourdieu (2005) and others (see, e.g., Hanusch 2013) have shown, the ideal of autonomy, including from commercial pressures, is still a widely 'shared belief' in the field of journalism (Bourdieu 1996c: 54; Zelizer 2013), including in the field of fashion journalism. For this field is at the intersection of two fields, that of fashion and that of journalism, and so is informed by dynamics pertaining to both fields. Bourdieu (2013) has commented on the intersectional dimension of fields, such as in his discussion of the field of literary criticism, which when it first emerged crossed the fields of art and literature and then, as it gained autonomy, that of journalism. Literary critics were subject to the forces and values at play in all three fields. Similarly, fashion journalists and the fashion media are subject to forces and values at play in both the field of fashion and that of journalism, and this includes being subject to the journalistic ideal of autonomy. Suzanne Menkes, former fashion editor at *The International Herald Tribune* and *Vogue International*, invokes it on her website, which reads: 'Frank, fearless and free from editorial constraints, she has built a reputation for having a strong and independent point of view' (https://suzymenkes.com/).

All fields are informed by struggles. In the field of fashion journalism, these are, for instance, the struggles between players to be acknowledged as a significant voice and authority in judgements of taste or the struggles for a position on the front row, which materialises and so reproduces the significance and dominance of one's authority (Entwistle and Rocamora 2006). Fields are also informed by struggles for the definition of their boundaries (see, e.g., Bourdieu 2015: 483–487). The 'symbolic competition' (Bourdieu 1996b: 16) and discursive struggles which, in the field of fashion journalism – as in the field of journalism more generally in recent years – have opposed established journalists from legacy media to bloggers is an instance of struggle for the definition of the boundaries of a field (see, e.g., on journalism Eldridge 2018; on fashion bloggers vs. fashion journalists, Cheng and Tandoc 2022; Rocamora 2016). The struggle for the definition of the boundaries of the field of fashion journalism has informed the work of scholars too. Whilst Hartley and Rennie

(2004), for instance, argue that fashion photography, as featured in fashion magazines, should be considered photojournalism in its ability to document life through images, Le Masurier (2020) makes a case for defining fashion photography as visual journalism. She gives the example of the work of photographer Steven Meisel to argue that fashion photography can 'perform the usually journalistic work of cultural, social and political comment' (p. 2).

Struggles take place amongst players located in fields that have national as well as cross-national boundaries. Indeed, although earlier I have referred to the UK field of fashion journalism, anchoring it to the boundaries of the British State, the picture is more complex, for the field of fashion media is transnational. In *Pascalian Meditations*, Bourdieu (1997: 119) refers to 'transnational fields' but does not elaborate on this idea, and although in his work on the journalistic field (which I return to in the next section) he (1996c: 41) suggests that 'to be complete' an analysis of a national field needs to account for its position in 'the global media field', it is not one he undertakes. In his work, the fields under analysis are largely inscribed in a national context (see also Bucholz 2016).

The space of fashion journalism and fashion media has always had a transnational dimension: one of the earliest fashion media, fashion plates, circulated across Europe in the 17th century to inform consumers of the latest Parisian trends and promote a Parisian aesthetic across national borders (Rocamora 2009); in 1909, publisher Condé Nast bought the US magazine *Vogue* and launched a UK edition in 1916, and a French one in 1920. However, at the end of the 20th century, the transnational dimension of the field of fashion intensified. In the 1980s and 1990s, fashion publishing, like media publishing more generally (Gershon 1997), underwent an intense process of conglomeration, globalisation and centralisation in the hands of fewer publishers (Duffy 2013; Nelson Best 2017). Transnational media corporations (Gershon 1997) extended their economic reach across the world by launching more local editions of established brands yet overseen by the centralising force of the publisher they belong too. Those processes of centralisation and globalisation find a recent illustration at Condé Nast in the appointment in 2023 of Anna Wintour (until then the Editor-in-Chief of US *Vogue* and global content advisor) as 'worldwide chief content officer and global editorial director' of *Vogue*. There are now 28 *Vogue* editions, whilst *Elle*, owned by Lagardère,[2] and *Harper's Bazaar*, owned by Hearst, come in 43 and 37 editions, respectively, on top of, like *Vogue*, a broad social media and online presence.

Although national issues offer content specific to the country they are associated with, the syndication of articles and images across the editions of a flagship brand contributes to the transcultural (Hepp 2015) nature of fashion media, and so does the magazines' aesthetic and branding. In her study of Indian *Vogue*, *Marie-Claire* India and *Harper's Bazaar* India, Arti Sandhu (2023), for instance, notes that the style and layout of those magazines often replicate those of their European and American counterparts, to the point that it can be difficult, at first glance, to distinguish them from each other. Editors are given a 'brand book' they are required to follow as well as articles and photoshoots for use to ensure similarity of aesthetic, tone and approach across editions (Sandhu 2023). In other words, local players must follow rules and values that extend beyond the confines of the nation in which they are located – rules and values set by large global publishing groups struggling for readership and economic dominance across the world.

To ensure local issues reproduce the agenda set by the flagship brand, Sandhu also notes that the editors of the Indian editions she looked at 'undergo training in the nuances of Western fashion, travel overseas to experience luxury brands and ultimately ensure the international team approves of their local issue's editorial vision' (Sandhu 2023: 113). This helps further establish the dominance of Western luxury brands across the globe (Sandhu 2023: 113). These are the fashion players that have enough economic capital to advertise in fashion publications across the world and the power, therefore, to influence content. This is not to say that local forces are not at play in the field of fashion journalism. Transnational and national fields can intersect (Sapiro et al. 2018). A comprehensive analysis of the transnational dimension of the field of fashion journalism and the fashion media is beyond the remit of this chapter, but later in this chapter, I explore these issues further when looking at online media and current changes in the field. First, however, I move on to Bourdieu's theory of field change.

Conceptualising field change

Bourdieu's work has often been accused of focusing on the idea of reproduction rather than change. That one of his books is titled *Reproduction* has not helped move readings away from this viewpoint, nor have statements such as 'the tendency to the reproduction of the structure is immanent to the very structure itself of the field' (Bourdieu 2000: 238). However, acknowledging forces of reproduction does not mean denying the idea of change. Not only does Bourdieu often refer to notions such as 'rupture', 'transformation', 'crisis' or 'revolution' throughout his writing, but also in books such as *The Rules of Art*, *Manet* and *The Social Structure of the Economy*, he theorises change at length.

There he makes a distinction between two categories of 'factors of change': internal and external, although they are hard to disentangle from each other (Bourdieu 1992: 416). The four main external factors of change he looks at are what he terms morphological, technical, social and economic factors of change. Internal changes are linked to the internal logic of fields such as, in the field of cultural production, 'the dialectic of distinction', which is a 'specific law of change of the field of cultural production' (Bourdieu 1992: 259). In the UK field of fashion journalism, an illustration is the emergence, in the 1980s, of style magazines such as *The Face*, which, favouring an aesthetic borrowed from fanzines, moved away from the polished looks of glossy titles to report on street style, as worn by urban dwellers (Rocamora and O'Neill 2008).

Internal struggles are also forces of change in a field. On the one hand, dominant players have the power to impose change: their dominant position allows them to set the rules of the game and impose their values (Bourdieu 2000), as mentioned above in the case of fashion publications. On the other hand, in wanting to differentiate themselves from established players, newcomers too can bring change to a field, such as by advocating for new values and practices (Bourdieu 2000). They can 'make history', that is, 'create a new position beyond established positions' (Bourdieu 1992: 261), as Bourdieu has shown of the revolutionary work of Manet, or as has been taking place in the field of fashion media in recent years, an idea I return to later.

Bourdieu refers to the arrival of newcomers in a field as a morphological factor of change, and he paid particular attention to the idea of the rise in the number of players, as in his study of the 19th-century French fields of art and literature. He argued that 'the rise in number of middle class and working young people with no money who went to Paris to become a writer or artists' led to a growth of the market for cultural goods and a concurrent crisis in the space of exhibitions and sales (Bourdieu 1992: 95, 2013: 433). In the French academic field, a morphological change represented an increase in the number of students since the

1960s. This led to an increase in the number of lecturers too and thus to a change in the power relations at play between faculties, disciplines and teaching grades (1996b: 129). The rise of the student population was itself linked to wider social changes such as the rise of the birth rate following the Second World War, an idea which draws attention to the link between morphological and social changes (Bourdieu 1996b: 129).

Morphological changes are tightly connected to other external factors of change such as technical changes, for newcomers may bring in new techniques that will have some effects on the field. In the 19th-century French field of art, new artistic techniques gave birth to new artistic forms (Bourdieu 2013). New technologies can be the basis for the reconfiguration of the power relations between dominant and dominated players, as Bourdieu also shows in his study of the field of housing, to such an extent that he talks about technologies as a form of capital. In this field 'technological capital plays a determining role': a 'technological mutation' can lead to cost reductions advantageous to smaller competitors, allowing them to outrank dominant companies (Bourdieu 2000: 249).

It is perhaps in his work on the field of journalism in *On Television* that Bourdieu elaborated most fully on the transformational effect of technological factors of change. The 'intrusion' in the 1950s of television in the French field of journalism deeply transformed its structure, he argues (Bourdieu 1996c: 2). Having become, by the 1980s, a dominant media player both symbolically and economically, television imposed itself as a space for the production and distribution of news, taking readers away from newspapers, which entered a crisis compounded by the lack of financial state support. Some titles disappeared, and others had to revisit their practices, such as by publishing more television-related content. TV became able to 'determine the order of the day for newspapers' (Bourdieu 1996a: 2). Bourdieu blames the Audimat, which, he contends, contributed to the further heteronomisation of the field of journalism. An instrument of measurement of audience levels introduced in the 1980s French television landscape, the Audimat played into the competition between channels to attract the largest number of viewers possible, and thus into the commercial logic that underpins television (Bourdieu 1996a). 'Through the Audimat the commercial logic imposes itself to cultural productions' (Bourdieu 1996c: 29). With digitisation, the struggle for attention has moved online and involves new practices and instruments of quantification as well as a broader constituency of media players – established as well as emerging – across borders, an idea I will return to later.

In the field of fashion journalism, technologies have for long been a factor of change. In 19th-century Europe, for instance, new technologies of printing – which made for an easier, cheaper and higher-quality printing process – and the development of the lithograph print supported a rapid increase in the number of fashion magazines (Nelson Best 2017). In the late 19th century and early 20th century, better photographic technology supported the development of fashion photography and coverage, whilst technologies of communication such as the telephone and cable allowed for an easier and faster reporting of fashion news from a wider geographical sphere (Nelson Best 2017). However, Bourdieu warns against technological determinism: technological factors of change, like morphological ones, are tightly linked to social and economic factors, and all are interdependent (Bourdieu 2013: 409). In the 18th- and 19th-century field of the fashion media, technological factors contributed to the consolidation and proliferation of the fashion press, but so did social and economic factors such as a growing female literacy and consumer culture (Nelson Best 2017). Industrialisation fuelled the development of the fashion industry, which also translated into stronger advertising revenue for the fashion media (Nelson Best 2017).

These are some examples only of the ways technological factors of change in tandem with social and economic factors of change have affected the field of fashion journalism. In the next section, I focus on digital technologies to carry on investigating the idea of field change, and thus recent transformations in the contemporary field of the fashion media. I qualify some of the morphological changes that have taken place in this field with digitisation in the late 1990s by looking at the types of newcomers they are associated with.

Digital technologies and the contemporary field of fashion journalism

The 1990s and early 2000s saw a series of digital innovations that facilitated a transformation of the field of fashion journalism and, as in the field of journalism more generally, 'lowered the barriers to entry' into the field (Marconi 2020: 25), resulting in its fragmentation into a broader variety and number of players struggling for a proportionally scarcer share of audience attention (Webster 2014). The public launch of the World Wide Web in 1991; the invention of new digital tools for publishing faster and at low cost, such as Blogger in 1999 and WordPress in 2005; the use of portable computers and smartphones and the arrival of platforms such as Twitter (now X), Instagram and TikTok have allowed a growing number of 'peripheral actors' and 'interlopers' to access cheaper ways of producing media for larger audiences and, in the process, to disrupt the field of journalism (Hanusch & Löhmann 2023; Quandt 2024; Eldridge 2018). Until then, it had been economically and professionally relatively stable (Quandt 2024; Eldridge 2018). Fashion bloggers, for instance, disrupted visions of fashion as circulated in legacy fashion magazines by featuring on their web pages bodies that departed from the dominant young, white, thin, non-disabled bodies of glossies or by discussing designers ignored by established magazines for want of the economic capital that would have given them access to advertising – and so editorial – space (Rocamora 2011).

Social media newcomers

In recent years, a new genre of fashion media players has emerged with the proliferation of digital platforms, contributing to the further fragmentation of the field of fashion media into a wider range and number of fashion information sources. Although present across the wider social media space, YouTubers, TikTokers and Instagrammers, the most recent newcomers, are, like bloggers before them, categorised through a reference to the platform they are most active on. This semantic melding of person and platform underscores the tight relation that exists between new media players and social media, and thus the tight relation between the field of fashion media and that of technology, an idea I return to later.

In statements contributing to their consecration, the established style magazine *The Face* calls those newcomers 'alternative fashion critics' (Cochrane 2023a). *System Magazine* calls them 'The new generation of fashion critics' (Prigent 2023), whilst Elle.com.uk ran an article titled 'These are the Next-Gen TikTok Critics Shaking Up fashion' (Cochrane 2023b). On their social media feeds, those new fashion critics discuss a broad range of fashion-related topics from fashion history to current issues such as sustainability or racism, whilst audiences can contribute to the comments sections. Often appearing on their posts using tones ranging from playful to serious, their home visible in the background or their image juxtaposed to a broad range of fast-moving visuals, with some shot by them, they produce original fashion media texts not only in content but in form too, through the mixing and layering, thanks to the multimodality afforded to social media, of written and oral commentaries alongside still and moving images as well as sound. At once editor, commentator, writer, photographer, videographer and researcher, and even sometimes model, they populate their feed with a succession of fast-moving fashion vignettes that can reach large audiences.

Amongst the new fashion critics listed in the articles are Kim Russell (aka thekimbino), who, *The Face* notes, has 'racked up 157K followers' on Instagram; TikToker Rian Phin (aka @thatadult) as well as YouTuber Odunayo Ojo (aka Fashion Roadman). All three are black people, a social category notoriously underrepresented in the field of fashion in the Global North, but who, having taken advantage of the lowering of the boundaries between users and producers on social media have carved a position for themselves in the field.

The Face's highlight of Russell's '157K followers' draws attention to the value attributed to metrics in the field of social media and to the logic of quantification that underpins it (see also Rocamora 2023). As *Vogue Business* writes, in a comment that also points to the significance of metrics in media's struggles for audience attention (Shin and Ognyanova 2022): 'On the site, Vogue's 2023 Red Carpet Gallery is now Vogue's most read and engaged story in the website's history, with 3.6 million unique visits and 31 million engaged minutes. Countries including Germany, India, Italy, Japan and Mexico also topped site traffic records for the regions' (Schulz 2023). In the field of fashion media, as in the media field more generally, engagement rates and numbers of followers and likes are forms of symbolic and social capitals that media players draw on to nurture economic capital and secure further recognition (Mau 2018; Grosser 2014; Rocamora 2022; Sadowski 2020). Sadowski (2019) talks about 'data capital'. In the case of TikTokers, YouTubers and Instagrammers, 'data capital' can lead to media coverage, as with the articles mentioned above, and thus to further symbolic capital, which in turn media players can draw on to secure paid work. In the field of journalism, metrics have become a symbolic resource and asset that journalists capitalise on (Christin 2020; Shin and Ognyanova 2022).

However, data matters also because it shapes journalistic practice and content, for in the media industry, metrics are put 'at work' (Christin 2020). A 2020 *Digiday* article explains 'How Vogue's international approach to audience data helped it reach record readers'. Data tracking across the titles' platforms indicated readers wanted 'Stories about altruism, culture, fashion history, sustainability and ethical production'. This was relayed to the editorial team, who produced content accordingly (Barber 2020).

Newcomers have emerged in an economic landscape that has contributed to the disruption of the field of fashion media. Indeed, being largely heteronomous, both the field of fashion media and that of the media more generally are part of the wider economic field and thus subject to its forces. Looking beyond technological factors, the discursive struggles that opposed fashion bloggers and fashion journalists, for instance, unfolded within the context of a wider 'crisis of journalism' (Alexander et al. 2016). This crisis has been linked to digitisation and the disruption of the traditional field of legacy media it has entailed, but it has also been brought about by a wider and persisting economic crisis, especially following the 2008 financial crash, and the ensuing recession (Alexander et al. 2016; Compton and Benedetti 2010). It has translated into declining advertising revenues for fashion titles, especially print legacy ones, with advertisers moving their budgets to platforms; circulations, subscriptions and profitability falling (Conti 2023; Majid 2022a, 2022b), and some magazines becoming digital only, such as *InStyle* in 2022 or *Marie Claire* UK and *Marie Claire* US in 2019 and 2021, respectively.

Furthermore, precarious labour is rampant in journalism (Zelizer 2017; Wahl-Jorgensen and Hanitzsch 2020) and notoriously so, both in the field of fashion and that of fashion media, where free labour is also often expected (Mensitieri 2018). Permanent positions are rare, and freelancer tariffs have been decreasing (Deuze and Witschge 2017), leading the *Press Gazette* to ask in 2023: 'Poor rates, unreliable payment and publications closing: is being a freelance journalist basically a hobby?' (Jones 2023). It might not come as a surprise then that individuals interested in making a position for themselves in the field of fashion media have opted to self-publish on digital platforms, not least since the data capital accumulated there might lead towards a broader range of remunerated works. For in the current precarious labour context fashion journalists often have a portfolio of activities that helps them secure economic capital. On her website, Berlin-based Brenda Weischer of @brendahashtag (205K Instagram followers) describes her work as 'fashion writer, collector, consultant and content creator … her consultancy work is based around personal branding, fashion journalism and storytelling' (https://www.brendahashtag.com/about). New fashion titles have emerged too, which also bridge editorial work with branding and consultancy, further blurring the distinction between editorial and commercial in the field of fashion media. *The Perfect Magazine*, for instance, describes their work in the following terms: 'We create multi-platform content for and with brands [...] developing and interpreting a brief to create their own perfect print issue' (https://www.theperfectmagazine.com/about).

Fashion journalists and the logic of entrepreneurship

In the current volatile economic context, established fashion media players too have had to find alternative ways of generating income. This has included new ways of publishing their work. Many have embraced what has become known as newsletter journalism, which consists in regularly sharing articles with readers through emails. Journalists often do so through a new genre of media publishers they have signed up to: digital publishing platforms such as Substack or Puck, which host journalists' writing against a fee. Readers can choose between different subscription packages. This mode of publishing allows journalists to produce content less constrained by the forces at play in existing journalistic institutions (Zilberstein 2022), such as, in the field of the fashion media, pressures from advertisers. It allows them 'to say what is typically left unsaid' as Laurent Sherman (formerly chief correspondent at BOF) puts it in her 16 November 2023 Puck newsletter Line Sheet. Amy Odell (formerly of *The Cut*) also invokes the journalistic ideal of autonomy when describing her Substack newsletter Back Row as 'The fashion and culture newsletter that publishes what legacy media can't' (https://substack.com/@amyodell).

Fashion journalists have drawn on their existing data capital to drive their audiences towards their newsletters. In August 2023, Alec Leach, for instance, announced on Instagram that he was joining Substack. A series of posts in his Stories convey the feeling of precarity fashion journalists' experience as well as journalism's value of autonomy. There he states:

> I've been writing about fashion for nearly ten years now, and in that time media jobs have become so precarious that it feels almost impossible to build a long-term career from writing, especially when you're critiquing the industry. The newsletter

format means I can write deeper and more consistently about the topics I care about, and Substack's subscription model gives me the chance to make a living from paid subscription.

(Leach 2023)

In her 1 May 2023 newsletter, Odell refers to herself as a 'journalist-entrepreneur', a term that draws attention to the logic of entrepreneurship that now informs the field of journalism (Wahl-Jorgensen and Hanitzsch 2020). This logic has long been at play in the field of legacy publishers and press barons (Neveu 2001), but now also underpins the work of individual journalists and their 'solitary' (Zelizer 2013) labour. A dominant ideology of neoliberal capitalism, it goes hand in hand with individualisation, including of the labour of fashion journalism. Self-branding becomes yet another business skill that journalists must master to acquire enough capital to survive in the field (Zelizer 2017).

Odell, along with other established fashion media players, is active across platforms, with 83.7K, 81.8K, 46.3K and 18.1K followers on TikTok, Instagram, X and Thread, respectively, as of April 2024. Being present on social media, and on Instagram especially – still the most popular platform in the field of fashion (Launchmetrics 2023) – has become a 'normalised' (Tandoc and Vos 2015) routine of fashion journalism: Tim Blanks, for instance, has 181K Instagram followers, and Suzy Menkes, 796K (30–04–2024). Like the newcomer 'fashion critics' discussed above, Odell and her colleagues have embraced a range of textual formats to publish the broad variety and volume of content key to the struggle for online attention in today's field of journalism (Leinonen 2022; Tandoc and Vos 2015). With both established and emerging media players having to accumulate data capital, what was once, as with television and the Audimat, an institutional responsibility and logic, tracking and attracting large audiences has become an individualised logic that has stretched across a broad range of agents.

Transnational fashion media players

New players and new publishing spaces have been emerging in the field of fashion media in a context of economic and media crisis. However, other forces that have participated in the conditions of possibility of their emergence have been at play. There are 'global collective causes' one must account for to understand change in a field (Bourdieu 2013: 419). The transnationalisation of the wider field of fashion is one of them. In the 1980s, the globalisation and corporatisation that informed the rise of transnational media groups in the field of the media also informed the field of fashion. The 1980s and 1990s saw its concentration in the hands of a small number of large transnational conglomerates, both in the field of luxury and in that of mass fashion (see also Nelson Best 2017) with the founding, most significantly, of fast fashion company Inditex in 1985 (seven high-street brands in 2023) and luxury groups Louis Vuitton Moët Hennessy (hereafter LVMH) in 1987 (now owner of 14 luxury fashion brands), and Richemont in 1988 (19 luxury brands in 2023). Alongside luxury group Kering (11 fashion brands), today they dominate the field of fashion. Endowed with a large economic capital, those global conglomerates have spread the reach of their commodities worldwide, in retail spaces as well as in the media. They are, in effect, producing transnational goods and brands. These are the goods and brands Instagrammers, TikTokers and other social media fashion commentators report on in the knowledge that, being familiar to their audience, such goods and brands make for posts that can reach the wide constituency of possible viewers, which the networked quality of online media grants them.

Transnational fashion goods are also now widely visible online through the brands' websites and social media platforms. Their online presence allows new media players to tap into a repository of fashion signs to which media audiences also have access across the world by just logging in on their phone or computer (see also Granata 2021), whilst the networked quality of the internet supports their transnational circulation, as it does that of news and information more generally (Gershon 1997).

Fashion events such as fashion shows also participate in the consolidation of this repository of shared signs, and in the increased transnationalisation of the fields of fashion and the fashion media. No longer aimed at a select group of gatekeepers and journalists only, whose reports would have been read long after the shows had taken place, those events have become spectacles live-streamed to audiences across the globe and designed to that effect (Rocamora 2017). Viewers can discuss them almost simultaneously in their social media feeds. Indeed, they are a regular topic of analysis amongst fashion commentators on Instagram, X and TikTok.

Brands' online and social media presence also points to the significance of digital media for allowing fashion companies to become media players in their own right (Rocamora 2018). Not only do brands and retailers alike produce content to circulate across online sites, but also various fashion companies have launched print and digital fashion publications too (Rocamora 2018). The online retail site Net-à-Porter, for instance, publishes online magazine *Porter* (1M Instagram followers, 14–12–23), and in 2020 swimwear brand Cuup launched digital-only title *BodyTalk*. Edited by a former *Vogue* fashion writer, it focuses on women's relationship with their bodies (Fraser 2020). These are only two of the many instances of the mediatisation of fashion companies (Rocamora 2018, 2017). Publications allow them to build not only their symbolic capital but their economic capital too, for 'Analysing the performance of articles can help inform everything from product development to marketing campaigns and brand positioning' (Mondalek 2021). Here, the fields of commerce, fashion and the media collapse into one another in a further blurring of the distinction between the commercial and the editorial.

Fashion companies' role as media players also takes the form of dominant fashion conglomerates having direct financial stakes in media groups, and thus a direct say in their fashion coverage. LVMH had shares in Lagardère and owns the French dailies *Les Echos* and *Le Parisien* – in 2020, French newspaper *Le Monde* called its owner Antoine Arnault a 'press baron' (Chemin 2020). The conglomerate's rival Kering (13 luxury fashion brands) owns the French magazine *Le Point*.

Fashion titles too have tapped into the logic of entertainment that informs the field of fashion (Rocamora 2023) by holding live events to attract viewers online in the hope of converting them into readers. *Vogue* runs *Vogue* World, a multimedia show and festival, and the Met Gala. Of the former, UK *Vogue* editor Edward Enninful (cited in Guthrie 2023) states that it is 'an opportunity for us to make an enormous amount of content', whilst the *Women's Wear Daily* notes of the Met Gala content' of 2022 that it 'notched 14 billion impressions' (Guthrie 2023), a comment that also underscores the importance of metrics in the field of fashion media. Such events are indeed widely covered by fashion media newcomers on their social media accounts, adding to the repository of shared signs and aesthetics they can draw on to produce transcultural fashion news and commentary and reach a transnational audience.

Social media affordances such as hashtags are key to this. Acting as vectors of transnationalisation and visibility, they are widely mobilised by media players in their struggles for attention. #fashioncommentary and #fashionanalysis, for instance, are commonly used, whilst *Vogue Business* credit the hashtag #metgala for having generated 12.3 billion impressions in 2023 (Schulz 2023). Although counting a large 48.5M followers on Instagram (30-04-2024), *Vogue Magazine* must compete for attention with a broad range of media players, from fashion brands that now produce content to established and new online and social media players such as Style Not Com (359K Instagram followers, 30-04-2024) or Diet Prada (3.4M Instagram followers, 30-04-2024). Both accounts post in English, the lingua franca of fashion, although Instagram's automatic translation affordance between languages allows for the bypassing of linguistic and, in the process, national barriers.

Tech companies

Bloggers, TikTokers and fashion companies are not the only newcomers to have entered the field of fashion media in recent years, so are the very companies that have granted them access: tech companies, for, today, not only is the field of fashion at the intersection of the fields of fashion and journalism, but it is at the intersection of the field of technology too. Social media players' work being platform-dependent means it is dependent on platforms' power to manage their activities such as through software designs or the implementation of notoriously non-transparent algorithms. Here, the rules of the social media game are governed by a handful of transnational tech companies that have the power to 'generate and manage attention' (Bucher 2012: 4), thereby becoming key players in journalists' struggle for attention.

Not only are Platforms such as Google and X sources which audiences turn to for news (in the United Kingdom in 2023, TikTok overtook BBC Radio 1 and Channel 5 as news sources (Majid 2023)), but they are also key in driving traffic towards media players, which must abide by their rules (Nielsen and Ganter 2022). Online titles, for instance, publish articles using strategic keywords and related content in the hope that platforms' SEOs will direct readers towards them (Duffy 2013). In the field of online fashion media, 'the best …' or 'the most…' are recurring clickbait headlines of what fashion journalist Amy Odell (2020) calls 'the relentless clicks-driven news cycle'. Platforms such as Meta and Google have in effect become 'gatekeepers' of the field of media, granting media titles audience reach in their own terms (Nielsen and Ganter 2022: 4). In this context, digital specialists have become key in the operations of online media titles and their struggle for attention (Duffy 2013). However, their involvement is not limited to software design only. They are involved in editorial and content decisions too, as Duffy shows of women's magazines at Hearst (Duffy 2013). Data analysts are indeed in high demand in the field of fashion (Rocamora 2023), including fashion media, as witnessed by an October 23 offer for a position of 'Editorial data analyst' at Hearst to 'support … editors and video creators' (https://www.builtinnyc.com/job/data/editorial-data-analyst/235073). Conversely, a job offer for the post of Fashion Writer at *Marie-Claire* UK in 2023 specifies that the applicants will need to have, among other things: 'Understanding of SEO best practices' and 'Ability to interpret data to inform content strategy' (https://uk.indeed.com/q-marie-claire-jobs.html?vjk=2bf139ead46b2db5).

Thus Wu (2023) argues that technological firms are 'new entrants' to the journalistic field. That is, the field of technology and that of the media intersect, and the boundaries between the two have become porous. In his work on the field of housing, Bourdieu (2000: 249) has acknowledged the 'crossing' and 'redefinition' of boundaries between fields, which technological change can generate. This field, he argues, has been disrupted by newcomers from the fields of telecommunications and information technology, two fields normally distinct from that of housing. A company can be in competition with other companies from its own field as well as with companies belonging to other fields (Bourdieu 2000: 249). A statement by *The Perfect Magazine* captures the intersection between the field of fashion media and that of tech. Guaranteeing 'full audience reach', they write that: 'our audience-first, platform-specific approach backed by data will always have an impact in the powerful confluence of technology and constantly-evolving consumer behaviours' (https://www.theperfectmagazine.com/about). The field of fashion media, like the media field more generally (Chadwick 2013; Witsche et al. 2016), has become a dispersed and fragmented space made of a diversity of players, including newcomers not usually associated with media work – bloggers, TikTokers, fashion brands, tech companies and data specialists – all involved in the struggle for audience attention and economic capital.

Conclusion

The field of fashion journalism has changed with the advent of digital media. In this chapter, I have argued for the value of Bourdieu's field theory to capture key changes. His is a complex framework of interrelated concepts and analytical layers developed to grasp the many dynamics at play in a social space. Bourdieu (2013: 413) acknowledges this complexity of both the theoretical and the social when, talking about his 'model' of field change, he writes that 'in theory it's easy to say but in practice it's difficult to do' for 'It's a very complicated multifactorial system' made of factors that determine each other when shaping that which they also determine. A chapter length essay can only start capturing the complexity of the field of fashion media, and this chapter is by no means a complete picture and analysis of this field, but it points to the value of the Bourdieuian framework for interrogating fashion journalism and its transformation. Future research could further unpack the field of fashion media and the way it has changed across time, looking at its genesis, for instance, as I have suggested in this chapter, and further analysing its transnational dimension. Such studies are needed to better understand the complex formation of both the field of fashion and that of journalism.

An analysis of the genesis of the field of fashion journalism would bring to light the players, dynamics and logics that have participated in its formation in particular geographical settings. This could form the basis for comparative analyses that would be useful for interrogating similarities and differences between fields as spaces that are both nationally and transnationally structured, bringing into the analytical equation, then, historical as well as geographical parameters. Such an analysis could also be narrowed down to the present time, through an investigation of the emergence and rise of the field of social media and new fashion media players, as the present chapter has started doing. A comparison between fields located in the Global North and the Global South, such as the UK and Brazil, for instance, could usefully identify the forces of globalisation and localisation at play in and across national fields. This could be by way of looking at how new fashion critics operate on TikTok, for example, mapping the local and transnational agents (individual as well as institutional) they are related to and dependent on, including for their consecration, and identifying the capitals needed to succeed. Bourdieu's analytical framework allows for an exploration of such national and transnational dynamics and for the ways spaces of cultural production emerge and evolve, giving the researchers tools for capturing change and complexity.

Notes

1 Citations from French texts are my translations.
2 Although *Elle* is owned by Lagardère, Hearst has the right to publish it in 13 countries following a 2011 deal between the two publishers.

Further reading

Bourdieu, P. (1996c). *Sur La Télévision*. Seuil. (Translated as *On Television*. Pluto Press, 1998).
Duffy, B. (2013). *Remake, Remodel*. University of Illinois Press.
Nelson Best, K. (2017). *The History of Fashion Journalism*. Bloomsbury.
Rocamora, A. (2022). Datafication and the Quantification of Fashion. *Fashion Theory*, 26(7), 1109–1133.
Sandhu, A. (2023). Fashion for a cause. In R. Findlay and J. Reponen (Eds.) *Insights on Fashion Journalism* (pp. 110–123). Routledge.

References

Alexander, J. C. Butler Breese, E. and Luengo, M. (eds) (2016). *The Crisis of Journalism Reconsidered*. Cambridge University Press.
Barber, K. (2020). *How Vogue's International Approach to Audience Data Helped it Reach Record Readers*. https://digiday.com/media/how-vogues-international-approach-to-audience-data-helped-it-reach-record-readers/.
Benson, R. and Neveu, E. (2005). *Bourdieu and the Journalistic Field*. Polity.
Bourdieu, P. (2015). *Sociologie Générale*. 1. Seuil.
Bourdieu, P. (2013). *Manet*. Seuil.
Bourdieu, P. (2005/1995). The political field, the social field, and the journalistic field. In R. Benson and E. Neveu (eds). *Bourdieu and the Journalistic Field*. Polity.
Bourdieu, P. (2000). *Les Structures Sociales de L'Economie*. Seuil.
Bourdieu, P. (1997). *Méditations Pascaliennes*. Seuil.
Bourdieu, P. (1996a). Actes du colloque fondateur du centre de recherche de l'Ecole Supérieure de Journalisme. *Cahiers du journalisme*, June, 1.
Bourdieu, P. (1996b). *Homo Academicus*. Polity.
Bourdieu, P. (1996c). *Sur La Télévision*. Seuil.
Bourdieu, P. (1995). *Sociology in Questions*. Sage.
Bourdieu, P. (1993). *The Field of Cultural Production*. Polity.
Bourdieu, P. (1992). *Les Règles de l'Art*. Seuil.
Bucher, T. (2012). A Technicity of Attention. *Culture Machine*, 1–23.
Buchholz, L. (2017). What is a global field? In *The Sociological Review*, 64(2), 31–60. Sage.
Chadwick, A. (2013). *The Hybrid Media System*. Oxford University Press.
Chalaby, J. (1998). *The Invention of Journalism*. Palgrave.
Chemin, A. (2020). *L'un des hommes de confiance de Bernard Arnault place des fidèles dans les médias de LVMH et Lagardère*. https://www.lemonde.fr/economie/article/2020/12/21/l-un-des-hommes-de-confiance-de-bernard-arnault-place-des-fideles-dans-les-medias-de-lvmh-et-lagardere_6064095_3234.html.
Cheng, L. and Tandoc, C. Edson Jr. (2022). From Magazines to blogs. *Journalism*, 23(6), 1213–1232.
Christin, A. (2020). *Metrics at Work*. Princeton University Press.
Cochrane, L. (2023a). *The Best Alternative Fashion Critics to Follow*. https://theface.com/style/fashion-critics-to-follow-this-year-the-kimbino-style-not-com-tiktok-style
Cochrane, L. (2023b). *The Are the Nexgen TokTok Critics Shaking Up Fashion*. https://www.elle.com/uk/fashion/a42826656/tiktok-critics-fashion/

Conti, S. (2023). Condé Nast international sees profits plummet in fiscal 2022. *WWD* https://wwd.com/business-news/media/conde-nast-international-division-sees-profits-plummet-fiscal-1235878023/

Deuze, M. and Witschge, T. (2017). Beyond journalism, *Journalism*, 19(2), 1–17.

Duffy, B. (2013). *Remake, Remodel*. University of Illinois Press.

Eldridge II, Scott, A. (2018). *Online Journalism from the Periphery*. Routledge.

Entwistle, J. and Rocamora, A. (2006). The field of fashion materialized. *Sociology*, 40, 735–751.

Findlay, R. and Reponen, J. (2023). *Insights on Fashion Journalism*. Routledge.

Fraser, K. (2020). *Marjon Carlos Tapped to Lead Cuup's Editorial Team*. https://fashionunited.uk/news/people/marjon-carlos-tapped-to-lead-cuup-s-editorial-team/2020110652039

From, U. and Kristensen, N. N. (2020). Unpacking lifestyle journalism via service journalism and constructive journalism. In L. Vodanovic (ed.) *Lifestyle Journalism* (pp. 12–24). Routledge.

Gershon, R.A. (1997). *The Transnational Media Corporation*. Western Michigan University.

Granata, F. (2021). Introduction. In F. Granata (ed.) *Fashion Criticism* (pp. 6–11). Bloomsbury.

Grosser, (2014), 'What do Metrics Want?', Computational Culture, 1–40. http://computationalculture.net/what-do-metrics-want/ (accessed on 05-10-19).

Guthrie, M. (2023). *Condé Nast Casts Itself as Arbiter of Culture*. https://wwd.com/business-news/media/conde-nast-new-front-vogue-world-anna-wintour-1235640935/.

Hartley, J. and Rennie, E. (2004). About a girl. *Journalism*, 5(4), 458–479.

Hanusch, F. (ed.) (2013). Broadening the focus. In F. Hanusch (ed.) *Lifestyle Journalism*, (pp. 2–11). Routledge.

Hanusch, F. and Löhmann, K. (2023). Dimensions of peripherality in journalism. A typology for studying new actors in the journalistic field. *Digital Journalism*. 11(7), 1292–1310. DOI: 10.1080/21670811.2022.2148549

Hepp, A. (2015). *Transcultural Communication*. Blackwell.

James R. Compton and Paul Benedetti (2010). Labour, new media and the
Institutional restructuring of journalism, *Journalism Studies*, 11(4), 487–499, DOI: 10.1080/14616701003638350

Jones, R. (2023). Is Freelance journalism becoming unviable? *Press Gazette*. https://pressgazette.co.uk/comment-analysis/is-freelance-journalism-becoming-unviable/

Launchmetrics. (2023). *Beyond Followers*. https://www.launchmetrics.com/resources/whitepapers/instagram-marketing-strategy-report?utm_source=Twitter&utm_medium=Social&utm_campaign=23-wp-ig-report_en

Leach, A. (2023). Big personal news: I'm launching a newsletter. *Instagram Stories*, Tuesday 29 August. Retrieved 29 August 2023. https://www.instagram.com/stories/alecleach_/

Leinonen, S.-R. (2022). Can journalists be influencers? How to engage hard-to-reach audiences on social media. In Polis, *Journalism at LSE*. LSE

Le Masurier, Megan (2020). Like water & oil? Fashion photography as journalistic comment. *Journalism*, 21(6), 821–837. DOI: 10.1177/1464884919860926

Majid, A. (2023). *Most Popular News Sources in the UK*. https://pressgazette.co.uk/media-audience-and-business-data/most-popular-news-sources-uk-tiktok-ofcom-news-consumption-survey/

Majid, A. (2022a). *Charted*. https://pressgazette.co.uk/publishers/magazines/uk-consumer-magazine-industry-charts/

Majid, A. (2022b). *Magazine ABCs for 2022*. https://pressgazette.co.uk/media-audience-and-business-data/media_metrics/magazine-circulations-2022-abc-print-digital/

Marconi, F. (2020). *Newsmakers*. Columbia U Press.

Mau, S. (2019[2017]). The Metric Society. Polity.

McDowell (2020). *The Truth About the Fashion World, Exposed*. https://www.businessoffashion.com/articles/colins-column/colins-column-andre-leon-talley-memoir-alexandra-shulman-grace-mirabella-fashion-books

Mensitieri, G. (2018). *Le Plus Beau Métier du Monde*. Découverte.

Mondalek, A. (2021). *Can a Brand Publish a Magazine People Actually Want to Read?* https://www.businessoffashion.com/articles/marketing-pr/can-a-brand-publish-a-magazine-people-actually-want-to-read/.

Nelson Best, K. (2017). *The History of Fashion Journalism*. Bloomsbury.

Neveu, E. (2001). *Sociologie du journalisme*. Découverte.

Nielsen, K. and Ganter, S.A. (2022). *The Power of Platforms*. Oxford University Press.

Odell, A. (2020). *How to Leave Your Old Media Job*. https://www.businessoffashion.com/articles/media/how-to-leave-your-old-media-job/.

Perreault, G. and Stanfield, K. (2018). Mobile journalism as lifestyle journalism? *Journalism Practice*, 13(3), 331–348. DOI: 10.1080/17512786.2018.1424021

Prigent, L. (2023). My problem has been not having a filter. *System*. https://system-magazine.com/issues/issue-19/survey-says.

Quandt, T. (2024). Euphoria, disillusionment and fear: Twenty-five years of digital journalism. *Journalism*, 25(5), 1186–1203.

Rocamora, A. (2023). Deep mediatization and the datafication of fashion. In K. Kopecka-Piech and G. Bolin (eds.) *Contemporary Challenges in Mediatisation Research* (pp. 63–79). Routledge.

Rocamora, A. (2022). Datafication and the quantification of fashion. *Fashion Theory*, 26(7), 1109–1133.

Rocamora, A. (2018). Mediatization and digital retail. In A. Geczy and V. Karaminas (eds.) *The End of Fashion*, 99–112. Bloomsbury.

Rocamora, A. (2017). Mediatization and digitization in the field of fashion. *Fashion Theory*, 21(5), 505–522.

Rocamora, A. (2016). Pierre Bourdieu. In A. Rocamora and A. Smelik (eds.) *Thinking Through Fashion* (pp. 233–250). Bloomsbury.

Rocamora, A. (2011). Personal fashion blogs. *Fashion Theory*, 15(4), 407–424.

Rocamora, A. (2009). *Fashioning the City*. I.B. Tauris.

Rocamora, A. and O'Neill (2008). Fashioning the street. In E. Shinkle (ed.) *Fashion as Photograph*, (pp. 185–199). Bloomsbury.

Sadowski J. (2019), 'When data is capital', *Big Data and Society*, 1–12.

Sandhu, A. (2023). Fashion for a cause. In R. Findlay and J. Reponen (eds.) *Insights on Fashion Journalism*, (pp. 110–123). Routledge.

Sapiro, G., Leperlier, T. and Brahimi, M.A. (2018). Qu'est-ce qu'un champ intellectuel transnational? *Actes de la Recherche en Sciences Sociales*, 224, 4–11.

Schulz, M. (2023). *The 2023 Met Gala by the Numbers*. https://www.voguebusiness.com/fashion/the-2023-met-gala-by-the-numbers.

Shangyuan Wu. (2023). A field analysis of immersive technologies and their impact on journalism: Technologist perspectives on the potential transformation of the journalistic field, Journalism Studies, 24(3), 387–402, DOI: 10.1080/1461670X.2022.2161931.

Shin, J. and Ognyanova, K. (2022). Social media metrics in the digital marketplace of attention. *Digital Journalism*, 10(4), 579–598.

Tandoc Jr. Edson, C. and Vos, Tim P. (2015). The journalist is marketing the news. *Journalism Practice*, 10(8), 950–966. DOI: 10.1080/17512786.2015.1087811

Vos, Tim P. (2016). Journalistic fields. In T. Witsche, C. W. Anderson, D. Domingo, and A. Hermida (eds.) *The Sage Handbook of Digital Journalism*, (pp. 383–396). Sage.

Wahl-Jorgensen, K. and Hanitzsch, T. (2020). *The Handbook of Journalism Studies*. Routledge.

Webster, J. G. (2014). *The Marketplace of Attention*. MIT Press.

Witsche, T., Anderson, C. W., Domingo, D. and Hermida, A. (2016). Introduction. In T. Witsche, C. W. Anderson, D. Domingo, and A. Hermida (eds.) *The Sage handbook of Digital Journalism*, (pp. 1–4). Sage.

Wu, Shangyuan, Tandoc, Edson C. Jr. and Salmon, Charles T. (2019). When journalism and automation intersect. *Journalism Practice*, 13(10), 1238–1254. DOI: 10.1080/17512786.2019.1585198

Zelizer, B. (2017). *What Journalism Could Be*. Polity

Zelizer, B. (2013). Tools for the future of journalism. *Ecquid Novi*, 34(2), 142–152.

Zilberstein, S. (2022). Digital platforms and journalistic careers. *Columbia Journalism Review*. https://www.cjr.org/tow_center_reports/digital-platforms-and-journalistic-careers-a-case-study-of-substack-newsletters.php

26
COACHES, GURUS AND INFLUENCERS AS SELF-HELP AND LIFESTYLE EXPERTS

From Insta therapy to becoming "that girl" on TikTok

Stephanie Alice Baker

Introduction

The 21st century has witnessed the proliferation of coaches, gurus and influencers sharing self-help and lifestyle advice online. Scrolling on social media, users are inundated by content creators sharing tips and secrets about how to improve their lives across three domains: health, wealth and relationships. In contemporary parlance, self-help is a genre that instructs consumers about how to improve their lives. Self-help encourages self-reliance rather than external support from an institution, organisation or a clinician. Initially a form of literature, the genre has become ubiquitous on social media where self-help is disseminated in digestible memes, posts and videos. Self-help acts as a guide to help the consumer achieve their goals and realise their potential. The genre has flourished under certain cultural, economic and political conditions, which conceive of the individual as the author of their own destiny. In *Lifestyle Gurus* (Baker and Rojek, 2020), we situated the rise of self-help in the context of de-traditionalisation (the loosening of tradition) and low institutional trust, both of which encourage a departure from the moral scripts dictated by organised religion, official knowledge and institutional expertise. Self-help, conversely, emphasises self-discovery and self-making under the guidance of coaches, gurus, and influencers who have become entrepreneurs in self-making (Baker, 2022a, 2022b; Baker and Rojek, 2019, 2020). This broader shift was foreshadowed by Antony Giddens' work on *Modernity and Self-identity* (1991), whereby the self in late modern society is conceived as a 'reflexive project', sustained through a continuous, revisable narrative of self-identity. Despite the new possibilities and freedoms afforded to individuals in late modern society, the imperative of self-improvement has come under critique by numerous scholars (Illouz, 2008; Orgad and Gill, 2021).

Critics of self-help revive a compendium of critiques of modernity (Illouz, 2008). Commentators have critiqued the rise of individualism at the expense of social bonds (Putnam, 2000), the flourishing of consumer society in late capitalism and the way it flattens political discourse (Debord, [1967] 2021) and recasts relationships as disposable commodities to be discarded when found faulty or unsatisfactory (Bauman, 2013). These themes persist in critiques of self-help. Philip Rieff (1966) and Christopher Lasch (1979) critiqued the rise of therapy culture in post-war society. They convey an impoverished view of Western culture and "psychological man," symptomatic of the individualistic culture they observed in the United States. Rieff (1966) associated 'the triumph of the therapeutic' in American culture with the shift from a religious sensibility to a therapeutic one. Whereas pre-modern and Christian societies found meaning and order in their commitment to divine authority, the modern self rejects authority altogether. Salvation is not found in the community that is upheld by either the authority of fate, honour and shame or the Church with its mediating authorities, symbolic systems and rites; rather it is found in the self, expressing its desires without restriction. Desire becomes the ultimate expression of freedom and identity. As Rieff (1966) declared, "Religious man was born to be saved, therapeutic man is born to be pleased." For Rieff, it is not simply that the Enlightenment's emphasis on science and reason has dispensed with religion; new individualistic forms of religion have emerged – those who self-identify as "spiritual, but not religious" – which offer a variety of therapies to soothe and satisfy the self, but one which is devoid of authority and communal purpose. Rieff foresees a future where rather than finding their true self in community or seeking truth at all, humans become virtuosos of themselves and the ordering of their desires, adopting whatever new religion or therapeutic method gives them pleasure and satisfaction. Although these commentators critiqued social relations in the late 20th century, they were not implying that society was ideal in the post-war period. Instead, Lasch and others believed these conditions originated in the 19th century (see Menand, 2002), a period which coincides with the birth of modern self-help. This chapter contextualises the rise of gurus, coaches and influencers in the history of self-help, tracing the development of self-improvement literature historically to the 21st century. In doing so, it contributes to previous research on lifestyle journalism. Lifestyle journalism influences self-identity and consumer behaviour (Hanusch and Hanitzsch, 2013), providing audiences with information and advice to cope with the challenges of everyday life (Eide and Knight, 1999). This chapter develops this literature by examining how self-appointed life coaches, gurus and influencers position themselves as experts in the domain of self-improvement and life planning to influence identity construction within the genre of self-help.

The history of self-help: Self-reliance and unofficial knowledge

Questions about how to live have endured throughout the centuries. The Greeks and Romans were preoccupied with questions about how to live a good life. Philosophers provided remedies to perennial questions about how to appraise our feelings, how to understand the nature of reality and how to navigate the vicissitudes of life. The Greco-Romans believed that good character was essential to individual excellence and cultivating a healthy *polis* (city-state) (Baker, 2022b). Virtue was conceived as a form of excellence concerned with cultivating the character traits essential to *eudaimonia* (human flourishing) (Adams, 2008). The main virtues of the time included practical wisdom (understanding how to act in a given situation), courage (how to act bravely), justice (how to treat people fairly) and temperance (how to act with moderation). The conduct manuals of the Renaissance society, analysed by the sociologist Norbert Elias (1978), encoded shifting canons of behaviour and affect. The long-term trend Elias observed towards emotional regulation and more refined etiquette and human conduct were identified as a consequence of changing social conditions and relationships. Elias proposed that as society became more complex, the "chains of interdependency" among people became "denser" and "longer," placing new standards of behaviour of the individuals who comprised them (van Krieken, 2017). In addition to conduct manuals spanning the medieval period to the mid-20th century, various texts circulated over the previous centuries have featured the daily habits, rituals and routines of successful individuals. These texts share much in common with original self-help literature by providing insights about how to cultivate character and achieve self-reliance and social mobility.

Self-help is the use of one's own resources and efforts to improve their life. The genre emerged in the 19th century with the publication of *Self-help with Illustrations of Character and Conduct* (1859), written by Samuel Smiles. The book provided practical advice about how to achieve social and economic success. For Smiles, success in life was predicated on individual conduct and character. The book instructed readers about how to improve their character through inculcating lessons from inspiring historical figures and Victorian values, including hard work, ingenuity, thrift and perseverance. Smiles' text was directed at young working-class men, whom he encouraged to apply themselves diligently to the right pursuits. Rather than depend upon institutions or the patronage of others, Smiles encouraged his readers to pursue self-reliance, a pursuit that reflected the spirit of individualism that permeated Europe during the 1800s, the transcendentalist movement of the mid-19th century and Smiles' personal disillusionment with bureaucracies' capacity to enact social reform.[1] The Scottish government reformer believed that progress would emanate from new attitudes rather than from new laws, which informed the practical advice he bestowed to individual readers about how to improve their character. The opening quote in *Self-help* (1859) is suggestive of Smiles' belief in the capacity of individuals to take control of their lives, quoting former UK prime minister Benjamin Disraeli as saying: "We put too much faith in systems, and look too little to men." *Self-help* (1859) became known as "the bible of mid-Victorian liberalism," reaching audiences across the globe. Despite promoting Victorian values, Smiles spoke to perennial desires to develop oneself and improve one's conditions in life. His message resonated with readers in the United States, contributing to the proliferation of the self-help genre in the 20th century.

Today, self-help is a global industry. The genre experienced several periods of growth in the United States in the 20th century. The first was in the early 20th century with the publication of several self-help texts including Wallace D. Wattle's *The Science of Getting Rich* (1910), Dale Carnegie's *How to Win Friends and Influence People* (1936), Napoleon Hill's *Think and Grow Rich* (1937) and Norman Vincent Peale's *The Power of Positive Thinking* (1952). The second was in the 1980s when the genre began to cater to women, who were entering the paid workforce at scale and negotiating new demands and opportunities regarding aspirations to "have it all" (McGee, 2005). The phrase "having it all" featured in a series of self-help books marketed to women at the time including Joyce Gabriel and Bettye Baldwin's *Having It All: A Practical Guide to Overcoming the Career Woman's Blues* (1979) and Helen Gurley Brown's *Having It All* (1984). Other self-help books aimed at women at the time focused on improving their intimate relationships, with titles such as Louise Hay's *You Can Heal Your Life* (1984) and Robin Norwood's *Women Who Love Too Much* (1985). As the market became more saturated, self-help texts began to market themselves to niche audiences (McGee, 2005). Many of the underlying principles remained the same, but the generalised reader was differentiated on the basis of age, occupation, sex, race and income. Self-help resonated with US audiences because it built on the American

Dream – the idea that anyone could be successful with discipline, determination and effort (Baker, 2022b). Whereas self-help in some non-Western countries is conceptualised collectively in terms of "mutual aid" (Davis, 2007: 180–181), in the modern West, self-help is predominantly an individual pursuit. Self-help literature promotes a meritocratic vision of success and an individualist approach to knowledge that resists official knowledge and institutional learning. The genre's emphasis on self-belief shares much in common with the quasi-religious New Thought movement and subsequent offshoot Christian Science, which spread across the United States in the 1800s (see Baker, 2022b). New Thought emphasised the power of the mind to create reality. The movement gave rise to the "law of attraction" – the belief that the energy you project into the world determines what you attract in all areas of life from health to wealth and relationships – and informed the preoccupation with "manifesting" that features in much contemporary self-help literature today from *A Course in Miracles* (1976) to the best-selling self-help book, *The Secret* (2006).

Despite the historical origins of self-help, there are important differences between how the genre has been conceived over time. When Samuel Smiles wrote *Self-help* in 1859, he sought to inspire his readers to develop the character to succeed in an uncertain world. Rather than fixate on fulfiling individual desires, Smiles' focus was on how to cultivate character to create the conditions for success in life. The individualist ethos and liberalism apparent in Smiles' work was part of the cultural zeitgeist of the time (Baker, 2022b: 86–87); however, Smiles' emphasis on individual character is quite distinct from the individualism that shapes much contemporary self-help. Similar to the practical wisdom traditions of ancient Greece and Rome, Smiles saw the virtues of individual excellence as indispensable from the flourishing of the State. The inexorable relationship between the individual and the nation is articulated in the opening chapter of Smiles' text, entitled 'Self-help National and Individual.' The chapter commences with a quote by the English philosopher John Stuart Mill in which he claims: 'The worth of a State, in the long run, is the worth of the individuals composing it' (Mill in Smiles, 1859: 1). Smiles (1859: 1) expands on this statement by explaining that 'The spirit of self-help is the root of all genuine growth in the individual; and, exhibited in the lives of many, it constitutes the true source of national vigour and strength.' Indeed, Smiles saw the individual and society as interdependent to such an extent that he claimed, 'the spirit of self-help' as exhibited in the action of individuals 'furnishes the true measure of our power as a nation' (Smiles, 1859: 3).

Much criticism of self-help today reflects the ways in which the genre encourages a pre-occupation with the self at the expense of society. Authors of self-help maintain an interest in learning, knowledge and growth about our inner lives and its relationship to feeling and action. However, there has been a shift in the 20th century from cultivating character, virtues and values to developing specific skills, habits and tactics geared towards the pursuit of individual happiness and self-optimisation. This shift is evident in popular self-help texts from the early 1930s that provide manuals about "how to" achieve wealth creation, status and material success. Popular titles including Dale Carnegie's *How to win friends and influence people* (1936) and Wallace D. Wattles' *How to Get What You Want* and *The Science of Getting Rich* (1910) promoted New Thought principles as the foundation of material success; 'Getting rich is the result of doing things in a certain way,' rather than a matter of environment, Wattles (1910) repeatedly reminds readers. These texts consider the laws of success, as described by great philosophers, but focus on individual rather than civic outcomes. Self-help texts written at the dawn of the depression also responded to the economic crises and anxieties of the time by explaining "how to" achieve financial success.

Modern self-help often rebrands and repackages ancient ideas through the language of psychology (Baker, 2022b). Psychological language gives self-help advice the veneer of scientific legitimacy. It also resonates with the therapy culture in which we live, which presents psychological vulnerability as the defining feature of personhood (Furedi, 2013). 'The therapeutic persuasion,' as Eva Illouz notes, 'is quintessentially modern and that it is modern in what is most disquieting about modernity':

> …Bureaucratization, narcissism, the construction of a false self, the control of modern lives by the state, the collapse of cultural and moral hierarchies, the intense privatization of life caused by capitalist social organization, the emptiness of the modern self severed from communal relationships, large-scale surveillance, the expansion of state power and state legitimation, and "risk society" and the cultivation of the self's vulnerability'.
>
> *(Illouz, 2008: 1–2)*

The emphasis self-help places on neoliberal pursuits of personal responsibility and self-making has come under critique for placing the burden of self-improvement on the individual at the expense of structural inequalities (Baker and Rojek, 2020; Orgad and Gill, 2021). Self-help advice targets both men and women; however, this lifestyle advice is marketed in different ways according to one's gender. Shani Orgad and Rosalind Gill (2021) critique the extent to which confidence imperatives are directed at women, who are called upon to "love your body" and "believe in yourself." Self-help produced by women for women has proliferated in recent years with the ubiquity of visual forms of digital communication. What is missing from much scholarly literature is a discussion of the ways in which self-help is transmitted on emergent technologies. Of particular note is the rise of short-form video platforms – TikTok, Instagram Reels and YouTube Shorts – in the past five years. These platforms have contributed to the proliferation of self-help in short video form with users algorithmically steered to certain content, which given their brevity can be consumed with greater frequency. In what follows, I examine how self-help advice is constructed, communicated and reinforced on short video platforms by analysing two dominant trends in contemporary self-help: becoming "that girl" on TikTok and Insta therapy. These trends dominate self-help content on video platforms and have popular appeal, making them timely topics to analyse the genre. Data were collected and analysed by tracing popular hashtags associated with these trends: #becomingthatgirl, #thatgirllifestyle, #instatherapy and #selfhealing on TikTok and Instagram. After analysing the short videos aggregated under these hashtags on TikTok and Instagram over a 9-month period from April to December 2023, the content was inductively coded using thematic analysis (Braun and Clarke, 2006) to identify how self-help content is communicated on short video platforms, the techniques of self-improvement promoted by content creators and the consequences of these portrayals.

#thatgirllifestyle: Becoming "that girl" on TikTok

Becoming "that girl" is a popular trend on social media. The movement is typically communicated in video form with content creators sharing short videos on TikTok, YouTube and Instagram documenting how to improve your life. Becoming "that girl" is a lifestyle. It involves carefully planning and optimising one's daily habits and routines, especially morning routines. A typical "that girl" video is recorded by a young female content creator in their home or bedroom. They usually speak directly to the camera while applying their makeup or visually recreate their morning routine: waking up early, making their bed, hydrating with a glass of water, exercising, meditating, journaling and consuming a coffee, green juice or a healthy breakfast. Thousands of videos depicting a similar routine are collated under the hashtag #becomingthatgirl, claiming to provide the ultimate guide to self-improvement. Content creators often assert that everyone's self-improvement journey is highly personal – "you keep what resonates with you and tailor it to your needs" – yet these videos depict a high degree of conformity. For example, one TikTok video assembled under the #becomingthatgirl hashtag lists a certain morning routine to be followed, while another video aggregated under the becoming "that girl" hashtag promotes a similar routine:

> Here are the five easiest ways to feel like the it girl, that girl, put together whatever the heck you want to call it. (1) make your freaking bed okay…your life will change; (2) keeping up with your nails; (3) planning out your days; (4) reading books: the right self-improvement and self-help book where you can learn about life and yourself, (5) start switching your mindset to quality over quantity.

"That girl" is aspirational, but it is not about becoming a different person; it is about aspiring to become the best version of yourself. "Being your best self" involves aspects of wellness culture (holistic health and personal responsibility – Baker, 2022b), but the trend is more firmly grounded in the self-help genre by instructing consumers about how to become more productive, optimised versions of themselves. These videos are premised on the idea that adopting a "that girl" lifestyle will improve your life. By becoming your best self, you will feel better and increase your capacity for success.

Becoming that girl is not only a lifestyle, but it is also an aesthetic. Videos typically convey females wearing matching active wear, with immaculate hair and make-up. These videos are recorded in a room or kitchen with minimalist decors, with drinks and meals prepared and served in aesthetically pleasing cups and breakfast bowls. "That girl" is well-kempt, depicting her confidence and aspirational self through her poised demeanour, orderly routine and complementary attire. Content creators repeatedly instruct viewers that "good posture is a sign of confidence." The objective is self-confidence and feeling good. As one "that girl" video explains:

> She is working on three things right now: herself, her life, her peace. Do not disturb. Lucyjane, 511.5K likes. #selfcareroutine, #aestheticmorningroutine #thatgirlaesthetic #thatgirllifestyle #wellnesstok.

Or, as explained by another,

> At the end of the day the only thing that really matters is…making life as pleasant as possible like that should be the goal is just to make life as enjoyable as possible – Danielle Nguyen, 122.5k followers.

Some commentators and content creators situate the "that girl" trend as part of wellness culture. This is somewhat of a mistake. Wellness culture is premised on three interconnected principles: holistic health, self-actualisation and personal responsibility (Baker,

2022b). Wellness culture is also firmly grounded in relation to health. The wellness movement emerged in reaction to what some practitioners perceived as a limited conception of health at the time – health as the absence of disease (see Baker, 2022b). Figures such as Halbert L. Dunn and Jack Travis promoted a more holistic conception of health – incorporating mind, body and spirit – as integral to 'peak wellness,' as Dunn phrased it. 'Becoming that girl' videos may incorporate ostensibly healthy meals and fitness routines, but these videos are less about health and more about self-improvement, self-optimisation and becoming one's "best self." The subgenre is better conceptualised as a contemporary subset of self-help insofar as "that girl" videos promise self-reliance and social mobility. They form part of the aspirational middle-class aesthetic we described in *Lifestyle Gurus* (Baker and Rojek, 2020), whereby figures such as Catherine Beecher and Isabella Beeton educated women in the 1800s about how to improve themselves – and their family – through efficient domesticity: espousing the advantages of early rising and an orderly, well-managed home. The emphasis "that girl" videos place on self-mastery and manifestation also shares much in common with contemporary lifestyle gurus, such as Oprah Winfrey, who evangelise our power to change our life by being in alignment with who we want to become (Baker and Rojek, 2020). As one "that girl" video explains:

> If you hate your life, physically write down concretely, clearly as detailed as you can your ideal dream life and then every day, as soon as you wake up!, ask yourself when you open up your piece of paper, what am I doing to make this my current reality? Laura Wizman 48.5K likes. #mindsettok, #wellnesstok, #thatgirllifestyle, #bossbabe, #mindsetmotivation, #motivational.

There is no mention of family or community in "that girl" videos. The emphasis is categorically on the self as a project to be constructed and improved upon (see Giddens, 1991). The common thread connecting these various lifestyle gurus under the rubric of self-help is the interweaving of self-improvement with social mobility and success.

Insta Therapy: Self-diagnosis, self-healing and self-identity

Another contemporary subgenre of self-help proliferating online is Insta therapy, which refers to the practice of influencers and content creators sharing mental health information online. Although the practice is not limited to Instagram, Insta therapy has become ubiquitous on the platform since the pandemic given that people were spending more time online due to stay-at-home orders and seeking advice to help them navigate the crisis (Basch et al., 2022; Şot, 2023). Some Insta therapy is created by certified therapists and licensed mental health experts. Much content, however, is shared by unlicensed professionals unqualified to provide mental health advice. This includes self-described coaches, gurus and healers who have established a career bestowing advice and recommendations about how to feel better and improve one's life (Baker and Rojek, 2019, 2020). Insta therapy is often packaged into digestible memes, charts and bullet points. Examples include: "4 Types of Emotionally Immature People And How to Deal [with them]," "5 Reminders to protect your peace" and "6 Reminders for recovering perfectionists." Much of this advice focuses on how to feel better and facilitate healing: "6 Healing Responses You Might Be Going Through," "3 Hard Truths When You're Healing" and "Affirmations for Healing the Father Wound." Consumers are informed about how to identify "toxic" people who impair their mental health – "How To Spot Someone Toxic Early On In A Relationship" – and the need to establish "boundaries." "You don't have to forgive. You need boundaries and self-care," as one influencer put it. Indeed, learning how to set healthy boundaries is a common technique shared by Instagram therapists. As one Insta therapist with the handle peaceful_barb explains:

> Normalize not feeling bad for removing yourself from anyone who doesn't feel bad for hurting you. Train your boundaries to be stronger than your soft heart.

The post was liked 20,153 times and received hundreds of comments. Commenters repeatedly thanked Barb for the reminder and "beautiful message," explaining that her post resonated with them. Advice around boundaries plays into metaphors of toxicity. One commenter stated: "Sometime they don't know they're toxic," to which another replied: "Hopefully, they will when they recognise you have some new boundaries." Barb's bio describes her as an author and meditation teacher. She is the co-creator of the podcast "Barb Knows Best," and her persona conveys the demeanour of an elderly kind and compassionate friend. Her use of the first-person singular highlights the "native expertise" she has acquired through lived experience that gives her the authority to advise others: "I'm proud of you," "I promise you someone rejecting you in the universe protecting you"; "Here are 3 hard truths I wish I had Unlearned sooner for my own peace of mind." Like so many Instagram therapists, it is unclear whether Barb has any clinical expertise as a mental health professional.

Another subset of Insta therapy encourages self-diagnosis by providing insights into mental health conditions. Consumers are commonly presented with a list of criteria or a series of questions, numerically itemised to identify their mental health conditions: "10 Red Flags You're Struggling With Your Mental Health, From A Neuroscientist," "6 signs you have ADHD" and "Is ADHD actually complex trauma in some people?" These posts are premised on the idea that certain feelings and behaviours ("If you do this…") are indicative of mental health conditions. Attention-deficit hyperactivity disorder (ADHD) and autism are particularly prevalent topics discussed by Insta therapists online, contributing to a series of consumers framing their experience as symptomatic of these neurodevelopmental disorders. Posts of this kind often suggest treatments and protocols for a range of mental health conditions. Some involve common sense knowledge and advice: hydrate, consume more fruit and vegetables, exercise, improve your sleep and reduce caffeine and alcohol. Other posts promote fringe products and miracle "cures" or advocate lifestyle changes as "natural ways to heal anxiety" and depression.

The proliferation of Insta therapy over the past decade has come under scrutiny. Searching for the hashtag #instatherapy on the platform presents a reactionary narrative, comprising a series of posts by accounts strategically using the hashtag to push back on the proliferation of Insta Therapy and what they perceive as the overuse and abuse of therapeutic discourse on the platform. At the time of writing this chapter, there were over 55,000 posts collated under the hashtag #instatherapy. Critics warn of "concept creep," the semantic expansion of concepts that refer to the negative aspects of human experience and behaviour and their meanings so that they now encompass a much broader range of phenomena than before (Haslam, 2016). Harm-related concepts, such as abuse, bullying, trauma, mental disorder and addiction, are particularly subject to this expansion (Haslam et al., 2021). In each case, the concept's boundary is enlarged, and its meaning is dilated by inflating the meaning of harm. Over the past century, the term "trauma" has been particularly subject to concept creep expanding from "somatic to psychic, extraordinary to ordinary, direct to indirect, and individual to collective" (Haslam and McGrath, 2020). Insta therapy exemplifies the increased prevalence and misuse of the term "trauma" to describe general instances of pain. "You will know what trauma to resolve based on your body's reactions," one Insta therapist explains. Or, as the self-described trauma educator explains, "Trauma healing doesn't make the wound disappear. It helps us become bigger than the wound so we don't lose ourselves in it anymore." In these instances, Insta therapy risks introducing ideas of trauma where there is none by pathologising everyday experience and "encouraging a sense of virtuous but impotent victimhood" (Haslam, 2016). This is because these terms do more than merely describe negative conditions: they are identity-conferring, describing the victim's identity (Furedi, 2016).

The commodification of community: From the wounded healer to self-healing

One of the defining attributes of self-help content is the emphasis on self-making. "That girl" videos characteristically feature the individual subject describing or reliving their daily routines. The message projected is that the individual is organised, intentional and in control of her life. While upon first glance Insta therapy seems more focussed on the domain of health, both trends maintain an underlying concern with self-making as a daily practice. This emphasis on the individual as the author of their own lives is exemplified by Insta therapists' multiple references to self-healing. Healing is portrayed as a daily practice, resembling the self-help genre's preoccupation with what Mikki McGee (2005) describes as the "belaboured self": a self subject to constant self-work in their quest to remain socially and economically viable in an uncertain world. In this context, Carl Jung's archetypal trope of the wounded healer, compelled to treat patients because the analyst themselves is "wounded," is re-cast into a universal wounded subject who must undergo constant self-discovery, self-healing and self-growth. It is tempting to dismiss these trends as highly subjective practices emblematic of the shift towards individualism. Similar critiques have been made about New Age spirituality, which is commonly described as an idiosyncratic collection of beliefs and practices, as indicated by references to "pick-and-mix religion" (Hamilton, 2000), the "spiritual supermarket" (Lyon, 2000) and "religious consumption à la carte" (Possamai, 2003). What critiques of this kind overlook, as Stef Aupers and David Houtman point out (2014), is the ideological coherence of such views premised on shared beliefs about the uncontested doctrine of self-spirituality, characterised by a sacralisation of the self set apart from profane social institutions. Hence, the elevation in much contemporary self-help of the "authentic" self – "uncovered" through a continuous process of self-discovery – in contrast to the "false" self, was perceived to be conditioned by society. As one testimonial shared by an Insta therapist online explains:

> Since joining [the Insta therapist's exclusive community] I have shed many layers of conditioning and continue to work on many more…
> *(Testimonial Instagram 1 January 2024)*

In this regard, coaches, gurus and influencers inherit, transmit and reformulate common scripts that reflect collective understandings of the self. On social media, it is not a private self seeking self-discovery and reflection, but a public self performed online *in relation* to others.

Part of what is novel about self-help content online is the way self-improvement is collectively constructed and steered in relation to others. The interactive components of self-help take several forms. On the one hand, gurus, coaches and influencers sharing self-help and lifestyle advice online commonly use hashtags to bring their audience into being (Baker and Walsh, 2018). In addition to giving their posts meaning and making their content discoverable, hashtags collate content under a common narrative. In our earlier work on health and wellness communities on Instagram, we demonstrated that "adopting a healthy diet on Instagram was depicted not only as an individual choice but as a means of collective membership into a community with other like-minded individuals" (Baker and Walsh, 2018). We argued that hashtags played a pivotal role in ritualised self-identity and that hashtags also commodify community with native advertising often featuring in the form of online tutorials and inspiring images accompanied by links to fitness programmes, cookbooks and health products. Self-help coaches, gurus and influencers continue this trend and monetise their audience by inviting them to join their exclusive online communities. One Insta therapist calls on her followers to join her private healing community, "if you're ready to wake up and heal." She published numerous testimonials by members of her inner circle on the platform, attesting to the benefits of partaking in this inner work collectively:

Being in the circle O makes me feel like I'm a part of something – a community. As someone that's always been ostracised her whole life amongst peers, this is super important and special to me. I just need to get back to the courses.
(Testimonial Instagram 1 January 2024)

There has been a clear shift in this regard from therapy as a personalised, private practice to a communal activity performed publicly online.

The ethics of Insta therapy

Part of the appeal of influencers is that their microcelebrity status is achieved online and bound up with utopian ideals of decentralised knowledge and democratic participation (Baker, 2022a, 2022b). In our previous work on lifestyle gurus, we demonstrated that influencers use performative displays of accessibility, authenticity and autonomy to establish trust and intimacy with their followers (Baker and Rojek, 2019, 2020). In a subsequent study on the proliferation of wellness influencers during the pandemic, I showed how the impression of being autonomous – an influencer's perception of being outside of the system – is instrumental to their appearance as trustworthy, credible alternatives to institutional authority (Baker, 2022a). While some of these shifts were observed prior to the pandemic, the social distancing and lockdown measures enforced by governments across the globe as a consequence of COVID-19, which resulted in people spending more time on their devices at home, saw the proliferation of coaches, gurus and influencers espousing self-help and mental health advice online (Baker, 2022b).

The parasocial relationship between Insta therapists and their followers raises a series of ethical issues. By virtue of the internet and the low barriers to entry to create a social media profile and build an audience online, fame is now available to coaches, gurus and influencers at an unprecedented scale. Many Insta therapists have become microcelebrities, using the same self-presentation techniques we described in *Lifestyle Gurus* (2020) to establish trust and intimacy with their followers. In addition to cultivating the impression of accessibility, Insta therapists provide greater access to mental health information, which may benefit those unable to access or afford a therapist.

Where the appearance of accessibility becomes ethically compromised is when Insta therapists strategically establish a parasocial relationship with their followers. A parasocial relationship is a "one-sided," "non-dialectical" relationship between a media figure and a spectator afforded by technology that fosters the impression of friendship and intimacy. The term was coined in 1956 by Horton and Wohl to describe salient characteristics of new mass media (radio, television, and film) that "give the illusion of face-to-face relationship with the performer," while being established at a distance. Language is crucial to parasocial interaction (Baker, 2022a). Insta therapists commonly establish parasocial relationships with their audience by expressing their "love" for their followers, whom they commonly describe as "friends" and "family." In addition to establishing a sense of community through the first-person plural ("us" and "we"), there is strategic use of the first- and second-person singular to relate the influencer's feelings ("I") to their follower's experience ("you"). Examples of these pronouns in the context of Insta therapy include Insta therapists expressing their love for their followers and telling them they are worthy: "I see you trying to heal. I'm rooting for you. Don't quit." Parasocial interaction is also transmitted through humorous memes that establish relatability and connection: for example, a static image depicting an exhausted individual accompanied by the caption, "Me after one day of healing." The problem is that despite the appearance of intimacy and connection, parasocial relationships are one sided. The advice shared by Insta therapists may resonate with their followers, and social media affords the capacity for direct communication in the form of comments and replies, but in most cases, Insta therapy is not a dialogue or conversation, as is characteristic of therapy.

There are notable differences between Insta therapy and therapy. Whereas therapy requires professional distance, Insta therapy is premised on connection. Therapy is personalised and anonymous. Therapists do not tend to speak in absolutes, given that people have different patterned responses based on their specific biography, history and cultural context. Insta therapy, conversely, tends to be de-contextualised and public. It repackages complex medical and mental health advice into digestible charts, memes and sound bites for a mass audience. The saturation of mental health advice has also contributed to concept creep and people self-diagnosing based on engaging memes, posts and short videos without the expertise of a clinician. This can lead to misdiagnosis, whereby users attempt to fit their experience to the label and undermine the experience of those with serious mental health issues. Part of the issue here is the conflation of lived experience and expertise endemic to the wellness industry (see Baker, 2022b). Insta therapy is an unregulated industry comprising untrained or uncertified mental health experts, many of whom possess limited or no professional credentials. Coaching and counselling is not a regulated field. Coaches, counsellors and healers may have acquired certification and training, but these professions are not regulated by licensing standards (Baker and Rojek, 2019, 2020). Unlike licensed professions, Insta therapists are not held to account by a license board for the information and treatment they provide. This lack of accountability is rife in the wellness industry and enables influencers to spread misleading and harmful information (Baker, 2022a, 2022b). What makes this industry particularly problematic are the ways in which qualified and unqualified mental health professionals occupy the same online platforms, making it difficult for users to discern trustworthy information.

Conclusion

A niche of industry of gurus, coaches and influencers, who have built a career bestowing self-help and lifestyle advice online, has proliferated online in the 21st century. The rise of this industry reflects the growth of lifestyle journalism and its preoccupation with self-identity in recent decades (Hanusch, 2014; Hanusch and Hanitzsch, 2013) and is situated more broadly in the global industry of self-help. The visibility of these entrepreneurs has been afforded by technological developments, including the ubiquity of smartphones and social media in the 21st century, which has lowered the barriers to entry to establish influence and expertise online (Baker and Rojek, 2019, 2020), especially photo- and video-sharing apps such as Instagram and YouTube. This chapter contributes to earlier discussions about the rise of "popular expertise" in the media (Lewis, 2008) and "native expertise"[2] on social media (Baker and Rojek, 2020) by examining the rise of self-help experts on emergent short video platforms. Short-form videos have risen in popularity since the launch of TikTok in 2017, which was followed by the creation of Instagram Reels and YouTube Shorts. These platforms allow users to create short videos around 30 seconds long. They also incentivise creators to share short video content through the promise of increased engagement and audience reach. Hence, while self-help has an established history dating back to the 1800s, short video platforms have contributed to the ubiquity of self-improvement content online and the variety of content creators who commercially profit from such advice.

In this chapter, I have analysed two popular subgenres of self-help on short video platforms: Becoming "That Girl" videos on TikTok and Insta therapy on Instagram. These trends are representative of novel forms of self-help proliferating on short video platforms. They demonstrate how self-help has expanded the genre's original emphasis on self-reliance to incorporate life coaches and gurus, who purport to instruct and mentor clients about how to achieve their goals, and therapists, who assist patients with internal psychological change. The genre's expansion has made self-help advice more accessible, enabling those unable to access or afford external support to acquire information about self-improvement and mental health. But this expansion also introduces a series of ethical issues, not least the difficulty in discerning reliable, trustworthy information from the veneer of authority and influence. Insta therapy incorporates a niche of self-described experts (coaches, gurus, psychologists, therapists and healers), who purport to help people on their healing journey. It combines those with lived experience – what we term "native expertise" (Baker and Rojek, 2020) – and those with clinical and certified expertise, making it exceptionally challenging for consumers to discriminate between the two. The recent incorporation of mental health information into self-help discourse makes this fusion particularly problematic. Short video platforms extolling self-improvement advice on a range of lifestyle issues from health, success to personal relationships frequently steer consumers to health and medical content, thus encouraging self-diagnosis on a range of neurodevelopmental disorders including autism and ADHD. The general audience to whom these posts are addressed are left questioning whether their experience is symptomatic of these conditions. Contrary to therapy which is contextualised and personal, the mass dissemination of mental health advice online treats the consumer as a universal subject. The fusion of therapy into the industry of self-help has contributed to concept creep, the expansion of the meaning of harmful concepts and the problematisation of emotional life, commonly labelling routine experience as a mental health disorder. Despite possessing no formal certification or mental health training, many content creators are encouraging healing remedies under the rubric of self-help. In a saturated market, diagnoses, claims and promises of self-healing have become more ubiquitous and extreme – often through the guidance of purchasing a book, a course or membership to their exclusive community. In this regard, the commodification of community and emotional experience raises serious ethical issues about the need for transparency and regulation in the self-help industry.

Future research could explore the impact that these technological shifts have on lifestyle journalism. Of particular significance is the impact that short video platforms are having on consumption habits and self-identity. Researchers could also examine how these technological developments have shaped lifestyle journalism as a field through encouraging journalists to produce brief, digestible content in short video form. This would include not only identifying novel trends and presentation techniques but also the risks and ethical consequences associated with the quest for engagement in an attention economy.

Notes

1 The transcendentalist movement was a philosophical, religious and political movement led by the American philosopher and essayist, Ralph Waldo Emerson. Together with other transcendentalists, including Henry David Thoreau, Emerson critiqued what he perceived to be uncritical social conformity, urging each person to find "an original relation to the universe" (see Baker, 2022b).
2 We use the term "native" to describe those lifestyle gurus who possess limited, or no certified qualifications, and hence, have no professional standing for claiming expertise in health and emotional management. Their skills and knowledge are those associated with ordinary people and everyday life; their perceived ordinariness itself part of their popular appeal. This description is not intended to be pejorative. Instead, it is used to highlight the forms of authority and influence based upon experience and folk wisdom rather than formal, certified training, which has given rise to an industry of lifestyle gurus increasingly placed in the same discursive category as trained doctors, psychologists and dieticians (Lewis, 2008).

Further reading

Baker, S. A., & Rojek, C. (2020). *Lifestyle gurus: Constructing authority and influence online*. John Wiley & Sons.
Giddens, A. (1991). *Modernity and self-identity: Self and society in the late modern age*. Polity.
Hanusch, F. (Ed.) (2014). *Lifestyle Journalism*. Routledge.
Illouz, E. (2008). *Saving the modern soul: Therapy, emotions, and the culture of self-help*. University of California Press.
McGee, M. (2005). *Self-help, Inc.: Makeover culture in American life*. Oxford University Press.

References

Adams, R. M. (2008). *A theory of virtue: Excellence in being for the good*. Clarendon Press.
Aupers, S., & Houtman, D. (2014). Beyond the spiritual supermarket: The social and public significance of new age spirituality. In S. J. Sutcliffe and I. S. Gilhus (Eds.), *New age spirituality* (pp. 180–202). Routledge.
Baker, S. A. (2022a). Alt. Health Influencers: how wellness culture and web culture have been weaponised to promote conspiracy theories and far-right extremism during the COVID-19 pandemic. *European Journal of Cultural Studies*, 25(1), 3–24.
Baker, S. A. (2022b). *Wellness Culture: How the wellness movement has been used to empower, profit and misinform*. Emerald Group Publishing Ltd.
Baker, S. A., & Rojek, C. (2019). The Belle Gibson scandal: The rise of lifestyle gurus as microcelebrities in low-trust societies. *Journal of Sociology*, 56(3), 388–404.

Baker, S. A., & Rojek, C. (2020). *Lifestyle gurus: Constructing authority and influence online*. John Wiley & Sons.
Baker, S. A., & Walsh, M. J. (2018). 'Good morning fitfam': Top posts, hashtags and gender display on Instagram. *New Media & Society*, 20(12), 4553–4570.
Basch, C. H., Donelle, L., Fera, J., & Jaime, C. (2022). Deconstructing TikTok videos on mental health: Cross-sectional, descriptive content analysis. *JMIR Formative Research*, 6(5), e38340.
Bauman, Z. (2013). *Liquid love: On the frailty of human bonds*. John Wiley & Sons.
Braun, V., & Clarke, V. (2006). Using thematic analysis in psychology. *Qualitative Research in Psychology*, 3(2), 77–101.
Brown, H. G. (1984). *Having it all*. Hodder & Stoughton Ltd.
Carnegie, D. ([1936] 2023). *How to win friends and influence people*. Good Press.
Davis, K. (2007). *The making of our bodies, ourselves: How feminism travels across borders*. Durham, NC: Duke University Press.
Debord, G. ([1967] 2021). *The society of the spectacle*. Unredacted Word.
Eide, M., & Knight, G. (1999). Public/private service: Service journalism and the problems of everyday life. *European Journal of Communication*, 14(4), 525–547.
Elias, N. (1978). *The history of manners*. Volume I. *The Civilizing Process*. Pantheon.
Furedi, F. (2013). *Therapy culture: Cultivating vulnerability in an uncertain age*. Routledge.
Furedi, F. (2016). The cultural underpinning of concept creep. *Psychological Inquiry*, 27(1), 34–39.
Gabriel, J., & Baldwin, B. (1979). *Having it all: A practical guide to overcoming the career woman's blue*. Holt & Company, Henry.
Giddens, A. (1991). *Modernity and self-identity: Self and society in the late modern age*. Polity.
Hamilton, M. (2000). An analysis of the festival for mind-body-spirit, London. In S. Sutcliffe and M. Bowman (Eds.), *Beyond new age: Exploring alternative spirituality* (pp. 188–200). Edinburgh University Press.
Hanusch, F. (Ed.) (2014). *Lifestyle journalism*. Routledge.
Hanusch, F., & Hanitzsch, T. (2013). Mediating orientation and self-expression in the world of consumption: Australian and German lifestyle journalists' professional views. *Media, Culture & Society*, 35(8), 943–959.
Haslam, N. (2016). Concept creep: Psychology's expanding concepts of harm and pathology. *Psychological Inquiry*, 27(1), 1–17.
Haslam, N., & McGrath, M. J. (2020). The creeping concept of trauma. *Social Research: An International Quarterly*, 87(3), 509–531.
Haslam, N., Vylomova, E., Zyphur, M., & Kashima, Y. (2021). The cultural dynamics of concept creep. *American Psychologist*, 76(6), 1013–1026.
Hill, N. ([1937] 2011). *Think and grow rich*. Hachette UK.
Horton, D., & Wohl, R. (1956) Mass communication and para-social interaction: Observations on intimacy at a distance. *Psychiatry*, 19(3), 215–229.
Illouz, E. (2008). *Saving the modern soul: Therapy, emotions, and the culture of self-help*. University of California Press.
Lasch, C. (1979). *The culture of narcissism: American Life in an age of diminishing expectations*. W. W. Norton.
Lewis, T. (2008). *Smart living: Lifestyle media and popular expertise*. Peter Lang.
Lyon, D. (2000). *Jesus in disneyland: Religion in postmodern times*. Polity.
McGee, M. (2005). *Self-help, Inc.: Makeover culture in American life*. Oxford University Press.
Menand, L. (2002). *American studies*. Farrar, Straus & Giroux.
Orgad, S., & Gill, R. (2021). *Confidence culture*. Duke University Press.
Possamai, A. (2003). Alternative spiritualties and the cultural logic of late capitalism. *Culture and Religion*, 4(1), 31–45.
Putnam, R. D. (2000). *Bowling alone: The collapse and revival of American community*. Simon and Schuster.
Rieff, P. ([1966] 1987). *The Triumph of the therapeutic: Uses of faith after Freud*. University of Chicago Press.
Smiles, S. (1859). *Self-help with illustrations of character and conduct*. Available at: https://www.gutenberg.org/cache/epub/935/pg935-images.html

Şot, İ. (2023). Scrolling TikTok to soothe and foster self-care during the COVID-19 pandemic. *Social Media+ Society*, 9(4), 20563051231213542.

van Krieken, R. (2017). Norbert Elias and figurational sociology. In B.S. Turner (Ed.), *The Wiley-Blackwell Encyclopedia of Social Theory* (pp. 1–3). Wiley. https://doi.org/10.1002/9781118430873.est0266

Vincent Peale, N. ([1952] 2006). The power of positive thinking. Orient Paperbacks.

Wattles, W. D. ([1910] 2020). *The science of getting rich: The complete original edition with bonus books*. St. Martin's Essentials.

27
EVERYDAY MULTICULTURALISM ON ASIAN AUSTRALIAN FOOD BLOGS

Tisha Dejmanee

Introduction

On the home page of her food blog *Recipe Tin Eats*, Japanese-born Australian blogger Nagi Maehashi publishes recipes for Irish Beef and Guinness Stew, Chow Mein, Beef Tacos and Lamb Shawarma Chickpea soup. Featuring lush food photography with glossy sauces, melted cheese and bright garnishes, each recipe is prefaced with Maehashi's friendly and emoji-laden commentary. Through her extensive recipe catalogue and chirpy dialogue, Maehashi has built an incredibly successful food blog brand, with a weekly global readership of 15 million people (Di Iorio, 2022). While these numbers situate Maehashi in the top echelons of all food bloggers, her global visibility as an Asian Australian woman is also a representational milestone, given the chronic underrepresentation of Asian Australians in mainstream media (Song and Maree, 2021; Law, 2009).

While food blogs originated as amateur "personal weblogs" in the late 1990s, the blogosphere has become increasingly professionalised throughout the 21st century. The production quality of food blogs is now indistinguishable from commercial lifestyle media, and there is a large degree of crossover between food blogging and lifestyle journalism. In this chapter, I explore the capacity for food blogs to portray negotiated and underrepresented cultural identities, examining how Asian Australian food blogs represent an "everyday multiculturalism" that centres the everyday, embodied and ambivalent narratives of Asian Australians. More broadly, this study analyses the potential of lifestyle journalism to illuminate counterhegemonic discourses from racially marginalised communities and, through doing so, to serve representational politics in the growing context of global multiculturalism.

I focus on two exemplar food blogs by Asian Australians – *Recipe Tin Eats* by Nagi Maehashi and *Cook Republic* by Sneh Roy. I explore a sample of their Asian recipe posts to thematically analyse the ways in which Asian Australian everyday politics – particularly the negotiation of hybrid cultural identities and the conceptualisation of cultural authenticity – are narrated through their narratives of everyday food work. I find that while Maehashi and Roy offer many contributions to the dialogue on Asian Australian experience, these representations remain focussed on the positive depiction on ethnic food as evidence of harmonious multiculturalism. While this finding does not void food blogs of their political value, this suggests that the structures of commercial media and the attention economy continue to frame and delimit user-generated representations of diverse lifestyles.

An overview of food blogs

Food blogs are "digital media texts that combine recipes and food photography with personal narratives and reflections…[that] showcase original or adapted recipes that are produced and photographed within the home of the blogger" (Dejmanee, 2023, pp. 3–4). The food blogosphere originated in the early 2000s as an amateur community that experienced prime popularity around 2011 (Lofgren, 2013) in conjunction with the rise of parallel genres such as fashion blogging, beauty vlogging and mommy blogging. Food blogs have often been distinguished from the large body of commercial food media that was also ballooning around the early 2000s (Miller, 2007) through their focus on the domestic space, feminine interiority and the mundane routines of "everyday" women (Dejmanee, 2016). The use of food blogs to share everyday intimacies has generated tightknit food blogging communities as well as close parasocial relationships with unknown readers (Dejmanee, 2023; Presswood, 2020). These assumed intimacies are communicated through a sweet and self-deprecating "girl next door" persona (Dejmanee, 2023) that is distinguished from the more sartorial tone of fashion blogging (Marwick, 2013) or the sardonic tone of the mommy blogosphere (Lopez, 2009).

The labour of food blogging can be understood as self-branding, a strategic act where "individuals develop a distinctive public image for commercial gain and/or cultural capital" (Khamis et al., 2017, p. 191). That is, even though food blogs ostensibly focus on personal intimacies, these self-representations become understood as a commercial branding practice that distinguishes individual food blogs from others on the market and narrates a unique and consistent selling point for the audience. Food blogs adhere to branding practices through using taglines, distinct aesthetics and/or a focus on particular dietary or cooking practices (for instance, seasonal, vegan or whole-food blogs). However, most importantly, for successful self-branding is the notion that food bloggers are "authentic," performed in the food blogosphere through sharing unique personal details, life milestones, memories and intimacies that help audiences relate to and empathise with food bloggers (see also Chapter 10).

The centrality of self-branding practices in the food blogosphere demonstrates how the growth of food blogging has been influenced by its commercialisation, as the potential to monetise blogging encouraged more individuals to participate, formalised the conventions of this genre and increased the standards of professionalisation across the blogosphere. Although the barriers to entry for food blogging are relatively low, the food blogosphere is built upon a hierarchy of visibility where a small fraction of food blogs are influential, successful and profitable, while the vast majority languish without much attention (Duffy, 2017; Matchar, 2013). The ones that have become profitable are, by and large, sponsored by corporate brands due to their ability to build media content that aligns the white, middle-class lifestyle values that most brands seek to replicate. Over time, this has eradicated the amateur origins and possibilities of the food blogosphere as the standards of food styling and photography have led to digital content that is largely indistinguishable from the production quality of mainstream lifestyle media. Additionally, this commercially sponsored hierarchy of visibility has created a homogeneity across food blogs that are mostly led by white, North American, middle-class, cisgender and heterosexual women who are married with children (Dejmanee, 2023).

In more recent years, social media platforms have enabled several additional kinds of food-based media, including YouTube, Instagram and TikTok, which all have spawned their own dedicated and prolific forms of food media communities and content. These developments in the digital landscape have rendered food blogging less popular, and the genre remains wedded to a particular generational audience. However, food blogs remain culturally and commercially influential, and their unique properties are worth examining in relation to their proximity to lifestyle journalism and the sociocultural opportunities they afford.

Food blogs in the framework of lifestyle journalism

Food blogs adhere to Hanusch's foundational definition of lifestyle journalism as "a distinct journalistic field that primarily addresses its audiences as consumers, providing them with factual information and advice, often in entertaining ways, about goods and services they can use in their daily lives" (2012, p. 2). However, drawing on interviews with French food bloggers, Sidonie Naulin (2019) catalogues some of the major differences between food bloggers and food journalists (see also Chapters 8 and 19). This includes that food bloggers are inspired by the qualities of passion and authenticity, which stands in diametric opposition to some of the foundational pillars of journalism; food bloggers represent more diverse socioeconomic and demographic profiles than food journalists; food bloggers invest significant amounts of time and money in food blogging as a leisure activity and seek to monetise their labour through related careers such as cookbook writers and cooking instructors, rather than to engage in paid professional food writing; the food blogger's audience is not simply hailed as consumers but often as fellow friends and bloggers, and the food blogger – as a perceived impartial hobbyist – is considered to be innately more trustworthy by readers than food journalists (Naulin, 2019).

However, it is worth noting that Naulin's findings are based on surveys of the food blogosphere in 2010–2011, and the professionalisation and commercialisation of the food blogosphere have increased exponentially since then. While I would agree that food blogs and food-based lifestyle journalism are distinct areas, the boundary between the two is porous, and there continues to be interaction and collaborations across these fields (see also Chapter 24). Food media corporations have historically played an important gatekeeping role in the hierarchical blogosphere. For instance, gourmet food magazine *Saveur* has for many years published a prestigious list of top food blogs in different categories, while the *Martha Stewart* company endorsed a select network of food bloggers. Over the years, commercial media have increasingly mined the food blogosphere for content, food trends, media hosts and personalities and branding opportunities. In contrast, many food bloggers seek to distinguish themselves and establish their credibility as bloggers by advertising media appearances on their blog sites, and most food bloggers rely on these endorsements from mainstream media outlets and commercial brands to become successful. This symbiosis sets up a close and, at times, competitive relationship between the food blogosphere and lifestyle journalism as food blogs have "occupied the margins of food journalism and... challenged its borders" (Naulin, 2019, p. 102). This perceived threat of social media influencers to food journalism is aptly demonstrated by Martha Stewart's dismissive comment on Bloomberg TV: "Who are these bloggers? They're not editors at *Vogue* magazine...I mean, there are bloggers writing recipes that aren't tested, that aren't necessarily very good, or are copies of everything that really good editors have created and done" (Brion, 2013). Such tensions between digital influencing and lifestyle journalism have also been documented in other lifestyle journalism studies (Arriagada and Ibanez, 2019).

In terms of the core lifestyle journalism attributes of "self-expression, the signification of identity, as well as consumption and everyday life" (Hanusch and Hanitzsch, 2013), all may be considered features of food blogs. However, at times, these features are obfuscated because food blogs have often been required to erase the evidence of their commercialisation. Audiences/followers are purposefully hailed as "friends," labour is presented as lifestyle and self-branding is styled as authenticity. While some early food blogs incorporated Google ads onto their pages, the current aesthetic requires food bloggers to work at the brand level to derive income through sponsored content and partnerships. Unlike parallel genres such as fashion blogging or beauty vlogging, which are self-consciously styled on reviewing/recommending consumer goods, food blogging's relationship with consumption practices is more subtle. While branded products are occasionally enfolded into recipes, the genre is much more aligned with domestic production than commercial consumption practices. Accordingly, tastemaking is largely practiced through postfeminist depictions that glorify the pleasures of domesticity and girlish femininity (Presswood, 2020; Rodney et al., 2017; Salvio, 2012). This aspirational lifestyle tenor has more to do with hailing a particular kind of gender performance through domestic production/consumption practices, rather than the more traditional consumption of commercial lifestyle products.

Nevertheless, the trust and aspirational relationship fostered by the intimacies of food blogging is highly valued for its 'organic marketing' potential, where brands are recommended in an unforced and natural way (Matchar, 2013). Audience interaction is actively solicited by food bloggers, particularly through the comments sections that typically appear under each post. Often, these comments are simply used to compliment the food bloggers, revealing that the primary function of such recipe posts is not necessarily pragmatic but is based on identification with the food blogger's public persona and lifestyle performance. This is one area in which the food blogosphere has clearly had an impact on food media. I have previously documented the ways that food television shows on the US cable channel *The Food Network* have increasingly adopted conventions from food blogging such as filming in the domestic, rather than studio, setting; structuring the narrative around family events and incorporating diary-like confessionals from the show host (Dejmanee, 2018). More broadly, as self-branding practices have become normalised through social media platform cultures, self-branding is now also considered to be a practice of journalists (Vodanovic, 2019; Hanusch and Bruns, 2017).

While it might make sense for lifestyle journalists to try and distinguish themselves from food bloggers (Arriagada and Ibanez, 2019), food bloggers continue to be invested in affiliations with mainstream media platforms/outlets as this continues to be recognised as a form of legitimation in the user-generated blogosphere. These affiliations may also help alleviate the burdens of labour and reputation that are faced by individual bloggers whose brands become synonymous with their identities, as opposed to lifestyle journalists who are generally backed by the outlets with whom they are published or associated. At the same time, this association with a masthead may come with a loss of freedom or identity – for instance, food blogger Maehashi publishes recipes regularly with national masthead *The Sydney Morning Herald*, but the narrative published in the newspaper is short and succinct, which is very different to the languorous and more personal writing style that comprises the majority of her blog posts. I examine these differences with a focus on how food blogging and lifestyle journalism may engage with the everyday politics of Asian Australian cultural identity.

Asian Australian food blogging in multicultural Australia

Australia is one of the most multicultural nations in the world with nearly 30 percent of its population born overseas (Australian Bureau of Statistics, 2022). This multicultural demography has been shaped by post-World War 2 immigration policies that were aimed at boosting Australia's population (Stratton and Ang, 1994). While the majority of immigrants to Australia come from England (Australian Bureau of Statistics, 2022), the proportion of Australians who were born in Asia has grown exponentially since the 1980s, with India, China, the Philippines and Vietnam contributing the largest populations of Asian-born Australians in 2022. In 2021, nearly 20 percent of people in the country self-identified as having Asian heritage (Australian Bureau of Statistics, 2022).

Reflecting these demographics, multiculturalism now serves as a cornerstone for contemporary Australian national identity. However, Jon Stratton and Ien Ang note that Australian multiculturalism centres the state's role in actively promoting "multicultural Australia as a 'unity-in-diversity'" (1994, p. 149), presenting multiculturalism as a national cultural policy that is imposed from the top-down. This policy has replaced the race-based (and racist) definitions of Australian national identity through the 20th century, punctuated by the White Australia policy which promoted an Anglo-European ideal for Australian immigration by explicitly banning immigrants of non-European origins – particularly Chinese and Pacific Islander immigrants – and was only revoked in 1973. While there is less explicit racism within contemporary state multiculturalism, Hage (1998) argues that state multiculturalism continues to operate through the notion of white nationalism, where ethnic others are welcomed by an assumed benevolent paternalistic state in exchange for the promise of their contribution to the economy, the labour market and consumable markers of cultural diversity. However, one of the main critiques of state multiculturalism is that it only ever grants conditional acceptance of non-white Australians contingent upon political and cultural dynamics, and when social and moral panics arise, this tolerance is revoked (Hage, 1998).

This conditional acceptance of Asian Australians can be seen at many points in Australia's history, but a flashpoint moment occurred in the 1990s with populist politician Pauline Hanson's ascent to fame on an explicitly anti-Asian platform that was amplified through widespread media coverage. The Hanson era inspired academic backlash through the formation of Asian Australian studies, which denotes "the critical analysis of the culture, history and politics of Australians of Asian descent" (Lo, 2006, p. 15). Some of the main political goals of this research area are to politicise Asian Australian communities and encourage their mobilisation in representational roles in order to interrogate the foundations of Asian Australian hybrid cultural identities and the ways in which they are wrought through hegemonic discourses of Asian/Australian binary difference and the homogenisation and Othering of Asians in Australia (Khoo, 2006; Ang et al., 2000; Lo, 2006).

Ang et al. (2000) note that in spite of state narratives of harmonious multiculturalism, there remains a deep-rooted fear of the "Asianisation" of Australia. Yet, this fear, and the bigotry it breeds, is rarely accorded public discussion, leading many non-Asian Australians to deny that this exists. For these reasons, many scholars have sought to find avenues for countering state multiculturalism with "everyday multiculturalism," which Flowers and Swan describe as including "conflict and racial intolerance that official multiculturalism occludes from its national pride stories...[as well as] intercultural and interethnic encounters that do not smack of triumphalism" (2012, p. 3). These banal and negotiated narratives centre the everyday, lived and embodied experiences of non-white Australians and include the experiences of racism and ambivalence that are not often accorded space within mainstream media depictions of harmonious multiculturalism. Australian food culture offers a productive site with which to explore everyday multiculturalism.

Several food scholars have explored the ways that food media and food cultures contribute to national identity (see also Chapter 19). Appadurai (1988) provided a foundational study in the ways that cookbooks were used to transform regional cuisines into a national Indian identity, while Duffy and Yang (2012) have noted that food media are used in Singapore to reassert government-promoted characteristics of national identity, such as resilience and self-improvement. Similarly, in Australia, food is liberally used as "a public pedagogy of multiculturalism...[where] educational policy makers, the tourist industry, government and media promulgate the idea that by eating ethnic food we can learn about ourselves, the Other and their culture" (Flowers and Swan, 2012, p. 1). Asian food, in particular, is conspicuous and generally well-integrated across the Australian foodscape and its corresponding food media landscape.

While surveys of representational diversity on screen routinely find that Asian Australians are underrepresented in Australian film and television dramas (Screen Australia, 2016, 2023; Law, 2009), Asian Australians are overrepresented in food media, particularly food television, which "have become one of the principal sites in prime-time Australian television for Asian faces to be seen as a matter of course" (Bonner, 2015, p. 103). Bonner argues that these performances of cooking ethnically marked foods can constitute everyday multiculturalism by "paying attention not to top-down normative desires and intentions, but rather to ordinary practices of interaction and exchange, and also rejection, in daily life" (2015, p. 104). However, this potential is always set against food media's aspirational lifestyle politics and their tendencies to conflate the positive reduction of ethnic difference to consumable (palatable) foods. There is little evidence that Asian Australian celebrity chefs – such as Kylie Kwong, Adam Liaw and Luke Nguyen – ever deploy their commanding media presence to integrate stories of ambivalent experiences within normatively Anglo-Australian culture, even though they routinely share stories about heritage, migration and cultural traditions.

Alternatively, food blogs offer greater potential for everyday politics due to their specific investments in personal disclosures and the documentation of everyday experiences. As I have previously found with Asian American food bloggers, while practices of self-branding often result in the commodification of race and ethnicity, there exist moments of rupture in the course of these reproductions of race that "give food bloggers the opportunity to 'speak back' to some of the racial microaggressions they regularly encounter" (Dejmanee, 2023, p. 48) and, in doing so, challenge the tendency to erase these encounters within hegemonic discourses of postracial America. I explore how and whether a similar political potential is present for Asian Australian bloggers in the context of Australian state multiculturalism.

Recipe Tin Eats and Cook Republic

Recipe Tin Eats by Nagi Maehashi and *Cook Republic* by Sneh Roy are two prominent food blogs created by Asian Australian bloggers. While neither blogger explicitly self-identifies as Asian Australian (unsurprisingly, as this term is rarely used in popular discourse), Maehashi (n.d.) describes herself as "born in Japan, raised in Sydney" and living in "beautiful Sydney, Australia," while Roy (n.d.) describes herself as "born in India…in bustling Mumbai (It was called Bombay back then)" and living in "gorgeous Sydney in Australia." These biographies unequivocally situate them as bloggers of Asian descent who are currently living in Australia.

Both Maehashi and Roy have professionalised their blogging, and their success is demonstrated by the accolades they have received for their work. Roy commenced blogging in 2003 and in 2013 was awarded the titles of Best Australian Blog and Best Lifestyle Blog by the Australian Writer's Centre. She published her first cookbook in 2014 and worked briefly as a food columnist for ELLE Australia magazine. Maehashi launched her blog in 2014, and her debut cookbook was the fastest-selling Australian cookbook of all time (Di Iorio, 2022). Maehashi employs a team of nine to help behind the scenes with her blog and its associated food bank (Maehashi, 2021b) and is a regular columnist for "Good Eats," the food section of Australia's most-read masthead the *Sydney Morning Herald* (SMH Still The Nation's, 2024). While these two blogs are not necessarily representative of the Asian Australian food blogosphere as a whole, in the hierarchically structured blogosphere, their success connotes high visibility and influence.

Although both bloggers cover a diverse variety of cuisines on their food blogs, they incorporate a significant number of pan-Asian recipes – particularly Chinese, Thai, Korean and Indian – that go beyond their ethnic backgrounds and reflect the popularity of these cuisines in the Australian foodscape. While Roy incorporates a number of Indian recipes, Maehashi has removed all Japanese recipes from her site and instead links to a sister site published in her mother's name that exclusively posts Japanese recipes. I focussed on the Asian recipes published on *Recipe Tin Eats* and *Cook Republic* to elucidate themes specific to Asian Australian everyday politics.

I randomly selected 50 posts from each blog that referenced Asian recipes or names in their titles. Drawing on a grounded theory approach (Glaser and Strauss, 1967), I performed a thematic analysis of post content, focussing on the textual narratives within the posts but reading them contextually within an understanding of the respective food blog brands, the site layout and the food blogosphere as a whole. Using the constant comparative method, similar themes were clustered and labelled with conceptual codes, which were then collapsed into abstract categories (Glaser and Strauss, 1967) that were relevant to Asian Australian cultural and political identity. This resulted in four dominant themes: (1) Rearticulating Western/Asian Binaries, (2) "Generically" Asian vs Specific Nations/Regions, (3) Authenticity in Ethnic Foods and (4) Cultural Adaptability.

Rearticulating Western/Asian Binaries

The concept of the Western/Asian binary is often evoked on *Recipe Tin Eats* and *Cook Republic* in ways that demonstrate the nuance and hybridity inherent to this relationship. Food parallels are often used to demonstrate the similarities and equivalences that take place across the imagined binary. For instance, Roy describes Pav Bhaji as "similar to the Sloppy Joe of the West" (Roy, 2011c) and Aloo Matar as her "Indian version of a quick mac and cheese" (Roy, 2011b). These metaphors emphasise the "intricate and heterogeneous entanglements and interconnections" (Ang et al., 2000, p. xix) between Asia and the West. In eroding the imagined Eastern/Western binary, such discourses challenge notions of un-assimilability, essentialism and mutual exclusivity that characterise dominant depictions of Asia in the West and have long been used to justify the alienation and exclusion of Asians in Australia (Ang et al., 2000; Lo, 2006). When the bloggers occasionally reproduce the Asian/Western binary, the assumption of Western superiority is inverted, as demonstrated by Roy's introduction to a recipe for Chicken Biryani: "Baking is an exact science. Indian Cooking is not. One of the most forgiving styles of cooking…Indian cooking is kind to the cook and takes on as many beautiful and delicious variations as there are cooks" (Roy, 2021).

This re-negotiation of the Western/Asian binary also takes place through the bloggers' meticulous instruction on consumption practices. Maehashi provides detailed accounts of where ingredients can be purchased, referencing Australian national grocery chains such as Woolworths and Coles; specialty grocers such as Harris Farms and, Asian, Thai and Indian grocery stores, performing hybrid cultural identity that is realised at the intersections of mainstream, speciality and ethnic consumption practices. Maehashi's references to Australian grocery chains punctuate the specificity of her influencing work to Asian *Australian* – as opposed to other Asian diaspora – communities, while the publication of this commentary on a food blog allows for more freedom to reference brands and chains without specifically being sponsored by them. For example, Maehashi publishes an image with a side-by-side comparison of two different brands of Chinese cooking wine, one available from a major grocery chain and the other from an Asian grocery store, noting their differences in size and prize. This image structure again alludes to the equivalence of products across the Western/Asian binary and the multiple possibilities for recreating Asian tastes within the Australian landscape through considered consumption practices. This involves finding or recreating appropriate substitutes through exploring a variety of grocery stores, road-testing different brands and offering at times surprising substitutes for products, such as ketchup, which Maehashi assures readers is prevalent in several "Chinese recipes you know and love (like Sweet and Sour Chicken!)" (Maehashi, 2022b).

Additionally, Maehashi's tastemaking encodes everyday politics. In her detailed descriptions of Asian ingredients and products, she celebrates the incorporation of a larger variety of traditionally Asian products and ingredients at grocery chains, which is seen as reflective of the growing acceptance and appreciation of Asian influences on Australian national culture. At the same time, her detailed instructions on how and why Asian ingredients are used – such as the differences between dark and light soy sauce or the distinctions between basil, Thai basil and Thai holy basil – demystify and translate Asian foodscapes in Australia, encouraging a cultural tolerance of what initially appears to be "foreign" in the Australian landscape. The result is a cultural hybridity in the sense conceived by Asian Australian and diaspora scholars (Ang et al, 2000; Hall, 1996; Lo, 2006; Bhabha, 1994), encompassing the notion that through straddling different worlds, exploring different cuisines and becoming intimately familiar with the products on offer at both Australian and Asian grocery stores that a unique and syncretic hybrid culture is created that challenges the gap and the boundaries drawn in cultural discourse between Asia and the West.

"Generically Asian" vs specific nations/regions

One of the core debates articulated within Asian Australian studies is the use of "Asian" to collectively reference the diverse range of ethnicities, experiences and politics of Australians of Asian descent. Referencing Spivak's "strategic essentialism" in the "strategic use of a positive essentialism in a scrupulously visible political interest" (1988, p. 205), Jacqueline Lo argues for the critical contextualisation required to "challenge and destabilise hegemonic discourses that marginalize Australians of Asian descent, while simultaneously acknowledging the internal contradictions and differences within the category of Asian Australian" (2006, pp. 15). This debate is echoed in the Asian Australian food blogosphere through discussion of the ways "Asian" is applied to recipes.

Maehashi posts several recipes that include the descriptor "Asian" in their titles, such as "Asian beef bowls," "Asian chilli chicken" and "Asian side salad." She acknowledges the imprecise use of this term, writing: "Calling a dish 'Asian'-something always feels a little generic, a lazy label that people seem to use loosely if a recipe happens to contain a dash of soy sauce" (Maehashi, 2021a). However, she justifies her considered use of this descriptor:

> Ginger, garlic, chilli, sesame, sriracha and lime juice all make the roll call of ingredients. While it may not be strictly traditional to any particular cuisine, the flavours still plant this quick chicken recipe firmly in the 'Asian' genre in my book.
>
> (Maehashi, 2021a)

In doing so, Maehashi draws attention to the range of different flavours that are considered common across parts of Asia – that go beyond the superficial "dash of soy sauce" – and generates a new category of recipes that celebrate these commonalities.

More frequently, however, great care is taken to point out the subtle distinctions between national cuisines – for instance, the absence of soy sauce that distinguishes Thai from Chinese or Indonesian fried rice or the many variations of Cendol that exist "in practically every street and home of Malaysia, Indonesia, Myanmar, Singapore, Vietnam and Thailand" (Roy, 2018). These distinctions are also applied to regional variations, with Roy exploring variations between North and South Indian recipes, differences between Indian, Singaporean and Malaysian curries as well as the cultural hybridity that takes place within India. For instance, Roy writes about Gobi Manchurian, "an Indo-Chinese dish that is said to have been invented by a small Chinese community living in eastern India by marrying classic Chinese techniques with Indian flavours" (Roy, 2020). Thus, regional variations are specific, historicised and contextualised, which are key projects of Asian Australian – and, more broadly, critical race and diaspora – studies.

Roy and Maehashi foreground food research to offer context to their recipes that challenges the dominant definition of "Asianness in Australia…[as] the lumping together of all of 'Asia' as if it were a monolithic entity" (Ang et al., 2000, p. xviii). Food bloggers take seriously the project of quantifying the simultaneous affinities and differences between countries and regions within Asia, modelling a notion of regional affinity that does not deny the specificity and heterogeneity that comprises Asia and Asian Australia.

Ethnic foods and authenticity in foodie culture

The concept of authenticity, which is so central to influencer culture, also has particular resonance in contemporary foodie culture. As Johnston and Baumann (2009) write, "foodie" culture is no longer distinguished through haute cuisine but through cultural omnivorousness, where high taste is marked through being discerning, informed and adventurous. In this context, authenticity "is a key element of how foodies evaluate and legitimate food choices" (2009, p. 69), and food is constructed or perceived as authentic "when it has geographic specificity, is 'simple,' has a personal connection, can be linked to a historical tradition, or has 'ethnic' connections" (2009, p. 70).

Maehashi and Roy each reference authenticity in different but attentive ways throughout their posts. Maehashi references authenticity by frequently engaging in in-depth discussions to justify her assessment of recipes as authentic or not. In her post on Pad Thai, she writes:

> Authentic Pad Thai on the streets of Thailand has a distinct fishy/prawny 'funk' (which sounds thoroughly unappetising but is actually completely addictive and the very essence of true Thai street food). If authentic is what you're after, try this Prawn/Shrimp version.
> *(Maehashi, 2023a)*

A more elaborate discussion takes place on Maehashi's recipe for Thai Panang Curry:

> This recipe … we created from scratch ourselves, using Panang Curry eaten in Thailand and at really reputable, authentic Thai restaurants here in Sydney as our benchmark. We referenced many recipes during the course of our research, notably from highly regarded Thai food experts including David Thompson and Sujet Saenkham of the acclaimed Spice I Am restaurants, and YouTube videos from Thai home cooks.
> *(Maehashi, 2023b)*

Across Maehashi's work, the need for authenticity is discussed and established through a reliance on research, chefs, local restaurants, local people (particularly mothers) and in-country eating experiences (particularly street food) as a gauge for authenticity.

Alternatively, Roy – who grew up in Mumbai – references the authenticity of her Indian recipes in more poetic ways, citing family members and contextualising recipes with vivid descriptions of India. Roy prefaces several recipes with vibrant scenes of Indian life, writing: "On the streets of Mumbai, especially around a large water body like the curve of a beach or a lake are colourful gypsy like carts selling *bhelpuri*" (Roy, 2013) and

> Decked up with garlands of dried lemons strung up around a highly colourful typographic sign, a man chopping and squeezing lemons at record speed and a steady crowd of locals and tourists greedily gulping down the sweet nectar from huge beer mugs, the *nimbu pani* cart is hard to miss.
> *(Roy, 2016)*

Such descriptions situate her knowledge of authentic recipes within her embodied knowledges, memories and experiences of India.

These different strategies serve similar objectives, which are to assure the reader of the authenticity of these recipes or to qualify why and how concessions can be made without impacting the taste of the dish too severely. Even though both bloggers identify as Asian, their attention to authenticity in the production of pan-Asian recipes invokes the sense that authenticity in this context is also drawn in contrast to the fear of reproducing "basic Westernised" approximations of these Asian recipes. As Maehashi continues in her post on Pad Thai:

> A quick Google is all it takes to find a myriad of basic westernised versions which are typically made with not much more than something sour (vinegar, lime juice), soy

sauce and sugar. These recipes will not taste like any Pad Thai you've had from a restaurant...[they] tend to lack the proper depth of flavour and are typically too sweet.

(Maehashi, 2023a)

In this sense, authenticity appears along a spectrum but invokes a binary between Western and Asian that haunts the bloggers and shapes their approach to recipe production.

Asian Australian identity as cultural adaptability

Bell and Hollows (2007) write that the valorisation of ethnic foods within Western foodie culture is contingent upon the celebration of "domestic and local culinary practices...as a site of tradition and authenticity in a globalized world" (p. 23) which generates "mythologized figures of domestic femininity [who are fixed in place] to anchor the meaning of idealized images of 'authentically' local culinary cultures" (p. 23). Discussing the valorisation of ethnic food as celebrated for both its tradition and its local specificity, Bell and Hollows argue that the colonisation of these knowledges by foodies in a globalised world has the effect of "fixing" these cultures and their people in time and place in service of the preservation of authenticity for Western audiences.

Even though Maehashi and Roy discuss authenticity extensively, as discussed above, their portrayal of Asian food is mired with the spirit and pragmatics of adaptability. There is an emphasis on their ability to recreate dishes, tastes, memories and experiences of Asian food and of being in Asia that creates more complexity to their well-researched and tested Asian recipes. Both bloggers generate many posts that are inspired by their experiences eating at Asian restaurants in Sydney. As Maehashi writes:

This prawn recipe came to be after I had a terrific Stir Fried Prawns in Chilli Jam at a modern(ish) Thai Restaurant... I tried to achieve the same flavours using a little bit of this, a little bit of that, a dash of this and a splash of that.

(Maehashi, 2022a)

This version of tastemaking shapes a new relationship to production and consumption, for although their recommendations are based on their expertise as knowledgeable consumers navigating a diverse foodscape, their translation of these experiences for home cooks encourages domestic production, not further consumption.

Moreover, this notion that recipes can be recreated and adapted underlines the cultural creativity and change that accompanies the mobility of diasporic women. This is most apparent through Roy's series of microwave Indian recipes – such as "5 minute microwave Besan Laddoos" and "Quick no frills lamb biryani" – that deliberately decouple "traditional" Asian recipes from their historic, pre-modern contexts. In her recipe for carrot halwa, Roy writes:

The typical Halwa like the one Mum makes, takes anywhere between 2–6 hours simmering away on the stove...Thanks to modern technology [microwave] and a lot of laziness [me], I have conjured up my own version of the Microwave Gajar Ka Halwa. It takes 20 minutes to cook and if you practice it enough number of times, it tastes as good as the lengthy version, I swear!!

(Roy, 2011a)

This seamless transition from her mother's traditional version to her microwave shortcut is asserted by Roy to remain both authentic and meaningful, emphasising the dynamism of recipes and the empowerment inherent in this ability to reproduce traditional dishes in changing times and locations. In a similar fashion, the adaptation of traditional recipes leads to the power to recreate meaningful moments in lives marked by mobility, as Roy recreates the Singaporean congee she regularly consumed while pregnant with her first-born son and, through doing so, relives the memories of this exciting period of her life.

The playful inventiveness that permeates Asian Australian bloggers' approach to pan-Asian recipes speaks to the experience of Asian Australian cultural identity as inspired by history and place but also evolving in the light of shifting contexts and influences. Presented in a negotiated relationship with authenticity, adaptability complicates essentialist notions of static, traditional ethnic foods. While the importance of authenticity is reinforced, different cooking styles, improvisations and the long notes on substitutions that are included in these recipes create a mix-and-match style of cooking options which alludes to the productivity of cultural hybridity and the novel possibilities for cultural formation that arise from earnest recreations of cultural practices and traditions.

Food blogging and everyday Asian Australian politics

Food blogs are a genre that hold the possibility of opening up spaces of dialogue for the representation and consideration of Asian Australian cultural identity in everyday life. In this analysis, I have identified several ways that Maehashi and Roy's food blogs engage in everyday Asian Australian politics, even though this is not an explicit or possibly even conscious intention of their sites. Through their discussion of foodscapes and grocery options within Australia, they inadvertently portray some of the everyday ways that hybrid cultural identity is wrought within mainstream hegemonic culture. Capitalising on foodie culture's valorisation of being informed about food contexts and histories, the bloggers use their positioning to translate and demystify Asian recipes, ingredients and brands, forging new possibilities for understanding the relationships between Asia and the West as one of parallels, equivalences and substitutions rather than mutual exclusivity. Moreover, this information helps contextualise and complexify "Asia" in mainstream Australian discourse as heterogeneous, situated and historical.

While Maehashi and Roy do not overtly hail an Asian Australian community, their references to Australian foodscapes – notably through their use of Australian terminology, brands and chains – situate them in Australia in a way that touches on the specificities of the Asian Australian experience, as opposed to the Asian American, Asian Canadian and Asian British experiences that are more common across the lifestyle blogosphere. This can be powerful in the context of the global influencersphere, where Australian influencers must engage a global audience to make their work visible, which typically means appealing to dominant markets in the United States, China and South Korea (Dejmanee, 2024). *Recipe Tin Eats* and *Cook Republic* focus on Asian foodscapes in Australia, providing a representational experience that has particular resonance for Asian Australians, even though their work is read beyond this community.

However, while I posited that the intimate disclosures of the blogosphere might support bloggers' portrayal of ambivalent experiences within multicultural Australia, there was little evidence of everyday multicultural narratives on these blogs. Maehashi and Roy both disclose personal references, experiences and family stories on their blogs. They include references to children's birthday cakes; siblings' honest responses to different Asian recipes and detailed glimpses into the bloggers' family lives and everyday routines. Maehashi incorporates a section titled "Life of Dozer" at the end of every post, which details stories and images of her golden retriever that is extremely popular with her audience and has become integral to her brand. Yet, ultimately, there is little deviation from upbeat and positive reflections on multiculturalism and the consumption and production of ethnic foods. This absence suggests the structural limitations that shape visibility and voice, particularly constraining non-white bloggers talking about race and ethnicity, in the food blogosphere.

Conclusion

The original excitement around food blogging centred on its possibilities for publishing and celebrating a greater diversity of voices, lifestyles and experiences than was represented in mainstream media, and the representational value of Maehashi and Roy as prominent Asian Australian women is clearly significant to situating the experiences of Australians of Asian descent and communicating the nuances of hybrid cultural identities. Moreover, given the global orientation of food blogs, their work travels transnationally, benefitting a global Asian diasporic community. However, as Maehashi and Roy have followed the common trajectory for successful food bloggers into the realm of food journalism through their affiliations with *ELLE magazine* and the *Sydney Morning Herald*, it is important to be mindful of the continuing structural limitations that guide these representations of lifestyle. In this study, I have found that while both Maehashi and Roy have generated substantial influence within Australian cultural dialogue and are able to illuminate aspects of their quotidian and domestic experiences as Asian Australians, without explicit attention to issues of race and everyday multiculturalism, there remains the risk of romanticising ethnic foods *as* multiculturalism, while continuing to ignore the racialised power dynamics of consumption, production and citizenship. This remains an ongoing project of everyday politics and, in reference to the ways that racial, ethnic and national identity negotiations take place through lifestyle blogs and journalism, a fruitful site for further research.

As the food blogosphere and lifestyle journalism continue to symbiotically evolve, the transition of food bloggers to influential national media platforms highlights the opportunities for user-generated content to provide a pathway for lifestyle journalism to incorporate diverse voices and alternative consumption practices that are then circulated through mainstream media channels. While these diverse voices may not in and of themselves constitute a radical politics, they serve as an important starting point for building affinities and alternative representations that begin to challenge hegemonic discourses, such as the whiteness that lies at the heart of Australian multiculturalism. However, the political potential of these representations continue to be constrained by commercial and structural limitations – in this case, through making Asian Australian consumption legible and palatable to non-Asian, global audiences; retaining a friendly tone that suppresses microaggressions and ambivalent racialised experiences; and at times contributing to hegemonic state narratives of harmonious multiculturalism. These limitations must be taken into account when exploring the political potential of lifestyle journalism's potential to represent racially diverse voices and audiences in a meaningful and productive way.

Further reading

Ang, I., Law, L., Chalmers, S., & Thomas, M. (eds.) (2000). *Alter/Asians: Asian-Australian identities in art, media and popular culture*. Pluto Press.

Dejmanee, T. (2023). *Postfeminism, postrace and digital politics in Asian American food blogs*. Routledge. https://doi.org/10.4324/9781003302278

Khorana, S. (2018). *The tastes and politics of inter-cultural food in Australia*. Rowman & Littlefield.

Lo, J. (2006). Disciplining Asian Australian Studies: Projections and Introjections. *Journal of Intercultural Studies*, 27(1–2), 11–27. https://doi.org/10.1080/07256860600607488

Phạm M.-H. T. (2015). *Asians wear clothes on the internet: Race, gender, and the work of personal style blogging*. Duke.

References

Ang, I., Law, L., Chalmers, S., & Thomas, M. (eds.) (2000). *Alter/Asians: Asian-Australian identities in art, media and popular culture*. Pluto Press.

Appadurai, A. (1988). How to make a national cuisine: Cookbooks in contemporary India. *Comparative Studies in Society and History*, 30(1), 3–24. https://doi.org/10.1017/S0010417500015024

Arriagada, A., & Ibanez, F. (2019). Communicative value chains: Fashion bloggers and branding agencies as cultural intermediaries. In: L. Vodanovic (ed.) *Lifestyle journalism: Social media, consumption and experience*. Routledge, 91–101.

Australian Bureau of Statistics. (2022). *Cultural Diversity of Australia*. ABS. https://www.abs.gov.au/articles/cultural-diversity-australia

Bell, D., & Hollows, J. (2007). Mobile homes. *Space and Culture*, 10(10), 22–39. https://doi.org/10.1177/1206331206296380

Bhabha, H. K. (1994). *The location of culture*. Routledge.

Bonner, F. (2015). The mediated Asian-Australian food identity: From Charmaine Solomon to Masterchef Australia. *Media International Australia*, 157(1), 103–113. https://journals.sagepub.com/doi/10.1177/1329878X1515700113

Brion, R. (2013, October 15). Martha Stewart on Gwyneth Paltrow: 'I started this whole category of lifestyle." *Eater*. https://www.eater.com/2013/10/15/6351805/martha-stewart-on-gwyneth-paltrow-i-started-this-whole-category-of

Dejmanee, T. (2024) "An Australian beauty-lover based in Singapore": Negotiating Asian Australian identity in the beauty vlogosphere. *Communication, Culture and Critique*, 17(4), 293–300. https://doi.org/10.1093/ccc/tcae009

Dejmanee, T. (2023). *Postfeminism, postrace and digital politics in Asian American food blogs*. Routledge. https://doi.org/10.4324/9781003302278

Dejmanee, T. (2018). The food network's heartland kitchens: Cooking up neoconservative comfort in the United States. *Critical Studies in Television*, 14(1), 74–89. https://journals.sagepub.com/doi/abs/10.1177/1749602018810923?journalCode=csta

Dejmanee, T. (2016)."Food porn" as postfeminist play: Digital femininity and the female body on food blogs. *Television and New Media*, 17(5), 429–448. https://doi.org/10.1177/1527476415615944

Di Iorio, M. (2022, November 18). How recipetin eats became Australia's star food blogger and changed my life for the better. *Pedestrian*. https://www.pedestrian.tv/bites/recipetin-eats-nagi-maehashi-interview/

Duffy, B. E. (2017). *(Not) getting paid to do what you love: Gender, social media, and aspirational work*. Yale. https://doi.org/10.12987/yale/9780300218176.001.0001

Duffy, A., & Yang, Y. A. (2012) Bread and circuses. *Journalism Practice*, 6(1), 59–74, https://doi.org/10.1080/17512786.2011.622892

Flowers, R., & Swan, E. (2012). Eating the Asian Other? Pedagogies of food multiculturalism in Australia. *Portal Journal of Multidisciplinary International Studies*, 9(2), 1–30. https://doi.org/10.5130/portal.v9i2.2370

Glaser, B. G., & Strauss, A. L. (1967). *The discovery of grounded theory: Strategies for qualitative research*. Aldine de Gruyter.

Hage, G. (1998). *White nation: Fantasies of white supremacy in a multicultural society*. Pluto Press. https://doi.org/10.4324/9780203819470

Hall, S. (1996). New ethnicities. In D. Morley and K. Chen (eds.) *Stuart Hall: Critical Dialogues in Cultural Studies*. Routledge, 441–449.

Hanusch, F. (2012). Broadening the focus: The case for lifestyle journalism as a field of scholarly inquiry. *Journalism Practice*, 6(1), 2–11. https://doi.org/10.1080/17512786.2011.622895

Hanusch, F., & Bruns, A. (2017). Journalistic branding on Twitter: A representative study of Australian journalists' profile descriptions. *Digital Journalism*, 5(1), 26–43. https://doi.org/10.1080/21670811.2016.1152161

Hanusch, F., & Hanitzsch, T. (2013). Mediating orientation and self-expression in the world of consumption: Australian and German lifestyle journalists' professional views. *Media, Culture & Society*, 35(8), 943–959. https://journals.sagepub.com/doi/10.1177/0163443713501931

Johnston, J., & Baumann, S. (2009). *Foodies: Democracy and distinction in the gourmet foodscape*. Routledge. https://doi.org/10.4324/9780203868645.

Khamis, S., Ang, L., & Welling, R. (2017). Self-branding, 'micro-celebrity' and the rise of Social Media Influencers, *Celebrity Studies*, 8(2), 191–208. https://www.tandfonline.com/doi/full/10.1080/19392397.2016.1218292

Khoo, T. (2006). Introduction: Locating Asian Australian cultures. *Journal of Intercultural Studies*, 27(1–2), 1–9. https://doi.org/10.1080/07256860600667243

Law, B. (2009). *The new lows: Representing Asian-Australians on Television (Screenplay & Exegesis)* [Doctoral dissertation, Queensland University of Technology]. QUT ePrints

Lo, J. (2006). Disciplining Asian Australian studies: Projections and introjections. *Journal of Intercultural Studies*, 27(1–2), 11–27. https://doi.org/10.1080/07256860600607488

Lofgren, J. M. (2013). *Changing tastes in food media: A study of recipe sharing traditions in the food blogging community*. [Masters by Research thesis, Queensland University of Technology]. QUT ePrints.

Lopez, L. K. (2009). The radical act of "mommy blogging": redefining motherhood through the blogosphere. *New Media & Society*, 11(5), 729–747. https://journals.sagepub.com/doi/abs/10.1177/1461444809105349

Maehashi, N. (2023b, August 7). Panang curry - real deal, from scratch. *Recipe Tin Eats*. https://www.recipetineats.com/panang-curry/

Maehashi, N. (2023a, July 30). Pad Thai. *Recipe Tin Eats*. https://www.recipetineats.com/chicken-pad-thai/

Maehashi, N. (2022b, November 26). Sticky baked Chinese chicken wings. *Recipe Tin Eats*. https://www.recipetineats.com/sticky-chinese-chicken-wings/

Maehashi, N. (2022a, October 11). Asian chilli garlic prawns (shrimp). *Recipe Tin Eats*. https://www.recipetineats.com/asian-chilli-garlic-prawns-shrimp/

Maehashi, N. (2021b, October 14). Pressing pause – feels like failure. *Recipe Tin Eats*. https://www.recipetineats.com/pressing-pause-feels-like-failing/

Maehashi, N. (2021a, January 21). Asian beef bowls (super quick!). *Recipe Tin Eats*. https://www.recipetineats.com/asian-beef-bowls/

Maehashi, N. (n.d.). About me. *Recipe Tin Eats*. https://www.recipetineats.com/nagi-recipetin-eats/

Marwick, A. E. (2013). *"They're really profound women, they're entrepreneurs": Conceptions of Authenticity in Fashion Blogging*. Proceedings of the International Conference on Weblogs and Social Media. https://tiara.org/wp-content/uploads/2018/05/amarwick_fashionblogs_ICWSM_2013.pdf

Matchar, E. (2013). *Homeward bound: Why women are embracing the new domesticity*. Simon & Schuster.

Miller, T. (2007). *Cultural citizenship: Cosmpolitanism, consumerism, and television in a neoliberal age*. Temple.

Naulin, S. (2019). Are food bloggers a new kind of influencer? In L. Vodanovic (ed.) *Lifestyle journalism: Social media, consumption and experience*. Routledge, 102–113.

Presswood, A. (2020). *Digital domestics: Food Blogs, postfeminism, and the communication of expertise*. Lexington.

Rodney, A., Cappeliez, S., Oleschuk, M., & Johnston, J. (2017). The online domestic goddess: An analysis of food blog femininities. *Food Culture and Society*, 20, 685–707. https://www.tandfonline.com/doi/abs/10.1080/15528014.2017.1357954

Roy, S. (2021, March 25). Hyderbadi chicken biryani with a modern dum. *Cook Republic*. https://www.cookrepublic.com/hyderbadi-chicken-biryani-with-a-modern-dum/

Roy, S. (2020, February 25). Gobi Manchurian - cauliflower fritters in Chinese garlic sauce. *Cook Republic*. https://www.cookrepublic.com/gobi-manchurian-indian-chinese-cauliflower-fritters-garlic-sauce/

Roy, S. (2018 September 5). Gula melaka syrup - palm sugar syrup. *Cook Republic*. https://www.cookrepublic.com/gula-melaka-syrup-palm-sugar-syrup/

Roy, S. (2016, February 29). Nimbu pani pops - lemon lime sherbet pops. *Cook Republic*. https://www.cookrepublic.com/nimbu-pani-pops-lemon-lime-sherbet-pops/

Roy, S. (2013, March 27). Chickpea bhel salad. *Cook Republic*. https://www.cookrepublic.com/chickpea-bhel-salad/

Roy, S. (2011c, August 18). Pav Bhaji - Indian sloppy joes. *Cook Republic*. https://www.cookrepublic.com/pav-bhaji-indian-sloppy-joes/

Roy, S. (2011b, August 8). Aloo matar Indian potato and pea curry. *Cook Republic*. https://www.cookrepublic.com/aloo-matar-indian-potato-and-pea-curry/

Roy, S. (2011a, May 25). Gajar Ka Halwa - Indian carrot pudding. *Cook Republic*. https://www.cookrepublic.com/in-search-of-a-quick-and-sweet-indian-treat/

Roy, S. (n.d.). About. *Cook Republic*. https://www.cookrepublic.com/about/

Salvio, P. (2012). Dishing it out: Food blogs and post-feminist domesticity. *Gastronomica, 12*, 31–39. https://doi.org/10.1525/GFC.2012.12.3.31

Screen Australia. (2023). *Seeing Ourselves 2: Diversity, equity and inclusion in Australian TV drama*. Screen Australia. https://www.screenaustralia.gov.au/getmedia/233e459c-e340-49bc-8de2-9f04a846632b/Seeing-Ourselves-2-Full-Report-Accessible-PDF.pdf

Screen Australia. (2016). *Seeing ourselves: Reflections on diversity in Australian TV drama*. Screen Australia. https://www.screenaustralia.gov.au/getmedia/157b05b4-255a-47b4-bd8b-9f715555fb44/TV-Drama-Diversity.pdf

SMH Still the Nation's Most Read Masthead. (2024, February 26). *Sydney morning Herald*. https://www.smh.com.au/business/companies/smh-still-the-nation-s-most-read-masthead-20240225-p5f7nh.html

Song, J., & Maree, C. (2021, February 24). The place, voice and portrayal of Asians in Australia. *Melbourne Asia Review*. https://www.melbourneasiareview.edu.au/the-place-voice-and-portrayal-of-asians-in-australia/

Stratton, J., & Ang, I. (1994). Multicultural imagined communities: Cultural difference and national identity in Australia and the USA, *Continuum, 8*(2), 124–158. https://doi.org/10.1080/10304319409365672

Vodanovic, L. (2019). *Lifestyle journalism: Social media, consumption and experience*. Routledge.

28
THE NEW LOOK OF LIFESTYLE GUIDES

Rethinking brand journalism for the digital age

Myles Ethan Lascity

Introduction

How to Build a Seasonless Wardrobe.
Testing the Limits of Surf.
A 100-Year Journey through Mickey Mouse's art style.

At first, these headlines might not seem to have much in common, but they are all examples of contemporary brand journalism. The first piece, written by Chris Lawrence for the sustainable clothing brand Everlane's *Everworld Stories* encourages the use of separates and utilitarian items that can be worn in various ways depending on the weather. The second, published by US workwear firm American Giant, discusses how an engineer developed custom surfboards unique to each surfer. And, the final headline for Uniqlo's *UT* magazine chronicles artistic renderings of Mickey Mouse since the character's inception in *Steamboat Willie* in 1928.

Although media publications run by brands and corporations date back to at least 1895 (Pulizzi, 2013), in the past decade or so, researchers have started paying closer attention to the genre (Bull, 2013; Cole & Greer, 2013; Greer, 2016; Lee, 2015; Swenson, 2012; Serazio, 2021a, 2021b; Yarnykh, 2023) under the nomenclature of customer magazines (Denner, Koch & Himmelreich, 2018; Dyson, 2007; Schijns, 2008; van Reijmersdal, Neijens & Smit, 2010) and the rise of native advertising (Amazeen & Muddiman, 2018; Ferrer Conill, 2016; Wojdynski & Evans, 2016). This academic interest has coincided with increased interrogations of lifestyle and related journalistic forms (e.g., Hanusch, 2012; Kristensen & From, 2012; Fürsich, 2012) and ongoing disruption of legacy brands by digital and social media (Duffy, 2013).

This chapter examines brand journalism produced by four fashion brands American Giant, Uniqlo, Everlane, and Suitsupply. Fashion brands are a poignant site to understand the impact of brand journalism since they have frequently relied on cultural constructions of meaning (Holt, 2004) like storytelling and lifestyles (Hancock, 2016; Saviolo & Marrazza, 2013) and because the entire realm of fashion media has been impacted by increased mediatization (Rocamora, 2012, 2017, 2019) and the increased presence of non-traditional media outlets, including blogs and influencer accounts.

As such, this chapter traces contemporary brand journalism practices onto postmodern and hypermodern brand practices. To do so, this chapter places "brand journalism" in the lineage of customer magazines and later magazine–catalog hybrids (also known as magalogs) before examining their contemporary form as digital publications. Through an analysis of several publications, it is possible to see how brand journalism can be used to create postmodern branding constructs, like image or market segment, and can also emphasize hypermodern brand needs like consumer education to support transparency and corporate responsibility. Finally, this chapter argues that brand journalism in the digital era does not threaten civic-minded journalism as it does not present itself as an unbiased news source and, instead, acts as an overt form of brand communication.

Brand journalism: Past and present

Brand journalism has been beset by definitional issues, even though the idea itself has a long history. Under the term "content marketing," Pulizzi (2013) cited the roots of brand journalism in the 1895 launch of *The Furrow*—a magazine produced by farm equipment manufacturer John Deere. The goal, Pulizzi writes, was not to sell equipment but "to educate farmers on new technology and how they could be more successful business owners and farmers." *The Furrow*, however, was just the beginning; other publications like *The Michelin Guide*, which helped drivers maintain cars and find lodging during road trips, was released in 1900, and the Jell-O recipe book, first published in 1904, was credited with contributing to the brand's $1 million in sales only two years later.

When automaker Ford Motor Company launched the *Ford Times* in 1908, it was part of a rising tide of public relations efforts done, at least in part, to combat muckrakers and anti-business journalism. However, as Swenson (2012) notes, the goal of the magazine was "to foster feelings of community and dialogue, to inspire readers to improve moral and societal ills, and to improve the standardization of communication amid corporate maturity and growth" (p. 57). By and large, the goal was to connect the various Ford stakeholders—e.g., dealers and customers — to share "information, values, and experience" (p. 57). Such publication was not only the brainchild of Ford: at least two other automotive manufacturers had produced similar magazines. Yet, over the course of its production, the *Ford Times* used journalistic principles to engage in "credible corporate storytelling" and helped frame the past and shape car culture as integral to American identity (Swenson, 2012, p. 192).

Company magazines would number in the hundreds by 1928 and collectively would have a circulation of more than 70 million by 1950 (Swenson, 2012, p. 10). In the 1960s, advertising executive David Ogilvy believed companies could garner better press by using advertorials—advertisements made to mimic the look and feel of the publication in which it is contained. The goal is to blend promotional content into the surrounding content and "capitalize on the credibility of the media organizations printing or broadcasting the sponsored information" (Greer, 2016). This process is akin to native advertising today.

The 1990s would see another turn in branded journalism content with the wide proliferation of the *magalog*—a magazine–catalog hybrid. Such publications were a way to cut through the clutter of catalogs while having the wider ability to include advertisements for outside products and "sell a certain image" to shoppers (Bird, 1997). Brands like Hermès had sold advertisements in their catalog as early as the late 1970s, and names like Williams-Sonoma, Land's End, and Abercrombie & Fitch would engage in the practice toward the end of the decade. As others have noted, Abercrombie & Fitch, especially, managed to use their magalog, *A&F Quarterly*, to blur the lines of everyday life and the mediated brand image (Engel, 2004). Thanks to lifestyle journalism articles that addressed everything from travel tips to drink recipes, risqué fashion photography from Bruce Weber and reviews of films, movies, TV shows, books and other consumables, like cars, the publication produced a "total commodity environment" that could tie a wide swath of consumption practices back to the intangible Abercrombie lifestyle (Engel, 2004).

More recently, researchers have used the term "brand journalism" to several different ends. Researchers theorize brand journalism as synonymous with native advertising (Ferrer Conill, 2016; Wojdynski & Evans, 2016), if not fully encompassing the latter process (Serazio, 2021b). Others extended the term to the work of professional journalists who understood themselves as a "brand" (Holton & Molyneux, 2017). Moreover, it has been suggested that the development and implementation of brand journalism today is thanks to "a specific set of cultural, institutional and technological contexts in which both journalism and commercial communication fields were undergoing changes in their forms and governing logic" (Lee, 2015, p. 27). This latter contention is often taken to mean that advertising and corporate communication practices have usurped or are inappropriately capitalizing on the form of civic journalism (Lee, 2015, pp. 36–37; Serazio, 2021b), yet as *The Furrow* and *Ford Times* shows, brand journalism has long existed in the form of customer magazines (Cole & Greer, 2013; Denner, Koch & Himmelreich, 2018; Dyson, 2007; Schijns, 2008). Yet, it is equally important to note that readers tend to be somewhat discerning and rate more commercial content as less credible (Reijmersdal, Neijans & Smit, 2010) and that many who produce brand journalism largely follow professional journalistic work routines (Koch, Viererbl & Schulz-Knappe, 2023).

Mediatization and the digital turn

Although brand journalism vis-à-vis customer magazines has been present for more than a century, its increased prominence is often assumed to be linked to the rise of the internet and digital communications. The digital turn complicated the professional media landscape, forcing publishers to think of themselves more as "brands" than single-medium publications (Duffy 2013) and undermining financial viability, pushing outlets toward new revenue streams like native advertising (Amazeen & Muddiman, 2018). Specifically, in the fashion realm, the rise of blogs (Findlay, 2015; Pham, 2015) and later influencers (Perdoni, 2022) has altered publication techniques; the affordances of digital technology include the ability to include multiple media types (e.g., text, photography, and audio–video formats), sometimes called hypermediacy (Bolter & Grusin, 2000), and also include hypertext and links (Rocamora, 2012), thus altering the way we consume media.

Drawing on wider studies on mediatization (e.g., Strömbäck & Dimitrova, 2011), Rocamora (2017) noted that digital communication reshaped the logic of fashion, writ large, and the media aspects related to it. Mediatization made three changes to fashion media. First, digital technology made fashion shows, once the exclusive realms of editors and the fashion elite, open to everyone (Rocamora, 2017, pp. 509–512). Second, increased use of technology by retail outlets, such as smart mirrors, in-store digital screens, and brand apps, have imbued media into everyday shopping experiences (Rocamora, 2017, pp. 512–515). Third, mediatization altered how people present themselves and their personal adornment online, allowing better production quality and easier photo manipulation (Rocamora, 2017, pp. 515–518).

Elsewhere, Rocamora (2019) theorized Net-a-Porter's *The Edit* as a "shoppable magazine" that allowed readers to click links and seamlessly purchase items from the web retailer. Other than the shoppable links, *The Edit* also included fashion photography, editorial stories, and other publication departments (p. 102). Yet, *The Edit* was not singular in mixing digital publications with shopping affordances—traditional magazines like *Vogue*, *GQ*, and *Harper's Bazaar* would follow suit, creating spaces where readers could purchase items and where editorial and commercial content merged (p. 103). More broadly, Rocamora suggests this blur helped unite shopping and entertainment but also that it helped turn all brands into media producers.

Brand processes: From post- to hypermodernity

To understand the role that contemporary brand journalism plays in the branding process, it is important to take a step back and understand exactly what branding is. Brands are the product of a complex semiotic system (Danesi, 2013; Conejo & Wooliscroft, 2015) that provides additional value and meaning to goods (Gardner & Levy, 1955; Levy, 1959). Brands have been equated to a "new media object" since the meaning and value of a brand are always in flux, and their diffuse nature allows them to appear differently to various stakeholders (Lury, 2004, pp. 6–8). As others have noted, brand messages targeted at specific communities can work in tandem with larger brand messages (Grow, 2008), an understanding that is even more pronounced today, thanks to various algorithmic functions (Beer, 2013; Turow, 2011).

That said, brands are often understood as a collection of their communicated texts (Wigley, Nobbs & Larsen, 2013), even if only a fraction of these texts can be read and interpreted by particular consumers (Christensen & Askegaard, 2001). Toward these ends, the most culturally impactful brands are often understood to provide some meaning that consumers can use in everyday life (Holt, 2004) or some narrative or storyline that items and their consumption can fit into (Hancock, 2016). The most pronounced have been deemed "symbol-intensive" brands and might promote an entire lifestyle for consumers to buy into (Saviolo & Marrazza, 2013). Nevertheless, such symbolically intensive meaning creation through brand communication is a hallmark of a postmodern communication environment whereby media messages both help construct the world around us and seduce us into that semi-fictional world (Baudrillard, 1994; see also Hancock, 2016, pp. 20–27 on postmodern advertising and branding).

Comparatively, today's media environment driven by digital communication and social media seems to be moving toward a post-postmodern situation (Reilly & Blanco F., 2021)—potentially toward hypermodernity, which has been defined by an increased buildup of ever-changing consumer trends and products and colored by anxiety and fear over the consequences of this ongoing consumption (Lipovetsky, 2005; Morgado, 2014). Theorists have suggested hallmarks of hypermodernity include an emphasis on individualization (Rendtorff, 2019, p. 194), corporate responsibility (Rendtorff, 2014 pp. 282–283), social instabilities including growing inequality (Charles, 2009, pp. 394–395), and an acceleration of time, whereby trends and life writ large move more quickly (Martineau, 2017, pp. 225–226). While some have suggested hypermodernity sees a re-emphasis on science and technology discourses (Rendtorff, 2014), especially within brand communication (Arnould & Tissier-Desbordes, 2005), this can equally be understood as a search for instruction, authority, and stability in an increasingly complex and ever-changing world.

As such, the following pages show how brand journalism treads a line between postmodern branding (e.g., the acknowledgment, creation, and seduction of intangible meaning constructs) and hypermodern brand practices underscoring information and education rather than intangible meaning creation. Within the fashion realm, contemporary brand journalism includes a mix of informational and instructional content that runs the gambit from product information to guidance on product care and maintenance, style advice, and holiday gift guides. The following four examples—*Giant* from American Giant, Uniqlo's *UT Magazine*, *Everworld Stories* by Everlane, and *The Journal* from Suitsupply—highlight the nimbleness of brand journalism as a corporate communication practice that can be used in both postmodern and hypermodern environments.

Giant by American Giant

While *Giant* from the U.S.-based workwear brand American Giant is the most recently launched publication of those covered in this chapter, it also best embodies the use of brand journalism to create a target market and provide intangible values to the brand. *Giant* has been dubbed "A Working Magazine," by the brand, which noted it has "produced catalogs that sold the things we made and loved. In them, we told stories of the men and women across America doing good work" (American Giant, n.d.a). The explanation says the stories being told in the catalog were the impetus of *Giant* and that the new publication could cover more narratives from working people. The introduction concludes: "Because we believe that hard work is a beautiful thing."

Unlike the other publications examined here, which are more substantial, *Giant*'s first two issues were limited to three stories each; thus, as of this writing, the publication consists of six profile pieces. Nevertheless, these stories highlight a host of "working" occupations, including firefighters, fishermen, mechanics, and home builders. Each story comes with one large photo, a headline, and a series of smaller photos illustrating the nature of the work (see American Giant, n.d.a, n.d.b). And while the stories are written to profile either specific individuals or a group of people, the narrative underscores that the work environment is difficult. For example, "A Legacy in Fire" profiles the "elite firefighters known as the Tahoe Hotshots." From the beginning of the profile, the tough working environment is highlighted. "Deep in the *rugged* terrain of California's Tahoe National Forest," the profile begins (emphasis added). The piece goes on to say that the Hotshots are "pushing themselves" because "peak physical condition is non-negotiable." The profile continues:

> To be a Hotshot means that you are one of the most skilled and physically fit firefighters in America, battling at the front line of wildfires that rake across North America every year. ... When the call comes, they could be sent anywhere in the country, dropping straight into the frontlines of the flames. During these grueling 18-hour days, they push themselves to the brink, physically and mentally.
>
> *(American Giant, n.d.a)*

There is a similar sentiment that underscores the other profiles as well. "Not everyone is cut out to fish," the lobster fisherman profile explains. "It takes years of training, often working on an established boat under an experienced captain to learn the trade ..." And when profiling the kitchen staff of Nashville restaurant Audrey, *Giant* reads, "In this kitchen, the inspiration makes the *tiring intense* work exciting" (emphasis added).

The profiles in the second issue (American Giant, n.d.b) also underscore work and manual labor but do so with a particular craftsmanship in mind. Here, readers are introduced to Elise Talley who, at age 25, has been driving Range Rovers for nearly a decade—learning to fix cars and bonding with other auto enthusiasts and mechanics along the way. While Talley continues to work on the car, the profile notes "That's a good thing" because Talley enjoys the "satisfaction and confidence" from completing a job. The theme of personal satisfaction is repeated in the profile of engineer-turned-surfboard designer Zouhair Belkoura. Although he took up surfing as a recreational pursuit, he began testing different boards and customizing them for riders. "Board shaping, like playing an instrument, is about feel," the profile reads, "it's personal, music coming from within." Again, when profiling Zach and Jas, who fix up old houses, the emphasis is on craft. The profile explains they aim to be "shokunin," a Japanese term for a master craftsman that emphasizes the lifelong "pursuit of mastery."

In both issues, the profiles from Giant are presented without shoppable links or even a much overt reference to American Giant products. The exceptions are "collections" hosted elsewhere on the American Giant website that coincide with the work of those profiled. In this way, *Giant* is most like earlier brand journalism efforts, in that it provides various faces of the brand but does not do so in an overtly commercial manner. While there is some intangible meaning to be gleaned from these profiles, the emphasis on work—and especially blue-collar work—feels more measured and less aspirational and seductive than other uses of brand journalism.

Uniqlo's *UT Magazine*

Comparatively, *UT Magazine*, produced by Japanese basics clothier Uniqlo offers fewer profiles and provides more information in relation to its extensive line-up of T-shirts, known as UT. In website promos, *UT Magazine* promises "curated stories, interviews with creators, the latest product news and much more," while the "About UT Magazine" page explains that graphic T-shirts "can tell you so much about a person" and closes its description with an anachronism. "By flipping through the pages of this magazine, we hope that you will discover the joys of UT and even a culture that you never knew existed" (Uniqlo, n.d.).

Nevertheless, the U.S. version of *UT magazine* is broken into multiple sections: "Latest," which includes the most recent content across the categories; "Interview," which focuses on creators whose designs are used in the lineup; "Look," which gives styling ideas; a "Keyword" section that uses various hashtags related to the content and T-shirt line, and a "Styling Book," that includes style photos from Uniqlo's wide array of offerings. (The Japanese version of *UT Magazine* does not include a "Styling Book," but does have a section for "Product" that claims to give a "behind the scenes" on how the T-shirt line is made). Although the content mimics some journalistic forms, it does not seek to produce the widespread meaning-making of postmodern branding, nor does it allow readers to forget that the content is largely an advertisement.

For example, the feature "Immerse Yourself in the Cinematic World of Sofia Coppola" is largely a question-and-answer interview with the filmmaker and her collaborator, Jeannie Sui Wonders. From the top of the webpage, a box on the right corner announces this is part of the "Celebrating Sofia Coppola"—"one of the leading female filmmakers directors [sic] of our time"—with a link to the product lineup. Moreover, after the introductory paragraph, another button prompts readers to "View the Collection." The interview itself is broken up by photos that display the products, and after the short interviews, the page contains five photos of T-shirts commemorating Coppola's films with a short explanation of the design and its relationship to the film, along with a link to the product page. It is not until the bottom of the page that photos of the interview subjects along with brief biographies are offered (Uniqlo, 2023d).

Other content here is more informative and less journalistic in nature. For example, "A 100-year Journey through Mickey Mouse's Art Style," a *UT magazine* labeled a "feature," is a timeline of the Disney character Mickey Mouse, from his introduction in 1928's "Steamboat Willie" through the "Mickey Mouse Works" version circa 1999–2000 (Uniqlo, 2023a). Again, the article includes links to the "Mickey Shines" collaboration between Uniqlo and Disney, offers to "view the collection," and promotes specific products throughout the story. Although this article provides authoritative information about Mickey Mouse, this piece does not conform to journalistic standards or the standards of postmodern branding; there is no confusion that the article is a piece of promotional content.

Perhaps the best example of postmodern brand journalism in *UT Magazine* is the article "A day in my life as an art student," which is a Q&A with seven Parisian art students (Uniqlo, 2023b). The students are prompted to respond to an array of questions such as "What is art?" "Where does your creative inspiration come from?" and "What do you like to do in Paris?". While each student is wearing a T-shirt from the UT line, the items vary from the Disney collaboration "Magic for All" to shirts produced with the Louvre Museum and others. Meanwhile, a second piece, "Fun Skateboarding" profiles five professional skateboarders in support of Uniqlo's "Skater Collection" (Uniqlo, 2023c). Unlike the Q&A articles, this piece is written in more of a journalistic manner, documenting the five skaters at a skatepark and linking them to the wider skateboarding trend hitting Japan. Collectively, these pieces — both of the art students and skateboarders — come the closest to providing an idealized user or constructed meaning for Uniqlo's products.

Even so, there is no immersive experience within these articles as they are continually broken up with shoppable links in various forms. There are also limited intangible meanings developed through this content; articles primarily give a history or perspective to the designs used on the garments. As such, *UT magazine* barely supports the development of an intangible brand construct and instead largely provides information or even education about the graphics used by the T-shirt line.

Everworld Stories for Everlane

In many ways, *Everworld Stories* by sustainable clothing company Everlane toes a similar line to *UT magazine*. *Everworld Stories* announces they are "on a mission to clean up a dirty industry," adding: "These are the people, stories, and ideas that will help us get there" (Everlane, n.d.b). The vertical is largely divided into two sections: "The Latest" with an ongoing list of stories that are updated often and "Our Progress," which is more educational and information-driven. This latter heading offers pages to the brand's "carbon commitment," which discusses carbon dioxide emissions and global climate change (Everlane, n.d.a); information about the brand's factories, including a list of comprehensive list of where products are made and how Everlane audits suppliers (Everlane, n.d.d); and an overview of all of Everlane's social responsibility, including environment certifications and the brand's efforts to limit waste and use recycled materials (Everlane, n.d.c).

Everworld Stories articles are labeled under three categories: transparency, people, and style. Similar to the "progress" links, articles tagged as "transparency" document Everlane's sustainable efforts. The story "Black Friday Fund 2023" discussed how the brand launched a fund in 2014 that has raised more than $1.5 million to create better wool and to support New Zealand farms and farmers (Lei, 2023a). Another article, "We won a Glossy Award," is an announcement that Everlane was named the 2023 Sustainable Brand of the Year by fashion outlet *Glossy*. The piece explains its selection, writing: "We were thrilled to be listed amongst other environmentally conscious brand leaders, such as von Halzhausen, Cleobella, For Days, Reformation, and VIVAIA" (Lei, n.d.). The piece goes on to cite Glossy's comments about the brand, thoughts from Everlane's director of sustainability, and an overview of other environmental accomplishments by the brand.

Meanwhile, the "style" tag provides a number of instructional information in much of a journalistic format. Articles like "Coordinate Your Style" (Gardner, n.d.) and "Thanksgiving Outfit Idea" (Gardner, 2023c) act as style guides informing readers of the appropriate attire for different situations. Of course, these articles provide photos of and include text links to various Everlane garments and have a carousel of items at the end of the article, complete with model pictures, descriptions, and prices. Meanwhile, other articles offer advice on how to "wash and maintain" outerwear (Gardner, 2023b) and how to care for sweaters (Gardner, 2023a)—aspects that support the brand's efforts to be environmentally friendly.

The final heading of the "people" gives face to those working on sustainable issues or otherwise in line with Everlane's social responsibility efforts. While not exclusively a practice in diversity, equity, and inclusion, many of these articles focus on people from marginalized backgrounds. For example, pieces dubbed "For the culture" and published around Latinx Heritage Month demonstrate the interview of the executive director of a San Francisco women-led community center (Macias, n.d.), focusing on a women-of-color-led clothing swap in Los Angeles (Lei, 2023d), and profile members of Latino Outdoors, which "supports a national community of leaders in outdoor creation, conservation and environmental education" and "provides leadership, mentorship and professional development opportunities for marginalized communities of color" (Macias, 2023a). Other pieces include an interview with an ACLU attorney for LGBTQ+ Pride Month (Macias, 2023b) and profiles of Everlane's AAPI community (Lei, 2023b). More environmentally focused pieces interviewed Everlane employees about their commitment to sustainability (Lei, 2023c) and people from Recology, a project that aims to recycle waste for new purposes (Lei, 2023e) This final article mixes information on recycling efforts with the subjects expressing what they like about Everlane, as well as questions about their style and making their wardrobe more sustainable. Interestingly, within the "people" tag, only the profiles of eco-conscious consumers include shopping links to recycled products; the stories that profile Latino, AAPI, and LGBTQ+ communities do not include shopping links; however, they do link out to the Latino organizations, the ACLU, and works from AAPI authors.

As such, these pieces walk a link between working to develop a target consumer—those interested in recycling, as well as the various marginalized communities—but do so in a way that highlights Everlane's corporate responsibility and focus on sustainability. Yet, while such pieces underscore the brand's messages, the articles are informative or educational about Everlane's environmental efforts and do not construct an intangible meaning in the same way that past brands have used similar communication. In fact, while such articles undoubtedly promote the brand, they can also be seen as an attempt to assuage concerns and fears that consumers have about the environmental impact of fashion; at the same time, they solidify Everlane's image as an eco-conscious producer.

The Journal by Suitsupply

Finally, unlike the other examples, *The Journal* hosted by Dutch formalwear maker Suitsupply does not profile consumers—or potential consumers—in any way and instead completely leans into information and more service journalism-style pieces. Several pieces under the heading "Behind Our Fabrics" detail both types of fabrics and the mills where the fabrics are made. For example, in an article about the "Tessilmaglia Mill," Suitsupply documents the history of jersey—from its use by fishermen in Jersey in the Channel Islands to its inclusion in women's attire by Coco Chanel—and the development of piqué, a woven material often used for polo shirts (Suitsupply, n.d.i). The mill uses specialized production processes for both fabrics: in the case of jersey, the mill has "specialized machines" and "stretch needles" that avoid damaging the fabric and "specialized looms" for piqué, which create "rich dense fabrics." Finally, the piece ends by declaring that Tessilmaglia Mill uses its "natural surroundings" in Italy, which allows it to "forgo chemicals" and ultimately be more eco-friendly (Suitsupply, n.d.i).

Multiple other articles offer similar profiles of the brand's factory partners. An article on the Weba Mill shows how a Swiss mill crafts "super fine Egyptian and Supima cottons" (Suitsupply, n.d.j), while an article on the Reda Mill traces the facility's 150-year history of "transgenerational excellence" and "artisan excellence" (Suitsupply, n.d.f) and another profiles "Italy's oldest silk weaver" (Suitsupply, n.d.b). Other "Behind Our Fabrics" pieces provide insights into Solaro, "a specifical type of fabric recognizable by its distinct colour and radiance," (Suitsupply, n.d.a) the craft behind creating Giro Inglese, a "highly specialized weave known and celebrated for its rich one-of-a-kind texture" (Suitsupply, n.d.d) and how wool production can be traced from a Tasmanian farm through the Italian weaving mill and the Chinese atelier (Suitsupply, n.d.c).

The rest of *The Journal* is filled with advice aspects including various guides (i.e., style guide and care guide), instructional information about wedding attire, and even explanations for understanding suit and shoe construction. Broadly, these pieces are educational rather than promotional and work to delineate and/or instruct consumers on "proper" or "best" dressing practices. For example, "The Suit Jacket Fit Guide" explains the differences between slim, regular, and relaxed fits including a breakdown of five Suitsupply product silhouettes and which fits they embody (Suitsupply, n.d.h). Similarly, "The Relaxed Trouser Guide" explains the types of fits—straight or tapered—possible waist details and provides "inspiration" photos (Suitsupply, n.d.g). Throughout these guides are links that allow users to shop the products mentioned and/or pictured. Two guides specifically were educational about appropriate wedding attire; one explains formal and semi-formal attire and even advises color selection depending on the season (Suitsupply, n.d.k). The second goes more in-depth, and in addition to breaking down classifications like Black Tie, Black-Tie Optional, Formal Attire, and Cocktail Wedding, the page also includes photo examples, shopping links, and links to a series of YouTube videos, whereby a stylist demonstrates the style on a model (Suitsupply, n.d.e).

While the informational aspect of these pieces works to support the brand image set out by Suitsupply, these articles do not attempt to do it through a meaning-laden construction. Instead, *The Journal* might be the best example of brand journalism in a hypermodern environment insomuch as it emphasizes instruction and information over developing target consumers. By teaching shoppers the proper way to wear a suit, how to tell if a product is high quality, and by sharing information about the company's supply chain, there is an explicit assumption that Suitsupply's products meet these requirements and, as such, the garments and the brand's custom tailoring offers are worth it.

Reconsidering brand journalism in the digital age

The four examples examined here—*Giant, UT magazine, Everworld Stories,* and *The Journal*—underscore not only the use of brand journalism for promotional activities but also how the practice has been changing in the contemporary, digital marketplace. *Giant*, the most traditional of the four products, continues to profile consumers and construct market segments, while the other three examples act as informative and educational aspects for brands; *UT* offers histories of creative works, while both *Everworld Stories* and *The Journal* offer extensive information about the products and supply chains. Moreover, *The Journal* goes so far as to teach consumers about fit and social categorizations vis-à-vis dress codes.

From a brand perspective, it is possible to see this transition between heavily emphasized, constructed lifestyles toward product information as being emblematic of a shift from postmodern to hypermodern brand communication. Brand managers are no longer trying to seduce consumers to purchase symbols for use in their daily lives, but rather brands are trying to be transparent about their production practices and social responsibility efforts including an acknowledgement of factory work and better information about the supply chain. Further, that these media products—like *The Journal*—feel the need to inform shoppers about dress codes and garment fits and share supply chain information supports the contention that hypermodern consumption is full of fear and uncertainty. Education guides that inform shoppers of how products *should* fit and articles that ostensibly show a brand's commitment to environmental responsibility can be seen as corporate communication means to lessen those concerns.

Additionally, today's brand journalism utilizes the additional affordances of digital communication (Rocamora, 2012, 2017, 2019), yet primarily does so in a way that underscores its place as a form of corporate communication, that is, as a means of ultimately selling more products. The most obvious example of this is the use of hyperlinks throughout these publications. Again, except for *Giant*, these publications not only provide information but also prompt shoppers to move to the sales pages and purchase items. These links take various forms—from the "shop now" links and buttons to a list of related products someone might be enticed to buy—but underscore the explicit nature of *selling products* and thus do not allow shoppers to become engaged with the journalistic stories and information in the same way. In other words, it is difficult to get lost here and the fact that these publications are by and for a retailer is omnipresent. Similarly, three of the publications—*Everworld Stores, Giant,* and *The Journal*—along with the content therein only present below a branded banner for the sponsoring retailer. Further, in the case of both Everlane and Suitsupply, there is not an easy back button to the publications, and the service article looks like just another piece of branded content—not part of a tangentially produced publication. Moreover, most of these publications do not even use traditional bylines; *Everlane Stories* is the exception. Instead, these articles imply they are authored or otherwise credited to the brands.

It is for this reason that some of the academic handwringing about brand journalism (e.g., Lee, 2015; Serazio, 2021a, 2021b) seems to be overwrought. Brand journalism, that content produced by and for branding efforts, is—and largely has been—overt in its connections to the brand that helped create it. While contemporary brand journalism seems to be drawing more from the service side of lifestyle journalism rather than profiles or other pieces, it remains clearly marked as a form of brand communication and

The new look of lifestyle guides: Rethinking brand journalism

not something someone is likely to confuse with civic-minded reporting. Today's brand journalism is not even fully attempting to entice shoppers into a fictional or exaggerated use of their product; instead, as the analyzed publications have shown, content seems geared toward informational efforts and transparency. That's not to say related concepts like native advertising are unimportant or unproblematic. However, brand journalism and content produced in the legacy of customer magazines have a long history of existing side-by-side with watchdog and other forms of civic and lifestyle journalism. Even if today's digital environment makes producing such content easier, and thus more available, affordances and conventions keep it clearly labeled as a corporate communication endeavor.

Yet, to some extent, the processes of advertising and branding are always changing and, as such, brand journalism is always in flux. As discussed throughout this chapter, brand journalism in the vein of customer magazines and content has served various purposes: building community, constructing brand meaning, and informing and educating consumers. This ever-changing environment is both a boon and an obstacle for researchers. On one hand, there will always be new brands to explore and new practices to interrogate. On the other hand, it's difficult to anticipate what is new or different until it has already changed. And, due to the increased media fragmentation, brand journalism efforts and publications may come and go without much fanfare, and only hard-core brand followers might notice.

Setting aside the unanticipated turns of brand journalism, there is certainly more work to be done on the production side, including further examinations of decision-making processes of brand managers and more thorough interrogations of writers, editors, and other producers. And, of course, on the consumer end, there will always be a desire to determine what type of brand content is most effective and persuasive for selling purposes.

Yet, what might be most interesting (and indeed what this chapter sought to begin to address) is how communication affordances and styles are changing the *product* of brand journalism. The shift from a print product to digital publications and social media content is remixing and imagining how *all* journalism works—including brand journalism. Consider, for example, cooking brand Tasty. Once a subsection of the media website BuzzFeed, Tasty revolutionized online recipes through its style of video content before becoming a standalone media brand *and* lending its name to a line of cookware sold at Walmart. This might be a case of the tail wagging the dog, but the transition represents a merging of journalistic-style production and brand culture that is emblematic of the contemporary media environment.

Finally, although social media content is not usually considered journalistic, influencer content produced at the behest of brands plays some of the same roles that customer magazines historically have. While examples of such content abound on social media, when dance influencers Twin Sauce (@twinsauce on Instagram) posted sponsored content for a brand of protein shakes, they both provided information about the product, what drinking it helped them throughout the day, and the content made them the face to potential consumers—aspects of brand communication once done (@twinsauce, 2024a). In another video, the dancers posted photos of their shopping haul from clothing brand Nice Laundry, including an unsolicited review of the products and imagery that mimicked the brand aesthetics (@twinsauce, 2024b). Both examples are forms of brand communication that previously might have fallen to publications—like the ones discussed in this chapter—yet are now being done by social media content creators.

Conclusion

In short, brand journalism, in the vein of customer magazines and today's online publications, has been a tool of corporate communications for well over a century. While past publications might have more seriously mimicked civic journalistic forms, the digital affordances of today's brand journalism underscore its role within corporate communications through both its form (i.e., the inclusion of shoppable links) and content, which prioritizes information and education about supply chains and brand offerings. As such, contemporary brand publications seem to be indicative of a hypermodern branding environment that prioritizes transparency and information above intangible meaning constructs. Nevertheless, brand journalism remains a potent and nimble form of promotion that can respond to media and trends in creative and yet-to-be-fully-determined manners.

Further reading

Arrese, Á. and Pérez-Latre, F. J. (2017). "The Rise of Brand Journalism." In G. Siegert, M. B. von Rimscha and S. Grubenmann (eds.), *Commerical Communication in the Digital Age*, 121–140. Berlin: De Gruyter.

Bull, A. (2013). *Brand Journalism*. Routledge.

Dyson, L. (2007). "Customer Magazines: The Rise of 'Glossies" as Brand Extensions." *Journalism Studies*, 8(4): 634–640. Doi: 10.1080/14616700701412159

Koch, T., Viererbl, B. and Schulz-Knappe, C. (2023). "How Much Journalism Is in Brand Journalism? How Brand Journalists Perceive Their Roles and Blur the Boundaries Between Journalism and Strategic Communication." *Journalism*, 24(4): 749–766. Doi: 10.1177/14648849211029802

Serazio, M. (2021). "The Other 'Fake' News: Professional Ideals and Objectivity Ambitions in Brand Journalism." *Journalism*, 22(6): 1340–1356. Doi: 10.1177/1464884919829923

References

Amazeen, M. A. & Muddiman, A. R. (2018). "Saving Media or Trading on Trust? The Effects of Native Advertising on Audience Perceptions of Legacy and Online News Publishers." *Digital Journalism*, 6(2): 176–195. Doi: 10.1080/21670811.2017.1293488

American Giant. (n.d.a). "A Working Magazine." *Giant*, 1. https://web.archive.org/web/20240823020617/https://www.american-giant.com/pages/giant-magazine

American Giant. (n.d.b). "A Working Magazine." *Giant*, 2. https://web.archive.org/web/20240823020617/https://www.american-giant.com/pages/giant-magazine-2

Arnould, E. J. & Tissier-Desbordes, E. (2005). "Hypermodernity and the New Millennium: Scientific Language as a Tool for Marketing Communications." In A. J. Kimmel (ed.), *Marketing Communication: New Approaches, Technologies and Styles*, 236–255. Oxford: Oxford University Press.

Baudrillard, J. (1994). *Simulacra and Simulation*. Ann Arbor: The University of Michigan Press.

Beer, D. (2013). *Popular Culture and New Media: The Politics of Circulation*. New York: Palgrave Macmillan.

Bird, L. (1997, July 29). Advertising: Beyond mail order: Catalogs now sell image, advice. The Wall Street Journal, B1, B3.

Bolter, J. and Grusin, R. (2000). *Remediation: Understanding New Media*. Cambridge, MA: MIT Press.

Bull, A. (2013). *Brand Journalism*. New York: Routledge.

Charles, S. (2009). "For a Humanism Amid Hypermodernity: From a Society of Knowledge to a Critical Knowledge of Society." *Axiomathes*, 19: 389–400. Doi: 10.1007/s10516-009-9090-3

Christensen, L. T. & Askegaard, S. (2001). "Corporate Identity and Corporate Image Revisited – A Semiotics Perspective." *European Journal of Marketing*, 35(3/4): 292–315. Doi: 10.1108/03090560110381814

Cole, J. T. & Greer, J. D. (2013). "Audience Response to Brand Journalism: The Effect of Frame, Source, and Involvement." *Journalism & Mass Communication Quarterly*, 90(4): 673–690. Doi: 10.1177/1077699013503160

Conejo, F. & Wooliscroft, B. (2015). "Brands Defined as Semiotic Marketing Systems." *Journal of Macromarketing*, 35(3): 287–301. Doi: 10.1177/0276146714531147

Danesi, M. (2013). "Semiotizing a Product into a Brand." *Social Semiotics*, 23(4): 464–476. Doi: 10.1080/10350330.2013.799003

Denner, N., Koch, T. & Himmelreich, S. (2018). "News Selection with Customer Magazines: A Quantitative Survey Among Editors-in-Chief in Germany." *Journalism Practice*, 12(7): 888–900. Doi: 10.1080/17512786.2017.1343092

Duffy, B. E. (2013). *Remake, Remodel: Women's Magazines in the Digital Age*. University of Illinois Press.

Dyson, L. (2007). "Customer Magazines: The Rise of 'Glossies" as Brand Extensions." *Journalism Studies*, 8(4): 634–640. Doi: 10.1080/14616700701412159

Engel, S. M. (2004). "Marketing Everyday Life: The Postmodern Commodity Aesthetic of Abercrombie & Fitch." *Advertising & Society Review*, 5(3). Doi: 10.1353/asr.2004.0009

Everlane. (n.d.a). "Earth's Climate Is Changing. We Are Too." https://web.archive.org/web/20240825132628/https://web.archive.org/screenshot/https://www.everlane.com/carbon

Everlane. (n.d.b). "Everworld." https://web.archive.org/web/20240825133028/https://web.archive.org/screenshot/https://www.everlane.com/everworld

Everlane. (n.d.c). "Our Environmental Initiatives." https://web.archive.org/web/20240825133216/https://web.archive.org/screenshot/https://www.everlane.com/sustainability

Everlane. (n.d.d). "Transparent Factories." https://web.archive.org/web/20240825133416/https://web.archive.org/screenshot/https://www.everlane.com/factories

Ferrer Conill, R. (2016). "Camouflaging Church as State: An Exploratory Study of Journalism's Native Advertising." *Journalism Studies*, 17(7): 904–914. Doi: 10.1080/1461670X.2016.1165138

Findlay, R. (2015). "The Short Passionate, and Close-Knit History of Personal Style Blogs." *Fashion Theory*, 19(2): 157–178. Doi: 10.2752/175174115X14168357992319

Fürsich, E. (2012). "Lifestyle Journalism as Popular Journalism: Strategies for Evaluating Its Public Role." *Journalism Practice*, 6(1): 12–25. Doi: 10.1080/17512786.2011.622894

Gardner, B. B. & Levy, S. J. (1955). "The Product and the Brand." *Harvard Business Review*, 33(2): 33–39.

Gardner, N. (2023a). "How to Care for Your Sweaters: 8 Tips to Keep Your Sweaters Cozy." *Everworld Stories*, October. https://web.archive.org/web/20240825133509/https://web.archive.org/screenshot/https://www.everlane.com/everworld/how-to-care-for-your-sweaters-tips

Gardner, N. (2023b). "How to Wash & Maintain Your Outerwear." *Everworld Stories*, October. https://web.archive.org/web/20240825133737/https://web.archive.org/screenshot/https://www.everlane.com/everworld/how-to-wash-&-maintain-your-outerwear

Gardner, N. (2023c). "Thanksgiving Outfit Ideas." *Everworld Stories*, November. https://web.archive.org/web/20240829130948/https://web.archive.org/screenshot/https://www.everlane.com/everworld/thanksgiving-outfit-ideas

Gardner, N. (n.d.). "Coordinating Your Style: Matching Outfits for Everyone." *Everworld Stories*. https://web.archive.org/web/20240825133709/https://web.archive.org/screenshot/https://www.everlane.com/everworld/coordinate-your-outfits-matching-looks

Greer, J. D. (2016). "Brand Journalism." In C. E. Carroll (ed.), *The Sage Handbook of Corporate Reputation* (pp. 82–83). Los Angeles: Sage. Doi: https://doi.org/10.4135/9781483376493.n39

Grow, J. M. (2008). "The Gender of Branding: Early Nike Women's Advertising a Feminist Antenarrative." *Women's Studies in Communication*, 31(3): 312–343.

Hancock, J. H. (2016). *Brand/Story: Cases and Explorations in Fashion Branding*. New York: Bloomsbury.

Hanusch, F. (2012). "Broadening the Focus: The Case for Lifestyle Journalism as a Field of Scholarly Inquiry." *Journalism Practice*, 6(1): 2–11. Doi: 10.1080/17512786.2011.622895

Holt, D. B. (2004), *How Brands Become Icons: The Principles of Cultural Branding*. Boston, MA: Harvard Business School Press.

Holton, A. E. & Molyneux, L. (2017). "Identity Lost? The Personal Impact of Brand Journalism." *Journalism*, 18(2): 195–210. Doi: 10.1177/1464884915608816

Koch, T., Viererbl, B. & Schulz-Knappe, C. (2023). "How Much Journalism is in Brand Journalism? How Brand Journalists Perceive Their Roles and Blur the Boundaries Between Journalism and Strategic Communication." *Journalism*, 24(4): 749–766. Doi: 10.1177/14648849211029802

Kristensen, N. N. & From, U. (2012). "Lifestyle Journalism: Blurring Boundaries." *Journalism Practice*, 6(1): 26–41. Doi: 10.1080/17512786.2011.622898

Lee, K. (2015). *The Rise of Brand Journalism: Understanding the Discursive Dimensions of Collectivity in the Age of Convergence.* [Doctoral dissertation, University of Pennsylvania]. ProQuest Dissertations Publishing.

Lei, A. (2023a). "Black Friday Fund 2023." *Everworld Stories*, November. https://web.archive.org/web/20240825133907/https://web.archive.org/screenshot/https://www.everlane.com/everworld/black-friday-fund-2023

Lei, A. (2023b). "The Everlane Team Celebrates AAPI Heritage Month." *Everworld Stories*, May 19. https://web.archive.org/web/20240825133955/https://web.archive.org/screenshot/https://www.everlane.com/everworld/the-everlane-team-celebrates-aapi-heritage-month

Lei, A. (2023c). "The Everlane Team Celebrates Earth Month 2023." *Everworld Stores*, April 19. https://web.archive.org/web/20240825134123/https://web.archive.org/screenshot/https://www.everlane.com/everworld/the-everlane-team-celebrates-earth-month-2023

Lei, A. (2023d). "For the Culture: Radical Clothes Swap." *Everworld Stories*, September. https://web.archive.org/web/20240825134456/https://web.archive.org/screenshot/https://www.everlane.com/everworld/for-the-culture-radical-clothes-swap

Lei, A. (2023e). "Transparent Conversations with the Recology Team." *Everworld Stories*, April 24. https://web.archive.org/web/20240826163552/https://web.archive.org/screenshot/https://www.everlane.com/everworld/transparent-conversations-with-the-recology-team

Lei, A. (n.d.). "We Won a Glossy Award." *Everworld Stores*. https://web.archive.org/web/20240826163703/https://web.archive.org/screenshot/https://www.everlane.com/everworld/we-won-a-glossy-award

Levy, S. J. (1959). "Symbols for Sale." *Harvard Business Review*, 37(4): 117–124.

Lipovetsky, G. (2005). *Hypermodern Times*. Malden, MA: Polity.

Lury, C. (2004). *Brands: The Logos of the Global Economy*. New York: Routledge.

Macias, N. (2023a). "For the Culture: Latino Outdoors." *Everworld Stories*, October. https://web.archive.org/web/20240825141728/https://web.archive.org/screenshot/https://www.everlane.com/everworld/for-the-culture-latino-outdoors

Macias, N. (2023b). "In Conversation with the ACLU." *Everworld Stories*, June. https://web.archive.org/web/20240825134717/https://web.archive.org/screenshot/https://www.everlane.com/everworld/in-conversation-with-the-aclu

Macias, N. (n.d.). "For the Culture: The Women's Building." *Everworld Stories*. https://web.archive.org/web/20240825134846/https://web.archive.org/screenshot/https://www.everlane.com/everworld/for-the-culture-the-womens-building

Martineau, J. (2017). "Culture in the Age of Acceleration, Hypermodernity, and Globalized Temporalities." *The Journal of Arts Management, Law, and Society*, 47(4): 218–229. Doi: 10.1080/10632921.2017.1369482

Morgado, M. A. (2014). "Fashion Phenomena and the Post-Postmodern Condition: Enquiry and Speculation." *Fashion, Style & Popular Culture*, 1(3): 313–339. Doi: 10.1386/fspc.1.3.313_1

Perdoni, M. (2022). "Two Decades of Fashion Blogging and Influencing: A Critical Overview." *Fashion Theory*, 27(2): 237–268. Doi: 10.1080/1362704X.2021.2017213

Pham, M. H. T. (2015). *Asians Wear Clothes on the Internet: Race, Gender, and the Work of Personal Style Blogging*. Durham, NC: Duke University Press.

Pulizzi, J. (2013). *Epic Content Marketing: How to Tell a Different Story, Break Through the Clutter and Win More Customers by Marketing Less*. New York: McGraw-Hill.

Reilly, A. & Blanco F. J. (2021). *Fashion, Dress and Post-Postmodernism*. New York: Bloomsbury.

Rendtorff, J. D. (2014). *French Philosophy and Social Theory: A Perspective for Ethics and Philosophy of Management*. Netherlands: Springer.

Rendtorff, J. D. (2019). *Philosophy of Management and Sustainability: Rethinking Business Ethics and Social Responsibility in Sustainable Development*. Bingley, UK: Emerald.

Rocamora, A. (2012). "Hypertextuality and Remediation in Fashion Media: The Case of Fashion Blogs." *Journalism Practice*, 6(1): 92–106. Doi: 10.1080/17512786.2011.622914

Rocamora, A. (2017). "Mediatization and Digital Media in the Field of Fashion." *Fashion Theory*, 21(5): 505–522. Doi: 10.1080/1362704X.2016.1173349

Rocamora, A. (2019). "Mediation and Digital Retail." In A. Geczy and V. Karaminas (eds.), *The End of Fashion: Clothing and Dress in the Age of Globalization* (pp. 99–111). New York: Bloomsbury.

Saviolo, S. and Marazza, A. (2013). *Lifestyle Brands: A Guide to Aspirational Marketing*. New York: Palgrave Macmillan.

Serazio, M. (2021a). "How News Went Guerrilla Marketing: A History, Logic, and Critique of Brand Journalism." *Media, Culture & Society*, 43(1): 117–132. Doi: 10.1177/0163443720939489

Serazio, M. (2021b). "The Other 'Fake' News: Professional Ideals and Objectivity Ambitions in Brand Journalism." *Journalism*, 22(6): 1340–1356. Doi: 10.1177/1464884919829923

Swenson, R. D. (2012). *Brand Journalism: A Cultural History of Consumers, Citizens and Community in* Ford Times. [Doctoral dissertation, University of Minnesota]. University of Minnesota Digital Conservancy, https://hdl.handle.net/11299/127279.

Schijns, J. M. C. (2008). "Customer Magazines: An Effective Weapon in the Direct Marketing Armory." *Journal of International Business and Economics*, 8(3): 70–78.

Strömbäck, J. & Dimitrova, D. V. (2011). "Mediatization and Media Interventionism: A Comparative Analysis of Sweden and the United States." *The International Journal of Press/Politics*, 16(1): 30–49. Doi: 10.1177/1940161210379504

Suitsupply. (n.d.a). "Discover the One-of-a-Kind Character of Solaro Fabric." https://web.archive.org/web/20230602160459/https://suitsupply.com/en-us/journal/solaro-fabric.html

Suitsupply. (n.d.b). "Fermo Fossati Mill." https://web.archive.org/web/20240825135126/https://web.archive.org/screenshot/https://suitsupply.com/en-se/journal/fossati-mill.html

Suitsupply. (n.d.c). "Fully Traceable from Sheep to Shop." https://web.archive.org/web/20240825135344/https://web.archive.org/screenshot/https://suitsupply.com/en-se/journal/fully-traceable-merino-wool.html

Suitsupply. (n.d.d). "Giro Inglese, the Height of Elevated Craftsmanship." https://web.archive.org/web/20230401105013/https://suitsupply.com/en-us/journal/giro-inglese-mill.html

Suitsupply. (n.d.e). "A Guide to Formal Wedding Attire for Men." https://web.archive.org/web/20240825135705/https://web.archive.org/screenshot/https://suitsupply.com/en-us/journal/formal-wedding-attire-for-men.html

Suitsupply. (n.d.f). "The Reda Mill." https://web.archive.org/web/20240825140025/https://web.archive.org/screenshot/https://suitsupply.com/en-se/journal/reda-mill.html

Suitsupply. (n.d.g). "The Relaxed Trouser Guide." https://web.archive.org/web/20240825135758/https://suitsupply.com/en-us/journal/relaxed-trousers-guide.html

Suitsupply, (n.d.h). "The Suit Jacket Fit Guide." https://web.archive.org/web/20240131074732/https://suitsupply.com/en-us/journal/the-suit-jacket-fit-guide.html

Suitsupply. (n.d.i). "Tessilmaglia Mill." https://web.archive.org/web/20230322214557/https://suitsupply.com/en-us/journal/tessilmaglia-mill.html

Suitsupply. (n.d.j). "The Weba Mill." https://web.archive.org/web/20240825140154/https://web.archive.org/screenshot/https://suitsupply.com/en-se/journal/weba-mill.html

Suitsupply. (n.d.k). "Wedding Attire for Men Explained." https://web.archive.org/web/20240825140335/https://web.archive.org/screenshot/https://suitsupply.com/en-us/journal/wedding-attire-for-men-explained.html

Turow, J. (2011). *The Daily You: How the New Advertising Industry is Defining Your Identity and Your Worth*, New Haven, CT: Yale University Press.

TwinSauce [@twinsauce]. (2024a, April 15). *A day in our lives with the new #QuestIcedCoffee* [Instagram video]. Instagram. https://www.instagram.com/p/C5yQ9Qnu090/

TwinSauce [@twinsauce]. (2024b, April 19). *Out @nicelaundry haul! We have been eyeing their stuff for a LONG TIME and finally pulled the trigger and bought some pieces to try*. [Instagram post]. https://www.instagram.com/twinsauce/p/C58t3h1uqTK/

Uniqlo. (n.d.). "About UT Magazine." https://web.archive.org/web/20240825140428/https://www.uniqlo.com/us/en/contents/feature/ut-magazine/about/

Uniqlo. (2023a). "A 100-Year Journey Through Mickey Mouse's Art Style." *UT Magazine*, November 6. https://www.uniqlo.com/us/en/contents/feature/ut-magazine/s191-mickeyshines/

Uniqlo. (2023b). "A Day in My Life as An Art Student." *UT Magazine*, May 23. https://web.archive.org/web/20240825140811/https://www.uniqlo.com/us/en/contents/feature/ut-magazine/s182-art-students-in-paris/

Uniqlo. (2023c). "Fun Skateboarding." *UT Magazine*, January 29. https://web.archive.org/web/20240825140929/https://www.uniqlo.com/us/en/contents/feature/ut-magazine/s158/

Uniqlo. (2023d). "Immerse yourself in the Cinematic World of Sofia Coppola." *UT Magazine*, May 23. https://web.archive.org/web/20240825125643/https://www.uniqlo.com/us/en/contents/feature/ut-magazine/s181-celebrating-sofia-coppola/

van Reijmersdal, E. A., Neijens, P. C. & Smitm, E. G. (2010). "Customer Magazines: Effects of Commerciality on Readers' Reactions." *Journal of Current Issues and Research in Advertising*, 32(1): 59–67. Doi: 10.1080/10641734.2010.10505275

Wigley, S. M., Nobbs, K. & Larsen, E. (2013). "Making the Marque: Tangible Branding in Fashion Product and Retail Design." *Fashion Practice*, 5(2): 245–64. Doi: 10.2752/175693813X13705243201577.

Wojdynski, B. W. & Evans, N. J. (2016). "Going Native: Effects of Disclosure Position and Language on the Recognition and Evaluation of Online Native Advertising." *Journal of Advertising*, 45(2): 157–168. Doi: 10.1080/00913367.2015.1115380

Yarnykh, V. (2023). "Brand Journalism Approach in Corporate Communication of Educational Organization." *International Journal of Mass Communication*, 1: 8–12. https://lifescienceglobal.com/pms/index.php/IJMC/article/view/9021

29
INTIMACY AND COMMUNITY BUILDING IN LIFESTYLE JOURNALISM 'DIALOGUES'

Lucia Vodanovic

Introduction

Both journalism research and industry practices have experienced a heightened interest in audiences in the past few years, responding to a general understanding that the public is crucial in dimensions as varied as the newsgathering process, the financial viability of the profession, or its social role, among several others. This has led to academic discussion and industry experimentation into participatory, interactive, or even collaborative pursuits, which, according to Hornmoen and Steensen (2014), emphasise the dialogical nature of journalism. In its current iteration, "dialogue" in journalism speaks of audience participation, the blurring of boundaries between consumers and producers, and between private and public spheres. It also speaks of the fact that the site of news production has moved away from traditional newsrooms (Hornmoen & Steensen, 2014) and that the audience is an intrinsic aspect of newsgathering activities as the boundary between professionals (very often freelancers, not loyal to a single news organisation) and non-professionals has also been blurred. "They [journalists] can no longer ignore audience feedback, but must relate to it in, for instance, comments to their stories, and their texts must increasingly relate to other texts in a dialogical relationship to hyperlinks" (Hornmoen & Steensen, 2014, p. 546). According to the authors, the digital era has opened a Pandora's Box of more and more opportunities for these "dialogical relationships between journalist and sources, text and sources, text and other texts, text and audiences, journalists and audiences, sources and audiences, and between audiences" (Hornmoen & Steensen, 2014, p. 546).

Even though those various dialogical relationships form part of the whole ecology of contemporary journalism, this chapter pays particular attention to the interaction of the journalist and their audience in forums facilitated or created by lifestyle journalists. 'Below the line comments, – about which I have written elsewhere (Vodanovic, 2019) – constitute one of the many forms of participatory journalism that have transformed the relationship between journalists and audiences, creating a space for engagement with the public and even the production of news content in a more collaborative fashion (Wright et al., 2020). Like other digital platforms, they provide opportunities for users to comment on, criticise, praise, clarify, or interrogate news content, while also allowing readers to like or dislike other users' posts and engage in direct conversations with them; the former has been characterised as "user-content interactivity" and is primarily a form of feedback, while the latter has been described as "user-user interactivity" and takes the form of a dialogue or conversation between commenters (Ksiazek et al., 2016). I am interested in how these interactions can facilitate people's public connection within groups based on the significance of sharing news, fostering communities, creating common terms of reference, and aiding social integration, forms of engagement that are arguably very visible in lifestyle journalism as audiences coalesce around niche interest such as food, fashion, and music. Forums that facilitate interactions between journalists and their audiences are not limited to 'below the line' comments, particularly in the case of freelancers who build these audiences across various platforms and very often outside – or alongside – news organisations that they might work for. These conversations are also to be found, for instance, under social media posts, on their websites, or in dialogues facilitated by newsletters, a contemporary format that is very often used by lifestyle journalists.

This chapter unpacks these dialogues by using the notion of "intimacy" and how it facilitates the creation of communities that coalesce around a journalist. It argues that lifestyle journalism is a particularly fertile terrain to explore these notions, given that lifestyle content often uses a mode of address characterised by personal narratives written in first person that invite those dialogues, in which the journalist is regularly cast as a "friend" or equal among other roles (Vodanovic, 2019), while also being a form of journalism in which freelancing and precarious work is commonly found. In this way, journalists create communities around themselves that they can bring to different media outlets and/or their entrepreneurial activities.

To do so, this chapter starts with a general overview of issues of audience engagement and reciprocity and how they are played out in lifestyle journalism. It then discusses the notion of intimacy in the journalist-audience relationship, arguing that the intersection of three elements in the work of lifestyle journalists contributes to the creation of a perceived and/or real community: self-expression and aesthetic content, confessional or first-person writing, and freelancing/entrepreneurial culture. It then further explores the concept of reciprocity, the forms it takes in contemporary lifestyle journalism, and how it could be illustrated with dialogues found around the work of three female lifestyle journalists, before finishing with some remarks about the directions that these practices might take in the future.

Contemporary perspectives on audience studies

There is an agreement amongst scholars that, until relatively recently, the audience of journalism was often disregarded both in industry and in research about the profession. Costera Meijer (2019) has explained this omission in academia by arguing that journalism research has traditionally been based on professional practices and newsroom activities, so if the "user" (audience) is not the main concern of the "producer" (news outlets and individual journalists), then readers, viewers, and listeners are not sufficiently studied. Additionally, being overly concerned with the audience was often associated with negative developments in the profession such as the popularisation of journalism and sensationalism. "Audience interests were thought to be trivial and superficial, and consequently listening to audiences was seen as inevitably leading to a decline of journalistic quality" (Costera Meijer & Groot Kormelink, 2019 p. 3). More recently, Costera Meijer (2020) has argued that this is no longer the case and that we are now experiencing an "audience turn" in journalism, even though the production-oriented focus has continued to exist or at least co-exist with this approach.

Contemporary research by different authors also speaks of an audience turn in both industry and journalism studies with various emphases, a topic that was covered in a special issue of the journal *Digital Journalism* in 2022. Hendrickx (2023), for instance, focuses on the notion of "agency" (of individuals, organised groups, and collective audiences) to develop a conceptual framework that might be helpful for the study of audiences, while Blassnig and Esser (2022) investigate this audience turn in relation to commercial logic, asking if a new "connection-strengthening audience logic" has emerged in addition to the commercial interests. Both authors and others such as Truyens and Picone (2024), who focus on what the audience thinks of this so-called audience turn; Vos et al. (2019), who write about "journalistic capital" in the context of audiences; and Carlson and Peters (2023), who research audiences' "sense making practices", situate the emergence of digital journalism as the moment from which the audience could no longer be ignored. Beyond the use of metrics in industry and research – how many visitors a news page has, how much time they spend on it, and do they share it or not – those practices of "making sense", and how they coexist with other media and discursive forms, are important for the notion of dialogues in lifestyle journalism that will be developed later in this chapter.

"Engagement" is arguably the most common notion found in discussions about audiences in journalism. "Audiences can be measured through a broad array of metrics, usually referred to as 'engagement', which includes clicks, shares, comments, time spent, likes, and return visits (Napoli, 2011). In this context, the "practice of commenting highlights an active user that is challenging, supporting, or at the very least reflecting on the news" (Ksiazek et al., 2016, p. 505). "Although the term engagement calls up positive associations with active citizenship like in the previous quote, it is aimed at making *news* more engaging rather than citizens more engaged", write Costera Meijer and Groot Kormelink (2019, p. 4). This understanding of audiences simply as metrics is also mirrored in some journalism research, which still focuses primarily on the production aspects of the profession (Carlson & Peters, 2023). "Research addressing news audiences still tends to talk more *about* audiences than *with* audiences", describe Swart et al. (2022, p. 8).

For that reason, Swart et al. (2022) have called for a more "radical" turn of audience studies, based on four points: decentring journalism so that it can focus on other news or non-news; broadening the understanding of audiences so that marginal audiences can be considered; paying attention to what people consider as informative; and regarding audiences as active. What counts as news, what "feels" like news, and what people do with it are included in this approach (Swart et al., 2022), which resonates with Costera's (2019) broader understanding of news as "social experience".

This wider preoccupation with audiences' perceptions of news and individual and social behaviour around it is important in the context of lifestyle journalism, particularly in the discussion of dialogues between journalists and audiences that exceed the strict values of what mainstream media might regard as newsworthy. Costera Meijer (2019) extends her argument by noting that, traditionally, the concern about a perceived or real quality decline if audiences are given "what they want" has been expressed in a desire for audiences to focus on "hard news" such as politics, economics, and current affairs at the expense of "soft news" such as travel, food, fashion, and the majority if not all, the beats associated with lifestyle journalism (a distinction that, nonetheless, has been challenged or problematised by some authors such as Lehman-Wilzig & Seletzky, 2010; Boczkowski, 2009). A focus on other dimensions of journalism, including the emotional and interactional aspects, the embodied and the material, such as the one proposed precisely by Costera Meijer (2019), could provide a frame for the study of the dialogues facilitated by lifestyle journalism, which, so far, has been omitted in contemporary discussions about audiences or, at least, has not been studied in its specificity.

In this vein, the concept of "reciprocal journalism", developed by Lewis et al. (2014) and Holton et al. (2020), might be more appropriate than traditional notions of audience engagement as metrics to discuss the exchanges between lifestyle journalists and their audiences and how they create offline and online communities through those exchanges. "*Reciprocal journalism*, as we call it, builds upon and yet departs from traditional notions of audience engagement and participation, capturing the range of dynamics through which journalists and audiences may exchange mutual benefit" (Lewis et al., 2014, p. 230). In their argument, if sustained over time, those relationships get clustered in communities, which constitutes an unrealised potential of participatory journalism. As a result, the authors see journalists as, potentially, "community-builders who can forge connections with and among community members by establishing patterns of reciprocal exchange" (Lewis et al., 2014, p. 236) and who are equipped to "catalyse patterns of reciprocal exchange—directly with readers, indirectly with community members, and repeatedly over time—that, in turn, may contribute to greater trust, connectedness, and social capital" (Lewis et al., 2014, p. 229).

Conceptions of audience as "community" are very visible in the lifestyle journalism ecology and appear regularly in the exchanges between journalists and audiences in various forums, particularly in social media and conversations to be found around newsletters, blog posts, and personal websites. This is arguably a result of the different roles that journalists adopt in these exchanges and of the audience's perception of their work, which ranges from top-down expert advice (product recommendations, "how to's") to horizontal relationships in which the journalist is cast as an equal and therefore responds to comments as if they were a friend, relative, or acquaintance of the audience member (Vodanovic, 2019). My previous research about the beauty section of the online site of the British news outlet *The Guardian* (Vodanovic, 2019), for instance, discusses how in some interactions between the beauty journalist Sali Hughes and her readers, the experiences of both parties come together to talk about similar and intimate affairs such as the death of a friend, the role of scent as a trigger for memories about people and events, body image, and other personal matters. This is also the Sali Hughes' interviewing style in her podcast *Beyond the Bathroom*, where she talks to women in the public eye about their appearance and the role that it plays, or not, in their lives. Very often, the journalist comments that she "feels the same" about something or that she has also had a similar experience to that of the interviewee, which is less likely to happen in other genres of journalism. In these interactions, the notion of a community of beauty lovers is often reinforced.

Critical issues and themes

Various scholars have noted that lifestyle journalism has not been as researched as other forms of journalism in academic publishing (Hanusch, 2019a, 2019b; Hanusch & Hanitzsch, 2013; Vodanovic, 2019), so perhaps it is not entirely surprising that the current "audience turn" described above has not paid enough attention to the specific nature of the journalist–audience relationship within this genre. It is a significant omission though because this is a particularly fertile terrain to explore this relationship, given that lifestyle content often uses a mode of address characterised by personal narratives written in first person that invite those dialogues, in which the journalist is regularly cast as a "friend" or equal among other roles (Vodanovic, 2019).

In her research about lifestyle magazines, for instance, Favaro (2017) argues that journalists from publications such as *Cosmopolitan* and *Elle* in the United Kingdom, and *grazia.es* and *nosotras.com* in Spain, describe their relationship with readers as "intimate" and state that they follow a "listening to a friend" approach when making editorial decisions. Positioning the reader as their "best friend" informs their work at all times: they research stories by paying attention to what is being discussed in social media (which the journalists interviewed described as a form of "audience research"). They also often use personal experiences as a narrative tool, and they see themselves as the "target audience" of their publications as if there was a match or symmetry between the journalists and their readers. In their interviews with the researcher, journalists "highlighted notions of 'camaraderie' and 'a fun community-esque thing'. Women's magazines were declared to render a valuable sense of 'being part of a gang' and 'part of a community', 'clique', 'tribe' or 'group'" (Favaro, 2017, p. 324).

According to Favaro (2017), this emphasis on stories that matter to readers at a personal level mirrors the focus on intimacy and authenticity of Web 2.0 cultures. The latter often exposes complex dynamics between the very personal stories shared and the very public displays of emotion between various parties, practices that have been described by Kaplan (2021) as a form of "public intimacy" or the performance of interpersonal ties in front of a third party. This happens when "friends" or "followers" respond to a post on social media, when people like each other's content and share it with a wider public, or indeed when journalists interact with their audience in a public forum that is then witnessed by other readers and members of the community, who then might like and leave a comment related to that exchange, and eventually develop a reader-to-reader interaction under the umbrella of the journalist who is acting as a host or community manager.

Intimacy, as a notion and a practice, invokes the aspiration of a shared story. Chambers (2017) identifies three moments in society's recent aspirations of intimacy: the "elective intimacies" of the mid to late 20th century, in which individuals became less determined by external frames of reference (family, religion, and national boundaries) and were able to choose relationships based on compatibility and friendship; a second phase of "fluid intimacy" with social dependency often based on transient connections and "families of choice"; and a third moment constructed around networks and loose systems of interaction in which individuals with shared interests come together and meet around values such as choice, agency, flexibility, respect, mutual disclosure, and companionship. This last phase, the author argues, exhibits two contradictory logics: "One emphasises exclusiveness and privacy, and the other emphasises social connectedness and sharing" (Chambers, 2017, p. 28). Chambers (2017) sees contemporary digital friendships (between people who might know each other or not in the offline world) as archetypical in this third moment of networked and mediated intimacy.

Three elements of lifestyle journalism coalesce to facilitate dialogues between journalists and their audience that can be characterised by this notion of networked and mediated intimacy. Firstly, this is a form of journalism that is often discussed in the context of "self-expression": "Since lifestyles carry an expressive component, they can therefore be understood as the expression – or even exhibition – of one's self along with one's individual 'way of life'" (Hanusch & Hanitzsch, 2013, p. 946). Given that our identities are not as determined by external terms of references as they were in the past, primarily but not exclusively in Western societies, the "self" becomes a project or a task to be produced and reproduced. This is what Ouellette (2016) has referred to as the "enterprising model of subjectivity" in lifestyle media. Several intermediaries, including journalists, come to help with this enterprise of creativity and self-expression, shaping tastes, aspirations, body and beauty ideals, and consumer preferences (Ouellette, 2016, p.7). In this context, the lifestyle journalist can adopt the "role perception of the friend, who may act as a companion or even therapist to help audiences 'navigate the task of identity work'" (Hanusch, 2019a, p. 197), as well as connecting audience members in their shared identity. This process of identity creation fosters identification with one group and differentiation with another group, resulting in the creation of off and online communities that come together around a particular interest such as fashion, food, gaming, or travel.

Secondly, both personal experiences and intimate accounts are often found in the lifestyle journalism space, alongside expressions of taste and identity of the journalists themselves, who often engage in influencer-adjacent content such as *"get ready with me"*, *"what I eat in a day"*, or *"my body acceptance journey"* in their social media interactions, revealing their preferences and routines. These personal narratives of expression and identity are examples of what has been termed "confessional society" by Rosalind Coward (2010). Coward's work (2009, 2010, 2013), with a focus on what she calls "confessional journalism", discusses the centrality of intimate stories about lived experiences and personal journeys in journalism. She defines it as a form of "autobiographical writing exposing intimate personal details [which is] part of [a] rapidly growing cultural trend towards the inclusion of 'real life' stories in the media and linked to exposure of ever more intimate personal details" (Coward, 2010, p. 224). While the confessional tone is not exclusive to lifestyle journalism, Coward (2013) argues that its presence in mainstream media is a consequence of the "feminisation" of journalism, which has now become more adept at discussing issues such as mental health, body image, sexuality, and relationship that in the past were only to be found in so-called women's pages. Journalism is not an isolated realm and therefore reflects societal trends like the growing preoccupation with subjectivity and emotions, yet Coward – an academic and a journalist who for years wrote a newspaper column about caring for her mother living with dementia – also acknowledges that this recent emphasis is a result of "the push of feminism and featurisation towards more personal and intimate subjects" (2013, p. 88).

Molyneux's (2019) research about the self "branding" of journalists has established that female journalists (the majority of those who work in the lifestyle field) tend to be more personal than their male counterparts in the way they speak about themselves and in their interactions with their audiences. This is evident in the social media accounts of various lifestyle journalists, which bring together professional or work-related posts – a recent work trip, a link to a magazine article, an industry award – with content from their personal or non-work lives – weddings and anniversary photos, milestones of their children's lives, pets, holidays, and the outfits worn during them. Aspects of this content exist in what Maares and Hanusch (2020) call the "twilight" of lifestyle journalism, a grey zone between what journalists and Instagram micro-influencers do on social media. Several of them are represented by talent agencies such as Insanity Group in the United Kingdom and the United States and are booked for brand events and as hosts of various functions.

Their web profiles on those agency sites list both their professional achievements and biographical information such as the city where they live or their relationship status. This speaks to the third element of lifestyle journalism that creates a very distinct relationship with its audiences: how the personal narratives described above coexist with commercial logics, entrepreneurialism, and branding practices. In a field heavily characterised by freelancing, lifestyle journalists need to develop strategies to demonstrate their added value to both employers and audiences.

> By developing a relationship with the audience is also part of the value proposition individual journalists make to their employers, both present and future: I can bring you this information, this writing expertise, and also this group of followers who are already interested in my content.
>
> (Holton & Molyneux, 2017, p. 199)

Audience maintenance is a significant dimension of these branding practices, which takes the form of answering queries in 'below the line' comments, responding to requests on social media, liking and sharing audiences' posts, and using journalists' personalities as the main currency. "Being 'personal' is crucial in building a personal brand by means of social media" (Hedman & Djerf-Pierre, 2013, p. 372). Authors such as Olausson (2018) have summarised these processes of self-production, commodification, and promotion within journalism with the notion of a "celebrified" journalist, while Markham (2012) has discussed how the use of headshots in online and print, the activity of journalists in comment forums, and the personal authorial voice in news writing allude to a form of agency that is primarily individualist and personal yet also constrained by larger industry pressures. "The notion that you cannot and should not write yourself out of your work is perhaps philosophically pragmatic, supported even by author-deconstructing thinkers such as Derrida", he writes (Markham, 2012, p. 188), suggesting both a demand for and a strategy built around these intimate exchanges, with ambivalent consequences for journalists, audiences, and the industry at large.

Current research and examples

Favaro's (2017) work on lifestyle magazines constitutes an example of these efforts in audience maintenance and their links to both commercial imperatives and readers' cravings for authentic and intimate content.

> Contributing to their success, women's online magazines offer free of charge content, and significantly greater opportunities for interaction. This includes 'internal' features in the form of discussion boards and/or comment sections under the editorial, along with the possibility to engage with social media by 'liking', 'sharing', 'retweeting' or 'pinning' content.
>
> (Favaro, 2017, p. 321)

The lifestyle journalists interviewed in her research state that these interactions with the audience motivate the readers to share the content through their networks, and so drives traffic. "Therefore, 'being real' content is the profitably shareable content, as required by a business model based on virality" (Favaro, 2017, p. 328), while also being content that audiences perceive as more real and less mass produced. These findings support earlier work about the social and business merits of audience participation, in terms of enhancing the user's ability to get and recall new information, leading to social engagement and creating roots for communities online (Meyer & Carey, 2014).

These audience practices in magazine culture and lifestyle journalism more broadly embody what was conceptualised earlier in this chapter, based on the work of Lewis et al. (2014), as "reciprocal journalism", a notion that speaks of the mutually beneficial relationships that journalists develop with their audiences. This reciprocity takes the shape of different forms of exchange: direct exchanges between the journalist and their audiences in a one-to-one fashion, for instance, when the journalist responds directly to an individual comment below the line or takes the time to respond to a direct message sent through Instagram or one of the other social media platforms; indirect messages intended for community benefit, as they are witnessed by third parties and so embody the notion of networked intimacy also described earlier; and sustained reciprocity, which is fostered through exchanges that occur repeatedly over time. Sustained reciprocity "resituates journalists in the network. It casts them in a community manager role" (Lewis et al., 2014, p. 167). The role of the community manager and advocate involves different and varied tasks, from providing a forum for readers' comments and questions to fostering and reinforcing that community of interest, while also engaging in more critical practices "advocating for audiences' interests, telling audiences about ethical and moral dimensions of certain lifestyles and experiences, and monitoring and scrutinizing businesses involved in the lifestyle industries" (Hanusch, 2019a, p. 201).

These different forms of mutually beneficial relationships between journalists and their audiences might even be taken offline. It is not uncommon for lifestyle journalists to host events, for instance, ticketed or not; invite their audiences to come and meet them personally; and attend book launches and signings. Various lifestyle journalists have been involved in commercial enterprises outside yet linked to their profession and expertise, so those interactions also become ways for them to promote their products in an informative manner (instead of a conventional sales pitch) and for audiences to engage in conversations about how much they enjoy them. Pandora Sykes, for instance, had a brand collaboration with swimwear range Hunza G when she was working as the fashion features editor at *The Sunday Times Style* in the United Kingdom; beauty and health journalist Nadine Baggott has done Beauty Box Sets with high street chemist Superdrug, in addition to her work for various newspapers, magazines, and television programmes. These commercial activities are further iterations of the intimate yet commercial logic that governs the journalist-audience relationship as described in the previous section.

It is important to note that research into journalist-audience interactions in general, and 'below the line' comments in particular, has highlighted that not all journalists have positive views about these exchanges. For instance, initial research by Hermida and Thurman (2008) speaks of "a clash of cultures" in UK newspaper websites concerning user-generated content (of which 'below the line the comments' is a significant dimension alongside other forms of participation such as polls and "have your say" sections). The authors argue that even though tools and opportunities for audience participation had become more available, in those early years, editors expressed doubts about their commercial value given that moderation has a cost and that the opportunity to monetise these interactions was unclear at the time. More recently, Wright et al. (2020) have researched *The Guardian*'s 'below the line' comments space and established that, while there is a considerable interest in comment spaces among readers, an exponential growth in user commenting and substantial engagement by some journalists – a dynamic that the author describes through the notion of "sustained reciprocity" that has been used here too –, journalists' responses to audience comments have recently waned. The reasons cited are to do with cost/benefit logics, concerns about abuse and uncivility, lack of clarity about the value added of these comments, and editorial changes (Wright et al., 2020). The negative effects of abuse and harassment from news audiences are often mentioned in the recent literature about the mental health and wellbeing of journalists (Šimunjak, 2023; Bélair-Gagnon et al., 2024; Storm, 2024). This can be made worse if work is precarious, as is often the case with freelancers and self-employed journalists (Van Leuven & Vandenberghe, 2024).

The lifestyle space of the news organisation reflects this change: for instance, the beauty section of *The Guardian* that I studied elsewhere (Vodanovic, 2019) is currently closed for comments after the columnist Sali Hughes was embroiled in a long series of Internet attacks that she documented in the BBC Radio 4 audio series *Me and My Trolls* (2020), with consequences for her mental health and personal life. Hughes has continued to engage extensively with audiences on her social media platforms though, where she shares a mixture of personal and professional content, promotes her skincare range Sali Hughes for Revolution, and answers questions from readers about her published work in various outlets, including her weekly column for *The Guardian*. It could be argued that this reflects Olausson's concept of "individualisation" in journalism, the "trend among the most active journalists to exploit social media to create personal brands and promote themselves as individual professionals rather than (or possibly in parallel with) their role as employees of a particular news organisation" (2018, pp. 2379–2380). Despite the longevity of her column (it has been published weekly for over 15 years), Hughes contributes to *The Guardian* in a freelance capacity, and therefore "digital disconnection" strategies – including muting or deleting social media accounts altogether – , which have been discussed as potentially beneficial for the mental health, work management, and wellbeing of journalists (Šimunjak, 2023), might have a financial cost for her. On social media, she does sponsored and non-sponsored beauty and lifestyle content (including Instagram "lives" filmed during family holidays) and also adds to and expands on her journalistic practice. This defence and explanation of why and how journalists do their work is identified by Wright et al. (2020) as one of the ways in which journalists have continued to maintain audience reciprocity despite the recent overall wane in their responses to the public. Arguably, it is also one of the most important contributions to the journalist industry that these spaces for dialogue can make, as there are few other spaces where this type of conversation can take place.

Lifestyle journalists, particularly those who are freelancers, invest heavily in audience engagement in their platforms, either alongside, or sometimes in place of, interactions on news and magazine sites. The use of newsletters – hosted either by Substack or other subscription newsletter platforms – for instance, has become a relatively recent but a very popular addition to the contemporary ecology of journalism. They have also been discussed as particularly useful for freelance journalists who want to interact with their audiences directly, build their personal brands, and foster and expand their communities (Andringa, 2022). Themes such as "imagined audiences", "reciprocal exchanges", and "parasocial relationships" have started to be explored in the emergent research into this area (Andringa, 2022), alongside the notion of a "digital epistolary" (Santos & Peixinho, 2017), which emphasises the dialogical nature of the medium. From an industry perspective, a recent report published by the Reuters Institute for the Study of Journalism (Newman, 2022) states that the top two recent audience-facing innovations according to publishers and editors were podcasts (80 percent) and email newsletters (70 percent), which speaks of the increasing popularity and relevance of the format. Substack, in particular, has been called the "New New Thing" in mainstream media (Naughton, 2023). Lifestyle sectors such as Food & Drink, Fashion & Beauty, and Parenting, among others, are heavily represented in the "Discover" section aimed at Substack (n.d) readers. The same platform has a separate link in the "For Writers" section aimed specifically at food writers (Substack, n.d.).

The type of content that Katherine Omerod creates is illustrative of how dialogues between her and the audience work in this new space created by newsletters. After a career of 15 years as a lifestyle and features journalist in publications such as *Grazia*, *Glamour*, and *The Sunday Times Style*, and a parallel one doing content for Instagram and working with brands, she launched her newsletter *Every Shade of Grey* on Substack, which was free for subscribers until November 1, 2023, and now has a membership model that allows readers to access a small portion of the content for free and paid subscribers to get full access. The trade-offs of this change are discussed by Omerod in the post "How desperate are you" (2023e), where she worries about what her audience will think of the new, transactional setup given the close bonds they have with her, talks about the likely decrease in subscribers and what would it mean for her career, and offers to gift a subscription to those readers who can't afford it (with no specification of a means tested process), which suggests a model based on loyalty and community, but also commercial value and privileged access.

Omerod's subscribers receive a weekly newsletter delivered to their emails and partial or full access to her website, where the dialogues between her and the readers take place. The newsletters encompass all aspects of everyday life, from health to relationships, careers, children, interiors, hosting dinners, and online safety, among others, often written in an honest and confessional tone that heavily resonates with readers who leave comments on her website. "Forget confidence: steadfastness is a far more realistic goal" (Omerod, 2023d), her newsletter from September 17th containing a mixture of life coaching advice and career tips, shows 'below the line' comments from readers such as "I have tears in my eyes reading this", which highlight how audience members feel that they are very seen in her experience. Similarly, her post about having a pregnancy termination for medical reasons contains a dialogue between an audience member stating "in it together" and Omerod replying "love you mate" (2023b). Another newsletter entry, "My children may kill each other, I've been told this is normal" (Omerod, 2023c), from August 6th, gets a reply that says "I will genuinely sleep better tonight so thank you", followed by a heart emoji, once again highlighting the similarity between the reader experience and that of Omerod. A third one, "Getting shit done doesn't make you a good person" (Omerod, 2023a) about being overly productive in all areas of life from career to parenting, to the detriment of oneself, published on January 15th, gets several comments about how it resonates with readers. One poster sends a message with the wording: "Sending you so much love, XXXX". In the 'below the line' exchanges under this third example, Omerod (2023a) expands on the topics already discussed, revealing, for instance, what she does when and if she manages to relax. She also likes readers' posts and writes hearts and other emojis with various face expressions. Interestingly, several of the posters also have their Substacks, so audience members who are witnessing and reading those exchanges can also click directly on the username and access the site of a different newsletter. 'Below the line' comments in the examples just cited come from content creators such as Emma Louise Boynton from the "Writers Swipe Right" newsletter; Louise Hallan, who writes "The Wisdom Path"; and Sarah Copeland, author of the popular food and travel newsletter "Edible Living" about recipes and travelogues.

A slightly different model is that of *That's Not My Age*, the fashion site and monthly newsletter founded by Alyson Walsh, dedicated to older women. Walsh is another freelance journalist and former magazine fashion editor and the author of the book *Know Your Style*. Various aspects of her site emphasise the notion of community described earlier in the chapter. For instance, there is an exclusive section for paid Patreon subscribers only (the rest of the content is available for free). The invitation to become one tells readers to "join the community" (Walsh, n. d.), whereas the phrase that encourages audience members to post comments reads "start a conversation" (Walsh, n. d.), also used by other digital lifestyle publications such as *Refinery 29*. Even though Walsh's content is primarily fashion and beauty (the subtitle of the site is "the grown-up guide to great style"), the website also includes stories about books, films, interiors, health, menopause, and others. The tone of her interactions with readers is less personal than in the previous example, yet Walsh comments on, likes, and responds to almost every comment from readers, at times with simple phrases that signal she agrees with or likes what is being said. Others contain longer paragraphs with memories about areas of London (where she lives), shops that she trusts, or retailers that have disappeared. Often, she uses the friendly humour and tone of phrases like "Steady on, Helen!" or "Nice one, Liz", stressing the name of her readers as if they were known acquaintances. These interactions coexist with the commercial dimension of her site, sometimes in the same post. There is a dedicated section called "TNMA Edit", a collection of items for sale that she has created in collaboration with independent designers; some stories are shopping lists with affiliated links. A selection of clothing comes with direct links to the sites of retailers.

Yet another example of dialogues facilitated by this format is *The Review of Beauty* (formerly known as *The Unpublishable*), the newsletter of freelance beauty culture critic Jessica Defino. Her reporting on how the beauty industry affects people, often in negative ways, has appeared in mainstream media such as *Vogue*, *The New York Times*, and *The Cut*, among others, and her newsletter has been highlighted by outlets such as *Forbes* and *HuffPost*. She calls it "The beauty industry's least favourite newsletter" (jessicadefino.substack.com, n. d.) as it often goes against the grain of the standard beauty coverage and gives reasons why audience members should stop buying products rather than presenting them with several options. Her "don't buy list"s include, for instance, various pink packaged products that are marketed during breast cancer awareness month every year; she suggests that readers could donate directly to cancer charities instead and read around the potentially harmful health effects of, for instance, petrochemical byproducts used in the beauty industry. During one of the Black Friday November sales (when retailers often choose to sell items at discounted prices), she wrote a "Don't Buy Day" column (Defino, 2021) and made all her "don't buy list"s freely available, while marking down the subscription price of her newsletter for a few days only. This is arguably an example of how different dynamics can coexist in the work of these journalists: on the one hand, Defino's following is likely to expect a column about how the consumer logic of the market permeates the intimate space of wellbeing and personal appearance, which she delivers; on the other, she is using the same Black Friday sales period to increase her subscribers and income.

Defino's newsletter from October 10, 2023, titled "When war sells serum", argues that beauty companies often use war metaphors in their press releases, quoting phrases such as "combat aging" or "battle acne", alongside others such as "skincare regime" or "army of products" that are also often found in journalistic copy about beauty. In the same piece, she interviews linguist Amanda Montell, who notes that a general "vocabulary of conflict" permeates this industry; other examples include talking about pimples or acne "colonizing your face" (in Defino, 2023c). Readers' comments under this newsletter post include phrases such as "standing ovation" or "round of applause", all of which are liked and directly thanked by the author, who says things such as "This made my day xx" (Defino, 2023c). Further dialogues between the journalist and readers include recommendations of books about the same topic in several conversations between the journalist and the reader and reader-to-reader interactions. As in Omerod's example, some of the readers are also Substack writers, so those conversations could, potentially, lead to other newsletters and other conversation threads. Another newsletter post, from May 19th, "Martha Stewart's *Sports Illustrated* Cover Means Next to Nothing" (Defino, 2023a), about the American entrepreneur who appeared on the magazine cover wearing a silver swimming costume at the age of 81, is followed by personal messages from readers talking about the negative effects of diet culture and what some, including Defino, see as the cynicism of some age-positive content. Readers describe how the author verbalises "all my feelings about this" or matches their reactions. Others tell stories of how they have seen their mothers, of similar age to Stewart, be unhappy for the whole of their lives due to extreme dieting; reply with their own, intimate experiences of eating disorders; or post comments about friends who have been unwell or died as a result of health complications after cosmetic surgery procedures.

On November 2, 2023, Defino started to do a monthly advice column for *The Guardian* with the title of "Ask Ugly". She informed *The Unpublishable* readers that she would share a preview of that column with her newsletter subscribers, who would also be able to access extra quick-fire questions not available to the rest; this suggests that Defino is interested in keeping some exclusive and intimate aspects of her smaller community, while also reaching a much bigger audience. That first column, "Should you be getting Botox? Welcome to Ask Ugly, our new beauty column!" (Defino, 2023b) from *The Guardian* website was not open for readers' comments.

Future directions

As this chapter has outlined, the recent "audience turn" in journalism studies and the industry of journalism has not paid dedicated attention to the relationship between journalists and their audiences in the specific field of lifestyle journalism, where notions of community and intimacy discourses coexist with commercial logic. As such, it is necessary to study the particularities of this relationship given those characteristics, which include "where" they take place – online and offline communities, 'below the line' comments, newsletters, and journalists' websites – what is the content of the interactions; and how they are performed. A change of paradigm in audience research that does not focus solely on metrics but rather on making sense practices, in emotional and embodied dimensions, and a notion of news consumption as "social experience", as outlined by Costera Meijer (2019), seems an appropriate approach that could inform future avenues of research.

The literature and examples discussed in the chapter demonstrate that the commercial logic and interest that underlie the lifestyle media sector and the fact that this journalist niche relies heavily on freelancers foster a form of interaction that could be characterised as individualistic, invested in the voices and authority of individual journalists who have built audience communities around themselves. As a result, forms of audience engagement value intimate experiences, authorial voices, and displays of personal identity; dialogues in different interactive forums bring together personal and professional content, conventional journalistic work, and entrepreneurial activities, across different platforms and modes of interaction. At the same time, this work is not free from traditional journalistic structures, the logic and commercial priorities of platforms, or the simple need to make a living in a precarious industry through a portfolio career.

This is a time in which several news organisations have limited the use of spaces for audience interactions, particularly 'below the line' comments, both for commercial reasons and for protecting journalists from abuse and uncivility (Wright et al., 2020). Women and people of colour appear to be particularly vulnerable to abuse and dismissive trolling regardless of what the article is about, as research from *The Guardian*, based on 70 million comments left on their sites, has established (Gardiner et al., 2016). "The tone of comments was also found to deter some readers—particularly women—from participating in comment threads", states Gardiner (2018), based both on her own experience as an editor and on academic research that discusses this. Some news organisations have closed those sections on their sites but have moved the interactions and moderation to the social media pages (Goujard, 2016). As discussed in this chapter, lifestyle journalists, who are often freelancers, reflect this trend as they do audience engagement work on their platforms and appear to invest significant resources in it.

Further research into what happens when these dialogues are increasingly being held outside mainstream news outlets (and often behind a paywall) is needed, particularly in the case of freelance lifestyle journalists who then become the only moderators and gatekeepers of those dialogues, unlike in the case of news organisations that have their policies, practices, and staff working on moderation. This has consequences for both journalists themselves – the workload, time, cost, and emotional labour required for this is significant, with potential impact on their mental health as mentioned in this chapter – and for the audience, who might have limited access to a diverse, meaningful, and enriching space for dialogue that is not fully controlled by the journalist who relies on their branded persona; these two aspects could be explored in research too. The access and visibility of marginal communities, a dimension that has been absent in audience studies anyway, is also something to be explored when interactions are held on individual sites that often bring together like-minded people with very similar interests and lifestyles. Lastly, the intersection and overlap between commercial, branded, and entrepreneurial work by lifestyle journalists, and their editorial and conventional outputs, require further examination too.

Further reading

Coward, R. (2013). *Speaking personally: The rise of subjective and confessional journalism*. Bloomsbury Publishing.

Favaro, L. (2017). Mediating intimacy online: authenticity, magazines, and chasing the clicks. *Journal of Gender Studies*, 26(3), 321–334.

Kaplan, D. (2021). Public intimacy in social media: The mass audience as a third party. *Media, Culture & Society*, 43(4), 595–612.

Swart, J., Groot Kormelink, T., Costera Meijer, I., & Broersma, M. (2022). Advancing a radical audience turn in journalism. Fundamental dilemmas for journalism studies. *Digital Journalism*, 10(1), 8–22.

Vodanovic, L. (2019). Journalism without news: the beauty journalist's private/professional self in *The Guardian*'s 'below-the-line comments. In L. Vodanovic (Ed.), *Lifestyle journalism: social media, consumption, and experience* (pp. 129–140). Routledge.

References

Andringa, P. (2022). *Email Newsletters and the Changing Journalist-Audience Relationship* (Doctoral dissertation, University of Oxford).

Bélair-Gagnon, V., Holton, A., Deuze, M., & Mellado, C. (Eds.) (2024). *Happiness in journalism*. Routledge.

Blassnig, S., & Esser, F. (2022). The "audience logic" in digital journalism: An exploration of shifting news logics across media types and time. *Journalism Studies*, 23(1), 48–69.

Boczkowski, P. J. (2009). Rethinking hard and soft news production: From common ground to divergent paths. *Journal of Communication*, 59(1), 98–116.

Carlson, M., & Peters, C. (2023). Journalism studies for realists: Decentering journalism while keeping journalism studies. *Journalism Studies*, 24(8), 1029–1042.

Chambers, D. (2017). Networked intimacy: Algorithmic friendship and scalable sociality. *European Journal of Communication*, 32(1), 26–36.

Costera Meijer, I. (2019). Journalism, audiences, and news experience. In K. Wahl-Jorgensen & T. Hanitzsch (Eds.), *The handbook of journalism studies* (pp. 389–405). Routledge.

Costera Meijer, I. (2020). Understanding the audience turn in journalism: From quality discourse to innovation discourse as anchoring practices 1995–2020. *Journalism Studies*, 21(16), 2326–2342.

Costera Meijer, I. C., & Kormelink, T. G. (2019). Audiences for journalism. In T. Vos and F. Hanusch (Eds.), *The International Encyclopedia of Journalism Studies*, (pp. 1–7). Wiley. https://doi.org/10.1002/9781118841570.iejs0002

Coward, R. (2010). Practice review: Journalism ethics and confessional journalism. *Journalism Practice*, 4(2), 224–233.

Coward, R. (2013). *Speaking personally: The rise of subjective and confessional journalism*. Bloomsbury Publishing.

Defino, J. (2021, November 24). Black Friday? More like don't buy day. *The Review of Beauty*. https://jessicadefino.substack.com/p/black-friday-beauty-sales?utm_source=publication-search

Defino, J. (2023a, May 19). Martha Stewart's *Sports Illustrated* cover means next to nothing. *The Review of Beauty*. https://jessicadefino.substack.com/p/martha-stewart-sports-illustrated

Defino, J. (2023b, November 1). Should you be getting Botox? Welcome to Ask Ugly, our new beauty column! *The Guardian*. https://www.theguardian.com/lifeandstyle/2023/nov/01/should-i-get-botox-advice-ask-ugly?utm_source=substack&utm_medium=email

Defino, J. (2023c, November 21). When war sells serum. *The Review of Beauty*. https://jessicadefino.substack.com/p/beauty-industry-response-israel-palestine-war

Favaro, L. (2017). Mediating intimacy online: Authenticity, magazines, and chasing the clicks. *Journal of Gender Studies*, 26(3), 321–334. https://doi.org/10.1080/09589236.2017.1280385

Gardiner, B. (2018). "It's a terrible way to go to work:" What 70 million readers' comments on the Guardian revealed about hostility to women and minorities online. *Feminist Media Studies*, 18(4), 592–608.

Gardiner, B., Mansfield, M., Anderson, I., Ulmanu, M., Louter, D., & Holder, J. (2016, April 12). The dark side of Guardian comments. *The Guardian*. https://www.theguardian.com/technology/2016/apr/12/the-dark-side-of-guardian-comments

Goujard, C. (2016, September 8). Why news websites are closing their comments sections. *Medium*. https://medium.com/global-editors-network/why-news-websites-are-closing-their-comments-sections-ea31139c469d

Hanusch, F. (2019a). Journalistic roles and everyday life: An empirical account of lifestyle journalists' professional views. *Journalism Studies*, 20(2), 193–211.

Hanusch, F. (2019b). Journalism and everyday life. In K. Wahl-Jorgensen & T. Hanitzsch (Eds.), *The handbook of journalism studies* (2nd edition, pp. 406–419). Routledge.

Hanusch, F., & Hanitzsch, T. (2013). Mediating orientation and self-expression in the world of consumption: Australian and German lifestyle journalists' professional views. *Media, Culture & Society*, 35(8), 943–959.

Hedman, U., & Djerf-Pierre, M. (2013). The social journalist: Embracing the social media life or creating a new digital divide? *Digital Journalism*, 1(3), 368–385.

Hendrickx, J. (2023). Power to the people? Conceptualising audience agency for the digital journalism era. *Digital Journalism*, 11(7), 1365–1373.

Hermida, A., & Thurman, N. (2008). A clash of cultures: The integration of user-generated content within professional journalistic frameworks at British newspaper websites. *Journalism Practice*, 2(3), 343–356.

Holton, A. E., Lewis, S. C., & Coddington, M. (2020). Interacting with audiences: Journalistic role conceptions, reciprocity, and perceptions about participation. In Allan, S., Carter, C., Cushion, S., Dencik, L., Garcia-Blanco, I., Harris, J., Sambrook, R., Wahl-Jorgensen, K. & Williams, A. (Eds.), *The future of journalism: Risks, threats and opportunities* (pp. 327–337). Routledge.

Holton, A. E., & Molyneux, L. (2017). Identity lost? The personal impact of brand journalism. *Journalism*, 18(2), 195–210.

Hornmoen, H., & Steensen, S. (2014). Dialogue as a journalistic ideal. *Journalism Studies*, 15(5), 543–554. https://doi. 10.1080/1461670X.2014.894358

Jessicadefino.substack.com. (n. d.). *The Review of Beauty*. https://jessicadefino.substack.com/

Kaplan, D. (2021). Public intimacy in social media: The mass audience as a third party. *Media, Culture & Society*, 43(4), 595–612.

Ksiazek, T. B., Peer, L., & Lessard, K. (2016). User engagement with online news: Conceptualizing interactivity and exploring the relationship between online news videos and user comments. *New Media & Society*, 18(3), 502–520.

Lehman-Wilzig, S. N., & Seletzky, M. (2010). Hard news, soft news, 'general' news: The necessity and utility of an intermediate classification. *Journalism*, 11(1), 37–56.

Lewis, S. C., Holton, A. E., & Coddington, M. (2014). Reciprocal journalism: A concept of mutual exchange between journalists and audiences. *Journalism Practice*, 8(2), 229–241.

Maares, P., & Hanusch, F. (2020). Exploring the boundaries of journalism: Instagram micro-bloggers in the twilight zone of lifestyle journalism. *Journalism*, 21(2), 262–278.

Markham, T. (2012). The politics of journalistic creativity: expressiveness, authenticity and de-authorization. *Journalism Practice*, 6(2), 187–200.

Meyer, H. K., & Carey, M. C. (2014). In moderation: Examining how journalists' attitudes toward online comments affect the creation of community. *Journalism Practice*, 8(2), 213–228.

Molyneux, L. (2019). A personalized self-image: Gender and branding practices among journalists. *Social Media+ Society*, 5(3), 2056305119872950.

Napoli, P. M. (2011). *Audience evolution: New technologies and the transformation of media audiences*. Columbia University Press.

Naughton, J. (2023, September 10). From me to your inbox: 33 of the best Substack newsletters. *The Observer*. https://www.theguardian.com/culture/2023/sep/10/inbox-33-substack-newsletters-culture-to-read-blogging

Newman, N. (2022). *Journalism, media, and technology trends and predictions 2022*. Reuters Institute for the Study of Journalism.

Olausson, U. (2018). The celebrified journalist. *Journalism Studies*, 19(16), 2379–2399. 10.1080/1461670X.2017.1349548

Omerod, K. (2023a, January 15). Getting shit done doesn't make you a good person. *Every Shade of Grey*. https://katherineormerod.substack.com/p/getting-shit-done-doesnt-make-you?utm_source=%2Fsearch%2Fgetting%2520shirt%2520done&utm_medium=reader2

Omerod, K. (2023b, February 19). My experience of termination for medical reasons. *Every Shade of Grey*. https://katherineormerod.substack.com/p/my-experience-of-termination-for

Omerod, K. (2023c, August 6). My children may kill each other, I've been told this is normal. *Every Shade of Grey*. https://katherineormerod.substack.com/p/my-children-may-kill-each-other-ive

Omerod, K. (2023d, September 17). Forget confidence, steadfastness is a far more realistic goal. *Every Shade of Grey*. https://katherineormerod.substack.com/p/forget-confidence-steadfastness-is

Omerod, K. (2023e, October 23). How desperate are you. *Every Shade of Grey*. https://katherineormerod.substack.com/p/how-desperate-are-you

Ouellette, L. (2016). *Lifestyle TV*. Routledge.

Santos, C. A., & Peixinho, A. T. (2017). Newsletters and the Return of epistolarity in digital media: The case of the Portuguese online newspaper Observador. *Digital Journalism*, 5(6), 774–790.

Šimunjak, M. (2023). "You have to do that for your own sanity": Digital disconnection as journalists' coping and preventive strategy in managing work and well-being. *Digital Journalism*, 1–20.

Storm, H. (2024). *Mental Health and Wellbeing for Journalists: A Practical Guide*. Taylor & Francis.

Substack (n.d). https://substack.com/

Swart, J., Groot Kormelink, T., Costera Meijer, I., & Broersma, M. (2022). Advancing a radical audience turn in journalism. Fundamental dilemmas for journalism studies. *Digital Journalism*, 10(1), 8–22.

Truyens, P., & Picone, I. (2024). Does the audience welcome an audience-oriented journalism? *Journalism*, 25(4), 735–754 doi: 14648849231170063.

Van Leuven, S., & Vandenberghe, H. (2024). Self-employment in the news industry. In V. Bélair-Gagnon, A. Holton, M. Deuze, & C. Mellado (Eds.), *Happiness in journalism* (pp. 157–165). Routledge.

Vodanovic, L. (2019). Journalism without news: The beauty journalist's private/professional self in *The Guardian*'s 'below-the-line comments. In L. Vodanovic (Ed.), *Lifestyle journalism: social media, consumption, and experience* (pp. 129–140). Routledge.

Vos, T. P., Eichholz, M., & Karaliova, T. (2019). Audiences and journalistic capital: Roles of journalism. *Journalism Studies*, 20(7), 1009–1027.

Walsh, A. (n. d.). *That's Not my Age*. https://thatsnotmyage.com/

Wright, S., Jackson, D., & Graham, T. (2020). When journalists go "below the line": Comment spaces at The Guardian (2006–2017). *Journalism Studies*, 21(1), 107–126.

30
PRECARITY, ALGORITHMIC VISIBILITY AND ASPIRATIONAL LABOUR IN THE CONSTRUCTION OF LIFESTYLE

Rob Sharp

Introduction

The lifestyle journalism field has been met with unique unforeseen challenges in recent years, given the context of the COVID-19 pandemic and its disastrous effects on the symbolic and material labour conditions of legacy media, as well as the long-term structural economic destabilisation with its short-term fluctuating profits and uncertain commercial advertising revenues. The impacts include the precarity of what is often a freelance career with its own heightened symbolic, economic, and psychological precarities; fewer permanent jobs in a changing sector, alongside the threat of furlough in traditional media organisations globally; and not to mention the accelerating growth of digital lifestyle content (Sharp and Vodanovic, 2022; Vodanovic, 2019; Hanusch, Banjac and Maares, 2020).

Lifestyle journalism is defined here as "a distinct journalistic field that primarily addresses its audiences as consumers…often in entertaining ways, about goods and services they can use in their daily lives" (Hanusch, 2012, p. 5). This comprises subjects including fashion, travel, style, and fitness. Given the increased hybrid roles taken by a hyper-precarious fluidly employed workforce, this chapter will take the lifestyle sub-field to also include journalism about the culture and creative industries, following Hanusch's definition of lifestyle as that which "provides factual information and advice" and as linked to what audiences might consume, including the arts, such as cinema, visual art, mass-produced literature, theatre, and music (Hanusch, 2012, p. 2). It is worth noting that some view arts and lifestyle journalism as distinct sub-fields with specific labour, practices, and values, although the conclusions here span both (Sharp and Vodanovic, 2022).

The negotiation of boundaries between so-called content creators on social media and lifestyle journalists has received recent attention for the ways lifestyle journalists and content creators' values may overlap or see journalists as being under increased commercial pressure from the advertising industry due to a "decline in traditional jobs following a collapse in advertising funding" (Maares and Hanusch, 2020; Hanusch, Banjac and Maares, 2020; Matthews and Onyemaobi, 2020, p. 1837). Precarity is also at the heart of a number of recent studies considering influencers (e.g., Duffy et al., 2021; Duffy, 2020; Glatt, 2021;

Glatt, 2022; Stoldt et al., 2019), including in relation to gendered divisions of work such as the erasure of female-gendered skills from discourses of labour (e.g., Jarrett, 2014). The hyper-precarity of content creation is hitherto underexplored in relation to lifestyle journalism in the context of this work around digital influencers and might usefully augment the existing lifestyle journalism-centred literature and vice-versa.

As such, this contribution argues for the centralisation of critical approaches to digital labour in considering the sub-field of lifestyle journalism given its rapidly changing nature. Drawing on recent interviews with lifestyle journalists in different global contexts, I argue there needs to be greater attention paid to three specific elements of precarity that are currently more generously explored in the literature around influencers. Firstly, the hybrid roles that lifestyle journalists often occupy across both content creation and journalism to battle against uncertainty; secondly, the entrenched dimensions of exclusion and visibility which might perpetuate among those dependent on the lifestyle journalism industries, and, finally, the dangers of labour practices that rely on free content.

These themes might usefully draw on literatures relating to how the logics of platformisation have created an uncertainty around content creators' understanding of platform algorithms. This includes the intersection between prominent content creators' precarity and visibility online insofar as they are relevant to the perspective of lifestyle journalism and journalists and the entrepreneurial pressure of the often unpaid labour of building audiences online through 'aspirational labour' (Duffy, 2016, 2020; Duffy et al., 2021; Arriagada and Ibanez, 2020, p. 2; Cunningham and Craig, 2019). In referring to this literature, we should be mindful of the unique characteristics of each of lifestyle journalism and lifestyle influencing, and the questions unique to how each workforce's own precarities and exclusions might expand the relevance of the literature around the other. At the same time, the various literatures can be augmented, forming a conceptual bridge between the two sub-fields as defined. In doing so, we should pay heed to those practitioners working in both sub-fields or switching between the two at different times. Influencers are defined here as those digital content creators whose opinions hold sway with networked audiences (Duffy et al., 2022, p. 1671).

I will argue for the centralisation of precarity as a conceptual tool for understanding lifestyle journalism in light of the aforementioned approaches, mapping out the similarities between the precarity of lifestyle journalists and the precarity of influencers and digital lifestyle content creators more broadly along the three dimensions outlined, describing along the way the extent to which the overlap in such dimensions of precarity has been explored within the relevant literatures, again mindful of their distinguishing features and the unique practices within each. I will argue for a theoretical reconsideration of precarity in light of the specificities of lifestyle journalists' labour along these terms, before arguing for a centralisation of these questions beyond a white, highly gendered and exclusionary Euro-American lens. In doing so, I will draw on a data corpus of interviews with 24 lifestyle journalists in 12 different countries around questions of professional identity, specifically as it relates to precarity within this context, and journalists' self-perception of their economic positions. This is inspired by a hybrid inductive/deductive approach to analysis, mindful of themes that might emerge in relation to precarity in lifestyle journalism when conducting my analyses (Fereday and Muir-Cochrane, 2006).

Uncertainty and hybridity within lifestyle journalism

Hardt and Negri's influential conceptualisation of precarity is a useful theoretical jumping off point regarding the uncertainty which surrounds the financial viability of lifestyle journalism for its workforce, with their concept of precarity defined as "…organizing all forms of labour according to the infinite modalities of market flexibility," or indeed, "…precarity is a mechanism of control that determines the temporality of workers, destroying the division between work time and nonwork time, requiring workers not to work all the time but to be constantly available to work" (Hardt and Negri, 2009, p. 146). This theory maintains a critical focus on the effects of neoliberalisation on the labour market. This operates through the elision of boundaries between the interests of transnational conglomerates structuring lifestyle content and the interests of a highly precarious lifestyle workforce producing this content and reproducing its importance through doing so (Vodanovic, 2019, p. 3).

As noted by Hanusch, Banjac, and Maares (2020), lifestyle journalists are under increasing commercial pressure from the advertising and public relations industries, with this sub-field being particularly susceptible to short-term economic headwinds. Scholars note that in the case of fashion bloggers "who work amidst greater economic precarity," the overlap between advertorial and editorial content is especially blurred (Hanusch, Banjac and Maares, 2020, p. 1039; see also Pedroni, 2015; Brydges and Sjöholm, 2019).

It is clear that such uncertainties are even more pressing in the algorithmic age, with algorithms and platform visibility functioning as a "contested terrain of control" around labour, with workers participating in systems that direct, evaluate, and discipline them (Kellogg et al., 2020). With journalists increasingly needing to curate content online and build personal audiences (Olausson, 2018), one might argue that such workers are caught between two stools of precarity: on the one hand, anticipating algorithmic change in order to gear their personal content towards it to competitively brand-build and on the other, such practitioners may work within or pitching to news organisations that might be themselves subject to algorithmic vicissitudes. This might include, for example, Buzzfeed News's loss of traffic from Facebook in 2023 as a result of Meta's strategic shift away from news in its recommendation algorithm, leading to Buzzfeed News's closure and the laying off of its staff (Majid, 2023). It might also include lifestyle brands, public relations firms, and other forms of subsidised labour, which are subject to their own market-oriented uncertainties.

My argument is that such precarisation and hybridisation make these forms of hybrid freelance work increasingly the norm within a broader, algorithmically uncertain economic landscape. Between 2000 and 2015, the number of freelance journalists in the United Kingdom increased from 15,000 to 25,000, an increase of 67 percent, with the proportion of journalists considering themselves as freelancers increasing from 25 to 35 percent (Spilsbury, 2021). More broadly, freelancers, including lifestyle freelancers, make up an increasing proportion of journalists overall at a time of media industry realignment (Bromley, 2019; Deuze and Witschge, 2020; Massey and Elmore, 2018). As noted in the literature and in my interviews, lifestyle journalism attracts a 'significant component' of freelancers (Hanusch et al., 2017, p. 147).

Dimensions of exclusion and visibility

Within this complex mesh of overlapping precarities, we can see clear parallels between the uncertainties faced by lifestyle journalists seeking to maintain professional visibility and the ways influencers might need to work across multiple platforms in order to maintain and build their own visibility among audiences in a metricised way and how this might affect some more than others (Duffy et al., 2021).

Duffy, Poell, and Nieborg (2019) have argued that the logics of platforms have radically changed the production, distribution, and monetisation of cultural content. These new logics necessitate influencers maintaining a visible presence on multiple platforms simultaneously, something that anecdotally at least is observable among lifestyle journalists maintaining profiles on multiple social media platforms: TikTok, Instagram, X (formerly Twitter), Facebook, and recently launched alternatives such as Mastodon, Bluesky, and Threads. Such visibility has long been instrumental to freelance journalists' lives, with freelancing being a significant component of lifestyle journalism; this might involve maintaining a presence for audiences or visibility with particular clients, publicists, or editors (Hanusch et al., 2017). Such regimes of visibility likely favour particular dimensions of subjectivity over others, particularly those palatable to the neoliberal economy in which this representation is contextualised—editors might like to pigeonhole lifestyle journalists of colour to encourage them to 'speak for' particular communities in ways in which they feel uncomfortable, for instance (Sharp and Vodanovic, 2022).

In addition, we should be mindful that precarity means different things in different global contexts, heeding the findings of Matthews and Onyemaobi (2020, p. 1836) regarding its Western biases, particularly instances of "precarious professionalism", including poor pay and working conditions that are locally contingent. Just as importantly, we should be conscious of the fact that algorithmic uncertainty is expressed along dimensions mirroring existing social inequalities. Sociocultural and commercial inequities along intersections of "race, class, gender, ability and sexuality" are expressed within the influencer industry, and barriers to entry are "staggeringly high" (Duffy, 2017, p. 223; Glatt, 2022, p. 3858). Thus, the uncertainty facing lifestyle journalists draws on a combination of these unique precarities—from the specificities of lifestyle journalism's immediate media economy on the one hand and algorithmic uncertainty on the other, on local, regional, and global scales.

Thus, neoliberal logics of visibility already provide the context to which the majority of lifestyle journalists operate—platformized and precarious labour, increasingly in a digital context—contingent on the particulars of the sub-field, including individual labour conditions, alongside nationally and culturally contingent factors influencing visibility. Furthermore, this occurs within the context of the ongoing and contested negotiation of the division between the sub-fields of lifestyle content and lifestyle journalism, which increasingly share the same digital spaces to win audiences and thus lie in mutual competition. Maares and Hanusch (2020) found in their study of professional Instagrammers' discursive constructions of journalistic boundaries and their role perceptions that such content creators often placed themselves within journalistic boundaries by aligning with journalism's values. At the same time, professional journalists are resembling influencers in their increasing reliance on self-branding, promotion, networking, and reliance on analytics, contributing to the sub-field's transformation. While these two sub-fields may still be distinct at least on the practitioners' own terms, neoliberal algorithmic logics are increasingly regulating the practices of both. The contingency of visibility on multiple platforms on this scale is a relatively under-researched dimension of such logics, the importance of which I present evidence for here.

Labour of building audiences

Moving to my third and final dimension of interest, Duffy defines aspirational labour as a "forward-looking, carefully orchestrated and entrepreneurial form of creative cultural production" (Duffy, 2016, p. 7), akin to the aspirational nature of consumption and consumer behaviour, for instance, through purchasing luxury goods to accrue cultural capital. Such aspirational labourers work with the hope that they will one day be compensated for their talents, ideally in their chosen media content profession of choice. Deuze has highlighted the increasing "merging of work, life and play" alongside the blurring between media consumption and production as affecting the way journalists construct their identities. Freelancers, particularly, are "forced to give meaning to their work and thus construct their own professional identity in the context of rapidly changing and often overlapping work contexts" (Deuze, 2008, p. 111). It is easy to see that this emerges within the context of structural labour conditions, with the associated labour of reporters "adopting different identities...across different platforms, organisations and roles" (Vodanovic, 2019, p. 43).

Regarding the extent to which Hardt and Negri's claims around 'market flexibility' ring true within the lifestyle sub-field, Perreault and Bélair-Gagnon (2024) have raised the question of the presence of aspirational forms of labour within lifestyle journalism, whereby reporters "do what you love," (Duffy, 2017; Perreault and Bélair-Gagnon, 2024, p. 2) whether or not they are financially compensated for it—a clear pitfall of a digital modern attention economy of "anxious-self-making" (Duffy and Pooley, 2019, p. 21). Such labour is often unremunerated, with the ever-renewing promise of financial or reputational reward just around the corner. As before, such labour intersects with content creators' experiences along lines of gender, race, and class (see North, 2016; Ross, 2001; Gregg and Andrijasevic, 2019; Irani, 2019). Although such free forms of labour are relatively underresearched with respect to lifestyle journalism, there is a more developed literature on unpaid work in the news sector (Bakker, 2012; Compton and Benedetti, 2010) and on the increasing role of freelancing among news reporters (Mathisen, 2017; Obermaier and Koch, 2015).

Such workers need to be 'always available' partly because of the nature of the industries upon which they report. They operate in highly network-based economies, often oriented around consumer-facing events, involving long hours and travel, with an abundant expectation of free labour from those looking to break into the industry, alongside competition from the subsidised labour of the public relations industry. These factors place pressure on such journalists to break down the boundaries between their personal and professional lives. Given the availability of so-called 'perks' and the behavioural norms within these industries, these journalists may be less likely to unionise, driving up competition for staff jobs, suppressing wages, and dampening the labour market. Within lifestyle journalism itself, there is an emerging literature on precarity due to the "decline in traditional jobs following a collapse in advertising funding" (Matthews and Onyemaobi, 2020, p. 1837).

We should note that the idea of aspirational labour draws on a combination of an understanding of 'invisible work' relating to traditional gendered approaches to labour as well as theories relating to value-generating labour, for instance—affective labour, in the form of building affective relationships with different communities— that are of increasing importance in the digital economy (Jarrett, 2014). While both men and women are subject to these logics, gendered exclusions within this economy are still prevalent and should be acknowledged as described.

Current contributions and research

Given the paucity of literature relating to these particular factors in this context, my argument for the increased centralisation of precarity in the terms defined draws principally on a data corpus gathered through interviews with global lifestyle journalists in 2021, presented alongside relevant contemporary literature (Sharp and Vodanovic, 2022). Lifestyle journalists working in major cities who had been employed regularly in their sub-field for longer than five years were selected for inclusion, with participants sampled for their diversity with respect to nationality, gender, sexuality, job role, medium of journalism (e.g. digital, broadcast, print, and/or video), genre, and ethnicity. They were chosen using a mixture of purposive and snowball sampling, with participants selecting others to interview of relevance (Bryman, 2016, p. 408).

Of 24 participants interviewed, six participants had contracts with major mainstream media organisations, with everyone else working as freelance. Ten of the journalists interviewed were female and 14 male. Speaking to questions of precarity, visibility, and hyper-flexibility in the workforce as described, almost none of the journalists only pursued one job, with many also working as novelists, curators, lecturers, in public relations, or in entirely unrelated fields. Among the participants, 14 were working in Europe (11 journalists working primarily in the United Kingdom, six of whom were journalists of colour; one journalist each was based in Poland, Kosovo, and Greece). Three were working in Latin or Central America (Chile, Costa Rica, and Brazil), three partly or full-time in Sub-Saharan Africa (two people from Ghana and one from Nigeria), alongside two in Iran, and one journalist each in the United States and China. Participants were transnationally mobile and worked in multiple countries, necessitating a strong awareness of digital labour practices (Sharp and Vodanovic, 2022, p. 1808).

Evidence for unique digital uncertainty

There is increasing evidence that lifestyle journalists occupy hybridised positions as platform content creators or public relations practitioners with a digital presence alongside their journalism. The boundaries between these workforces are porous, constantly changing, and subject to negotiation, interrelating as part of the unique neoliberal logics of precarity highlighted above. This builds on literature relating to contested boundary work between traditional lifestyle journalists and amateurs producing digital content, amateur bloggers, or semi-professional content creators (e.g., Maares and Hanusch, 2018). As we will see, this occurs in similar ways in different national media contexts, alongside practices unique to different regions.

Games journalism has been a particular area of growth which also serves as a useful case-study regarding uncertainty with respect to precarious platform logics alongside the precarities of journalism. Such a genre of lifestyle journalism is beholden to the 'uncertainty and lack of control' whereby the next "Big Job [is] right around the corner" (Neff et al., 2005, p. 319) despite the rapid expansion of a global industry set to be worth $312bn by 2027 (PwC, 2023). In the following interview with a British male games writer, journalist, and publicist, the interviewee noted the evolving role of subsidised digital content creators in the gaming industry, with a significant number heavily sponsored by the producers of the games they feature. These creators may receive payments to play specific games and may even be offered subsidised travel to the developers' offices for on-site gameplay. Equally, they are subject to algorithmic vicissitudes in order to get their work seen.

> They want to produce, they want to get their audience onside, but they are also, quite often, heavily sponsored by whatever they're producing. They're paid to play

> particular games by the producers of those games. They may be flown out, much like journalists used to be on junkets, to the offices of the game developers to play the game on-site. That exclusive thing has gone to them now. Again, they may report it, they may put a little thing on YouTube or wherever they're producing it to say sponsored, but it's small text and they're telling their audience this is great, this is the next big thing. So, they've become part of the marketing machine rather than necessarily being part of the objective reporting. There are still good ones out there who do objective reporting, but they have much smaller audiences than the people who just play games and scream at the screen. The kind of excitable, Radio One journalism rather than the Radio Four journalism.—British gaming writer.

The interviewee highlights a shift towards content creators becoming integral to games industry's publicity machinery and thus beholden to their logics of promotion, as well as the logics of platform production. The comparison is drawn between creators who primarily play games and engage in energetic, excitable content and those who maintain a more 'objective reporting' or 'thorough' approach, equating these approaches to two BBC radio stations, Radio One—which has a target audience of 15–29—and Radio Four's older audience. Yet while the interviewee acknowledges that 'objective reporting' may still be desirable as a normative value, he suggests that creators with a focus on entertainment often garner larger audiences within this hypercompetitive landscape, through the production of the kind of emotive, audience-focused sensationalist content that is known to perform well algorithmically.

The games writer also describes how the market for games-related lifestyle journalistic content has balkanised, with traditional print-first lifestyle journalism forming a small legacy minority within a broader sphere of digital content creation—a sector with its own specific uncertainties.

> So, the market has shifted again. The print side of journalism has died off mostly. The print circulations in my lifetime have gone down from, maybe, in the UK as an example, the top magazine selling 100,000 to 200,000 copies a month at £4 or £5 an issue, they may be selling, at most, 15 to 20,000. I've not looked at it recently, but it's very low, the print side. They are almost acting more as content feeds for the online side for those magazines. So, those magazines, all that stuff they produce is then repurposed online. And online is where they make their money, through curated advertising markets and, very rarely, subscription services. Not many of the games websites manage to make money from having registered users.—British gaming writer.

While it is no surprise that legacy lifestyle media circulation is in steep decline—that "the market has shifted again"— it is of note that the commercial imperatives of both online and offline games journalism are now explicitly geared to the priorities of algorithmic online-first media regarding traffic and advertising, subject to its own vagaries of different platforms falling in and out of favour (Meese and Bannerman, 2022). These add to the broader uncertainties surrounding commercial platforms, shaped significantly by the values and interests of advertisers (Brock, 2013). This speaks further to long-running concerns regarding employment patterns within the culture industries shifting away from stability towards an emphasis on a neoliberal worker subject, with "profound experiences of insecurity…about finding work…and 'keeping up' in rapidly changing fields" (Gill and Pratt, 2008, p. 14).

Within this structurally insecure landscape, a significant proportion of lifestyle content is now created by gaming streamers, as opposed to traditional forms of journalism. In this case, journalists' influence has been eroded among its audience, although this lifestyle journalist's views on that are uncertain and ambivalent.

> So, you'll have a streamer like Ninja who is sitting on Twitch with millions of followers, and who is, basically, an independent celebrity who will be earning millions of pounds a year from sponsorship deals, from the platform even paying him to be on there, because he has so many independent followers. PewDiePie is another one. There's an interesting thing going on there because, obviously, we expect the journalistic side to be independent, objective, all of those positive credentials that we've associated with 400–500 years of media. You produce something which is meant to be pushing towards truth, and these streamers have no responsibility for that.—British gaming writer.

The interviewee talks of influencers clearly competing with traditional journalists for coveted sponsorship or advertising revenue and the uncertainty that it creates. On the flipside, the participant clearly values what he calls journalistic 'objectivity' and does not frame influencer culture in terms of its broader precarities—focusing on the most famous influencers, as opposed to the long tail of content creators with fewer followers. Either way, the promise of 'objectivity' is no match for the hyper-precarious uncertainty faced by this industry's workers and their constant struggle for visibility.

Within a broader context of algorithmic uncertainty, journalists interviewed across broadcast, digital, and print platforms in different global contexts raised the need for increased visibility to multiple clients through 'moonlighting'; the taking on of other non-journalistic work to supplement their income, and the associated algorithmic risks. This included the production of sponsored digital content, digital or otherwise, albeit often in the 'long tail' of relatively anonymous media workers, as opposed to influencers. "It might happen that you develop a career as a journalist and spend 20 years and so on as a writer and so on and then you become a curator or a programmer or whatever," said one Costa Rican lifestyle writer. "In Costa Rica, given that the field is so small…because there isn't that much money, that probably means that we are involved in some other way in the cultural sector". He said that the country's lifestyle journalism was outcompeted not by local digital media content but the crowding out by Spanish and English-language titles from global economic centres, that was algorithmically more available.

> They read Vice from Spain for the cultural journalism. That's a preference. It's very interesting that we don't read that much from Chile or from Argentina or from Mexico or even from Colombia, which you would guess would be much closer to our experience, and the case is that not even from Panama. Not even from Nicaragua.

Thus, the specifics of this media economy contextualise precarious personal brand building across industries that structure practitioners' occupational self-identification, and its negotiation by them.

In Ghana, the lack of long-term stable employment in legacy lifestyle journalism meant that some lifestyle journalists have always juggled sponsored content and unpaid blogging, alongside jobs entirely outside the media. A male music blogger based in Ghana said that his shifting between different forms of unpaid and paid digital labour was constantly being negotiated with clients. "The labels work with the streaming sites, right...when they approach you as a music person or a private person not working for the company, sometimes you get paid," he said of his subsidised blogging work. "Some of them do get back to you. Others might not come back because there are a lot of people doing the same business".

Another male lifestyle journalist based in Ghana, who also worked as a lecturer and blogger, said that within media institutions, there were already commonplace instances of subsidised lifestyle journalism. "There's a type of arts commentary you'll find in the newspapers here, which is the sponsored kind," said the journalist. "So I pay you money, you say good things about my event or my record, etc. And that had problems because obviously, he who pays the piper calls the tune. It means that there is no culture of criticism." A third of the country's media outlets are owned by politicians or those associated with dominant political parties; its top five most read newspapers are all affiliated in some way with prominent politicians (Asante, 2020). This sponsored content is displayed both on institutional and social digital content platforms (Sharp and Vodanovic, 2022, p. 1810). Again, this hyper-precarity of structural and algorithmic uncertainty is subject to the contingencies of particular global media economies and practices, though still present across all of them.

Exclusionary dimensions of visibility within lifestyle content

Within this flexible economy, individual journalists' experiences depended ambivalently on dimensions of nationality, gender, sexuality, and race. Within European contexts, many lifestyle journalists from minority backgrounds working across different digital platforms felt like they were misrecognised as colleagues or feared being misrecognised more broadly by audiences, and these concerns coalesced around their self-identification. These concerns mirror those of content creators from historically marginalised groups who are punished by peripheralization in the algorithmic creator economy (Bishop, 2021)—suggesting precarity and the need for hyper-flexibility hit particularly socially marginalised groups harder. As we will see, those beyond Europe expressed additional concern regarding structural exclusion, including visa and travel restrictions.

One LGBTQIA+ Kosovan journalist said there was a tendency for LGBTQIA+ lifestyle journalists to be labelled by their sexuality, leading to "a reluctance to engage with LGBTQIA+ stories" for fear of further misrecognition within broader publics, digitally or otherwise (Sharp and Vodanovic, 2022, p. 1813). In Kosovo, the majority of the population are Muslim ethnic Albanians, with few openly LGBTQI+ people (Agence France-Presse, 2018).

Meanwhile, two female lifestyle journalists in the United Kingdom expressed concerns that their expertise might be misrecognised as relating to their identity, as opposed to their journalistic value. "It's actually almost insulting, that because I'm from [a particular country] that I'm necessarily going to be an expert on all things [from that country] and therefore I would be the right person to write this article", said one journalist. A second journalist based in the United Kingdom said they similarly had an experience of being misrecognised as relating to their ethnicity, with both journalists expressing ambivalence around feeling recognised for their identities above their professional expertise. This points to a structural need for senior editorial gatekeepers to pay attention to such concerns within broader media ecosystems (Sharp and Vodanovic, 2022, p. 1814). Given that this also exists within a broader digital economy whereby such content is shared, liked, and clicked, we should be mindful that racialised exclusionary discourses may be entrenched, under the cover of such platforms evincing their democratic potential.

These racialised exclusions also occur transnationally, as we might expect from the transnational ways that lifestyle content is produced, shared, and consumed. Due to this increasingly digital transnational marketplace for editorial content, one lecturer and lifestyle journalist from Accra, Ghana, commented on a digital economy divided between local digital content subsidised by journalists and a global shift in interest in Black music culture supplied by the Global North—entrenching neocolonial axes of editorial influence.

> There's a global interest in African arts and culture at the moment from Afrobeat to Beyoncé. That creates opportunities for local writers to be on international platforms. Let's say Vogue wants to do an interview with someone here. They might employ someone locally through contacts or through their work. That's happening with greater frequency. When it happens, that translates well locally because the local currency is weak. In reality it should be possible for [a] writer to sustain themselves well. The problem is demand. I can't think of many people who are [full-time] culture correspondents for this region–Journalist working in UK and Ghana.

The journalist describes a local journalism economy "beholden to a Western drive" towards questions of racial diversity, increasingly commissioning local journalists and paying them in dollars or pounds sterling (Sharp and Vodanovic, 2022, p. 1811). For those who can access such networks, this is economically beneficial; however, this clearly also functions along the dimensions of a digital divide between those who can and can't access these commissioning networks. Necessarily, this is mirrored in the use by influencers in the Global South of platforms—YouTube, X, or Facebook—beholden to Western capital (Sinha and Srivastava, 2023). Agreeing with this perspective, a second male Ghanaian lifestyle journalist said the expansion of transnational digital platforms in Ghana is creating some opportunities for work—but not for all.

> So, with some blogs for example, I know that [Ghanaian music blogger] Swayye Kid now partners, he's the Ghana representative for Boomplay. And Boomplay are one of the biggest music distributors on the African continent. So, think of them as an Africa-based iTunes. And so, he's become their Ghana rep, simply through being a blogger. But he's always had a day job. I think he's an accountant somewhere, this young guy.—Ghanaian lifestyle journalist.

Thus, it is significant that lifestyle reporters in Ghana, though suffering from local forms of financial precarity, are beholden to regulated opportunities stemming from Chinese investment in international streaming services (Sharp and Vodanovic, 2022, p. 1812). These mirror the structural dimensions of algorithmically mediated content more broadly, whereby platform owners hold significant power in establishing users' institutional conditions of labour (Burgess and Green 2009).

This transnational production process, while superficially democratic, masks broader structural inequalities relating to financial stability, as well as mobility and the ability to produce content at different transnational sites. Indeed, a female British-Nigerian lifestyle journalist interviewed—a broadcast journalist working in English—agreed this "global interest in African culture" cemented the structural advantages of 'passport privilege'. "I hold dual nationality–British and Nigerian–so I know the ease of jumping on a plane if invited to a biennale to cover it", she said. "While someone else would need at least a month or two in advance to gather all the documentation, there is still no guarantee that they would get a visa. That affects your ability to expand your storytelling". Thus, those lifestyle journalists in Nigeria who might seek to work internationally, for instance, within the European Union, might be "disadvantaged by difficulties around visa paperwork" (Sharp and Vodanovic, 2022, p. 1811). In this respect, we might think of how various travel conglomerates' use of influencer marketing may reinforce such hierarchies or differences—it is remarkably easier to visit Dubai from North America or Europe than it is from Africa or South Asia, for instance.

This obvious sense of precarity across different national digital contexts, modulated by specific local realities, necessarily intersects with contingencies relating to gender, nationality, sexuality, and ethnicity. Given the importance of how local and international questions interrelate, the lack of research into lifestyle creators' precarity beyond Western European contexts should be a source of concern, particularly given the different ways such lifestyle journalists and content creators may be forced to compete within broader transnational digital economies. This cements a need to study the sub-field beyond local questions and to think about how these visibility concerns contribute to and are influenced by nationally dependent challenges, along with global flows of labour and capital.

Free labour within lifestyle content

Finally, I will consider briefly how lifestyle journalists are increasingly dependent on free labour in their need to maintain visibility online. Journalists have long been expected to maintain a presence across social media platforms, interact with audiences, and distribute and market their content, in ways that are difficult to monetise. They are reliant on maintaining relationships with peers, audiences, and potential clients, the economic worth of which is difficult to assess. There is some evidence to suggest that journalists' success is judged according to the number of likes and followers they attract, with freelancers most acutely affected by the need to become self-branding entrepreneurs (Simon, 2019). This entrepreneurial sensibility is redolent of aspirational labour observed within the digital culture industry more broadly (Duffy, 2016, p. 443).

The games art writer noted the aspirational melding of professions within this broader economy, with gaming content creators engaging in aspirational labour on social media in the hope of someday monetising their content to broader audiences. "I logged on to Twitch the other day, and there was one person streaming to two people," he said.

> So, there are people who are just streaming in the hope of making something if it, and then there's a whole curve up to these people who have got millions of followers. So, yes, it's a whole new world. It's amazing to watch.

Though this 'long tail' is presumably largely unmonetised, the journalist frames this aspirationally, as opposed to in relation to precarity.

In interviews with a Kosovan lifestyle journalist and a female British visual arts writer, we see the elision between reporters' professional and personal lives, the sense they need to be 'always on' in maintaining their self-branding on social media and to be producing content for multiple platforms alongside their traditional reporting roles with no additional financial compensation. However, we also see the emergence of monetizable channels including Patreon, where those reporters with sizeable social media followings can charge for content. Again, both journalists frame these changes in positive ways, rearticulating entrepreneurial discourses of 'empowerment'.

I think in Twitter I saw that now it's more than ever, journalism is a lifestyle. People live as journalists. They write for it, they live for it, they write for it, it's a bit more complex than it used to be because back in time you would write an article and then you would go home and there were very few social media but still it was not that empowered as it is right now.—Kosovan lifestyle journalist.

I would add that Patreon and websites like Ko-fi are making individuals more able and empowered to write for themselves without having to rely on advertisements or arts funding. This is something happening across the creative industry as a whole to many different degrees and outcomes, but I think the culture of a collective direct patronage (and with such ease) is something still fairly new and should be noted when considering writing in the context of recent years.—British visual arts writer.

We see here the emergence of different strata of uncertainty within this broader neoliberal logic, one that is reminiscent of the differing levels of stability available to cultural producers in the broader digital economy. While all reporters in this section speak of the influence associated with a large social media following, this is decontextualised from the broader structural barriers that still situate the majority of freelance lifestyle journalists in precarious positions that force them into these new revenue streams, about which they maintain ambivalence, and adopt with varying degrees of success (Hanusch et al., 2017).

Future directions

In this chapter, I have argued that the underexplored realm of precarity within the sub-field of lifestyle journalism might be better understood in relation to the broader digital economy and its associated research disciplines. The seismic shifts in traditional job structures, compounded by the collapse of advertising funding, have left lifestyle journalists grappling with financial disruption, income instability in freelance careers, the ongoing impact of the global pandemic, and heightened competition due to the blurring lines between digital lifestyle content and formal journalism. The urgent call to theorise the labour dynamics in lifestyle journalism thus becomes more pressing, particularly in the context of critical examinations of content creators' own precariousness.

While influencers represent direct competition to lifestyle journalists' work, this is based on the idea that journalists only pursue one role at a time, as opposed to constantly renegotiating the boundaries of their sub-field (Perreault and Hanusch, 2024). While there are strong arguments to say that lifestyle journalists police the boundaries of their own work, especially in relation to content creators, there is still a significant hybridised and shifting workforce spanning the two sub-fields. Thus, alongside policing boundaries, a hyper-flexible workforce is forced to 'moonlight' in different roles at different times in order to make ends meet and is subject to multiple forms of uncertainty and precarity: those relating to visibility, which affect different people in different ways, and the pressure to cross-subsidise work digitally. As noted by Hanusch, Banjac, and Maares (2020) in the case of fashion bloggers 'who work amidst greater economic precarity', the overlap between advertorial and editorial content is blurred (Hanusch, Banjac and Maares, 2020, p. 1039; Pedroni, 2015; Brydges and Sjöholm, 2019). Beyond this, lifestyle journalists increasingly engage in relationally driven forms of free and aspirational labour. Future research should seek to retheorise the relationship between these currently siloed practices, whether historically, ritualistically, or sociologically, relating to their political economy, or their sociocultural meaning, or all of the above, given the clear similarities within their workforces, working approaches, demographics, sources of income, and increasingly, their form.

By aligning this discussion with emerging literature on the precarious nature of digital content creators and influencers, this chapter emphasizes the need to critically analyse the intersections of platformisation, algorithmic uncertainties, discrimination, visibility, and the imperative to contribute to multiple platforms for financial viability. The introduction of the concept of aspirational labour further enriches our understanding of the pressures faced by lifestyle journalists in contemporary contexts, unravelling the hidden nature of their precarious employment. This conceptual bridge, connecting lifestyle journalism to the broader discourse on labour precarity in content creation, not only addresses a critical gap in the existing literature but also underscores the importance of placing different global contexts at the centre of this discussion. As ever, there is significant room for further work in expanding the global focus of this work. In doing so, we must caution against imposing Western perspectives on precarity onto local sites as a crucial reminder to acknowledge the nuanced impact of factors including media ownership and local working conditions on these phenomena. As we navigate these complexities, we might ultimately encourage a more comprehensive understanding of the challenges faced by those constructing lifestyle globally and pave the way for fresh theoretical nuance.

Further reading

Drenten, J., Gurrieri, L., & Tyler, M. (2020). Sexualized labour in digital culture: Instagram influencers, porn chic and the monetization of attention. *Gender, Work & Organization*, 27(1), 41–66.

Duffy, B. E., Pinch, A., Sannon, S., & Sawey, M. (2021). The nested precarities of creative labor on social media. *Social Media + Society*, 7(2), 20563051211021368.

Glatt, Z. (2024). The intimacy triple bind: Structural inequalities and relational labour in the influencer industry. *European Journal of Cultural Studies*, 27(3), 424–440. https://doi.org/10.1177/13675494231194156

Mehta, S. (2019). Precarity and new media: Through the lens of Indian creators. *International Journal of Communication*, 13, 5548–5567.

References

Agence France-Presse. (2018). *Being LGBT in Kosovo, a Battle to Come Out from the Shadows*. Available at: https://www.france24.com/en/20180923-being-lgbt-kosovo-battle-come-out-shadows (Accessed 23 March 2022).

Arriagada, A., & Ibanez, F. (2020). "You need at least one picture daily, if not, you're dead": Content creators and platform evolution in the social media ecology. *Social Media + Society*, 6(3), 1–12. https://doi.org/10.1177/2056305120944624

Asante, N. (2020). *How Free Is Ghana's Media?* Oxford: Reuters Institute for the Study of Journalism, October 5. Available at: https://reutersinstitute.politics.ox.ac.uk/how-free-ghanas-media (Accessed 23 March 2022).

Bakker, P. (2012). Aggregation, content farms and huffinization: The rise of low-pay and no-pay journalism. *Journalism Practice*, 6(5–6), 627–637. https://doi.org/10.1080/17512786.2012.667266

Bishop, S. (2021). Influencer management tools: Algorithmic cultures, brand safety, and bias. *Social Media + Society*, 7(1). https://doi.org/10.1177/20563051211003066

Brydges, T., & Sjöholmm, J. (2019). Becoming a personal style blogger: Changing configurations and spatialities of aesthetic labour in the fashion industry. *International Journal of Cultural Studies*, 22(1), 119–139. https://doi.org/10.1177/1367877917752404

Bryman, A. (2016). *Social Research Methods*. Oxford: Oxford University Press.Brock, G. (2013). *Out of Print: Journalism and the Business of News in the Digital Age*. London: Kogan Page.

Bromley, M. (2019). 'Who are those guys?' The challenge of journalists' identity. *Journalism* 20(1), 13–16. https://doi.org/10.1177/1464884918806737

Burgess, J., & Green, J. (2009). *YouTube: Online Video and Participatory Culture*. London: Polity

Compton, J. R., & Benedetti, P. (2010). Labour, new media and the institutional restructuring of journalism. *Journalism Studies*, 11(4), 487–499.

Cunningham, S., & Craig, D. (2019). *Social media entertainment: The new intersection of Hollywood and Silicon Valley*. New York University Press.

Deuze, M. (2008). The professional identity of journalists in the context of convergence culture. *Observatorio (OBS*)*, 2(4).

Deuze, M., & Witschge, T. (2020). *Beyond Journalism*. Cambridge: Polity

Duffy, B. E. (2016). The romance of work: Gender and aspirational labour in the digital culture industries. *International Journal of Cultural Studies*, 19(4), 441–457. https://doi.org/10.1177/1367877915572186

Duffy, B. E. (2017). *(Not) Getting Paid to Do What You Love: Gender, Social Media, and Aspirational Work*. New Haven, CT: Yale University Press.

Duffy, B. E. (2020). Algorithmic precarity in cultural work. *Communication and the Public*, 5(3–4), 103–107. https://doi.org/10.1177/2057047320959855

Duffy, B. E., Miltner, K. M., & Wahlstedt, A. (2022). Policing "fake" femininity: Authenticity, accountability, and influencer antifandom. *New Media & Society*, 24(7), 1657–1676. https://doi.org/10.1177/14614448221099234

Duffy, B. E., Pinch, A., Sannon, S., & Sawey, M. (2021). The nested precarities of creative labor on social media. *Social Media + Society*, 7(2). https://doi.org/10.1177/20563051211021368

Duffy, B. E., Poell, T., & Nieborg, D. B. (2019). Platform practices in the cultural industries: Creativity, labor, and citizenship. *Social Media + Society*, 5(4). https://doi.org/10.1177/2056305119879672

Duffy, B. E., & Pooley, J. (2019). Idols of promotion: The Triumph of self-branding in an age of precarity. *Journal of Communication*, 69(1), 26–48.

Fereday, J., & Muir-Cochrane, E. (2006) Demonstrating rigor using thematic analysis: A hybrid approach of inductive and deductive coding and theme development. *International Journal of Qualitative Methods*, 5(1), 1–11.

Gill, R., & Pratt, A. C. (2008). In the social factory? Immaterial labour, precariousness and cultural work. *Theory, Culture & Society*, 25(7–8), 1–30. https://doi.org/10.1177/0263276408097794

Glatt, Z. (2021). "We're all told not to put our eggs in one basket": Uncertainty, precarity and cross-platform labor in the online video influencer industry. *International Journal of Communication*, 16(2022), 3853–3871.

Glatt, Z. (2022). Precarity, discrimination and (in)visibility: An ethnography of "The Algorithm" in the YouTube influencer industry. In E. Costa, P. Lange, N. Haynes, and J. Sinanan (eds.) *The Routledge Companion to Media Anthropology* (pp. 546–559). New York: Routledge.

Gregg, M., & Andrijasevic, R. (2019). Virtually absent: The gendered histories and economies of digital labour. *Feminist Review*, 123(1), 1–7. https://doi.org/10.1177/0141778919878929

Hanusch, F. (2012). Broadening the focus: The case for lifestyle journalism as a field of scholarly inquiry. *Journalism Practice*, 6(1), 2–11.

Hanusch, F., Banjac, S., & Maares, P. (2020). The power of commercial influences: How lifestyle journalists experience pressure from advertising and public relations. *Journalism Practice*, 14(9), 1029–1046. https://doi.org/10.1080/17512786.2019.1682942

Hanusch, F., Hanitzsch, T., & Lauerer, C. (2017). 'How much love are you going to give this brand?' Lifestyle journalists on commercial influences in their work. *Journalism*, 18(2), 141–158. https://doi.org/10.1177/1464884915608818

Hardt, M., & Negri, A. (2009). *Commonwealth*. Cambridge, MA: Belknap Press/Harvard University Press.

Irani, L. (2019). *Chasing Innovation: Making Entrepreneurial Citizens in Modern India*. Princeton, NJ: Princeton University Press.

Jarrett, K. (2014). The relevance of 'women's work': Social reproduction and immaterial labour in digital media. *Television & New Media*, 15(1), 14–29. https://doi.org/10.1177/1527476413487607

Kellogg, K. C., Valentine, M., & Christin, A. (2020). Algorithms at work: The new contested terrain of control. *The Academy of Management Annals*, 14(1), 366–410. https://doi.org/10.5465/annals.2018.0174

Maares, P., & Hanusch, F. (2020). Exploring the boundaries of journalism: Instagram micro-bloggers in the twilight zone of lifestyle journalism. *Journalism*, 21(2), 262–278. https://doi.org/10.1177/1464884918801400

Majid, A. (2023). As reach warns of traffic slowdown: How Facebook referrals to publishers have plummeted. *Press Gazette*. Available at: https://pressgazette.co.uk/platforms/how-far-facebook-referral-traffic-to-news-sites-has-plummeted/ (Accessed 4 January 2024).

Massey, B. L., & Elmore, C. (2018). Freelancing in journalism. In H. Örnebring and H. Wasserman (Eds.), *Oxford Research Encyclopedia of Communication*. Oxford: Oxford University Press. https://doi.org/10.1093/acrefore/9780190228613.013.818.

Mathisen, B. R. (2017). Entrepreneurs and idealists. *Journalism Practice*, 11(7), 909–924. https://doi.org/10.1080/17512786.2016.1199284

Matthews, J., & Onyemaobi, K. (2020). Precarious professionalism: Journalism and the fragility of professional practice in the Global South. *Journalism Studies*, 21(13), 1836–1851. https://doi.org/10.1080/1461670X.2020.1797524

Meese, J., & Bannerman, S. (Eds.) (2022). *The Algorithmic Distribution of News*. London: Palgrave Macmillan.

Neff, G., Wissinger, E., & Zukin, S. (2005). Entrepreneurial labour among cultural producers: "Cool" jobs in "hot" industries. *Social Semiotics*, 15, 307–334. https://doi.org/10.1080/10350330500310111

North, L. (2016). 'The gender of 'soft' and 'hard' news'. *Journalism Studies*, 17(3), 356–373. https://doi.org/10.1080/1461670X.2014.987551

Obermaier, M., & Koch, T. (2015). Mind the gap: Consequences of inter-role conflicts of freelance journalists with secondary employment in the field of public relations. *Journalism*, 16(5), 615–629. https://doi.org/10.1177/1464884914528142

Olausson, U. (2018). The celebrified journalist: journalistic self-promotion and branding in celebrity constructions on Twitter. *Journalism Studies*, 19(16), 2379–2399. https://doi.org/10.1080/1461670X.2017.1349548

Pedroni, M. (2015). Stumbling on the heels of My Blog": Career, forms of capital, and strategies in the (sub)field of fashion blogging'. *Fashion Theory*, 19(2), 179–199. https://doi.org/10.2752/175174115X14168357992355

Perreault, G. P., & Bélair-Gagnon, V. (2024). The lifestyle of lifestyle journalism: How reporters discursively manage their aspirations in their daily work. *Journalism Practice*, 18(7), 1641–1659.

Perreault, G., & Hanusch, F. (2024). Field insurgency in lifestyle journalism: How lifestyle journalists marginalize Instagram influencers and protect their autonomy. *New Media & Society*, 26(7), 3767–3785. https://doi.org/10.1177/14614448221104233

Pw, C. (2023). *Perspectives from the Global Entertainment and Media Outlook 2023-2027*. Available at: https://www.pwc.com/gx/en/industries/tmt/media/outlook/insights-and-perspectives.html (Accessed 5 January 2024).

Ross, K. (2001). Wo men at work: Journalism as en- gendered practice. *Journalism Studies*, 2(4), 531–544. https://doi.org/10.1080/14616700120086404.

Sharp, R., & Vodanovic, L. (2022). Professional and personal identity, precarity and discrimination in global arts journalism. *Journalism Studies*, 23(14), 1802–1820. https://doi.org/10.1080/1461670X.2022.2112907

Simon, F. M. (2019). What determines a journalist's popularity on twitter? *Journalism Studies*, 20(8), 1200–1220. https://doi.org/10.1080/1461670X.2018.1500491

Sinha, M., & Srivastava, M. (2023). Augmented reality: New Future of social media influencer marketing. *Vision*, 1–12. https://doi.org/10.1177/09722629221147124

Spilsbury, M. (2021). *Exploring Freelance Journalism*. London: NCTJ. Available at: https://www.nctj.com/wp-content/uploads/2021/08/EXPLORING-FREELANCE-JOURNALISM-FINAL.pdf (Accessed 5 January 2024).

Stoldt, R., Wellman, M., Ekdale, B., & Tully, M. (2019). Professionalizing and profiting: The rise of intermediaries in the social media influencer industry. *Social Media + Society*, 5(1). https://doi.org/10.1177/2056305119832587

Vodanovic, L. (2019). *Lifestyle Journalism: Social Media, Consumption and Experience*. London: Routledge

INDEX

Note: Page numbers followed by "n" denote endnotes.

Adam, Ansel 229
  advertising 4, 10, 347–349; attracting 283, 304, 309, 326, 347; and editorial content 17–18, 56, 108, 348; funding 363, 455, 459, 466; goods 76; green 307; influence of 347; media's 158–159, 409; native 348, 366, 401, 423–425, 433; in news industry 16, 342; paid 348, 361; and publicity 111; revenue 347, 378, 381, 383, 462; self-improvement 271; and tourism industry 222; travel magazine 175–176
  advertorial stories 348
  aesthetics 386, 408; aspirational objects 121, 124, 142; and authenticity 140, 142; commercial or capitalist 161; in context of journalism 122–123; contributions and research 128–129; cultural consumption 7, 33, 121; defined 122–123; expertise 94; with food journalism 7; future directions 129–130; genre traits from previous studies 125–127; issues 127–128; lifestyle work 124–125; object 124; popular 95
  agency(ies) 347, 441, 443; industrial 103; marketing 194; news 287; political 220, 305–306; and power 198; regulatory 283; self-agency 271, 280; state 39–40; talent 290, 444; tourism 118; travel 227
Almheiri, Mariam 291
Amanpour, Christiane 3
amateur bloggers 190, 365, 460
Anderson, C. 141

Anderson, Mary 278
Andres, Jose 286
Ang, I. 411
anthropological tourists 77
anthro-tourism 76, 77, 83, 87
Archer, L. 173
Arık, E. 155
Arnold, M. 274
Arriagada, A. 144, 145
artificial intelligence (AI) 18–19, 130, 147
artistic identity 144
Ashe, I. 142
Asian Australian identity 417–418
aspiration(al): of audience 108, 172; conceptualizations of 173; for culinary adventure 118; doxic 172, 174–177, 179–182; elements 123; emerging/emergent 172, 174, 180–183; goals 173; habituated 172, 174, 178–180, 182; and habitus 177–178; and hope 198; identity work is 8; and imagined futures 180–182; of intimacy 443; labour 127, 212, 318, 337, 365, 368, 456, 458–459, 465–467; of lifestyle journalism 77, 123, 142–143, 171–183, 410; luxury 51; market 111; narratives 137; navigational capacity 171; objects 124, 129–130; politics 181; social class 172; taste of 182
Asquith, Herbert 48
audiences: aspiration of 108, 172; boundaries by members 369–370; as community 442; contemporary perspectives 440–442; engagement 441; entertainment

471

for 240; hard news 323–325; labour of building audiences 458–459; perceptions of news 441; radical turn 441; studies 108, 172, 440–442
Aupers, S. 400
Australia 56, 141, 151, 239, 364; commercial influences 346–347; empire trade in 46–47; food blogs *see* food blogs/bloggers, Asian Australian; Great Depression 47; newspapers in 50, 52, 113; travel magazines in 175, 240, 304, 352
authenticity 189–190, 334, 415; and accuracy 211; and authority 141–143; and credibility 138; cultural 407; and digital media 143–145; distinctive 136; emotional 190, 197; existential journalism 140; experiences 138; in foodie culture 415–417; identities 286; illusions 138, 146; influencer 196; infrastructure 139; institutional 138; and integrity 24; labor of 145; in lifestyle journalism 7, 19, 128, 136–141; mediated 138, 146; perception of 211; political 138; work 138
Ayurveda: beauty practices 206; commerce and class 211–215; consumption 212–214; food 206; identity 207–209; as lifestyle choice 207; medicine 211–214; Ministry of AYUSH 205; modern 209–211; reviews on 203; role of 8; wellness 207

Bagehot, W.: *The English Constitution* 31–32
Baker, S. A. 10, 144, 203, 336
Baldwin, B.: *Having It All: A Practical Guide to Overcoming the Career Woman's Blues* 394
Baldwin, Stanley 56
Bali, R.N. 156–158
Banet-Weiser, S. 143, 145
Banjac, S. 8, 61, 77, 78, 87, 110, 143, 152, 182, 194, 236, 245, 317, 364, 369, 370, 457, 466
Banks, Tim 377
Barnhurst, K. G. 16
Baumann, S. 415
Baumgarten, Alexander 122
Beard, James 115
Beckett, C. 139
Beck, U. 253
Beecher, Catherine 398
Beeton, Isabella 398
Bélair-Gagnon, V. 188, 189, 196, 319, 459
Bell, D. 304, 308, 417
Bendy Bananas 45
Bennett, Arnold 51

Beres, D. 336
Berger, R. 205
The Best Families (Blæsbjerg) 94
Biddle, B. J. 236
Bilefsky, Dan 159
Binkley, S. 305
biomoral consumerism 205–206, 213
Bishop, S. 144, 145
Bissell, K. 175
Black culture 176
The Black Dwarf (Wooler) 270
#Black Lives Matter 40
Blackmore, Richard Doddridge 279
Blæsbjerg, Kim 97, 100–102: *The Best Families* 94
Blassnig, S. 441
bloggers: amateur 190, 365, 460; digital lifestyle 109, 137, 346; fan 256; fashion 346, 365, 368, 378, 382, 383, 457, 466; food *see* food blogs/bloggers, Asian Australian; hatebloggers 145; micro 194, 361–362, 364–367, 369; online 351; rising competition from 141; roles performed 112; science 256; second wave of 365; travel 142, 349, 368
Bluesky 458
blurred boundaries 10, 13, 15, 21, 24, 75, 94, 104, 115, 118, 125, 155, 187, 189, 195, 203, 252, 286, 366, 367
Bonner, F. 412
bookishness 100, 101
book reviewing: changing interaction and promotion 102–104; defining features 93, 96–99; future directions 104–105; historical overview 93–94; in (media) historical perspective 94–96; on Instagram 94, 99–102
Bookstagram 125
Boorstin, D. J. 222
Bordo, S. 215
Borges-Rey, E. 140
boundaries: by audience members 369–370; blurred 10, 13, 15, 21, 24, 75, 94, 104, 115, 118, 125, 155, 187, 189, 195, 203, 252, 286, 366, 367; class 269, 272, 274; conceptual 15, 75, 399–400; between consumers and producers 439; content creators on social media and lifestyle journalists 455; cross-national 379; of cultural and lifestyle journalism 7, 14; definitional 75, 145, 377, 378; emotional labor 190; between fact and fiction 128; between food TV and journalism 115–116, 287–288; between hard and soft news 80, 110; between health, lifestyle and wellness journalism 9, 332, 337;

between highbrow and popular culture 96; between journalism and media 109; journalism as occupation 362–363; between journalists and influencers 189, 190, 362; between lifestyle and political 197; of lifestyle journalism 364–365, 367–368; linguistic, national, and sectarian 36; between literature and journalism 220; personal 188–189, 459; between private and public spheres 439; professional 127, 188–189, 459; soft 260, 314, 315; subject 15; between work and lifestyle 314–315, 337, 342, 345, 346; work from peripheral actors 368–369
Bourdain, A. 44, 116, 287, 288
Bourdieu, P. 15, 16, 66, 87, 143, 154, 173, 174, 179, 315, 376–381, 388; field theory 376
Boynton, Emma Louise 448
brand journalism: in digital age 432–433; *Everworld Stories* 429–430, 432; fashion brands 423; *Giant* 427–428, 432; *The Journal* 431–432; media publications 423; mediatization and digital turn 425–426; past and present 424–425; from post-to hypermodernity 426–427; Suitsupply 431; Uniqlo's *UT Magazine* 428–429
Brennan, M. 182
Briggs, C. L. 332
British culture 276
British newspaper press 45
Bro, P. 23
Brüggemann, B. 113
Brun, Malou Wedell 103
Brydges, T. 307
Burgess, J. 144

Cakir, B. 152
Canada 17, 49, 55–56; empire trade in 46–47; Great Depression 47; Instagram content creators in 145; newspapers in 50, 175
Carey, J. W. 323
Carlile, Richard: *The Prompter* 270; *The Republican* 270
Carlson, M. 141, 146, 441
Carnegie, D.: *How to Win Friends and Influence People* 394, 395
Cartney-Morley, Jess 377
celebrity culture 136, 204, 268, 273, 279; news journalism 6, 61–70, 274
Ceppos, J. 138
Chambers, D. 443
Chartism 280n1

Chattopadhyay, Swati 57n2
Cheng, L. 367
Chew, M. 367
Child, Julia 115
China 110, 241, 346–347, 353, 411, 418, 460
Chipungudzanye, Tatenda 80, 85
Chong, P. 97, 188, 190, 192
Christians, C. G. 238
clash of culture 446
class boundaries 269, 272, 274
Cleave's Weekly Police Gazette (1834–1836) 271
Clinton, Bill 285
Clinton, Hillary 325
Clinton, William J. 285
Cocking, B. 8
Cohen, B. C. 235
Cohen, E. 222
Coleman, R. 9
collective action 41, 286, 291, 293, 295
collective identity 35
commercial: advertising 347–349; agents 94; branding 213, 408, 409; classes 38; conflicts of interest 112, 118; consumption 410; context and consumption 21, 161, 307, 309; culture 306; defined 342; fiction 28; food 46–47, 408; impacts on lifestyle journalism 6–8, 14, 24, 64, 108, 407; incentives 332; influences 108–113, 115, 212, 341–343, 346–347, 364, 369–371; interests 17–18, 155, 306, 314, 330, 332, 345, 349, 368; issues 108; logic 14, 381, 441, 445, 446, 450; media 16, 153, 156–159, 162–163, 408, 409; news 22, 61; pressures 9, 17, 114, 241, 341–342, 346–347, 353, 378, 451, 455, 457; public relations 349–350; television 108, 118
Conboy, M. 269, 270
conceptual boundaries 15, 75, 399–400
confessional society 444
Conlin, L. 175
conspicuous consumption 32–33, 76, 156, 161, 162, 172, 212; *see also* consumption
constructed certitude of identity 128
constructive journalism 22–23
consumer culture 6, 18, 93, 95, 96, 125, 154, 157, 158, 162, 164, 286, 301–302, 333, 364, 381
consumerism 63, 68, 128–129; biomoral 205–206, 213; and capitalism 162; and citizenship 68; commercial media 157–159; and culture 187; expansion of 96; Islamic 154, 159–160, 163; and service journalism 80

consumption 4; authenticity 144; Ayurvedic 212–214; choices 124, 129–130; commercial 410; conspicuous 32–33, 76, 156, 161, 162, 172, 212; cultural 7, 11, 14, 94–96, 102–104, 121, 190, 242, 244; domestic 19, 410; ethical 300, 304–306, 308; everyday 195, 198, 305; food 191, 292; green 308; group 15; habits and self-identity 404; home 37; idols of 63; inconspicuous 172; individual 15; issues of 22; and lifestyle journalism 7, 88, 122, 151; mass 16; media 15, 275, 459; of others 211; patterns 24, 96, 152, 153, 158, 162, 163, 302; politics of 86; of products 175–176, 239; unsustainability of 305; upper-class 162; value 97; Western style of 156–158
content creators 455
Cook Republic (Roy) 407, 413, 418
Copeland, Sarah 449
Cordúa y Cruz, G. 112
Coren, G. 113
cottagecore 125
COVID-19 pandemic 250, 253; awareness of value of health and wellbeing 204–205; challenges 455; health and wellness journalism 330, 337; issues 9; lock down 228; role of hard news 335; wake of 254–255, 295, 322
Coward, R. 44, 139, 444
Craft, S. 324
Craig, Elizabeth 47, 51, 54
Craig, G. 9, 21, 293, 304, 305, 308, 309
crime news 61–63, 65, 66, 68–71, 71n1, 271, 272
cross-national boundaries 379
cultural consumption 7, 11, 14, 94–96, 102–104, 121, 190, 242, 244; *see also* consumption
culture/cultural 15; American 393; Black 176; British 276; capital 173; celebrity 136, 204, 268, 273, 279; citizenship 19; clash of 446; commercial 306; consumer 6, 18, 93, 95, 96, 125, 154, 157, 158, 162, 164, 286, 301–302, 333, 364, 381; democratization of 16, 352; digital 136, 144, 204, 212; DIY 19; everyday 15–16; foodie 415–416, 418; freelancing/entrepreneurial 440; highbrow and lowbrow 95, 121, 179; hybrid 414; Indian 205, 207, 210; identity 121, 138, 214, 220, 277, 407, 411, 413, 414; intermediary 35; Italian 226, 230; magazine 446; mass 63, 67; material 100; Ottoman 159; parlour 272;

popular 14, 29, 95–96, 115–116, 129, 152, 159, 178, 267, 301, 344; public 19; therapeutic 187, 194, 393, 396; Turkish 223; uncultured 176; Web 2.0 443; wellness 8, 202, 204, 205, 215, 397–398; Western 393
Curran, J. 270
Curtis, L.P. 274

Dağtaş, E. 158
Daily Express 46–56
Daily Mail 45–56
Daily Telegraph 45
Dalai Lama 188
Dale, R. 37, 394, 395
dance influencer 433
Danish legacy media 7
dark academy communities 125
Davis, M. 111
Debord, G. 274
Deere, John 424
definitional boundaries 75, 145, 377, 378
Defino, J. 449, 450
Dejmanee, T. 10, 11
democracy 19, 23; capitalist 9, 38, 267, 268, 279–280; and citizenship 317; constructive journalism 23; cultural journalism 195; elective 40; historical evolution of 361; role of journalism 62; Western 220
democratic culture 352
Denisova, A. 348, 349
Deuze, M. 18, 139, 294, 344, 345, 459
dialogical relationships 438–439
digital culture 136, 144, 204, 212
digital epistolary 447
Dinç, C. 160, 163
Disney+ 117
Disraeli, Benjamin 394
DIY culture 19
domestic consumption 19, 410; *see also* consumption
doxic aspiration 172, 174–177, 179–182
Dubied, A. 6
Duffy, B. E. 145, 337, 387, 412, 458
Dunn, Halbert L. 398
Durkheim, E. 321
The Edinburgh Review (1802–1929) 272
editorial content 17–18, 29, 54, 56, 108, 154, 175, 346–348, 457, 464, 466
Eide, M. 9, 22, 68
Elgesem, D. 23, 242
Elias, N. 393, 394
Elle 377, 379, 389n2

Elliott, T. 114, 344
emerging/emergent aspiration 172, 174, 180–183
emotion(al): aesthetic or moral 186; authenticity 187, 189–190; cultural and lifestyle journalism 195–196; defined 186; emotional turn 186; exceptionalism of lifestyle journalism 186–188, 190, 197; genres 61–62; and identity 240, 242, 245; joy, passion and love 187–189; labor 187, 190–192, 197, 451; narratives 7; news 68–69; and subjective experiences 98, 104, 187–190, 404; well-being 8; work 187, 192–195
empire crusade 48–49
'Empire Loaf' campaign 48–49
Empire Marketing Board (E. M. B.) 47
empire trade 46–47
The English Constitution (Bagehot) 31–32
English, P. 7, 110, 112
Enli, G. 138
Enninful, Edward 386
entertainment 6, 14, 16, 330; for audiences 240; blurred boundaries 21; choices 153; consumerism and culture 187; elements of 110; factual 126; fictional 127; food television 115–118; hard and soft news boundaries 80; home consumption or general 37; and inspiration 176; market 29; mass 33; media 29, 288, 305; narrative 29; news 303; pleasure-seeking consumers of 30; programmes 157, 304; and relaxation 239, 243, 368; reporting 84; reviews and ratings 111
entrepreneurship, logic of 384–385
environmental journalism 302
Ergul, I.N. 152
Erkilet, A. 159, 161
Ernaux, Annie 97, 100, 101; *The Years* 94
Esser, F. 441
ethical journalism 338; and commercial influences 342–343; consumption 300, 304–306, 308; issues 109, 341, 346, 353, 401, 403–404; principles of 29–30; theory 343–345
Ethical Journalism Network (EJN) 29–30
ethnic identity 83–84, 138, 205
Evans, David 276
Evans, Matthew 117
Evening Standard, London 45, 46, 49–55
Everworld Stories 429–430, 432
everyday life 240, 250–253; aestheticization of 16–17; citizen-oriented 71; consumption 195, 198, 305; culture 15–16; dimensions of 171; everyday politics 418–419; issues 23, 45–46, 63, 69, 286; and narrative 65–68; politics of 137, 154, 177, 236, 238, 242, 280, 285, 289, 294–295, 302, 407, 411, 414, 419
exclusion: dimensions of 456–458; identity 128; and inclusion 172, 178–179; issues of 268; from questionnaire 80; racialised 463–464
expertise: aesthetic 94; communication of 13; construction of 256–259; crisis of scientific expertise 251; democratization of 251–252; explosion of 251, 252; future directions 259–260; institutional 392; lifestyle experts 255–256; multiplication of 252; native 399, 403; in pluralistic knowledge societies 254–255; popular 403; professional 140, 370, 463; specialized expert knowledge 252–254; specific 363

Facebook 457–458, 464
Fakazis, E. 9, 44, 45, 109, 111, 113, 116
fan bloggers 256; *see also* bloggers
Faramarzi, S. 76
Farrell, J.G. 36
fashion 29, 31, 40, 51, 64, 74, 76, 123, 141, 152, 154–156, 243, 272, 278, 304, 310, 316, 333, 344, 346, 350, 352, 353, 440–441, 444, 455; brands 10, 302, 371, 376, 385–388, 423; companies 386, 387; critics 382–385, 388; digital 386; events 386; Islamic 159; magazines 128, 159–160, 163, 175, 346, 382; media 347, 376, 382, 384, 386–388, 423, 425; photography 425–426; of politics 325; shows 365–366, 425; soft news 313; stylish 158; transnational media players 385–387
fashion bloggers 346, 365, 368, 378, 382, 383, 457, 466; *see also* bloggers
fashion journalism 13, 75, 126–127, 220, 313, 349, 376–382, 384–385
Favaro, L. 443, 445
Featherstone, M. 302
"feel good" pieces 352–353
feminist theories 316–318
Fenn, George Manville 276
Ferrucci, P. 241
Ficara, G. 241
Financial Times 377
Findlay, R. 365
Finland 348–349, 353
First World War 44–48, 61
Fiske, J. 20, 75
Fisk, Robert 3

Index

FitTuber (male influencer) 214
Flay, Bobby 115
Fleischman, D. 7, 110, 113
Fløttum, K. 23, 242
fluid intimacy 443
food among others 174, 176–178
food blogs/bloggers, Asian Australian 10; *Cook Republic* 407, 413, 418; ethnic foods and authenticity 415–417; everyday politics 418–419; in framework of lifestyle journalism 409–411; in France 112; "Generically Asian" *vs.* specific nations/regions 414–415; identity as cultural adaptability 417–418; in multicultural Australia 411–413; overview of 408–409; personal weblogs 407; rearticulating Western/Asian Binaries 413–414; *Recipe Tin Eats* (Nagi Maehashi) 407, 413, 418; *see also* bloggers
food consumption 191, 292
foodie culture 415–418
food journalism 3, 5, 13, 127; commercial ingredients 108–118; competitive reality cooking 116; as cultural critique 286–289; diversifying 289–291; ethics of care 343, 352; food television, rise of 44, 115–118; future directions 294–296; issues 21, 55; journalists in 109–111; news stories in 44, 113–115; political relevance 9, 45, 49, 283–296; restaurants, reviewer ratings of 112–113; reviews 7, 111–113; roots of 284–286; and sustainability 291–294
food travel 118, 141, 174, 310
food TV 109, 115–118, 347
Foucault, M. 205, 215
Franklin, J. 3, 331
freebies 319, 350–352
Freedman, H. 313
free labour 117, 384, 459, 465–466
freelancing/entrepreneurial culture 440
free press 39
French Revolution 32
From, U. 7, 16, 22, 23, 75, 86
Fürsich, E. 15, 20, 44, 45, 70, 75, 109, 111, 113, 116, 136, 141, 221, 222

Gale, T. 175, 182
Gardiner, B. 451
gender identity 352
generative AI 337
The Gentlewoman 377
Ger, G. 157, 161
Germany 151, 239, 241, 346, 353, 383; commercial influences 346; newspapers in 113; PR in 350

Giant 427–428, 432
Giddens, A. 392
Gieryn, T. F. 363
gifting 351
Gilligan, C. 343
Gill, R. 396
Giroux, H. A. 79, 87
Givhan, Robin 325
Goddard, Arabella 276
Goffman, E. 77, 138
Google 13, 97, 337, 387, 410, 416
Great Depression 44, 47, 49
green advertising 307
green consumption 308
Green, J. 144
green lifestyle journalism: evaluation 304–307; journalism of 302–303; media research and future of 307–309; relationships between 300–301; types of 303–304
Green, M. 38
'greenness' of nature 301
Greenpeace 301
Gregory, S. 139
Groot Kormelink, T. 441
group consumption 15
group identity 77, 138, 362
Grundmann, R. 250, 252, 254
The Guardian 109, 111–112, 292, 313, 377, 442, 446–447, 450–451
Guillier, Maitre 55
Gürgen, V.S. 152
Gyldensted, C. 22

habituated aspiration 172, 174, 178–180, 182
habitus 177–178
Hackett, E. 9
Hage, G. 411
Halfpenny Magazine of Entertainment and Knowledge (1840–1841) 271
Hallan, Louise 449
Hallin, D. C. 332
Hamid-Turksoy, N. 223
Hamilton, M. 51
Hanitzsch, T. 4, 17, 110, 154, 158, 163, 194, 234–240, 243, 323
Hanson, Pauline 411
Hanusch, F. 14, 17, 29, 61–62, 67, 77–78, 87, 110, 143, 152, 155, 158, 163, 182, 188, 194, 236, 238–241, 243, 245, 256, 267, 314, 317, 323, 368–370, 409, 444, 455
hard news 3; advocacy 322–323; audience commitment 323–325; for campaigns 34; challenges 9; defined 317; division between quality 317; ethical issues in 346; food journalism 108, 113, 284,

476

287–288; general 84; of green lifestyle stories 303; health journalism 331, 335; hostility 318–319; labor 319–320; in lifestyle journalism 4, 5, 9, 154, 286, 314–315, 318–319, 330, 341; market pressures 320; and political life 4, 176–177, 303; repackage 86; social cohesion 320–322; and soft news 62, 68, 75, 80, 242, 314–315, 364, 441; stories about climate change 310; traditional journalism 344–346

Hardt, M. 456, 459
Harper's Bazaar 379
Hartley, J. 5, 6, 16, 19, 191, 277, 303, 378
hatebloggers 145
Having It All: A Practical Guide to Overcoming the Career Woman's Blues (Baldwin) 394
Hay, Louise: *You Can Heal Your Life* 394
Hayes, A. S. 138
health journalism: beauty standards 180; challenges and opportunities 337; for female and family 123; hard news 331, 335; historical review of 330–333
Hearst, W.R. 32, 379, 387
Hellmueller, L. 237
Hendrickx, J. 441
Heřmanová, M. 189, 190, 192, 193
Hermida, A. 446
Hetherington, Henry 270, 271
Hetherington's Twopenny Dispatch and People's Police Register (*Twopenny Dispatch*, 1834–1836) 271
highbrow culture 33, 95–96, 121–122, 176, 178–179, 272
Hill, Napoleon: *Think and Grow Rich* 394
Hill, A. 9
Hitler, Adolf 48
holistic wellness 203
Hollows, J. 304, 308, 417
Holt, K. 140
Holton, A. E. 9, 442
home consumption 37
Homeopathy 205
homogeneous identity 162
Hornmoen, H. 439
Horton, D. 275, 402
Houghton, W.E.: *The Victorian Frame of Mind* 272
Houtman, D. 400
How to Get What You Want (Wattles) 395
How to Win Friends and Influence People (Carnegie) 394, 395
Hulu 117
Hund, E. 145, 203, 211

hybrid culture 414
hybrid identity 7, 164, 419
hypermediacy 425

identity 76, 209; American 424; artistic 144; Asian Australian 417–418; authentic 286; Ayurvedic 207–209; collective 35; constructed certitude of 128; cultural 121, 138, 214, 220, 277, 407, 411, 413, 414; and emotion 240, 242, 245; ethnic 83–84, 138, 205; gender 352; of green lifestyle journalism 304, 309; group 77, 138, 362; homogeneous 162; hybrid 7, 164, 419; Indian 208, 412; influencers' 209; Islamic/Muslim 152, 156, 161, 163; journalistic 363; national 24, 44, 175, 176, 205–206, 209, 213, 215, 267, 285, 411, 412, 419; organizational 196; people's 8; personal 157, 188, 303, 316, 451; politics 21, 74, 76, 81, 283, 287, 289, 413; professional 196, 220, 456, 459; racial 179; religious 205, 208; secular 161; self-identity 270, 274, 277, 392–393, 398; sense of 'vlog life' 230; social 9, 224, 229, 295; status 138; sustainable 21; travel 224; work 4, 8, 10
ideology of authenticity 144
"i-docs" 126
Illouz, E. 396
The Illustrated London News (1842–2003) 273
imagined community 35, 143, 268, 285
inconspicuous consumption 172
India: Ayurvedic identity 207–215; cooking and recipes 414, 416–417; culture 205, 207, 210; food coverage 49–53, 56; identity 208, 412; influencer 204, 208; Modern Ayurveda and biomedicine 209–211; national identity and homegrown traditions 205–206; *Vogue*, *Marie-Claire* and *Harper's Bazaar* (magazines) 379; wellness influencing in 8, 202–207
Indianness 208, 215
"individualisation" in journalism 447
Indonesia 415
industrial agencies 103
"Industrial Attachment" 81
influencer 365, 392–393, 400–401, 425; authentic 196; Ayurvedic consumption 213, 214; blurring boundary 189, 337; brand engagements 213; creep 337; culture 462; dance 433; defined 456; on digital platforms 14, 17, 137, 142, 143, 146, 147, 362, 456; ecosystem 18; identity 209; imaginary 144; Indian 204, 208; Instagram 189, 194; male influencer,

FitTuber 214; marketing 18; national 17–18, 49; online lifestyle 17–18, 127, 243, 251, 256, 259–260, 366, 367; professional lifestyle Instagrammers 142, 336; social and economic capital 190; social media 10, 74, 94, 109, 112, 143, 189, 192, 194, 197, 203, 211, 275, 302, 336, 350, 409; wellness 9, 203, 206, 210, 331, 334, 336–337, 401; women 145
Instagram 10, 14, 18, 93–94, 112, 117, 182, 219, 259, 302, 366, 382, 396, 403; book(ish) and affective reviews on 99–102; content creators 145; fashion commentators 386; followers on 383, 385–387; hashtags 396; health and wellness communities on 401; influencer 142, 189, 194, 243, 336; micro-influencers 444; photo-sharing platform 99; recipes and recipe blogs 287; reels 396, 403; reviews 100–104; rise of entertainment 330; Twin Sauce 433; use of 'Paid Partnership' tag 18; works and reviews 7
Insta Therapy: ethics of 401–402; self-diagnosis, self-healing and self-identity 398–400
institutional expertise 392
interlopers 142, 197, 336–337, 382
The International Herald Tribune 378
internship 81–82, 84, 341
intimacy 10, 127, 138, 193, 268, 275, 401–402, 439–441; fluid 443; public 443; sympathetic 276
invidious comparison 31–33
Irish Republican War 46
Irving, Henry 276, 278
Islamic consumerism 154, 159–160, 163
Islamic identity 152, 156, 161, 163
Italy 224–226, 285, 383, 431; culture 226, 230

Jaakkola, M. 7, 99, 100, 195
Jackson, K. 275
Jacobs, S. 181
Jaffrey, Madhur 115
Janowitz, M. 235
Japan 46, 383, 413, 428–429
Jenkins, J. 7
Johnson, B. K. 144
Johnson, S. 30
Johnston, J. 415
Jones, J. P. 343–345, 352
Jones, S. 44, 112, 304, 308
Joosse, S. 307
Jost, J. S. 95
The Journal 431–432

journalism scholarship 3–4, 6, 11, 129, 234, 260, 320, 365
Jung, Carl 400

Kaltmeier, O. 32, 33
Kaplan, D. 443
Kasturi, S. 8, 11
Kavoori, A. P. 221, 222
Khalikova, V. R. 205, 208, 213–215
Kim, B. 321, 322
Kirkwood, K. 109
Knight, G. 9, 22, 68
knowledgeable society 252, 255
Knudsen, E. 23, 242
Kohlberg, L. 343
Kotišová, J. 8
Kristensen, N. N. 6, 14, 22, 23, 162, 191
Kruiper, Dawid 86
Kruiper, Veitkat 86
Kuenssberg, Laura 3
Kuipers, G. 223
Kunert, J. 113
Kylie Kwong 412

Lagasse, Emeril 115
Lahav, H. 256
Lanza-Abbott, J. A. 112
Lasch, C. 393
Lascity, Myles Ethan 10
Lauerer, C. 110, 158
Lau, Susanna 361
Lawrence, Chris 423
Lawson, Nigella 115
Lee Ajussa 80, 82
Lee, S. S. 144
leisure 6, 14, 16, 29, 31, 69, 74; activities 273–274, 276, 278, 303, 409; 'celebrity sphere' 63; experiences 219; lifestyle choices 117; time and hobbies 123, 155, 157, 220, 221, 239, 242, 245, 267, 269, 272, 301, 342; travels 77, 177
Leitão, J. 226–228
Le Masurier, Megan 379
Le Mercure Galant 377
Lethlean, J. 112, 113
Leupold, A. 321
Lewis, T. 19, 251, 255, 258, 442, 446
Liaw, Adam 412
Lifestyle Gurus 392
lifestyle journalism: addressing issues of public concern 21; African academics' views of 80–83; boundaries of 364–365, 367–370; commercial entanglements of 17–19; conceptualizing 6–7; and consumption 7; cultural dimensions of 14–15; defined 13–14, 40, 75–78, 254,

301, 323, 333, 455, 457, 458; emotion and identity 8–9; ethical dilemmas in 17; field theory in 315–316; fillers of 86–87; future scholarship in 24–25; on historical continuum 22–23; historical evolution of 15–16; impact on societal norms and values 16–17; insider/outsider distinction 30–31; issues 365–366; Journalists' perceptions on African 84–87; new economy and neoliberalism 18–19; new horizons in 10–11; permeable boundaries 362–363; political and public dimensions of 19–20; public utility of 9; and semiotics 83–84; strategic coffeehouses 37–39; within theory of value 78–80; weekenders 271–274
Lindén, C.-G. 189
Littler, J. 305
LiveJournal 365
Livingstone, S. M. 258
Lloyd, Edward 273
Lloyd George, David 48
Lloyd's Weekly (1842–1931) 273, 274
Löhmann, K. 256, 363
Lo, J. 415
Lončar, M. 175
Lonsdale, S. 6, 69, 109
Lotman, Y. 29
lowbrow culture 95, 121, 176, 178–179
Luebke, S. M. 138
Luhmann, N. 321
Lunt, P. 251, 258

Maares, P. 10, 110, 188, 336, 368, 444, 457, 458, 466
MacCannell, D. 222
Madsen, O. J. 194
Maehashi, N. 407, 410, 413–419
magazine culture 446
Malaysia 48, 415
Marie-Claire India 379
marketing 13, 15, 16, 141; agents 96, 194; content 424; direct 18; influencer 18, 465; organic 410; products 86; tourism 227
market journalism 6, 31, 34, 40; collective action 41; and cultural institutions 104; entertainment 29; expansion of 35–36; information 37; labour market 457, 459; mass market 33; print market 13; target market 427; wellness market 203–205
market pressures 318, 320
Markham, T. 140, 445
Marwick, A. E. 208
Marx, Karl 34
mass consumption 16

mass culture 63, 67
mass press 61–62, 67, 69
Mastodon 458
material culture 21, 100
Matthews, J. 458
Mazzucato, M. 79
Mbembe, A. 87
McDowell, Colin 378
McGee, M. 400
McIntyre, K. 22
McKay, G. 19
media consumption 15, 275, 459
media moguls 39
mediated authenticity 138, 146
mediated intimacy 443
Meijer, I. C. 20, 65, 68, 75, 342, 440–442, 450
Mellado, C. 237
Menkes, Suzanne 378
Merrill, J. C. 140
Meşe, I. 160, 161
Meta 387, 457
#MeToo 40
Mhiripiri, N. A. 7, 11
micro bloggers 194, 361–362, 364–367, 369; *see also* bloggers
Miller, K. 196, 318
The Million (1892–1895) 275–276
Mishan, L. 287
Moeran, B. 128
Møller, Kristian F. 102
Molyneux, L. 444
monotony/variety 52
Moody, Dwight 277
Morimoto, Masaharu 115
Morin, E. 63, 67
Morris, C. 151
Morris, William 277
Murdoch, Rupert 33, 35
Murphy, Andi 288

national identity 24, 44, 175, 176, 205–206, 209, 213, 215, 267, 285, 411, 412, 419
national influencer 17–18, 49
native advertising 348, 366, 401, 423–425, 433
native expertise 399, 403
Naulin, S. 112, 409
Ncube, Lyton 80, 82, 83
Negri, A. 456, 459
Nerone, J. 16
Netflix 117, 126
networked intimacy 443, 446
"The New Journalism" 274–275
Newnes, George 274–276, 278

news: agencies 274, 287; analysis 322; consumption 179, 450
newsletter journalism 384
New York Times 45
New Zealand 53, 54, 430; empire trade in 46–47; Great Depression 47; green lifestyle journalism 303; newspapers in 50, 56; travel vlogs 228
Ngomba, T. 324
Nguyen, Danielle 397
Nguyen, Luke 412
Nichols, J. 288
Nieborg, D. B. 458
The Nineteenth Century (1801–1930) 272
Nölleke, D. 9
The Northern Star and Leeds General Advertiser 271
Nothstine, W. L. 130
novelty/luxury 55

Obama, Michelle 285
O' Brien, James Bronterre 270
Odell, A. 384, 385, 387
Ojo, Odunayo 383
Olausson, U. 445, 447
Oleschuk, M. 175
Oliver, Jamie 109, 115, 250, 251, 259, 285
O'Loughlin, Marina 111
Omerod, K. 448, 450
O'Neill, M. 289
online lifestyle influencer 17–18, 127, 243, 251, 256, 259–260, 366, 367
On Television 381
Onyemaobi, K. 458
OpenAI 338
Orgad, S. 396
organizational identity 196
Ottoman culture 159
Ouellette, L. 19, 444
Öztürkmen, A. 152

Pagot, Maitre 55
paid advertising 348, 361
Paine, Thomas 36, 38, 269
Palin, Sarah 325
Paramount Plus 117
parlour culture 272
The Penny Magazine (1832–1845) 272
People's Weekly Police Gazette (1835–1836) 271
Pepper, S. C. 124
The Perfect Magazine 388
peripheral actors 234, 243, 245, 256, 362–363, 366–371, 382
'perks' 459
Perreault, G. P. 9, 188, 189, 196, 241, 318–320, 459

persona-driven journalism 189
personal boundaries 188–189, 459
personal identity 157, 188, 303, 316, 451
personal weblogs 407
Peters, C. 441
Peterson, R. A. 138
Petrini, Carlo 285
Philpott, Tom 288
Phin, Rian 383
Picone, I. 441
Pınar, L. 158
Pirolli, B. 222, 368
Poell, T. 458
political agencies 220, 305–306
politics: acts of 242, 364; Asian Australian 418–419; aspirational 181, 412; of being 268, 279–280; of civic life 295; of consumption 9, 86; critics 116; of everyday life 177, 280, 285, 289, 407, 411, 414, 419; fashion of 325; of food 284, 285, 287–288, 294; of green consumption 308; identity 21, 283; issues of 289; of knowledge 211; of lifestyle 154–155, 192, 286, 294; and media 77; and national identity 44, 76; of nationalism 205; of ordinariness 294; personality 32; of presentation 122, 127; as prestigious section 81; sensationalising 33; soft and hard news of 303; Turkish 153
Politkovskaya, Anna 3
Pollan, Michael 286
Poole, E. 152
popular culture 14, 29, 95–96, 115–116, 129, 152, 159, 178, 267, 301, 344
popular expertise 403
popular news 20, 75, 152, 179
populist partisans 40
Potter, S. 39
Potts, J. 38
Poutanen, P. 348, 349
The Power of Positive Thinking (Peale) 394
precarity 10–11, 187, 195–198, 302, 455–460, 464–466
Premika, A. 8, 11
Pressman, J. 100
press parasociality 275, 280
private news *see* soft news
professional boundaries 127, 188–189, 459
professional expertise 140, 370, 463
professional identity 196, 220, 456, 459
The Prompter (Carlile) 270
public: broadcasting 156; concerns 19–21, 61, 64, 65, 283, 317; culture 19; intimacy 443; quality 20–21, 70, 75; relations 349–350
Puck 384–385, 447–450
Pulizzi, J. 424

quality *vs.* popular journalism 20

racial identity 179
   Ramdev, Baba 206, 208, 210, 213, 214
   Ramsay, Gordon 115
   Rao, Akshara 206
   Rayner, J. 114
   Ray, Rachel 115, 285
   Recipe Tin Eats (Nagi Maehashi) 407, 413, 418
   reciprocal journalism 442, 446
   reciprocity 276, 440, 446–447
   recognition 5, 24, 30, 34, 116, 146, 210, 229, 303, 309, 368, 383; of amateur bloggers 365; of green lifestyle journalism 308; lack of 245; newsroom 315–316; of privileged positionality 40; social 173, 178
   refeudalization 33
   regional affinity 205, 208, 415
   Reich, Z. 256
   Reimer, J. 321
   Reinemann, C. 316
   Rennie, E. 378
   The Republican (Carlile) 270
   review genre 93–96, 98, 102–104
   Reynolds, G.W.M. 273
   Reynolds's Weekly Newspaper (1850–1967) 273, 274
   Richardson, J.E. 152
   Ricoeur, P. 65, 66
   Rieff, P. 393
   Robinson, Jamila 288
   Robinson, S. 139
   Rocamora, A. 10, 425, 426
   Rojek, C. 144
   role conceptions 345–346
   role orientations: attitudinal and performative dimensions 237–238; empirical studies 240–242; future directions 243–245; in journalism 234–236; political and everyday life 238; theorising in lifestyle journalism 239–240; theorizing journalistic roles 236–237
   Rosenkranz, T. 349
   Roy, S. 407, 413, 415–419; *Cook Republic* 407, 413, 418
   Rusbridger, Alan 292
   Russell, Kim 383

Sadowski J. 383
   Saeed, A. 152
   Saenkham, Sujet 416
   Salanga, Janelle 290
   Sandhu, A. 379
   Sandikci, Ö. 157, 161

Santos, C. A. 222
Sayan-Cengiz, F. 160, 161
Schmitz, R. M. 176
Schneider, Gabe 290
Schudson, M. 19, 66
The Science of Getting Rich (Wattle) 394
secular identity 161
self-agency 271, 280
self branding 444
self-expression 239
self-healing 400–401
self-help: content 400–401; critics of 392–393; gurus 10, 392; history of 393–396; rise of 392
Self-help with Illustrations of Character and Conduct (Smiles) 394
self-identity identity 270, 274, 277, 392–393, 398
Sellar, S. 182
semiosphere 29
Sen, M. 286–288, 291
service journalism 22, 80
sex journalism 198
Shakespeare, William 36
Sharp, R. 10
Sherman, Laurent 384
Siddha 205, 208
Silsüpür, Ö. 158
Sine, R. 158
Singapore 142, 175, 244, 353, 412, 415, 418
Singer, J. B. 138
slimming/health 54–55
Smiles, Samuel: *Self-help with Illustrations of Character and Conduct* 394
social cohesion 321; hard news 320–322
social identity 9, 224, 229, 295
social media influencer 10, 74, 94, 109, 112, 143, 189, 192, 194, 197, 203, 211, 275, 302, 336, 350, 409
social media newcomers 382–384
soft boundaries 260, 314, 315
soft news 3–4, 75; expense of 441; as fashion 313; feminist theories 316–318; field theory 315–316; formats 5; as green lifestyle journalism 303; *vs.* hard news 6, 14, 21, 24, 62, 68, 75, 80, 242, 314–315, 335, 364, 441; in lifestyle journalism 23, 86, 155, 314–316, 333–335, 376; or private news 23; popular forms of journalism 177; reporting 367, 370
Soronen, A. 192, 193, 196, 197
South Africa 46, 48–53, 55, 56, 77–78, 80–81, 143, 162, 172, 181, 242, 244–245
Spain 116, 352, 443, 462
specific expertise 256, 363
Sprengelmeyer, L. 113

The Stage (1814–1816) 270
Stage, Carsten 7
state agencies 39–40
status identity 138
Stead, W.T. 274, 275, 277, 278
Steensen, S. 321, 439
Steenveld, L. 79
Stehr, N. 250, 252, 254
Steiner, L. 316
Stewart, Martha 115, 409, 450
Stone, Curtis 115
The Strand Magazine (1891–1949) 275–276, 278
strategic journalism 31, 34, 39–41
Stratton, J. 411
Stupart, R. 188, 189
subject boundaries 15
Substack 384–385, 447–450
sustained reciprocity 447
swadeshi/homegrown 205, 213
Swart, J. 441
Swenson, R. D. 424
symbolic competition 378
sympathetic intimacy 276

Tagore, Rabindranath 36
talent agency 290, 444
Tandoc Jr., E. C. 237
taste, concept of 143
taste-making, in media 94, 98
Taylor, B. 44, 112
Taylor, L. 258
tech companies 387–388
technology: advancements 13, 18, 333; AI-powered 130; communication 96, 157, 381; determinism 381; digital 100–101, 193–194, 319, 323, 376–389, 425; of enchantment 128; factors of change 381–383; gadgets 7; internet 226; issues 86, 87; machine-learning 130; new technologies 10, 129, 320, 332, 337, 381, 424; personal 14, 98, 242, 244, 347, 350, 364; photographic 381; of self 198; transformations 10, 219
The Telegraph 377
textual modernity 28–30
therapeutic culture 187, 194, 393, 396
Think and Grow Rich (Hill) 394
Thomas, R. J. 141
Thompson, David 416
Thread 458; followers on 385
thrift/economy 53–54
Thumala Olave, M. A. 104
Thurman, N. 446
TikTok 10, 14, 117, 182, 219, 223, 302, 330, 336, 366, 383, 387–388; fashion commentators 386; fashion critics 377, 382; followers on 385; hashtags 396; rise of short-form video platforms 396; #thatgirllifestyle 396–398; travel vlogs 228–230
Time Magazine 276
Tirodkar, M. 208, 209, 211, 214
Tit-Bits (1881–1984) 275–276
Titz, K. 112
Tlhankane, Mompati 80, 84, 85
Tomaselli, K. G. 7, 76, 77, 81, 83, 87
transcendentalist movement 394, 404n1
transnational fashion media players 385–387
travel 3, 6, 14, 15, 29, 31, 157, 160, 303, 316, 333, 344, 350, 352, 353, 364, 455, 459; campaigns 366; companies 366; exploration of studies 77; features about 272; learning through 116; locations 321; magazine 175; narratives 86; news on 74; reporting on 141; story 353; writing 228
travel agency 227
travel blogging/bloggers 142, 226–229, 349, 368; *see also* bloggers
travel destinations 121, 128, 347
travel identity 224
travel journalism 3, 5, 8, 13, 17, 127; analysing 223–224; authentic adventures 180; British 222; contributions and research 221–223; elements of 115; examples on 75; experiences or places 111; exploration of 21, 116; free or subsidized trips 341; in growth of mass tourism 220; historical perspectives 220; issues in 220–221; journalist's experience 225–226; lifestyle beats 240; motivational aspects of 222; news on 74; newspaper-based 227–228; nomadic revelations 226–228; non-artistic beats 197–198; origins of 220; political dynamics 75; proliferation of 230; Tabloid travels 224–225; traditional print-based forms of 219; in United States 349; #wilderness_addict 228–229
travel vlogs (TikTok) 223, 228–230
Travis, Jack 398
Trump, Donald 32
Truyens, P. 441
Tulloch, J. 138
Turkish: advertisers 158; case of lifestyle journalism in 7, 151–152, 155; consumer culture and lifestyle journalism 158; culture 223; high-circulation newspapers in 1990s 157–158; Islamic consumerism in 159–161; lifestyle portrayal in

157–159; media 153–159; media's advertising influence and consumerism 158–159; politics 153–155
Türksoy, Nilüfer 7, 11
"twilight" of lifestyle journalism 444

Ülken, F.B. 157, 158
Unani 205, 208
uncertainty 19, 195–197, 250, 253–254, 276, 308, 432, 456–458; digital 460–463; within lifestyle journalism 456–458
uncultured culture 176
unemployment 46–47
Uniqlo's *UT Magazine* 428–429
United Kingdom 17, 151, 285, 349, 446, 457; aspirational culture 173; cost of living crisis 225; fashion journalism 377; Insanity Group 444; lifestyle magazines 443; media genres 377; newspapers in 113, 349; Yoga magazines in 175
United States 46, 54, 61, 109, 113, 115, 151, 393–395; content creators in 145; counter-culture movements of 203, 205; culture 393; far-right populist authoritarianism 40; Federal Trade Commission 17, 351; "Feed Me Better," school meal reform campaign in 285–286; food blogs in 418; food journalism 284, 289; Green Living 304; health journalism in 332, 335; identity 424; Insanity Group 444; Instagram content creators 145; mass shootings in 322; Men's Health and Women's Health 175; travel journalism in 349–350; Washington Post's 325; wellness culture 203, 205; Yoga magazines in 175
Ureke, Oswelled 80–82
Urry, J. 222
Usher, B. 9
Usher, N. 244
Utkan, O. 158

value 78–79; commercial 153, 446, 448; cultural 16, 152, 163–164, 226, 306; ethical 191, 319; Islamic 161, 164; news 40, 79, 158, 188, 235, 303, 336; people's 80, 293; political 31, 408; social 4, 69, 239, 305
Veblen, T. 31, 35, 161
Verlogieux, Maitre 55
Verriet, J. 258
The Victorian Frame of Mind (Houghton) 272
Victorian "weekender" publications 268, 271–272

Vietnam 116, 411, 415
Vincent Peale, N.: *The Power of Positive Thinking* 394
visibility 387, 403, 407–408; exclusionary dimensions of 456–458, 463–465; of groups of people 129; and growth 206; hierarchy of 408–409; in media 256; public 163; quality of 31
vloggers 100, 109, 228–230, 364–365
Vodanovic, L. 5, 10, 138–140
Vogue International 378
Vos, T. P. 4, 141, 154, 234–238, 240, 324, 441

Wahl-Jorgensen, K. 139
Walsh, A. 449
Walters, Barbara 3
Waters, Alice 285
Wa Thiongo, N. 87
Wattles, W.D.: *How to Get What You Want* and *The Science of Getting Rich* 395; *The Science of Getting Rich* 394
Weaver, D. H. 235
Web 2.0 cultures 443
Weber, Bruce 425
Webster, Richard 276
Weekly Dispatch (1801–1928) 273
Weekly Dispatch (1801–1961) 271
Welles, Orson 32
Wellman, M. L. 9
wellness 203, 207; culture 8, 202, 204, 205, 215, 397–398; holistic 203; industry 334; influencer 9, 203, 206, 210, 331, 334, 336–337, 401; journalism 330, 333–335, 337
Western culture 309, 393
Western style of consumption 156–158
West-Knights, I. 114
The Whigs 271, 280n2
Whipple, K. 15
White, Marco Pierre 114, 115
white nationalism 411
Wilkes, John 29, 36
Wilkinson, Ellen 51
Williams, R. 268
Winfrey, Oprah 258, 398
Wohl, R. 275, 402
women: concerns 343; influencer 145; magazines 15–16, 44, 98, 109, 125, 128, 136, 159, 161, 175, 194, 284, 387, 443, 445; modern 163; pages 31, 45, 51–53, 55, 284, 343, 444; White working-class 174
Women Who Love Too Much (Norwood) 394
Wood, R. 111
Wooler, Thomas J.: *The Black Dwarf* 270

The Working Man's Friend (1832–1833) 270
Work Related Learning 81
Worlds of Journalism Study 235
Wright, S. 446, 447
Wu, Shangyuan 387
Wyn, Silikat van 86

X 387, 458, 464; arrival of 382; fashion commentators 386; followers on 385; news content on 221

Yang, Y. A. 412
The Years (Ernaux) 94
Yosso, T. J. 178

You Can Heal Your Life (Hay) 394
YouTube 116, 126, 259, 366, 382–383, 403, 464; community guidelines 204; cooking videos 287; culture 126; food-based media 409; Shorts 396, 403; wellness influencers on 203, 206
Ytre-Arne, B. 194

Zelizer, B. 4, 19, 139, 238
Zimmern, Andrew 288
Zipin, L. 172, 174, 177, 178, 180–182
Zonfrillo, Jock 114
Zoonen, L. Van 223